THE ECONOMICS OF COMPETITIVE ENTERPRISE

ECONOMISTS OF THE TWENTIETH CENTURY

General Editors: Mark Perlman, *University Professor of Economics, University of Pittsburgh* and Mark Blaug, *Professor Emeritus, University of London; Professor Emeritus, University of Buckingham; and Visiting Professor, University of Exeter*

This innovative series comprises specially invited collections of articles and papers by economists whose work has made an important contribution to economics in the late twentieth century.

The proliferation of new journals and the ever-increasing number of new articles make it difficult for even the most assiduous economist to keep track of all the important recent advances. By focusing on those economists whose work is generally recognized to be at the forefront of the discipline, the series will be an essential reference point for the different specialisms included.

A list of published and future titles in this series is printed at the end of this volume.

The Economics of Competitive Enterprise

Selected Essays of P.W.S. Andrews

Edited by

Frederic S. Lee

Principal Lecturer in Economics
De Montfort University, Leicester, United Kingdom

and

Peter E. Earl

Professor of Economics
Lincoln University, Canterbury, New Zealand

EDWARD ELGAR

Published by
Edward Elgar Publishing Limited
Gower House
Croft Road
Aldershot
Hants GU11 3HR
England

Edward Elgar Publishing Company
Old Post Road
Brookfield
Vermont 05036
USA

British Library Cataloguing in Publication Data
Andrews, Philip Walter Sawford
 Economics of Competitive Enterprise: Selected Essays of P.W.S.
 Andrews. – (Economists of the Twentieth Century Series)
 I. Title II. Lee, Frederic S. III. Earl, Peter E. IV. Series
338.6

Library of Congress Cataloguing in Publication Data
Andrews, P.W.S. (Philip Walter Sawford), 1914–1971.
 The economics of competitive enterprise: selected essays of
P.W.S. Andrews/edited by Frederic S. Lee and Peter E. Earl.
  p. cm. — (Economists of the twentieth century)
 Includes bibliographical references and indexes.
 1. Competition. 2. Business enterprises. I. Lee, Frederic S.,
1949– . II. Earl, Peter E. III. Title. IV. Series.
HD41.A648 1993
338.6'048—dc20
                93–15394
                 CIP

ISBN 1 85278 891 7

Printed and bound in Great Britain by
Hartnolls Limited, Bodmin, Cornwall

Contents

Contents

Preface

P.W.S. Andrews (1914-1971), the founding editor of the the *Journal of Industrial Economics*, was for many years a fellow of Nuffield College, Oxford, and later was Professor of Economics at the University of Lancaster. He was a pioneer of fieldwork-based analysis of the behaviour of firms and of the normal-cost/mark-up approach to pricing in oligopolistic markets. He also played a significant role in debates about competition policy in the UK in the 1950s and 1960s. Most aspects of his work are represented in the essays reprinted or published for the first time in this volume. The book should be of interest to a wide range of readers in economics departments and business schools, including microeconomic analysts, industrial economists, historians of economic thought and marketing theorists.

This collection is a result of over a dozen years of correspondence between the editors about the work of P.W.S. Andrews. During this period three main factors led us to believe that a book of collected papers by Andrews might be a desirable and feasible publishing proposition. First, we both changed our academic affiliations several times and thereby became aware of the differences in university and polytechnic libraries in terms of their holdings of Andrews's works. Newer institutions tended not to have copies of his out-of-print books or early volumes of the journals in which he published. In these environments, it is difficult to teach about Andrews's work or conduct research into it without spending much time at photocopiers and in arranging inter-library loans. We soon discovered that we were not the only scholars of Andrews's work who found themselves lamenting the absence of a volume which contained his key papers — there was a growing number of relatively young economists who had discovered Andrews and felt his contributions warranted serious discussion.

Secondly, when Fred Lee was in Oxford in 1986 doing some research, Oliver Westall invited him to Lancaster to look at Andrews's papers. On doing so, he was excited to discover that this included unpublished lectures and case study work by Andrews as well as correspondence between Andrews, his friends and some of his critics, about his work and its implications for mainstream marginalist thinking. From the standpoint of the history of economic thought, these documents are doubly interesting: they include Andrews's analysis of why price theory was developing along lines which he felt was unfortunate; they also reveal something of the processes of academic discourse shortly after the Second

World War. On top of this, these papers and letters seem in some cases like missing links that can help make clear the integrated vision of the workings of competitive process that Andrews developed but failed to present in a single work. After digesting this material, Fred Lee assembled the long essay on Andrews's career that forms the Introduction to this volume and suggested which papers and letters might be assembled to provide a comprehensive guide to Andrews's work.

A third factor which encouraged us to set about trying to relaunch Andrews's work was the contestable markets revolution in monopoly analysis in the early 1980s. In 1984, before Fred Lee moved to the UK, Peter Earl left the UK for Australia and shortly after arriving there attended the annual conference of the Economic Society of Australia. He found this a most unsettling experience: many papers were applications or reviews of contributions to the contestability literature, yet none referred to Andrews's work. This was indeed odd and seemed somehow unjust, for Andrews had reached similar conclusions to contestability theorists as part of a far richer vision of competitive processes that involved fewer restrictive assumptions and less technical complexity. In a bid to put these concerns on the record, Earl presented a paper on this theme at the next conference of the History of Economic Thought Society of Australia, intending eventually to publish it as a journal article. Several years later, while he was still trying to find time to incorporate feedback from referees and other Andrews scholars, Lee suggested that the paper might make an appropriate Epilogue to the Andrews volume. While Earl continued to struggle to make time available to polish up the Epilogue, Lee set about scanning/key-entering the Andrews papers and obtaining reprint permissions. Having at last caught up, Earl used Clarisworks and an Apple Macintosh to perform the final tasks of turning Lee's DOS disks into typeset, camera-ready output and preparing the indexes.

The works of Andrews that have thus ended up sandwiched between the editors' Introduction and Epilogue are organized as follows. Chapter 1 gives a taste of the kind of case study work that Andrews engaged in as well as serving as an invaluable document for economic historians interested in industrial structure in the textile industry during the inter-war period. Chapter 2 presents, in an extended article, many of the ideas on costs and price-setting that were developed into Andrews's best-known and controversial book *Manufacturing Business*. Chapters 3 to 5 reveal Andrews's Marshallian sympathies and criticial views on the ways that the theory of the firm and competitive analysis developed following the rise of theories of imperfect and monopolistic competition in the 1930s. Chapters 6 and 7 extend the theoretical analysis from manufacturing to the retail sector and are especially rich in insights about the ways that markets work as information structures and the dangers of looking at structural changes in terms of 'snapshots' rather than from an evolutionary perspective. Chapters 8 to 10 deal mainly with investment behaviour and how it is affected by processes of 'internal competition' in organizations. Finally, Chapters 11 and 12 are essentially methodological essays that reveal something of Andrews's vision of how industrial economists ought to operate and of how economists and managers in academia and industry might best interact to learn from each other's research and experience.

As with many books of collected essays, there are overlapping passages among the various chapters. We could have produced a rather shorter book by adopting a more radical approach as editors and removing instances of duplication. However, our own experiences of coming to terms with Andrews's work implied that such a strategy could well prove counter-productive. Andrews wrote in a style with which it takes quite a while to come to terms and this, coupled with the fact that he is often demanding that his readers make a shift away from their conventional point of view, means that important points can easily be missed or misunderstood on first or second readings. Moreover, the full impact of many of the details of Andrews's work comes after one has grasped the broader context into which they fit: the complexity of Andrews's view of the competitive process can sometimes make reading about it seem like a mental act of juggling, yet quite simple unifying themes emerge as the juggling process goes on. The Introduction and Epilogue attempt to bring out many of these key themes, but they are no substitute for reading Andrews in the original and gradually coming to terms with what he was saying.

Acknowledgements

The editors would like to thank the University of Lancaster, acting on behalf of the estate of P.W.S. Andrews, for permission to reprint or publish works by P.W.S. Andrews as listed below. We also wish to thank the following archives and publishers of the original versions of these works:

The Warden and Fellows of Nuffield College, Oxford, for granting permission to inspect archives held at the College, and to publish, from the G.D.H. Cole Papers, Andrews's 'Report from the "accountancy" side of the pilot inquiry into the relative efficiency of small- and large-scale business';

The Librarian of the British Library of Political and Economic Science at the London School of Economics and Political Science for granting permission to inspect the P.W.S. Andrews Papers and publish from them various items of correspondence along with the following papers by Andrews: 'The legacy of the 1930s in economics' and 'The Netherlands lectures';

Oxford University Press, for permission to reprint the following articles by Andrews: 'A reconsideration of the theory of the individual business', from *Oxford Economic Papers* 1 (new series), January 1949, pp. 54–89; 'Industrial analysis in economics — with especial reference to Marshallian doctrine', from *Oxford Studies in the Price Mechanism*, edited by T. Wilson and P.W.S. Andrews, published by Clarendon Press in 1951; and 'Some aspects of competition in retail trade', *Oxford Economic Papers* 2 (new series), June 1950, pp. 137–75;

Macmillan Accounts and Administration Ltd, for permission to reprint pages 40–84 of *Fair Trade* by P.W.S. Andrews and F.A. Friday, published by Macmillan & Co. Ltd. in 1960;

The Textile Institute, for permission to reprint Andrews's 'Some aspects of capital development', from the *Proceedings* of the *Journal of the Textile Institute* **44**, September 1953, pp. 687–97;

The Institute of Petroleum, for permission to reprint Andrews's 'Competition in

Acknowledgements

the modern economy', which appeared as pp. 1–42 of George Sell (ed.) *Competitive Aspects of Oil Operations — Report of the Summer Meeting of the Institute of Petroleum, held at Scarborough, 4th–6th June 1958*;

The Graduate School of Management, University of California, Los Angeles, for permission to reprint Andrews's lecture 'Industrial uses of economic theory';

Blackwell Publishers for permission to reprint the following articles by Andrews: 'Industrial economics as a specialist subject', *Journal of Industrial Economics* 1, November 1952, pp. 72–9; 'Business profits and the quiet life', *Journal of Industrial Economics* 11, November 1962, pp. 72–8 (written with Elizabeth Brunner).

For permission to reprint letters written by Andrews or received by him we would like to thank the following: John Presley (on behalf of the estate of the late Sir Dennis Robertson); Lady Roberthall (on behalf of the late Lord Roberthall); Michael Fogarty; Henry Harrod (on behalf of the estate of the late Sir Roy Harrod); David Papineau (on behalf of the estate of the late Lord Kahn); The Earl of Stockton (on behalf of the estate of the late Harold Macmillan, The Earl of Stockton); Monique Chamberlin Spalding (on behalf of the estate of the late Edward H. Chamberlin).

Every effort has been made to trace all the copyright holders but if any have been overlooked inadvertently the editors and publishers will be pleased to make the necessary arrangement at the first opportunity.

Introduction: Philip Walter Sawford Andrews, 1914–1971

Frederic S. Lee[1]

Early life, 1914-1937

Andrews was born in Southampton on 12 March 1914 into an upwardly mobile working-class family. His mother was the daughter of an agricultural and iron stone labourer and had been a domestic servant before her marriage. His paternal grandfather was a ship's steward and stevedore, and his father rose from being an able seaman and railway shunter to retire as Chief Inspector, Traffic Department, at Southampton Docks. After attending elementary and secondary schools in Southampton, Andrews entered University College, Southampton as an Open Foundation Scholar in 1931 to read for a London University external degree.

Since the London School of Economics dominated economics at London and its lecturers and professors were the examiners for the external B.Sc. (Econ.) examinations, that institution's lecture syllabuses and recommended reading lists were adopted by P. Ford and R.A. Hodgson who made up the economics teaching staff at Southampton. Thus, the readings in economic theory at Southampton, for example, included Cannan's *Wealth*, Knight's *Risk, Uncertainty and Profit*, Wicksell's *Lectures on Political Economy*, Marshall's *Principles of Economics*, Pigou's *Economics of Welfare*, and Keynes's *Treatise on Money*. In particular, Andrews read and took notes on L. Von Mises's *The Theory of Money and Credit*, read Pigou, Cannan, Hayek, and Robbins; and later at his examination did a question on the monetary theory of the trade cycle. Consequently, the education Andrews received at Southampton was similar to that received by students at the L.S.E.

Driven by a desire to improve the economic world he lived in, Andrews specialized in economics, taking courses from Hodgson and Ford. Hodgson lectured on money, banking, public finance, international trade, and applied

(1) I am grateful to Juli Irving-Lessmann, John E. King, R.A. Hodgson, O. Westall, R.C. Tress, and Peter Earl for comments on an earlier draft of the Introduction. I am also grateful to S.W. Davies for his explanation of the workings of the editorial board of the *Journal of Industrial Economics*.

economics and taught statistical methods for which Andrews was grateful, because it enabled him not only to become the Chief Statistician for the Nuffield College Social Reconstruction Survey but also to tackle any statistical problems that came his way.(2) Ford lectured in a broadly homiletic style on economic theory from an historical perspective in the style of Edwin Cannan. At the time Andrews did not enjoy this way of teaching:

> Some of us were mad with Ford; he did not teach economic theory in the sense of a single body of analysis but insisted that we thought of it in terms of Ricardo, Jevons, Marshall, etc. — in terms of questions and environments which varied secularly (Andrews, 1964a).

However he later realized that Ford's approach to economic theory forced one to realize the importance of methodology. In particular Andrews learned 'that one could be wrong, not in any sense of an error of logic but in the more difficult to detect sense of an error in the approximation of the whole of one's model to the whole one was thinking about.' So in later years, he considered Cannan to be his academic grandfather (Andrews, 1964a; Tress, 1990; Hodgson, 1990; and King, 1988), and he came to lecture in a similar style.

In 1934 Andrews graduated with a second-class external London degree in economics, although he felt that he might have done better if he had been given the 'textbook' or a more conventional analytical approach to economic theory. Awarded a research grant by Southampton, he remained there for the next three years as a research student, a temporary assistant lecturer at the College, and as honorary tutor-organizer for the Workers' Educational Association. As lecturer, he gave a few lectures for Ford who had obtained a Leverhulme Grant to do some research on retail trade.(3) In 1934, Andrews was a British Association Exhibitioner, which meant he attended the 1934 Aberdeen meeting of the British Association for the Advancement of Science. At the meeting, he listened to D.H.

---

(2) In this context, Andrews noted that, given the statistical background he picked up from Hodgson, he knew enough to read his way through an econometric paper and then be able to 'judge by smell'. He further noted that if this were not possible, he would work harder at learning about econometrics; but 'except for an early work by Koopmans, the seminal work by Tinbergen, and some work by Johnston, I rarely get tempted.' Thus it is not surprising that M.A. Adelman noted that as the American editor of the *Journal of Industrial Economics* he sent Andrews more econometric papers than he cared for (Andrews, 1964a; Adelman, 1991)

(3) Ford apparently obtained the grant based on his research on the retail trades in Great Britain and used it to further his research (see, e.g. Ford, 1935 and 1936; and Ford and White, 1936). Ford's interest in empirical research apparently had an impact on Andrews.

2

MacGregor, the Drummond Professor of Political Economy at Oxford, giving a paper on joint-stock company registrations as part of his contribution to a session on economic planning. Andrews greatly enjoyed MacGregor's presentation and met him afterwards. MacGregor not only encouraged him to carry out research on joint-stock companies, but also to attend Oxford as a postgraduate. Thus, trying to make up for his disappointing second-class, Andrews returned to Southampton where he began research on joint-stock companies which culminated in his first publication (Andrews, 1937 and 1964a; Tress, 1990; Robson, 1990; and Lee, 1989).(4)

Like many other young adults in the 1930s, Andrews saw himself as a socialist. However, his socialism was a kind of humanism (for example, he was a pacifist supporter of the League of Nations Peace Pledge Union) that was directed very much by his reading of economic history, by his desire to eliminate unemployment, and by the theory of imperfect competition which suggested that prices were very much the consequence of non-economic, non-competitive elements and that there was great scope for inefficiency of which British business took full advantage. The emergence of Keynes's *The General Theory*, however, pointed the way towards a non-socialist solution to the problem of unemployment and poverty. Moreover, his association with the Oxford Economists' Research Group, his work on the Nuffield College Social Reconstruction Survey, and his research into manufacturing businesses led him to repudiate the theory of imperfect competition and its welfare implications, and to conclude that the horrors of nineteenth-century capitalism were not generally present in the twentieth. Thus Andrews took a more positive view of capitalism and the businessman and therefore ceased to be a socialist, but not a humanist. This ideological shift, as we shall see, caused him much trouble in the late 1940s and early 1950s when many academic economists in Great Britain still considered themselves socialists (see Chapter 4; and Andrews, 1964a).

---

(4) Andrews was greatly assisted in his research when another researcher in the field, H.A. Shannon, was unable to continue his research and turned over his material on limited companies to him. In three published papers, Shannon had carried out an extended investigation on the history of limited companies up to 1883. He started first with the evolution of the limited company and its law in the first half of the nineteenth century, and then dealt with the registration, duration, and dissolution of limited companies that took place between 1856 and 1883 (Shannon, 1931, 1932, and 1933).

3

Oxford and the Oxford Economists' Research Group, 1937–1939

In the Spring of 1937, perhaps through the intervention of MacGregor, E.H. Phelps Brown asked Andrews whether he was interested and available to work on a company accounts project at the Institute of Statistics in Oxford. Because he had already decided to go to Oxford to pursue a D.Phil. degree and was interested in joint-stock companies, Andrews responded positively. Phelps Brown hired him as his research assistant on 17 May 1937. Later Phelps Brown also became Andrews's doctoral supervisor. Initially, Andrews worked on the company accounts at his home in Surrey, but in July he moved to Oxford and began working at the Institute. His dissertation (and Phelps Brown's project) was to study the profit-and-loss accounts and balance sheets of some three thousand British public companies over the period 1924 to 1936.(5) The objective of the dissertation was to provide information on earnings by industrial groups, on business policy with respect to the distribution of profits and allocations to reserve, and on changes in balance-sheet liquidity through cyclical and other changes in trading conditions. However, with the advent of war in 1939, he put aside this work and never returned to it.(6)

Although housed at the Institute of Statistics, Phelps Brown's company accounts project was under the auspices of the Oxford Economists' Research Group (OERG). When Andrews arrived in Oxford, Marion Bowley was the Group's secretary and had her office in the Institute. In December 1937 Bowley resigned to take a teaching position in Scotland and her place and office was officially taken by Andrews from 1 January 1938, although he was already functioning as the Group's secretary. Initially he received a £50 honorarium, but from 1 July 1938 he received £251. His job was to take extensive notes of the interviews conducted by the OERG, to distribute the notes to the members of the Group and to the interviewees for their comments, to distribute reports written by Group members relating to the meetings, and to handle the correspondence and other sundry details.

As a member of the OERG, Andrews became enthralled at seeing economists actually finding out what businessmen did instead of assuming that

---

(5) This study was conceived as part of Phelps Brown's general investigation into British trade fluctuations. Other projects directed by Phelps Brown included R. Goodwin's study on the stock and flow of money in Great Britain and G.L.S. Shackle's study on trends and fluctuations in British economic activity, 1924–1938.

(6) Andrews made his data available in 1945 to Ronald Hope, who used it in his D.Phil. thesis, 'Profits in British Industry from 1924 to 1935'.

they already knew.(7) His participation in the Group included preparing a summary of the replies by the businessmen who were interviewed by the Group to questions regarding the influence of interest rates on their decisions to undertake capital investment or to hold stocks of raw materials (Meade and Andrews, 1938). Andrews later undertook, on behalf of the OERG, a mailing of a questionnaire to businessmen regarding the influence of the interest rates on their investment decisions (Andrews, 1940). However, it was the Group's inquiry into price determination which really caught Andrews's interest and was destined to have a major influence on him.

All of the members of the OERG, including Andrews, but excepting MacGregor and H. Henderson, were confirmed marginalists and accepted the imperfect competition/monopolistic competition approaches to prices and price setting. On the other hand, the information they received from the businessmen indicated that the latter thought of prices in terms of some relationship to average total costs and totally ignored the marginalist approach to pricing. In fact, even penetrating questioning by the Group failed to uncover any evidence that the businessmen paid any attention at all to marginal revenue or costs in the sense defined by economic theory, and that they had only the vaguest ideas about anything remotely resembling their elasticities of demand. This shocked the Oxford economists. However, what caught their attention even more was the relative stability of prices over the trade cycle and this became the phenomenon which really needed to be explained. Robert Hall in particular brooded about this, i.e. why a firm's price based on a cost-plus formula could be stable if it faced a downward-sloping demand curve. This dilemma was resolved when he hit upon the idea of the kinked demand curve. Its virtue was that it appeared to reconcile the logic of marginalism with the empirical evidence of cost-plus (or full cost) pricing and price stability. In focusing their attention on price stability and the kinked demand curve, Hall, Andrews, and the other Oxford economists did not pay significant attention to the full-cost pricing procedures themselves. This, Andrews later realized, not only contributed to obscuring the Group's findings with regard to price-fixing over the trade cycle and the extent to which full-cost prices were incommensurate with marginalist prices, but also left him in the clutches of marginalism, from which he would not escape until after he carried out his investigations of manufacturing businesses in the rayon and boot and shoe industries, some ten years later (see Chapter 5).

---

(7) It was at this time that Andrews realized that this was a point which Ford had tried to get across to his students through lectures and readings (Andrews, 1964a).

Wartime Oxford, 1939–1946

With the outbreak of war in 1939, the OERG decided to suspend its work and agreed with the Institute that the company accounts project should be discontinued with Andrews aiming at quick publication of at least some of his research. This never occurred. Instead, the Institute decided that Andrews — who was a conscientious objector and thus remained in Oxford (in charge of undergraduate students at New College) — should make an analysis of the profit-and-loss accounts and balance sheets of British companies during the war.(8) In November 1939, the Institute also decided that its members should co-operate in producing a diary of economic events every two weeks. So beginning on 25 November, the Institute produced the *Diary* which initially consisted of a few pages which covered such areas as finance, foreign exchange, trade and shipping, commodities and industry. From March 1940 lengthier records of, and comments on, changes in the British economic system under the stress of war conditions were added to the *Diary*. Also at this time, a new section presenting excerpts from company reports was added. Although the *Diary* listed no name with this section, it is highly probable that Andrews was assigned the task of producing this section. In June the *Diary* was expanded to include articles and in October the *Diary* was completely reorganized and renamed the *Institute of Statistics: Bulletin*. Andrews contributed to the Institute's reporting on the war economy with articles on food policy and industrial development appearing in the *Diary* and the *Bulletin* (Institute of Statistics, 1940; Social Science Research

---

(8) Andrews was not called up for military duty because he was a conscientious objector, registering as such with the Military Service in May 1940, though in any case he was unfit for military duty (Fogarty, 1981; Andrews, 1964a).

Committee, 1935–1945, p. 77).(9)

On 8 February 1941 the Nuffield College Committee established the Nuffield College Social Reconstruction Survey Committee which in turn oversaw the Social Reconstruction Survey. The Committee appointed G.D.H. Cole as the director of the Survey. Cole's and the Survey's initial concern was to make a study of the probable post-war location of industry and distribution of population. However, the Survey quickly widened its scope and complexity to include the post-war economic and social prospects of the main industrial regions of Great Britain, and to formulate proposals about general problems of social and economic reorganization after the war. As a consequence, over the next two years the Survey directed its energies towards exploring the effects of war conditions on the working of the public social services and the social services provided by voluntary agencies, developing a comprehensive post-war educational policy, and exploring the ways in which local government carried out its activities and recruited its work force.

To carry out the activities of the Survey, Cole established a national office at Oxford which was organized into various departments, including Special Investigations headed by H.A. Silverman and the Local Surveys Department headed by M.P. Fogarty. Cole also established a Statistical Department and invited Andrews to be its chief statistician. Andrews accepted the offer, which also meant that he became a senior member of the Nuffield College research staff, and left the Institute in February 1941. His role in the Survey was to act as resource-person for all its activities. Consequently, he assisted all of the

---

(9) The relationship between Andrews and the other members of the Institute was not very close after the war started. This was in part due to the rapid and heavy influx into the Institute of left-wing economists, such as Josef Steindl and Michael Kalecki, at a time when Andrews was beginning to have more respect for the businessman. While in Oxford, neither Kalecki nor Steindl discussed their work with Andrews. There appear to have been a variety of reasons for this. Aside from the political differences, Kalecki considered Andrews too untheoretical and thus ignored him. In addition, for the period in which Kalecki was at Oxford (1940–1944), Andrews had not yet begun his work on normal-cost pricing, thus making their interaction even more unlikely. Steindl, on the other hand, had been at Balliol College as a lecturer since 1938; and in 1940 he joined the Institute. However, aside from their relationship at the Institute, Steindl and Andrews never engaged in a mutual discussion of their work, in spite of Steindl being engaged by the Courtauld Inquiry and writing *Small and Big Business* (1945) and *Maturity and Stagnation* (1952). The reasons for this were perhaps the same as Kalecki's, but it may also have been due to the cool reception members of the Institute gave Andrews in 1945 when he gave a lecture based on his work with the Courtauld Inquiry (Lee, 1985; Steindl, 1981; and Bellamy, 1981).

departments; however he was most heavily involved with those activities that were most closely linked with economics. For example he assisted the Survey's inquiries into the costs of housing development in the Greater London area and wrote a memorandum on the international economic conditions needed in connection for full employment in Great Britain. In addition he supervised Elizabeth Brunner, who had come to work in the Statistical Department at the end of 1942, when she wrote *Holiday Making and the Holiday Trades*. However, it was the activities associated with the post-war location of industry and population with which he was most heavily involved (Progress Reports, 1–14, 1941–1944; and Brunner, 1945).

Concerned about the large geographical variations in rates of unemployment observed in pre-war Britain and the long-term impact the war might have on them through its distributional impact on industry and population, the Survey initiated an investigation on the location of industry and regional development. This included regional and town surveys, interviews with large firms and trade associations, and particular industry studies.(10) The digesting and merging of the surveys into a publishable monograph on industry location and regional development was the responsibility of Fogarty, while the industry studies were carried out by a number of individuals but under the supervision of Silverman. Andrews assisted both Fogarty and Silverman in a variety of ways, ranging from statistical help to assisting Silverman in his work on the boot and shoe industry. However his most intensive involvement with their work came in 1944 when he reviewed their material for publication. In May 1943, the Nuffield College Committee established a committee to examine the allegations that the work of the Survey was not of high enough quality for an Oxford College and to see whether any of the material accumulated by the Survey was publishable. The committee refuted the allegations and stated that it felt that much of the material was publishable. Consequently, the Nuffield College Committee established the Industrial and Planning Sub-Committee in December 1943 to carry out the task

---

(10) Cole utilized two other approaches in carrying out the Survey's investigations. One consisted of preparing special reports and memoranda relating to a large number of questions, either based upon the Survey's own initiative or, at the request of various Government Departments. The second approach consisted of the sponsorship of private conferences held at Oxford on various topics dealing with post-war reconstruction and general economic and social policy to which industrialists, trade unionists, academics and government officials were invited. Andrews attended all of the wartime conferences, including the six that dealt with post-war employment. The conferences continued after the war, including one in 1948 on 'the government's controls of industry and trade' and one in 1949 on 'the problems of large-scale industrial organizations including the nationalized industries'. Andrews attended both of these conferences and spoke at the latter.

of reviewing the industrial findings and reports accumulated by the Survey for publication. The outcome of the Committee's work was the publication of *Prospects of the Industrial Areas of Great Britain* (Fogarty, 1945) and two volumes of studies in industrial organization, *Studies in Industrial Organization* (Silverman, 1946) and *Further Studies in Industrial Organization* (Fogarty, 1948). Andrews's role in this affair involved reading closely each chapter of each book and suggesting various changes and amendments. (Chester, 1986; Progress Report, 12 May 1944; Fogarty, 1981; Worswick, 1960; and Industrial and Planning Sub-Committee Minutes, 24 February, 17 March, 21 April, 8 June, and 17 June 1944).

In early March 1943, Cole received a letter from Samuel Courtauld, a visiting Fellow at Nuffield College and chairman of the board of Courtaulds, the rayon manufacturing firm, expressing some doubt over the dictum 'bigger is better', i.e. the bigger the firm or plant the more efficient it would be. Rather, Courtauld expressed a long-held belief that if the opportunity of buying and borrowing more cheaply were swept away, then the optimum size of the firm and plant would be reduced significantly. If this were in fact the case, he argued, then it would be possible to arrange conditions under which the small competitor could effectively compete with the larger firms. Because he did not believe that any thorough investigation into the economics of large-scale production had been carried out, he asked Cole whether it would be possible to establish such an investigation. Courtauld suggested that the investigation, which he would finance in part by paying the salary of the investigator for a few years, would involve collecting evidence directly from firms with the help of their cost accountants (Courtauld, 1943a; and Cole, 1943).

Cole responded to Courtauld immediately, saying that his proposal would be discussed at the next meeting of the Nuffield College Social Reconstruction Survey Committee. At the same time, he circulated a copy of the letter among the Oxford staff. Andrews, along with Fogarty and Silverman, responded to the letter by drawing up a draft proposal for a pilot study in which they emphasized the need to investigate the cost accounts of various firms while at the same time carrying out a survey of the literature. They sent the proposal to Courtauld, who responded in a letter to Cole saying that the proposed pilot study was too grandiose. Rather he argued that all that was necessary to get the desired information was to investigate one or two representative firms, not necessarily of the same industry. To iron out these differences and to deal with other matters, Cole scheduled a meeting with Courtauld on 3 April 1943 which Cole, MacGregor, Andrews, Silverman, Harrod, and others attended. After much discussion, it was decided that an exploratory six-month investigation be established which would analyse the theoretical material bearing on the optimum sizes of plants and firms, review the factual material available from studies made in Great Britain and the United States, and draw up a list of questions to be given to Courtauld's accountant, to be followed up by an analysis of the costs of Courtaulds from the standpoint of the economies of size of plant and firm. It was also agreed that, at the end of this part of the investigation, the results would be reviewed to see whether it would be continued (Andrews, 1943a; Courtauld, 1943b; and Discussion with Mr. Courtauld, 1943).

In June 1943, after obtaining the consent of the directors on the board of his firm, Courtauld agreed to support the exploratory investigation through a personal gift, although the gift was not payable until the research was completed so that its quality could be ascertained. Thus the Courtauld Inquiry was established and placed under the supervision of the Courtauld Sub-Committee, which in turn answered to the Nuffield College Committee. At the first meeting of the Courtauld Sub-Committee in October, it was decided that, in addition to his duties with the Social Reconstruction Survey, Andrews would take charge of the statistical and accounting side of the investigation, while the theoretical investigation into the optimum sizes of plants and firms and the review of the factual material would be carried out by Josef Steindl and J.R.L. Schneider, respectively (Courtauld, 1943c; and Courtauld Sub-Committee Minutes, 8 October 1943).

Andrews set to work almost immediately and, with Elizabeth Brunner's assistance, interviewed Courtauld, his accountant, and his statistician.(11) He also talked with the managers of Courtaulds's Preston Works, the firm's newest and biggest rayon plant, from which he derived much technical information about the economies of scale in the production of viscous continuous filament

---

(11) Elizabeth Brunner was Andrews's principal assistant in all his empirical studies and lifelong collaborator. Brunner obtained a degree in English in 1942, so, after she joined the Survey, Andrews taught her economics. Later, when faced with facts that did not seem to be consistent with marginalism, Brunner insisted that Andrews should try to keep to the marginalist framework that he had taught her and not slide around the facts. From this Andrews learned that the precise question which he asked was as important as the answer and that it was too easy to roll answers into one's preconceptions. Brunner's professional career consisted of being a member of the research staff at Nuffield College (1945-1967) and then subsequently being a senior lecturer, reader, and Professor of Economics at the University of Lancaster. As many economists who knew Brunner have noted, she was completely self-effacing to the point where people overlooked her entirely. But the fact of the matter was that she ensured that Andrews's interests proceeded in a businesslike way and that the *Journal of Industrial Economics* was running properly. Some have even suggested that she was the real origin of much of the work, at least in the latter part of his life, with which Andrews was credited (Andrews, 1964a; Carter, 1990; and Adelman, 1991).

yarn.(12) Putting this material together, Andrews produced a major report on the relative efficiency of small- and large-scale rayon producers for the May 1944 meeting of the Courtauld Sub-Committee (see Chapter 1). In summarizing his report to the Committee, Andrews noted that Courtaulds's actual accounts had been investigated and technical and commercial factors had been examined. In addition, Courtauld had supplied him data for a hypothetical firm of the same size as the smallest rayon producer in Britain. When comparing the actual and hypothetical data, he found that Courtaulds's most efficient plant — the Preston Works — had costs which were significantly less than the hypothetical firm, but this difference decreased significantly when based on Courtaulds's rayon business as a whole since it included works which were older and hence more costly than the Preston Works. Thus Andrews concluded that small rayon firms survived because of the technical inefficiency of Courtaulds's older plants. The Committee accepted his report, as well as the reports by Steindl and Schneider, and sent them to Courtauld along with an introduction. The Committee also agreed that the Inquiry should continue, that a better picture of economies of scale in the rayon industry would be obtained if the accounts of a smaller rayon firm were examined, and that perhaps it should be widened to include similar fields of investigation (Andrews, 1943b, 1943c, 1943d, 1944a; and Courtauld Sub-Committee Minutes, 11 May 1944).

Upon examining the reports, Courtauld reacted favourably to the quality of their work. Andrews's work was especially liked because he had put together Courtaulds's accounting data quite well. On the other hand, Steindl's work was not as well received because Courtauld disagreed with his conclusion that oligopoly leads to a reduction in the rate of technological progress. However, finding the work of acceptable quality, Courtauld entered into an agreement with Nuffield College in July in which out of his personal funds he would give £2000

---

(12) Beginning with his investigation of Courtaulds, Andrews developed over time a highly sophisticated method of investigating individual manufacturing businesses: 'I (Andrews) do not go to a business with a questionnaire nor do I rely just upon statistics supplied by the business. In fact, in my experience, ready made statistical evidence is of less importance than that which results from my detail interviews. I keep practically verbatim records of all conversations that I have inside businesses, and do not handle a business unless I am completely free to go where I like, to question whom I like and to call for and examine any documents whose existence I discover, which are relevant to my work. The facts which I am after are, therefore, generally speaking, facts of situations checked and rechecked by cross-questioning of individuals within any one business, with the protection that my notes of interviews are not shown to any other person even within the business — and also checked by probing into the experience of competing firms in the critical situations disclosed by any one other firm' (Andrews, 1953; also see Chapter 5).

a year for seven years to continue the inquiry. Once the question of the continuation of the Inquiry was settled, Andrews dealt with the Committee's second concern. Armed with introductions from Courtauld and Henry Clay, the Warden of Nuffield College, he visited two of Courtaulds's smaller competitors in September and October (Bingham, 1944; Courtauld, 1944; and Andrews, 1944c and 1944d).(13)

Once it was decided that the Inquiry was to be continued, it then became important as to what path it should take. Clay wrote to Courtauld later in July suggesting that Andrews's work be continued, since the question of scale raises fundamental issues of industrial organization and had not been subject to any thorough quantitative examination. Courtauld accepted Clay's suggestion, thus establishing the terms of reference of the Inquiry as investigating the relative efficiency of small- and large-scale business and allied problems of industrial structure and organization. Later in August, Clay invited Andrews to draw up a memorandum stating the lines of inquiry which he thought the Inquiry should take. In the memorandum, which was presented at the October 1944 meeting of the Courtauld Sub-Committee, Andrews argued that his line of research be continued and be expanded to include the Bradford Dress Goods Industry and the Boot and Shoe Industry; he also suggested that the Inquiry be enlarged to include research into the reasons for the survival of small-scale firms in retail distribution and agriculture; finally he suggested that Steindl's theoretical line of work be discontinued until further empirical results were collected, partly because the results could be used to test the previous work and partly in order to suggest the lines for further theoretical work. The Committee largely accepted the suggestions in Andrews's memorandum, with the result that Andrews began to contact firms in the boot and shoe industry (Clay, 1944; Andrews, 1944b; and Courtauld Sub-Committee Minutes, 12 October 1944).

At the January 1945 Sub-Committee meeting Andrews noted that no real further progress could be made examining the rayon industry; therefore he suggested that a final report be written up and that his primary attention should be directed at the boot and shoe industry. The Committee agreed with him. By December 1945, Andrews had paid visits to the secretaries of the employees' and

---

(13) Before being Warden of Nuffield College (1944-1949), Henry Clay had been the Stanley Jevons Professor of Political Economy at the University of Manchester (1922–1930). In 1930 he joined the Bank of England and in 1933 became the economic advisor to the governor of the Bank of England. In 1938 he helped establish the National Institute of Economic and Social Research; and then in 1941 he left the Bank to become economic advisor to the Board of Trade and later to the Ministry of War Transport. Then in 1944 he left Whitehall to become the second Warden of Nuffield College.

manufacturers' organizations, trade union officials, the British United Shoe Machinery Company, and nine firms which were subject to a full-scale study. At this point he concluded his visits and began producing his report on the industry. In March he was preparing to visit firms in other industries, such as the High Wycombe furniture and the Bradford dress goods industries. A start was also made on parallel studies of the extent to which large businesses have complementary as well as competitive relationships with smaller businesses. However, before these inquiries got started, Courtauld suffered a severe attack of pneumonia in May 1946. As soon as he was fit to do so, he began making plans to resign as chairman of Courtaulds; this more urgent and important concern meant that Courtauld ceased to be actively interested in the Inquiry. Although Courtauld died in December 1947, funding for the Inquiry continued until 1949 when it was brought to a close with the publication of *Manufacturing Business* (Courtauld Sub-Committee Minutes, 16 November 1944, 25 January, 3 May and 11 October 1945, and 7 March, 20 June, and 12 December 1946; Coleman, 1980; and Nuffield College, 1948).

The road to *Manufacturing Business*, 1946–1949

In 1946, Andrews was appointed an Official Fellow of Nuffield College. He had been connected with Nuffield as a member of its research staff since 1941, and it is likely that his elevation to the Fellowship would have upset many of his contemporaries — particularly those who had not been conscientious objectors and who were still waiting to be demobbed from the armed services. As will later be seen, his lack of popularity certainly made the renewal of the Fellowship at the end of its first seven-year term a rather controversial affair.

By this stage in his career, Andrews had realized that his work on the rayon industry could lead to a book which examined the chances of small firms in British industry. In particular he saw the book as a general report surveying the problem of how far the efficiency of an individual business was affected by its size and considering how far large-scale business did or did not enjoy real advantages which would not be available to smaller-scale businesses, even with appropriate changes in the organization of industry and in the economic environment of business. In addition, the book would pay special attention to the reasons for the survival of relatively small businesses in industries where they were important and thus indicate contributions that smaller-scale businesses made both to their own industries and to the economy of Great Britain as a whole. Finally, Andrews felt that it would be possible to publish reports on some of the industries on which the book was based and for which the disclosure of information would not lead to the identification of specific businesses in the industry. Consequently, he advocated the publication of the report on the boot and shoe industry because it was possible to mask the individual firms who were investigated, but not on the rayon industry, because the clear dominance of Courtaulds made it impossible to mask its data (Andrews, 1944a and 1944e).

Work on the book progressed to the point that, in August 1946, Andrews had drawn up an outline of it which included chapter titles such as 'the ownership of business', 'the reckoning of business income', 'markets and prices (a) selling', 'markets and prices (b) buying', 'technical factors and the efficiency of business', 'the size of businesses', and 'business and the community'. At this point he saw that the theme of the book had changed to a study of the effects of environment and organization on the running of manufacturing businesses. Andrews sent the chapter on 'the reckoning of business income' along with the outline of the book to Harold Macmillan, who apparently reviewed the material on his own without any consultation with academic economists. Macmillan liked what he saw so well that he agreed to publish it.(14) In November 1948 he completed the book and Macmillan published *Manufacturing Business* in June 1949.(15) As for the publication of the report on the boot and shoe industry, which Andrews had originally planned to accompany the book, Margaret Cole in 1946 made a speech in Northampton, the home of the boot and shoe industry, in which she mentioned the possibility of nationalizing the industry based on the research being carried out by Andrews. Consequently, the firms with whom Andrews was dealing asked that their data not be published; thus the planned report was left uncompleted and unpublished (Andrews, 1946a, 1946b, and 1948; and Brunner, 1979).(16)

The road to Manufacturing Business also included an intellectual revolution

(14) This most likely is the reason why Andrews was able to write Manufacturing Business in a manner accessible to businessmen but foreign to economists. The peculiar style, however, did affect the book's reception by academic economists.

(15) Between June 1949 and 1956, a total of 3135 copies of Manufacturing Business had been sold, and of that number 478 had been sold overseas. A different set of statistics have the number of copies sold from 1956 to 1982 as 2674, with 2489 being sold in the UK and 109 being sold in the US. Manufacturing Business was in print until 1982 (Handford, 1990).

(16) The political context of Cole's speech was the lead article in Northampton's Chronicle & Echo on 19 September 1946 where it was reported that the Council of the National Union of Boot and Shoe Operatives would advocate nationalization of the boot and shoe industry if the general advancement of the industry on a planned basis, as suggested in the Board of Trade's Working Party Reports: Boot and Shoes (1946), was impeded by lack of support from the manufacturers. As it turned out, nationalization never happened and concern about it soon subsided.

in Andrews's theoretical view of the firm and neoclassical price theory. As a result of his research on manufacturing businesses, Andrews accumulated a great deal of data which, when viewed with an open mind, produced conclusions that were quite inconsistent with many of the propositions found in the theories of monopolistic competition and imperfect competition. For example, his investigations of Courtaulds, where the production of rayon was a tightly specified chemical process, and of the boot and shoe industry where production was arranged in terms of teams of machines led Andrews to view the organization of production in terms of plant segments which consisted of a specific combination of capital equipment, and material and labour inputs needed to produce a specific flow rate of output.(17) Consequently, if a firm constructed a plant that included many identical plant segments, then its short-period average direct cost curve would be horizontal, not upward sloping as depicted in neoclassical theory. In addition, Andrews adopted MacGregor's position that managerial organization was a technique which could be altered as the firm's scale of production increased (see Lee, 1989). Thus the firm's average managerial costs would decline not only in the short period when the managerial technique was given, but also in the long period when it could be altered. Therefore Andrews concluded that the firm's short- and long-period average total cost curves declined instead of being U-shaped as in neoclassical theory. One implication was that the neoclassical notions of the optimal size of the firm and firm equilibrium had no theoretical (or empirical) validity.

Through his analysis of the data, Andrews also became dissatisfied with the downward-sloping firm demand curve and its implication that manufacturing businesses could in some way control their sales through their price policy. In particular he rejected downward-sloping marginal revenue curves (and with them downward-sloping firm demand curves), and denied the relevance of the concept of short-period price elasticity of demand for analysing the price behaviour of

---

(17) Andrews was also familiar with Silverman's work on the boot and shoe industry, in which production was described in terms of plant segments. Plant segment production was also mentioned in the chapters on the lace and jute industries in *Studies in Industrial Organization* (Silverman, 1942 and 1946).

firms.(18) Rather it appeared to Andrews, in the light of his data, that goodwill was the decisive factor which determined a firm's *share* of market sales, while the level of national income determined *total* sales in the market in question. In addition, he became convinced by his analysis of the data that competitive markets need not be defined in terms of competition between firms producing identical products; that oligopoly was the normal characterization of markets; and that oligopolistic markets were competitive irrespective of the number of firms in them. Finally, as a result of his investigations, Andrews came to believe that manufacturing businesses did not think that it was a good policy to play about with their prices in the search for maximum profit, and that they did believe that their normal-cost pricing policy gave them the correct prices subject to the emergence of actual competition. Thus when trying to analyse the rayon industry in terms of conventional oligopoly theories such as the kinked demand curve and Joan Robinson's theory of imperfect competition and the boot and shoe industry in terms of Chamberlin's theory of monopolistic competition, he found that they simply did not fit the facts.(19) So Andrews began rejecting marginalism and replacing it with a more realistic analysis of costs and a new theory of the relation of businessmen to their markets (see Chapters 1–3 and 5; Andrews, 1953).

Drawing in part from his experiences with the OERG and the Nuffield College Social Reconstruction Survey, from his research with the Courtauld

---

(18) It was commonly argued during the 1930s and 1940s that the primary basis of the downward-sloping demand curve for the firm was consumer irrationality. Andrews rejected this argument not only for consumers but also for industrial buyers, who were generally the consumers of manufacturing businesses. Regarding industrial buyers, wholesalers, and retailers, he noted that it was illogical to assume, as neoclassical economists did, that firms acted rationally when setting prices and maximizing profits, but irrationally when buying their inputs: 'We cannot evolve falling demand curves on the basis of irrational preferences, without falling foul of the presumption of rational business behaviour which is required by all our analysis on the cost side' (Andrews, 1965, p. 4). Moreover, both groups of buyers, he argued, shopped around comparing prices, thus ensuring that all markets were both oligopolistic and competitive. By rejecting consumer irrationality, while simultaneously asserting that all industrial and consumer markets were oligopolistic, Andrews could clearly argue that the downward-sloping firm demand curve had no theoretical validity and must thus be discarded.

(19) Andrews rejected Chamberlin's theory of large-group monopolistic competition because he found that the six hundred firms in the boot and shoe industry operated in chains of oligopoly relationships (see Chapter 9). It is interesting to speculate, in this regard, whether J.N. Wolfe obtained his idea of chain oligopoly from Andrews — see Wolfe (1954 and 1981).

Inquiry, and from MacGregor's work on the firm, Andrews struggled to develop a new and different theory of the manufacturing business which included theories of normal-cost pricing and prices, explanation for price stability, and a delineation of the firm's environment.(20) In particular, his intellectual debt to Hall, Hitch, and the OERG was to their documentation of the widespread usage of cost-plus pricing systems by businessmen and of the 'ethical' arguments espoused by businessmen to defend the price they set as the 'right price'. Andrews came to realize that both sets of data implied a range of theoretical ideas regarding price-fixing and prices which were incommensurable with marginalism. However, the data collected by the OERG were not sufficient in themselves to enable Andrews to develop his theory of manufacturing business. What he lacked was detailed knowledge of individual manufacturing businesses. This was corrected through his work with the Survey and the Courtauld Inquiry.

During this period he became aware of the compatibility of his analysis with Marshall's theory of prices as applied to industrial markets (see the appendix to Chapter 2).(21) This awareness was reinforced through his relationship with MacGregor.(22) Andrews viewed MacGregor as a 'true-blue' pupil of Marshall and hence a source of an interpretation of Marshall that was uncontaminated by Pigou's equilibrium firm and Joan Robinson's theory of imperfect competition (both of which he felt were a betrayal of the Marshallian tradition). Moreover, MacGregor's own research on the firm provided Andrews with an example of Marshall's method of analysis in action, and with particular insights into the working of the firm which could not be found elsewhere.(23) Thus Andrews considered his theory of the manufacturing business to be the

---

(20) In the 1949 Hilary Term, Andrews gave a series of lectures on the theory of manufacturing business.

(21) It is of interest to note that in 1949 Andrews, in his tutorials, discussed *Manufacturing Business* as a critique of monopolistic competition and imperfect competition as applied to industrial pricing, and its links with Marshall's *Industry and Trade* were mentioned (Ford, 1981). At the same time, Andrews wrote a letter to Harold Macmillan saying that it was a shame that Marshall's *Industry and Trade* was out of print since the judgements Marshall made in the book still held true (Andrews, 1949a).

(22) Andrews renewed his contact with MacGregor when he first arrived at Oxford in 1937. This occurred partially through their participation in the OERG, their involvement in the Survey and the Courtauld Inquiry, and perhaps also by Andrews attending MacGregor's lectures on Marshall during the 1939 Hilary and Trinity terms.

(23) Thus, it is not surprising that Andrews dedicated *Manufacturing Business* to MacGregor who, in turn, valued the compliment and, in return, stated that 'few people could have done a piece of work like this and you have really done it' (MacGregor, 1949).

only legitimate descendant of Marshall's theory of prices as applied to industrial markets (Irving, 1978).

Andrews's first presentation of his theory of the manufacturing business appeared in an article in 1949 in *Oxford Economic Papers* (see Chapter 2), while the more complete version appeared later that year with the publication of *Manufacturing Business*. However, Andrews could not claim that he had produced a theoretical alternative to marginalism. In particular his analysis of the manufacturing business lacked a grounding in a theory of markets, a discussion of industry and markets, an analysis of retail trade and consumer behaviour, a discussion of firm investment decision-making, and a critique of marginalism.(24) Between 1950 and 1966, in a series of books and essays — the most notable being *Capital Development in Steel* (with Brunner, 1951), 'Industrial Analysis in Economics – With Especial Reference to Marshallian Doctrine' (1951), 'Competition in the Modern Economy' (1958), *Fair Trade* (with Friday, 1960), and 'Proof of Evidence' in the Net Book Agreement Case (1966) — Andrews corrected these omissions and by doing so transformed his theory of manufacturing business into a theory of markets, including industrial, retail trade and consumer markets, which will be denoted as the theory of competitive oligopoly. Incorporated in it were more general versions of his theories of normal cost pricing and prices.

Theory of competitive oligopoly, 1950–1966

The first task undertaken by Andrews in developing his theory of competitive oligopoly was to provide his analysis of manufacturing business with a more analytical grounding within Marshall's theory of prices. This included both a positive restatement of Marshall's theory and an extended discussion of the 'Marshallian' aspects of his theory of manufacturing business, and a critique of the Cambridge interpretation of Marshall and the subsequent development of microeconomics (see Chapters 3–5 and 9).(25) In particular, Andrews argued

---

(24) Early in the process of writing *Manufacturing Business* Andrews had thought of including a detailed review of marginalism; however he decided to delete the review in favour of a strictly positive presentation of his theory. This may also explain why he did not include any extended criticism of marginalism in his 1949 *Oxford Economic Papers* article (Andrews, 1948; and King, 1988).

(25) During the 1950 and 1951 Michaelmas Terms, Andrews lectured on 'the theory of price: Marshall and after' and on the 'theory of the firm', presenting normal-cost pricing as a development of ideas found in Marshall and revived by Hall and Hitch (Hallett, 1981).

that Marshall's deductive supply and demand theory of prices, which Pigou and the Cambridge economists latched on to, was only appropriate for those raw materials and agricultural markets in which firms faced increasing costs when expanding output, atomistic competition prevailed, and goodwill played no role between buyers and sellers. In such markets, equilibrium of the firm would be the basis of market equilibrium. However, when dealing with industrial markets, Andrews argued, Marshall found that his deductive theory was no longer appropriate and thus did not use it. As a result, market equilibrium was reduced to price uniformity among the firms, but in doing this, Andrews concluded, Marshall was left with no theory of the firm that was consistent with his analysis of industrial markets.

Finding Marshall's analysis of markets compatible with his theory of manufacturing business, Andrews sought to integrate both:

> ... referring to Alfred Marshall's theory ... so far as the industry goes, I see no essential difference. Where I differ from Marshall is that I have provided a theory of the firm which fits into his theory of value, and which is flexible enough for practical use (Andrews, 1953).

In doing so, he defined an industry along Marshallian lines, i.e. in terms of processes instead of products; this permitted the existence of more than one firm in any market and of potential competitors. The end result was a theory of industrial markets in which Andrews's theory of manufacturing business provided the firm-theoretic foundation for a Marshallian market equilibrium, or what Andrews called a 'steady-state' situation in which market prices were stable. He then extended his analysis of industrial markets to include explanations for market instability or breakdowns of steady-state situations. With these additional developments, Andrews extended his theory of industrial markets beyond Marshall (Irving, 1978; Andrews, 1964b; and Andrews and Brunner, 1975).

Simultaneously with his reinterpretation of Marshall, Andrews developed a critique of Pigou, Joan Robinson, and the modern developments in microeconomics:

> I (Andrews) think that one of the biggest disasters in English economic theory has been the abandonment of the general Marshallian view of the working of manufacturing industry, and the adoption of the misleading doctrines of monopolistic competition — misleading because they appeal, first of all, to a concept of pure competition, which cannot apply in manufacturing industry: if you imagine any manufacturing industry operating as competitively as possible then the ordinary doctrines of pure competition could not apply. Things do not work that way (Andrews, 1949b, p. 8).

He began this in the late 1940s, while writing *Manufacturing Business*, with a lecture on 'Post-Marshallian Developments in the Theory of Business Behaviour' which he gave at Southampton University College, and further developed it in the 1950s (see Chapters 3–6, and 9). However, his most systematic discussion occurred in 1964 with the publication of *On Competition in Economic Theory* (Andrews, 1964b).(26) Andrews argued that the works of Pigou, the Cambridge economists, and E.H. Chamberlin were misdirected when they applied their version of Marshall's deductive system to industrial and retail or consumer markets. In addition, he directly challenged marginalist equilibrium methodology, dismissing not only demand curves for the firm, but also reversible cost curves, the independence of cost and demand functions, and the *equilibrium of the firm*, which he considered to be the fundamental principle of marginalism. Thus, Andrews argued, manufacturing and retailing businesses neither maximized profits along marginalist lines, nor could be captured by models based on equilibrium of the firm.(27) Finally, he dismissed subsequent developments in oligopoly theory because of their reliance on marginalist methodology.(28) Thus, in carrying out his critique, Andrews reinforced his claim that he was the true heir of Marshall, and differentiated his theory of competitive oligopoly from marginalism (Irving, 1978; Nuffield College, 1950; and Andrews, 1964b).

The second undertaking by Andrews in developing his theory of competitive oligopoly was to extend his analysis of industrial markets to retail trade and consumer behaviuor. His first attempt in this area was an article on retail trade in 1950 (see Chapter 6); he returned to the topic briefly in 1958 (see Chapter 9) and more extensively in 1960 (see Chapter 7) and in 1964 and 1966 (Andrews, 1964b and 1966a). Interspersed among his comments on retail trade were many statements on consumer behaviour that, when put together, constituted a significant development of his theory of competitive oligopoly. Andrews recognized that retail markets differed from industrial markets, not because of differences on the side of firms, but because of differences among the buyers. That is, he saw no substantial difference between manufacturing and retailing businesses in terms of pricing and entrepreneurial motivation. However,

---

(26) The book was in print from 1964 to 1976 with total sales of 4611, of which 2312 were in the UK and 1335 in the US (Handford, 1990).

(27) What Andrews was dismissing was the assumption that the actual behaviour of the firm can be captured by firm equilibrium models. Without this assumption, marginalism has nothing to say about the real world; this was Andrews's position.

(28) Andrews also found fault with the behaviouralist approach to the firm because he believed it would allow economists the comfort of teaching static marginalism as relevant to a more efficient world (Andrews, 1964a, 1964b.

Andrews did recognize that the rationale of consumer buying behaviour was different from the behaviour of industrial buyers, with the result that the form of retail competitive behaviour was somewhat different from that found in industrial markets. In particular, he saw consumer choice as based on a hierarchical process, given a level of income or budget. That is, the consumer would simplify the task of making choices by thinking at various mental levels of preference, one of which involved forming budget ranges to act as a filter for goods of inferior quality or excessive costs. Thus consumers would plan on visiting those stores whose prices, in past experience, promise to enable them to obtain a larger basket of acceptable quality goods, and hence a higher standard of living, than others. Consequently, price competition on particular goods among competing retail businesses should not be seen, Andrews argued, as a means of boosting net earnings on the individual products in question. Rather, such price competition should be seen as aimed at changing the stores which consumers were most likely to visit on their shopping expeditions.

The last undertaking by Andrews involved developing and elaborating particular features of his theory of competitive oligopoly. One such endeavour involved an extended discussion of competitive oligopoly in practice, the intrinsic competitiveness of large firms, and the role of internal management competition in driving the manufacturing and retailing business to be more efficient and competitive in the market (see Chapters 9 and 10). A second endeavour involved delineating private and public market organizations, such as cartels, price leadership, and government agencies, through which firms collectively fixed market prices. Elaboration on this point became necessary once Andrews had explicitly situated his manufacturing and retailing businesses within a market which included other firms. To this end, he briefly discussed cartels and price leadership with regard to collective price-fixing (see Chapters 5, 6 and 9, and Andrews and Brunner, 1951).(29) Andrews also made detailed studies of restrictive trade agreements in the water-tube boiler and book industries which were designed to support industry price stability and hence the stability of the structure of industry or the size distribution of the firms producing the goods in question (Andrews, 1966a; and Andrews and Brunner, 1975).

The third feature of the theory that Andrews developed concerned capital development and the factors which influenced management when making investment decisions. In his initial presentation of his theory of manufacturing business, Andrews did not discuss the factors which influenced the growth of the

---

(29) Andrews engaged in a systematic study of an international cartel in the 1950s, but the work was never published. It should also be noted that Andrews did not delineate any general statements about collective pric- fixing, thus making it one of the less developed features of his theory.

firm. In particular he presented no discussion of the investment decision-making process or the factors which determined the kind of capital development desired by the firm. To rectify this he undertook a case study of the capital development of a British steel company, *Capital Development in Steel: A Study of The United Steel Companies Ltd.* (Andrews and Brunner, 1951) and further developed his ideas in his lectures on investment decisions given during the 1951 Hilary term and in a lecture to the Lancashire Section of the Textile Institute (see Chapter 8). In his discussion, Andrews argued that one of the important factors affecting the direction and pace of the firm's capital development was the ability of management to adjust to the requirements of the new technology being put in place. As for the investment decision-making process, he noted that the level of desired investment was an increasing function of present sales, that the decision to undertake specific investment projects was based on existing cash resources and an earnings criterion, and that neither the level of the interest rate nor variations in that level affected management's decision on any specific investment project.

The failure of a promise

Upon the publication of *Manufacturing Business*, Andrews's theory of normal cost pricing was subject to withering criticism from neoclassical economists. The story of this controversy has been dealt with elsewhere (see Irving, 1978; and Lee and Irving-Lessmann, 1992; also see the appendix to Chapter 5), but it is interesting to note that many orthodox economists advised him to confine his attention to an empirical description of particular industries. In this light, it is important to note that it occurred at the same time (1950–1953) as J.R. Hicks and N. Chester were trying to prevent the renewal of his Nuffield Fellowship which came up for renewal in 1953. At issue were Andrews's qualifications as an economist and, perhaps, his unpopular personal beliefs, that is being a conscientious objector during the war, and his positive view of capitalism and the businessman. Concurrently, D. Champernowne was keen on getting Jack Downie as a Research Fellow and had convinced Chester of the idea. Thus it appears that Andrews and Downie were competing for the same position, and in spite of the low opinion Chester, Hicks, and even Hall (who was no longer at Oxford) had of his abilities, Andrews did retain his Fellowship partially through the helpful intervention of Clay. Clay's intervention on Andrews's behalf was unsurprising, since he was a Marshallian in the MacGregor tradition and therefore felt that it was a tragedy that so much theoretical speculation went on without continuous and natural contact with the everyday business of life.

Andrews's reaction to this institutional attack probably contributed to his reluctance to defend his theory publicly; it may have also contributed to his turning away after 1953 from systematic development of his theory of competitive oligopoly to work more with businessmen. For example, he published (with Brunner) a biography of Lord Nuffield and a business history of an Oxford manufacturing company (Andrews and Brunner, 1959 and 1965). He also developed a considerable expertise in anti-monopoly legislation and between 1958 and 1962 acted as a consultant in cases before the Restrictive Practices Court (Andrews, 1961 and 1966a; and Andrews and Brunner, 1975). Consequently, Andrews never wrote a book in which he presented his theory of competitive oligopoly in a systematic manner, especially in the light of work done by sympathetic theorists, such as the work by H.R. Edwards and P. Sylos-Labini on the determinants of the costing margin, (30) and G. B. Richardson on co-operative price-fixing.(31) Thus the promise of a well-developed alternative to marginalism, which seemed quite imminent in 1952, never materialized (King, 1988; Andrews, 1954 and 1964a; Hall, 1989; and Wilson, 1971).

Other activities, 1941–1971

Andrews did not spend all of his energies or time developing his theory of competitive oligopoly. In 1947, Harrod and he revived the OERG. Continuing its prewar traditions, the chairman would invite a businessman or trade unionist to Oxford for dinner and then have him face the questions of the Oxford

---

(30) Andrews never formally commented on Edwards's and Sylos-Labini's work; however he did correspond with Sylos-Labini about it. The correspondence suggests that Andrews did not think that Sylos-Labini added much new to the 'theory' of the determination of the costing margin. In particular, he claimed that he had further developed his treatment of the costing margin in Manufacturing Business in an unpublished paper (written in 1951) entitled 'A Note on Some Economic Limits to the Attainment of Maximum Technical Efficiency in a Manufacturing Industry'. He further noted that many of the ideas in the paper later appeared in 'Competition in the Modern Economy' (see Chapter 9) and in a 1956 article in *Revue Economique*. However, such claims have not been accepted by economists sympathetic to his work (Andrews, 1966b and 1966c; and Sylos-Labini, 1966).

(31) *Studies in Pricing* appeared after Andrews's death in 1971 and consisted in part of three essays written by Andrews between 1958 and 1967 — one essay on the crisis in microeconomic theory, a second on the restrictive trade agreement of the Water-Tube Boilermakers' Association, and the third on the building industry; however, they did not present his theory in any systematic manner. The book stayed in print from 1975 to 1981 and 1082 copies were sold, 433 in the UK, 6 in the US, and 643 elsewhere (Handford, 1990).

economists. The post-war OERG was not so interested in theoretical issues; rather it concentrated initially on topics suggested by the performance of the post-war British economy, such as industrial productivity, the pricing policy of exporting firms with respect to changes in exchange rates, and the theory of investment decisions. Later, other topics, such as pay settlements, were explored. Members of the Group also presented papers for the members to discuss and criticize. Andrews was the Group's secretary until 1952, at which point Brunner took over the position; and he remained a member until 1957 when other demands on his time forced him to resign. The Group's inquiries on productivity and the theory of investment decisions was of particular help to Andrews's own work on capital development and the investment decision-making process. In 1949, he presented a paper on investment theory to the Group (Andrews and Brunner, 1950; Streeten, 1986; Champernowne, 1981; Clegg, 1981; and Hargreaves, 1973).

Andrews also devoted some of his energies to making the empirical study of industry a respectable academic activity and to making economic theory relevant to the needs of the businessman (see Chapters 11 and 12). In pursuance of the latter objective, Andrews helped to found the Oxford Management Club and became involved with numerous committees concerned with management education. To achieve the former objective, in 1952 he resigned as secretary to *Oxford Economic Papers* in order to establish the *Journal of Industrial Economics*.

The purpose of the *Journal* was to encourage both academic and industrial economists to use economic analysis when writing on industrial and commercial topics.(32) Being a journal devoted to industrial economics, it did not have the stature of the leading journals, such as the *Economic Journal*, the *American Economic Review*, the *Review of Economics and Statistics*, and the like; however among industrial economists, it was widely read and regarded as the leader for the subject area, as evident by the fact that circulation increased from a little over two hundred in 1952 to over eleven hundred in 1964. In fact, it laid the groundwork for much that came later in 'managerial' economics. As General Editor of the *Journal*, Andrews devoted much energy to getting good work into print and discussed. His use of referees and advisors, combined with his reliance on his editors, ensured that the academic quality of the *Journal* was, by and large,

---

(32) The *Journal* also provided Andrews and other economists who were sympathetic to his theory of competitive oligopoly with a place to publish their papers, since many economic journals were virtually closed to them.

respectable.(33) After his death, the General Editorship of the Journal was taken over by Brunner, who held it until shortly before her death in 1983 (Carter, 1990; Preston, 1991; and Adelman, 1991).(34)

As well as being a research economist, Andrews was also a teacher. Beginning in 1941, he took over tutorial responsibilities at New College from E.H. Phelps Brown, who had gone off to war. He obtained the position with Phelps Brown's help and with the backing of the acting warden of New College, A.H. Smith, and retained it after the war when Phelps Brown returned until

---

(33) However, Andrews was disappointed at how few papers from Continental Europe were sent to the *Journal* for consideration and, when considering the few that were sent, he was inclined to lower the standards a bit in order to publish them (Adelman, 1991).

(34) After Andrews's death, the content of the *Journal* became more and more based on neoclassical price theory. According to both D.A. Hay (General Editor from 1983 to 1988) and S.W. Davies (General Editor from 1988 to the present), this drift towards neoclassicalism was not consciously planned; rather, the *Journal* was following the state of the discipline in which industrial economics was being simply a branch of applied neoclassical microtheory. As Hay has argued:

[I]t was evident by the late 70s that the quality of the material being published was slipping, and that was beginning to show in circulation figures and in the esteem in which the *Journal* was held within the profession. Submissions were also falling. My response to this situation, encouraged by the publishers, was to take steps to promote the *Journal* generally, and to encourage more authors to submit articles. This was also the line taken by Larry White in North America, when he took over from Michael Mann. In practice, of course, an Editor has to rely on the material submitted, and in the mid-80s the *Journal* was not in a position to be particularly choosy. We published the best of what we got. There were very few submissions that reflected Andrews' position, and the quality was invariably low. So we did not publish them. I had no great personal enthusiasm for some of the more theoretical pieces submitted which we in fact published. But they were well done, and received good referee's reports. A particular disappointment for me was the lack of good 'industry' or 'business' studies. But I believe that may have been a passing phase in the discipline, and more recent empirical work is focusing attention on 'case studies'. To sum up, I think the Journal reflected the state of the discipline in the 70s and 80s, and that was not particularly favourable to the approaches favoured by Philip Andrews (Hay, 1991).

However, since the General Editors have a typical '*JIE* reader' in mind when deciding on what papers to publish and have created a cohort of referees based on personal acquaintance and contacts at conferences, the *Journal*'s move towards neoclassical price was immeasurably quickened. As unfortunate as it was to those economists who favour Andrews's approach to industrial economics, the move did pay off, for subscriptions are now around two thousand.

1948.(35) During this period Andrews lectured on statistical method, the theory of value, and the economics of manufacturing industry. After 1948 he specialized in graduate work, lecturing on Marshall, investment decisions, and the theory of the firm, while at the same time developing a graduate seminar in the economics of industry.(36)

By most accounts, Andrews was not a good lecturer, although to some he was charismatic. This perception may have been due to his approach in teaching economic theory, in which, following Cannan and Ford, he worked from the perspective of the evolution of the theory. His graduate seminar, on the other hand, was quite successful. As D.A. Hay recalls,

> I attended his graduate seminar in his last year at Nuffield, and I owe to him my own interest in industrial economics. I recall particularly his enthusiasm for the subject, and his insistence that the subject should address issues arising from the actual workings of business and markets, and not pseudo problems invented by theorists (Hay, 1991).

Moreover, as a tutor he was outstanding (Hargreaves, 1973; Hallett, 1981; Andrews, 1964a; and Brunner, 1971). This contrast in effectiveness as a teacher is brought out in the following passages by Alan Bevan, who was a student of Andrews at the University of Lancaster between 1969 and 1971:

> His (Andrews's) lecture style was not popular. He did not normally impart information, but rather sought to awaken understanding. Many gave up note-taking in despair, and from a few lectures I would sometimes have only a half a page or less of notes. Often, especially when heard for the first time, his lectures were hard to follow. There was something elusive and baffling, though always stimulating, in his style, which stirred the mind, but, except for a telling phrase or unexpected illustration, left little in the memory. But there would sometimes come through to us a sense of fellowship in exploration, for his manner was easy, and he seemed supremely happy in the lecture room. He brought notes, but I doubt if he really followed them. He would often begin a lecture by announcing what it would be about, and then at the end you were left with a slight feeling of having been cheated, for he invariably did not talk about what he said he would

---

(35) In 1948, Andrews applied for a fellowship in economics at New College, but the position was awarded to Peter Wiles. It should be noted that one benefit Andrews received while at New College was that he could talk with Isaiah Berlin about his methodology (Andrews, 1964a).

(36) According to Brunner, Andrews refused to teach his theory at Oxford because a senior Oxford economist suggested that he would indoctrinate students. Since Andrews was teaching his theory up until at least 1952, his refusal must have occurred after this date (Brunner, 1971).

— often chasing after a new line of thought or reminiscing about meetings with various economists and, particularly, businessmen. Occasionally he would invite questions or ask for answers — and always there was the embarrassing silence, for no-one dared speak up knowing that even if the question was good or the answer correct, he would go on to show how even a correct answer was in a way, wrong. No, few people were bold enough in such circumstances to speak under Andrews' intent and expectant gaze.

He gave one seminar a week to the same group of six students chosen at random at the beginning of the Session. I was lucky enough to be in his group for the first two terms of the 1969/70 Session. We met in his room each Monday afternoon for an hour. The room was clustered with objects of art — statues, paintings and sculptures (many of which he had probably made himself, for oil-painting and sculpture were amongst his most favourite pastimes) — and thick with the odour of pipe tobacco. It was in such informal meetings that his magnetic personality really showed through. He had an uncanny feeling for what each of us was thinking and would often stop what he was saying in mid-sentence and ask one of us by name, to say out aloud the question that had just begun to puzzle us. He loved to puzzle and perplex you and then suddenly dazzle you with unexpected light. Indeed the style of his lectures may be well described as 'Ages of darkness and moments of vision'. What one brought away from such lectures depended a lot on what one already knew. I found little in them the first time through, but when I went along for a repeat the next year (these were second year under-graduate lectures) I enjoyed them much more because I could then understand a few more of the oblique references and innuendoes. It was thus during this second hearing that I began to understand the source of his real genius. Alas this second Session (1970/71) saw him much sicker than the first. He gave most of the lectures in the Michaelmas term, but only one or two at the beginning of the Lent term. Miss Brunner took over from then on, and he died early in March, 1971.

His lectures certainly did not impart any ordered knowledge of economics, and not enough for passing an examination. Those in the audience who really thought with him each Tuesday morning, came away mainly with an awakened interest, a little more insight, the memory of some moment of illumination and a sense of the importance of economics. Few can have remained unaffected however, by his unbounded enthusiasm, dedication and personal integrity.

While visiting Harvard in the Spring of 1966, Andrews became seriously ill; he was later disgnosed as having cancer. The illness left him lethargic and unable to carry out all the work he wanted to do, but it did not stop him from taking on new duties. In 1967, he left Nuffield College to become Professor of Economics at the University of Lancaster, whose founding Vice-Chancellor was Charles Carter, the distinguished economist and editor of the *Economic Journal*. This move was, in part, prompted by the unfair and even discriminatory treatment of Brunner by Nuffield College, but it also gave Andrews the chance to appoint many young staff in a rapidly growing department and shape its pattern of teaching. Thus although the move meant that Andrews no longer had to contend with the kinds of pressures that Oxford had presented, it was hardly a stress-free environment in which he chose to live out the last few years of his life. However, he could at least be relaxed in the knowledge that, unlike most senior British academic economists, Charles Carter shared his enthusiasm for case study work industrial economics and his doubts about standard theories of investment decision-making (see Carter and Williams, 1958). Andrews threw himself at his administrative load with gusto, making it quite clear that it was what he had wanted (Westall, 1992). But his time was rapidly running out: less than five years after he moved to Lancaster, Brunner and some of his friends were looking for ways to ensure that his work would not be forgotten.(37)

---

(37) As a tribute to his memory and in an attempt to foster the development of Andrews's life work in industrial economics and theory of the firm, Brunner and a number of Andrews's friends established three awards at the University of Lancaster. With a donation from the Resale Price Maintenance Co-ordinating Committee, the Philip Andrews memorial book prize was established in 1973. The prize consisted of books to the value of £10 (later increased to £25) to be awarded to the undergraduate with the best performance in Part I economics. In 1972, the Philip Andrews memorial studentship was established which would provide free residence at Lonsdale College, University of Lancaster, for a student reading for the degree of Ph.D. Finally, in 1971, the P.W.S. Andrews memorial essay prize (initially for £100, but later increased to £300) was established to be awarded for the best original essay by a young scholar within the general field of industrial economics and the theory of the firm. In addition the essay had to be made available for publication in the *Journal*. The prize was first advertised in 1973 and was first awarded in the same year. From 1973 to 1985 the prize was awarded eight times to nine individuals, including T.J. Hazledine (1973), K.E. Scott (1975), D.W. Carlton (1977), D. Fixler (1979), L. Young (1979), R.L. Smith (1980), M.R. Burns (1981), S. Lanning (1984), and H.D. Dixon (1985). The essays by Hazledine (1974), Scott (1976), Carlton (1979), Smith (1981), and Burns (1983) also appeared in the *Journal*, while a variant of Fixler's paper appeared in *Economica* (Fixler, 1983) and Dixon's paper appeared in *Oxford Economic Papers* (Dixon, 1986). However, it is by no means obvious that the accepted and published essays in fact fostered the development of Andrews's life work in industrial economics and the theory of the firm; rather it would appear that the essays fostered the developed of mainstream industrial economics of which he was not a part. It is also important to note that the link between the essay prize and the *Journal* was established and maintained by Brunner; consequently, with her death the relationship became more tenuous and eventually ceased to exist. As a result, the *Journal* ceased to advertise the prize, thus severing the last link with its not-so neoclassical founder (Cockburn, 1992; and McClintock, 1992).

Despite its tragic aspect, the move by Andrews and Brunner to Lancaster can be judged successful in both instances, especially with regard to the deserved professional advancement and recognition awarded to Brunner (Carter, 1990; and Phillips, 1991). But the move epitomized Andrews's place within the economics profession. Considered to be far outside the mainstream of industrial economics, he had no real hope of advancement at Oxford or of a worthwhile move to an economics department in any other well-established university dominated by mainstream thinkers; thus any change from his Oxford appointment necessarily meant a move to a new university. The move could not be expected to have a major impact on the status of Andrews's work in the eyes of mainstream industrial economists, and with the growing formalism of modern industrial economics his style of research might have appeared doomed to be ignored. However, in the two decades since his death, increasing tendencies towards methodological debate in economics were followed by a steady growth of interest in Andrews's work, particularly among younger scholars, many of whom teach at newer universities. After discovering his contributions (often purely by chance), this younger generation of heterodox economists has tended to take the view that Andrews's research output was potentially revolutionary in its content and deserved to have made a bigger impact, especially with regard to developing a non-neoclassical theory of markets. This selection of readings is an attempt to foster progress in this direction.

References

Adelman, M.A. (1991) Personal communication, 13 May.

Andrews, P.W.S. (1937) 'Post-war public companies: a study in investment and enterprise', *Economic Journal* **47**, September, pp. 500–10.

Andrews, P.W.S. (1940) 'A further inquiry into the effects of rates of interest,' *Oxford Economic Papers* **3**, February, pp. 32–73.

Andrews, P.W.S. (1943a) 'Objects', 6 March, G.D.H. Cole Papers, Nuffield College, Oxford.

Andrews, P.W.S. (1943b) 'Notes on meeting with Mr. S. Courtauld and with Mr. R.A. Kinnes of Courtauld Ltd. 19 October 1943', 20 October, G.D.H. Cole Papers, Nuffield College, Oxford.

Andrews, P.W.S. (1943c) 'Report of meeting with Mr. R.A. Kinnes (Director and Accountant) and with Mr. H.A. Bingham (Statistician) at Courtaulds's London Office. 8th November 1943', 9 November, G.D.H. Cole Papers, Nuffield College, Oxford.

Andrews, P.W.S. (1943d) 'Notes on economies of scale in the viscous continuous filament yarn section of the rayon industry', 17 November,

G.D.H. Cole Papers, Nuffield College, Oxford.

Andrews, P.W.S. (1944a) 'Report from the "accountancy" side of the pilot inquiry into the relative efficiency of small and large scale business', May, G.D.H. Cole Papers, Nuffield College, Oxford.

Andrews, P.W.S. (1944b) 'Some suggestions on the future programme of the Courtauld inquiry', September, G.D.H. Cole Papers, Nuffield College, Oxford.

Andrews, P.W.S. (1944c) 'Report on visit to British Enka Limited, at Aintree. 11–14 September 1944', October, G.D.H. Cole Papers, Nuffield College, Oxford.

Andrews, P.W.S. (1944d) 'Report on visit to Breda Visada Ltd., at Littleborough. 9–11 October 1944', October, G.D.H. Cole Papers, Nuffield College, Oxford.

Andrews, P. W. S. (1944e) 'Inquiry into the relative efficiency of small and large scale business,' December, G.D.H. Cole Papers, Nuffield College, Oxford.

Andrews, P.W.S. (1946a) Letter to Henry Clay, 6 September. P.W.S. Andrews Papers, London School of Economics, London.

Andrews, P.W.S. (1946b) Letter to H. Macmillan, 17 August, P.W.S. Andrews Papers, London School of Economics, London.

Andrews, P.W.S. (1948) Letter to H. Macmillan, 25 November, P.W.S. Andrews Papers, London School of Economics, London.

Andrews, P.W.S. (1949a) Letter to H. Macmillan, 15 January, P.W.S. Andrews Papers, London School of Economics, London.

Andrews, P.W.S. (1949b) 'Comments', Nuffield College Twenty-Fifth Private Conference: 'The Problems of Large-Scale Industrial Organisations Including the Nationalised Industries. Session IV', July 1–3, Nuffield College, Oxford.

Andrews, P.W.S. (1949c) *Manufacturing Business*, London, Macmillan.

Andrews, P.W.S. (1953) Letter to A. Silberston, 23 March, In the possession of A. Silberston.

Andrews, P.W.S. (1954) 'Sir Henry Clay', *Journal of Industrial Economics* 3, December, pp. 1–8.

Andrews, P.W.S. (1961) 'The Registrar's Report', *The Lawyer* 4, Trinity, pp. 15–20, 44.

Andrews, P.W.S. (1964a) Letter to R.A. Hodgson, 1 December, P.W.S. Andrews Papers, London School of Economics, London.

Andrews, P.W.S. (1964b) *On Competition in Economic Theory*, London, Macmillan.

Andrews, P.W.S. (1965) 'Fundamental errors in the orthodox theory of the firm', P.W.S. Andrews Papers, London School of Economics, London.

Andrews, P.W.S. (1966a) 'P.W.S. Andrews: proof of evidence', in *Books Are*

Different, pp. 513–607, edited by R.E. Barker and G.R. Davies, London, Macmillan.

Andrews, P.W.S. (1966b) Letter to Paolo Sylos-Labini, 16 July, P.W.S. Andrews Papers, London School of Economics, London.

Andrews, P.W.S. (1966c) Letter to Paolo Sylos-Labini, 9 September, P.W.S. Andrews Papers, London School of Economics, London.

Andrews, P.W.S. and Brunner, E. (1950) 'Productivity and the business man', *Oxford Economic Papers* 2, June, pp. 197–225.

Andrews, P.W.S. and Brunner, E. (1951) *Capital Development in Steel*, Oxford, Basil Blackwell.

Andrews, P.W.S. and Brunner, E. (1959) *The Life of Lord Nuffield*, Oxford, Basil Blackwell.

Andrews, P.W.S. and Brunner, E. (1965) *The Eagle Ironworks Oxford*, London, Mills & Boon.

Andrews, P.W.S. and Brunner, E. (1975) *Studies in Pricing*, London: Macmillan.

Bellamy, R. (1981) Personal communication, 10 September.

Bingham, H.L. (1944) Letter to Samuel Courtauld, 10 July, G.D.H. Cole Papers, Nuffield College, Oxford.

Board of Trade (1946) *Working Party Reports: Boot and Shoe*, London, His Majesty's Stationery Office.

Brunner, E. (1945) *Holiday Making and the Holiday Trades*, London, Oxford University Press.

Brunner, E. (1971) 'Prof. P.W.S. Andrews', *London Times*, 20 March, p. 14.

Brunner, E. (1979) Personal communication, 5 March.

Burns, M.R. (1981) 'An empirical analysis of stockholder injury under section 2 of the Sherman Act', *Journal of Industrial Economics* 31, June, pp. 333–62.

Cannan, E. (1914) *Wealth*, London, P.S. King & Son.

Carlton, D.W. (1979) 'Vertical integration in competitive markets under uncertainty', *Journal of Industrial Economics* 27, March, pp. 189–209.

Carter, C.F. (1990) Personal communication, 23 November.

Carter, C.F. and Williams, B.R. (1958) *Investment in Innovation*, Oxford, Oxford University Press

Champernowne, D.G. (1981) Personal communication, 20 July.

Chester, N. (1986) *Economics, Politics and Social Studies in Oxford, 1900–85*, London, The Macmillan Press Ltd.

Clay, Sir Henry. (1944) Letter to Samuel Courtauld, 26 July, G.D.H. Cole Papers, Nuffield College, Oxford.

Clegg, H.A. (1981) Personal communication, 11 August.

Cockburn, G.M. (1992) Personal communication, 13 January.

Cole, G.D.H. (1943) Letter to Samuel Courtauld, 4 March, G.D.H. Cole Papers, Nuffield College, Oxford.

Coleman, D.C. (1980) *Courtaulds: An Economic and Social History*, Oxford, Oxford University Press.

Courtauld, S. (1943a) Letter to G.D.H. Cole, 3 March, G.D.H. Cole Papers, Nuffield College, Oxford.

Courtauld, S. (1943b) Letter to G.D.H. Cole, 9 March, G.D.H. Cole Papers, Nuffield College, Oxford.

Courtauld, S. (1943c) Letter to G.D.H. Cole, 4 June, G.D.H. Cole Papers, Nuffield College, Oxford.

Courtauld, S. (1944) Letter to G.D.H. Cole, 12 July, G.D.H. Cole Papers, Nuffield College, Oxford.

Courtauld Sub-Committee (1943-1946) Minutes, G.D.H. Cole Papers, Nuffield College, Oxford.

Discussion with Mr. Courtauld (1943) 3 April, G.D.H. Cole Papers, Nuffield College, Oxford.

Dixon, H. (1986) 'Strategic investment with consistent conjectures', *Oxford Economic Papers* 38, November, pp. 111–28.

Fixler, D. (1983) 'Uncertainty, market structure and the incentive to invent', *Economica* 50, November, pp. 401–23.

Fogarty, M.P. (1945) *Prospects of the Industrial Areas of Great Britain*, London, Methuen & Co. Ltd.

Fogarty, M.P. (1948) *Further Studies in Industrial Organization*, London, Methuen & Co. Ltd.

Fogarty, M.P. (1981) Personal communication, 29 October.

Ford, A. (1981) Personal communication, 10 September.

Ford, P. (1935) 'Excessive competition in the retail trades: changes in the number of shops, 1901-1931', *Economic Journal* 45, September, pp. 501–8.

Ford, P. (1936) 'Decentralisation and changes in the number of shops, 1901-1931', *Economic Journal* 46, June, pp. 359–63.

Ford, P. and White, G.V. (1936) 'Trends in retail distribution in Yorkshire (West Riding)', *Manchester School of Economics and Social Studies* 7, pp. 119–25.

Hall, R. (1989) *The Robert Hall Diaries 1947–53*, edited by A. Cairncross, London, Unwin Hyman.

Hallett, G. (1981) Personal communication, 7 September.

Handford, J. (1990) Personal communication, 5 October.

Hargreaves, E. L. (1973) *Memoirs*, Oxford, Bocardo Press.

Hay, D.A. (1991) Personal communication, 14 October.

Hazledine. T. (1974) 'Employment and output functions for New Zealand manufacturing industries', *Journal of Industrial Economics* **22**, March, pp. 161–98.

Hodgson, R. A. (1990) Personal communication, 2 November.

Industrial and Planning Sub-Committee (1944) Minutes, Nuffield College Social Reconstruction Survey Papers, Nuffield College, Oxford.

Institute of Statistics (1938) *Annual Report for the Academic Year 1937–38*, Oxford, Oxford University Press.

Institute of Statistics (1939) *Annual Report for the Academic Year 1938–39*, Oxford, Oxford University Press.

Institute of Statistics (1940) *Annual Report for the Academic Year 1939–40*, Oxford, Oxford University Press.

Irving, J. (1978) 'P.W.S. Andrews and the unsuccessful revolution', D. Phil. thesis, The University of Wollongong.

Keynes, J.M. (1930) *A Treatise on Money*, London, Macmillan.

Keynes, J.M. (1936) *The General Theory of Employment, Interest and Money*, London, Macmillan.

King, J.E. (1988) *Economic Exiles*, New York, St. Martin's Press.

Knight, F.H. (1921) *Risk, Uncertainty and Profit*, Boston, Houghton Mifflin.

Lee, F.S. (1985) '"Kalecki's pricing theory": two comments', *Journal of Post Keynesian Economics* **8**, Fall, pp. 145–8.

Lee, F.S. (1989) 'D.H. MacGregor and the firm: a neglected chapter in the history of the Post Keynesian theory of the firm', *British Review of Economic Issues* **11**, Spring, pp. 21–47.

Lee, F.S. and Irving-Lessmann, J. (1992) 'The fate of an errant hypothesis: the doctrine of normal cost prices', *History of Political Economy* **24**, Summer, pp. 273–309.

MacGregor, D.H. (1949) Letter to P.W.S. Andrews, 14 June, P.W.S. Andrews Papers, London School of Economics, London.

Marshall, A. (1920) *Principles of Economics* (8th edn), London, Macmillan.

McClintock, M.E. (1992) Personal communication, 9 April.

Meade, J.E. and Andrews, P.W.S. (1938) 'Summary of replies to questions on effects of interest rates', *Oxford Economic Papers* **1**, October, pp. 14–31.

Mises, L. von (1912) *The Theory of Money and Credit* (3rd English edn, 1981), Indianapolis, Liberty Press.

Nuffield College (1948) 'Annual reports and accounts, 1946–7', *Oxford University Gazette* **78**, 23 January, pp. 421–5.

Nuffield College (1950) 'Report for the year 1948-9 to the Hebdomadal Council and the Trustees', *Oxford University Gazette* **80**, 10 March, pp. 601–4.

Phillips, A. (1991) Personal communication, 20 May.

Pigou, A.C. (1920) *Economics of Welafare* London, Macmillan.

Preston, L.E. (1991) Personal communication, 6 June.

Progress Report (1941–1944) Nuffield College Social Reconstruction Survey Papers, Nuffield College, Oxford.

Robson, K. (1990) Personal communication, 23 October.

Scott, K. (1976) 'Investment in private industrial research and development in Britain', *Journal of Industrial Economics* 25, pp. 81-99.

Shannon, H.A. (1931) 'The coming of general liability', *Economic History* 2, January, pp. 267–91.

Shannon, H.A. (1932) 'The first five thousand limited companies and their duration', *Economic History* 3, January, pp. 396–424.

Shannon, H.A. (1933) 'The limited companies of 1866–1883', *Economic History Review* 4, October, pp. 290–316.

Silverman, H.A. (1942) 'The optimum firm in the boot and shoe industry', *Oxford Economic Papers* 6, April, pp. 95–111.

Silverman, H.A. (ed.) (1946) *Studies in Industrial Organization*, London, Methuen & Co. Ltd.

Smith, R.L. (1981) 'Efficiency gains from strategic investment', *Journal of Industrial Economics* 30, September, pp. 1–23.

Social Science Research Committee (1935–1945) Minutes, Oxford University Archives, UDC/R/9/1.

Steindl, J. (1945) *Small and Big Business: Economic Problems of the Size of Firms*, Oxford, Basil Blackwell.

Steindl, J. (1952) *Maturity and Stagnation in American Capitalism*. Oxford, Basil Blackwell.

Steindl, J. (1981) Interview, 2 September, Trieste, Italy.

Streeten, P. (1986) Personal communication, 18 September.

Sylos-Labini, P. (1966) Letter to P.W.S. Andrews, 3 September, P.W.S. Andrews Papers, London, London School of Economics.

Tress, R.C. (1990) Personal communication, 13 October.

Westall, O. (1992) Personal communication, 12 November.

Wicksell, K. (1935) *Lectures on Political Economy*, London, Routledge and Kegan Paul.

Wilson, T. (1971) 'Philip Andrews: editor and colleague', *Journal of Industrial Economics* 20, November, pp. 3–5.

Wolfe, J.N. 1954. 'The problem of oligopoly', *Review of Economic Studies* 21, pp. 181–92.

Wolfe, J.N. (1981) Personal communication, 14 October.

Worswick, G.D.N. (1960) 'Cole and Oxford 1938–1958', in *Essays in Labour History*, pp. 25–40, edited by A. Briggs and J. Saville, London, Macmillan & Co. Ltd.

1 Report from the 'accountancy' side of the pilot inquiry into the relative efficiency of small- and large-scale business[1]

1 The purpose and content of this report

Mr. Courtauld has suggested that Nuffield College might undertake an investigation of the nature of the advantages arising from the scale of business and that one of the objects might be an inquiry how far changes in economic organization and the environment of business might improve the survival chances of small-scale businesses in industries where technical economies of large-scale production do not give a preponderant advantage to the large business. During the past six months, a committee of the College has been responsible for preliminary research. This report is concerned with the work that has been done on what has generally been referred to as the 'accountancy side'. Here, the approach to the general problem has been seen in terms of an intensive examination of the position of particular large businesses in different industries, in order to investigate the relative weight of the advantages that they may derive from their size. Up to the present, we have been concerned solely with the viscose yarn section of the rayon industry, and have made use of data provided by Messrs Courtaulds.

This report should, of course, be regarded as preliminary, in so far as fresh work may still be done, for there is a possibility that Mr. Courtauld promised to look into — that we may be able to secure access to a relatively small-scale firm producing viscose rayon.

The possibility of future work is discussed later, but we should point out that our great indebtedness to Messrs Courtaulds has a bearing on this question. They have co-operated to an extent that we believe to be new in academic economic research. A substantial share of the work has been done by their staff in providing, and commenting upon, the data that we have been using. We have also felt quite unrestricted in access to any data that existed and that was likely to

(1) Reprinted with permission of Nuffield College and Lancaster University, acting on behalf of the estate of P.W.S. Andrews, from the G.D.H. Cole Papers, Nuffield College, Oxford.

have a bearing upon the problems that interested us. The committee will naturally consider the extent to which we may expect such full co-operation in the future.

The extent of Messrs Courtaulds' collaboration also makes it essential that this report in its present form should be regarded as secret and confidential to the committee that is controlling the inquiry. An undertaking has been given that it will be so regarded, and the report will need extensive editing before it can be used for a wider circulation, if that should be considered at any time.

The plan of this report is as follows: In the next section we discuss the general characteristics of the rayon industry that seem relevant to our inquiry and in the third section we state the questions that we should like to answer. The next three sections are given to a discussion of the potential efficiency of large and small businesses in the best conditions of technique, etc., that existed at the outbreak of war; the fourth section is concerned with technical economies of the scale of plant, the fifth with the non-production economies related to the scale of the firm, and the sixth briefly relates both types of economies to specific sizes and types of firms. The seventh section then looks at the industry as it actually was before the war and reviews our discussion of potential advantages in the light of the level of efficiency that existed in practice — mainly with reference to Courtaulds. The eighth section then follows with a brief statement of the kind of future work that might be done on the 'accountancy side', if it should be decided to go on with the major inquiry. Further details about technical conditions, labour-skills, etc., are being collected where it seems that they will be relevant, if at some later stage we should be concerned with comparing conditions in the rayon industry and in other industries. They are not written into the present report, since they have not directly contributed to its conclusions.

2 The British rayon industry before the outbreak of war: the general characteristics

Mr. Silverman's report upon the British Rayon Industry is already available in Nuffield College. Here, we outline the most important characteristics of the industry from our present point of view. We shall draw freely upon Mr. Silverman's report, supplementing and correcting it in the light of our own information.

This report is concerned almost exclusively with the production of viscose continuous filament yarn. This is, however, only one branch of the British artificial fibre industry and both it and the British industry itself must be seen against a wider background. The artificial fibre industry is located in all the major industrial countries of the world. Mr. Silverman quotes estimates of annual world production from *Rayon Organon*, and it appears that, immediately before the war, the United Kingdom produced about 11 per cent of the world's output of yarn and about 6 per cent of that of staple fibre (about 8 per cent of the world's output of yarn and fibre together).(2) The United Kingdom producers had a protected home market, and had, in several cases, established relationships with competing foreign producers.(3)

Eleven producers were operating in the United Kingdom in 1939. Only one of these produced staple fibre. All produced continuous filament yarn (only indirectly competitive with staple fibre). The yarn was produced by three quite distinct processes: viscose, acetate and cuprammonium, the resulting products being competitive but not perfectly so.(4) Six firms produced only viscose yarn, three only acetate yarn, one cuprammonium yarn, and the largest firm, Courtaulds, both viscose and acetate, principally the former (it was also responsible for all the production of staple fibre).

The United Kingdom industry is, on the whole, dominated by Courtaulds, but Courtaulds' leading competitor — British Celanese — is predominant in the production of acetate yarn. It would appear that the viscose yarn industry should be seen as oligopolistic, with only slight market imperfections,(5) the viscose industry as a whole being competitive with acetate producers with a fair amount of imperfection due to complementarity, special suitabilities, etc.(6)

Later in this report, we shall give some estimates for costs of production in firms of given sizes, in hypothetical conditions of efficiency. It will be useful to have some idea beforehand of the relative sizes of the firms actually present in the industry.

---

(2) All percentages are reckoned upon weight produced, ref. H.A.S. p. 22, table 7 (p. 318, table 77). [Silverman's report was written for the Nuffield College Reconstruction Survey in 1943; it was later published in Silverman (1946). The corresponding pages in the published version are set in parentheses.]

(3) H.A.S. p. 42 *et seq.* (pp. 332–348).

(4) H.A.S. p. 12 (pp. 310–313).

(5) The viscose product is substantially all manufacturer's material and is subject to working up before coming into the hands of the final consumer. It resembles a chemical product rather than a normal run of textile yarn, in so far as it is subject to accurate specification. We are thus presented with the conditions of uniformity of product and absence — here perhaps weakness — of buyers' preferences which make for oligopoly. Theoretically the viscose industry may be described roughly as an oligopoly with a single dominant firm.

(6) For example, complementarity due to different reactions in the dye bath.

Approximate proportion produced of:

Firm	(1) Viscose Yarn	(2) Acetate Yarn	(3) Total output, all yarns (including Cuprammonium)
Courtaulds	up to 2/3	up to 1/4	1/2
British Celanese and 2 other Acetate producers	3/4	–	1/5
6 non-Courtauld producers of Viscose Yarn	1/3	–	1/4
1 Cuprammonium producer	–	–	1/20

Table 1.1

Confidential production data from Courtaulds show that, since 1933, the firm has produced more than 45 per cent but less than 50 per cent of the total United Kingdom output of yarn as estimated in the *Rayon Organon* figures quoted by Mr. Silverman. On the basis of Mr. Silverman's estimates of the percentage share of total output held by viscose and by its competitive processes,(7) it would seem that (1935–9) Courtaulds produced up to two-thirds of the total output of viscose yarn, and that in 1939 it produced about a quarter of the total output of acetate yarn. We consequently estimate that in 1939 all three purely acetate firms, *including* British Celanese, produced not more than one-fifth of the total output of rayon yarn. Table 1.1 sums up our view of the strengths of the various firms.

Despite the early importance of patents, it would appear that the rayon industry, and particularly the viscose section, has been tolerably easy of access to new producers since the last war. As we have seen, the 1939 industry consisted of eleven firms. These were survivors of a larger number, most of which had entered the industry after 1924,(8) of which there were 25 firms in existence in 1929. The rush of producers into the industry was only one instance of the general tendency during the second half of the 1920s (reinforced by the imposition of favourable customs duties in the case of rayon) to seize upon and invest (or rather 'float' investment) in new products regardless of actual

(7) H.A.S. p. 24 (p. 320, table 79).
(8) H.A.S. p. 44 (pp. 336–341).

prospects. It would appear that those that have disappeared were principally firms of quite small size. But we must reckon with the fact that, excepting in such periods of high enthusiasm for new investment, the high initial capital investment that is needed will be a deterrent to new enterprise.

In the viscose yarn section, the seven 1939 producers were *Courtaulds*, with five factories located at Coventry, Flint (two factories), Wolverhampton, and Preston, at which production had been commenced in 1904, 1917, 1922, 1929 and 1939 respectively; *British Enka*, Liverpool, 1926; *Harbens*, near Warrington, 1926; *Kirklees*, Bury, 1926; *North British*, Jedburgh, 1929; *Breda-Visada*, near Manchester, 1932; *Lustrafil*, Nelson, 1932. Courtaulds produced about 60 per cent of the total output of viscose yarn (80–90 million lbs), British Enka may have produced about 10 per cent (that is, it was about one-fifth smaller than Courtaulds' Preston factory), leaving the five remaining firms with about 30 per cent of the total output. The average output per *firm* was about 12 million lbs, for the industry as a whole, and about 8 million lbs per *plant*. Courtaulds alone produce about 50 million lbs annually and had an average output per factory of about 10 million lbs.(9)

Thus, not only is the viscose section broadly a case of oligopoly; the relatively few firms had greatly differing annual outputs (the range of annual output per *firm* being, approximately, from 2–50 million lbs; per factory, approximately 2–10 million lbs). We might thus expect *a priori* to find a natural price-leadership on the part of the large firm, subject to strain in bad times (failing price-agreements). At the same time, in view of its predominant share in the rayon market, Courtaulds would appear to gain more from a relatively stable market than from upsetting that market in attempts to drive out competing firms through aggressive selling not related to its cost levels. (Another influence in this direction is the fact that its product is still several stages from the final consumer.) It has, however, an obvious interest in preventing new entrants.

These generalizations are consistent with the account that Mr. Silverman gives (p. 45 *et seq.*) of price policy in the rayon industry and of the price-stabilization effect of the British Viscose Association set up in 1937. (We would also suggest that the close of the patent litigation and the entry of Courtaulds into the production of acetate yarn on a scale equal to a quarter of the total output of this yarn is sufficient to account for the 1939 agreements stabilizing prices, including acetate yarns.)

Later in this report we discuss the relative efficiencies of small versus large firms in this industry. It seems worth pointing out as a fact that, before the war, smaller firms were surviving alongside the large business and that they appear to have been doing so with some profitability. For 1939, a relatively good year, we

---

(9) These figures give a general impression based upon yearly data 1933–8.

have the accounts of six out of the ten non-Courtauld firms in the rayon industry. Two of these are non-viscose firms and should, therefore, be excluded from our present consideration. Three of the remaining four non-Courtauld viscose firms (including a small one of £250 000 capital) were making profits, the other (relatively large with a paid-up capital of over £500 000) made a loss of £12 000 after, but a profit of £8000 before, charging depreciation.

Finally, we must say something about technical processes in the making of viscose cellulose. In view of the details available in Mr. Silverman's report, our description may be quite brief. In the manufacture of yarn in the form in which it can be handed over to the weaver-consumer, four process-stages are involved. In the *first*, the viscose is made by successive chemical and mechanical treatment of wood pulp (usually, although other natural sources of cellulose may be used and have been used during this war). In the *second* it is spun, this process consisting of the mechanical drawing out and collection in a revolving spinning 'box' of viscose threads made up of filaments obtained through the extrusion of alkaline viscose into acid. The *third* stage consists of finishing — washing and drying the thread created (in hank or cake form) at the previous stage. The *fourth* stage is processing the finished thread. As distinct from those that have gone before, this need not be carried out at the rayon producer's factory. It includes the winding of warp threads upon bobbins or cones, and the pirning of weft threads (winding them upon cardboard tubes), and also the drying of the thread. Yarn is sorted into classes of deniers — a denier being a measure of the weight in grammes per unit length of 9000 metres. The denier measurement thus moves inversely to the cotton 'count', a high denier denoting a coarse yarn.

In this report, our main discussion is confined to the actual production of rayon thread, covering the first three stages described above but excluding the fourth. This exclusion is on the grounds that, although Courtaulds do process their own yarns, this is not a necessary part of the industry, is not done by all the smaller firms, and is often done by cloth or knitwear manufacturers and by small specialist firms of middlemen. We have been given details of processing costs for Courtaulds and an analysis of these will be prepared and kept so that it will be available for future use if necessary, but our general discussion of economies of scale does not take cognisance of processing costs.

3 A list of questions to be considered in this inquiry

A. *General question*: To what extent would technical conditions be likely to attract small firms (defining small in terms of actual sizes in the industry) in terms of the following particular questions:

The relative efficiency of small- and large-scale business

1. How do costs of production per unit vary with the size of *plant* (all sizes presumed to be operating at optimum capacity)?

2. To what extent does an increase in the size of the technical unit of production mean a relative reduction or increase in the amounts of variable factors of production (materials and labour)?

3. How great a proportion of the total costs for various sizes of plant are fixed costs (overheads including depreciation, management, some labour, possibly some materials)? (This last question is relevant to effect of departures from optimum conditions).

4. To what extent, and in what way, is the technique of production different or constant for plants of varying sizes (what is the relative scope for intensive craftsmanship and mass-production)?

5. To what extent is there a technical optimum unit, and how sharply do costs rise beyond that size?

B. *General question*: To what extent do non-technical cost conditions vary with the size of the firm?

1. To what extent are economies in the purchase of materials realized with increases in the scale of the firm?

2. To what extent are there other non-technical economies of scale (cost of obtaining capital, etc.)?

3. What scope is there for improvements in the organization of industry reducing any relative disadvantages they may be found to accrue to the small firm under (1) and (2)?

4. What are the relative weights of the incidence of technical and non-technical economies?

C. *General question about divergence between actual and hypothetical conditions.*

1. How far do the actual efficiencies of firms of various sizes differ from those

found to be hypothetically open to them?

2. To what extent do marketing conditions affect the extent to which firms of various sizes are able to reach their optimum scale, and to what extent do they make for excess capacity?

4 Technical economies of production

In this section we are concerned with economies arising out of the scale of production — with the scale of the *factory* unit or plant, and not with the scale of the *business* unit or firm.

The technical conditions of production are fairly rigidly determined for viscose rayon yarn. Production is better seen as a chemical process than in terms of ordinary manufacture and the industry really consists of mass-production of a chemical product. There is very much less scope for changes in the broad technique of production than is normal in ordinary manufacturing industry. Certainly, nothing compares to the small-scale hand-craftsmanship that is sometimes possible in other industries. No doubt, exclusive patents and secret methods will affect the details of production (they appear to have been important in the days when the industry was first established in this country) but our impression is that the general effect of these is not very important now.

For these reasons we turn to some data provided by Courtaulds with reasonable confidence that they will give a fair idea of the relative strength, and direction, of the variation of cost of production with changes in the scale of plant. They are intended to help to answer our first question — the extent to which advantages resulting from the scale of production favour the *setting up* of large units of production as against smaller units.

At the outbreak of war, Courtaulds' Preston factory was just coming into production and it may, therefore, be taken as embodying the most efficient production methods available at the time of its design. It has 12 500 spindles, with an output of about 10 million lbs of yarn a year when it is operating at reasonably full capacity.

The smallest independent units surviving in the industry before the war were believed to be producing about two million pounds of yarn a year, which is about one-fifth of Preston's 'normal capacity' output. Experts in Courtaulds were asked by Mr. Bingham what they thought would be the costs of production for a small factory one-fifth the size of Preston (that is, with 2500 spindles), on the basis that the small factory was to be 'similar to Preston in date, construction, equipment and indeed in all respects except size'. The small unit is, therefore, assumed by Courtaulds' experts to be producing its smaller output as efficiently as possible.

We can compare the costs for this hypothetical small unit with those for the Preston factory. The latter's costs are actual data. They are, in general, taken for the first quarter of 1940 'when the factory was operating for the first time at reasonably full capacity', but raw materials used — the only items whose costs were materially affected by war conditions — are costed on the basis of representative periods in 1939. The costs of the smaller unit are constructed in comparable fashion.

We propose to make the cost-comparison under four separate heads — 'Work and Administrative Overheads', 'Materials', 'Labour' and 'Cost of Waste', and shall incorporate some notes, supplied by Mr. Bingham with the data, which explain the differences between the costs for the two scales of factory.

(a) *Works and administrative overheads*

The items here are depreciation — given separately for the production of steam and electricity and for the rest of the factory — and general overheads, which comprise rates and insurances, and administration, including salaries (of persons engaged in general administration as distinct from factory management).

The estimates of cost given imply a certain peculiarity in this industry that we shall find mirrored in the raw material costs. The technical conditions of production apparently require that total overhead capital costs are roughly proportional to output — that average overhead costs of capital are approximately constant whatever the scale of production. Therefore, if both units have the same depreciation policy, the cost of writing off capital will be the same in each. As Mr. Bingham's note puts it: 'similar machinery would wear out or become obsolete at the same time whatever the size of the factory, and so no change was assumed for the cost of this item (depreciation)'.

The note just referred to goes on: 'It was realized that a small firm might not write off its assets at so quick a rate as Courtaulds did, but it was thought that this would place it at a disadvantage in the long run. It was, therefore, decided to leave the items unchanged', with the exception that a small allowance has to be made for an increased depreciation under steam and electricity for the small firms due to relative inefficiency.

We wish to make some reservations here, coming back to them later, since they are more relevant to our second question than the one that we are presently considering. Members of Courtaulds have informed us (1) that repairs costs cover wear and tear *sensu stricto*, (2) that the depreciation allowance is really obsolescence, (3) that allowance has been generous in the light of past conditions, although there were signs that real obsolescence was beginning to equal the rate assumed in the costing figures for depreciation. It is a well-known accounting aphorism that 'Depreciation depends upon policy', and we wish to reserve judgement for the moment upon the aptness of assuming an equally large write-off for the smaller unit of production, even though it employs equal amounts of capital per unit of production. We shall certainly not agree with the assumption when considering the bearing of this upon our second question — that relating to the *survival* as distinct from the institution of small-scale units.

Whilst considering the question of capital-needs, this seems a suitable place to remark that both factories are assumed to generate their own electricity. The production of steam is so essential a part of the production of rayon that the generation of electricity tends to become a by-product, and the small unit was thought by Courtaulds' engineers 'to be large enough to generate its own electricity profitably, using small extraction-type turbines'. (We take the word 'profitability' to mean having regard to any price at which the small unit is reasonably likely to be able to purchase electricity.)

Due to ambiguities in accounting practice, we treat *factory* salaries as a cost of labour, but no change in cost, both of this and of the items 'rates and insurance' and 'administration' was assumed. The accompanying note states 'whilst it has often been said that the large firm spends a lot in administration, since Courtaulds' costs were so small for this item, the firm's experts did not believe that a small concern could do better'.

The following 'overhead' costs are assumed to be the same for both small and large factory when producing 150/27 Bright Viscose yarn at reasonably full capacity (all in pence per pound spun): rates and insurance 0.17; administration, including salaries 0.17; (also factory salaries 0.91); general depreciation 1.31. The technical inefficiencies of producing steam and electricity in the small factory referred to previously lead to its cost of depreciation and 'other expenses' under steam and electricity being 0.35 and 0.08, against 0.31 and 0.07 for the large factory. Average 'overhead' costs at capacity are thus estimated to total 2.03 pence per lb. for the large factory and 2.08 pence for the small factory (or 2.22 and 2.27 pence, respectively, if factory salaries are included).

(b) *Materials*

Here technical conditions are also assumed to imply identical rates of consumption of materials, with the exception of the coal used in the generation of steam and electricity. In the latter case, Courtaulds' engineers considered that the small unit would use its coal less economically. It appears that the relative waste of coal would be large and would amount per lb. of product to about 27 per cent of Courtaulds' consumption. With this exception, if purchasing advantages are not taken into account (and they are not relevant in this section), materials costs would be identical and would be as follows, if costed at Courtaulds' 1939 purchase prices:

1. *Raw materials* 4.32 pence per lb. (made up of pulp: 1.87 pence; caustic soda: 1.05 pence; carbon bisulphide: 0.44 pence; sulphuric acid: 0.42 pence; others: 0.54 pence);

2. *Repairs, materials, etc.* 0.50 pence. To these we may add:

3. *Coal used for steam and electricity* (costed at Courtaulds' prices) large factory: 0.92 pence; small factory: 1.17 pence.

(c) *Labour*

We have already noted factory salaries — assumed to be invariant at 0.19 pence per lb. For other labour items special estimates were made by Courtaulds' staff. The estimates allowed, where possible, for 'the combination of jobs by one individual in a small factory which would be done by different people in a large unit'. We are assured that in the production of viscose yarn there is a definite limit to the extent to which this can be done and that a substantial part of the labour force cannot be cut proportionately with a decrease in the scale of output.

Mr. Rupert Jones, the Assistant Manager at Preston, estimated that 'for a factory one-fifth the size of his own, he would need 32.7 per cent of his existing *manufacturing and general* labour; that is to say, assuming standard wage rates, the labour cost would be increased in the ratio 32.7 to 20' — this illustrating the general fact that 'in a large factory you can use labour more economically'.(10) In the generation of *steam and electricity* it was thought that attendance costs would be higher in the small unit than in the large, 'because, to a considerable degree, the same labour can look after boilers and power plant, whatever their size'. This item, therefore, also shows greater costs for the small than for the large factory as does the cost of labour engaged upon *repairs*, where the Preston Assistant Manager considered 'that for a factory 20 per cent the size of Preston he would need 37.5 per cent of the existing engineers'; the labour cost of repairs per lb. would, therefore, be increased in the ratio 37.5 to 20. It is recognized that there is some element of conjecture in the last estimate, since the commentary says 'possibly a small factory might save something by having repairs done outside, but this is difficult to estimate, and, in any case, the factory, with its complicated machinery, would need a considerable body of engineers for

---

(10) The quotation is from Mr. Jones's comments. It will, however, be apparent that more than the general fact of economical use of labour in a large factory is involved. The extremely great rise in cost of labour in the small firm is due to the peculiar difficulty in rayon manufacture of cutting the labour engaged in particular processes if the scale of production is cut, so much of the labour employed being of a supervisory kind.

maintenance work'. (Mr. Kinnes told us that in many industries we should find that small businesses could make savings not available to the larger business in the purchase of machinery. An owner-manager would find it worth his while to hunt round for second-hand machinery and get it reconditioned. This was not thought likely to be significant in the rayon industry.)

It is convenient to include with labour costs the item 'factory sundries'. These are 0.18 pence per lb. for the large factory, and are estimated to be 0.20 pence for the small unit. The accompanying note states 'this item in our costing set-up includes national health, unemployment and workmen's compensation insurance, hence, as these items vary with labour, we have made a small addition for the small factory's cost'.

The resulting estimates of labour cost of production are given below in Table 1.2. As before stated, we think that factory salaries, although invariant and theoretically overhead, should be added in here, because the division between this and other labour costs is ambiguous in practice.

The small factory would, on the basis of these estimates, have a two-thirds greater labour cost than the large factory. In the previous interim report we queried if proper allowance had been made for the possible combination of jobs in the small factory that had been done by several specialist individuals in the large factory. We are assured that this is so, and accept that, with the proviso that we should like to inquire if, since the estimates are separately made for the main departments, allowance has been made for such combination between departments. In any case, there appears small room for scaling down the difference by any large amount. Certainly, we think that the absolute difference in costs must be of the order of 1.5 pence per lb. against the small factory.

	in:		
Cost of: (pence per lb.)	A. *Large factory*	B. *Small factory*	B as % of A
Wages, manufacturing & general	1.76	2.88	164
Steam & electricity wages	0.17	0.32	188
Repairs wages	0.54	1.01	187
Factory salaries	0.19	0.19	100
TOTAL cost of labour	2.66	4.40	166
TOTAL cost of labour including 'Factory Sundries'	2.84	4.60	162

Table 1.2

(d) *Cost of waste*

The rigidity of the technical process apparently implies the same rate of physical wastage of products. The monetary allowance for waste, therefore, depends upon money costs of production. It follows that the cost of waste will be higher in the small unit than in the large, since waste results in the sacrifice of more costly product in the former than in the latter. The cost of wastage in the large factory is given as 0.19 pence per lb., and, ignoring as we are in this section differences in the cost of raw materials, we think that this means a cost of wastage in the small factory of 0.21 pence per lb. of product. From the documents loaned us by Messrs Courtaulds, our personal opinion is that physical wastage *might* be smaller in the small factory, since, besides the element of wastage due to the chances of production (assumed to operate equally in both units), there is obviously an element due to oversight and other managerial factors. The small unit might be more efficient here, but we cannot give numerical effect to our judgement.

It is now possible to give some sort of answer to our general question — the effect of the scale of the unit of production upon costs — and it will be useful to give a table epitomising the data that we have so far presented. It will be borne in mind that, in terms of the question that we wish to answer, it is assumed in these costs that the small unit can buy its materials as cheaply as Courtaulds (the removal of this assumption is relevant to our next section).

	A. In large factory	B. In small factory	B. minus A.	B. minus A. as % of A.
Total Materials(11)	5.74	5.99	0.25	4
Total 'Wages'	2.84	4.60	1.76	62
Total Depreciation	1.62	1.66	0.04	2
Other Charges & Overheads	0.41	0.42	0.01	2
Total 'Overheads'	2.03	2.08	0.05	2
Cost of Waste(12)	0.19	0.21	0.02	11
Total Factory Cost	10.80	12.88	2.08	19

Table 1.3: Summary of Costs (pence per pound of product)

---

(11) All costed at Courtaulds' prices.
(12) Includes materials costed at Courtaulds' prices.

On balance, then, if it had access to materials upon the same terms as the large Preston factory, the small unit would have been producing yarn at a relative cost disadvantage of 2.08 pence. For it to cover its estimated costs, the price of its product would have to be high enough to yield a 19 per cent margin to the large factory. A 1/4d. of the difference in costs would be due to the small unit's relative inefficiency in the use of coal, the balance would arise from increased labour costs.

The cost discrepancy would, of course, be less if the estimates of labour cost in the small firm were pessimistic. We think that the method of calculation would tend to produce pessimistic error, but do not think that this is likely to be of anything like the same order as the difference in costs. Mr. Bingham, when reporting the engineers' calculations of relative coal consumption, appeared to think that the extent of that difference would be more than sufficient to cover any errors in labour costs. It follows that the cost disadvantage would not be reduced below 1.83 pence — 17 per cent of the large factory's costs.

The difference in costs is also estimated subject to the assumption that the small unit will adopt the same depreciation (obsolescence) policy as the large one. At present, we are asking whether the technical economies are sufficiently large to prevent the *setting up* of small units of the given size. It would be absurd to suppose that the potential owner of the small unit would not charge something on obsolescence account, if he were trying to answer this question, but, even in this extreme case, his other costs would still be greater than the large factory's costs by 0.42 pence, on the basis of the given estimates, and 0.17 pence, if we allow the maximum possible amount for pessimism in the framing of labour-cost estimates.

Our conclusion is, therefore, that the technical conditions of production are against it being economical to set up in the rayon yarn industry units of production of the size of the smallest firms at present existing. This conclusion is based solely upon cost comparisons for the production of rayon yarn, and is subject to our later discussion of processing and to the existence of market imperfections. Apart from processing, and if the industry were perfectly competitive, the most efficient small units of the same size as the smallest existing firms could not compete successfully with large units of the size of Preston. (It is interesting to note that since our estimates in Section 3 give the six non-Courtauld firms in this industry a total 1939 production of not more than 30 million lbs per annum, it follows that the whole of their 1939 output could be produced by three units of the size of Preston, or not more than four units, if we reckon the other firms to have been working at the same degree under-capacity as was Courtaulds.)

Intermediate sizes of plant and the optimum

What of intermediate sizes of plant, between our hypothetical small unit and the 'Preston' size of unit? To what extent, and at what level, is there an optimum for the unit of production? Our answers here cannot be given numerically, but, after correspondence and discussion with Mr. Bingham, we have come to the following opinions.

First, Preston is certainly not over the limit of size for the realization of production-economies, and costs of production would be reduced progressively as the scale of the factory increased from that of our imaginary small unit up to the size of the Preston plant. This means that, at some size within the interval of the range of output from 2 to 10 million lbs that we have been considering, a plant smaller than Preston might compete successfully, if it adopted a less liberal write-off policy and if there are errors of pessimism in the estimates of labour cost. For example, assuming that average cost of production varies in a linear fashion over the whole of the range, it would fall by 0.26 pence for every million lbs increase in the scale of production. If no write-off were charged by the smaller firm, it would have a cost of production of 10.08 pence per lb. or less when it exceeded the 32 million lb. scale, and could, therefore, compete successfully with Preston. If it wrote off at *half* the Preston rate, the requisite cost level would be reached on passing the 54 million lb. scale. (These calculations are approximate and ignore the possibility of errors in the calculation of labour costs; if these exist, the scales of possible competition would be lower than those stated.)

When considering the question of an optimum size of plant, we should like to quote the following from Mr. Bingham: 'Preston is a small factory compared with some in the USA which are three times its size. I do not think there is much more to be saved by expansion beyond the 10 million lbs per annum level (except that we understand that there is some economy in the very latest Power equipment, which could not be utilized in a factory smaller than about twice the size of the existing Preston factory), but, on the other hand, no known American factory is so large that it loses efficiency on that account. The most I think can be said is that for maximum efficiency the existing Preston unit is about the minimum size, while the maximum is undermined'. It should also be noted that Preston was built for twice the number of spindles it has as yet.

On the basis of these considerations, we would chance the personal opinions that costs probably continue to fall, but not so steeply, beyond the Preston size; that the optimum is probably larger having regard only to production factors — ie apart from management factors. it might also be suggested, having regard to the problems of management in a multiple factory organization such as Courtaulds, that an independent single-factory firm might well find that it paid it to run a larger factory.

Note on the effects of specialization of output

In the previous cost-estimates both factories have been assumed to be designed for and producing a single count or denier of rayon yarn (150 denier). The production of yarn as a commercial proposition must mean that a *firm* will not be able so to specialize its output. It is feasible for a large firm such as Courtaulds to have one of its factories specializing to the extent that Preston did, but such specialization would not be possible for a firm of the size either of Preston or of the hypothetical small unit. In the previous interim report, this led us to doubt the determinateness of the cost comparison. In normal industries less specialization would mean a significant rise in costs, and we could not *a priori* determine the relative effect of this for *firms* with plants of the two sizes involved in the comparison.

Our attitude was based upon impressions derived from consultations with Mr. Bingham, and we were led to the conclusion that a small firm of the imagined size would be even less efficient as compared with *Courtaulds'* Preston than the cost data indicated. Since the last report, we have had a further discussion with Mr. Bingham, and, as a result of his looking further into the matter, he has produced a note of the effect of changes in denier.

We will not go into detail here, but the upshot for our present purpose is this: the plant may be seen as designed for a particular denier. If the *average* denier is greater than this, then the spinning department (and with it the processing department, with which we are not at the moment concerned) will be working under capacity. Similarly, if the average denier is less than that for which the plant was designed, then the viscose and finishing departments will work at less than their capacity. A change in average denier thus causes an important rise in costs. If, however, the *average* denier is not changed, the production of a variety of deniers will leave unaffected the balance of production between the departments. An expert in Courtaulds has given his opinion on the effect on cost of producing a single denier in a factory and of producing seven or eight deniers at the same time. 'He calculates that, provided the average denier is not changed, the difference in cost amounts to about 2 per cent on producing departments' labour and nil on other elements of cost'. Mr. Bingham notes 'the costs in our hypothetical small factory would, therefore, be further increased by only a negligible amount if, instead of being all on 150 denier, it were on a number of deniers averaging to 150. Hence perhaps the costs in our quasi-Preston are not quite so unrealistic as at first appears.'

5 Non-production economies of scale: with a note on some aspects of the question of management

In the preceding section, the scale of output of the individual unit of production — the plant — provided the background for the discussion of the incidence of the technical economies of production. Here the unit of reference is changed: the incidence of 'non-production' economies must be related to the size of the unit of enterprise — the firm — and it is necessary to discuss how these economies will vary with the scale of the output produced by the firm as a whole.

A complete consideration of non-production economies would involve their consideration under three heads: the acquisition of the goods and services required in the manufacture of the product; the selling and marketing of the product; the general question of management. In this report we can proceed only with the discussion of the first class, the only one where available quantitative data appear adequate for us to reach reasonably valid conclusions. If this research were extended, it might be hoped, from the consideration of a sufficient variety of firms and industries, to give adequate consideration to the second class, with quantitative information as a basis. The third class is not likely to lend itself to quantitative treatment, but here again a wider background of experience might fructify in a body of generalizations of a qualitative kind.

To return to the first class of non-production economies: based as it is upon the experience of a single large firm, the discussion of the effect of variation in the size of firm has to be conducted *a priori*. The purchase-price of labour is, therefore, assumed to be the same for large firms and for small firms. Our attention is, for this reason, confined to materials, and we shall study the way in which their prices are estimated to vary with the scale upon which they are purchased.

Our data consist of a comparison of the prices of materials for the Preston factory (10 million lbs output of product a year) with estimates, made by Courtaulds' experts, of what those prices would be if orders for materials were placed on the scale appropriate to a firm with an annual output of 2 million lbs.

The actual size involved on the 'Preston' side of the comparison is not consistent from item to item. As we shall see, nearly all of the items are not affected only by the size of the Preston business but they are also affected by the size of Courtaulds' viscose yarn business as a whole, by the size of all the Courtaulds' business based upon 'viscose' materials, or even by the size of the firm of Courtaulds as a whole with all its complex of activities. To disentangle completely the various effects of these is impossible.

It will be easier to proceed, if we first state the cost comparison as we have it, with notes explaining how the estimates have been made, and then take the principal items separately, analysing what size of 'firm' is involved in each

51

comparison. We shall then find that the costs as given exaggerate the relative buying advantage of a *firm* the size of Preston and so exaggerate the extent to which changes in 'industrial organization' in this field might help the smaller firms.

	A. *To Preston*	B. *To small factory*	*Increase in cost to* B. *due to purchasing disadvantages*(13)
Raw materials:			
Pulp	1.87	1.99	0.12
Caustic soda	1.05	1.16	0.11
Carbon bisulphide	0.44	0.53	0.09
Sulphuric acid	0.42	0.45	0.03
Others	0.54	0.54	-.--
Total raw materials	4.32	4.67	0.35 (8%)
Coal for steam & electricity	0.92	1.22	0.52(14) (5%)
Repairs materials:	0.50	0.57	0.07 (14%)
Effect of dearer materials on			
cost of waste (estimated)	-.--	0.02	0.02
TOTAL MATERIALS	5.74	6.23(14)	0.49 (9%)

Table 1.4: Costs of Materials (pence per lb. of product)

The following are the comments given to us with the data from which Table 1.4 was drawn up:

1. The figures are based on representative periods in 1939.

2. *Raw materials*: The 'small' company in our industry is probably not small enough to have the advantages of the little business where the owner buys with the help of local contacts and the spur of self-interest. In any case, it is

(13) Note: in general this column is the difference between B and A, but in the case of coal 0.25 pence is deducted. This was the allowance for extra cost of coal at *Preston* prices due to the lower coal-efficiency of the smaller plant, and has been allowed for when comparing production costs in the previous section; 0.2 pence of the amount charged against coal allows for the effect of higher purchase prices upon this wastage.

(14) From these items 0.25 pence for waste of coal at Preston prices has been deducted.

doubtful if these advantages apply in an industry where the most important materials come from overseas or from large chemical manufacturers. The 'large' company gained in normal times through the reductions in prices obtained in large orders, which reflect the saving in cost thereby brought to the suppliers. Our purchase department estimate that on *pulp* we save £1 per ton (or about 6 per cent). For *caustic soda* we have a contract under which the price is progressively reduced for each 10 000 tons per year bought; a small company would pay what we pay for the first 10 000. *Carbon bisulphide* and *sulphuric acid* are manufactured by us at Trafford Park; the profit on manufacture has been deducted from the 'large' factory's cost. The remaining chemicals are bought in fairly small quantities, and the rebates obtained consequently inconsiderable.

3. *Coal*: The purchase department consider we save (at present) about 1/- per ton of coal as compared with a small firm in the same locality buying the same coal. (An adjustment was, therefore, made in the small firm's costs allowing for the corresponding saving at 1939 prices.)

4. *Repairs materials*: Our Purchase Office say we save approximately 12.5 per cent by being able to obtain merchants' terms, dealing direct with manufacturers, whereas a small buyer would have to go to the merchants.

To what extent is the relative lowness of Preston's costs under each head due to its size, and to what extent is it due to the size of Courtaulds' business as a whole, or of Courtaulds' viscose business as a whole?

It appears to us as quite definite that the prices at which Preston buys raw materials are considerably lower than would be achieved by a *firm* the size of Preston. Pulp and caustic soda are not bought for Preston only. They are required for the other yarn factories as well as for Courtaulds' other viscose products (principally staple fibre and cellophane — which is also viscose-based). Courtaulds in 1939 had a total output of about 50 million lbs of yarn and about 60 million lbs of staple fibre. Common raw materials would naturally not be negotiated for piecemeal for the separate factories; it follows that the terms upon which Preston acquired them would be available only to a concern as large as Courtaulds. A firm as large as Preston would, no doubt, get them cheaper than would our 'small' firm, but since Preston's 10 million lbs output is only 20 per cent of Courtaulds' 1939 viscose yarn output (and only about 9 per cent of its combined viscose yarn and fibre output) the net advantage would be considerably smaller than the 0.35 pence shown in the estimates.

Similarly, the saving on carbon bisulphide and sulphuric acid, which is due to Courtaulds having their own chemical factory, must be seen as an economy of

Courtaulds' whole business, and it would not be likely to be available to sensibly smaller organizations.(15)

No doubt, the same argument applies in the case of repair materials. Here, it is also possible that it is not only the size of Courtaulds' viscose production that enables them to obtain 'merchants' terms'; possibly the size and prestige of the firm as a whole has helped in securing and maintaining this concession.

Coal is the only case where costs reflect the saving to a firm of the size of Preston. Coal is ordered locally and the price obtained probably depends mainly upon the size of the individual factory's contract (subject to the extent, if any, to which the prestige of a firm of Courtaulds' size may influence even purely local negotiations). The relative saving is fairly important, but we must note that the cost of coal is only about one-sixth of Preston's total cost of materials.

The comparison of the costs of materials is, therefore, applicable only over a much wider range of firm-size than it actually purports to cover — these costs for the 'large factory' are really the costs of a factory such as Preston when it is an integral part of a firm the size of Courtaulds. We shall come back to this point immediately and shall sum up our total costs-evidence as if for Courtaulds *versus* the small firm. Meanwhile, we may note that, despite the great differences in size of the parties really being considered, the costs of materials to the small firm will be only 9 per cent higher than Courtaulds' materials costs at Preston (only 5 per cent on Preston's total costs of 10.80 pence). This leads to an important conclusion, highly relevant to Mr. Courtauld's original terms of reference, namely, that changes in the organization of the smaller-scale firms, such as the setting-up of co-operative buying of raw materials, could not, in any conditions, give them very substantial aid in their competition with Courtaulds.

For example, suppose that the entire saving in costs of materials results, as we think it does largely, from the relative scale of Courtaulds. If the latter is rightly measured by total viscose yarn production, all the non-Courtauld firms produce only 60 per cent (in 1939 when their share in the market was apparently unusually large) of Courtaulds' output; if by total yarn plus fibre, only 30 per cent. Then, by common buying, we do not expect them to reduce materials costs to less than 2 per cent or so above Preston in the first case; nor to less than 3 per cent in the latter.

---

(15) We have been given to understand that, as it is, the chemical factory does not provide for the whole of Courtaulds' needs in these chemicals. This emphasizes the validity of the above generalization.

6 Hypothetical Courtaulds v. imaginary small firm

When discussing technical economies in Section 4 we were concerned with factories; the non-production economies of Section 5 were related to firms. Our inquiry is concerned with firms, and we can best sum up the position so far by posing a hypothetical large firm, producing its output in specified factory conditions, against our imaginary small firm. This is done in Table 1.5.

	I 'Courtaulds'	II Small Firm	I minus II	I minus II as % of I
A. *Running costs*				
Materials[1]				
at Courtaulds prices	5.74	5.99	0.25	4
difference due to 'buying factors'	-.—	0.47	0.47	--
Total	5.74	6.46	0.72	13
'Wages'[2]	2.84	4.60	1.76	62
TOTAL	8.58	11.06	2.48	29
(of which 'buying factors'[1]	-.—	0.47	0.47	6)
B. *Overheads*[3]				
Administrative & general	0.41	0.42	0.01	2
Depreciation	1.62	1.66	0.04	2
Total	2.03	2.08	0.05	2
C. *Cost of waste*[4, 5]	0.19	0.23	0.04	21
(of which 'buying factors'[1]	-.—	0.02	0.02	11)
Total all costs	10.80	13.37	2.57	24
(of which 'buying factors'[1]	-.—	0.49	0.49	5)

(1) Source: pp. 44–5 and Table 1.4;
(2) Source: Table 1.2;
(3) Source: p. 44;
(4) Source: including both 'running and overhead costs';
(5) Source: p. 47.

Table 1.5: Summary Comparison of Costs (pence per lb.)

This large firm is supposed (a) to be of exactly the same size as the real Courtaulds — thereby deriving all the saving in costs of materials described in Section 5; (b) to be producing all its output from factories as large, as modern, as efficient as Preston, and each working at the 'reasonably full capacity' of the Preston of our cost data — thus reaping the production economies of Section 4.

The small firm is, as before, producing an output one-fifth of that of Preston (about one-twenty-fifth of 'Courtaulds'), and using a single plant to do so. The table repeats our previous data in summary form — as before, each firm's factories are supposed to be designed for, and operating at, an average denier of 150. In the table 'running' and 'overhead' costs do not correspond to the distinctions normally made in economic analysis. It is clear, from the comments on the wages data, that wages costs include a substantial element of overhead labour, but we have not been able to separate this out.

Our conclusions are (a) that the weight of costs, as estimated in this table, is against the profitable setting up of a small firm of the size assumed;(16) (b) that the large firm should be in possession of very real and not fortuitous advantages; (c) there would seem to be little scope for the chances of the small firm being improved by changes in the organization of industry. We do not think it likely that such things as common buying by small firms of their raw materials would reduce the buying disadvantages to nil, but, in this extreme case, the discrepancy between total costs would be affected only by one-fifth.(17)

Firms larger than the small firm would have better prospects. If they were as large as Preston, their factory costs would be identical with 'Courtaulds' and they would be left with something less than 5 per cent buying disadvantage, which means that with a less liberal depreciation policy they could hope to compete successfully at any price which paid Courtaulds. Firms of this size, however, would each be producing an output equal to 12 per cent of the entire output of viscose yarn in 1939 and could hardly be described as small. We are not inquiring into the general possibility of competing firms existing profitably in the viscose industry, but into the prospects for small firms.

If, however, small firms were established in our hypothetical conditions, then it does appear likely that they might survive over the period during which their fixed capital wore out (a long period in view of the adequacy of repairs) or

(16) Even if the small firm charged no 'depreciation' at all, its costs would still be 0.91 pence per lb., (8 per cent) above Courtaulds', and in this industry some depreciation would normally be charged.

(17) We have not brought into account the relative ease of obtaining capital, but have assumed implicitly that each business is equally favoured. In practice, Courtaulds finances its own developments and a smaller business would be in a relatively disadvantageous position, any possible improvements are irrelevant to our conclusions.

until improvements in technical progress introduced new methods whose total costs were less than their costs apart from depreciation — since depreciation costs are irrelevant in this circumstance.

So far, all businesses have been assumed to be working at 'capacity' and producing the denier for which their factories were designed (assumed at 150). We accept the expert evidence that a number of deniers may be produced without greatly affecting costs, provided that the average denier is that which the factory was designed to produce. It is obvious, however, that the large multi-factory firms will be less affected than the small firm by the increase in costs, however small, due to producing several deniers. Further, it appears likely that the large firm can more easily produce at a non-optimum average denier, since it could 'marry' the viscose spinning and finishing (and processing) departments in the different factories, so as to keep all as nearly at capacity as possible. The large firm could thus produce more easily for a wider market (in terms of range of deniers) and would be able to meet changes in the balance of market demand with greater flexibility.

If the industry were working below capacity, however, the small firms would be in a relatively less disadvantageous cost position than appears from our data. This is because variable costs are a higher proportion of their total costs than they are for the larger firm.

7 Some data for Courtaulds' viscose business as a whole and their bearing upon actual pre-war conditions of competition(18)

We think that the previous discussion has answered the general questions in which this inquiry is interested. The viscose rayon yarn industry does not appear to be a good field for small-scale enterprise and there appears to be little scope for changes in the organization of industry that would be likely to benefit smaller firms.

The argument and answers have been hypothetical, for they assume all units of enterprise to be working with the greatest efficiency available for units of their particular sizes. With our present knowledge, it would be foolish to attempt answers on other assumptions, for we have no basis for generalizations about the effects of its size upon the ability of an actual business to realize the efficiency

---

(18) This section is written very close upon recent work, of which it incorporates such part as seems relevant for the present report. It is naturally subject to our more leisured review, and, on reflection, further work may be seen as likely to be profitable.

theoretically open to it. Failing such a basis of discussion, the admittedly hypothetical approach that has been adopted appears to shed the clearest light upon the actual prospects for small-scale enterprise.

At the same time, there is no intention to neglect any opportunity of collecting data bearing upon actual efficiency. It is possible that we may ultimately be able, by comparing actual conditions with hypothetical optima, to make some generalizations about the extent to which size affects the ability of a business to achieve maximum efficiency.

In this section, therefore, we analyse such information we have about the efficiency of the viscose industry as it actually existed before the war and do not proceed beyond this analysis. If, however, future work is carried out upon the conditions in other industries, it may lead to further generalizations that will be highly relevant to the central core of our inquiry. Meanwhile, this section is written for its own immediate interest.

Of course, we cannot expect any of the existing firms to have been so efficient as previously imagined. The Preston unit is the latest in the Courtauld organization, and came into production only in 1939. The latest of the previous Courtauld plants dates from ten years earlier (ref. Section 2, p. 37); the youngest of the firms competing with Courtaulds dates from 1932; — this is an industry where technical progress has been very marked in the decade or so before the war. Whatever the extent to which minor improvements may be carried out, it appears to us that the technical conditions of the industry make the date of lay-out of preponderant importance in determining the efficiency of a plant.

Our actual cost data relate only to Courtaulds; — of the smaller firms we know only that it is most unlikely that their costs will have been so low as those of our hypothetical small firm and, at the same time, that there is evidence (ref. Section 2, pp. 37–9) that some of them were producing rayon with profit before the war. In this section, actual data for Courtaulds as a whole are used, (a) to compare the actual pre-war efficiency of the viscose section of the firm with the optimum efficiency available to it, and (b) to show what conditions in the Courtauld organization may have helped the smaller firms to survive. At first, we restrict ourselves, as before, to the *production* of viscose yarn, and later, with especial reference to the survival of small firms, we discuss also the processing and selling of the yarn.

We shall make frequent reference to Table 1.6, which gives in its first column a summary of Courtaulds' actual costs for the year 1939.(19) The Preston factory is included but we should remember that, whilst it came into

---

(19) The figure for cost of waste is an approximate estimate made by us on the basis of data for individual products and factories of Courtaulds. The other costs have been adjusted proportionately to compensate for the extraction of this item.

| | A
Estimate of costs for Courtaulds' viscose business as a whole — 1939 | | | B
Estimate of costs comparable with column (3) | |
	(1) Actual 1939 costs when average denier = 133.5	(2) Approximate 1939 costs if average denier =150	(3) Estimated 1939 costs, if 'at capacity' with average denier =150	(4) For 'Preston' alone when at capacity	(5) For hypothetical 'small-firm' at
Raw materials	4.83	4.83	4.83	4.32	4.67
Manufacturing and general wages	3.44	3.22	2.90	1.76	2.88
Steam and electricity	2.01	1.87	1.68	1.47	1.97
Repairs and maintenance	1.60	1.44	1.28	1.04	1.58
Factory sundries	0.25	0.23	0.21	0.18	0.20
Factory salaries	0.51	0.46	0.40	0.19	0.19
Cost of waste	0.29	0.27	0.25	0.19	0.23
Rates, insurance, and administration (including salaries)	0.37	0.34	0.27	0.34	0.34
General depreciation	1.46	1.34	1.28	1.31	1.31
(Estimated depreciation included in steam and electricity)	(0.40)	(0.37)	(0.35)	(0.31)	(0.35)
(Estimated total labour cost* including above)	(4.41)	(4.10)	(3.67)	(2.47)	(4.21)
TOTAL COST	14.76	14.00	13.10	10.80	13.37
If Sundries and Factory Salaries are included, the figures would be:	(5.17)	(4.79)	(4.28)	(2.84)	(4.60)

* Excluding sundries and factory salaries.

Table 1.6: Comparative Estimates of Average Costs (pence per lb. of product)

production during the first quarter of 1939, it was not fully in operation until comparatively late in the year.

It will be seen that in 1939 the average denier was 133.5, whereas up to now our cost comparisons have assumed the production of 150 denier yarn. If the average denier is changed, costs will also be affected (ref. Section 4, p. 42). A firm producing an average denier other than that for which its plant was designed will have higher costs per unit than it would have if its yarn averaged to the denier for which the plant was laid out. Courtaulds' plants were all laid out for a denier of 150 and, therefore, the 1939 actual average costs must be *reduced* in order to make them comparable with the 150 denier costs that we have been considering up to now.

In the earlier draft of this report the correction required by the preceding paragraph was made upon the basis of a reported rule of thumb that average costs decreased by 0.5 pence per lb. for every 10 denier increase in average denier and a diagram giving estimates of the average of producing outputs of differing average deniers.(20)

Over the range 133.5 to 150 deniers the estimates of the diagram were consistent with the 'rule of thumb' (giving a decrease of 0.81 pence against the latter's 0.83 pence). In the previous draft we adopted a correction for the required change of average denier of 0.83 pence and deducted that amount from the actual average cost for 1939, with corresponding deductions from the individual items making up that cost. Since those estimates were made, Mr. Bingham has been able to revise the primary estimates of cost on the basis of further work. Consequent modifications have been made in the individual items of cost that we are now considering and the total correction is now estimated to be 0.76 pence, which is still near to that suggested by the rule of thumb.

After this correction has been made, the 1939 average cost of Courtaulds' viscose yarn output as a whole is still 14.00 pence, which is 3.20 pence per lb.

---

(20) It is of interest to remark here that, failing this information, we should have hesitated to make any adjustment to costs for change of denier. An analysis of monthly details of costs and deniers for Courtaulds' viscose production as a whole for the years 1933–1939 provided us with the following estimates of the extent to which costs fell on the average for each 10 denier increase in the average denier: 1933, 0.1 pence; for each 10 denier increase in the average denier: 1933, 0.1 pence; 1934, 0.1 pence; 1935, 0.6 pence; 1936, 0.3 pence; 1937, 0.4 pence; 1938, 2.0 pence; 1939, 0.1 pence. These calculations were, of course, valid only over the actual range of variation of the average denier in these years (the maximum value of the standard deviation of average denier was 5.5 denier for 1933). With the exception of 1935, none of these values could be accounted significant. The estimate for 1935 happens to be consistent with the 'rule of thumb', but we should point out our conclusion that, while a change in average denier *tends* to have a precise effect, *in practice* this effect has often been swamped by other causes of change of cost.

(30 per cent) greater than the average cost of Preston, when that factory is at reasonably full capacity, and 0.63 pence (5 per cent) greater than our hypothetical small firm.

It follows that, at any given market price, firms of the smallest size extant in 1939, *if* they were of maximum technical efficiency, would have been relatively more profitable than Courtaulds to the extent of 5 per cent on their costs. Now, we have argued that it is not possible to believe that the small firms were at anything like this efficiency, so far as the processes presently considered are concerned, and this relative inefficiency of Courtaulds must be seen as only one factor contributing to the profitable survival of smaller units, amongst others, some of which we attempt to assess later. In any case, 5 per cent would appear too small a margin to allow for the extent to which the actual cost conditions in the smallest firms appear likely to depart from those of the hypothetical optimum.

At the same time, the extent of the variation in costs that was thought to be possible for intermediate sizes of plant (ref. Section 4, p. 42) appears to justify the conclusion that the discrepancy in Courtaulds' costs may be sufficient to account for the profitability of small units which are yet substantially larger than the 'small firm'.

It will have been noted as implicit in the preceding argument that the smaller firms are assumed to be working at or near their optimum capacity. We do not know the extent to which this is true, but we give later on reasons for thinking that they were probably nearer their optimum than Courtaulds. Those reasons are largely based upon considerations of price policy not relevant at this stage, and so we postpone this discussion until later in the section.

To return to Courtaulds, as Column (2) of the Table 1.6 shows, the 1939 costs, when corrected for an average denier of 150, remain higher than the corresponding cost for Preston, when that factory is at capacity. There are two reasons for this. First, the Courtauld viscose yarn organization in 1939 was producing an output seriously below its optimum capacity — Mr. Bingham estimates that output was at least 30 per cent below capacity.(21) This sub-optimum working of Courtaulds has certainly been more or less typical since 1933, the earliest year for which we have data. Second, a large part of Courtaulds' output came from units that were older and less efficient than Preston. Even if Courtaulds were working at 'capacity', the average cost would be greater than for Preston alone.

---

(21) And, on the basis of a study of detailed cost data and reports, we should not put the deficiency below 20 per cent, at the very least, allowing for extensions not fully utilized in 1939 but not necessarily intended to be in use at that date — this 20 per cent not being a 'statistic' but an opinion.

The second column of our table, giving the 150-denier basis 1939 costs (for the sub-optimum output of that year) combines the effect of both of these departures from conditions of maximum efficiency. It provides a fair basis of comparison with the 'capacity' costs of Preston (which we have been using as standard for the best cost conditions open to Courtaulds) and with those of the small firm, when we are interested in assessing the potential competition from efficient smaller units.

We are, however, interested in answering another question as well. If, in 1939, Courtaulds had been producing its *optimum* output, with a consequential reduction in its costs, what possibility of competition would there have been between it and the other units of enterprise with which we are concerned? A comparison between Courtaulds' actual 1939 costs and the level at which its cost would have stood if it had been producing at capacity, will provide a measure of the extent to which marketing and other 'strategic' factors caused a worsening in Courtaulds' competitive ability.

The third column of the table is due to Mr. Bingham, and provides an estimate of what the average 1939 costs of Courtaulds would have been if its output had been increased up to capacity. On the basis of this estimate, such an increase in output would have resulted in costs being reduced by about a penny — to about 13.10d. Thus an increase in output from 75 per cent to 100 per cent capacity would have meant only 6 per cent reduction in costs.

As we have seen, Courtaulds' average costs, when producing at the 1939 sub-capacity output-level would be 5 per cent above those for the hypothetical small firm. Even if Courtaulds were producing at capacity, the present table shows that the hypothetical small firm's costs would have been only 2 per cent above the Courtauld level. It would thus appear that a small firm of maximum efficiency might produce profitably alongside of Courtaulds so long as market price yielded Courtaulds a margin exceeding 2 per cent. A small firm actually in existence in 1939 would need a larger margin, since they would not be so efficient as in our imaginary example.

Even at 'capacity' in 1939, Courtaulds' average costs would still be considerably higher than the level at which they would stand if Courtaulds has been organized in the most efficient technical manner. It will be seen that its capacity cost is estimated to be 2.30 pence (21 per cent) above Preston's capacity cost. This is a measure of the second type of inefficiency, to which Courtaulds were subject in 1939 — that due to the advance of technical knowledge after investment had taken place in the bulk of their plant. This inefficiency was not within Courtaulds' control. It cannot be regarded as an economic inefficiency unless all costs of the new plant that would be needed, if Courtaulds generally were to be as efficient as at Preston, were less than the *prime* cost of operating with the older, less efficient units. We have seen already that overheads form a considerable proportion of costs in this industry and it is clear, therefore, that this would not be the case. Equally clearly, however, is it a penalty of Courtaulds' early start and dominant position in the industry that, as it is in fact organized, it would be subject to the effective competition of considerably smaller enterprises, if they were organized in the most efficient manner.

The other type of inefficiency — the rise in costs resulting from the firm not producing at capacity — was strictly within Courtaulds' control. If we look only at the costs side of the situation, then Courtaulds in 1939 was suffering from considerably higher costs, which could have been reduced if the firm had produced an output more nearly equal to capacity. It is, however, only in the theoretical case of pure competition that questions of efficiency can be settled exclusively with reference to costs of production. Courtaulds, as we have seen, is best described as a leader in an oligopolistic industry. It produces, as stated in Section 2, up to two-thirds of the total output of viscose yarn. If it had increased its output by the 40 per cent necessary in order to reach capacity, the output of the viscose yarn industry as a whole would have thereby been increased to the extent of 28 per cent. In this situation, Courtaulds' output policy must not take account only of the favourable effects of an increase in output upon its average cost of production; it must also look at the unfavourable effects upon market price. If we look only at the direct effects of Courtaulds' increase in output up to its capacity level, there would appear small doubt that the reduction of a penny, of 6 per cent, in its costs would have been achieved at the cost of a fall in market price considerably greater than this amount, since the market would have had to be induced to absorb 28 per cent more viscose yarn.(22)

We must also look at the indirect effects of a price cut by such an oligopolistic market leader as Courtaulds; a fall in its prices would have had indirect effects upon the terms on which smaller firms would be prepared to compete. A price cut in a falling or a stable market might well result in

(22) It will be seen that this conclusion would be valid even if the demand for viscose rayon yarn had a relatively high degree of elasticity. We might note, at the same time, that it appears to us as likely that, although the total market demand for rayon has certainly been subject to a relatively rapidly rising trend over the last 20 years, it is not very responsive to price decreases at any given point of time. A reduction in the price of viscose rayon yarn would, of course, attract customers away from acetate yarn as well as inducing an increased demand for rayon as a whole, but, since in 1939 the output of acetate yarn was only about one-third of that of viscose yarn, it would be necessary for a reduction in price to attract the bulk of the users of acetate rayon yarn, if Courtaulds were to be able, profitably, to sell the increase in their output needed in order to achieve capacity. We must also remember that Courtaulds were themselves producing acetate rayon and to that extent had an interest in the maintenance of its price.

excessive competition, since it would induce the smaller firms to offer their output at prices down to prime costs.(23)

Courtaulds' policy of working below capacity in 1939 is thus justifiable on broad theoretical grounds (24) and a similar explanation may be suggested of the fact that it produced a finer average denier than its plants were designed for. As the dominant firm in the viscose market, it has to produce for the market as a whole. For reasons of prestige, it cannot choose what denier it will produce but has to produce whatever its market requires at its quoted prices. (25) The general tendency of the rayon market has been to require increasing proportions of finer deniers. Courtaulds also pays a great deal of attention to its export markets, selling in those markets up to 10 per cent of total weight produced, and fine deniers are relatively more important there than they are in the home market.

Despite this increasing importance of the trade in fine deniers, it paid Courtaulds in 1939 to introduce a *new* plant designed for the production of 150 denier, because this was the most important single denier that it produced, accounting for about a third of its total output. It was, therefore, profitable to concentrate the advantages of the newer technical economies in the production of this denier.

Another factor is, however, relevant here. Courtaulds have quoted prices which generally yielded a lower profit margin on fine than on coarse deniers. We understand that this was, to some extent, based upon costings that were erroneous in so far as they did not show a sufficient rise in cost for the fine

(23) This does not mean that it would not pay Courtaulds to cut prices on a rising market. We suggest that the theory of leadership in oligopoly, plus falling short-period average costs, is sufficient to account for the fact that puzzled Courtaulds' competitors (ref. Silverman's memorandum) — that it paid Courtaulds to cut prices in 1933 on a rising market.

(24) Since this report considers the 1939 position in particular, we should draw attention to one special factor restraining Courtaulds from producing nearer to capacity in that year — the large size of unsold stocks carried over from 1938, which was a relatively bad year, and which resulted in 1939 sales being considerably larger than output.

(25) Its price-quotations will, of course, influence the strength of market demand for different denier-classes of product. To a large extent, however, different deniers are required by quite distinct classes of consumers and a higher price for finer deniers would not in itself produce a greater demand for coarser deniers. It will be of interest to future work to note here that Courtaulds' pricing policy is apparently intended to be neutral as between different deniers (we mention later on that there is evidence that its methods of costing inadvertently favoured finer deniers) and that it appears to price on a cost-at-normal-capacity-plus-profit basis of the kind discovered to be prevalent during the pre-war inquiries of the Oxford Economists' Research Group (ref. the article by Hall and Hitch in *Oxford Economic Papers*, Number 2.)

deniers. To some extent, however, the nature of Courtaulds' market again affords some justification. Its viscose is competing with acetate yarn, the total production of which is dominated by another firm, which although considerably smaller than Courtaulds is yet the second largest firm in the rayon industry as a whole. It appears that it is in the finer denier trade that competition is most acute between the two kinds of rayon, the same field where apparently foreign competition is most important.

Thus, given the size and nature of Courtaulds' investment in plant, marketing and strategic factors help to account for its producing below capacity. We suggest that, seen against the background of its oligopolistic industry, Courtaulds is only inefficient with reference to strictly technical conditions. Its excess capacity results from its strategic adaptation to its market.(26)

A very extensive knowledge of technical conditions and of the intimate history of the industry and of Courtaulds would be needed before it would be possible to criticize the policy which has led to Courtaulds developing plant capable of producing a much greater output than is normally required. D.H. Robertson and other writers have suggested that where the process of investment is 'imperfectly divisible' an expanding demand may well lead to 'excess' capacity being required in order to meet that demand. It might be possible to consider the establishment of such generalizations upon a factual basis after further work had been done upon conditions in other industries. For the present, we may leave the topic with the suggestion that, at any given time in an industry which has a trend developing so rapidly as the rayon industry has had, the leading firm must always plan to have something in hand by way of reserve for any unusually great accession to demand. The goodwill attaching to its central position will be essentially dependent upon its meeting its market.

The factors in Courtaulds' output policy which we have noted as tending to lead it to produce below capacity may also be seen as helping the smaller firms to produce at a profit. It appears reasonable that a minor firm in an oligopoly, selling in a market where price is mainly determined by the policy of the dominant firm, will tend to run more nearly at capacity. Such figures as are available suggest that, from 1933–1939, the non-Courtauld firms in the viscose industry at least maintained their share in total production. In competing with the leading firm they will have the advantage of its interest in the stability of its price. Further, they will be more free than the leading firm to develop the trade

---

(26) It is worth calling attention to the fact that in the modern theory of 'imperfect' competition little attention has been paid to this short-period excess capacity. The discussion has been almost entirely conducted in terms of long-period cost curves — ref. Chamberlin, etc. — and if the present inquiry proceeds it appears that those working upon the purely theoretical side might do useful work in this field.

in relatively coarse deniers, on which the profit margin is relatively large. We also understand that some parts of the coarse denier trade offer special opportunities for smaller firms in that the demand here is often made up of orders for relatively small quantities. At the end of this section quotation is made of some suggestions from Mr. Bingham about the reasons for the small firms competing profitably with Courtaulds, and those corroborate the present argument.

The general conclusion is that the small firm has been helped to survive by the facts of the market compelling Courtaulds to work in conditions of relative technical inefficiency, and to produce a relatively large proportion of the less profitable range of deniers (reducing its over-all profit margin and, at the same time, increasing its costs through its departure from optimum denier).

Two other factors remain for consideration. The first is the actual Courtauld profit margin in the home market. Since the non-Courtauld firms produce mainly for that market, the higher the margin here the more easily they will survive. At the same time, Courtaulds' zeal for the competitive foreign market will mean lower margins there, and, therefore, a higher margin in the home market than would be taken if both markets could be treated as one. This was certainly true for 1939. In that year, Courtaulds' average receipts were 22.72 pence per lb. in the foreign market and 31.29 pence per lb. in the home market. Their profit margin on viscose yarn after deducting all costs including processing and selling was 3.74 pence per lb. and was greater than this on the home trade alone. Before arriving at this margin, special costs of 1.16 pence per lb. have also been deducted (idle capacity, depreciation, etc. on extensions, special repairs and maintenance, and other special expenses and credits) which appear to us to have dubious claims to be entered as competitive costs. We may, therefore, use as an approximate figure Courtaulds' 'gross margin' of 4.90 pence per lb. This is after charging not only our previous cost of production of yarn of 14.77 pence per lb. but also the costs of processing and selling the yarn, making a total cost of 25.56d., on which the gross margin amounts to 19 per cent (and the 'net margin' to 15 per cent). Margins of this order (necessarily higher in the home trade, which is strictly more relevant, where at the selling price of 31.29 pence per lb. they amounted to 5.73 pence gross or 4.57 pence net, 22 and 18 per cent respectively) appear to afford considerable room for smaller firms competing successfully, taken into account with Courtaulds' relatively high costs through working below capacity.

Before we can balance this up, we must take into account selling costs and processing costs. Are these likely to be higher for the small firm than for Courtaulds? — in which case the discrepancy would eat into the margins just stated. For selling costs, we have at present no idea of the answer, but we note that 0.4 pence out of Courtaulds' selling costs of 1.55 pence are represented by advertising, a factor which is certainly of negligible importance for the smaller firms, giving them some room for relative inefficiency in actual sales costs. For processing costs we have it as Courtaulds' experts' opinion that the smaller firms would be able to have their yarn processed as cheaply as they themselves could. Apart from Courtaulds, the general practice is for yarn manufacturers not to process, the processing being done by the customer. For the moment, we regard the smaller firms as at least as efficient as Courtaulds here. We should welcome a chance of getting further evidence upon this, and meanwhile details of Courtaulds' processing costs have been collected so as to be available if we have further evidence.

To sum up, our general conclusions are (a) that the survival of the small firms, which we found to be very much against the weight of technical factors, is to some extent due to the fact that Courtaulds' production as a whole comes from factories with markedly lower efficiency than the level theoretically open to the firm and achieved in their newest unit at Preston. On that account, the survival of the smaller firms is tied up with the history of the industry; (b) that, at the same time, technical reasons do not appear to be most important. The survival of smaller units has been very largely the result of Courtaulds' marketing and price-policy. The nature of the market for rayon and their own dominant position in it have led to profit margins being established which give room for the profitable survival of firms considerably less efficient than Courtaulds. Further, as we have seen, the smaller firms are free to devote themselves to the more profitable parts of the general market for rayon and have no obligation to sell to the market as a whole — here, the very fact of a single large firm in such a market appears to make it possible for a few smaller firms to live alongside it.

It would also appear that the prospect of the profitable survival of smaller firms will be strengthened after the war by the operation of the agreements for stabilizing outputs and prices concluded before the war. It will in any case be aided by the well-known live-and-let-live attitude of Courtaulds, exemplified in the various speeches explaining their price policy that Mr. Courtauld has made from time to time.

At the same time, the industry appears to offer dubious opportunity for the creation of new smaller firms. It has been possible in the existing set-up for smaller enterprises to survive. Their long-run survival, in view of the weight of the technical factors, is much more a matter of conjecture. The introduction of new enterprises would only be profitable if the pre-war stability of the marketing factors continued to afford pre-war margins, and the entry of new firms might well cause a change in the inter-firm relationships in the industry that would be to their disadvantage. Mr. Courtauld has on at least one occasion stated the policy of his firm to be to discourage the entry of new 'speculative' capital and the basic facts of the industry appear to offer a justification. Even on the technical side, we must remember that Courtaulds' efficiency may be expected to be greatly improved with Preston fully operating at its low costs. They will also have been enabled to improve the general efficiency of the firm by the rebuilding of Coventry. New firms would thus come into an industry where the scales of both technical efficiency and marketing strategy appear to be weighted against them.

We had originally intended to include here a more detailed study of the relative efficiency of Courtaulds' individual factories, but we have decided that that is not so relevant to the main progress of our argument. We have been provided with detailed information from Courtaulds and this will be kept, together with some analyses based upon it, in case it should be needed in any comparison of the rayon industry with other industries that may be studied.

Some notes from Mr. Bingham on how the smaller firms contrive to make profits:

(a) I do not think they can save anything appreciable in management and administrative overheads, because Courtaulds' cost of these items, taken on the large production, is already so low.

(b) They certainly save in advertising, which in 1939 cost Courtaulds 0.4 pence/lb. of viscose yarn, and unless other items of selling cost are higher (which may be the case if the average size of the individual sale is smaller) they will make a net saving on their S. & D. cost.

(c) In pre-war days, owing to the particular market conditions prevailing, profit margins were better on some deniers than on others, and were relatively small on the 'bread and butter' yarns which necessarily formed the bulk of Courtaulds' production. The small firms, I believe, had more than their proportionate share of the more profitable lines required in relatively small quantities, such as the coarse denier yarns for embroidery, braids, ribbons, etc.

(d) Some of the small firms are known to have a high reputation for quality, which in some ways may be easier to control in a small organization. This may have helped them to avoid some of the large fluctuations in demand from which Courtaulds suffered.

(e) In 1939 as a whole, Courtaulds' viscose c.f. spinning departments as a whole worked at slightly under 70 per cent capacity. At other times this figure has been as high as 90 per cent or as low as 60 per cent. If a small firm can contrive to keep to a higher and steadier level of working capacity, owing to market connections or reputation for quality or non-dependence on export or any other reason, its savings not only in fixed overheads but in such cost items as repairs and maintenance will in the long run be considerable.

(f) Courtaulds are the only rayon yarn manufacturers doing any appreciable export trade. This has advantages in that export orders increase the bulk of saleable production, and sometimes lines that prove unsaleable in the home market can be profitably disposed of abroad, but there are disadvantages: the profit margin is generally lower than in the home trade, and one is at the mercy of foreign competitors and trade conditions in all parts of the world. So there is a possibility that, as suggested in (c) above, firms not interested in export may sometimes keep on a more even keel than those so interested. However, considerable investigation would be necessary in order to arrive at a reliable conclusion on this point.

(g) It is possible that the small firms may contrive to make *average* deniers closer to those for which their factories were planned than can Courtaulds. This point has an important effect on cost. If you make an average denier of 100 in a factory planned for 150 or in one planned for 60, it will cost more than if you make it in one planned for 100. Now, we have suffered in this respect from the fact that though our factories were all laid out for 150 denier we have generally had to produce average deniers finer than this. The small firms may have been able to keep closer to their planned average deniers than we have, and three reasons for this opinion are our export trade (deniers being on the whole finer abroad than here), the small firms' larger proportionate share of some of the coarse denier trades (noted in (c)), and the possibility that the small firms may be able to select the types of product they will make to a slightly greater extent than a large one.

(h) Courtaulds have generally had 'white elephants' in the form of factory buildings not yet brought into use, on which depreciation has to be charged and on which some maintenance is necessary. (There is still half the Preston factory which has not been fitted with machinery.) Such charges are excluded from costings but affect Courtaulds' net profit, whereas a small firm with one factory would not have them.

8 Some considerations of possible lines for future work

In this section, our aim is to provide a brief statement of the way in which the work on the 'accountancy side' might develop, if it is decided to proceed with the general inquiry. We refrain from stating any opinion as to whether or not that inquiry should proceed, since the decision in question is essentially one of policy, taking into account the possible value of the work and also the chances that the work will be successful and considering at the same time the alternative projects to which the College might devote its attention. It should, however, be useful for the College, when considering whether or not to carry on with the inquiry, to have a statement available of the methods by which the present investigation might be extended and the sort of results to which it might lead.

Before coming to our own field, there is one problem arising in the field of economic theory, of which we have become conscious during our present work and to which it might be worth some attention being paid if the general inquiry is proceeded with. This is the question of depreciation and obsolescence policy. We suggest that it would be useful to have an economist considering the extent to which depreciation or obsolescence is a cost in the case of monopolistically competitive firms (for example, the cases discussed by Chamberlin and Triffin). A firmer basis of economic theory in this matter would greatly help the sort of realistic inquiries upon which we have been engaged.

To turn now to our own field. Our general terms of reference have been: to consider the relative weight of factors affecting the efficiency of large and small businesses. The method of research is (a) to make an intensive investigation of the accounts of particular businesses, (b) to find the relative weights of various factors inside and outside the production field as shown in those accounts, from this it is hoped eventually to make generalizations concerning those factors, specifying the types of circumstances that would make one factor more important or less important, etc.

It will be obvious that if these terms of reference were taken generally, then this inquiry might well become too large for a team of any practical size but of an infinite number of investigators. We do not think such a *magnum opus* is called for and would suggest the following:

(1) that the Committee controlling the inquiry should select half a dozen or so industries (these need not all be selected at the outset) where the kinds of factors that appear to be important for our investigation are present in varying degrees;

(2) that in each of these industries a very limited number of firms be selected for examination. In general, one large and one small business would be all that is required;

(3) there is no need to worry about the difficulty of defining industries since we do not see it as necessary to cover widely defined industries for the purpose of the present work. That would seem to lead us to the *magnum opus* that we, personally, should like to reject. Thus, for example, we might take a small firm in the Dress Goods Industry, and not worry about the fact that

such firms produce for very special markets, and, therefore, that other small firms will be producing for a quite different market. The important thing will be to determine, for the small firm with which we are concerned, the way in which the specialization of its market is connected with its size and the extent to which the various efficiency factors favour or are disadvantageous to its retaining that market as a small firm;

(4) at each stage of the inquiry — that is, as large and small firms selected for parallel examination are investigated — reports should be prepared dealing specifically with the particular firms concerned on the lines of the lines of the present report, being related to, and discussing any conclusions in the light of, previous research;

(5) the final results of the work on the 'accountancy side' would be (a) a detailed statement of the factors affecting the relative efficiency of small businesses in terms of industrial processes, techniques, markets, and so on; (b) a statement of methods by which changes in the organization of industry could help to maintain small firms in existence without prejudice to efficiency;

(6) at this stage, the report on the 'accountancy side', together with the results of the theoretical work that it may be hoped to have proceeding at the same time, could be used for an extensive examination of leading British industries, using the Censuses of Production and other material, and it seems to us that it might then be possible to deal with the position of small firms *a priori* on the basis of previous intensive work.

The final results of all this work would then be a book, examining the chances of the small firm in British industry generally, and this book could be produced without disclosing the confidential material that we should have had to use in order to reach the basic generalizations — that is, it seems to us that these generalizations once reached could be defined in detail but without having recourse to secret data of individual firms. Up to this stage the 'accountancy side', at all events, would be producing a series of reports, the details of which would have to be kept secret and confidential to the Committee controlling the inquiry and to the research workers engaged upon it.

The present work has been concerned with an industry where the product is technically uniform and the market is substantially common to both large and small firms, where non-production economies are relatively slight in incidence (due perhaps to the bulk of the materials being imported) and where there are sharply increasing economies of scale due to the rigidity of methods of production. It would seem desirable that at the next stage we should examine an industry where the product is not so uniform (although there should be a substantial common technical element) where marketing economies are likely to

71

be more important, and so on. We would ourselves endorse the suggestion that has already been made — of an examination of the Bradford Dress Goods trade, as likely to fulfil these requirements; also, because we could utilize our acquaintance with Courtaulds for an introduction to the technical side of weaving. At the next stage we would suggest either brewing or boots and shoes, or some industry of this kind. We would suggest that the decision as to the particular firms and industries to be investigated should not be made too far ahead, since it seems desirable to let new contacts grow out of the results arrived at in previous stages.

At present the staff on the 'accountancy side' has consisted of P.W.S. Andrews and Miss E. Brunner (approximately half-time each) and Miss Cooper (approximately quarter-time). During the immediate past the first two have been working at nearly full-time. If the enquiry goes on we suggest that Miss Brunner be allocated full-time,(27) that P.W.S. Andrews be allocated full-time, subject to his acting in a consultative capacity for the other research work of Nuffield College, and that Miss Cooper be allocated half-time (we have had some discussion with Mr. Fogarty, and it would appear that this would be a convenient allocation of Miss Cooper's time over a period, with provision for her working full-time on general Nuffield work as occasion arose and making the Courtauld work good by compensating full-time work subsequently). This staff seems adequate to us for the accountancy work during the early stages of the inquiry, ie whilst we are building up techniques of interview and research. If finance were available, we think that the inquiry would be strengthened if there could be added to this staff a person with good qualifications in statistics and with a good knowledge of industrial organization, and that such an appointment is desirable. If such a person could not be found, then it would be better not to increase the staff, but, given time to look around, we believe that it should be possible to find such a person by the time that he or she was required.

---

(27) It is relevant here to note that Miss Brunner's Bursarship expires about the end of October.

2 A reconsideration of the theory of the individual business[1]

1 Introduction

This paper puts forward the outlines of a theory of the individual business.[2] Its generalizations have been reached in the course of detailed investigations of individual businesses during an inquiry into the factors affecting the relative efficiency of small- and large-scale businesses. This research, which is still proceeding, was suggested initially by the late Mr. Samuel Courtauld while a Visiting Fellow of Nuffield College, and encouraged practically by his generous gift to the College. It would be inappropriate to let a footnote carry the burden of the author's debt to Mr. Courtauld or to the many business men who, by their generosity with their records, their time, and their patience, have made the research possible.

The theory with which this paper is concerned was originally arrived at piecemeal, in successive attempts to describe one business so as to compare it with another. Other writers have already put forward some of the propositions, even if only as possibilities, but the whole theory has been worked out independently in order to account for the business behaviour that I studied. The upshot of the theory certainly differs considerably from that of the theories of such economists as Kalecki. They think in terms of monopoly where I think in terms of competition, and I do not see the gross profit margin as a simple index of monopoly power.[3] To me, personally, the chief extraneous interest of the theory is that it tends to reinstate the Marshallian view of competition and to justify Marshall's ideas about normal price.

The theory of the individual business, which is so much the core of traditional analysis in this country, has become more important, rather than less, despite the recent preoccupation with the problems of social behaviour, the

---

(1) Reprinted with permission from *Oxford Economic Papers* 1 (January, 1949), pp. 54–89.

(2) A more detailed account of the theory will be given in a later book.

(3) Kalecki's analysis also seems to assume (constant) short-run elasticities of demand, which I deny as relevant, and do not need to suppose the business man to know.

theory of aggregates, and the technique of social accounting. Its importance is shown by the contemporary discussion of industrial efficiency, of the impact of nationalization, and of the uncertainties affecting the relation between business behaviour and social strategy or between private and public investment. The theory of business needs restating in terms such that it can be conveniently incorporated into social accounting theory.

According to the views put forward here, the theory of the individual business has been frustrated by two things in particular. The first is the neglect of the existence of short-run reserve capacity (for no obvious reason in view of the writings of Sraffa, Clark, and Harrod), which appears to have led to errors in the theory of costs for an individual business in normal situations. The second is the neglect (to which Hall and Hitch have called attention)(4) to take time into account in the theory of demand. It is, in retrospect, surprising that economic theory should not have considered the long-run behaviour of demand, which is so clearly a factor in the business man's behaviour, whilst giving great attention to the theory of long-run costs, which, as I shall argue, is less important.

This paper, therefore, falls naturally into two parts, the first dealing with the theory of costs, while the second discusses the important question of the determination of prices. The analysis is necessarily abstract, since the theory is intended to have general application, and it will not be possible to go very far into the detailed modifications that are necessary when one is looking at a particular individual business producing given products at a given time. The separate parts of the paper will each carry its own set of assumptions, but there is a general reservation which should be made before we turn to the detailed arguments.

When an individual business is being studied in isolation an adequate account of its behaviour can usually be given from two points of view — the market situation in which it is working and the organization which it has available in order to meet that situation. Any peculiar features of its history can usually be treated under these heads as they arise. But when one wishes to compare one business with another, it is usually necessary to introduce a third topic which can be left implicit in the earlier type of analysis, i.e. the relevant characteristics of the main personalities who have played their part in each business.

This is always a key element in the two factors of situation and organization which the observer has otherwise to take as given. Even when one would consider them to be of equal efficiency on balance, business men usually differ in the interest that they take in particular aspects of their functions, and their

---

(4) *Oxford Economic Papers*, Number 2, May 1939, 'Price Theory and Business Behaviour'.

personal predilections and abilities leave their mark on the business. This personal equation is especially important in determining the size to which a given business has been allowed to grow or towards which it is straining. The attitude which the business man takes up affects both the market situation and the kind of organization which he evolves. To refer to another aspect of the same problem: while it is true that the immediate aim of the business man is to make profits, and that his business is where he gets his living, it is also true that it is his way of life, and that the profit-getting motive will be affected and moderated by his personal preferences as will any other man's income-getting motives. This paper conforms to the usual theoretical custom of abstracting from the personal idiosyncrasies of business men, which is justified in the broad treatment of social phenomena in economic theory, but it is an important omission in the theory of the individual business as such.

2 Costs in the individual business

i. Assumptions

This section discusses the way costs of production in an individual business may be expected to change as the business changes its output. Cost curves, as drawn in current text-books, are thought to be misleading when applied in the study of individual manufacturing businesses. In particular, it will be asserted (1) that it will be normal for a manufacturing business to experience decreasing short-run costs; and that the rising branch of the short-period average-cost curve is irrelevant; (2) that the rising long-run cost curve, as usually drawn, is based upon a wrong conception of the way in which management factors affect costs.

The firm considered is imagined to be engaged in manufacturing as ordinarily understood, i.e. businesses engaged in extractive industries or in commerce are formally excluded, although the bulk of the conclusions will apply to undertakings engaged in commercial activities.

Secondly, the business is supposed to be manufacturing a single product of a homogeneous specification at any one time and will make only such changes in specification as are called for by the new production methods which naturally accompany any changes in the scale of production.(5) To make the business so rigidly single-product is indeed to take away the flavour of reality, but it would add unnecessary complexity to discuss a multi-product business, and it would not alter the broad conclusions.

---

(5) The qualification is necessary because it is usually true that one cannot make precisely the same product by large-scale methods of production as by small-scale methods. A product usually has to be redesigned for mass-production.

Thirdly, the business will generally be assumed to be operating a single plant.

Fourthly, as a previous paragraph has indicated, we shall be concerned with *production* only, and shall not discuss selling costs.(6) Some assumptions will, however, be made about the markets for the firm's factors of production, since the prices of those factors will affect the costs of production.

ii. Short-run costs of production

Costs of production are of two classes — direct and overhead costs. The actual content of the terms cannot be clearly defined unless they are referred to the appropriate scale of output, but the distinction does more or less correspond to the prime costs and overhead costs of normal theory.(7) All forms of direct costs have this in common, that they are directly incurred in, and can be directly related to, the production of each particular unit of product. They are of three kinds: (a) direct materials costs; (b) direct labour costs, which may include other expenses besides wages; (c) direct expenses, which are the other expenses of production which vary directly with the output of the product: an example is the running costs of power used for operating process machinery.(8)

Overhead costs comprise all other expenses of the business's operations. They include *(a)* overhead materials costs — the costs of materials not used directly in the production of the product and the use of which does not vary with changes in output; *(b)* non-process labour costs — the wages of all workers not actually employed on process work, such as yardmen, labourers employed for internal transport, etc.; *(c)* the wages of foremen and other supervisory grades of management;(9) *(d)* the wages and salaries of office staffs; *(e)* the salaries paid to management personnel; *(f)* rent, rates, and insurances; *(g)* the costs of repairs to machinery, renewals of loose tools, etc. The remaining type of overhead costs *(h)* consists of the 'financial' costs of writing down capital equipment on account of depreciation and obsolescence, so that the expenses laid out on the equipment

---

(6) A theory of the behaviour and consequences of selling costs will be given in my book.

(7) Direct costs are, in any case, the important part of prime costs from the point of view of price-determination, as will be seen in Part 3.

(8) It should be clear that, granted the assumption of a single-product business, it is not necessary to distinguish variable overheads; they have to be given special recognition only where it is necessary to distinguish between the output of a single product and the output from the plant as a whole.

(9) In small businesses, of course, some of these may also be engaged on process work, in which case their wages may more conveniently be reckoned in with direct costs.

shall all have been charged as costs by the time that it is expected to have ceased to be useful to the business. There is a big difference between this class of overheads and those listed earlier, since they carry no necessary obligation to pay out currently actual sums of money away from the business, while the others are all '*paying-out*' costs, and, unless covered by current earnings, will deplete cash balances.

When analysing the effects of changing outputs and sales on a business's financial position, it is useful to add to the strict costs the current obligations by way of interest payable for loans to the business. Failure to earn sufficient to cover them will not involve the same consequences as failure to cover the classes of overhead costs *(a)* to *(g)*, but they will represent a current need for cash, and default may well cause a change in the ownership of the business or of some of its assets. In fact, *payment* of them may well be made in preference to providing for the 'financial' costs listed under *(h)*.

Since overhead costs are not directly related to particular units of product, the way they are charged as costs will depend upon accounting procedure. The items *(a)* to *(g)* (and also the current interest obligations) will appear in the accounts as given amounts per period and, for our single-product business, may be assumed to be simply divided by the number of units of output produced in a given period, to give the appropriate average costs per unit. The amounts written off the value of capital equipment will be determined by an accounting procedure the exact basis of which may vary between businesses, and the speed at which the equipment is written down will, ideally, depend upon the probable life of the equipment — in practice, it depends upon the policy of the business man, the write-off having *some* basis in real cost but no necessary relations being statable. We may assume the business which we are discussing to employ a consistent policy, which will yield it a determinate sum per unit of time as chargeable to the accounts.

As already noted, it is necessary to make assumptions about the prices at which the business buys its factors of production. It will generally be assumed that they will not vary at all with changes in the size of the business's demand for them. Although no change in basic wage-rates will be allowed, it will be reasonable to assume that higher wages would be paid if the business produced a higher output by getting an existing labour-force to work overtime. This will mean that, for the period during which overtime is worked, the existing wage-rates will be increased by a definite proportion, such as one-quarter.

It will not be possible to discuss very fully the generally accepted theory of costs, which rests upon a Marshallian basis (modern usage, however, largely derives from the articles by Harrod and others during the famous *Economic*

Journal controversy on costs, and from an article by Viner).(10) On the usual assumptions, the static law of diminishing returns is held to justify the short-run average-cost curve being drawn as U-shaped. The rising branch of the U, in particular, is justified by the assumption that there will be an optimum dosage of the direct cost factors, after which average direct costs rise and, in the end, more than counterbalance the effect of the falling overhead-cost curve.

However, the rising part of the average direct-cost curve, and hence of the average total-cost curve, even when it would exist, is not relevant to normal analysis. The normal situation is that the business man will plan to have reserve capacity, his average-cost curve falling for any outputs that he is likely to meet in practice, and his average direct costs, which the second part of this paper will treat as of crucial importance in the theory of pricing, normally being practically constant for very wide ranges of output.

The present theory differs from accepted doctrine precisely in that it considers the constant level of average direct costs, and the reserve capacity on which it is based, to be normal phenomena, *irrespective of the degree of competition which the firm has to meet*. It has been urged previously that 'excess' capacity may be normal, but the claim has been put forward on the basis of the assumed effect of falling marginal revenue curves, and a consequent *falling* long-run cost curve. It is here argued that short-run costs will normally be falling even if the long-run cost curve is rising, and however competitive may be the market for the individual business.(11) In any case, the existence of short-run reserve (usually called 'excess') capacity has been ignored in most of the recent pricing theory. In Chamberlin's analysis, for example, the cost curves are clearly long-run.(12)

The reserve capacity which is so evident in the real world is not just long-run, as in Chamberlin, showing itself, in too many firms, each of which is too small for really efficient management. It is largely short-run in character, the

(10) We would cite particularly the article by R.F. Harrod, 'Decreasing Returns', *Economic Journal*, Dec. 1931, and J. Viner, 'Cost Curves and Supply Curves', *Zeitschrift fur National-Oekonomie*, 1931–2.

(11) This implies a rejection of the principle of tangency invoked by Professor Viner's draughtsman and others. That principle can be attacked on general grounds, and it is certainly not necessary for the long-run cost curve to be defined in such a way as to imply tangency with any short-run cost curve. But if the business man is assumed to plan for reserve capacity, the curves cannot be tangential, for the long-run cost curve will necessarily cut the falling short-run curve, whatever its slope.

(12) This neglect of the feature of short run, 'excess', capacity is perhaps surprising in view of the original Marshallian discussion, the article by Sraffa (1926) which started off the *Economic Journal* controversy, and the plea by Harrod at that time that it may be normal.

manufacturing business having typically a capital equipment which could produce a larger output than it normally expects to produce so that its average costs would fall if it produced more from that equipment.

Such extra capacity has no necessary connexion with falling marginal revenue curves. A business man will always lay down his plant with a certain output of completed product in mind,(13) but, whatever the output, he will not invest in exactly the equipment which would theoretically produce just that output when fully utilized. As a general rule, the business man will not wish to produce at all near the theoretical capacity of his plant. Accidents happen to the best-looked-after equipment, and machinery will have to be repaired or renewed in any case. Many things, therefore, may cause a proportion of the plant to be idle at any one time, and a reserve, over and above the equipment which is strictly necessary for the planned output, will have to be kept to allow for these contingencies.

Quite apart from such allowances for repairs and breakdowns, the output which a business man plans into his equipment will normally be greater than the output which he expects to produce when he lays down the plant. He will generally hope that in course of time, by accretion of goodwill(14) and continuity of service, he will face an expanding market. Further, he is producing in an uncertain world and will be liable to fluctuations of output. While he will be prepared to suffer his reverses, he will wish to take advantage of the occasional extra demands for his product. His capital equipment will be especially constricting unless he allows a margin in his plans — the margin being greater where the particular equipment is most likely to become a source of constraint.

The business man will, therefore, plan to have reserve capacity in order to get the elbow-room that he needs. He will also need some reserves in management personnel and overhead labour, but will not need so much, since emergencies can be met by working overtime, and since, subject to training time, his overhead personnel can be extended more easily.

In order to consider the effects of these reserves, it will be useful first to consider a relatively simple case, where the business man is operating a single process, for example, where the plant is producing a chemical in one process, the sole nature of which is continuous chemical reactions between materials fed in in

---

(13) His choice of the method of producing that output will be considered when the behaviour of long-run costs is discussed.

(14) This, of course, does apparently introduce 'monopolistic competition', but it is not to be taken as committing us to any belief in falling marginal revenue curves, as necessarily relevant to the analysis of such cases. That proposition is denied in the next part of this paper.

their raw state at one end and delivered chemically combined at the other. The only direct costs will be the costs of the raw materials — all other costs will be overhead, i.e. the cost of the building housing the process, the cost of the vessels or chambers in which the process is taking place, and the costs of the supervisory labour and management.

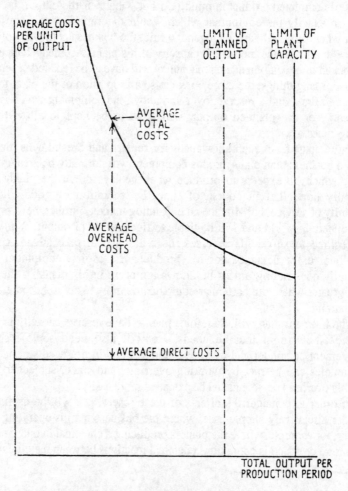

Figure 2.1

Total overhead costs, so far as plant and buildings are concerned, will be constant, and average overhead costs per unit of product will, therefore, fall hyperbolically as his output increases. His overhead labour costs will be constant in total for fluctuations in output not calling for overtime and will, therefore, fall on the average as output increases within that range. If overtime has to be worked, his labour overheads will rise by a fixed amount per production period and then remain constant. The average overhead labour cost curve will thus be on a higher level during the period of overtime, but will fall for increases of output.

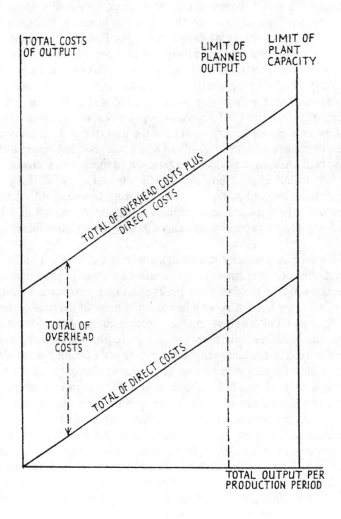

Figure 2.2

Unless the plant is being operated at so low a level that some wastage of materials takes place (as it would in a chemical plant designed for a certain through-put of materials), or at so high a degree of capacity that the quality of the product cannot be so well controlled, the average direct costs may be expected to be invariable and constant, since the plant will use the specified quantities of raw materials per unit of product.

Figure 2.1 shows the situation thus imagined for this simple case. Over the whole range of the capacity of the plant the business is shown as having constant average direct costs of production. The line showing the level of these costs is stopped abruptly because there will be a physical limit to the capacity of the plant. Average overhead costs are shown as falling continuously up to the same limit; the rise in the level of these costs due to working overtime has not been shown, since the difference would be small and it is desirable to keep this diagram simple. Figure 2.2 shows the same situation in terms of total costs. This type of diagram is very useful for the analysis of the effects of varying outputs or prices on the profitability of a business. For that reason it tends to be used by business men in practice, for example, in 'break-even' charts.

Most manufacturing businesses will, of course, be working in a more complicated situation. A typical manufacturing business will certainly have several process stages and some, usually an important part, of its labour-force will be engaged on process work, and will accordingly contribute to the direct costs.

When he is planning the equipment to produce a particular output of finished product, the business man will take each stage of production and assess the capacity of the machinery and equipment that is involved. From the present point of view the machinery may be ranged in order of the relation between the capacity of each unit-machine and the projected output. At the lowest level there will be the machines whose capacity will be the lowest proportion of the planned output; at the other will be the machinery or plant the individual items of which have the largest capacities in relation to that output. For each type of machine some reserve will have to be kept in hand to meet emergencies due to repairs. The repairs allowance may very well be largest for the small-capacity machines, since these are frequently the ones with the fastest moving parts and therefore most frequently need running repairs and maintenance attention.(15) The allowance to be made for possible increases in production will, however, be lowest here. First, a temporary but possibly large increase in output may be possible at the expense of deferring running repairs. Second, there will be a hidden reserve due to the possibility of working overtime. Third, deliveries of

---

(15) Of course, where this is so, the reserve may be partly in the form of spare parts.

new units of such machinery can frequently be obtained without too long a delay. It will be here that the equipment of any industry will be most standardized, tending to be available as ready products from the machine-making industry. (For this reason, reserve capacity will usually be less where this equipment is rented.) Fourth, the installation of extra units of such machinery will not usually be a very great problem. Some allowance for the possibility can usually be made when the building is being designed. It will certainly not involve the major changes in layout, etc., that may be caused by additions to the bigger machinery. A business can therefore plan to develop in a more piecemeal fashion with this type of equipment.(16)

In the case of the most restrictive processes, the reserve capacity will have to be proportionately larger. To give one obvious instance, a business generating its own electrical power will naturally want to have a plant adequate for its needs — the economies of scale in the production of electricity are very large. But it will have to have a stand-by plant at least sufficient to cover a large proportion of its needs.

Further, it is frequently true of the more bulky heavier capital equipment that it has a relatively long life. The business man will, therefore, tend to look ahead and plan for reserve capacity here just because of the nuisance any limitation may become if his business grows. For example, he certainly will not wish to be installing fresh power-plant at frequent intervals with the waste that will occur from scrapping efficient plant which the normal development (and all business men hope for growth as a normal development!) has made too small.

The larger the output of a machine or plant the more likely it is that the business will plan to have reserve capacity. It will not be so easy to make piecemeal extensions. Such equipment tends very frequently to be made to the specification of the business, and additions to it frequently mean major reconstructions. These conclusions will still apply even if the machinery is worked on a continuous three-shift basis so as to get the most use of it before it becomes out of date or worn out. In that case, of course, overtime working is not available.(17)

As output expands, apart from the relief obtained by working overtime, the business will approach the limits set by its equipment. The first limits — those set by the relatively small-capacity process machinery — may be met by

---

(16) This is more likely to the extent that it is generally true that there is a tendency for whole departments to be dominated by machines of a particular class in terms of the relative importance of their capacities.

(17) In order to get the maximum degree of flexibility here the units of such large-scale machinery may be deliberately kept rather smaller than the technical optimum so that a large number of units is employed. See pp. 93–4.

extensions to equipment, each increment of which may be relatively minor. Up to this point, average overhead costs will be falling continuously. At this point, new machinery will cause the level of the overhead costs to rise. Ultimately, the business will run against the more fundamental limitation of its basic equipment and further output will not be possible without major reconstructions.

The way the other overhead factors are affected may now be considered. Labour is the most important of these from our point of view. At every stage of production there will be some supervisory labour, and the larger the relative capacities of the plant, the bigger the proportion of the labour-force that will, in effect, be overhead. If a large-capacity machine is working at only a part of its capacity, it will frequently require very much the same labour-force. Here, again, there will normally be some reserve capacity. Overtime may be worked, and people are also able to carry heavier responsibility for short periods of time than they can carry as a regular matter. For any short increase in output, then, it may be possible to carry on with the same supervision. If the output is sustained at the new level, then extra supervisors will have to be trained, but their absence will certainly not be the bottle-neck that a piece of machinery can be. For other grades of overhead labour the extra output may be carried on the basis of working overtime with the effect on costs analysed in the simple case.

The management of the business will normally be able to cope with increased responsibilities but may be augmented if those responsibilities become permanent.

Overhead costs thus are to be seen as fixed in total over broad stretches of output, and certainly over the range of output which the business expects as usual. It has not been necessary to make any significant change in the conclusions drawn from the simplified model. How about direct costs?

In the simple case, the only direct costs were raw materials. In the normal case, as has been said, the firm will have process labour. How will the cost of that vary with the output that is being produced? Can we assume that direct labour costs per unit of output will remain constant, subject to the usual qualification of a rise in the level of such costs for periods when overtime is being worked? We obviously can do so when labour is engaged on repetitive work and is being paid on a piece-rate basis. In many cases, however, labour is engaged on more varied duties, involving the application of individual skill, and so cannot be paid piece-rates. In other cases, for whatever reason, piece-rates are not paid, the labourer being on a time basis.

In the real world, of course, there are great differences in the skill and energy of individual workmen, but it is not a very unreal assumption that the actual performance differences between individual labourers on time-work in any one business will not be so great as the potentialities of the workmen, and for the present analysis it is suggested that it would be a legitimate simplification to assume that the *average* productivity of labour in the business is constant. It may be said without cynicism that, although new-comers to a business may display unwonted energy or lethargy, they will not long continue to work significantly away from the average when day-wages are being paid. If they do not come up to something near the normal working pace of the department in which they are engaged they will be dismissed; and if they work much harder, the normal forces operating inside a workshop will induce them to moderate their zeal.

So long, then, as a firm is varying output by working short time(18) or by taking on or standing off workpeople who are normally on its books, it may be expected that average efficiency of labour will remain unchanged. If a business were free always to discharge the least efficient workers, then a reduction in output might mean a fall in the average cost per unit of direct labour; but, in practice, businesses are usually compelled to share out short-period stoppages fairly evenly.(19)

As in the simplified model, therefore, average direct costs will be constant so long as it is not necessary to work overtime. The output will be limited, even when overtime is worked, by the capacity of the equipment, process equipment imposing a narrower limit than the less divisible machinery, etc. If at the earlier limit extra process machinery is acquired, this will cause average overhead costs to rise when the machinery is acquired, falling thereafter as they are spread over larger outputs. The effect of overtime will be that the (marginal) direct costs of the additional output will rise to the new constant level appropriate to overtime wages, the average direct-cost curve rising gradually to the marginal level. This increase in costs will, however, not affect pricing policy. Diagrams III and IV illustrate these conclusions.

iii. Long-run costs

The theory of long-run costs is concerned with the way in which costs of production will change with changing outputs when the business is completely free to change its methods of production and to adapt them specially to the

---

(18) If a guaranteed week exists, then, of course, costs will be affected if short-time is worked.

(19) Of course, if the reduction in employment coincides with a general fall in employment in the area from which it draws its labour-force, then there may be a rise in the average intensity of effort of day labour — and the business may be more free to discharge the less efficient. There will then be a consequent fall in the level of the average direct-labour-cost curve. Equally, the existence of full employment in that area may cause a fall in labour productivity and a rise in the level of the average direct-labour-cost curve. This paper however, is restricted to considering changes in cost due to changes in the output of the individual firm.

production of each particular output. The theory is therefore fully applicable only to the costs of a new firm constructing and operating a plant suitable for the output concerned. It will be convenient to restrict discussion to this case for the present. The case of a business which is already in being with a given organization and with a plant of a given size(20) is discussed in the appendix to this part of the paper.

It is usual to make a special assumption about the choice of methods of production, and the long-run cost curves of the text-books may be regarded as attempting to answer the question: What will be the cost of production of each output *when the business is so organized as to produce that output in the most efficient manner?*, and long-run costs so defined are, therefore, assumed to be the lowest costs at which the particular outputs can be produced. That assumption will be questioned later on,(21) but, given it, the theoretical cost curve is a reasonable concept. The business man could list various methods of production by which each output could be produced, and would be able to make forecasts of the costs of establishing and operating a plant using any of these methods.

The older texts refrain from making a single generalization about the shape of the long-run cost curve for an individual business. Three distinct possibilities are described — increasing, constant, or decreasing long-run costs. In more recent literature, the shape of the long-run cost curve is, however, brought within a single generalization, and such cost curves are usually drawn U-shaped with minimum average long-run costs at the point of optimum scale for the individual business.

The falling branch of the U is justified easily enough. There must be some outputs which, however efficiently they are produced, involve a plant which is on too small a scale to make use of available technical economies. Similarly, some sizes of a business will be too small for efficient management, the managers being too little specialized (e.g. engaged on process work and other non-managerial duties) or under-employed. It is the rising branch of the U that is more difficult to justify and, since that is usually justified by reference to management conditions, let us look at that side of the question first.

---

(20) The establishment by such a business of a completely new and separate plant, although outside the scope of this paper so far, might seem sufficiently a new venture to fall within the theory that is being discussed, but decisions about the size and structure of such a plant would not be taken without reference to the plant already being operated and the conditions which are desirable in a complementary plant may well be quite different from those which would be preferred if the new plant were an independent entity.

(21) It has already been implicitly denied, see footnote 11.

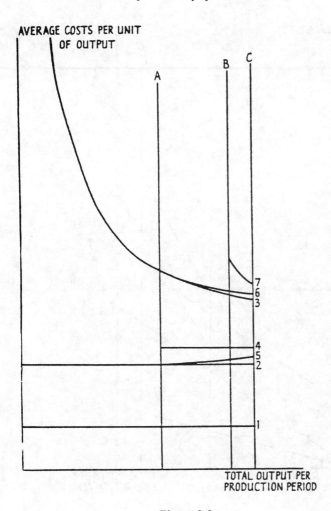

Figure 2.3

1 = Average direct material costs. 2 = Average direct costs with no overtime. 3 = Average total costs with no overtime. 4 = Marginal direct costs with overtime. 5 = Average direct costs with overtime. 6 = Average total costs with overtime. 7 = Average total costs with new process machinery working overtime.

A = Assumed limit to output from normal direct labour force. B = Assumed limit to output from process machinery. C = Assumed limit to output from machinery with the greatest reserve factor.

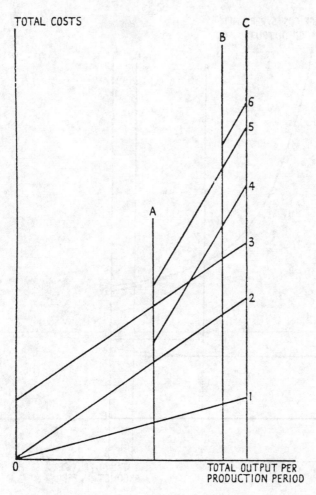

Figure 2.4

1 = Total direct material costs. 2 = Total direct costs, no overtime. 3 = Total costs with no overtime. 4 = Total direct costs with overtime. 5 = Total costs with overtime. 6 = Total costs after new process machinery, and assuming overtime.

A = Assumed limit to output from normal direct labour force. B = Assumed limit to output from process machinery. C = Assumed limit to output from machinery with the greatest reserve factor.

Management's task is to run the business, supervising the non-managerial factors of production. A lowering or a raising of managerial efficiency may, accordingly, show itself *either* in a rise or fall in the level of these non-managerial factors per unit of product, *or* in a less or more than proportionate increase in the number and expense of managers. It seems probable, in particular, that a lowering or raising of managerial efficiency will show itself particularly in a rise or fall in the level of direct costs of production, but that involves the short-run cost curves with which we are not now concerned. For the present purpose we can imagine a technical cost curve showing the average costs of production when the non-managerial factors of production are employed at the optimum level of managerial efficiency,(22) and can allow for changes in the efficiency of management by constructing a curve of average managerial costs, *it being understood that those costs may, in fact, show themselves elsewhere than in the costs of management proper.* The managerial cost curve is thus conceived as addable to the technical cost curve in order to get the effective cost curve.

As has been said already, the rising branch of the long-run cost curve is normally justified by management being regarded as, in the last resort, the one really indivisible factor of production, and, whilst the introduction of new personnel is admitted to allow of increasing specialization of the manager (who will become in the end simply the planner and chief sayer of 'yes' and 'no'), the fundamental indivisibility of his ultimate function is thought to remain. Accordingly, the law of non-proportional returns, to use Gide's term, is invoked to justify the concept of an optimum scale of business, so far as the management factor is concerned. Beyond this scale, diseconomies of management are thought to set in, and this will mean that, in the end, whatever the technical economies of scale, the cost curve must turn up and increasing costs be experienced for the business as a whole.

The generalization is frequently defended by implied appeals to 'experience', for example that, in fact, it is well known that large businesses are unwieldy and that there are decreasing returns to the factor of co-ordination, but the implicit assumption — that management will get continuously and progressively less

----

(22) The costs being calculated, e.g., as such estimates usually are, with the help of assumed figures for the capacities and performances of the various factors of production. A correspondent with wide experience of business projects says: 'I have seen a good many estimates of "technical long-run cost curves" (though not so described) offered as a reason for providing finance for large-scale reorganization or mergers. They usually turned out to be the less convincing kind of fairy-tale.' I quote this to emphasize that such a curve is a theoretical concept and to reinforce my later statement that, in fact, no business succeeds in producing at those costs — i.e. no business is 100 per cent. efficient.

efficient — should be questioned.(23)

Management should *not* be seen as a single factor combined in varying proportions with other factors and, therefore, subject to the simple law of non-proportional returns. There are *levels* of management. This is well known in everyday life, and it is possible to distinguish kinds of management techniques appropriate for different scales of output (varying with the type of business: that is to say, in one industry the atmosphere of really large-scale management will be encountered at a far smaller size, measured either in value of output or in number of employed, than in another). Changes in the type of management will be called for only at discontinuous intervals, and it may reasonably be held that those intervals get farther apart with increasing scale. To give a crude example: in a particular industry there may be one system of management for a plant with under 100 workers; the next system of management technique may be applicable to the scale from, say, 90 to 500 workers, the next from 400 to 1200 employees, and the growth in scale may then involve a system which is applicable to sizes from, say, 1000 to 5000, and so on. At each critical point in the scale the management will have the choice of being stretched to the limit or adapting itself to the new larger-scale technique (which will mean adding some personnel which will be overhead for the new range of scale — thus introducing one factor, however small its relative importance, which will make for decreasing costs over the new scale). Whatever the degree of inefficiency at any particular level of managerial scale, the business will probably be able to carry on without any notable decrease in average efficiency until near to the limit of its system of management, when it adopts the technique of management appropriate to the larger scale on which it is entering.

The way the efficiency of business varies as between the various levels of management must differ from industry to industry (and particularly with complexities arising on the selling side — outside the scope of this part of the paper). Management may well continue to get progressively less efficient at each higher level. Equally it *may* not, and we would put forward as a fairly plausible proposition that, even if we accept the usually assumed decrease in managerial efficiency, the rate of decrease will slow down with successive levels of management. *Still accepting the text-books' generalizations* then, we suggest that the 'management' average cost curve should be seen as a series of plateaux, each wider than its predecessor and each at a lesser height above its predecessor than that was in turn above its, the rise being steepest when the business gets too large for the personal management of the business by a single manager —

---

(23) It has to my knowledge been questioned by Harrod and by Kalecki, and Kaldor has pointed out that the usually assumed fall in managerial efficiency with scale could hold only under dynamic conditions.

this particular limit varying significantly according to the industry. If it is producing a single product, the business must have been so much organized already, at some scale, that larger scale will be simply a matter of routine. The management would then be able to carry on reasonably near to its existing level of efficiency. There is a general feeling that, at some very large scale, a business becomes so much of a routine that it suffers from not being able to adapt itself quickly to the vagaries of everyday life.(24)

Our generalization, then, excludes, by reason of ignorance, the business which is so large that it becomes more akin to Civil Service than to business management, when the common opinion is that it would be relatively inefficient, even though the Civil Service has admittedly developed efficient techniques for managing organizations which are too large to be efficient!

As a matter of fact, firms appear to come up against the problem of systems of management much more usually when there is a change in the management due to the passing of the persons who brought them to the scale at which they are operating than through any simple further growth whilst those persons remain in charge. A person managing a business of a given size has usually a good idea of how to run it as efficiently at a relatively larger size. In any case, he sees the business as his child, and will have at least that reason for being an efficient manager and, in addition, will have built up his technique around himself. His successors always find it difficult to adopt the technique that would be appropriate to management on a still larger scale to simplify the problems of the changeover and to reduce the management more nearly to a routine.

So far as *technical* factors are concerned, it is usually assumed that there is an optimum scale of plant, this being justified by examples of businesses employing factors of production with given indivisibilities, e.g. employing units of machinery and plant of given capacities. The optimum size is then that of the plant producing an output which is the least common multiple of the

---

(24) We have heard this alleged to be the case for one very large British manufacturing business, but we do not know the facts. On the other hand, it should be said that there ought to be some economies available to this very large business — for example, through the employment of specialists, and that, for this reason, the foresight of the business may well be more efficient than it could be for a business not of its large scale. One may cite the example of the employment of professional economists — surely profitable on a full-time basis only for a very large firm, but certainly profitable for a business whose output is a significant proportion either of the National Income or of the world output of its product, but it may, of course, be said that the employment of such experts will bring economies only to businesses engaged in a much more uncertain and complex world than that postulated for the cost curve of a single-product business under static conditions!

various machine-capacities.(25) In terms of this concept, technical factors imply no more than constant long-run average costs of production once the optimum scale of plant has been reached, so long as the increase in scale takes place by duplicating the optimum combination of factors.

If the growth in scale is by a smaller amount, then, of course, average costs will rise until it is again possible to utilize fully an optimum unit. But this undulating curve, as Stigler calls it,(26) cannot have the rising trend required by the theoretical curve. Further, at a sufficiently large scale, the finite increase in scale necessary to get once more to the optimum combination of factors can be treated as relatively so small as not to impair the continuity of the curve, in which case the average technical cost curve could be regarded as reasonably approximating to the conditions of constant cost.

The previous two paragraphs have accepted the assumption that there *is* an optimum size of plant from the technical point of view. It is difficult to accept the assumption, however, especially for the single-product plant, that growth means merely an enlarged plant, which is just a recombination of the machinery and equipment used at the smaller scale. A continuous increase of scale must always carry further technical economies at some point.

The larger the output going through the works, the more likely it will be that some process or other could be further mechanized. The introduction and elaboration of mechanical methods in ancillary operations such as internal transport is another possibility. Again, economies in maintenance and repair are likely to be always available to some extent with an increase in scale. Whatever the scale of the plant, maintenance and repair will necessarily be carried out on a smaller scale, and a large part will frequently be in the handicraft stage. Increasing scale, by increasing the runs of repair jobs of particular kinds, will enable some further economies to be achieved. There seems no reason to suggest that costs of maintenance do anything but fall continuously (although probably not sharply) with increasing scale.

Further, the single-product assumption relates to the end-product; the business is certainly not to be restricted to a single process, and continued growth may mean that it will become more attractive to manufacture for itself some of the goods that it previously purchased, when the technical economies of

(25) E.g. H. A. Silverman, 'The Optimum Firm in the Boot and Shoe Industry', *Oxford Economic Papers*, Number 6, 1942.
(26) G. Stigler, *The Theory of Price*, 1947.

scale in that line of business will be added to it.(27)

Apart from the management factor, still assuming that the prices of the factors of production are not affected by the growth of the firm, it is, therefore, contended that the long-run cost curve should always be seen as falling with increasing scale. A rider should be added, however — that the larger the scale already, the less important *relatively* will be the incidence of further technical economies.(28) The fundamental redesign of equipment, or changes in layout and methods of production, will give way to the relatively less important development of mechanization of parts of the individual processes, etc. The more spectacular gains from increased scale will be exhausted first, and the technical economies of a still larger scale frequently consist of the further development of what has been done already. The reduction in the relative strength of technical economies as the plant grows must mean that, at a relatively large scale, the further economies available must seem of greatly diminished significance.(29)

But there is one further criticism of the theoretical long-run cost curve — the assumption that, for any given output, the business man will choose the method of organization that will enable him to produce at least costs must be questioned. The necessity for strategical reserves will affect the long-run cost curve as well as the short-run and will show itself in the nature of the business man's long-range plans and the general lines of his productive organization. This will make him seek for flexibility in order to be able to meet any likely need of varying his output (and his product). It will therefore not cause only short-run reserve capacity, but will also affect the type of organization and, therefore, the *types* of overhead factors of production employed. For example, in choosing

---

(27) Of the same kind, perhaps, are the gains from undertaking its own research, both that which is simply devoted to the more effective control of the business's processes and the more fundamental kinds. In this field, economies of scale are notoriously likely always to be present, although in fundamental research they are perhaps not relevant to the single-product business of our assumption. Such gains will, strictly, affect the level of the cost curve from the point of scale at which they operate.

(28) The weakening of the force of the technical factors making for the expansion of the size of the plant is one reason why conditions in the labour market will tend to induce large businesses to operate separate plants in different labour markets. Where a business is producing many products, of course, the fact that economies of scale will first arise in, and be mainly available in, the common processes or services will be a restraint on any tendency to split up the plant, but, at a certain size, the possibility of economies through turning a plant entirely over to one product or to a more restricted range of products may be disintegrative.

(29) Especially when taken alongside the effects of the short-run excess capacity which this paper stresses as being so much a normal occurrence.

managers he will seek for men with flexible minds rather than those relatively better at routine (i.e. whose efficiency is greater *given* the size and nature of the output to be produced). Similarly, in the choice of maintenance labour he will prefer a craftsman who is good at turning his hand to anything rather than one who will be better if his work is completely a matter of routine. But he will be *especially* restricted in his freedom to change his plans in future by his choice in the matter of investment in equipment. Although the short-run reserve capacity that is postulated will mean that the capital investment will be pushed farther than necessary for the particular output that is expected, it will not be pushed so *deeply* as if it were certain that neither product nor output would be varied.(30) It follows that, in terms of the short-run cost curve, average overhead costs and average direct costs will each be higher than they would be in a less uncertain world, and if there were all the infinity of choice postulated by the normal cost curves.

The effects of this will be particularly marked in the relatively more capitalistic industries (in the Austrian sense of employing more round-about processes) or those which have the greater expectation of fluctuations in output. Reserve capacity is, therefore, most marked in the capital goods industries. *Within* an individual business, the effects will be most marked in that part of the plant where the units of equipment are largest in size relatively to turnover. Each unit of equipment will tend to be organized on a smaller scale than would be ideal for the output that is planned, in order to get the flexibility of a larger number of smaller units and to reduce the minimum desirable excess capacity. Where output is especially liable to fluctuate, particularly indivisible processes may be operated by, say, four or five units of equipment, when costs could be reduced if they were replaced by a single unit taking care of the whole through-put. Such an elephant would be economical only when running relatively near to capacity; it would have to be duplicated to some extent to get reserve capacity, and its operation would be seriously less efficient than the smaller units as the through-put declines — which situation could be better met by completely closing down one or more of the smaller units that are the alternative.

The desire for flexibility will also mean that ancillary processes such as

(30) So far as the first of these factors is concerned, the author has several times had the instructive experience of visiting factories, one of which was run by a producer facing the normal risks of the particular product's market, and the other of which was run by a business that was really operating in the next stage. It was frequently the case that the latter business would deliberately plan for a factory considerably smaller than its usual needs, so that this could be operated full out with all available economies. The difference in the efficiency of the two types of factories, as measured by costs of production and as illustrated by the methods of production, has to be seen to be believed.

internal transport will be far less automatic than they might be. Conveyors and such-like equipment will always be used relatively sparingly, since they are frequently sunk in a particular manner of producing a particular product.(31)

The removal of the least-cost assumption clearly makes it still more likely that technical costs of production will fall with increased scale of production — and, therefore, that they will be available, to some extent, to counteract any decreased efficiency in management, especially since they may well operate continuously, whereas management has been thought of as likely to become less efficient only at critical points in its scale, maintaining its efficiency over the intervening range.

Whereas Chamberlin's long-run 'excess' capacity appears to consist of management which is not fully extended at the given scale, we should expect that in the real world reserve capacity will exist in capital and other overhead equipment. This type of reserve capacity is 'excess' only in terms of theoretical criteria based on the postulate of the minimization of current costs of production, and it has been argued that it does not involve waste in the fluctuating conditions of the real world, nor does it necessarily result from monopoly.

The shape of the long-run cost curve will be the result of adding together the average managerial cost curve and the curve of average technical cost per unit of product. It is certainly not possible to make any very precise statement about its over-all shape. The technical cost curve should fall continuously,(32) although it will probably get less steep as scale increases. The managerial cost curve will fall for part of the range, and will probably rise again, at least for a time, after which it may or may not level off. What happens to management as scale increases is thus very much a matter of conjecture and will probably vary from industry to industry. Even if management should continue to get less efficient with increasing scale, that will only be as between levels of management, and the consequent rise in managerial costs will probably diminish as the scale of management rises. Two very broad conclusions, however, do follow: (a) that at a very large scale of output the business will get as near as matters to the condition of constant long-run costs of production — if we had not accepted the assumption that management becomes less efficient for all increases in management scale, then the weight of the technical factors would lead to decreasing long-run costs once management was at the routine level of efficiency; (b) that over any given scale of management the business will be in a condition of decreasing long-run costs.

---

(31) This effect will, of course, operate especially for the multi-product plant with which we are not now concerned.

(32) Its fall may become sharper at critical points where the business becomes large enough to embark on new kinds of technical economies.

It may be noted that, where diseconomies of management are most likely,(33) e.g. for a product where, for whatever reason, the processes are largely in the hands of hand-craftsmen (this will include industries where the machines are really power-driven tools), or, again, where the costs of the raw material are a large part of the total costs, so that continuous supervision of its use may be necessary, economies of scale are likely to be less important, because other circumstances limit the degree of mechanization. Conversely, in industries where technical innovations come most easily — where mass-production methods can be used — the sheer production side of management is most amenable to routine methods, and diseconomies to management are likely to be less important. Accordingly, a business will be more likely to be in a position of decreasing long-run costs the larger is the typical firm in its industry. But, however much costs may decrease with increasing scale, we should still expect that long-run economies of scale will be relatively unimportant compared with the falling slope of the short-run cost curve.

It will be seen that firm generalization cannot be made about the over-all shape of the curve of long-run marginal costs. It will fall over the early stages in the growth of a business; over any level of management, it will be below the long-run average cost curve, possibly rising at the limit of one level of management and falling at the commencement of the next; and it will approximate to the long-run average cost curve for very large scales, when the business will be approximately in a condition of constant long-run costs. Much more important in our view, however, is the curve of marginal long-run technical costs appropriate to the business which is under consideration. This curve will never rise above average technical costs; it will generally be falling, although it may have stretches where it is more or less constant. In actual conditions it will probably not tend to be very low in relation to the curve of average technical costs.

It is difficult to discuss in the abstract the way changes in scale, i.e. along the long-run cost curve, will affect the short-run situation in which the business man will find himself, but a few generalizations may be attempted. If businesses employed the same technical processes at all sizes, the slope of the short-run cost curve should diminish with growth of scale, since, thanks to the reduced importance of indivisibility, the relative degree of reserve capacity would diminish, but, as we have already argued, growth will probably mean an intensification in the use of capital and other overhead factors. Accordingly, the

---

(33) It must be remembered that this part of the paper does not discuss the selling side of the business at all, and ignores the fact that limitation of the market for one product may frequently lead to a business adding to the complexity of its management by becoming multi-product.

degree of reserve capacity may well increase, and, therefore, the slope of the short-run cost curve may be steeper for larger sizes of the business. Certainly, in practice, in industries where economies of scale are important, the reserve capacity of the bigger business is often greater than that at which smaller businesses operate, but marketing strategy plays its part in this situation.

Restricting ourselves to technical factors and to the effects of technical economies available only to plants of larger sizes, capital and other overhead factors of production are characteristically substituted for direct factors of production (particularly for direct labour), and a growth in scale accordingly will usually mean a fall in the level of the short-run average direct-cost curve. A large-scale business will, therefore, usually have lower average direct costs per unit than will a smaller-scale business, even if its average total costs are the same. This means that it will be more easily able to survive in any period of low prices.

Appendix to Part 2: some observations on costs in practice
This appendix will consider some aspects of the behaviour of costs of production as they are encountered in practical analyses; the heading refers to its contents as 'observations' to emphasize the fact that systematic generalization of the kind that has been made so far will not be possible, which is why the normal theoretical discussion stops where it does. In the actual examination of an existing business it need not be left there, since the data usually make it possible to decide what factors should receive special attention and what should be ignored, and it is frequently possible to assign limits to the strength of the factors in which one is interested. Certainly one can, in practice, usually maintain a level of generalization which is appropriate to the business. Here, in a general paper, one can make only general observations.

The assumption of a constant price-level for all factors of production is one which must, to some extent, be unrealistic. Although it may be tolerably acceptable for any change in output which is appropriate for a given short-run cost curve, it is more questionable for changes in scale, since some change could be imagined for any business which would make that business so large that it would have an appreciable share of the market for at least one of its factors of production, and, in that case, the price of that factor could not be assumed *a priori* to be unaffected by the size of the business.

With present knowledge, little general correction can be made. So far as concerns raw materials in wide industrial consumption relative to the size of the business, however, it seems that, perhaps contrary to received opinion, purchasing economies proper are likely to be unimportant over quite a wide range of scale as compared with technical economies. In one particular case, which seemed as likely to afford purchasing economies as could be imagined, they existed, but only for so great a disparity of business size as made it certain that so small a gain was not worth taking into practical account in the factors accounting for the growth of the large business, and they were certainly negligible against the economies of scale on the technical side.(34) To the extent to which such economies exist, of course, they *will* reinforce the effects of technical economies and make it more likely that the cost curve will fall.

The labour market is, perhaps, the one where firmer generalizations can be made, as it is the one where the effects of increasing scale are most important, especially since they will go against the weight of the generalizations which have been made on the basis of the usual fixed-price assumptions. In the short-run, it is nearer the truth to say that a business has a unique labour-market than to say that it shares its labour market with other businesses. The established business will have relations with a group of workmen whom it normally employs, and who normally look to it for employment, even though, at any one time, they may be temporarily unemployed. These will be available to it without the standard rate of wages being affected, and the degree of their utilization may be increased, as has already been said, by overtime — which will affect the levels of the cost curves but will not greatly affect their slopes. In the short-run, then, a business will increase its output by overtime, from its normal labour-force, and a growing business may work on an overtime basis for the whole period during which it is growing.

There will be a more floating body of persons who are not so clearly attached to any one firm, and who may be attracted if they are offered the prospect of full-time employment.(35) These again will come to it gradually without the standard rate of wages for the business necessarily being altered. So far as unskilled labour is concerned, in large industrial areas such as that around Birmingham, there may be a relatively large pool of labour of this kind normally available, if time is given for them to get to know the prospects. *If* the business wishes to expand beyond this or at a faster rate than the extra labourers come to it at its existing wages, it will have to bid away workmen who have a preference for remaining where they are already. Accordingly, the further we push our long-run cost curve *during a given interval of time*, the more likely it will be that there will be an upward pressure on the business's wage-rates. But it does not follow that a business will let itself get into this position. First it will have good reasons against mere wage-competition; and these will not be the simple monopsonistic reasons that may naively be adduced. As a continuing business, it has an interest in settled relations with its workpeople, and too great a

(34) It is frequently forgotten in discussing purchasing economies that some are available only to the small business. A small engineering business, for example, can well make use of occasional bargains in the second-hand machinery market, refurbishing them for its own service, but it would not pay a large business to do so, since the small lots that turn up would not be of much use; another example is the small business in the boot and shoe industry, which can similarly make use of odd parcels of leather.

(35) The existence of overtime, by the way, is never a deterrent to new-comers in ordinary times. In its own interest, the business will keep it within reasonable limits, and regular overtime is some sort of guarantee of future prospects, being regarded as one of the signs of a business which is vigorously growing.

rate of growth, especially if induced by the wage-packet, is liable to bring disturbing factors here. A continuing business will wish the new-comers to settle down in the business and cannot be so sure of this if it makes too rapid a development or if it gets its labour by snatching tactics.(36) Taking the cost curve as it is usually described, there must be some scale beyond which the growth of a business in a given time period must mean a rising wage-level, which, in turn, must cause the long-run cost curve to rise if still larger scales are achieved in the same period. We do not think that this part of the cost curve has any relevance to practical conditions. Growth does not usually come in such great spurts relative to the existing size of the business, and in the rare case that it does the business usually becomes multi-factory, locating an additional plant in some other area where it will have a new chance to grow.

If the normal idea of the long-run curve is retained, it must be seen as non-reversible. A declining business will be left with at least some equipment and organization which is too large for its short-run output. Accordingly, its long-run cost curve will lie above that which was appropriate to that output during its previous growth. This case is relevant only in the analysis of the pathology of business strategy, and would take the argument into wider questions.

When the actual behaviour and experience of a given business in a given market situation is being considered, it is, of course, the short-run cost curve that the business man sees as immediately relevant and which he acts on. In analysis, therefore, and particularly with reference to practical pricing policy, it should be our starting-point. Given the data, at least a working approximation of the short-run cost curves is easily constructed. At any given time a fairly satisfactory division can be made between overhead costs and direct costs (most businesses are multi-product, and

---

(36) It is not possible, without stating detailed cases, to consider the effects of the fact that a business does not work in isolation — that, quite apart from circumstances which are peculiar to it, it will share many events in common with other businesses who are working in its product-market or who share its factor-markets. The labour market does, however, lend itself to at least one simple generalization. The trade cycle will generally exercise a depressing or an expansionist influence on all businesses simultaneously. In any case, granted the fact of the localization of industry, a business will frequently be sharing its labour market with other businesses producing similar products, and those will certainly have similar experiences over the trade cycle. It follows that all the businesses in a particular labour market will be wishing to expand their output at the same time. When there is such a general pressure on the market for labour of a particular sort, the course of wage-rates will be upward, even for the existing labour-force. Once a certain degree of full employment has been reached, wages will start to rise, and increased pressure to get output will cause them to rise still further. In the trade cycle, therefore, direct costs will rise with the rise in general output. It is, perhaps, for this reason that the normal short-run cost curves have appeared to be useful weapons for the social analysis for which they are used, but that is no justification for their use in the analysis of the behaviour of individual businesses.

variable overheads present a little difficulty, but allowance for them can usually be made with a fair degree of approximation). The direct costs can then be assumed to remain at their current level, and the total overheads can be taken as constant. From this, one can construct fairly reliable estimates of the effect on the business of normal fluctuations in output, i.e. those allowed for in the organization of the business. In rare cases more elaborate statistical methods will enable us to make better estimates. A good example of these is given in the evidence presented by the United States Steel Corporation to the Temporary National Economic Committee. It may be observed that the statistical curves conform to our generalizations, since a straight line gives a good fit to total costs over the period, as estimated free from entangling considerations such as the changes in factor-prices. It follows that marginal direct costs are estimated to have been constant for the very large fluctuation of output over the period covered by the statistical study. However, the kind of procedure that has been outlined frequently serves the business man in his policy-determination.

We are now concerned with how the actual long period looks from the starting-point of the short period, and how it differs from the theoretical concepts. As already indicated, the hypothetical curve of long-run costs is of nothing like the importance that it is in the broader analysis of social conditions for which it is used in the text-books. However, the business man will usually have at least a hazy idea of the opportunities open to him from continued expansion, but they will be hazy, and the haziness will increase with the time that it would take to make a given increase in scale.

Looking at it from the business man's point of view, suppose that current output gets to the limit of the usual range of fluctuations, and that the pressure on output has come consistently enough to look like persisting. Some adjustments will have to be made, and, as already indicated, one of the first effects will be the working overtime of personnel — this will usually occur before the limit of the plant has been reached, overtime being worked in the 'bottle-neck' departments. That will mean a rise in the level of the direct-cost curve for the enlarged output which is being produced.(37)

If the high output persists, then the business man will start to make more permanent adjustments. He will be willing to take on and train extra labour, and, since this will mean working his process machinery more fully, he will probably order extensions here — which, assuming the growth only of the particular business with which we are concerned, will usually be possible without too much delay in normal times. The probable pressure on his labour supply will also make him regard with favour the deepening of his capital structure, using equipment to eke out labour. He will certainly be guided by his knowledge of, or guess at, his long-period technical cost curve, the general properties of which have already been discussed. It is worth stressing that *it is his technical cost curve which is relevant to the planning of*

(37) Such a rise in costs will not affect pricing-policy as a rule. Overtime will be seen as a temporary expedient, and granted the existence of the overhead costs, the larger output will still be profitable without distributing the price-situation, even at the high direct costs (i.e. labour will normally be costed up at non-overtime rates.)

the business man. No business man would expect to be a less efficient manager at a larger scale; he will tacitly assume that he will remain as efficient as he is for any increase in scale that he is likely to make. Realized costs may, therefore, differ from the expected costs on which he plans, but that cannot affect his planning. It follows that to a business man long-run costs will usually be expected to fall with the growth of the business, and, therefore, that rising long-run average costs are ruled out of the analysis of business strategy, though they may be relevant to the analysis of a business's history.

Time is of the essence of the business man's thinking. There will be a limit to the rate at which he will be prepared to grow. He normally views a new scale as a position which once taken calls for consolidation. He will expect his costs at first to be higher than they will become when he has achieved that consolidation — in fact, for any given scale, he will expect, other things being equal, that his cost curves will fall over time. that he will always be able to make some improvements in the light of experience. The idea of an optimum size of business is outside his usual way of thinking. A reasonably efficient management will always expect to be able to manage a bigger business at lower costs if it is given due time in which to make adjustments, and it will take all the time that is necessary.(38)

One final observation may be of interest. We have discussed the provision of an empirical content to the short-period cost curve; how far is it possible to do the same for the long-period curve? In some industries, where technical reasons make it possible to convert even multi-product output into equivalent units of a standard product, it is possible to use expert advice to construct a hypothetical technical long-run cost curve(39) which may be used as a criterion against which to assess the degree to which an existing business achieves a degree of efficiency which is thus thought to be *potentially* open to a business of its particular size, on the basis of the most up-to-date technical information.(40) Such a curve, of course, will extend over a far wider range than will be relevant to the planning of any particular business. The business man will usually have a good enough idea of the shape of his technical long-run cost curve in the neighbourhood of his existing size, but that will be only the beginning so far as he is concerned. Non-technical factors affecting efficiency frequently turn

---

(38) In our experience business men take a good deal of time to make long-run decisions such as are entailed in major extensions. They therefore try to make them in advance of their becoming urgent.

(39) But see page 91, footnote 24.

(40) The construction of such a curve has led us to evolve the concept of a practicable optimum which we have found useful in explaining the survival pattern of an industry. This will be at the scale, varying with the industry, where further economies of scale will be relatively negligible except for a very large increase in plant. In view of the flattening of the long-run technical cost curve in this neighbourhood, considerably smaller businesses could survive for relatively long periods if they adopted a relatively less generous obsolescence policy than the larger businesses.

101

out to be of even greater importance than technical considerations, even for industries where technical economies seem spectacular relatively to other industries. These other factors can only be analysed in the light of the details of the business's marketing strategy, and of the development of its market, but, where the empirical technical cost curve can be constructed, it provides a help in assessing the relative strength of the other factors, and as a starting-point for the detailed questions which will uncover some of those factors, even if only in a qualitative way.

3 The determination of prices

i. Introduction and general assumptions
This part of the paper gives the outline of the theory of the normal price-policy of an individual business; a general analysis of situations in which that policy breaks down is reserved for later publication.

The assumptions and reservations which will generally be made are as follows:
(1) As in Part 2, the business is assumed to be a manufacturer.
(2) The analysis will be restricted to the product-market.
(3) The business is first assumed to be single-product.
(4) The conclusions of the earlier part will be taken over as assumptions — i.e. *(a)* that average direct costs are constant for all outputs, *(b)* that since long-run pricing policy can be based only on the expectation of business men, average long-run costs of production will, at worst, remain constant, but will probably decrease at a slackening rate with the growth of a business. For this reason the business man will use his existing (short-run) costs as a basis for his long-term pricing policy.

ii. Normal price-policy
A business man producing an article with a given specification will normally base his price on his costs of production.(41) He will be able to make fairly accurate estimates of his average direct costs, and, in order to get the quoted price, these will be grossed up by a definite amount, which following accounting usage we shall call the average gross profit-margin required per unit of product. The addition will equal the average contribution that the business man will

---

(41) Similarly if, as with some consumers' goods, he has to work to a conventional price, he will determine the specification of the product on the basis of his costs. It is for this reason that the length or weight of towels produced to be sold in some markets would provide a so-far unexplored index of the trade cycle, since they have varied according to changes in the prices of materials or in wages, shortening in the boom and lengthening in the slump.

require each unit of product to make towards covering the overhead costs of the business and making a profit. Whether the accounts for any period will actually show a profit or loss on balance will depend, of course, upon the extent to which the total sales(42) in that period have sufficed to cover the total overheads charged in the accounts as well as the direct costs.(43)

The exact method by which the average required gross profit-margin is calculated will vary between businesses, but the details do not affect the present analysis.(44) It is necessary only to take it as generally true that a definite addition will be made to current direct costs in order to get a price which will normally be adhered to (subject to relatively minor modifications or to short-term aberrations, one kind of which is discussed later). The amount added will formally include an allowance *as for* profit, although, as noted, the actual earning of a profit will depend upon the sales actually achieved.

Given, then, the business's costing rules and given the current level of its direct costs, the price which it will *normally* charge will be determinate, and will bear a definite relation to average direct costs. This principle of pricing will be called the *Normal Cost Principle*, since the business man, in fixing his price in this way, appears to act on the idea that such a price will normally enable him to cover his costs. The principle appears first to have been stated in economic literature in the article by Hall and Hitch, reporting some of the results of the inquiries of the pre-war Oxford Economists' Research Group.(45)

This costing-practice is stubbornly adhered to, as will be agreed by all who have discussed price-policy with manufacturers. Departures will certainly not be made for the sake of short-period gains but only in abnormal situations, and need not be regarded as weakening the normal cost principle as a general rule of behaviour.

---

(42) We ought, strictly, to refer to output rather than sales because additions to stocks will also result in credits in the accounts. However, output decisions depend upon sales, and, since stock-policy is not considered here, it will be simpler to assume that stocks remain constant, when total output and sales will be equivalent.

(43) Given the price, the line showing total receipts will cross the curve of total costs at the point where sales would be just sufficient to break even with costs. This is the break-even level of output.

(44) The differences are, of course, important in practical work, and the reasons why a business should choose one particularly will be considered in my book.

(45) 'Price Theory and Business Behaviour', *Oxford Economic Papers*, Number 2, May 1939. The authors there named the principle as the Full Cost Principle. I have reluctantly changed the name, because the earlier term suggests, wrongly, that prices always tend to equal the full average costs of all business men. Even if they do so normally, they will not do so when output is running at a low level. The change in terminology has, at least, brought relief to one pedagogue.

Granted that the principle is is generally adhered to in manufacture, the mystery is that it has not yet emerged as a *postulate* of economic analysis. It should obviously be an accepted principle in pricing-theory.(46) Those economists who have thought about it have been too concerned with trying to explain it on the basis of the existing theory, instead of accepting it. Any explanation, of course, is wanted only for the purpose of constructing other and wider generalizations which will enable the principle to be incorporated more closely into the general framework of economic analysis. Scientific method would suggest that the right thing to do at the existing state of knowledge would be at least to accept the principle as a basis for further theory in its own field — the analysis of price-policy. An explanation is offered in the rest of this section, but it should be stressed that the validity of the principle as a theoretical postulate is independent of the argument.

As the Hall–Hitch paper has shown, business men offer at least the outlines of a rudimentary theory when questioned as to the reasons for their conduct. Economists have, perhaps, paid too little attention to the practical theorizing of business men — especially when produced in answer to the economists' own questions. Two things stand out in particular — the business man normally thinks long-run, and views the world he functions in as a *much* more competitive world than the modern economist is prepared to concede. In fact, a business man quite normally thinks that business is, in the long run, so competitive that there is a 'right' price, and that any serious departure from this will not be profitable in the long run, however attractive may be the gains of short-run price-changes.

In the long run, it is thought, a business which charges a higher price must have the ground cut from under its feet with the incursion of rivals into its market, and a lower price is thought to be unprofitable because the rightness of the price results from its representing normal costs. The business man therefore uses his costs as a guide from which to determine the right price in this sense, is sure that it will not pay him to charge more, and will only charge less when

---

(46) Economic literature had to wait for the inquiries of the Oxford Research Group and for the publication of the subsequent paper by Hall and Hitch for even a statement that it was the general practice. One would have thought that enough persons trained in economics had gone out into the business world for someone at least to have been impressed by the lack of any explicit marginal analysis and to have reported back from his frontier observation post that this is the custom, and that economic argument might at least consider adopting it as a principle of analysis. Further, it is now nearly a decade since the Hall–Hitch paper, and no attempt has been made to deny the general application of the principle which they then put forward, yet general economic analysis is still unaffected.

convinced by experience that only a lower price will keep him in his market, because he is less efficient than the rivals who are threatening him. Equally, while he will not normally cut his price *for the sake of competition*, he will be quite willing to offer a lower price than his rivals if he can justify it on his own costing rules, and will do so then because he will think himself able to sustain his attack on their position and to consolidate his own, his business thus being able to grow just because its lower costs will support it.

In more technical language, the business man is thus seen as thinking of his long-run demand curve as being infinitely elastic for a certain level of price, in the sense that any attempt to maintain a higher price will mean the loss of his market, since other producers will find it profitable in the long run to continue to supply the market at that price. We must recognize that modern theory has led to erroneous views about the marketing situation confronting a typical manufacturing business. It is, of course, strictly true that no two businesses will produce exactly the same product. Even when the two products have identical specifications, they will be sold by different people, and all the personal circumstances surrounding the sale will be different. In fact, the multi-product business of the real world will usually specialize in some way, and any speciality will frequently be differentiated in specification.(47)

The fact of this separability of the market of individual businesses appears to justify labelling the individual producer as a monopolist, rather than as a competitor, but the demand for the products of an individual producer is thought of far too much in terms of the short-run demand curves of the text-book consumers' market. Where the private consumer is concerned, it may not be false to regard his attachment as meaning that, in the short run, the individual seller will not lose all of his customers if he raises price. Equally, if he lowers price, he will not, in the short run, be able to attract all customers away from the rival

---

(47) This is frequently the consequence of the way in which the founder set about getting *his* market and building up *his* goodwill, by doing anything which came his way in his line of business and, at the same time, looking round for any product on which he could specialize, in order to get buyers to give him more than the casual order and thus to become his 'customers'.

sellers.(48)

However, leaving the consumers' market on one side, the text-book view of preferences will not be true even for most makers of consumers' goods, let alone for the maker of producers' goods. The typical customer of a manufacturing business is another *business*, and, whilst such customers are no less subject to personal habits and preferences than the final consumer, they cannot, even in the short run, be as indifferent to the price which they are offered. To buy identically specified articles at a higher price than they could get them elsewhere would expose them in the long run to effective competition from those who buy more cheaply. Such business customers, moreover, are much better informed about costs and prices, and have a measure of any irrational preferences in the effects on their profit-and-loss account position. It is, accordingly, essential in the normal manufacturing business that its price should not be significantly higher than that which other businesses would quote for the same, or substantially similar, goods. Even where specialities are concerned (ruling out the case where they are protected by patent) they will normally be producible by other businesses — in fact, frequently are being produced, perhaps as non-specialities.

Apart from the businesses actually producing his type of article, a manufacturer will have two other potential competitors — new businesses, and new enterprise on the part of businesses who are producing other goods at the moment, but whose equipment and organization could be turned over to producing his type of product, if the gross profit-margin available to them were sufficiently attractive. The latter type of competition is important.

In an established business there will often be some drive from an existing department to expand by taking on new products which suit it. The mass of mature business leaders may be as conservative as are most men, but it is a characteristic of the business world that its rewards do attract the innovating mind, and in any industry there will usually be some up-and-coming young men with ideas who will force their way. In this way all efficient mature business is often subjected to expansionary pressure from its younger men. As one business

---

(48) Even in the consumers' market proper, however, the seller cannot rely upon the long-run support of his customers' preferences and habits. If he charges too high a price, rival sellers may well think it worth their while to incur the selling costs that would be necessary to transfer customer-attachments. Too high a short-run price thus means that his short-run demand curve will shift to the left in the long run, i.e. that the long-run demand curve will be elastic, its elasticity probably increasing with the height of his short-run price. This is one of the reasons why the Normal Cost Principle is found to be observed in retail pricing. It is realized that our general argument implies the abandonment of Chamberlin's 'large-group' analysis and the assertion of a kind of 'oligopoly' as normal. This will be defended in detail elsewhere.

man put it, looking back over the growth of his business, 'you have to expand to keep your young men'.(49) It should also be noted that many new ventures on the part of established businesses have been caused by the desire to keep a key department more fully occupied in the face of a temporary depression in trade for the main product.

In economic literature a lot is made, and rightly, of the difficulty of new businesses getting sufficient capital and, hence, of the fact that established businesses may make large profits before new businesses start coming into the industry. When, however, the detailed history of individual businesses is examined, one becomes aware how normal it is for an established business to take on new products requiring broadly the same equipment, even if only in one department. In the course of time it is possible, in this way, for shifts in emphasis to lead to a business changing its typical product, and crossing the frontier from one industry to another. In fact, the frontiers of an industry are rarely fixed so firmly as they appear when, at any moment, one looks at the perhaps small number of apparently securely established businesses. Over a period one can often find a story of several attempts to expand into that product's market, some succeeding, some failing.

In short, the business man when he reports his world as competitive is generalizing from his experience and from his own attitude. A clue to the main characteristics of his approach, and of his innate competitiveness, is given at once when he is seen with the product of another business in his hand. It need not be at all the same product as he makes himself, so long as he has some acquaintance with the processes by which it is made. It appears almost an instinctive reaction for him, given the price at which the product is sold, to form a rough idea of the gross profit-margin which would be available to him, getting first an estimate of the cost of materials and then, if the net product seems attractive, of the direct labour cost. If the proposition continues to look attractive, there will follow at least the rough idea of the sort of additional equipment that he would need if he went for the new market. The process may well be left there in most cases, but there will remain the possibility of action being taken when circumstances are favourable, and a sufficiently attractive margin will always lead to action being taken somewhere. Of course, mistakes are made in the process, but innovation and the mistakes of innovation are part

---

(49) This paper has deliberately used the term business man in place of the term entrepreneur — it is a pity that some hardening of the linguistic arteries has removed the fundamental idea of enterprise from the traditional name. The characteristic of a business which is alive is the enterprise of its managers. The interest of the job is always tending to spill out in playing with new ideas and the idea of a new product quite naturally comes into the game.

of the essence of business life.

In this way, the focusing point of competitive action is the gross profit-margin, and competition results, in the end, in stabilizing gross profit-margins in sections of industry which involve fundamentally the same sort of organization. So stable is it that, whilst one cannot make good guesses at the net profit-margin of a business, quite frequently after a walk round a works one finds oneself putting the business mentally in the same class as another which one knows, although that may produce a very different product and, on this basis, it may be possible to make surprisingly good guesses at the gross profit-margin.

It may help a little to understand the emergence of a business's costing rules if we consider the case of a brand-new product introduced exclusively by a particular business (it may, of course, be protected initially by patents). Theoretically, the new producer can charge what price he thinks best. He certainly will pay attention to short-run conditions of demand, especially if he is exploiting a patent valid only for a limited period of time. He may well set a very high gross profit-margin (but note that even his initial price-policy is reflected in his margin, which becomes the explicit part of his policy). There will be limits set to it by competition even here. Too high a margin will give an incentive for other business men to get round the patent, or even risk the chances of actions for infringement. The fountain-pen market appears to have known this sort of successful competition on occasion. If the product is not patented, or on the expiry of the patent, the product will be considered by other business men and some of them may come in, probably cutting away a bit of the original producers' market. To protect his position he will have to lower his price, i.e. granted that the specification of the article does not change he will have to reduce his gross profit-margin.

The competition of the new-comers and their zeal to get in, possibly counting on anticipated economies of scale to see them right when once they are in, will cause a fall in the gross margin. It may be set too low, in which case, sooner or later, some marginal businesses will be squeezed out, and it will be possible for the remaining producers to set a more remunerative margin. Granted the increase in their trade, and the reduction of costs through greater experience and technical development of the product, they may be able to get a higher margin whilst price is not raised. This has been apparently the normal story on the setting up of some of the modern British industries. The upshot is that, in the end, the gross margin of each producer will be set at such a level as preserves him from long-run competition in price by other producers, but which is at the right level for him to be able to continue to offer it in the long run against the others who might otherwise wish to come into his market.

Where the product is very standardized, and where technical conditions of production are similar for the producers, each of them will have very much the same rule relating his price to his direct costs, for price will not be able to differ appreciably for articles with identical specifications, and they will have very similar direct costs (there are usually minor differences in what are included in direct costs, resulting from differences in bookkeeping practice rather than differences in principle). The more efficient firms will be charging a higher allowance for net profit, and at the given level of price they will tend to improve their financial position relatively to the other businesses.

In normal circumstances, price will be cut only when that is justified by reductions in direct costs. Once a normal cost rule has emerged in a business, price will be cut when these costs fall, for the producer will expect the lower price to continue to be profitable in the long run, and will regard any consequent cut in the prices of his rivals' products with equanimity. It is in this way that an efficient business emerges as the price leader in its market; the market will follow its price policy just because the price is lower than the competing firms would prefer to set on the basis of the normal costing rules and their higher direct costs. Where such price leadership has emerged, the leader has also been known to justify it on the grounds that a more generous margin would jeopardize the long-run position of the existing industry, in so far as it would provide a constant temptation to new entrants. Such a price leader will also try to prevent prices from being cut below the level given by its costing rules, but it will not be able to maintain that position very long if other businesses have in fact developed lower costs.

It may have more success against the price-cutting war of the kind described in the text-books, because it is generally recognized that this kind of price-cutting pays no one in the long run. It is recognized that any cut in price, if persisted in by any business, will lead to a general fall in prices — i.e. to a general cut in the gross profit-margins charged to get price. In the end, then, all producers merely get their share of the usually inelastic total market for the product, but the general level of price has fallen to a level which will not cover costs in the long run. Why, then, does such a situation occur? — usually because of the relatively desperate position of what is rightly called a weak seller. Given the prices at which a particular group of products is being sold, the general reduction in output which takes place in a slump will tend to bring at least some businesses to the point at which they are not covering their overheads. If their receipts do not cover the *paying-out* overheads such as overhead wages and salaries, their cash balances will be progressively depleted. It is then that a producer in a weak financial position, in danger of having to cut his organization or even to leave the market, while some at least of his rivals are in a stronger position, may try the remedy of cutting prices, knowing that there will probably be reprisals and that in the end he will lose his relatively improved share of the market, but hoping that the short-term increase in his receipts will enable him to hang out a little longer. In this way a depression, especially in industries with heavy overhead costs, may cause a departure from the normal costing rules. It may be noted that in such industries the costing rules themselves are usually based upon such a way of charging overheads as to permit of some relaxation, and thus to offer a deterrent against an abandonment of the rules.

Because such price-cutting does not pay, there are often attempts to prevent it by agreements, occasionally with financial sanctions. In view of the low elasticity of total demand, such agreements are not necessarily against social policy, provided that the gross profit-margin which they seek to enforce is only normal — and only in exceptional circumstances will it be possible to maintain an excessive gross profit-margin. It is to the community's interest that price should normally cover cost, and the normal pricing rules of business not only prevent price-cutting, they also prevent attempts to snatch temporary advantages from price rises in booms. If they prevent the share of profits from falling in the depression even more than it does, they also prevent it from rising so much as it would in a boom. A general departure from them in a depression would result in businesses cutting down their organizations, and dismissing overhead staffs when there is little prospect of alternative employment.

It is therefore suggested that the normal attitude to price agreements needs reconsidering. They are not necessarily anti-social, and it would be possible for social action independently to encourage the latent competition which generally exists. It would then not be possible for too high a profit-margin to be taken. In our experience it is difficult for price agreements alone to ensure that the participants retain excessive profits. Rings sooner or later bring into existence vigorous outsiders who grow and strengthen their position on the basis of finding it profitable to charge a lower price.

This is not to deny that what may be called monopolistic forces — the forces making it difficult to enter a particular market — will not affect the size of the margin which is taken as normal in the industry concerned, but it is possible greatly to exaggerate the size of the resulting monopoly net profits. In some at least of the industries usually referred to as quasi-monopolies (including cases where price agreements are known to operate), the figures for net profits do not appear to be large, bearing in mind the risks that necessarily attend industrial investment. British industrial history shows that there may well be some uncertainty about the security of investment in any industrial enterprise, however secure its position appears to be. The taking of only a reasonable gross profit-margin is one of the business man's ways of *reducing* that uncertainty.

Profits sometimes seem generous in the cases of well-established businesses which have been able to build up for themselves a rather specialized market, even

110

in what may appear to be a competitive industry. Experience, however, suggests that such cases do not last, and that long-term forces do readjust the size of the margin. The tide of competition may leave little pools of abnormal profit behind it, but in the end they tend to disappear. In general, then, experience of industry does suggest that the business man is right when he sees his gross margin and his price as competitively determined. In our view, the newer developments in theory have caused economists to be too ready to regard manufacturing industry as a network of monopolies, and of deliberate restriction of output.

Certainly, on the basis of the theory which has been outlined here, the attempt to define as the degree of monopoly, the difference between marginal cost and price must fail. The horizontal nature of the direct-cost curves makes nonsense of any idea that in a purely competitive market (in Chamberlin's sense) equilibrium price would be that which equalled marginal prime costs — the standard for reference has therefore fallen to the ground. Equally it is necessary to attack the pricing rule which has been suggested for socialized industry — to make price equal to marginal costs would mean perpetual losses, and the nonsense of the rule would be obvious if all industry were socialized, for then how should we pay for the overhead factors in any industry?

These are wider topics, and a fuller treatment of them must be reserved for another occasion, some of them, in any case, calling for further research. It seemed, however, fitting at least to record the sense of competition which has emerged from the research which led to the theory which this paper has put forward. The firm conclusion for analysis is that the theory of normal behaviour should describe the business man as offering his product at a fixed price according to his cost rules, changing it only when his costs change. At that price the amount that he will sell will largely be determined by the National Income. The consequences for his profit-and-loss account will depend upon the amount that he sells, his total net profit increasing, or his net loss decreasing, with any increase in his sales. The gross margin that he takes in his price will depend upon competition, and hence upon the level of direct costs for the most efficient competitors. There is no reason to suppose that, in the case of the great majority of manufacturing businesses, competition will not keep that margin down to a reasonable magnitude. The theory of the gross profit-margin should be one of the central parts of economic analysis, and should be formulated in terms of competition.

Appendix: letters on 'A reconsideration of the theory of the individual business' and *Manufacturing Business*(50)

From ROY HARROD, *24 July 1948*

My dear Philip,

I was most interested in your article. I think you are not submitting it for *E.J.* for which anyhow it would be too long.

I was a little saddened by it. If you had treated your old friend, Harrod, as the best authority on this subject, instead of whoring after Viner, your article would have had to be differently worded. I noticed in an American journal some time ago a note by Prof. Schumpeter taking me to task for not having taken more trouble to establish my claim to authorship of these doctrines; and Prof. Knight told me the other day, when in Oxford, that he only used my *Q.J.E.* article, in preference to Chamberlin or Robinson, in his seminars at Chicago, on the ground that it was more free from error.

In *E.J.* June 1930 I published the marginal revenue curve and in December 1931 I gave the formula for it which has always been used since. These were both new, except, according to Joan Robinson, for an article by Yntema in *J.P.E.* in 1928 (which I am afraid I never looked up). I did actually submit marginal revenue to Keynes, early in 1928, but it was not published as he had some criticisms and I was preoccupied with other things and could not get around to it till 1930.(51)

In the 1931 article I gave the correct relation of the long period to the short period cost curve which was later incorrectly given by Viner in the article you quote. I *should* like you anyhow to alter your wording in the first paragraph of III on p. 7 since this slightly implies priority for Viner(52) — compared with 'various works that make use of its constructions.' I worked out all this before Viner, and got this particular point right while he got it wrong. But one is not a prophet in one's own country.

Now according to my construction — not Viner's — the entrepreneur will usually plan capacity the optimum use of which will be in excess of what he expects to produce. This is the same as what you say. My statement is entirely formal. The

---

(50) Reprinted from the P.W.S. Andrews Papers, London School of Economics, London. Reprint permissions for individual letters are listed in the Acknowledgements at the start of this book.

(51) Editors' note: Harrod appears to be glossing over the fact that the adverse referee's comments he received from Keynes (actually made by Frank Ramsey) came as such a severe blow that he suffered a nervous breakdown and it was a year before he saw that the strictures were due to a misunderstanding and resubmitted his paper — see p. 9 of E.H. Phelp-Brown (1980) 'Sir Roy Harrod: a memoir', *Economic Journal* **90**, March, pp. 1–34.

(52) Editors' note: the reference here is to an earlier draft; see pp. 77–8 and footnote 10 for Andrews's subsequent treatment of Harrod and Viner.

reason is not that given by Chamberlin. I did not concretise the matter as I wanted to give solutions which could be proved theoretically and was diffident of going into practical questions, about which my knowledge might be deficient. It may be that your point about wanting to have something in hand to meet unexpected demand increases is additional to mine. I am not, however, sure that it is. I am rather inclined to think that it is merely filling in my theory which remained at a high level of abstraction. I should therefore feel that that part of your article was filling in my point, tho' it may be rebutting an assumption made by inferior writers!

As regards the long period question I say in the article approved by Knight (*Q.J.E.*, May 1934 — this was of course much later than the *E.J.* articles — p. 449): 'The upward slope in the later stages is due to the increasing difficulties of coordination and control. The universal validity of this second part of the assumption may indeed be challenged; it will appear that it is not necessary to make it in analysing the equilibrium of imperfect competition.' So I feel that I am fully safeguarded. After all in some cases increasing costs of management will appear; it is a question of how often. Anyhow I did not make the assumption which you rebut.

I like your article and think you have brought together some useful points. I hope I have made plain the reasons why I feel a little unjustly attacked.

The *E.J.* article of 1931 unfortunately made a mistake in not making the demand curve tangential to the cost curve in fig. 1. As the whole thing was path-breaking at the time, perhaps, I may be excused for the error.

Yours,

ROY [HARROD]

To ROY HARROD, *26 July 1948*

Dear Roy,

Your letter came this lunch time. I have had to be out all the afternoon, so this is the first chance that I have had of replying. May I first say that my article honestly gave the origin of my theory — i.e. a negative reaction to Viner and to Chamberlin. I had been brought up on their ideas, and, as you know only too well, they have now become the received doctrine. I remember reading your articles, 'Notes on Supply', and am sorry that it slipped out of my conscious mind. I had never seen your *Quarterly Journal of Economics* article.

May I say at once that I have known for a long time that your work on marginal revenue had been unjustly ignored; I had not realized how much your work on costs, also, had become part of accepted doctrine. The only thing that really concerns my article is the fact that you insist so much that excess short run capacity may well be the normal case, although I think that you give the wrong reasons for it i.e. my contention is that it must be recognized as normal irrespective of the degree of competition. By the way, in a footnote to the final

113

version of my article, which goes to the printers this week, I have queried the assumption of tangency between short and long run cost curves. I do not think that it is legitimate to supply infinitesimal calculus to the curves for the individual firm, the finite differences that exist make the long run curve merely a series of points appropriately defined on the short run cost curve; my points of excess capacity are basic to my definition. However, I have already said that for these reasons: some writers have urged that a falling long run cost curve implies that the short run curve falls, but note that on my theory the short run curve must fall even if the long run cost curve is rising.

I am thinking now that I shall rewrite the first part of my article, and shall give you certainly a fair place in it, where I do make references, but I must insist that, taken as a whole, what I say on costs is original. I am the first to assert, as necessary, what my experience in business has shown me to be correct — that the average direct costs must always be regarded as constant, and that a rising marginal cost curve cannot exist in practice.

When you see the second part of my article, that dealing with marketing strategy, which I have decided must be published together with the first as a single, you will realize that this theorem plays an essential part in a theory of pricing which I feel to be reasonably complete. I have, by the way, abandoned completely the idea of falling marginal revenue curves as irrelevant to pricing policy as a normal thing.

I hope that you do not mind my stressing what I felt sure is my own originality — in the sense that I am for the first time stating the economic theory which is relevant to the business man's normal behaviour. I owe it to those who have financed me for several years, and to friends like yourself who have given me much needed encouragement (I will not forget, indeed have never forgotten, all that I have been told of what some people regarded as your very courageous defence of me at a crucial stage in my career) — I owe it to all those I should assert my own priority; it is the one theoretical reward which you and those others will have for giving me the opportunity of doing the fundamental research work. May I say that I, too, am a little hurt that you have not recognized my article as more than just filling in. As I told you, all my ideas are simple and I am sure that the theoretical situations that I envisage have somewhere or another been seen as *possible* by a good many people. What is original is the argument and statement that they are necessary conditions. I have just spent some time re-reading all the articles which you mention, and I must say that to me my article still stands as something new in the essentials. I had hoped that you at least would see it like that.

As I have said, I will take care in my redraft to remove the impression that no-one has thought about short run excess capacity, but I must leave any impression of a claim to originality for the major contention.

I have written, since that was your own means of communication. I hope that you will give me a 'phone call as soon as you can, and arrange to see me. I shall have few tranquil nights until I have your personal assurance that you do not regard me as one of those aggressive younger men who like to take a kick at the shoulders they stand on.

Yours very sincerely,

PHILIP [ANDREWS]

From ROBERT HALL, *24 October 1948*

Dear Andrews,

Thank you very much for the proof of your article on the theory of the individual business. I have read it rather quickly and enjoyed it very much, but hope to be able to read it more carefully later on.

As you know I am very much in sympathy with the general line of thought you follow, and in particular I entirely agree with the importance of the theory of the individual business. We are learning so slowly how business men behave, and the one thing we do know is that the strength of the profit and loss motive, which allowed us to make assumptions about the conformity of the individual to a pattern, has been enormously reduced in this country. (I am not sure that one ought not to specify the country in future titles!)

I will not try to discuss all the points that interest me, but would like to put one or two to you. While I agree that the typical direct cost curve is constant over a much wider range than most textbooks suggest, some of what you say seems to imply that it would rise if the business in fact had to work for long towards the right hand end. e.g. 'Accidents happen ... and machines will have to be repaired or renewed', 'He will also need some reserves in management personnel and overhead labour.' The implication seems to be that if he tried to work flat out, he would get interruptions and so his costs would be higher after all. I do not deny however, that the costs are constant over a range and that the typical business is not near the end: but it might be argued that the cost curve would turn up for some time before it became vertical because it was at capacity. This would be the probable normal cost curve, not the actual one for a short time if all went well.

I could pursue these ideas further if I had time, but must go over to the second part, where I agree very much with what you say, though I sometimes feel very uncertain about how much there are actual agreements and how much influence these have on keeping all firms from expanding in certain ways. My own theory on all this is that it is selling costs which cause the cost curve to rise and bring the firms into equilibrium. But I have a somewhat private view of the nature of competition, where there are selling costs. This is that such competition is *necessarily* oligopolistic, and that the price is always indeterminate until we know which type of behaviour is being

115

followed by the competitors. This is very much in accordance with the theory of duopoly, where the equilibrium reached or not reached depends on what each competitor thinks the others will do in response to his own action.

I shall look forward to your book.

Yours ever,

ROBERT HALL

From D.H. ROBERTSON, *14 February 1949*

Dear Mr. Andrews,

Many thanks for sending me your article, which I am very glad to have in separate form as well as in the *O.E.P.* volume. I have given it a first reading (skipping for the moment the Appendix) and shall certainly go back to it. I have never done any independent thinking in this field, my efforts having been confined to attempting to understand and correlate the contributions of others. What isn't apparent to me on a first reading is how, postulating a perpetually falling cost curve and a competitive market, you evade the old dilemma — that apparently under such conditions any firm which once gets a start will capture the whole market. Is the secret that, like Hall and Hitch, you really suppose the producer to live in a condition of what I have ventured in lectures to call 'oligopolistic pessimism', i.e. to believe himself faced with a demand curve which is elastic to the *left* but inelastic to the *right* of the 'normal cost' price? That is how I interpret p. 83 [pp. 105–6 here], but I am not sure if I am right.

It may amuse you, and serve to exhibit my general sympathy, if I transcribe the sentence with which, in my general lecture course, I conclude the lecture in which I gallop through the various models of 'monopolistic competition'.

The Hall-Hitch model is thus perhaps a contribution to a medium run rather than either a true long run or a very short run theory of value. But within its limits it is a valuable correction to the tendency, generated alike by the Pigouvian model of pure competition and the Chamberlinistic model of monopolistic competition, to exaggerate the extent to which the maximisation of net revenue is at every moment the conscious objective of entrepreneur policy. In this respect, it has affinity rather with the work of Marshall, who, at the cost of some laziness of language, interlards his mathematical marginalism with frequent reminders of the way in which, under what is ordinarily thought of as competition, the individual producer is preoccupied with the calculation and covering of average full cost of production — thus short-circuiting as it were the results of the competitive process as foretold by the more logical but less realistic theory.

In fact, having hacked our way through the jungle of monopolistic competition, we seem to find old Marshall, representative firm in hand, awaiting us on the other side!

116

And the following lecture, on the short period, ends thus:

> We can give a rough idea of the result, as Marshall seems to suggest (*Principles*, 374-7) by portraying each producer as retracting, when demand falls, not along his marginal variable cost curve but along a curve lying above it and containing some allowance, arrived at in a more or less arbitrary manner, for fixed charges; and we can conceive, as he does, of a short period supply curve for the industry compounded of such individual curves. Modern analysis, with its formidable jargon, is attempting to give greater precision to these results; but nothing can surpass the clarity and emphasis with which Marshall sixty years ago hammered in the main truth that long-period considerations enter into the determination of short-period value and output.

All the same, I can't help suspecting that entrepreneurs are readier than they always admit to depart, both upwards and downwards, from the 'normal cost' principle. They like to have the accountant's statement of what they 'should' do — but when the accountant's back is turned, they follow their own hunch and go and do something a bit different! But you have mixed with entrepreneurs much more than I have, and will be better able to judge whether there is anything in this suspicion.

Please don't regard this half-baked effusion as needing any answer, and forgive my handwriting!

Good wishes for your book.

Yours sincerely,

D.H. ROBERTSON

To D.H. ROBERTSON, *17 February 1949*

Dear Professor Robertson,

Of course I shall reply to your letter. My reprint was sent to you just because I thought that I should like you to have it. I am very pleased that it provoked you into writing at such length, and shall treasure your letter.

There are two specific points that I should like to take up. You will, of course, appreciate that my theories have come out of realistic thinking about particular problems. It is not easy then to present a sort of general philosophy which is carefully buttoned up at every point — there is also the fact that I feel too great an insistence upon a complete model to be dangerous. In economics — or at least in the economics of the firm — it has been only too easy to develop general theories which end by being too remote from the practical situations with which they have to deal. But it is not only this diffidence which is responsible for what I now believe to be obscurities in my article. I hope the greater length of the argument in my book will make my position clearer.

117

The first point is, how I evade the old dilemma — n.b. it was not a dilemma to Marshall. He merely saw that it might lead to unstable short-run equilibrium — that with a perpetually falling cost-curve and a competitive market, any firm which once gets a start will capture the whole market. The answer is that I think the definition of a competitive market was wrong, in so far as it did not recognize (Marshall did) the fact of buyers' preferences *at*, and only at, a given price (the modern theory of monopolistic competition is wrong, I think, in so far as it believes that the normal demand for a manufacturing business will exhibit preferences against lower prices); also that the discussion of the problem in the 1930s was really thinking in terms of the sharp fall of the short-run cost-curve. The long-run cost-curve, I think, falls at a decreasing rate with increases of scale. Further, in the cases where long-run costs fall most steeply, capital costs will generally be important and will increase in their relative importance as scale increases. Now, if any one firm cuts, hoping to justify the price-cut through the increase in its market (and, ultimately, in its long-run scale), it will find that its demand will not increase very much in the short run. The other businesses will at once cut their price to meet its — for failure to do so will tend to lose them the whole of their market. They can afford to cut right down to the level of their average paying out costs — and this alone would generally mean a substantial cut in price. They will even go below this if they have the cash reserves. The price-cut which the prospective change in costs of the large business would justify is unlikely to be so large as this. It will be looking long-run, by hypothesis, and hoping to cover its costs. Further, the other businesses may be able to meet the lower price for quite a while — especially if the larger business is charging substantial amounts on account of obsolescence. All this means that the price-cutting firm finds that it gets only its share of the total market at the lower price, and, in so far as the demand for its product as a whole will generally be price-elastic, the cut will not pay it. It will tend to cut price as its actual costs change, for, by definition, it will be covering its costs and so can justify the price-cut in the long-run; equally, the position of its smaller competitors will be worsened, and, if all the businesses are of equal efficiency, apart from the scale factor, such a price-cut will tend to squeeze them out in the long run. So far as the larger business is actually getting reductions in costs, then I do not find that there is any 'oligopolistic pessimism' — it will charge its normal costing margin, lower its price and sit back, knowing that it has strengthened its position but it will not gamble on reductions in prices which will only be justified by *substantial* increases in scale.

The gentle slope of the cost-curves (long-run) at moderately large scale is shown by the following instance which I must ask you to treat as confidential — since the business could be identified by some of my business men friends. I am thinking of one business which, on technical grounds, seemed the most favourable possible case for increasing economies of scale. In fact, an increase of 25 per cent in the already very large output would have brought a cost reduction per unit of only 10 per cent, and, by reason of the way in which the calculation had to be made that 10 per cent included the short-run gains through using up the reserve capacity of the business — i.e. a business which was 25 per cent larger would plan to produce at a higher average cost than is assumed in the calculations: in fact, I guess that the reduction would not be more than about five per cent. For the business to get that extra capacity, even if the other businesses had not increased their absolute outputs, market price would probably have had to have fallen by more than 10 per cent. Whilst long-run substitution for other products might have improved the position, it is doubtful if total demand would have expanded sufficiently to justify the reduction in price. Meanwhile, the other producers would certainly have cut to the new level and could have kept in production for quite a while.

By the way, that the business will normally take a long-term view and cut at once if, in fact, its costs fall, is the reason why the low cost producers tend to set the level of price for the whole market. The gross margins of the other producers will be determined by the price which the leading business would quote.

To take up your second point: You will see that, whilst I am ready to agree that a business will always depart downwards from its normal cost policy if competition forces it to do so, I do not think it normal that a business will revise its margin upwards. It will believe that it will meet successful competition if it does so. Certainly, in all the cases that I have examined, the business men act as if upward revision would be folly. I am impressed by the extent to which they have held out against upward revisions of prices even in conditions of war-time markets, when in some cases their customers would have liked more expensive goods to swell their turnover. If in such circumstances a business produces more expensive goods to meet the demand, then the specification is revised, so that the normal cost principle will still hold.

I am going on much too long, and I do hope that you will treat this long letter merely as a sign of the great pleasure that your letter gave me, and not as meaning that I have impertinently taken advantage of the opening that you offered for a good ride on my hobby horse — I am keeping a firm hold on the reins!

Thank you very much for the quotations from your lectures. I do agree that, whenever in my field one gets down to realistic thinking, there is Marshall already. I wish that I had been trained to use the representative firm — by Marshall — I am sure that it was an important tool in his thinking, and that great book *Industry and Trade* — completely and undeservedly neglected here, how is it in Cambridge? — shows how good his thinking was. I have often

119

thought that I was catching a glimpse of what the representative firm meant to Marshall, but have not yet managed to get so that I can put the position clearly. I am only aware that in my industrial studies some similar shadowy concept seems to be developing, but am not yet at the stage when I can disentangle it from the details of my case studies.

Thank you for listening to me so long. I shall inflict a copy of my book on you and shall be completely satisfied with moderately diminishing returns in your response to that.

Yours very sincerely

PHILIP ANDREWS

From RICHARD A. LESTER, *12 July 1949*

Dear Mr. Andrews:

It was very thoughtful of you to send me a copy of your book on *Manufacturing Business*, which has been forwarded to me here where I am vacationing. I have started to read it with real interest. It is encouraging to see that many of the younger economists both in your country and here are improving and developing the theory of business behavior. Encouraging also is the fact that business men are themselves lending aid to our endeavors. I am sure that out of all our searching a much more realistic and intelligent theory will result. Again let me thank you for the opportunity to read your book so soon after publication.

Sincerely yours,

RICHARD A. LESTER

From M. FOGARTY, *29 July 1949*

Dear M. Bye,

I was very much interested during the Semaine Sociale to see the emphasis laid by many speakers, including yourself, on imperfect competition and oligopoly as developed in recent theory. A number of us at Oxford have become rather suspicious of the value of this theory for interpreting actual conditions. I would be very interested to know what you think of the enclosed book which has just been published by one of my colleagues, Mr. P.W.S. Andrews, and which I think puts the whole of this field in a new light.

The background of the book is that, two or three years before the war, a group of economists was formed with Andrews as Secretary to discuss with business men the basis on which their decisions are actually made. You probably know the preliminary results of the Group's work, which were published in *Oxford Economic Papers* No. 2 in 1939. During the war the Group was disbanded, but Andrews continued a certain amount of related work. In 1944 Samuel Courtauld offered to sponsor an enquiry into

120

the relative costs of large and small-scale business, and Andrews undertook this. With Courtauld's backing he got complete access to the books of firms in the rayon industry, which is, as you know, one of the most highly oligopolised. By way of comparison, he also made a similar and equally detailed study of the Boot and Shoe trade, which is highly competitive.

These studies were made without any intention of leading to a general revision of economic theory, and the first results were written up on the basis of accepted theory of the Joan Robinson–Chamberlin type. This, however, proved unsatisfactory and Andrews was led step by step (helped by his experience with the Group) to drop imperfect competition theory and return to a theory on Marshall's lines, re-stated in a form which reconciles it with the criticisms made by the imperfect competition theorists.

The chief new points in Andrews' theory fall under four heads:

(a) he re-states economic theory in terms compatible with the normal business accounting practice; which, of course, from the point of view of econometrics is an extremely important development.

(b) he re-defines monopoly in terms not merely of identity or otherwise of product but of identity or otherwise of process and business experience; i.e. a competitor is not a firm engaged in selling the same product but one capable of moving without serious difficulty into the same market. The practical importance of imperfect competition is thus immensely diminished.

(c) Andrews has produced a new (or rather improved Marshallian) theory of the relation of business men to their markets, bringing out the essential difference between the long-term market, which in manufacturing industry is normally completely elastic, and the short-term market in which there is always, or almost always, some possibility of exploitation.

(d) In view of the very high elasticity of most markets in the long run, even in an industry such as rayon, business men normally tend to act even in the short run in accordance with long-run considerations, except for those businesses which do not in any case have to remain in existence for any length of time. Such businesses will naturally exploit the short-run possibilities to the best of their ability, and will behave in accordance with the Joan Robinson type of theory. This theory is, in fact, as Andrews describes it, the theory of the Black Market.

The value of all this lies I think particularly in two directions. First the lectures at the Semaine left me feeling that there was an unsolved contradiction between the desire for decentralisation and the almost universal assumption that competition could not be an effective mechanism of control. Decentralisation, the establishment of each enterprise as an independent community, and all the rest of it, can be carried through completely only if there is a decentralised method of control linking the business directly to the consumer without the intervention of a higher authority. Andrews' discussions, I think, show that competition can be used as a mechanism of this sort to a far greater extent than we have in recent years supposed.

Secondly, while Andrews' theory does not, of course, do away with the need for central intervention, it does throw a good deal of light on the type of intervention which is likely to be satisfactory. Monsieur Vedel in his lecture referred to the type of leadership provided by the T.V.A. This is essentially voluntary. It derives its force partly from moral pressure but partly also from the fact that the T.V.A., from the point of view of the farmer or small business man who benefited from its attentions, was chiefly engaged in pointing the way down a path along which competition is a force which may make itself felt at very different speeds, and intervention is desirable to accelerate it; but Andrews' discussions, I think, show how intervention on the lines of the T.V.A. or of our own Cotton Board and Development Councils can be effective. That is, it tilts the balance between authoritarian intervention and intervention which merely educates and gives a lead to competitive forces.

I think that the two lectures at the Semaine which touched most closely on this was your own and Monsieur Leduc's and I have therefore also written to him in the same terms. I believe myself that Andrews' book and the work of the Oxford Economists' Research Group represent a turning point in economics of much the same importance as the developments in the theory of imperfect competition around 1930.

Yours sincerely,

M. FOGARTY

3 Industrial analysis in economics — with especial reference to Marshallian doctrine[1]

1 Introduction

Until very recently, the theories of monopolistic or imperfect competition which were evolved in the nineteen-thirties appeared to have swept all before them. It is true that distinguished economists have expressed disagreement or dissatisfaction with these doctrines, especially in recent years.[2] It is equally true that a remarkably long period has passed without any counter-theory being proposed, or without any restatement of the older theories as an alternative body of doctrine, apart from the now almost ignored contributions made by Robertson and Shove in the controversies in which the modern theories originated.[3]

The principal 'victim', of course, has been the Marshallian analysis of price determination in the 'ordinary run' of manufacturing industries. The consequences, however, have been much wider than the simple attainment of Sraffa's objective — that Marshall's theory 'should be abandoned'.[4] A whole department of economic analysis has disappeared into the gulf that he opened up.

(1) Reprinted with permission from *Oxford Studies in the Price Mechanism*, edited by T. Wilson and P.W.S. Andrews (Oxford, Clarendon Press, 1951), pp. 139–72.

(2) Shove, 'The Place of Marshall's Principles in the Development of Economic Theory', *Economic Journal*, December 1942; Robbins, 'The Economist in the Twentieth Century', *Economica*, May 1949; Stigler, *Five Lectures on Economic Problems*, Longmans, 1949; MacGregor, *Economic Thought and Policy*, O.U.P., 1949. (This contains an important restatement of Professor MacGregor's position and a very critical examination of post-Marshallian theory, largely in terms of its own concepts.)

(3) Robertson, 'The Trees of the Forest', in 'Symposium', *Economic Journal*, 1930; Shove, 'The Representative Firm and Increasing Returns', *ibid*. The other reference to Shove above shows that, at the most, he would in 1942 have given the newer theories a not-proven verdict, and I hope that Professor Robertson will not mind my adding, on the basis of private correspondence, that, like Professor MacGregor, he still deems to stand where he did.

(4) Sraffa, Rejoinder to Robertson in 'Symposium', *ibid*.

Industrial analysis has been virtually abandoned as a meaningful occupation in theoretical economics, and the only solid legacy has been a revised version of the theory of the individual business with which the whole revolt started, together with some use of that theory in the analysis of social aggregates. Modern analytical economics finds no firm ground anywhere between the individual business and society as a whole. The theory of inter-business relationships has acquired all the indeterminacy of the old duopoly analysis, which has shown a great capacity for spreading like a fog over any theoretical attempts at group analysis, and has recently begun to blur the edges even of the theory of the individual business itself.

The result has been a greater gulf between theoretical analysis and practical thought than can have existed during any other period since before Mill. Practical thought continues to show that an industry is a meaningful concept for its purposes: governments insist on administering in terms of industries, business men persist in thinking against an industrial background, and our official statistics continue to be collected on the basis of definitions of industries which, although they vary from source to source, nevertheless agree in significant details. If it is to have any 'bite', theoretical analysis needs to be capable of statement in industrial terms.

'Old Marshall' at least supplied an analytical framework within which everyday life seemed to take on an intelligible shape. In this sense, his industrial analysis 'works' for the purposes for which it is constructed. Marshall's analysis has certainly not been pushed aside because it fitted its subject-matter worse than the newer analyses, or because it was less reliable as a basis from which to predict the behaviour of actual industrial groupings of businesses; the world of competing monopolies has no industrial syntax. The case is, rather, that Marshallian theory has, it is thought, been convicted of internal inconsistencies. His analysis of industrial equilibrium was proved to be inconsistent with a theory of the equilibrium of the individual business which evolved from the 'Marshallian tradition' and which was believed to be basic to Marshall's own concept of competition. The difficulty has been resolved by dropping industrial analysis and retaining the static equilibrium theory of the individual business. It would have been equally legitimate to have abandoned the latter.

My empirical studies during the last 12 years have forced me to reconsider the whole position of business economics. Naturally enough, my first approach to the individual business was in terms of the modern theories of monopolistic competition. It was soon obvious that the business man made no explicit reference to marginalist concepts, but it was a long step from that to rejecting a theory which had become so strongly established. It was much easier to assume the implicit validity of the theories in terms of which one was trained to think, indefensibly weak though that procedure seems in retrospect. With increasing familiarity with business behaviour, this way of thinking became progressively less tolerable. On several points one became aware of explicit differences in conduct and outlook, which produced an increasing sense of strain and an awareness of the danger of twisting facts so that they might conform to the theoretical approach to which my generation had been brought up. I was therefore forced to work out a theory of the individual business which did satisfy me as far as I could take it.(5) This lent itself quite naturally to thinking about industrial groupings and thus satisfied both requirements of practical research as I saw them. On returning to empirical work, I was aware how Marshallian my broad analysis was becoming, with the advantage, as it seemed to me, that it was now possible to think consistently in terms of the individual business, whereas Marshall did not push individual analysis beyond a few limited generalizations. The theory of the equilibrium of a competitive industry as presented by Marshall seemed meanwhile to take on the firmness which it must have had for him.

In this paper, therefore, I shall plead for a reconsideration of Marshall's theory of competitive industry, which is, in fact, not inconsistent with what Marshall says about the individual business; he stopped himself from going too far in a theory of the equilibrium of the firm. At the same time, I shall urge that it is now possible to construct a theory of the behaviour of an individual business which is consistent both with the phenomena which it purports to describe, and with Marshallian analysis.

In general, the argument will be restricted to long-run conditions — sufficient time being presumed to allow the entry into an 'industry' of any businesses whose founders consider this likely to be profitable.(6) To save tedious differentiation of cases, the analysis will formally be restricted to manufacturing industry. This restriction of the argument is justified since the modern rejection of Marshall's theory originated in a dilemma (first posed by Marshall himself) in the theory for the individual business in this class of industry. Subject, however, to what I regard as minor changes, the analysis will be applicable to commerce and to retail trade as well.(7)

---

(5) *Manufacturing Business*, by P.W.S. Andrews, Macmillan, 1949.

(6) Whatever the case 60 years ago, it is now unrealistic to imagine that new entrants consist only of brand-new businesses undertaken with all the uncertainties involved. As I have pointed out, we must allow for the new enterprise which in favourable conditions will always be available from businesses established in other lines of industry.

(7) Cf. 'Some Aspects of Competition in Retail Trade', *Oxford Economic Papers*, Vol. 2, No. 2, June 1950.

2 Marshall's Industrial Analysis

Marshall distinguished two classes of industry — competitive industries and monopolies. When we study his competitive markets it appears that the basis of the distinction is whether or not it would be possible for other businesses to produce a commodity with the same technical specifications as the product of any particular firm, and to offer it for sale to that firm's customers. This is a much wider concept than the purely competitive market of later theory with its assumed absence of all buyers' preferences and its stress on homogeneity of actual products.

It is significant that Marshall's principal example of a monopoly is that of a public utility with statutory privileges. A monopoly exists when technical, legal, or other reasons make it impossible for other businesses to offer the same type of commodity to a business's customers.(8) In such a case, the business will have a determinate demand curve of its own, of the kind analysed by Marshall in Book III of *Principles*; granted, of course, that no technically distinct commodity is a sufficiently close substitute for the monopolist to have to take it into account when he is framing his own policy, and given the usual Marshallian assumption that the total receipts of the business will not form a large proportion of its customers' total expenditure.

In so far as the monopolist followed strictly the motive of maximizing his net profits, his output and price policy would be affected as much by his demand curve as by his cost curve. Marshall's analysis of this case (p. 480) is formally equivalent to the modern doctrine that marginal revenue will equal marginal cost and that the latter will be less than price by an amount which will vary inversely with the elasticity of the demand curve. There will be no *a priori* connexion between the price on which the monopolist will settle and the average cost of the output which he will sell at that price.

Marshall thought the case to be completely different for the ordinary run of industry, and he draws no fine distinction here, such as is drawn by later theory, between purely competitive and imperfectly or monopolistically competitive industries. So long as entry into the industry is possible, it will be competitive in Marshall's sense; his analysis now refers to agriculture and now to particular manufacturing industries, without any sign that he is uneasy about putting them

---

(8) Marshall also recognized the case of a 'partial monopoly' where a business's wares are better known than 'others which are really equally good' (p. 60 footnote). (All page references so given are to *Principles*.) But for the class of industries with which we are concerned, these cases cannot be analysed on quasi-monopoly lines.

in the same fundamental class.(9)

In such competitive industries, Marshall thought that the possibility of entry of other producers would ensure that long-run price would be equal to the normal average cost of production. This is in striking contrast to the theory of monopoly. The contrast is equally strong with the modern theories of the determination of price in 'normally competitive' manufacturing industries.

Where an industry is normally competitive, in this sense of being open to the entry of new producers, Marshall's analysis runs in terms of industrial demand and supply schedules. On the demand side, later theorists have persisted in interpreting the analysis in terms of a perfectly competitive market, on the lines of the simple markets discussed by Marshall at the beginning of Book V. This seems to me to be a mistake. It is quite true that Marshall does start his analysis of the markets for competitive industry by an examination of the type of market which has provided the model for post-Marshallian analyses of pure competition — the great primary markets of the world, the large stock exchanges, etc. In these, with their completely undifferentiated products, not only is there but one price at any one time, but each seller provides so small a part of the total supply that he may be presumed to meet an infinitely elastic demand at the prevailing level of price.

It seems, however, quite clear from Marshall's subsequent discussion of manufacturing industries that the only characteristic of those purely competitive markets that we should take as required by Marshallian analysis is that which has reference to price: i.e. in the long run, at least, no business would be able to get a higher price than any other business would take for an identical product as delivered to the particular customer. It would be as unrealistic as it would be inappropriate, in view of Marshall's later analyses, to require that an individual business should be able to sell any amount at the ruling price. In fact, such businesses will not commonly be able to sell all that they would like to sell at that price. Accordingly, I suggest that we should presume Marshall's competitive analysis for manufacturing industry to imply identical prices for identical commodities, but not individual demands of infinitely large extent at those prices.

The previous paragraph has referred to identical prices for identical commodities; this calls our attention to an important abstraction of Marshall's.

---

(9) Marshall was worried about the case of an industry which had come to be in the hands of a few giant businesses (p. 805). He suggested that this should be treated analogously to monopoly, but he goes on to admit that 'even in such cases competition has a much greater force, and the use of the term "normal" is less inappropriate than seemed probable *a priori*'. The Cournot type of analysis of this case is, of course, unrealistic so far as manufacturing industry is concerned.

He analysed ordinary manufacturing industries as if an identical commodity were produced throughout the industry. He must have known this for the abstraction it was; otherwise, with his knowledge of the world, he could not have referred, for example, to the boot and shoe industry, or to the woollen industry. A number of realistic asides would justify our assuming him to have known that the typical products of individual producers would quite frequently differ in their technical specifications, their producers thus specializing to meet the demands in different sections of the broad 'market' with which Marshall was concerned. Similarly, it would be common knowledge that, on a strict analysis, the individual business itself would be multi-product, producing a 'range' of products with differing technical specifications, even though it was a specialist within, or on, that range.

I cannot recall that this abstraction of Marshall's has been discussed at all, and, so far as I am aware, Marshall did not call attention to it himself. Once it has been stated for what it is, however, the probable Marshallian justification appears obvious enough. The Marshallian industry will consist of businesses with a sufficiently common technical equipment, knowledge, experience, etc., for them to be able to turn over to making any 'range' of the given commodity or any of the particular commodities within the 'range'. Further, the business men can be assumed to be sufficiently 'in' the general market to be aware of the prices secured by producers of other types of commodities within the market. In this sense, the producers of electric motors would constitute a clearly defined industry, and in an only slightly more diffuse sense the producers of light electrical engineering products might also be analysed as belonging to the same industry.

Granted this, the analysis which Marshall provides for the larger aggregates that he chooses to call industries would apply with even greater strength to the firms producing in any sub-market within the industry, for that would be even more readily open to new entry than the broad market for the 'industry' as a whole, of which it forms a part. The gross earnings of management would tend to be equalized over the whole industry when analysed into its separate elements — payment for the capital employed, and for the work of the managers (p. 313). For each sub-market we could therefore take Marshall as imagining a 'representative firm' (this concept will be further examined later; meanwhile it may be accepted without comment). The proportion of long-run price which would be taken by the gross earnings of management of a representative firm would vary with differences in the normal intensities of management between the sub-markets, but subject to that, the relationship between the normal prices for the different 'grades' or types of the industrial product would be strictly determined by differences in the normal average costs of production (i.e. the costs of the relevant representative firms).

Given these assumptions, the complex of commodities produced by an actual industry could be imagined as reducible to a cost-equivalent standard commodity, and Marshall could use the concept of a demand schedule for this 'product' of the industry, giving the corresponding hypothetical demand curve the negative slope of the demand curves proper of Book III, where the analysis is formally in terms of simple uniform commodities.

Marshall's supply schedule is the analytical counterpart of the demand schedule. It relates various amounts of total output to the prices which would have to be paid if these amounts were to be forthcoming in a stable fashion over an indefinitely long period (pp. 343, 345). 'This is the price the expectation of which will just suffice to maintain the existing aggregate amount of production; some firms meanwhile rising and increasing their output, and others falling and diminishing theirs; but the aggregate production remaining unchanged.' Supply price being defined so as to imply a stable supply, the Marshallian concept of long-run equilibrium price follows. At that price the amount taken from the market will equal the amount supplied and the equilibrium will be stable whether the supply curve rises or falls with expansion of the industry's long-run output, so long as, in the latter case, the demand curve has a steeper slope.

In order to understand the inter-war rejection of Marshall, it will be necessary to consider his concept of a supply schedule in a more detailed fashion. Given Marshall's assumptions of the uniformity of market price and of free entry, his conclusion that market price cannot be higher than the level which will bring new businesses into the industry seems a familiar result of modern theory as well. It has, however, a different significance in Marshall. He defines the long run in terms of the stability of industrial output and not in terms of the stability of individual businesses. He therefore does not require that all firms in a given industry should be covering their costs, and thus have their survival assured, even in a position of long-run equilibrium.

For one thing, Marshall refuses to take as 'given' the level of efficiency of the businesses assumed already to be operating in an industry. Of course, Marshall recognizes, as must any realistic thinker, that there would be unsystematic changes in their relative positions; for example, those resulting from the constant pitting of one business man's wits against another's so that one business may make an innovation and go ahead at one time, but others will catch up later and the initiative will pass to a different business man. Theoretical analysis, however, might well smooth this out as a 'random' factor, even though to do so would be to miss an important practical manifestation of competition — in fact, its essence on any dynamic view. But Marshall also thought of the relative efficiency of business men as varying systematically over their lifetime. With his eye on the private business rather than on the great public company, he states this primarily in terms of the contrast between a new business and an old and settled one. It is, however, a more general position that he takes up — that an individual business man will have increasing vigour and grasp of the situation as he matures in his industrial experience.

Over its early years, then, Marshall thought that a business's costs of production would tend to decline for this reason alone. With increasing age, the efficiency of a business man will tend to slow down, will become stationary, or even decline. This generalization is not weakened by the case of a large public company, and Marshall's statements on this are not so tinged with doubt as some of his inter-war interpreters suggested. He thought that such businesses were less likely to be forced to the point of actual death, and recognized that they had one relative advantage, in so far as they provided opportunities for organizing ability not associated with the ownership of capital. On the other hand, of course, they would suffer from a weaker association between ownership and control than in the smaller business. Quite apart from this, however, although the survival of the business will not be so dependent upon the efficiency of a particular business man, the management group in control can surely be imagined as having a similar life-history to Marshall's independent business man; their efficiency waxing and waning, and the tides of fortune accordingly flowing to them or ebbing from them. When we are engaged on the realistic study of actual industries, and see how important over a period is the cumulative effect of quite minor changes, this general view of Marshall's becomes very important. It is easy to overlook this in any static survey of an industry which will concentrate attention on the advantages of the powerful positions of existing businesses at any one time. There can be tremendous changes in the position of individual businesses without actual failure.

Accepting this view of Marshall's, it follows that, at any time, even the stable long-run output which is being presupposed for the industry may well include a declining proportion from established businesses which are slipping back, and even making actual losses. This factor may be compensated by the output coming from new entrants; Marshall's definition of long-run supply price requires such a compensation if the increasing output from the more successful existing businesses is not sufficient. It would not be realistic to require that, on entry, they should be able to get normal profits. They will expect higher costs in the beginning than they will achieve later as they get experience, and will hope for increasing goodwill to enlarge their share of the market. Their entry into the industry will be decided on the basis of estimates of what they can hope to achieve at some relatively more mature stage. Their ideas of this will be derived from what seems to be happening to existing businesses. New businesses will come in so long as they can reasonably expect to cover their running costs in the short period before they have exhausted any spare liquid resources, provided that it seems likely that they will get established at a later stage, achieve a sufficient level of output, and get their average costs down to a sufficiently low level to be able to make satisfactory profits then.

Marshall's analysis is therefore conducted in terms of a representative business whose size and opportunities might thus be taken as the target which attracts the efforts of new-comers. The price which would give this firm a sufficient level of profits to call in the output from new businesses which is required by Marshall's stability assumptions is his long-run supply price for the industry. It seems quite legitimate to follow Robertson in refusing to interpret the situation for the new business in terms of any actual level of normal reward for the particular levels of efficiency which their founders have.(10) Prospective new entrants will not know their actual efficiency until they are in the industry, and they may make optimistic estimates both of the size of the market which will accrue to them and of the level of costs at which they could produce that output. In the event, a large proportion of new enterprise may not make the normal level of profits whose prospect attracted them, and a fair proportion may do so badly as to fail in the long run. Market price, accordingly, will not be determined by this factor but by the 'representative' costs on the basis of which new entry takes place.

Marshall therefore interprets long-term price in terms of the normal costs of a representative firm. This might be thought of as having a real existence at any given point of time. In so far as such actual firms are taken as representative by newcomers, new entry will keep market price at such a level that the representative firm will only make the normal level of profits in terms of which the Marshallian new businesses act. The supply schedule, accordingly, traces out the normal costs of the representative firm for the various levels of output. The supply curve may fall, rise, or, alternatively, remain constant with increasing long-run outputs from a given industry, and an increased demand could therefore be met by a decreased, an increased, or an unchanged price in the long run. We shall argue later that Marshall would ordinarily expect a falling supply curve for a manufacturing industry.

Early in this section we referred to Marshall's contrast between a competitive industry which is open to new entry and a monopoly. This is clearly justified on his analysis. The monopolist's price would have no necessary connexion with his average costs. Long-run price for an industry with free entry which behaved in a Marshallian manner would have a determinate relationship with costs. The force of this contrast is strengthened if we make the assumption that the relative efficiencies of businesses remain constant, which has become usual in post-Marshallian attempts to give a Marshallian analysis in terms of the

---

(10) Robertson, 'The Trees of the Forest', *loc. cit.*

behaviour of individual businesses.(11) On that assumption, there will be a determinate relationship between price and average costs for each individual business, the relationship, of course, varying with the business. If these relative efficiencies are thought of as remaining stable between points of long-run equilibrium, market price will be a determinate function of the costs of any individual business.

It is this assumption of modern theory which gives analytic determinacy to the concept of the marginal firm, and when we reason in terms of the full equilibria of individual businesses, long-run price is easily analysed in terms of the normal costs of such a firm. The long-run supply curve will then be derivable from a particular expenses curve, suitably modified to take account of the effect of external economies.(12) Marshall refused to take the initial step, and warns us against any confusion of particular expenses curves with supply curves. Although his objection relates formally to an increasing returns industry, the reasoning is of general application; this is not the only instance where the blunt facts of increasing returns saved Marshall from the use of constructions which would otherwise appear admissible, yet — if the reasoning is general in its application — would have led to misleading conclusions. In Marshallian analysis, the marginal firm, in the sense of a business which is only just managing to hold on in the industry, is not to be seen as the firm whose costs determine total supply and hence prices.(13)

3 Marshall and the individual business

Marshall's treatment of the individual business in a competitive industry is much more confused than his treatment of the industry and of the 'representative' business. This is because his analysis of the firm is overshadowed by the concept of static equilibrium, which he was anxious to accept, but which he was, in fact, forced to reject at every decisive point in his analysis where a manufacturing business had to be integrated with its industry. Marshall's very evident desire to ground his analysis on this concept is easily understood. Partial equilibrium analysis was one of his most useful weapons, and continual use made it very difficult to prevent his thoughts from flowing into that mould. (To

---

(11) Shove, *Economic Journal*, 1930, *op. cit.*; Viner, 'Cost Curves and Supply Curves', *Zeitschrift fur National Okonomie*, 1931–2.

(12) Ref. Marshall, p. 810, n. 2. The particular expenses curve for an industry producing a given output with given economies of production ranges the existing producers' outputs in order of their particular expenses of production.

(13) Ref. MacGregor, *Economic Thought and Policy*, p. 44.

later theorists, of course, an analysis based upon atomistic equilibrium within the industry had pedagogic attractions, since it made possible an elegantly generalized view of the whole social mechanism.) There is the related point that a static theory of the distribution of income had proved possible only on the basis of such a concept, and Marshall's theories in that field required it for their full validity.(14)

Lastly, the adoption of this concept would have given the supply schedule a meaning by which it would have become the full complement of the demand schedule. The demand schedule resulted from the decisions of individual consumers as to the amounts that they would purchase at the given price; the concept of full equilibrium for the individual business would have enabled the supply schedule to be interpreted as resulting from similar atomistic decisions to supply the commodity. Marshall's supply schedule has generally been so interpreted, but that is an error. Marshall would certainly have liked to have constructed a supply schedule which would be explained formally as the integration of determinate supplies from each individual business. He was, however, compelled to define his supply schedule in such a way as to make it refer only to the terms on which the market could get varying amounts from the industry as a whole. In manufacturing industry, his individual businesses are obviously often quite willing to supply more at the existing market price than the market will take from them at that price. That Marshall does not put the matter in this way is due to his shadow-preoccupation with particular equilibrium analysis, but the conclusion comes out clearly enough when he is talking about realistic industrial situations.

In the event, the principle of substitution was the one general guide to the conduct of the individual business, whether in the short or in the long run, that Marshall insisted on. He thus retains the concept of an equilibrium in the distribution of a business's resources between possible alternative expenditures; but in the text, as distinct from the Appendix, he gives no clear view of an equilibrium determination even of short-run output, and, despite obvious heart-burnings, his analysis leads to no determination of long-run equilibrium size of the individual business. In the Mathematical Appendix, as elsewhere when the concept does momentarily emerge, he stresses the danger of pushing mathematical analysis farther than the economic logic warrants, and this is but a further denial of the concept itself, however much he may be tempted to affirm it. His equilibrium analysis for the industry runs, as we have seen, in terms of

---

(14) If this concept is rejected, the theory of distribution will need a complete overhaul. The theory of wages and of employment, in particular, needs to be freed from formal dependence on theories of marginal productivity. Ref. *Manufacturing Business*, pp. 215 ff.

an individual business whose size and opportunities are taken as representative by new entrants, so that their profits would be satisfactory if they achieved the same; there is, however, no sense in which this gives an equilibrium of output for individual firms, so that more or less would not yield the same or a greater level of profits.

When Marshall was considering a wheat farmer in Book IV he could make his analysis run in terms of the equilibrium of the individual business, whether or not its ability was representative. Subject to the requirements of rotation, he could imagine the production of the crop as being subject to decreasing returns in both the short and the long run. In view of the nature of the market, he could, and did, go on to describe a state of equilibrium (p. 153, etc.); but it was the peculiarity of the market which enabled him to take this step quite as much as the assumption of diminishing returns. The analytical method was attractive, and he found it difficult to explain why he could not use it as a general rule. But, although he might explicitly reject this view of a firm when it conflicted with the realistic analysis later in *Principles*, at the back of his mind there was always the concept of an individual business taking all decisions and deciding its whole position — including its output and scale — in such a way as to maximize its profits.

His ultimate refusal to persist with this view arose from difficulties which he encountered when trying to apply it to manufacturing industries. The initial difficulty as it arises in Marshall is a long-run matter — resulting from the fact that such industries tend to be in a state of increasing returns. But, once it had been recognized, this fact led him on to make other observations concerning such industries, and especially concerning their markets, which would themselves be inconsistent with the equilibrium theory that he would otherwise have erected. It is misleading simply to accept his view that mathematical complexities stand in the way of the generalizations which he seems to have thought that his readers would expect (ref., *inter alia*, Mathematical Note XIV) — it was much more a question of logical difficulties that could not be settled at all by partial equilibrium analysis of the individual business.

In formal terms, Marshall analysed short-run conditions as though decreasing returns were universal. In my view, this is a major error of Marshall's analysis — and of post-Marshallian analysis of pure competition — for short-run average total costs in a manufacturing business always decrease up to the limit of their short-run capacity. Even apart from this point, for Marshallian theory to apply it would be necessary for the markets of manufacturing businesses to be of the primary product character in the short run, although Marshall refuses them this quality in his long-run analysis when he has to face the problem of increasing returns.

Where Marshall faces the problem of short-run equilibrium of the individual business and its relation to long-run analysis he argues rather loosely in terms of the fishing industry, whose market can be taken as resembling the market for wheat. I have argued elsewhere that these primary markets necessarily differ significantly from industrial markets, and that the differences result from the nature of the market rather than from the degree to which any level of competition exists. I shall also argue later on that such significant differences must also be taken to be presumed by Marshall's analysis, if we argue backwards from his methodology and his conclusions to the implicit rather than the explicit premises (or the premises which are traditionally taken as having been stated explicitly). With a theorist of Marshall's calibre, I do not see it as false piety to refuse to convict him of errors of reasoning which do not get carried over into his final conclusions. The view put forward is accordingly that Marshall was prevented both in his short- and in his long-run analysis from achieving a clear statement of the matter because his vision of the equilibrium of the individual firm constantly got in the way.

In the case of his short-run analysis, however, his conclusions are so vaguely worded that the defects of the reasoning almost amount to error. His main analysis is in terms of markets for primary products, where the buyers can have no reason for preferring one source of supply to another, at the same price. Further, the market organization for such undifferentiated products is such that there is no room for personal contact between the producer and his customers — and little point in it if there were. Such producers sell to the market as a whole, and a single producer need feel no limitation on his market, but can dispose of his whole output without affecting price.

The essence of the market for a manufacturing industry is otherwise. Marshall analysed such industries as if they were producing a uniform product. We have already presumed him to have known which way the truth lay, and have suggested an analytical justification for such a procedure (pp. 127–8 above). In fact, the total output will consist of a mass of more or less specialized products, catering for the orders of particular customers or classes of customers. On my view, even Marshall's theory should be seen simply as insisting that such customers will not willingly pay more for a particular product than they need pay elsewhere. At any given price, they will usually have goodwill towards particular suppliers, and personal contact and familiarity with conditions and requirements on both sides of the bargain will produce the individual business's 'share' of the market. It must be admitted that this view of Marshall did not occur to me until after I had produced my own theory of the firm, but when I became aware how Marshallian a view of industry I was favouring, it seemed to me impossible to make sense of Marshall's analysis on other terms. This might be taken as reading a theory into Marshall in other than the literal sense, but I am glad that I can now cite the high authority of Professor MacGregor as indicating that Marshall's views were consistent with my interpretation, and that he may be presumed to have reached at least a closely similar conclusion:

[Marshall] was fond of emphasizing to his pupils that efficient (or representative) business has always some element of monopoly; that is the 'custom' or trade connexion of the business. But this by itself is not a power to raise prices; it is nothing but the fact that the demand can be split up in various ways, one of which is to add to the parts of the demand supplied by each supplier (*Economic Thought and Policy*, pp. 39–40.)

This view — that 'goodwill' limits the market available to the individual business at a given level of price — will, accordingly, be taken as fully Marshallian. Marshall did not state it in *Principles*, but it is certainly consistent with the general position into which he was forced when he recognized the fact of increasing returns in manufacturing. Marshall's theories will, therefore, generally be interpreted with its help. It seems worth stressing that, once this is accepted, there can be no use for the concept of static equilibrium for the individual business, in manufacturing, whatever the state of returns in the particular industry which is under discussion. Even if the business were producing at increasing costs, it could be only a matter of accident that the output that it produced would be such that marginal cost equalled market price.

It is not, therefore, very surprising that Marshall's realistic sense prevents him from finalizing the issue, even in the short run, where he does argue that we may rely upon increasing costs to the firm and implies that static equilibrium analysis is applicable; he never quite perpetrates the explicit nonsense with which later interpretation would credit him. As already stated, the general case is given in terms of a primary industry — fishing — and the analysis uses the concept of marginal supplies to the industry rather than that of the equilibrium of the individual fishing business. Here it makes sense to analyse, as Marshall does, in terms of the costs of the marginal short-run supply to the industry as a whole.

When Marshall turns to manufacturing industry, and wishes to make use of the notions of prime and supplementary costs, whose importance in practical thinking he stresses, he does not, in fact, proceed to a rigorous analysis of the situation in terms of price and the marginal prime costs of the firm. He is clearly aware that, in reality, short-run prime costs, average or marginal, are frequently a good deal below price (p. 375). At several points he also appears to be aware that, excepting at rare boom periods when the whole industry might be extended, and the total output might be less than the market would take, it would be normal for manufacturing businesses to be able to produce additional output at decreasing costs even in the short run. It must surely have been rare, even in

Marshall's day, for all the businesses in a competitive manufacturing market to have such pressure on their total resources as he represented as normal in the fishing industry.

To take care of these difficulties of actual cases, Marshall could not use the notion of a representative firm,(15) but something very like representative marginal costs makes a shadowy appearance (pp. 372, 376, etc.). It is surprising that this analysis of Marshall's received so little critical attention later. This is probably due to the apparent cogency of his reasons for decreasing returns in the short run in the stationary state, in terms of which most of Marshall's critics have preferred to argue, and for which they wished to use similar constructions in their own generalizations about the shapes of the cost curves for individual businesses. It is an interesting feature of the history of this branch of economic thought that generalizations which later theorists used as the basis for their cost curves of the firm were originally required in order to make workable a theory which it was their own concern to attack on allegedly realistic grounds.

When it came to long-run analysis, Marshall *had* to face up to the issue of increasing returns. In the famous Chapter 12 of Book V he tried to state his theories in such a way as to meet the requirements of himself and other analysts, and made an effort to achieve the theory of the equilibrium of the firm which the general analysis of the pricing system and the neoclassical theory of distribution required. This chapter has, of course, to be read with Appendix H. Both are still imbued with the notion of the individual business as, in some sense, able to determine its own output, but we should ignore any particular manifestations of this idea which are inconsistent with the rest of Marshall's analysis. In the end we are left, as already foretold, with no theory of the static equilibrium of the individual business. The market for the individual firm is certainly limited; Marshall's reference to the fact that its growth will take time is to be taken as referring to the dynamic process of establishing and enhancing 'goodwill'; the limitation of the market makes Marshall's references to a firm's particular demand curve only formally correct and that 'curve' becomes analytically useless. Further, the type of demand curve which is consistent with Marshall in long-run analysis must certainly be 'kinked', for we have the overriding Marshallian rule that price cannot be higher than that charged by any other business.

It must be admitted that all this is a *reading* of Marshall, but it does make sense. It perhaps remains a puzzle why he did not state it formally. On the negative side the cogent reasons seem to be that he would have liked to make a formal statement of individual equilibrium, and the generalizations which he gives are not inconsistent with a formal marginal statement, even if they render it meaningless. Marshall saw that clearly enough, and when pressed to describe

---

(15) Since he was concerned with short-run analysis.

the situation in terms of the marginal costs which determine price, he falls back finally on the representative firm (p. 460). This, however, is unconvincing. The representative market must share the characteristics of the atomistic markets which it represents; it, peculiarly, cannot be given infinite expansibility at the given market price.

The positive reason why Marshall did not go farther is that in his historical studies he was more concerned with industrial development, and he had achieved a firm enough theory of the industry with the help of the concept of the representative business. It is not recorded that Marshall ever worked empirically on the problems of individual businesses as such. If he had, his interesting references to the average-cost-plus-standard-net-profit basis for fixing a reward in an arbitration case (p. 617 and note 1) would surely have leapt to life in his hands instead of its being dismissed because of inconsistency with notions of equilibrium rates of profits. These latter, again, are adhered to because of the fascination of the marginalist theory of the firm which Marshall had assumed elsewhere and wanted to justify in his industrial theory, but had in the end to reject, because it came into conflict with reality and the phenomenon of increasing returns.

Accordingly, it is submitted that a careful reading of Marshall, whilst leaving us with no clear statement of the theory of the firm which would be consistent with his industrial analysis, must lead us to reject any notion of the equilibrium of the firm as an integral part of his analysis. All that we can carry over as clearly Marshallian into the theory of the individual business in a competitive manufacturing industry are his generalizations about the behaviour of its costs if, in fact, its output increases. In this connexion, although Marshall formally argues in terms of rising short-run costs, there is at least a strong suspicion that we should assume that even short-run costs may normally be falling — this would be required by realistic analysis, as I have argued elsewhere.(16) There is no doubt that the long-run costs of the individual business in the Marshallian manufacturing industry should normally be taken as falling. Quite apart from the effect of external economies and the final balance which they make with external diseconomies (i.e. making the usual assumption that the prices of the factors be taken as given), its cost curve will be falling with any sustained increase in its output. Coming to the industry as a whole, Marshall thought that for industries of the normal kind where the original costs

---

(16) See p. 136 above. For some increases in output I have suggested that short-run costs should be imagined as lying below the appropriate long-run costs, whilst both would be falling; however, this is another matter, not relevant to Marshall, but inconsistent with a good deal of post-Marshallian analyses and, no doubt, productive of mathematical complexities in the Marshallian sense.

of primary materials are not a high proportion of the firm's manufacturing costs (p. 318) the net effects of decreasing returns on account of rises in factor prices would be negligible. Accordingly, when we are considering the growth of the whole of such an industry (in response, for example, to an increase in demand) the levels of costs would certainly fall as output increased.

First, any growth will tend to widen the market for all businesses, each obtaining its share of the enlarged output, which is why the representative firm is assumed to grow. Accordingly, the firms making up the industry will reap the consequent internal economies and, at the same time, there will probably be further external economies. For this reason, the growth of an industry will enable the individual firms to produce at a lower cost than if each had merely made the expansion on its own, and the representative firm's costs will always fall faster than would those of an equivalent business growing in isolation. Marshall therefore expected the supply price of an industry, such as those with which we are concerned, to fall with increases in industrial demand.

The upshot of this paper so far is that Marshall's theory of price determination in a manufacturing industry runs in terms of industrial equilibria, long-run price in such an industry being analytically tied to average costs of production in the representative business postulated by the analysis. As already noted, if we make the assumption which has become usual in later theory (because necessary for the static theory of the individual business) that the relative efficiencies of the firms in an industry remain constant and given, which Marshall himself would not make, then, of course, the relationship between long-run market price and average costs in each individual firm will similarly be determinate.

In the next section of this paper it will be useful to examine briefly what has happened to the theory of the individual business since Marshall. Its development was initially related to a particular view of Marshallian industrial equilibrium which we have already rejected, but it has led to an alternative body of doctrine, and it is desirable that we should reconsider this before returning to the concept of industrial analysis which these recent theories rendered suspect.

4   Business theory after Marshall

It would be interesting to know precisely what happened to business theory at Cambridge between the date of Marshall's *Principles* and the attack by Sraffa in 1926 upon Marshallian theory. In the interval, economics had grown up as an academic subject, and this fact alone seems sufficient to account for most of the details that may be inferred. So long as each set of problems was dealt with as fully as possible in its own right, any inconsistencies between the various hypotheses would be of no great consequence. For all Marshall's desire for consistency of vision, his sense of reality, when confronted with a problem, set limits to how far he would go to achieve it in his analyses. A teacher, on the other hand, has to have regard to conceptual difficulties and tends to develop generalized syntheses in which the maximum of apparent reference is made with the minimum of tools. It would be natural from a teaching point of view that Marshall's distinction between monopoly and competition should become a clear division in analysis, and that this should start with a correspondingly general dichotomy of markets. Pedagogic reasons would also make it desirable to argue in terms of the behaviour of individuals, so that the full contrast could be drawn between the two hypothetical states.

The theory of competitive business could most elegantly derive from the theory of the primary markets, which Marshall himself states as examples from which the chief characteristics of competitive behaviour could be grasped most readily. It was unfortunate for the subsequent development of business theory that the demand in such a competitive market as a whole was interpreted simply in terms of the consumers' demand curves of Book III. Marshall had himself analysed markets as if the price of the relevant commodities were those at which they reached the final consumer (pp. 341–2). This led to some confusion in his analysis, but the consequences were to be worse in an academic treatment which, I think, is prone to argue from diagrams, which are too readily taken as both established and understood.(17) The demand curves for all commodities in theoretical economics have been given the general attributes of consumers' demand curves, making it a natural step to argue as if all markets were simply consumers' markets.

Given the total supply to the 'market', demand would determine the 'equilibrium price'. The demand for the products of the individual business can be very simply treated: variations in the amounts put by it on the market will not have any significant effect upon market price; it may, therefore, be considered to have an infinitely elastic demand at any given level of market price. The Marshallian concept of equilibrium in the market as a whole then came to be 'mirrored' by a general concept of the equilibrium of the individual business. Since he can sell what he will, the producer's problem is to determine how much he will produce. Given constant price, the condition for a determinate equilibrium, whether short run or long, is that marginal costs should be rising. Granted the assumed nature of the market and also the concept of individual equilibrium, it could too easily be assumed that such a condition had to apply, with the result, perhaps, that it became impossible to examine critically the reasons that traditional theory adduced for the existence of increasing costs.

---

(17) See MacGregor, *Economic Thought and Policy*, p. 35.

No difficulty seems ever to have been suspected in postulating increasing costs in the short run for all types of industries; the simple use of the concept of fixed factors of production, analogous to the 'field' in theoretical agriculture, plus the law of 'non-proportional returns' seemed to yield increasing costs as an irrefutable consequence. It followed, of course, that when economists had to recognize the existence of decreasing short-run costs, this could too easily be analysed as the consequence of imperfections of competition rather than as a necessary characteristic of many manufacturing industries in normal times. In long-run analysis, the dynamic difficulties which Marshall had adduced as besetting the management of a growing business, when once it got beyond a certain size-stage, made it possible to call in a factor which 'must' eventually cause the static cost curve of the individual business to turn up, whatever the technical economies which were otherwise available. Accordingly, both in short-run and in long-run analysis, the problem of the behaviour of the individual business, given its efficiency, etc., could formally be solved in terms of its supply curve — traced out by the relevant rising curve of marginal costs.

In the analysis of the firm, the ability of the producer would naturally be taken as given, and his cost curve would necessarily be drawn on the assumption of given prices for the factors of production. It was easy enough to take care of any effect of external economies or diseconomies, as the whole output of an industry grew, by letting this affect the supply curve for the industry and imagining the individual cost curves as shifting accordingly. In the long run, full equilibrium was reached when market price equalled the marginal costs of the supply from each individual firm and from the industry as a whole. It would also be equal to the average costs of the firms when all rents were included. All this is so familiar an interpretation of Marshall's theory of competitive equilibrium that it is understandably difficult to turn one's mind round to criticizing it in its own terms; and it was this construction which served as a basis for the attack upon Marshall, for thinking that increasing returns, and especially decreasing costs for the firm, could be present in any market which could properly be analysed as competitive.

Space will not permit of our making the detailed review of the development of the inter-war controversies, which would otherwise be interesting. They started with a statement of the dilemma which faced a teacher when he confronted the logic of the pseudo-Marshallian theory of competition with the cases which Marshall analysed. In so far as increasing returns in an allegedly competitive industry resulted from decreasing costs in the firm, they were incompatible with equilibrium of the kind normally envisaged by the theory. Why did not the individual business just go on growing, until either it ran into a stretch of increasing costs or the competition in its industry had disappeared into a monopoly situation? This dilemma might be evaded by appealing to external economies, but these would militate against the partial analysis of the industry, unless they were of the internal–external type which seemed only doubtfully capable of real content. The restatements of Marshall's theory which were attempted by Pigou, by Shove, and by Sraffa appeared unsatisfactory in so far as they did not challenge the theory of the market for the competitive manufacturing business, which lay at the heart of the dilemma. Robertson's contribution remained most close to Marshall's original formulation, but, because he did not bring this issue out as one which the critics themselves had to face, he was too easily regarded by the inter-war generation as 'downed' by Sraffa's skilful pricking of his analogies.

The solution upon which economists eventually agreed, and practically everything else which was subsequently written on the theory of the equilibrium of the individual business in imperfect competition, was contained in the original article by Sraffa, but it took a good deal of discussion before it was worked out fully. It was eventually accepted that decreasing costs, in both the short- and the long-run senses, were a normal feature of many manufacturing industries analysed by Marshallians as competitive. It was rightly discovered that Marshall's uniform market was, in fact, not uniform, and that producers normally produced differentiated commodities. It was here that the phenomena of consumers' preferences were so easily invoked. We have already commented on the weakness of this solution, but the reason for it seems clear: it was essential for the analysis that was to be developed that the buyers' preferences to be invoked should not be related to inherent qualities, for the latter would be reflected in costs, and it was analytically desirable to counter falling costs in the firm by some independent penalty to expansion. Stresses upon the role of advertising and other selling costs made it possible to credit the consumer with irrational differentiation of the market into more or less distinct 'commodities'. It was now possible to bring in the theory of monopoly.

This was done in the contributions made by Harrod and by Mrs. Robinson in the *Economic Journal* controversy.(18) Let the fact of consumers' preferences be taken as conferring upon the business its own demand curve, with consequently falling marginal revenue. (Similar demand — and cost — curves would yield similar prices which would be stable with falling costs.) It was now understandable that it was possible for the firm to stop short at an output or

---

(18) R. F. Harrod: 'Notes on Supply', *Economic Journal*, 1930; 'The Law of Decreasing Costs', *ibid.*, 1931; J. Robinson: 'Competition and Falling Supply Price', *ibid.*, 1932.

scale with falling costs.(19)

Chamberlin, who had been working independently at the problem, developed similar conclusions, and his large-group analysis had formal relevance to industries where businesses were numerous and where the products were sufficiently comparable technically for them to be produced under similar cost conditions. In such an industry, free entry in the Marshallian sense (new businesses coming in so long as they can get normal profits) plus the necessity of existing businesses covering average costs in order to survive in the long run, gave a Marshallian equilibrium, with businesses earning normal profits but with decreasing costs.

Chamberlin also provided the outlines of a theory for the case where the firms were not so numerous that cross-elasticities of demand could be neglected by them. In an ingenious piece of analysis he provided what should now be recognized as a general background to the theory of the 'kinked' demand curve. Starting from any given position of price and demand for an individual business, he imagined two demand curves: (20) the one tracing out its share of the market, if all businesses followed its price policy; the other, tracing out its demand, if it varied its price but the other businesses with whom it was competing held theirs stable. With the aid of these tools Chamberlin analysed the various possible solutions to what was essentially a parallel to the old oligopoly problem, but in which the solutions could be seen in terms of the differentiated market which the newer theories were assuming.

The large-group analysis of Chamberlin did seem to provide a formal solution for the Marshallian dilemma where numerous businesses were competing with one another without serious apparent disparities in their profits and where decreasing costs occurred for the individual businesses. It had, however, involved assumptions which Chamberlin himself called 'heroic' and which did not seem particularly to fit many of the industries to which the analysis should apply. Both this and his small-group analysis came under fire from the theorists of the Walrasian school. Triffin, in particular, launched a

---

(19) Further, as Harrod showed, if conditions in an industry, with this differentiation of the product, were such that the businesses got only normal profits, they would necessarily be producing at decreasing costs in both the short run and the long. For, by definition, the price which they got for their product would equal their average cost, and the tangency of the curves that was thus postulated would mean that costs were falling. In such a situation price would exceed marginal cost, and excess capacity — which the economists of the thirties had experienced as a real phenomenon — emerged as the normal condition of such an industry in such a position.

(20) I have found it useful to call these the 'share-of-the-market' demand curve and 'particular' demand curve respectively.

critical attack upon the whole concept of an industry, which Chamberlin had preserved with such strenuous efforts. Even in the hands of its founder, the analysis seemed to be wilting under this criticism when the late war broke out, and it began to appear that Triffin's cry of triumph had been justified,(21) and that the old concept of an 'industry' had disappeared for ever from economic theory, although it might be possible to tolerate the empirical worker using such an admittedly vague idea. The theorist was delivered over to a Walrasian world where everything is determinate but nothing can ever be determined.

At the same time, however, a new attack on the problem developed from quite a different angle. Realistic inquiries at Oxford had elucidated the facts that business men, when quoting prices, did not think explicitly in terms of marginal revenues and costs, and that a general method of pricing was to add a margin as for net profit to average short-run costs. Further, business men appeared to adhere firmly to this method of pricing and to be reluctant to cut or increase their prices for the sake of short-term advantages. The important article by Hall and Hitch reporting this research gives a fair summary of the comments of the business men concerned, but the speculative part of the article devotes more attention to the stability of prices than to possible theoretical explanations of the pricing practices disclosed. Businesses were taken as fixing their prices on the 'full-cost' basis, their reluctance to alter them was explained by a very ingenious use of a demand curve of the kinked kind incorporating a segment from each of the demand curves which Chamberlin devised for his small-group analysis. Here, within wide limits, any existing price would be justified; within a possibly large range, marginal revenue would be indeterminate. A rise in price would not be followed by competitors, and sales would shrink along the appropriate elastic 'particular-demand' curve; a cut in price would be countered by other businesses, and output would increase only along the inelastic 'share-of-the-market' curve.

The reason why the 'kink' should occur at the full-cost (better termed 'normal-cost') level of price was not adduced, and the rationale of the costing rules that produced that price were left unanalysed. If anything, the determination of prices appeared even less rational than before, even though, for the first time since the doubts of the inter-war period, economic theory seemed at last to be taking a stand upon what people actually did. Theoretical attention concentrated upon the apparent fact of the kinked demand curve, price appeared to be determinate neither upon a competitive nor on a monopoly basis, but to be a matter of strategy, or of various excursions into actual warfare, if the strategies of the individual businesses diverged. The concept of the price-leader had emerged from the basic empirical research, but otherwise the net result was to bring in the theory of oligopoly as a general method of analysis.

---

(21) Triffin, *Monopolistic Competition and Equilibrium Theory*, p. 52.

The analytical merit of the approach made by Hall and Hitch was that it preserved intact the old approach via the static equilibrium of the firm. It was still possible to think in terms of marginal revenues and costs, only the indeterminacy of their point of intersection accounted for the vagueness of the resulting theory and the paucity of empirical data. For the teacher, the approach was attractive since it lent itself to the systematic development of the theory of business behaviour from the Marshallian cases of perfect or pure competition and monopoly, through the concepts of monopolistic competition, to a theory which had apparent reference to real procedures whilst retaining at least the forms of marginal analysis.

Harrod, when introducing the results of the Research Group of which he had been Chairman, which were discussed by Hall and Hitch, suggested that the full-cost principle must have its rationale since it was so firmly established. Unfortunately, the fact of the 'kink' appeared to provide a negative sort of reason — the principle gave prices which normally did not provoke the serious competition of other businesses, and the kink explained why such prices were maintained once fixed. Nevertheless, Harrod was right in his wider plea. In fact, a careful examination of the original Hall and Hitch paper will show that the business men who had given evidence themselves offer some of the major elements of a theory which yields a determinate analysis of the normal-cost price, when once the theory of costs is put on a better empirical basis. As has already been said, my empirical studies have forced me to construct such a theory of the firm, and it is in the light of that theory that we shall now reconsider the concept of an industry in the Marshallian sense.

5 The 'industry' reappears[22]

After the post-Marshallian revolution it is desirable that business analysis should start from and be centred upon the theory of the individual business; the concept of an 'industry' will be acceptable only if it should emerge as a natural extension of the theory of the firm. It is the contention of this paper that it does so, when the basis of price-determination in manufacturing businesses is clearly understood.

It is convenient to commence with the static analysis of a business which is producing a given range of products — only, for simplicity's sake, it will be imagined to produce a single product. At any given time the business will be organized in a definite manner, i.e. it will possess a given equipment and overhead organization run by a management with a given level of ability, energy, etc.; its output will be obtained by the use of amounts of the variable factors of production (including materials) which will vary with the size of that output, and it will be supposed to obtain these at given prices.

Other things being equal, the average direct costs of such a business will be constant over a fairly wide range of actual output, and its average total costs per unit of output will therefore fall as output increases, due to the reduced weight of the fixed indirect costs. There will be a definite limit to the output that the business can produce, given its fixed factors, but as a purely temporary measure it will be able to produce a larger output than it could maintain indefinitely, for it can temporarily 'overwork' its overhead factors of production — especially its personnel. A business man will, however, normally plan to operate within this limit, and, in this sense, a business which is running at its full planned capacity will normally have some reserve capacity available for short-run increases of output. If its output increases so that it can normally produce a larger output than is desirable with its present organization, then the business will reorganize

---

(22) It will be understood that the elements of the theory of the firm can be stated much more baldly when we are concerned with the analysis of industrial groupings of firms than would be appropriate when our attention is more narrowly concentrated upon the individual business. In the same way, when we are examining an actual business our thought-pattern has to be much more complex than would be appropriate for a theoretical discussion even of individual businesses. Further, since the aim of this paper is to discuss a normal pattern of analysis for manufacturing industry, even the industrial analysis can be presented in stark outline without bothering overmuch about the differences between one industry and another which concern us in empirical work. Some aspects of each of these more complex questions have been discussed in *Manufacturing Business*, and a more detailed discussion of them will be provided in a later book which will be concerned with empirical studies as such.

to produce these larger outputs. It is assumed that the average costs for larger outputs will be less than for smaller outputs, the business being appropriately organized in each case.

The individual business will, therefore, produce at decreasing costs per unit, both short and long run. But whereas short-run average costs will decline relatively sharply as output increases over the relevant range of production, the long-run costs will decrease relatively more gently in the case of an established business. It would normally take a substantial increase of output to enable it to run at substantially reduced long-run average costs.

We shall see that, in fact, market conditions are not likely to permit such large relative increases in output to result from factors which are within the control of the business, such as price cutting. But, even if this were not so, it would be wrong in a realistic theory of price-determination to let long-run cost changes have the full force that abstract theory might suggest that they possessed. In actual conditions costs will always be liable to chance fluctuations, and the uncertainty within which the business man plans is such that his estimates will be tentatively used. More important, perhaps, is the consideration that it will always take time for a business to consolidate itself at a significantly enlarged scale, and some time must elapse before actual costs can be got down to the level which the business man may have estimated as possible in the end. Meanwhile he could not postulate that the other factors in his calculations would remain unchanged.

It will, therefore, be very reasonable for a business man to take his present costs as a good guide to his probable costs of production for most increases in output that appear likely. If his output does increase, and he maintains it, then he can count on reductions in costs improving his position, other things being equal.

What about the marketing side of the picture? First, let us assume that at given prices an individual firm will have a definite clientele, given that it retains its 'goodwill'. Other things being equal, its customers will prefer to deal with it rather than with other businesses; a brand-new business, similarly, may be imagined as building up its clientele out of the custom that it gets at seasonal or other times of pressure of demand for its type of products. The *ceteris paribus* clause, however, reminds us that all this is subject to the condition that in the long run no business will be able to charge a higher price than another business would for a product which is technically identical with its own, as delivered to a particular customer. In the long run, therefore, all businesses producing the same product will have to charge the same price, and a business which is producing a speciality will not be able to charge a higher price than another business would charge to produce it, provided that the business has not got a monopoly in the strict original Marshallian sense. In the short run, a business may be getting a higher price, but as the knowledge of this circumstance spreads it will face a decreasing demand for its products, the lower-pricing businesses gaining, until in the long run its demand would disappear altogether — but it will revise its pricing policy long before that happens.(23)

In practice, a business man knows this and reasons accordingly. He will, therefore, try to avoid quoting a price which he could not maintain in the long run. It should be remembered that he is assumed to be a manufacturer who has sunk a good deal in investment which will take some time to justify itself. Goodwill is too precious a commodity, and takes too long to build up, for it to be thrown away on a wrong pricing policy. And on the other side of the picture, the fact of decreasing costs will mean that all businesses will gladly accept extra orders at a price which is no lower than they are getting already. Price-regulating competition does not, therefore, in normal times, involve so long a run as might naively be imagined on the old notion of existing businesses all working to capacity, when new competition could come only from the slow development of absolutely new firms.

What determines the competition which a business man will thus have to meet, and the price at which he will meet it? It will pay any existing business, with suitable production facilities, to quote against him, if a lower price would enable it to cover its estimated average costs of production plus a fair profit.(24) Similarly, it will be attractive to set up a new business, if its founder calculates that, in the long run, he may hope to get a total output which would suffice to leave him in a favourable position at the given price.

The experience of a business man in an established business will give him a fair idea of what level of price is likely to be dangerous; and any mistake, if he should be mistaken, will soon show itself in a relatively shrinking demand. But we must not regard him simply as thinking about the right price; it is rather that he adopts a costing-up policy which on his experience will yield him the right price, or, at least, no higher price. This pricing policy will enable him at once to quote a price for a new product at which he can feel reasonably safe against the competition of other businesses.

(23) One reason why this theory here differs so substantially from generally received doctrine is, as I have pointed out, that the typical customer of a manufacturing business is another business.

(24) It will be noticed that here and elsewhere I refer to the business as quoting a price; this recognizes the fact that different businesses frequently produce different products; and, in any case, it is quite usual for the precise nature of the product to be specified by the customer. In practice, then, a manufacturing business is more often in the position that it formally quotes a price than that it sells at a price which is impersonally quoted on a market. That does not prevent businesses from being in competition with one another.

An established business in a stable or growing market will normally fix its price quotations on the basis of a detailed estimate of its actual costs of production, direct and indirect separately, adding to these a margin as for net profit. Alternatively, quoted price may be reached on the basis of a much more explicitly rule-of-thumb basis of average direct costs plus an allowance for gross profit. I say 'explicitly', for, of course, any allowance as for net profit in the more detailed costings will be no less on a rule-of-thumb basis. In either case the business can be presumed to have an idea of the level of net profits which it is safe for it to take in its line of manufacture, and this has special significance in any dynamic view of profits; but the significant elements (from the static point of view generally assumed for this section of the paper) in the analysis of price-determination, are average direct costs and the gross profit margin which makes up the balance of the quoted price. In price-equilibrium, each business will find that it is able to charge safely only on the basis of a definite level of gross profit, since it will have a definite normal level of average direct costs. And the gross profit margin that it can get will seem to be limited by the competition which is actually or potentially present in its market.

At this point it will be convenient to break off for a discussion of the effect upon quoted prices of changes in a business's costs of production, although it will not be possible to avoid straying a little from our static assumptions strictly interpreted. A manufacturing business will normally be quick to lower price if its costs fall by reason of reductions in the prices of raw materials or in the wages of labour. These will affect other businesses as well, and to neglect to make consequent adjustments in prices will be to invite successful competition in one's market. Moreover, the buyers will normally be fairly well acquainted with the fact and extent of such changes, and will expect a reduction whose size they will often be able to estimate — in fact, where a business is selling to expert buyers, they will frequently have as shrewd an idea as it of the 'right' price, at which they could get such a thing made elsewhere. Similarly, it will generally be fairly easy to revise prices upwards in the event of increases in the prices of such factors; in general, they will occur only during a rising market for such factors, buyers will expect them, they will not affect the strength of the final market, and the competitive normal price will be similarly affected.(25)

It remains to consider the effects of autonomous changes in a business's costs — those due to changes in its output or to changes in its efficiency. An increase in average costs due simply to a reduction in output will, of course, have no upward effect upon price. Whether it is due to a weakening of the business's relative hold over its market, or to a general decline in the demand for its sort of products, to raise price will make matters worse and present its goodwill to other businesses who will be only too anxious to enlarge their sales at the ruling price. The same will be true of a rise of costs due to a decrease in the productive efficiency of the business.

Weak businesses which are only just holding on, or making very low profits relatively to the rest of their industry, will not reduce prices on account of any autonomous decline of costs. Their long-run position will be in danger, and they will both need and be seeking such cost changes in order to ensure that they have the means of continuing in being. The position is very different with the relatively stronger businesses: those which at the given level of price are selling a sufficiently large output and working at such a level of efficiency that they already get satisfactory profits. They will reduce prices fairly promptly if their cost levels fall because their market has expanded and enabled them to produce at lower costs, or if their level of costs for the same output falls because of improved efficiency. It will be borne in mind that the shape of the long-period cost curve will normally require a substantial increase in output before costs are substantially affected. In the latter case, the way that costings are drawn up will generally ensure a fairly prompt reduction if average direct costs fall; a fall in overheads may take a little time to make its presence known, or at least for it to be taken as likely to continue, but once it shows itself in the costings, it will

---

(25) In practice, a business may not be able to make minor changes in price, which sometimes can be changed only by conventional amounts; it is also generally true that buyers will not like too sensitive a price policy leading to too frequent relatively minor changes in price. It is, therefore, frequently the custom for businesses to delay price rises until they have become increasingly justified over a period; and if a rising trend in factor prices is expected to continue it may be allowed for to some extent in the rise of price that is made. There will be a stronger inducement to do something quickly about a fall of costs, but minor changes may be allowed simply to have the effect of improving the quality of the product, or of associated services, or be ignored.

tend to lead to price reductions.(26) It is in this way that a growing efficient business will be one of the chief forces of competition in its market, determining what we have called equilibrium price in its market.(27)

The inducement to reduce price will not only be that it may be able to retain some of any short-period increase in relative sales that it gets from the initial price cut, but that it will certainly increase its long-run hold on its market, continuing to get satisfactory profits which will enable it to have the wherewithal for growth and for innovation, whilst the long-run hold of its rivals will be weakened, if their efficiency remains relatively unimproved. A failure to make such a reduction will carry corresponding dangers and, as has been said, the normal costing rules will tend to cause such a downward reduction to take place.

To return to the static analysis with which we are mainly concerned at present, the upshot so far is that the price quoted by a manufacturing business is to be seen as competitively determined; at that price, at any given time, it will be able to sell only what the market will take. This statement, in itself, means the implied abandonment of any definition of equilibrium output for the individual business, in the sense of the achievement of a balance between marginal revenue and marginal cost. This concept of a deliberately planned (restriction of) output is, it may be observed, one of the major intellectual difficulties in the way of a trained theoretical economist when he turns to empirical studies. We shall return to this aspect of static theory later, for, to some extent, the static method in general has similar disadvantages, although I do not think them so grave as those that flow from this particular static concept. Meanwhile it will be noted that the analysis given here is in terms of an equilibrium of *price*, and not of individual *outputs*.

An existing business will continue in production at the given level of price so long as it can cover all the outgoings that have currently to be met. In the short run, it may be prepared to run at a loss, so long as it is covering at least its direct costs — and the pricing rules will evidently tend to ensure this for businesses which are not surprisingly inefficient or unlucky in the matter of

---

(26) All this, of course, is presuming rather more normal times than we have known recently, in the sense that it must be possible for an efficient business quickly to get the additional equipment, etc., that it will need in order to extend its output; it must also be free to extend in the most appropriate way, The position is very different when an industry is held tightly controlled by outside factors.

(27) When an industry is loosely defined, as it is in most official statistics, it is too easy to be impressed by the large size of the largest business and easy to invoke the modern jargon of oligopolistic price-leadership. When we study the matter from the inside, we find frequently that it is not here that leadership is to be found; the level of prices is much more often determined by the vigorous, medium-sized or small, relatively specialist, business which is bent on growing.

organizing their direct factors of production. In the longer run it will not be able to carry on at all unless it covers all its paying-out costs, for continued production will otherwise imply steadily depleted cash balances. These paying-out costs will in the long run include the costs of the maintenance and replacement of its capital assets as well as the wages of management and other overhead personnel, which will have to be met more continuously. Provided that the business does cover its paying-out costs, it will be able to carry on, even if it is not earning anything by way of interest on its capital; if they are not covered, it will become less efficient, have rising levels of costs, and in the end will be forced out of business.

A new business, of course, will not start up unless it is thought to have a reasonable chance that in the long run it will get a sufficient output to enable it not merely to survive but also to earn satisfactory profits. It would be misleading, however, to make the usual full-static-equilibrium assumption that all businesses which are producing a given product must cover their costs and get normal profits. This would be unrealistic even if additional capacity for the production of a particular product could come only from the starting of a new business. A new business will start too small from the long-run point of view, and will usually 'get by' initially only in the favourable circumstances of a trade boom or with extraordinarily hard work on the part of its management. It will allow for these difficulties by taking as its target some idea of what it may reasonably hope to achieve when it gets established. It will get this idea by guessing or estimating what is happening to established businesses making similar products and, thence, what its own fortune is likely to be. Looked at from the point of view of their actual results, new businesses will, therefore, often have taken an optimistic view. Accordingly, where capital requirements make it relatively easy for new businesses to produce a particular type of product, it is understandable that a substantial part of the output of such types of products should be produced at a loss, when all costs are allowed for.

In the world as it is, however, competition from new businesses is often not the most important source of competition. Granted the limitation of their primary markets, established businesses will normally be looking around for related products which they can take on. Here again, the decision to do so will be related to the chance of the experiments justifying themselves ultimately, rather than upon immediate results. The more narrowly we define a product, in fact, the more normal it will be to find that a proportion of the output is being produced at a loss; but if we considered the business possessing the appropriate type of production facilities, the proportion of these making losses would be smaller, many businesses will be sufficiently established with their main products to cover the costs of their output as a whole, but will be making current losses on the products where they are trying the market, or tentatively establishing themselves.

Although no formal warning has been given, it will no doubt have already been realized that we have slipped away from the strict analysis of the individual business into talking about groupings of businesses which are apparently playing the same analytical role as the old Marshallian 'industry'. (In the same way, the previous two paragraphs will have suggested the shadowy reappearance of something very much like a 'representative firm'; but it has not, in fact, appeared, and its usefulness will be discussed below.) In fact, we cannot erect the concepts which are needed to understand the behaviour of the individual manufacturing business without at the same time conceiving of the relevant grouping of competing and potentially competing businesses — the 'industry' — through which the forces of the economic environment of the business act and react upon it. From now on, we explicitly define an 'industry' as any grouping of individual manufacturing businesses which is relevant when we study the behaviour of any one such business. The discussion of this paper, however, will formally be restricted to the consideration of product markets; we cannot consider the analogous, but not necessarily coterminous, groupings of businesses which come into view when the markets for their factors of production are analysed.

In the product markets, what is the chief characteristic of an industry? It is largely a matter of technique and processes; an individual business must be conceived as operating within an 'industry' which consists of all businesses which operate processes of a sufficiently similar kind (which implies the possession of substantially similar technical resources) and possessing sufficiently similar backgrounds of experience and knowledge so that each of them could produce the particular commodity under consideration, and would do so if it were sufficiently attractive.

The scope of such a definition will widen as we increase our understanding of the economics of the production of the particular commodity. At first, attention will be concentrated upon all commodities with very similar technical specifications, sold in circumstances entailing that similar services are rendered to the customer. Thus we may consider the producers of fractional horse-power motors or the producers of fitting shoes. Within such narrow groupings our price-equilibrium analysis applies most simply: Technically similar products must have identical normal prices, or normal prices whose differences will be explicable on the basis of a difference in normal costs of production.(28) This narrower definition of an industry will include all the businesses which are in most active competition with one another on any short-run analysis. But,

_____

(28) Compare Mr. Leyland's note on prices in the lightweight bicycle industry: 'A Note on Price and Quality', *Oxford Economic Papers*, June 1949.

studying the way in which competition actually emerges, we become aware of the significance of a much more widely drawn boundary to the industry — to include all those who possess such facilities, etc., that they could well turn over to the production of our narrowly defined product in a rather longer run, since they will take more time to enter its particular market. Our analysis then runs in very broad terms: 'the boot and shoe industry'; 'electrical engineering'; even, on occasion, 'the leather and footwear industry'; or 'engineering'.

These wider definitions of the industry which are relevant to longer-run analyses will, as already argued, normally be separable into sub-industries each producing its relatively narrow grade or type of product. The typical gross margins, and net profit margins, of these will differ between themselves(29) — but normal differences in such margins will tend to be established; for example, as between different 'ends' of the boot and shoe industry; and these will be found to differ with differences in the costs that are normally involved. Even these wide definitions of industries thus take on a sense of reality for economic analysis.

When we are teaching the principles of economic analysis as they are applicable to manufacturing industries, it will, therefore, seem appropriate to do as Marshall did, to use the concept of 'an industry', and to analyse it as if it, in fact, involved producing an identical commodity. In empirical analysis we shall have to break down such a general concept and obtain realistic definitions of the industry which will vary both with the type of commodity with which we are concerned and with the purpose of the analysis; even the same inquiry may therefore use a definition which shifts in its scope as between different parts of the analysis. For general analysis, and for teaching purposes, however, the matter can be left very much in Marshallian terms.

For the hypothetical commodity which will be the subject of such analyses we can postulate a Marshallian demand curve — which should perhaps be given with the realistic warning that it should generally be taken as inelastic in the neighbourhood of existing price (except perhaps after a really long period has elapsed after a change of price, so that the full indirect effects may have been realized). This analytical concept of 'the' demand curve for the industry will have some empirical validity even for an industry which, in fact, produces a great variety of actual products, because they will often be subject to the same broad historical influences (their demands, for example, broadly rising and contracting together). Such a combination will have some meaning from the point of view of producers, because the individual commodities will be alternative products in the long run; it will also frequently be the case that they are all in some sort of competition as substitutes for one another.

----

(29) And within such sub-industries gross margins will differ between businesses according to the levels of their average direct costs.

At a given level of price the total demand will be analysable, at any one time, into definite amounts demanded from individual businesses and not available to others, unless the favoured business cannot in fact supply all that is demanded of it — which should not be presumed in a long-run analysis starting with some situation of equilibrium. The market will be in equilibrium as long as the total demand at the given price is within the capacity of the industry and of the individual businesses, and as long as the price is equal to the normal cost of producing the commodity, so that on balance any loss of capacity due to businesses being driven from production is made up by extensions to existing capacity or by the entry of new capacity.

If demand increases at the given price, there will be a general increase in the amounts demanded from the individual businesses. In normal conditions they will meet these up to the full extent of their short-run capacity, price remaining unchanged, and they will extend if their limited capacity makes it desirable to do so. Short-run increases in demand will generally be met at normal price, on our assumptions. (It will be understood that we are maintaining the assumption that factor prices will not have changed; this will not be valid, say, for an increase in demand which is part of a general cyclical increase of trade.) In the long run, however, such an expansion of existing businesses will enable them to reorganize and get the benefit of lower costs. Normal price will, therefore, fall in the long run. An increased demand for manufacturing products will therefore be met eventually at a lower equilibrium price.

In any full analysis of such a change we should have to allow for any effects upon costs which may be due to causes outside the organization of the individual business but due less directly to such a change in demand. These will be any diseconomy to the industry due to the prices of primary factors of production rising with the increased pressure of the demand for them, and also any economies which the larger-scale production may produce in other industries. These will have their effect upon the normal-cost price which will be established in the particular industry which we are analysing, and may cause the trend of normal price for the industry to differ from what we should infer from a knowledge of the behaviour of costs in an individual business considered in isolation. It will be recognized that this parallels familiar points in Marshallian analysis, but these are simply other instances of the way in which the theory of the firm which has been discussed here may be used to provide a very fair parallel to the Marshallian description of long-run equilibrium in a manufacturing industry, on static assumptions.

In the process of making the analysis, however, the supply curve concept has dissolved in the same way as we have earlier suggested occurred on a strict interpretation of Marshall's own analysis. We are left with the concept of a given stable demand being supplied at a normal-cost price, of an extension to that demand being met in the short run by increased supplies at the same price, and in the long run at a decreased price. The number of businesses in an industry will adjust themselves to demand in the long run.

One ingredient from Marshall has been prominently absent so far in this section — that is, the representative firm. It has been represented to me that it may usefully be accommodated in the analysis as a concept summarizing the factors which are relevant to long-run competition. Others may like to use it; I myself find it difficult to handle in conditions where we must assume that a good deal of the latent competition will be from businesses which are already in existence, even if not producing the particular product. It owed its origin to the necessity of relating the supply curve to the behaviour of individual firms, when the general tenor of the analysis was in conflict with fundamental notions of individual businesses as tending to be in marginalist equilibrium. It seems to me possible to do without it.(30)

The foregoing analysis has generally been made upon static assumptions, but to an economist who has experience of empirical studies of businesses there is bound to be some sense of strain in the use of such analysis, and this should be recognized here. Static theory is quite adequate for the purposes of general economic analysis, and is useful in training pupils to get the general view of industrial behaviour which will give the broad conceptual basis for empirical work. For an industrial economist as such, however, there is something much more seriously wrong with static analysis of industries than with that of the individual firm from which the wider analysis is built up.

In the case of a given business it seems a natural procedure to take things as they are and work out the implications in terms of the business's long-run capacity to compete and to survive, assuming other relevant factors to remain unchanged. But it is impossible to do this without being well aware just how dangerous it is to take for granted the relative level of efficiency which exists at a particular time. Businesses which are in a very strong position often lose it through becoming complacent, losing such firm control over overhead costs, etc., and losing the drive to be 'just that step ahead' which is necessary in a world where it will be rare for a business to be able to go on making just that particular product in such-and-such a particular way. Equally, a business which is

---

(30) Although I do not advocate the use of the concept of the representative firm in teaching industrial analysis, it should be noted that representativeness is a real enough quality when we are concerned with empirical work. When studying an 'industry' it is useful to get preliminary ideas of the types of business situations, with regard to technique, to marketing, to labour supply, etc., that are to be met with in practice, and then to select for study businesses which seem likely to provide good case-studies from these points of view.

doing badly has so much incentive to do something about it. As has been said before, it is out of the constant passing to and fro of industrial leadership that the essence of actual competition arises.

When we are studying actual businesses we break the bounds of static assumptions fairly easily. The histories of actual individual businesses and their competitors soon make us aware that an important factor in competition is the cost-reducing enterprise of individual business men. It is easy to lose sight of this in static industrial analyses; the concept of an industry is abstract anyway, the static analysis enables us to grasp certain essential elements of a right view, but it is difficult to realize that the theory may be seriously misleading. We may try to remove static assumptions which get explicitly in the way, but the broad picture of astatic competition still clogs thinking.(31)

Life does not run with the smoothness that economic theory can legitimately assume for general analysis or for teaching purposes. The very ups and downs of the trade cycle contribute their own element making for the increased efficiency of business over time, but the individual business will also get its share of minor setbacks. Something always remains from the enforced ideas of economy and novelty to which business men are driven by such forces. Innovation and the rest of such factors will mean that the forces of competition, apparently so easily impounded in static analysis, will cause the level of normal-cost price always to fall. It sometimes seems that the whole clue to the history of economic civilization is missing from static analysis.

The abandonment of the concept of static equilibrium for the individual business, which has been urged in this paper, would mean some improvement since it is certainly one of the major elements in his thought-pattern which prevents an academic economist from understanding what is happening in business life.(32) Even so, granted that its disappearance will leave our static theory on a better basis, it will still not be good enough. We need some different patterns of analysis. But these will have to be built up out of empirical studies,

---

(31) See Hayek's stimulating essay 'The Meaning of Competition' in his book *Individualism and Economic Order*.

(32) I cannot resist telling the story of a cohort of undergraduates at the last stages of their training who were invited to spend a period in a Midlands works. They spent the whole time not in seeing what did go on, and then trying to interpret it for themselves, but in the much more interesting pursuit of trying to 'prove' that the business man must be mistaken, or at least unaware of the implications of some procedure which their persistent questioning would bring out, when he said that he did not price with any calculations of marginal revenue, marginal cost, or of the right output which would maximize his net profits. They were unconvinced at the end of their stay, and were probably wondering exactly what had been hidden from them. Abstractions in economics sound very much like descriptions!

just as Marshallian concepts were largely informed by their founder's studies of historical processes. No amount of spinning-out of logical chains of analysis based upon static concepts will help in this task. The need is for more empirical studies, and for the co-operation of business men and academics in their making. Before such co-operation can be fruitful, however, economic theory must not be positively wrong in its approach, and I would conclude this paper by suggesting that that was the negative effect of the inter-war rejection of Marshall.

4   The legacy of the 1930s in economics[1]

When I was making definite arrangements to speak to you, I was told of your intended change of name and that carried my thoughts back to your predecessor — the Politics and Economics Society of pre-war days — and thinking back to the 1930s, I determined on my subject: the legacy which we have inherited from that decade which, looking back, we can see to have been so important in the history of economic thought.

You know, we knew it was important at the time. As modern sales jargon puts it, Economics then seemed to have reached an all-time peak. In many departments of analysis, definite results seemed at last to have been attained and those whom we then regarded as the leading modern economists applied the results of that analysis with very great confidence to the problems of the day. Such semi-fossil survivals from the earlier periods of thought as appeared before your predecessor were listened to respectfully of course, and their audience dealt with them kindly in discussion. At the same time, we pitied them for the hardening of the intellectual arteries which prevented them from seeing how many of their problems had been solved — and from appreciating the clear light which economics had begun to throw on the political problems of our own day.

Thinking back over this, it was natural to me to come once more to the question of the legacy of the 1930s, with which I find myself so often preoccupied. Before coming to this subject, I should like to say one thing. I can't avoid being somewhat controversial. Indeed, the breadth of the canvas I shall have to cover might well make me accentuate the tones, as it were. I shall, therefore, present the controversial points more sharply than I should if we were discussing the matter in a leisured correspondence. No doubt we shall be able to soften the outlines a little in the discussion. Further, in view of my special interest, I shall say rather more about the theory of prices than about other matters, which are no less interesting in their own rights.

Beginnings, in history, are always shifting affairs, according to our points of view. If we stand in imagination in 1930, we cannot but be conscious of the 1920s at our back. I certainly cannot, for I began to study economics in 1929,

(1) Presented to the Politics and Economics Society, Oxford, Hilary Term, 1952. Reprinted with permission from Lancaster University, acting on behalf of the estate of P.W.S. Andrews.

and so was taught by economists who were themselves largely educated in the 1920s. Further, the academic descent of my tutors led me to be aware of the influences in my training which came from pre-1914 Cambridge and from pre-1914 Austria.

If you will let me select boldly the characteristics of the 1920s, from an economist's point of view, I shall say that they are two: the serious troubles of our basic industries and the beginnings of Economics as a professional subject.

Take first the question of economics: As an academic discipline, Economics had hardly arrived before the first World War — in England at all events. We had had first-class Economists for three centuries but no regular output of professional, academically trained economists, such as we have become accustomed to since. At London, my academic grandfather, Edwin Cannan taught the history of economic doctrine in a school whose students, if they were academically inclined, largely studied economics as a subsidiary subject to economic history. The new school at Cambridge had achieved its first great pedagogue, Professor Pigou, and had already produced some very great products — Professors Robertson and MacGregor, for example. At Oxford, we had one of the oldest chairs of Political Economy in the country. In their wisdom, however, our ancestors left the Drummond Professors without a School, so that even Professor Edgeworth had to rely upon the extent to which he could entice undergraduates who were reading schools whose main interest lay elsewhere. Lord Beveridge and Sir Henry Clay may remind us of the quality of the product so casually achieved.

By the first World War, although there were, here and there, a few scholars professionally practicing Economics, the subject still retained its nineteenth century flavour of a discipline followed by gentlemen with private means or by amateurs, whose main jobs had led fairly naturally to an interest in economics.

The war of 1914–1918 made great use of such economists of standing as then were. These showed how useful in public affairs at such a time were the broad teachings of classical economists concerning prices and also the sound monetary doctrines which had been inherited from a still more remote past. During that war, economists moved over from being general advisors of politicians, to being departmental administrators. The general importance of economic issues, and the interest which these aroused, led to a new view of economics as a desirable academic subject, and 1918–1920, saw a flood of new appointments in the Universities, ever ready, as these always are, to produce a supply to meet any genuine demand for persons who are to be taught any teachable subject.

The 1920s gave those gentlemen a lot to think about. I am passing over the monetary upheavals. Economists certainly acquitted themselves well in that field, for monetary economics with its traditions and doctrines went back some four centuries at least, and that part of our subject had already well-made foundations. It was on the non-monetary side that economists began to run into trouble.

Until the war, England's prosperity had always been seen as bound up with certain basic industries — coal, iron and steel, cotton and wool textiles, shipbuilding and heavy engineering. These had given us our bread and butter — and even earned us the cake, while the ameliorative tradition of English politics looked forward to distributing even more fairly through the gradual diffusion of more equal opportunity.

We all know what happened to these industries — how high costs at home, increased by our deflationary policy, met lower prices abroad, aided and abetted by inflation and by dumping, plus the new protectionist division of markets.

Since those industries had been our mainstay for so long, and since their troubles were so serious — the more so because of their localization — the woes of our basic industries dominated our thinking. No one had an eye for the developing modern industries such as rayon, chemicals, motor vehicles and light and electrical engineering, and so on.

This led to a fairly widespread pessimism about the basic industrial position of this country. It was therefore natural that the voice of the planners began to be heard in the land — not yet primarily from economists as such. I'll come on later to some of the reasons why we had not yet discovered this most fascinating hobby of the modern economist. Facile comparison with foreign industries and false notions of technical efficiency led to the beginning of the damning of our industrial methods in our basic industries. This view of them as needlessly inefficient was later to extend in popular thought to our whole industrial system. The Economists in the 1930s were to play a part in that. Meanwhile this industrial pessimism played its part in the background of those economists who were then growing up and helped to establish their own unconscious presuppositions.

At the same time of course, the localization of these depressed basic industries led to our experiencing the problems of structural unemployment on a scale experiencing the problems of structural unemployment on a scale unknown since the mid-nineteenth century. Since then, this country had been hardened by prosperity and our industrial structure and had become less flexible with the growth of various social restrictions on the movement of labour.

Let's come back to the development of economics. In my view that had been making it very difficult for its practitioners to tackle these big problems of industrial life. The 1920s produced some very able studies of our miseries culminating in the poverty and depressed areas studies of the early 1930s. When it came to the remedies, however, the typical recently trained economists were unprepared to tackle them and their pupils were very conscious of their inability to agree on what should be done.

That is a pretty sweeping generalization, but I'll hold to it with perhaps one or two qualifications. When thinking of economics as a whole, however, we should bear in mind that I am not dealing with monetary economics — which, as I've already indicated had a separate life from other branches of economics. Also, in the other main department, the neo-classical view of price formation was broadly useful when we were thinking of the whole system of prices.

It was in the special features of this latter theory — in the theories concerning outputs and particular prices — that economics had shown the least satisfactory development. I have written about this elsewhere, and I shall be publishing at greater length one of these days; so tonight I may indulge in the luxury of being very terse and, perhaps, very provocative.

What happened, briefly, was that economics became an academic subject taught by professionally qualified men, instead of a few geniuses, and pedagogic economists became aware of the attractions of deductive theory. This, of course, is a natural danger in theoretical economics and practically pure deductive systems of economic analysis triumphed on the continent long before they gained the day in England. It is rather ironic that the whole-hog deductive school in England so frequently pretended the parentage of Alfred Marshall. His *Principles* came to be treated as the rather muddled work of a great thinker to whom later pedagogues rendered the service of presenting in a more systematic fashion the deductive analysis which underlay it.

In fact, of course, *Principles* was the sort of text-book which Marshall intended it to be. His Economic Theory was mainly intended to provide guiding concepts for the major work on Economic History he always hoped to get down to. *Principles* set out his theories in systematic form and was written so as to be intelligible and useful to the practical men who also were concerned with the more dynamic world of real life — business men, trade unionists and politicians.

Later writers have frequently implied their contempt that Marshall should have written with this strange audience in mind. Although this has, on occasion been magnanimously explained by the fact that Marshall never was a tutor in our modern sense, this is to overlook the fact that he was clearly aware of the danger likely to arise when his book was used as an academic text-book. I am thinking of the warnings about the danger and difficulties in carrying deductive reasoning too far. Marshall, with Cambridge in mind, usually links this up with too simple an application of mathematics.

Marshall himself was as good at deductive reasoning as the next man. Sraffa and the others in the 1930s, who so easily indicted him of a slip in reasoning which would have been unpardonable in a sixth-former, never seem to have thought it a puzzling contradiction that he had been 2nd Wrangler — and second to Lord Rayleigh at that. Marshall, the great eclectic, applied any deductive system only so far as he thought it safe to go.

In the theory of prices and of business behaviour, Marshall distinguished rather sharply pure monopolies and competitive industries. In the case of pure monopolies, which he defined rather rigidly, he simply made use of a quite elementary marginal model. He never carried the theory very far since he reserved the problem of monopoly for separate treatment in a later treatise.

The bulk of *Principles* is concerned with competitive industries. The deductive system of analysis of which Marshall made most use was that of the perfect competition type already developed by his classical predecessors and very thoroughly explained by his continental contemporaries. He used it fairly thoroughly where it had obvious application — to the primary industries where its postulates of increasing costs, of atomistic competition and of the total absence of goodwill, seemed reasonably applicable. It is for those industries that his pure analysis of short and long period values is developed. In Marshall's hands the marginal analysis of price and output formation in such conditions was of such elegance that in England the theory of perfect competition will always be associated with his name.

In *Principles*, however, that system of thought provides only a basic approach to the analysis of competitive *manufacturing* industries. Here Marshall carries over the principle of substitution as the basic rule of conduct, as well as that of the notion of equilibrium between Demand and Supply Factors. He nowhere suggests that he regards ordinary manufacturing as less competitive simply because it has goodwill elements, and recognizes the prevalence of decreasing costs and increasing returns conditions. In fact he invented the remarkable device of the representative firm to be the analytical vehicle whereby he might preserve the concept of equilibrium in the balance between demand and supply conditions, and might also still use the parallel analysis of the ways in which marginal forces will work in an industry.

Seen in this way, *Principles* has indeed a conceptual unity, but is not a unity of systematic deduction, but rather of the application of similar broad ideas in varying contexts.

Pedagogic Economists, however, with mistaken analogies drawn from natural sciences — determined as it were to copy the glories of physics or chemistry without the nuisance of centuries in the laboratory — saw its goal as the speedy creation of a general deductive system. In such a system a few basic concepts and postulates should serve as foundations for a general system of analysis. Academic Economics in the 1920s accordingly centred round the analysis of perfect competition. This could be used to give a seeming explanation of the whole pricing system, and when it was turned inside out, gave a no less complete theory of the distribution of income. Thus partly from the welfare interests of Professor Pigou this model was taken to be *the* Marshallian model, with the natural consequence that it was easy to saddle Marshall with Pigou's mistakes.

The erection of this perfectly competitive model into the academic theory of prices for industry, generally had three very unfortunate results.

First, it led to a view of the pricing system as a marvellous machine with whose workings it was difficult to advocate interference on economic grounds. Some of the best theorists of the 1920s thereby became too pure for practical problems. The sort of interference which was advocated on Pigovian welfare grounds put up impractical criteria and gave the glow of vicarious political improvement without any danger of practical results.

Secondly, the very generality of this economic theory led to its not being very useful for practical work. At the same time, to be adroit in applying the marginal passe-partout became the essential qualification for a good honours degree in Economics. To a considerable extent, the resulting professional prestige led to the better men becoming theory specialists and the difficulty of application led to some scorn for practical work.

By the 1930s economists were too often to be divided into empirical men — misleadingly called *applied* economists — and theorists. Where theory *could* be applied, excellent work might be done. I am thinking of Mr. Rowe's notable achievements in the field of primary commodities, where theory had a fairly ready application under the guidance of a very competent man.

Elsewhere, in the ordinary world of manufacture and commerce, applied economists were concerned with more stubborn facts. So their work lacked theoretical interest and was, in truth, often rather dull anyway; for it is difficult to do good empirical work without a useful theory. As Collingwood has said 'All knowledge is really answers to particular questions' and it is the job of theory to supply questions to which an answer can be made. The theorists gave no help, even if they did provide beautiful poems — I speak without reproach as one who rather enjoyed teaching poetry.

Thirdly, the most serious consequence at the time was the complete inability of Economists to tackle the problem of mass unemployment and of excess capacity. It is interesting to note that one theorist whose works had a considerable vogue even produced a theory of the trade cycle which, strictly analysed, assumed full employment. Similarly a wages theorist seems, in retrospect, to have been unduly concerned with the extent to which the employers contribution to social insurance might have been a serious cause of unemployment.

That roughly was the state of affairs when I was trained in Economics. Leaving on one side, monetary economics and forgetting, for the moment the commonsense maxims with which the best class of economists advanced their theories, all the practical guides which flowed from economic analysis consisted of the applications of the theory of value to primary commodities, some unexceptionable conclusions about the abstract virtues of free-trade, and the welfare propositions of the Pigovian school — which last as Clapham unkindly pointed out, were quite useless without a copper-bottomed classification of industries according to the actual state of their returns.

So far as apparent applicability in the real world was concerned, economic theory was to make up for this with a vengeance in the decade to which I now turn. To understand the enthusiasm with which many of us fell upon the newer doctrines which I shall now refer to, we must remember the reasons why most of us had taken up the study of economics. A few became economists because of some kind of interest or special calling; some no doubt because of a hope of understanding and perhaps improving the economic world we lived in. To paraphase Pigou, we were after fruit as well as light.

Two revolutions in thought marked the decade in which we came to maturity. The first in time was the development of the modern theories of imperfect competition and of monopolistic competition. Both owed their origin to the questioning of the Marshallian doctrine of price formation as expounded by Professor Pigou. To take the Cambridge revolution first, it began early in the 1920s, with a questioning of the practical validities of the state of returns classification of industries but burst into a real attack as soon as the aged Marshall was dead, and the whole Cambridge doctrine of price and output in ordinary manufacturing industries could decently be attacked — with the gloves off. Sraffa at once exposed the problems of stability of price in decreasing cost industries. The subsequent so-called controversy in the *Economic Journal*, apart from rude remarks addressed to Professor Robertson, chiefly consisted of leading young theorists' explanations of the consequences of assuming fairly complete differentiation of product and a U-shaped cost curve for the individual firm.

Modestly claiming the conclusions as simply another contribution to the economists' tool box, Joan Robinson set them out in her *Imperfect Competition*. We were not deceived by the modesty. The book, itself, as did her original *Journal* article, set out some very interesting results or general conclusions, even if some of her assumptions were not too clearly stated. At one bound we had a theory which explained excess capacity and so translated the misery of the 1920s into a permanent phenomenom. At the same time it gave us a theoretical world in which businesses were *assumed* to produce diverse products, and so increased its apparent reality. Further her marginal revenue and cost tools gave a new lease of life to the concept of elasticity of demand and enabled us to deepen the complexity of our general analysis without making it more difficult.

Almost simultaneously appeared Chamberlin's great book. This had an origin in the early controversies around the Cambridge doctrines via Allyn

Young, who had joined Clapham as a questioner of concepts. According to Chamberlin's latest statement he himself learned nothing from the keen battle in the *Economic Journal* during the six years in which he was revising his theory. Chamberlin's book was a really exciting event. It didn't use so much implicit assumption as Mrs. Robinson's but gave us an elegant general analysis in which the wastes of ordinary competition were presented as but a simple consequence of the irrationality of ordinary consumers, the existence of selling costs and the ability of the advertiser to build up consumers' loyalty for his employers.

Deductive analysis took a new lease of life. It was now possible to teach pupils what seemed to be a general marginal theory of price formation, and at every stage welfare conclusions could be drawn, provided one did not inquire too closely into the precise meaning and possible real existence of the marginal concepts which were employed. The recent exchanges between Professor Robinson and Mr. Farrell have brought to light one of the obscurities we then glossed over so lightly. Really this amounts to a too rigid handling of the time concept. Harrod had once made a valiant effort to compel us to face it on the cost side, but in the end economic orthodoxy persisted in making the easy analyses which were facilitated by a sharp distinction between the short and the long period. In demand analysis we avoided still more difficulties by applying short-run demand analysis to long-run situations.

We did not face up to the serious methodological difficulties inherent in our theory, because we were so pathetically sure that we were on the trail of reality; at last we had a model in which business produced differentiated commodities, in which it would be logical for costs to be decreasing, and in the same model there was excess capacity and businesses were not so efficient technically as they might be in the ideal situation. Were not all these phenomena to be found in the real world, and had they not been difficult to account for on the basis of the perfect competition approach to pricing?

Since we saw the new monopolistic competition theories as being essentially realistic, logical, but unverified, deductions from our theories led us to infer more detailed facts about the reality we presumed to study. I shall come back to some of the legacies we have inherited here when we have discussed the impact of Keynesian theory to which I now turn. This, of course, produced the second great theoretical upheaval of our decade.

When trying to trace the varied elements in our rich legacy from the Keynesian revolution, we should really draw a more careful distinction between Keynes and the Keynesians than I shall be able to maintain tonight. Keynes's *General Theory* was as important as the parent of a system of thought as it was as a source for particular theories. Indeed, its generality accounted for a good deal of untidiness seen as a systematic treatise and was partly responsible for its difficulties. Such a treatise owed a lot to its contemporary expositors for its rapid adoption as the classic of its time. The best of these naturally enough were as much concerned with applying Keynesian theory as with expounding Keynes. To draw the distinction which I am suggesting is made a little difficult because the really important expositors were either themselves distinguished Cambridge economists who had been closely associated with Keynes during the writing of the *General Theory*, or like Lerner, they stated that they had Keynes's approval for what they wrote.

Keynes's work was important in two fields — in monetary theory and in what we may now call the theory of social aggregates. In the first, he insisted on bringing the rate of interest over squarely into the theory of money, his liquidity preference doctrine insisting on treating it as a purely monetary phenomenon. The rate of interest had previously led a double life. In real, or non-monetary, theory it had appeared as the classical regulator of investment and was treated as being determined by savings and investment schedules. In monetary theory it was treated as the price of securities of a given currency and status. The neo-classical theory treating the rate of interest as the price of loanable funds acted as a sort of bridge between the two analytical territories, softening the transition for the student when, after his term's Principles he moved on to a term's Currency and Banking. Keynes, the monetary theorist, insisted on blowing up that bridge and was followed by all the Keynesian expositors.

The effects of mental dynamite, however, are ideological and not material and depend upon the point of view. When Keynes stood on the real analysis side of the river, we should note that he still gave the rate of interest its classical importance in the sphere of investment decisions. This was rather naughty of him and many have seen it as a puzzling inconsistency. For, as Hicks and Lerner have pointed out, if the rate of interest is an independent determinant of investment, then the Liquidity Preference doctrine is consistent with the Loanable Funds theory and Keynes does wrong to insist on the primacy of liquidity preference. Keynes did, however, insist. I'll come back to what I think are the reasons for the anomaly in a moment. Meanwhile we may note that the Keynesian legacy, thanks to the Hicksian gloss, has been a little ambiguous in the monetary field which is just where he clearly intended no ambiguity.

In the second sphere — the theory of aggregates — Keynes's triumph has been undoubted. Non-professional cranks had already experimented with this type of analysis but Keynes really created the analysis of aggregates as a professional discipline. The essence of this analysis is, having defined in a consistent manner the social aggregates in which it is interested, then to proceed to study the accounting relations which exist between them *ex post*, if change should have occurred in the dimensions of any one such aggregate on the basis of simple assumptions about the functions of governing them.

One of our most important positive legacies from the 1930s has thus been due to Keynes. This is the improved status of national income studies. Previously these had been chiefly concerned to build up totals, to be interpreted with the aid of index numbers and subject to all the qualifications of welfare theory. The parts now became of greater importance than the whole — which was a gain since we are more sure exactly of what we are measuring there — and at first under the personal stimulus of Keynes himself, these analyses have been of great importance as a guide to governmental budgetary and planning problems in War and Peace. Nowadays our foreign office has even found it to be productive of goodwill to be able to offer rather backward countries the advisory service of economist-statisticians who will teach the local organizations how to carry out similar analyses with whatever statistical straw is available on the spot.

The result which interested us most at the time — and probably the most important absolutely — was the creation of a general theory of employment in terms of the effective demand for the total national output, and in terms of consumers' outlay and investment decisions. There have, of course, been anticipators of Keynesian doctrine but there is no doubt of its originality taken as a whole. And its impact was equally striking. From getting bogged down in circular reasoning about the effects of demand changes and of price rigidities, we seemed at one bound to come to grips with reality. Where we found most difficulties was where Keynes had tried to link his social generalizations with *ex ante* deductive theory of the traditional marginal kind. The social generalizations themselves as *ex post* generalizations seemed broadly right and yielded results of a verifiable kind. His *ex ante* analysis of the effects of possible public interventions to increase employment by sustaining effective demand gave theoretical basis for the kind of attack upon our miseries to which most of us were sympathetic.

Here I am sure that we were indeed put on the right lines but I must call attention to two features of Keynesian analysis which have had important effects. The first is the relative neglect of the problem of inflation. Believing as he did that organized labour was more indifferent to real wage changes than to changes in money wages, Keynes left unexplored the great problem of how a free democracy is to prevent inflation whilst preserving a high level of employment — high enough for present unemployment to play no part in the fears and strategies of organized labour. This in turn has proved to mask a deeper problem — how far sustained full employment is compatible with the maintenance of our real national income. In a closed economy it is simply a question of the extent to which you can take full advantage of technical and other changes which would allow of increased prosperity. In an open economy, it is necessary to do this to a significant extent if your real national income is to be *maintained*, let alone increased. These problems did not seem so important to us before the war; after the great slump of the 1930s inflation would have seemed a negligible danger.

It is, however, more easy to acquit Keynes of responsibility for the present over concentration of popular and political argument upon full employment and the neglect of the inflationary danger than it is to acquit the Keynesians. A lot of responsibility seems to me to lie with the development of the over-simple Keynesian theory of the trade cycle, in which Keynes's *ex post* analysis is used overconfidently in the propounding of remedies.

Keynes himself did not put forward a systematic theory of the trade cycle. To the deductive minds of the 1930s however, all the elements were there and the theory rapidly developed beyond the tentative 'Notes on the Trade Cycle' as put forward by Keynes. Very rapidly we had created for us a complete model of the capitalist trade cycle, in which the villain was the inherent instability of investment and the only remedy which the Government Prince Charming need apply was the creation of additional investment.

Such models, of course, were in terms of a closed economy and, using *ex post* concepts *ex ante*, nothing can stand in the way of the full employment we desire. Once you open the model and think of a country dependent on international trade, of course, the inflation — which is the unsolved problem, but which is compatible with full employment in the closed system because it may there be restrained by physical controls — is quite capable of causing a complete breakdown of employment. The paradox arises, of course, because exports are the equivalent of investment and this country needs quite a lot of exports to keep going. To export, one's costs must at least keep in line with those of other countries.

But am I not being unfair to the Keynesian followers of the late 1930s — did they not state all their qualifications? Indeed they did in their technical writings. Their more popular expositions, however, played an important part in fixing in the minds of the leaders of Labour the notions that, in future, full employment — taken alas very literally — could be avoided by little short of criminal carelessness. These, together with the bitter memories of the 1930s, long dwelt on in more prosperous times, have left us with full employment at all costs — even if at the cost of concealed and useless idleness.

But before pursuing the general popular legacy of 1930 economics, I must refer in passing to one technical legacy from Keynes, which I believe to have been unfortunate. This concerns the theory of expectations. When handling the theory of investment at the level of the individual firm, Keynes still handled the matter in terms of the traditional stimuli of productivity and the rate of interest. In what follows, I shall refer to these as the traditional indicators in respect to which the individual business man is supposed to act. I have already shown that this statement led to a stress on the importance of the rate of interest which is anomalous in view of Keynes's treatment of it in monetary theory. I believe he did this just because this was traditional doctrine and because as a monetary theorist Keynes had never much worked in the real analysis field.

He needed to include some treatment of atomistic analysis to convert his *ex post* analysis into *ex ante* analysis, but above all he needed some such vehicle in order to suggest a change in the method of traditional theory. He wished it to take more full account of uncertainty and by this use of the marginal efficiency of capital he re-introduced the Marshallian concept of discounted marginal productivity. I believe this to have been thoroughly mischievous. When we have got our indicators right — when we have found those which the business man really uses — we shall not need to introduce any theory of discounting. Keynes backed the wrong indicators, and his treatment of future risks has merely led to a spurious new department of economics in which many nimble minds are getting lost.

There is one other legacy to which I should call attention, which is perhaps even more serious: the effect of Keynesian doctrine, taken together with the new doctrines of monopolistic competition, upon the attitudes adopted by economists towards private industry and (even where there are no formal attitudes) upon the implicit assumptions with which economists have tended to work. So far as Keynes himself was concerned, his view of employment and the trade cycle was neutral as between free enterprise and a socialized state. He saw free capitalism, because of the separation and specialization of investment activity, as liable to periods of general unemployment. But in his view planned action on the investment side of the problem gave a remedy which was quite compatible with private enterprise.

I have already said that many of us younger economists started off with a prejudice against the economic system in which such a slump and in which the continued misery of the 1920s were possible. We were socialist planners potentially long before we got down to our economics. Keynes's analysis in the hands of the Keynesians became a final criticism of the private enterprise world.

I should make it plain that in my view this could not have happened if the newer monopolistic theories had not had their triumph first. These, because they were the only available theories assuming product differentiation, and adducing the consequences of falling costs and excess capacities, were taken as explaining the world in which we lived. To their demonstration of excess capacity and waste of resources as a normal feature came the Keynesian view that such a system could not even avoid wasting available labour without considerable support from state planning. Further, the Keynesian doctrine also showed that the existence of profits in themselves might be thought to be one of the most serious factors leading to the breakdown of the boom. Undistributed profits were thought to be an evil, preventing effective demand from being maintained at full employment level. This sounds very ironic at the present time when we see them as being one of the bulwarks against inflation, without which full employment would be politically impossible.

If you think I exaggerate, look at Mrs. Joan Robinson's W.E.A. study outline where the full theoretical implications of profits during the trade cycle are clearly drawn. You may like to take that pamphlet also as an indication of the force of the subconscious prejudice against private enterprise and all its works which these two modern theoretical revolutions had achieved.

For of course you will find this attitude even more clear in the popular pamphlets of the 1930s. This, roughly speaking, was the time when the first large secondary school generation came of age. So that, for the first time, we had a large audience not only wishing to understand what was going on around them, but capable of reading and reflecting on a sustained argument. In such a generation the economic problems around them soon created a market for popular expositions of economics. The Left Book Club supplied them in a ready-coloured form, but it really was a Gollancz age. Gollancz is not really to be accused of publishing versions of economic doctrines which had been twisted round to suit political prejudices. In the field of unemployment, the trade cycle, and price theory, the sentiment of the younger theorists was really left wing anyway.

What would have happened normally is that we should have had a natural period of reaction during which economists digested the full implications of the presuppositions of their theories; in which they got to know their assumptions better and were not led astray by this first initial excitement due to getting a model which had some of the features which most concerned them in the real world. The war came just at the wrong time: it prevented this process of digestion whilst sustaining the strong popular interest in the economic problems of the inter-war period. And, of course, the only views that were available were these pessimistic views of the situation of our country and of the private enterprise system which it had so far developed. Until very recently the widespread scepticism of our industrial system among people who hold natural positions of leadership was itself one of the most serious political consequences of the 1930s. It was serious for economics itself in so far as the clouds left over by the climate we engendered then get in the way of fresh thinking over a very wide field.

A period of reaction was inevitable so far as price theory was concerned. Granted that earlier theory had been so fruitless for empirical studies of individual businesses and that the new theories of monopolistic and imperfect competition looked excitingly realistic, some theorist sooner or later was bound to make the mistake of trying to apply them in order to refine and extend the theories themselves. The newer welfare economics offered also to such a theorist the inducement that he might actually be able to lay down concrete rules for actual firms and industries concerning the price and output policies which they should

171

adopt in the interest of economic welfare.

The breach in the dyke, however, did not come about in that way, and by an accident Oxford was to see the start of the counter-revolution. I say by an accident. The now famous inquiries of the Research Group in Economics started with an intention to do research into the experience and behaviour of business men over the trade cycle, in order that the realistic fruits of Keynes's theories might be swiftly reached in the next depression. If you look at the gazettes for 1935 onwards you will see that the Rockefeller grants which were obtained for the support of the Institute of Statistics, which was founded by the same group of people to be a home for statistical research and teaching — all these grants are for the study of trade cycles.

In the course of asking about the trade cycle, the Research Group received a series of shocks. All its members were traditional marginal theorists. With the exception of MacGregor who was a Marshallian *pur sang*, all accepted the monopolistic competition approach to prices — although Sir Hubert Henderson had some canny reservations about the political nonsense which some of us derived therefrom.

You will know of the shock the Group had when it discovered that however important the rate of interest might be in general it was not important through any direct connexion with entrepreneurs' investment decisions. The parallel discoveries in connexion with prices was also a by-product of the trade cycle inquiry. Here the war came too soon for the Research Group to follow this up with the detailed special inquiry which it planned. But we had already got far enough to issue the reports by Harrod and by Hall and Hitch. This was of great importance in so far as it did produce the generalization that manufacturers thought of prices in terms of some relationship with average costs. Alas, the importance of this and of our evidence was obscured even for ourselves. Instead of trying to explain this average-cost approach to prices — and especially instead of paying much attention to the business men's own explanations — we were far too full of the newer marginal doctrines and really we took the relative stability of prices as the factor to be explained. We were more than content with Hall's and Hitch's kinked demand curve. Now since this led to the conclusion that business men would accept *any* level of prices once established, the curious thing is that it involved the abandonment of the marginal analysis. But it did not look like that. The causes for the abandonment were expressed in marginal terms — the indeterminacy of marginal revenue — which was satisfactory in so far as we thought it explained why business men did not pay much attention to marginal revenue-elasticity calculations. In our teaching, therefore, it was possible to proceed quite smoothly through all the maze of pricing theory until we came to pricing in practice which was dealt with in a factual basis and with the quiet abandonment of our tools — the marginal analysis explained why they should be blunted, and we and our pupils were satisfied with a denouement which left our marginal edifice untouched for examination purposes.

The sterility of the kinked demand curve taken by itself is then one professional legacy of the 1930s. The Hall/Hitch paper itself had one unfortunate legacy — the use of the term Full Cost and the way that price fixing practices were explained led many people who had not been on the inquiry to think that business men actually managed to fix prices which would always cover costs. If you heard Mrs. Joan Robinson's discussion with Mr. Chambers on the radio last term you may have noticed the preconceived notion on her part. She explained this in terms of the breakdown of the pure competition which she said applied in the nineteenth century and the rise of individual businesses so large that they fixed prices for their market. She therefore kept asking Chambers to justify why business men should determine what prices they should charge and also why they should be the arbiters of what was a fair margin of profit. Chambers's explanation of the way the market ultimately determined all this fell on stone deaf ears. In the discussion of my own theories I find this to be one of the most irritating legacies of the 1930s.

I have left until near the end one of the most significant of our legacies of the 1930s — the cynicism with regard to affairs in ordinary manufacturing industry. I have referred to the cynicism which the world of the 1920s tended to create regarding the applicability of economic theory to the real world which it pretended to discuss. This continued through the 1930s, in view of the deepening crisis of employment, until the advent of Keynesian theory. By then, however, it seems to me that economists were, however, unconsciously preparing their revenge. Remember, the ground was prepared by the attack on our basic industries as technically backward in the 1920s, to this the Robinson–Chamberlin revolutions added the theoretical conclusion that, given the assumptions which their creators thought necessary in order to make the theory of prices conform to certain basic characteristics of the real world (notably, differentiation of prices and decreasing costs), it would follow that competitive manufacturing firms *necessarily* produced at less than optimum technical efficiency. To those of us who were leaning towards socialistic planning anyway, this seemed an enormous reinforcement of our ideology. To those who were not, it represented a powerful obstacle besides which any arguments about the defects of planning seemed of slight account. To put them forward was to put possible defects of a hypothetical world against a glaring defect of the present one.

Keynes's demonstration of yet one more inefficiency of unplanned capitalism — that it was inherently unstable and inclined to underemployment — seems now but the final keystone of the arch through which younger economists were trained to see reality. The attitude which was thus engendered was carried by many of us outside the field of professional economics. We have a large part in the responsibility for the current attitudes of middle-aged people towards British industry generally, since economists of the 1930s with apparently full doctrinal authority did so much to confirm the deep rooted suspicions which the economic troubles of their generation had produced.

Finally, the 1930s was a theorist's decade and this brings me to the last, exclusively professional, legacy. The marginal analysis applied with full blooded confidence and elementary mathematics has led economists to erect many complex theoretical propositions from which derived many propositions of seemingly great practical application — for example, ranging from propositions concerning the prices which should be charged by nationalized industries to propositions concerning the iniquity of zoned or basing point prices. Any attack on the basic analysis and especially on the sensitive ramifications of elasticities of one sort or another leads to a natural bewilderment or even hostility. It is natural that such attacks should be fiercely resisted. But as the attack is pressed home, a different issue is occasionally raised — it is almost made to appear that it is the moral obligation of any attacker to help hold up the facade after he has blown away the foundation. At least two of our leading economists have said to me, if you are to destroy all this, you *must* put something in its place. One man even said we cannot *afford* to lose welfare economics. This seems to me to be perhaps the most annoying legacy of all to anyone who is concerned with the truth or falsity of some of our basic assumptions. I personally have decided to leave these Emperors of the 1930s to continue to wear in public their nice new clothes — and trust to the keener eyes of the children eventually to lead to a recognition of the precise fabric from which those suits have been constructed.

But what a pity it is that we push deductive analysis so far without intermediate testing against reality that our very important subject seems so doomed to provide revolutions in which suppressed aspects of truth have to force themselves to the light of day.

5 The Netherlands lectures[1]

Lecture 1

My college at Oxford, Nuffield College, is a very new college; its permanent buildings are still going up. But in New Inn Hall Street, not five minutes away from my rooms, is a reminder of ancient academic contacts between your country and mine to which it seems appropriate that I should refer. It is an old gateway of grey stone, dating from about 1430. I often stop as I go down that street and look inside the gateway at the traces of the porter's lodge of a vanished college — St Mary's College, a college of Austinian canons which came to an end with the suppression of the monasteries. There, according to tradition, stayed Erasmus of Rotterdam. He came to Oxford to see his 'friend and correspondent' Willian Grocyn, Fellow of New College, my other college at Oxford. We may recall that Grocyn, himself one of the humanists who contributed to the revival of learning in Europe, when no young graduate but a man of 35 or so, travelled for two years in Italy with Linacre, and studied with Politianus.

The gateway of St Mary's has thus special associations with the Netherlands, but there are many other things in Oxford which bring back vividly a picture of the vanished past, when it must have been so much easier than it is today to feel the universe of universities, the republic of letters extending beyond one's own college and university, and of which these are but a part. Despite all the difficulties of travel and communications, in the middle ages and during the renaissance, there seems to have been a very significant interchange of university teachers. And as the examples of Erasmus and Grocyn remind us, if a scholar went abroad to teach, he went no less to learn. If we have gained much over our ancestors, we have also lost a lot in some ways. We have certainly lost the universal facility in Latin of educated men, which gave our universities a common tongue. I feel that particular limitation very powerfully today, when here I am condemned by my ignorance of your language to rely upon what we in England take as an undoubted fact — alike a compliment and a reproach to us — that all Dutchmen speak and understand English!

It is good that the Western world is now making rather more easy the visits

(1) Presented at the University of Groningen, May 1952. Reprinted with permission from Lancaster University, acting on behalf of the estate of P.W.S. Andrews.

which are so essential for the close interchange of ideas we all desire. I am grateful for the arrangements between the British Council and the Government of the Netherlands which have made my own visit possible, and I wish to emphasize that I am very sensible to the honour which your Faculty of Economics has done me by inviting me to give these lectures in the University of Groningen.

The train of thought which I have been following so far suggests that formal teaching should be only a part of such visits. In my lectures, of course, I have to stand before you and put forward my own ideas in a formal fashion. Apart from that, I hope to have the chance of informal meetings at which some of us will exchange ideas generally. In particular, I hope to learn more of what you are doing at Groningen — and especially what it means if an economist has been trained at your University. I look forward very much to that part of my visit, and to the acquaintanceships I shall make during my stay with you.

I turn now to my subject — economic theory and the study of business behaviour. I use the phrase 'business behaviour' and not just 'business', because my main preoccupation is with the study of individual businesses and I shall not be directly concerned with the statistical study of business aggregates, important though that may be to economics. I shall further deal primarily with the interconnections between economic theory and the study of business behaviour in terms of English economic theory, provided that I am allowed to include the work of Professor Chamberlin in the school to which he seems to me to belong.

The distinction between English and other economics is made in no chauvinistic spirit. Economics *is* essentially the same subject the world over. In England as elsewhere the theory of the individual business was originally but an ingredient of the general theory of value. Thanks largely to the work of Alfred Marshall, however, the theory of value as taught by most economists in England developed certain characteristics which focused attention on industrial groupings of businesses. I am, of course, referring especially to partial equilibrium analysis. The Marshallian attempt to differentiate in general analysis between industries according to the state of returns — according to whether they displayed increasing, constant, or decreasing returns — led to realistic criticism of the theory of the individual business. Out of this came a new basic approach to the general theory of value which was developed variously in terms of imperfect competition or monopolistic competition. My own work has been done against this background, and in order to explain my views as they have developed I shall have to retrace the story of the developments in the theory of the individual business as taught in English schools of economics to which I have just referred.

I have said that the theories of business behaviour which were developed in the inter-war period came particularly as a reaction to Marshallian theories as then understood. For that reason, and also because I believe that their basis was

176

an *erroneous* interpretation of Marshallian economics *as taught by Marshall himself*, I shall have to give an account of Marshallian theory as I see it. I shall try to do this so as to enable us to understand how Marshall's critics saw him, whilst not following them into what I now see as their errors.

Let us first put Marshall himself against the general background of the development of theory in Europe and in America. Looking at economics as a whole, we may distinguish two broad fields; monetary economics, which is concerned with the consequences of the conditions on which the means of payment are available; and non-monetary economics, which has so far chiefly been concerned with analysing the broad structure of values and outputs which tends to be created in response to the various underlying economic forces in our society. The theory of the value of commodities is therefore the dominant body of analysis in this second field. In very broad terms, it is an exceedingly old doctrine. It is surprising, for instance, how modern some sections of the *Wealth of Nations* appear if, when we read them, we happen to forget the too hasty judgement that Adam Smith simply expounded the labour theory of value!

In a very real sense, however, the general theory of value was a nineteenth century creation, for it was only then that the theory of demand was fully developed, as a result of the work of Jevons, Marshall and the Austrian theorists.

By the end of the nineteenth century, the theory of value consisted of the two sets of analyses — the analysis of competitive value and that of values in conditions of monopoly. Generally speaking, the latter applied only in special circumstances and the theory of competitive value was treated as much more generally applicable. In fact, it was *the* general theory of value, and was everywhere treated as the basic theory for the understanding of the non-monetary forces influencing prices and for the understanding of the free pricing system as a whole.

Both in England and elsewhere, this basic theory of competitive value was a static theory, in so far as its method of analysis was to presume that all relevant economic forces were of given strength and direction, and then to work out the consequences in terms of the equilibrium relations of the various prices which it distinguished, studying subsequently the consequences of particular specified changes in underlying forces.

So far as commodity values were concerned, the resulting analysis was conducted in terms of demand and supply schedules for a particular commodity as a whole, and the value of a commodity was explained in terms of equilibrium relations between these two forces. In its most elegant form, however, the theory of competitive value proceeded in terms of full equilibrium, not only for social aggregates such as the demand and supply for a commodity class as a whole, but also for the individual enterprises involved in those aggregates. I use the term 'individual enterprises' to cover both individual producers and individual consumers.

At the level of the individual enterprise, the basic assumptions were such as to give either the individual producer or the individual consumer full freedom of choice in disposing of his resources in order to produce or to obtain individual commodities at given market prices, in conditions where such prices were unaffected by his particular decisions.

For such analysis, a necessary postulate was that of a universal and effective tendency to diminishing returns. In the consumer's enterprise this was secured by postulating diminishing marginal utility; in the producer's enterprise, by postulating increasing marginal costs or diminishing returns. The resulting analysis lent itself to the most elegant generalization and mathematical summarization. It could be turned round into a general theory of the employment of factors of production by individual producers and thence to a general theory of factor prices. Here marginal productivities were but reflections or analytical counterparts of the marginal costs used in the analysis of commodity values. From this it was but a step to a full analytical solution of the ancient problem of the distribution of income between classes of factors of production.

When this had been achieved, economics had won through to a general view of the whole pricing and income system such as had never been achieved before. The value of this intellectual achievement is shown pragmatically by its results. In every country we may number among our academic grandfathers some giants who were trained in it, and whose practical achievements in using it to pick their way through the shifting phenomena of everyday life helped to give economics the prestige which it had gained by the end of the first World War — so that economics has become a respectable academic subject, despite all the jokes about the quarrels of economists when faced with the vexed questions of the day.

Nevertheless, if I may, I should like in passing to comment a little upon the methodological validity of this body of inter-related theory of the price and income structure. Pedagogically, it had and continues to have tremendous importance. The whole analysis is so inter-related that it lends itself beautifully to the training of young economists. At every stage they are using similar tools — the weapons of the marginal analysis — and through a unified intellectual approach they get a view of the inter-connections between all prices and values in an economic system which is of great value. When we come to its scientific validity, I want to make one or two qualifications.

Economics, of course, is a social science and as such it is its job to provide valid generalizations about the social phenomena — the price levels, outputs and incomes etc. — with which it is concerned. The test of the validity of a generalization must be, that we must be able, better with its aid than without, to predict changes in the variables with which we are concerned. A realistic criticism of what I call a first order theory can thus come only by looking at the results we get when we use that theory. Judged on this basis, the general competitive theory of commodity prices *was* a successful theory. It is beside the point to criticize it on any ground that its particular assumptions are unrealistic. In any science, whether physics or economics, the test of reality must be applied only to conclusions.

Of course, there is another stage in scientific reasoning — what I call second order theory. We may not always be able to verify our conclusions in every field as well as we can in some particular part of our subject. In that case, it is legitimate to proceed on the basis of arguing from *results* already tested elsewhere in the manner I have indicated.

I feel much less happy, however, about a characteristic procedure in economic methodology — to take the assumptions upon which accepted generalizations have been constructed in one department of analysis and to use these as the basis for a different set of analyses. In this case, I feel, we cannot take the validity of particular conclusions as a test of the general validity of assumptions. Surely the assumptions themselves need verifying, i.e. we need to construct an independent set of first order generalizations.

For this reason, although as I have indicated, I think that the broad picture of the whole economic system which we get on the basis of traditional marginal competitive analysis is broadly right, I think that its general use, for example, in the theory of wages, may well have led us into errors which we might have avoided had we given up our straining after such a general body of theory and tried, say, to construct our theory of wages independently. I am, on methodological grounds, disturbed by the piling of a theoretical Pelion upon a hypothetical Ossa, which is involved in assuming the full atomistic equilibrium of the firm as the basis for a theory of wages, and still more for the general theory of income distribution. For these reasons I welcome the work in America of Professors Lester and Dunlop.

I am more than disturbed — I am profoundly antagonistic, when we come to apply this procedure in welfare economics, where it is almost *de rigueur* to use untested hypotheses in order to produce untestable conclusions, which are nevertheless pressed home in the advocacy of political consequences.

How does Marshall fit into this picture of the general competitive theory of value and the general economic analysis derived from it? My work has led me to rather different interpretations of Marshall, from that which was normal in the inter-war years, although on several points it is consistent with the position sustained by two of Marshall's pupils — Professors Robertson and MacGregor. Looked at as a whole, his *Principles of Economics* is, of course, one of the great original textbooks of the marginal school in England and its general structure is a thoroughgoing marginal one. There is no doubt whatever that Marshall regarded atomistic competition theory as yielding the general principles of

179

economic analysis as a whole in a form suitable for the training of economists, and the subject, for that purpose, simply to qualifications which would improve the student's powers of handling the greater complexity of reality when he came to grips with it. His mathematical appendix may be taken as exposing the bare bones of this structure of thought which underlies Books III and VI. When we come to the theory of competitive values of commodities, however, that very appendix exposes some uncertainty of treatment. In particular there are some positive statements which should put us on our guard if we wish to treat the corresponding section of *Principles* — chiefly Book V — along what have now become traditional lines.

In Book V Marshall tried to present the theory of competitive value in a very practical form. His basic unit of analysis is the industry. In his abstract analysis an industry is defined as a group of firms employing similar processes — in fact an industry in the ordinary everyday sense. Marshall is trying to give a broad structure of analysis which can be applied to the determination of prices in such industries. The model to which he is trying to work is, given all external circumstances, in terms of the equilibrium between the forces of demand represented by a demand schedule and those of supply which he also represents diagrammatically by a supply schedule. These two curves are, so to speak, the end-products of his analysis, summarizing his view of price determination.

For the industry as a whole, the demand schedule is assumed to bear everywhere the same general form, established for the consumer's demand curves of Book III. The supply curve is assumed to be capable of either falling, or rising, or, in the limit, remaining at a constant horizontal level according to the conditions of supply.

The *basic* model for the supply schedule is established for primary commodities; here a large number of sources may be required as producing commodities which are either homogeneous or can formally be taken as being so, thanks to market grading operations. Further, there can be no such thing as goodwill for such commodities; a consumer has no interest in maintaining a connection with any individual producer; the conditions of such markets ensure that he will be able to get what he wants from any source on the market terms. In view of the basic conditions, the terms upon which a commodity will be sold are not capable of being affected by the operations of either an individual consumer or an individual producer.

I am reminding you of some very familiar analysis so as to emphasize some differences in Marshall's theory. The one general law of a producer's behaviour which Marshall assumes right through his book is that he will obey the principle of substitution. In the case of the primary commodities of the basic model, such a producer can also be taken as freely determining how much of his commodity he will place upon the market — since he will be able to sell all that he will produce, which is the necessary assumption for atomistic equilibrium. The supply curve for primary industries is then simply the aggregation of the individual supplies. Individual suppliers, since their supply-sales will be limited only by cost considerations, will determine their supply with reference to their marginal costs of production, and we have the rule that market price must equal the marginal cost of the supply coming forward. In the long run, we also have the rule that the full equilibrium of the industry, prices must cover costs. It is interesting that Marshall never seems to have asked himself the question whether such a rigid definition of long-term equilibrium was necessarily a satisfactory one from a realistic point of view. Even for primary industries it is *possible* to imagine conditions such that total supply is stable but that individual businesses fail, being replaced by others who are sufficiently optimistic to imagine that they will succeed. Circumstances, however, made Marshall see this as possible in the case of manufacturing industry. So far as supply curves *in general* are concerned, his only warning against assuming that they can be got by integrating the supply curves of the individual firms is based upon the effects of economies of scale to the industry (in raising or lowering those individual curves as the output of a whole industry changes).

In primary industry, on the basis of his assumptions, Marshall could imagine the individual firm as always confronted by rising costs. The supply curve for the whole industry would rise in so far as it was affected only by the internal conditions of the constituent firms; in so far as the expansion of the industry would press more heavily upon scarce factors of production, the consequent rise of factor prices would be an additional reason for the supply curve rising. In the event of the expansion of the industry making external economies of scale possible, the rise of the supply curve would be mitigated and it might even, for a stretch, fall.

Marshall uses this basic analysis of primary markets at each stage of his argument, to give the main outlines of his analysis. Thus the great primary markets are used at the beginning of Book V, to give the archetype of the competitive market, the particular characteristic of these markets — that individual firms could dispose of whatever they chose to produce at the given market prices — not being clearly distinguished from the general characteristic which Marshall uses for all competitive markets — that no producer can get a higher price than another producer for whatever it is that he does sell. It is this last characteristic which is to be taken into Marshall's discussion of manufacturing markets.

In these latter manufacturing markets, Marshall uses the same apparatus of demand and supply schedules, the latter being either rising, falling or constant, and market price in the long run being determined by normal costs for the commodity in questions. Marshall, however, in order to get the stable supply condition postulated by his supply curve, does not in these cases use the concept of price having to cover actual costs for the individual firms employed in the industry. Nor does he assume that costs must always be rising for the individual firm. The whole purpose of his analysis was that it should provide a useful introduction to the practical study of industries. His analysis is therefore implicitly dynamic in the Schumpeterian sense.

Marshall retained the idea of a supply curve, and of a stable equilibrium between demand and supply conditions because such an idea conformed to reality, in so far as actual prices were stable in given conditions; also because, given changes in demand conditions, changes in the levels of market prices could be explained on the lines of systematic changes in supply conditions according to changes in the underlying cost conditions. But he could not retain the idea of full atomistic equilibrium of the firm. He did retain the notion of a competitive parity of price as between individual producers. But he had to recognize in manufacturing industries not only that costs would fall with the expansion of the industry owing to the increased exploitation of external economies, but that costs also fell because of the existence of internal economies. Many passages show that he was well aware that in actual fact manufacturing businesses would not tend to have higher costs if they could expand their sales but would frequently have lower costs.

He gets the stability of output by introducing a form of limitation of the market of the individual manufacturing firm. He recognizes that the general market for a manufactured commodity must analytically be resolved, at any one time, into separate markets. But he does not couple this with any power to maintain more favourable prices as a long-term phenomenon. Indeed, MacGregor has recently said that Marshall in fact stressed the danger of this misinterpretation of the effect of goodwill when discussing it with his pupils.

Granted the fact that Marshall, despite the existence of goodwill, found it possible to refer to manufacturing markets as if the general analysis of the more purely competitive primary markets applied, I have suggested that the essential characteristic of Marshallian competition was not an infinite elasticity of demand for the individual firm but the rule of uniformity of price for identical products. In this way I assimilate his market theory with that which is propounded on the lines of my theory of the individual business.

In such manufacturing markets, Marshall used the concepts of demand and supply curves for the market as a whole, which were naturally developed for primary markets. I have suggested that the analytical aggregation into a single demand curve of the demands for many different commodities stemming from the same types of processes, can be explained on the lines of my normal-cost theory. Marshall's supply curve, granted the limitation of the market which Marshall obviously saw as the effect of goodwill, can recognize frankly the existence of falling costs within individual businesses.

In these circumstances, Marshall gets the stable relations between prices and costs for the industry as a whole, which he needed for his 'supply curve' to be a usable concept, by relating prices to the levels at which new businesses would come into the industry.

I have suggested that, when interpreting this, we have to forget the notion of the supply curve for the whole industry as being the simple aggregation of all that the individual businesses would like to supply at any given price — which is how it is easy to interpret it in primary industry. We must recognize, as Marshall obviously did, that, in manufacturing industries, businesses would often be quite glad to sell more than they can at the ruling price level. The supply curve simply records the terms upon which the consumers can get, in a stable fashion, such and such a quantity when the industry is at a given scale of organization. Similarly, in view of the composite nature of the real demands and supplies summed up on Marshall's Demand and Supply schedules, we must not simply interpret new businesses as those which are entirely new to the industry, but must include in the price-regulating competition, competition coming in any section of the market from businesses already established in the industry but selling in another section, if market price here should get out of line with its normal-cost relation elsewhere. This is more than a simple interpretation of Marshall; I think that he never saw this clearly in relation to the aggregate phenomenon, although his reference to market inter-connections within the general market show that he was aware of it as a real phenomenon.

In these conditions, Marshall's long-run supply price is determined, as I have said, by the levels of prices which are attractive to new businesses. He gives this concept analytical meaning by imagining that such possible competitors look at the costs of representative established businesses and come in if existing prices seem to be yielding abnormal profits to these. In his analysis, then, the level of his supply curve is related to the costs of a representative firm, and will, or course, incorporate not only changes in these costs due to internal economies but also the effects upon such representative costs of *par-passu* changes in the scale of the industry.

These analytical devices enabled Marshall to treat the whole theory of commodity value in competitive conditions, whether for primary or for manufacturing industry, along the same general lines and to present his answers in terms of the same apparatus of demand and supply curves.

To summarize where we have got so far in this glance at Marshall, his effective definition of competition was not that of perfect competition as we have come to know it in later textbooks or as it was already being presented in continental textbooks. His definition was not in terms of homogeneous commodities sold in markets where preferences did not exist, but simply in terms of the fundamental assumptions of freedom of entry and of parity of prices. Pure competition should be seen as only a special case of Marshallian competition. The latter is the general case which he differentiates from pure monopoly, where freedom of entry was impossible and so the parity condition could not apply.

I should like to pause for a moment and comment on Marshall's short-period theory. I think we have to differentiate sharply the conditions in primary markets, dominated in the short-run by dealers' demand and supply conditions, from the conditions in manufacturing markets. In fact, Marshall's analysis of such short-period conditions, with the conclusion that prices will rise or fall to the level of short-period marginal costs, is invariably given in terms of primary markets. He was very fond of his clarification of the effects of time in such markets. However, when passing on to manufacturing markets, apart from important qualifications here and there, he gave no explicit recognition that it was a positive error to apply this analysis except possibly as indicating the possible limits to short-term prices. Goodwill would restrain the exploitation of short-run rises of demand provided that entry was genuinely free, and short-run costs would not rise in the typical manufacturing case as they might be assumed to rise in primary industry. It seems to me that in the short-period analysis of value we can accuse Marshall of errors of omission which add up to errors on his part, and a responsibility for the errors which others were to commit in his name. The fact that some of his particular qualifications would *not* justify *them*, does not excuse *Marshall*.

To come back to Marshall's long-run competitive theory: As I have indicated, Marshall himself uses the more rigid analysis of pure competition, of a primary commodity market kind, as the foundation for his second-order analysis of factor prices and of the distribution of income. Even there, however, he does not use his model rigidly but subjects it to all the qualifications, footnotes and moralizings which have made him, for several generations, the despair of young economists eager to get on with the business of learning the marginal analysis, and this has caused his great book eventually to give way to more streamlined products which have suited their consumers better.

You will have gathered that I interpret this part of Marshall (Book VI) apart from his qualifications, as simply an elegant exposition of traditional competitive theory and I would accuse him of risking methodological error in carrying over the rigorous analysis of pure competition into fields where its assumptions needed independent verification, granted that he had found himself so unhappy about using that analysis for its primary purpose — the explanation of commodity values.

Later generations, however, have interpreted the whole of Marshall in terms of pure competition analysis and have convicted him of error in the one field where he now seems to me to have been so original. The genuine inconsistency in Marshallian analysis of value, had it been accepted and maintained, might have provided some very valuable grit, the irritation of which might have helped to produce equally practical and effective theory elsewhere. The assumption that the whole of 'scientific' economic theory should be internally self-consistent seems to me to be a very dangerous and debilitating one. As it was, Marshall came to seem not merely muddled and long-winded but wrong, and his errors were traced back especially to his analysis of the determination of competitive prices for manufactured products. It was just here, however, that his analysis of value differentiated from the great marginal theorists of the continent from Menger, Wieser and Bohm-Bawerk down to Walras. Their economic analysis rested far more strictly upon the assumption of full atomistic equilibrium — in consequence their theories of competitive value postulated, as I have already indicated, increasing costs to the firm.

We can tell by its results in publications down to the 1920s that Cambridge analysis continued for some time to reflect the effect of Marshall's teaching, in so far as it embodied the partial analysis of industries which was basic to Marshall, and which was so well-designed to give a theoretical framework for practical economic speculation in England.

It seems to me now that Professor Pigou played a special part in the subsequent development of Cambridge doctrine, which was marked by the avoidance of any detailed contact with the actual world. Mrs. Robinson's preface to her recently published *Collected Economic Papers* in which she recants her interpretation of Marshall, seems to me some corroboration of the views which I had previously reached. Mrs. Robinson there blames Professor Pigou for misleading her and others into accepting the static view of Marshall. I should observe, by the way, that since she chose to reject Marshall's theory so bluntly, and since as an adult person she was free to read him and form her own conclusions, I do not think that she is morally entitled to blame someone else. Only an outsider, I think, is entitled to give that sort of verdict. Nevertheless it seems clear that Pigou played a significant part in this development.

Pigou's interpretation of Marshallian analysis necessarily had a high authority both at Cambridge and among readers of Marshall everywhere. A pupil of Marshall, he had been chosen to be Marshall's successor at Cambridge. What he taught was regarded as fully Marshallian. It was only in the 1920s that Robertson and MacGregor woke up to the implications of Pigou's position for the standing of Marshall's work. By then the hunt was up, and economic theory had moved on too far to come back and look at Marshall freshly.

Pigou must be seen as a systematic economist with an interest in extracting practical or welfare conclusions from abstract economic analyses of possible situations. His economic analyses ran in terms of two fundamental conditions —

perfect competition and complete monopoly. In this context, perfect competition supplies a normative assessment of the wastes of monopoly. Within competitive systems, Pigou preserved the Marshallian classification of industries into increasing, decreasing, and constant returns industries. Here again he drew welfare conclusions about the divergence of industrial output from social optimum conditions, so that one could discuss the advantages of taxes or subsidies in correcting and adjusting the distribution of social resources between such industrial classes. Further, he developed the welfare implications of the notion of optimum scales of production for the industrial firm, which followed in the static world of pure competition theory, once one had accepted the notions of a balance between increasing and decreasing cost conditions in the firm.

These welfare criteria of Pigou have lived on in English economics; the theory of perfect competition being taught for the sake of those critical standards of perfection long after it had been abandoned as a guide to the formation of prices in the real world.

The point I wish to call attention to now is that Pigou developed a vested interest in the atomistic equilibrium of the individual business which underlay all his welfare analyses. The fact that his work at first had a Marshallian form was only incidental to this. In subsequent controversy, Pigou was concerned to defend this method of analysis rather than to defend Marshall pure and simple. Thus, to give an example, when the pure competition analysis of increasing returns was under attack, Pigou utilized the notion of an equilibrium firm which bore a shadowy resemblance to Marshall's representative firm, but which was to be conceived as determining its output with reference to marginal costs and revenues. In defending himself so ingeniously he did not further his analysis very much, for the criticism of the basic assumptions was too severe, but he did help further to discredit the work of Marshall. His exposition of the equilibrium firm was widely regarded as the best defence of Marshall's representative firm that could be put up, which in terms of the controversy was not good enough. It thus got in the way of the re-reading of Marshall that Robertson was pleading for; had that been done it would have been seen that Marshall's representative firm was constructed in order to avoid his analysis of manufacturing industry depending upon atomistic equilibrium in the firm.

I have taken all this time over the exposition of Alfred Marshall, because I want you to realize that the development of our modern theories of imperfect or monopolistic competition started, not from Marshallian theory proper, but from the systematic application of the theory of pure competition to all ordinarily competitive manufacturing industries. Here the basic unit — the individual business — was conceived to be in full equilibrium whenever its industry was in equilibrium. If that was so, then its marginal revenue had to equal its marginal cost. But the terms of pure competition theory meant that the individual business had an infinitely elastic demand curve, and that its marginal revenue would equal current price whatever the output which it chose to put upon the market. In these circumstances, the individual firm could not be facing decreasing marginal costs without indefinite expansion. Therefore, pure competition could not apply in conditions of decreasing costs.

This was where Sraffa's famous article came in. It was well recognized that in the real world competitive manufacturing industries showed more or less stable conditions of market prices with falling costs to the individual firm. It followed from the logic of marginal revenue equals marginal costs, that the limitation to the firm's output could not come from the cost side, but must come from the demand side. I have shown you that it is possible to interpret Marshall in such a way as to justify his solution that an industry might display parity of prices between firms and yet those firms might be in a stable condition with falling costs. On this interpretation goodwill both protects and limits the individual firm's market but does not confer any power of raising prices *vis-a-vis* its competitors. The solution which the newer theories were to adopt was to give each firm its separate demand curve. But that takes me into the topic of my next lecture.

In my next lecture I shall set out the chief propositions concerning the individual business which were evolved during these newer theories in such a way as to show not only why they were evolved against the background of the controversy, and the use which was made of them, but also so as to bring out the presuppositions which they involve concerning the behaviour of the individual business. That will enable us to look at them critically in the light of conditions in the actual world, to which our theories must provide a guide, and so will give us a good platform for the structure of my third lecture, where I shall be concerned with more positive suggestions about the sort of theory of the individual business we may expect to have some real justification, and about the present importance for economic theory of empirical studies of individual businesses.

To conclude, may I call your attention to the methodology underlying the attack upon Marshallian doctrine as understood at Cambridge. As I indicated at the start of this lecture, for the purpose of the general theory of value, the correctness of particular assumptions about the behaviour of individual businesses, from the point of view of reality, was irrelevant to the purpose of the theory — to provide generalizations about the behaviour of market prices. The validity of the detailed assumptions has, however, become relevant for the other structures which have been erected upon them. It was important for welfare theory that its assumptions about individual businesses should be realistic. In the event the methodology of the Cambridge theory of the individual business was retained — all problems were approached on the assumption that individual businesses were in full marginalist equilibrium — but the theoretical environment of individual businesses was modified so as to get certain phenomena thought to be characteristic of actual businesses in the real world. These hypothetical environments were themselves then invested gratuitously with the attributes of reality. The real world, in short, was to be interpreted as a monopolistically competitive world in all senses of the theoretical description of monopolistic competition.

Lecture 2

Today I am going to discuss the modern theories of business behaviour which approach the problem of market value through the theory of monopoly. These theories were developed in England and the United States during the 1920s and early 1930s. I shall not discuss the historical development of these theories although it makes an interesting story watching the interplay of the various personalities involved, sometimes with an appreciation of motives which stretched further than the particular issues which were being argued. As a matter of fact, I have found this so interesting that, for the last three years, I have lectured on this development, and hope, perhaps next year, to publish a small book on it. Interesting as it is, however, to go into it at any length would require considerably more than one lecture. For our purpose, we can tackle the matter more directly. What I propose to do is to confine myself to the methodological issues which were involved. A select bibliography which I have circulated will list the main points in the development of the theories with which we are concerned, if any of you would like to trace the story for himself.

It seems desirable that I should start by summarizing the methodological characteristics of the traditional theory of value from, or against which, the modern theories developed. As we saw yesterday, with the exception of Alfred Marshall's analysis of competitive manufacturing industries, traditional or neo-classical theory as it is sometimes called, developed on the basis of the static equilibrium of the individual business and any market equilibrium was thought to involve that as an essential ingredient.

The two traditional analyses using this concept were the theory of pure competition and the theory of pure monopoly. In each, the concept of atomistic equilibrium required that marginal revenue should equal marginal costs, whether short or long run.

So far as the theory of the individual business in conditions of pure competition was concerned, the analysis assumed that each business competed with other businesses all producing identical products and offering them for sale to the same customers. It also assumed that each business produced so small a proportion of the total output of its commodity that any changes in its output would be negligible when measured against total supply. It followed that, given the total supply already coming from other businesses, any one business could dispose of the whole of its output without affecting market price, whatever the level of that. Market price was therefore analysed as constant in relation to the conduct of an individual business. In formal analysis, therefore, the concept of marginal revenue did not need to appear explicitly, but was represented by market price or average revenue to which it was formally equivalent.

For equilibrium to be possible in these hypothetical conditions it was necessary for marginal costs to be rising to the individual business.

As you will know, given the assumption of free entry into such an industry, the final long-run equilibrium price would be equal to the average costs of the individual firms, including rents.

Given its assumptions, whether these were realistic in themselves or not, the theory of pure competition produced a model of a market situation which had the following characteristics, which *may* be considered fairly realistic in their possible application of the broad analysis of the whole market for any class of competitive industry, including manufacturing industry — I break off to explain that I define a competitive industry realistically simply as one which comprises a fair number of businesses and to which there is fairly free entry. Also, by the term realistic I mean simply that an economist using pure competition theory would be likely to be broadly correct in his anticipations so far as they depended upon the characteristics I shall now list: identical prices for identical products; an equality of profits when these have been referred to their two dimensions according to the capital intensities of the businesses concerned and to any normal relative complexities of management at their scales of operation; lastly, a stability of prices given general conditions of demand and given factor prices. As a proof of the realistic virtues of this sort of theory intelligently applied, I may cite the success which Sir Henry Clay's *Economics for the General Reader* has had for many years in England, with business readers and with other practical men.

As far as manufacturing industry is concerned, the following characteristics may be thought to be *un*realistic — I do not refer to agricultural industry since I have not studied that especially although I may say that my first point at least seems to apply to dairying to judge from some evidence reported to me by a Canadian economist: the assumption that costs are rising to the individual business; the neglect of the goodwill factor and the assumption of unrestricted access to the whole market; the conclusion that prices would change with short-term changes in demand, or, indeed, in response simply to changes in demand by themselves — i.e. unaccompanied by changes in factor prices. I think also, as will appear later, that it was unfortunate that the definition of a purely competitive industry was in terms of the competition of firms producing identical products — that this imposed an unnecessarily stringent limitation on the sources of price-determining competition. I may mention that a recognition of this fact is one of the starting points of my own theories of price.

To turn to the theory of monopoly, this related strictly to one business only. Three conditions had to be fulfilled for it to apply. The first is that it had to be impossible for any other business to produce an identical product and to offer it to the particular customers with whom the monopolist business was in contact — in realistic references the examples given usually involved legal limitations on freedom of entry. The second condition is really similar to the first — it is that no single substitute of alternative application of the consumer's spending power, should be sufficiently close for changes in the price of either the monopolized produce or the alternative to affect substantially the total outlay upon the monopolized commodity — so that the monopolist could ignore the interaction between his prices and other prices. Thirdly, the commodity in question had not to absorb more than a small proportion of the total outlay of its customers over all commodities, or that changes in their outlay upon that commodity should cause only relatively small changes in their total outlay elsewhere — these are the normal conditions for it to be possible to construct a Marshallian demand curve or a portion of such a curve.

The theory of monopoly obviously did not have high claims to realistic validity, but it has sometimes been attacked unjustly as an unrealizable concept — as I have defined it, I think it is perfectly possible.

In conditions of monopoly, the equilibrium of an individual business would be formally compatible with falling marginal cost curves, since the basic assumptions would imply a falling demand curve and hence would entail a falling marginal revenue curve. In traditional analysis, the theory of monopoly price-output policy was often presented geometrically, so that it could be expounded with reference to the maximization of the area of net profit, and marginal revenue did not appear explicitly. It did appear in mathematical analysis of the case but was not a separately distinguished economic concept. To that extent, my present reference to it is an anachronism.

Intermediate to the theory of monopoly and that of pure competition, of course, traditional theory distinguished the case or oligopoly — generally duopoly. There a small number of businesses offered identical products to the same group of consumers. In the circumstances, changes in the output of any one producer would not have a negligible effect upon market prices and each would therefore be affected by the price-output policy of the others.

The theory of oligopoly did not pretend to great realistic validity — especially where it discussed the behaviour of manufacturers with zero, or constant, costs of production! But it did discuss one phenomenon which appeared in real life but which could not occur in the theoretical worlds or pure competition and monopoly — price-cutting. For this reason, economists have tended to see actual price-cutting too much in terms of theoretical oligopoly — i.e. as resulting from conditions producing high cross-elasticities of demand. In reality, price-cutting results more usually from the existence of certain supply conditions — from, that is, conditions internal to the individual business. Demand conditions make it *possible* — and such conditions are much more general than is assumed by traditional analysis, but being more or less permanent, such demand conditions cannot be credited with being the cause of price-cutting which is sporadic and occasional, and systematic only with relation to supply conditions as I have defined them.

The case of oligopoly could not be solved with the same type of assumptions as were used in the other two traditional analyses, but required special assumptions about inter-product psychology. Any of the classical 'solutions' involved special assumptions about inter-producer psychologies, and therefore was open to dispute. But the formulation of possible solutions has been a traditional recreation for active minds with a mathematical bent.

So much for the background of traditional theory. I now turn to the modern theories themselves. As you will know, these derived from a recognition of the logical difficulty of using the theory of pure competition in the analysis of industries in a Marshallian fashion — in particular, the use of falling supply curves. It came to be recognized that external economies, in so far as they were compatible with the partial analysis of market price for an industry, were unlikely to be important. Internal economies, on the other hand, were known to be important, but these were inconsistent with the basic assumptions of the analysis.

(Looking at the matter historically, it is a great pity that the recognition of this dilemma did not break out a few years earlier when Marshall would have been alive and in a position to explain his analysis authoritatively — it had obviously been building up for some years. I do not think that the attack upon the realistic applications of pure competition analysis to decreasing costs industries could have been made so easily to appear an attack upon Marshall for logical errors which I do not think were involved in his system of analysis. I have pointed out elsewhere that for Marshall to have been guilty of such a simple error of logic should have been found more surprising at Cambridge than it seems to have been, considering that he had been one of the outstanding mathematicians of his generation and second wrangler to Lord Rayleigh! Anyway, as you will know, the attack was launched in 1926, when Marshall was already dead, and was carried initially in Sraffa's powerful article being overtly an attack upon the Marshallian analysis and tradition.)

Looking at the development of the new theories from a methodological point of view, we may say that they were concerned to produce a body of theory which would be capable of the following realistic reference:

> It must result in a model of a market situation in which the individual businesses could normally have falling costs and yet in which market prices were stable.
>
> Also as a rough approximation to many normally competitive industries, the equilibrium of the individual business should be formulated in such a way as to be compatible with an industrial equilibrium in which similar products would have similar prices and the profits of individual businesses would work out at the sort of equality, when suitably analysed, which was to be found in real life.

The main aim of the new theorists had to be to receive the dilemma of competitive theory as they saw it — to reconcile falling costs to the individual business with stability of prices in an industrial situation where entry was free and where individual businesses were free to seek expansion by cutting prices. Now, it is clear that falling costs imply that there is no limitation to the expansion of the business on the cost side — i.e., no internal limitation. One hindrance in seeing clearly the methodology of this situation is that in traditional theory output and sales have been taken as formally interchangeable terms so far as equilibrium analysis is concerned. We must agree that the idea of falling costs implies that a business has an internal inducement to expand, and therefore that there must be some external limitation which can come only from the demand side. This solution need not in itself go much farther than that — we could attribute the stability of a business in these conditions simply to limitations on the business's market with no other implications for the quality of the equilibrium. If we did this, then, of course, we should see that we needed to make special inquiry into just how this market limitation arose in practice. Crudely put, this is the methodology involved in my own theories although I could not see it in these general terms until I had evolved those theories.

The revolutionaries of the 1930s, however, went a good deal further in the assumptions which they postulated rather than justified. In approaching the problem they were prisoners of the idea of full equilibrium in the individual business which had dominated the older traditional theories. This implied that all features of the industrial equilibrium which they were to describe had to be capable of being explained with reference to the decisions of the individual business. In particular, the supply to an industrial market as a whole had to be analysable, as the aggregation of the supplies deliberately put on the market by the individual business. Whereas the more general approach I have suggested as the only methodological necessity would simply require that, in order for a business not be in disequilibrium, its marginal costs should not exceed its marginal revenue; the atomistic full equilibrium approach required that its marginal revenue should equal its marginal costs. If, therefore, a business was supposed to have falling marginal costs, it was necessary for it to be confronted by a falling marginal revenue curve, if it were to reach equilibrium in the output which it planned to place upon the market. This required a falling demand curve. The traditional theory which produced such a demand curve for the individual firm was, of course, the theory of monopoly. Sraffa, in his article which sounded the trumpets for the English revolution, saw clearly enough that this was the methodological solution if the problem was to be solved on the basis of the equilibrium of the individual firm, and his article in fact outlined what was to become the general Cambridge theory of imperfect competition, to be more fully worked out in Mrs. Robinson's book of that title, although it was to take the long discussion in the *Economic Journal* to disentangle the issues which were involved, to assess their relevance to the methodological problem, and to get them separately accepted.

(Since I am not going over the details of the *Journal* discussion, I shall, in passing call attention to the exploration of the analysis of the cost curve of the individual firm, whose conclusions were to become a firm part of the newer theory, and from which many welfare conclusions were to be drawn about the effects of the type of competition which the newer theories claimed to analyse. It is interesting to recall that the U-shaped curve, which emerged as orthodox, was not submitted to any realistic justification, or rather that was provided *a posteriori*, the U-shaped cost curve rather being accepted because it was required in order to make the theory of pure competition with atomistic equilibrium work, through providing ultimately increasing costs to the individual business, despite the existence of internal economies of scale. I should add that, had Harrod been able to work his own views up in a more elaborate fashion, it is clear that the orthodox theory of costs might have remained more open-minded than it was to become.)

For my present purpose, I shall confine myself to the chief substantial product of all this theoretical discussion, so far as England was concerned — Mrs. Robinson's *Economics of Imperfect Competition*.

This followed the precedent of her contribution to the *Journal* discussion, by going straight for the 'monopoly' solution and side-stepping most of the analytical difficulties involved in applying it. Those difficulties chiefly concerned the application to an individual firm in an industry open to free entry, of the notion of a determinate particular demand curve, which the theory required. One of the chief difficulties was caused by the possibility of oligopoly — of such strong cross-interactions between businesses' price policies that any one firm might not be able to conclude anything about its own desirable price policy, even given the prices of others, unless it knew policies which these would pursue once its own policy had been settled. Mrs. Robinson side-stepped that difficulty by simply postulating that the individual business, which was the basic unit of her theorizing, knew enough about all possible interactions to take account of them, and by requiring that the demand curve for such a business should be deemed to have been drawn so as to take all such interactions into account, and leave the business with the net output shown by the curve.

In fact, of course, a producer could only have these stable expectations if serious cross-relationships did not exist or if he were the price leader whom others followed (to refer to a 'realistic' solution of the oligopoly dilemma). Mrs. Robinson, although she recognizes the problem of cross-elasticity of demand, has thus dodged it by assuming that the theoretical problem has been solved — a methodological trick which belongs to the class which Leontief, in a general criticism of the Cambridge school has called 'implicit theorizing'. The question of advertising, which must have raised the difficulties to which I have referred, in an acute form, is not discussed by Mrs. Robinson, on the grounds that its theory had not been sufficiently established at the time when she wrote.

Her general method, then, is to take the falling demand and marginal revenue curves for granted, and to analyse the consequences for the individual firm with various cost possibilities. She shows, of course, that, given the assumptions, such a firm might well be in equilibrium with falling costs.

As a whole, the book is more concerned with the concept of the marginal revenue curve as an analytical tool, and with the theoretical possibilities involved in its use, than it is with the construction of a body of theory which meets all the questions aroused by the case of imperfect competition which Mrs. Robinson is concerned to recognize. Nevertheless, it does provide a body of theory whose formal resemblance, so far as its stated conclusion goes, has a resemblance sufficiently close to one of the major cases which Professor Chamberlin has analysed for it to irritate him, in the same fashion that the worship of Mithras is stated to have irritated the early Christians.

This general case of an imperfectly competitive industry, as the Cambridge school calls it, is analysed in an implicit fashion. All businesses are assumed to produce similar products and the distribution of preferences is supposed to be such that they face similar demand curves. Free entry to the industry is supposed to imply that industrial equilibrium will obtain only if existing firms are making normal profits, which are included in the cost curves. In these circumstances, the corresponding equilibrium of the individual firms will involve tangency of demand and cost curves, all firms will have falling costs and all firms will be of less than optimum size. To this last characteristic, Mrs. Robinson attaches much more welfare importance than does Professor Chamberlin, because of her appeal to a 'norm' of perfect competition. The same is true of the implications which she draws for the theory of distribution of income, which does not concern us today.

I turn now to Professor Chamberlin's book. This was also evolved during the period of the *Journal* discussion, having been started as a post-graduate thesis in 1925–7. It had an independent origin, except in so far as Chamberlin also was preoccupied with the dilemma of pure competition analysis in the face of falling costs and in so far as his supervisor, Professor Allyn Young, was himself interested in the English controversy to which he made an important contribution.

Chamberlin is concerned with long-term equilibrium. His demand curves are constructed on the basis of his assumptions about consumers' preferences as between various producers, even when offering identical goods. His early formulation relied heavily upon irrational preferences. More recently, in his *Economica* article, he has stressed an alternative approach through what he calls 'spatial monopoly' — basing preferences upon a (rational) preference of a consumer for a particular producer who is nearer to him than are others. I should say, in passing, that Chamberlin has not so far been able to take full account of the differences which his new emphasis would entail for his theory of selling costs.

Consumers' preferences, in his view, are influenced by differences in price, so that the existence of cross-elasticity of demand is formally taken into account, and limiting degrees of oligopoly may be expressed in terms of his analysis. In this, Chamberlin proceeds in terms of a group of producers all offering similar products; his group was therefore easily translated in terms of an industry as handled in traditional theory.

His demand curves are of two kinds. The first, which I call the *particular demand curve* for an individual business, is based on the assumption that all other relevant producers hold their prices constant whilst the business in question varies its price. The second, which I have called the *share-of-the-market demand curve*, traces the sales of the business on the assumption that it, and all relevant producers, vary their prices together.

Having just referred to Chamberlin's group — the unit of analysis from the point of view of the share-of-the-market curve — I should say that even in his early formulations, Chamberlin recognized that his groups might be interpreted realistically as including the producers of commodities which were very disparate from the production viewpoint, provided that they were close enough substitutes from the point of view of the consumer.

This analysis came under heavy fire from Triffin, from a general equilibrium theory standpoint. Triffin pointed out that the 'group' had a very shadowy existence, if Chamberlin's concessions were extended realistically, and held that the partial equilibrium economists' notion of an industry could not withstand criticism. In his latest treatment, Chamberlin seems to have given way to Triffin, and his group relationship is no longer to be interpreted in industrial

195

terms. In fact, he seems quite willing to abandon the concept. Since he has not given any full account of the modifications which he would make in his entire structure of thinking, and since the formulation in *Monopolistic Competition* has an independent interest, I shall in this particular, follow the older Chamberlin. I may say, in passing, that, while I recognize the force of Triffin's criticism *vis-a-vis* Chamberlin, strictly interpreted, it has no force against the definition of an industry which I myself use and which I think was also basic to Marshall's analysis. But I shall be discussing that tomorrow.

So far as the cost curve side of the analysis goes, I shall not discuss this in any detailed fashion. Chamberlin takes over the U-shaped cost curves which, as we have seen, were required for methodological reasons in the analysis of pure competition, but has developed a rather different justification from that offered by the Cambridge theorists. He explains that eventual upward tilt of the average cost curve on the basis of the increasing complexity of management, whereas the latter school explain it on the basis of the indivisibility of the management factor.

As you will know, Chamberlin analyses the behaviour of an individual business and the equilibrium of it and its group in terms of three variables — price, quality, and selling costs. His only completely determinate analysis is that of the large group; this concept defined from the standpoint of the individual business whose equilibrium is the basic methodological assumption is a group of competing businesses large enough and with preferences sufficiently evenly distributed between them for changes in the policy of any one business to have a negligible effect upon the situation of the others — by the policy of the business, I mean its decisions with respect to any of the three variables.

In the large group it follows that oligopolistic reactions can be ignored from the point of view of long-term equilibrium and that only its particular demand curve is relevant to the decisions of the individual business. With respect to all three policy variables, quality, selling costs, price, the business is assumed to reach full marginalist equilibrium. Whatever the output which results, the general conclusion is drawn that price must be higher than would cover the fully competitive costs of an article of the given quality, together with the costs involved in selling it.

The competition from new entrants is assumed to limit the markets available at any given price to businesses already within the industry, and so to limit their profits. In the *general* case no conclusions can be drawn about the behaviour of individual businesses' costs when the group markets as a whole are in equilibrium. They may have falling or rising costs, and their outputs may be more or less than the theoretical optimum defined by the postulated cost curves.

Chamberlin, however, stresses the analysis of a special case — where the commodities produced within the group are identical with respect to costs of production, so that such differentiation as exists does not affect costs, and where preferences are evenly distributed. Page 150 may be quoted to show that he regards this as an approximation to an important real-life case. Hence, he tends to stress the conclusions which he reaches for this case as if they have some general practical significance in actual industrial situations. Here, all prices will be at the same level, the particular demand curves of the individual firms being tangential to their average cost curves, so that all firms will have falling costs and all will be producing at less than their optimum scale of production.

I suggest that besides Chamberlin's practical reasons for stressing the real possibility of this case, and in addition to his pedagogic reason (that it is easier to approach more complex cases through this particular model) he has also a methodological one which is important in view of his desire that his theory should have as general a relevance as possible. This is, that his simple model of the large group reproduces important analytical features of the old pure competition model — notably uniformity of prices and of profits, whilst also recognizing differentiation of the product.

As I have indicated, Chamberlin gives no determinate solution to the oligopoly problem — where the group is so small, or where preferences are so distributed, that there was significant cross-elasticities of demand between pairs of producers. He makes, however, brilliant analytical use of his two demand curves to establish the limits to the possible equilibrium of the individual firm when it is in such a situation. It is interesting that, so far as I can recall, he never hit upon the combination of these two curves in such a way as to produce a single kinked demand curve so that the oligopoly situation became determinate just because all producers would accept whatever level of prices had become established. (This is the contribution of Hall and Hitch, to which I shall refer later.)

In the general Chamberlin case of oligopoly, we need to know more about individual producers' price policies than can be inferred from their demand and cost curves. Chamberlin himself explores various possibilities on the basis of appeals to their actual occurrence in real life.

I shall come back to this question of oligopoly later on. At this moment it seems to me convenient that I should refer to Professor Chamberlin's latest formulation of his doctrines. In his *Economica* article he invokes 'spatial monopoly' as the genus-type by which to establish buyers' preferences of a rational character. The new model is put up alike for pedagogic convenience and for reasons of its practical importance — I suspect also because Chamberlin has become worried by the stress that has been laid upon the significance of irrational preferences. The fundamental idea of his model now becomes that customers are separated from producers, so that each producer will have a spatially protected market.

I should like to criticize this straight-away, and shall distinguish manufacturing from retail trade. In a forthcoming article, Miss Brunner has pointed out that in the case of manufacturing trade, it is not realistic to imagine producers and consumers as being randomly distributed within a country — rather it seems very unrealistic to imagine this for producers. In most industrial countries, manufacturing industry of various kinds tends to be concentrated in definite localities. Surely, if we must have a simple model, it would be better to imagine producers as being located at a single point and so equally distant from all customers. If we set up a model of this kind, we get at least an oligopolistic model, if not a purely competitive one, unless we also assume other kinds of preferences, irrational in so far as they do not relate to the inherent qualities of products or their transport costs.

In the case of retail trade, the new model may seem very realistic — if we simply think of the shop which is near to us but far from someone else. But do we never walk about? It does not require a large proportion of the population to refuse to stay paralysed at home, for there to be a large body of *floating custom*, and once again, on the assumptions of the model, we need to invoke less rational preferences to get a Chamberlin model with the old analytical firmness. I conclude that his reformulation has raised fresh difficulties which he has not fully faced. You may feel, no doubt, that these are realistic criticisms of the kind with which I shall be concerned in my next lecture. I shall plead that Professor Chamberlin's new model departs from the general methodology and is based upon a special assumption; his differentiation between the assumptions he previously employed and his selection of this one can only be defended on realistic grounds. I should like to give here one further detailed criticism of Chamberlin's model, which is relevant to his analysis as a whole, and to irrational preferences.

Chamberlin himself, in one passage, recognizes the probable existence of at least a proportion of any market who are skilled buyers and rational in their buying — this is where he recognizes that some customers will be only lightly attached to their present suppliers. Does this not vitiate his large group case, at all events? Surely, it is not necessary for such customers to be a large proportion of the total body of consumers for them nevertheless to be very significant in relation to the market of any single firm. If this is so, then any business will have the possibility of a very elastic demand curve for a reduction in price This, once again, would destroy the determinateness of Chamberlin's solution in such a case.

With this criticism, we seem to tremble once more on the brink of oligopoly. Surely when we look squarely at their theories, we should suspect that oligopolistic situations will be very much more important than either of the theorists we have been studying would suggest — so far as Mrs. Robinson is concerned, she does not deal with oligopoly at all; in Professor Chamberlin's case his stress is upon the importance of the large group model.

This consideration, no doubt, accounts for the fact that economic theory since Chamberlin and Robinson has been very pre-occupied with the analysis of oligopolistic relations. Professor Kahn's 1937 article is one instance of this.

The interest in the indeterminate small group case has also received much stimulus from reports of researches into pricing policies in actual businesses. My principal reference here must be to the work of the Oxford Economists' Research Group. I shall take up their detailed findings later on. All that is relevant just now is that the Research Group became very interested in the stability of prices in the actual world, given factor prices etc. When business men were pressed as to why they did not independently cut or raise their prices, their answers showed a great reluctance to alter their pricing policies, without any justification on the costs side. The reason seemed to be the widespread existence of a state of oligopoly. Business men were reluctant to cut prices because others would quickly follow, and they would not gain much increase in demand in a reasonable period. At the same time, if they raised their prices, unless there were good reasons of a general character on the cost side, others would not follow and they would have a marked decrease in sales.

Messrs Hall and Hitch, who wrote the paper reporting the work of the Research Group in this field, then worked out the idea of the kinked demand curve — virtually segments from each of Chamberlin's demand curves — so that one had discontinuous marginal revenue curves, these in turn implying that any given price would be the most profitable for quite a range of marginal cost curves. Thus was produced the curious result of marginal concepts being used to explain the stability of prices in normal circumstances through the non-applicability of the marginal calculus in a deterministic form.

Other realistic researches have increased economists' awareness of the importance of the small group case and the result has been, as I have said, to magnify the importance of the theory of oligopoly with all its indeterminancies, and we have already seen that here was the analytical lacuna in the newer theories of the 1930s.

I shall not go into any detail concerning the various treatments of oligopoly relationships which have been evolved. I want to suggest that they have all been far too much concerned with short-period price-cutting to have general relevance to the problem of normal prices, since price-cutting is not a normal phenomenon. Secondly, taking them from a short-term viewpoint, they have been too preoccupied, I think, with the effect of demand conditions, and have rather neglected what I believe to be the more direct importance of supply conditions of a temporary kind. One of the witnesses of the Research Group said: 'There is always a fool who cuts!' If we are to understand why the fool cuts, we must look at the internal conditions which distinguish him from his fellows who do not cut, rather than to the demand situation which they have in common.

At their most abstract level — as in Von Neumann and Morgenstern's *Theory of Games* — they seem to me to have little relevance to price formation as ordinarily developed in established industries. I think they have more relevance to the bluff and strategy of various personal relations — as when two people are competing for the same post in a situation where it would be fatal to the ambition of the first player to put his hand on the table.

I think that we can develop a theory of oligopoly which meets our practical needs in price theory — but only by taking account of practical facts. If the clue to price-cutting in oligopolies in the short-period lies on the supply side, the clue to price stability in normal times lies on the demand side. But this would take me into my next lecture. For the moment I propose to leave the small-group questions on one side, simply as the blind-spot in the theories which were developed in the inter-war period, and come back to certain methodological questions of a more general character.

Looking at these modern theories from the methodological point of view, two matters seems to be of especial importance. The first is the basic methodology which they shared with the older theory — of proceeding in terms of the atomistic equilibrium of the individual business. It was because older theory assumed this that it became involved in inconsistencies when discussing competitive industries with falling supply curves. Because the broad results of the theory were generally useful, older economists either ignored the inconsistency or, in Marshall's case, got round it by a special analytical device.

The more modern theories called attention to the dilemma and, as we have seen, resolved it by invoking the theory of consumers' demand for a commodity class as a whole and applying it to the product of an individual business.

To take this second aspect first, in view of the analytical implications of applying conventional demand and cost circumstances, individual businesses behaved like pure monopolists — this step was not justified simply because, with its aid, we could explain falling costs in stable conditions in an industry where the market was formally open to new enterprise. As I indicated at the start of these lectures, that result might have been obtained by a less stringent assumption — that of a simple limitation of the market for an individual business without implications as to its exploitability by the business man. It follows that, even in its own setting, this device needed independent justification, which I suggest would have had to be sought in realistic studies of the behaviour of individual businesses. I shall have a good deal to say on this when I come on to the discussion of my own theories.

Now, above all, I wish to put a large question mark against the basic assumption of atomistic equilibrium which is common to both sets of theories, and the strict application of which, in purely competitive market, had led to the original theoretical dilemma.

This is the most difficult of all theorems to question, because we have been brought up under its influence for so many generations. I may say that I find that this vested interest in the employment of this assumption, to be one of the chief obstacles to the critical understanding of my own theories. As a matter of fact, it was a serious obstacle in my own development of those theories — so that for some time I had developed various parts separately and yet could not see that they fitted together and made a consistent whole, because that would be in conflict with the basic assumption of atomistic equilibrium in terms of which I was still thinking.

Now this assumption has, from time to time, been questioned on realistic grounds. It certainly is one part of the mental equipment of economists which most bothers the business man who tries to read economic theory, and it leads to complaints that the real world does not give him such a nice control over what is going on, as we assume. On the whole, however, those questioning it have generally been those who are opposed to theory as such. That nihilistic standpoint must be unacceptable to any economist who is aware how valuable are the results which economics has got by persisting in seeking generalizations. The remedy for bad or incomplete theory must be better theory, not the abandonment of theorizing. The consequence of this justifiable attitude has been that insufficient attention has been paid to the theoretical standpoint implicit in such overtly empirical protests.

So far as I recall references by economists to the static method of analysis with its assumption of full atomistic equilibrium, the justification, generally speaking, has not been that it is realistic, but that it is useful. The usual justification is that, whilst economic life is a matter of flux, we are usually interested in forecasting the effects of some particular change or other, and that the application of the conclusions of our static analyses will enable us to forecast at least the *direction* in which either consumers or producers will tend to move; so long as they are actuated by the particular change in question. That argument seems to me to be impeccable.

It does not seem to me, however, that this valid justification is of much significance, as relating to the actual use which many economists have made of such static theories. If questioned on realistic grounds, many economists would protest rather indignantly that they were well aware that the actual world was not ordinarily in a state of equilibrium. In fact, however, and despite this, economists persist in looking at the real world and talking about it as though it were always in equilibrium. For example, I have found that one cannot report actual pricing practices without economists interpreting those practices at once in terms which imply that those businesses can best be studied under the assumption that, at any one time, they are actually in a position of atomistic equilibrium. (I may refer here to Mr. Wiles's article 'Marginal Analysis and Empirical Research' in the *Economic Journal*, September, 1950.) Thus, also, in America, basing point prices are explained on the assumption that each business employing them is maximizing its profits. Or again, Mr. Kalecki, in development of imperfect competition theory, explains the distribution of the national income of the United States and of Great Britain, after a period of years, by an analysis which assumes the full and continuous equilibrium of the individual business. Other examples could be cited, and it would seem that, like the sorcerer's apprentice, we have become the victims of our own devices. In consequence, it does become relevant to demand realistic justification of this basic analytical assumption. My own theories deny it, and further suggest considerable doubt as to whether it really has even the directional utility which older methodologists have claimed for it.

The point of these remarks, of course, has been to suggest that our accepted methodology is not, even in its own terms, the flawless logical construction we sometimes think it to be. I have also tried to remind you of its methodology, in terms which will help you to make significant critical comparisons with my own theories which I shall be expounding tomorrow.

Lecture 3

What I have said so far would suggest very strongly that, even in its own terms, the modern theory of business behaviour seems to need more detailed empirical verification than it has ever established. Today, I shall suggest that the empirical study of business behaviour, in fact, tells against any theory based upon atomistic equilibrium of the individual business.

I should, at this point, refer again to the inquiries of the pre-war Oxford Economists' Research Group, which I mentioned yesterday. We were then concerned only with the extent to which its findings supported the idea that oligopolistic relations were of practical importance, and with the idea of the kinked demand curve which Mr. Hall and Mr. Hitch invented, in order to explain a stability of market prices despite this relationship.

This Research Group was formed largely on the initiative of the late Sir Hubert Henderson and Mr. Roy Harrod. It consisted of teachers of economics at Oxford, who were interested in the experience of business men during the trade cycle. Its method was to invite selected business men to come down for interview, generally by the whole Research Group. A general question paper, which was revised at intervals, was used, not as a questionnaire in the usual sense but rather as a series of headings to start the business man off and to guide the members in his interrogation.

It was only incidental to the question of the trade cycle that the Research Group asked about the rate of interest and about prices, the two topics where its work has achieved results which have attracted such attention.

I shall not have time to discuss the rate of interest work in any detail, but it is tolerably well known. Its findings are very relevant to the theory of the individual business — they are that rates of interest had been of negligible importance as factors affecting business men's decisions concerning their investment in plant and equipment, or, so far as manufacturing was concerned, even their investment in stocks. The actual availability of credit, quite apart from the terms on which it might be available, did seem to have been of importance at particular times for a fair proportion of businesses. The mention of this last matter is a reminder that the Research Group did not, as it sometimes believed, discover that the rate of interest had no effect at all upon business; its findings are relevant to the direct effects of the direct decisions of business men *vis-a-vis* the rate of interest.

The side of the Research Group's work with which we are more directly concerned, related to the formation of prices. The chief fact which emerged was just how customary it was for business men to approach the problem of fixing prices via their average costs. The exact methods used in estimating prices varied but they nearly all had this in common, that the business man looked at his average costs and, for any one product at a given period or time, had a price policy which fixed the quoted price in some stable relation to average costs — either in relation to average prime costs or in relation to prime costs plus some allowance as for overhead costs, and the latter might be reached by simple rule-of-thumb accounting operations or by elaborate cost-accounting methods. I shall not now go into this question of price-fixing methods in any great detail. In fact, I shall argue later that this is not necessary for the purposes of broad theory. Nor shall I, for the moment, discuss the cases where the business men were not themselves fixing the prices which they quoted, but were overtly following prices fixed by outside bodies.

The Research Group were interested in the prevalence of this approach to prices and it should be said that severe questioning failed to show that our business men witnesses paid any attention to marginal revenues or costs in the sense defined by economic theory, and that they had anything but the vaguest of ideas about anything remotely resembling their particular elasticities of demand.

The other chief fact which the Group reported was that, as previously said, short-run prices as fixed by average-cost policy tended to be very stable. As we saw yesterday, this led to the chief theoretical construction in Mr. Hall's and Mr. Hitch's paper — the kinked demand curve. This, whilst of considerable interest, had the demerit of suggesting that it was not necessary for actual prices to have any rational basis at all. However they were fixed, business men would find that it paid them to adhere to them unless underlying cost circumstances got completely out of line.

So far as the average-cost basis of prices itself was concerned, the conclusions of the authors also were of a non- or even anti-theoretical kind. For in our discussions within the group we had fastened upon not the average-cost basis itself but on the attitude of mind with which the business men defended the ethics of their position when under attack from us. It transpired that most of those we questioned believed that, as a matter of principle, prices should normally cover their average costs and leave them a 'reasonable' margin of net profit. The precise relevance of this principle to their practice varied from businesses in a very depressed competitive industry, where it was a pious hope to businesses in a strong position where the principle was used, to set upper limits to the net profits included in their pricing calculations.

So far as I remember, Mr. Hall and Mr. Hitch reflect faithfully the general feeling of the research group, when they regard this attitude as rather a matter of ethics than of economics, and as fundamentally lacking rationality, although Mr. Harrod's introductory paper, when the report was published, does stress the feeling that, despite appearances, there might be a general rationality which eluded us. Our troubles over the full-cost principle led us, I think, to pay insufficient attention to the reasons for their pricing methods, which the business men themselves put forward. But of course, our basic tools with which to apprehend their reasoning were those of marginal theory.

The preoccupation with the full-cost principle had, however, one very unfortunate result. There has been much indication (e.g. a footnote by Mrs. Robinson in her latest book on dynamic economics) that our results have been regarded as naively asserting that businesses necessarily succeeded in getting prices which would cover their costs, whatever they were, and yield them what the business men themselves would consider only a reasonable margin of profit. As Mrs. Robinson said in a radio talk, why should business men themselves decide what is a reasonable margin of profit. This, of course, is nonsense, but the widespread development of this belief makes it very difficult to get a fresh approach to the rationale of average-cost pricing. After all, costing techniques are as much a matter of convention as of science, and there is nothing sacrosanct about the fact that a business's accounting costs are at such and such a level.

I have myself found that this misunderstanding gets seriously in the way of an understanding of my own theory, I have termed it the normal-cost theory and have drawn it up in such a way as to make it clear that there is no presumption that any one business will cover its costs, however defined, when market prices are stable. Nevertheless, because I justify the individual business approaching the price it should quote through its experiences in the light of its own costs, I am regarded as a 'full-costite', and held responsible for all the errors of reasoning into which my critics fall when they read me with that assumption firmly fixed in their minds.

The work of the Oxford Economists' Research Group has been an important factor in my experience, but my main work has been studies of individual businesses. These have not been what I have called business biographies, concerned with the individual businesses as for its own sake, but primarily have been part of some research into a problem of interest of economics. Thus my leading question has been the extent to which the efficiency of a business depends upon its size; others have been about the policy of a cartel, and of individual businesses in relation to it; or the factors which have affected the capital investment and development decisions of individual businesses. Sometimes I have been studying a number of businesses in a directly competitive relation one with another, at others I have been concentrating upon one particular business as an interesting specimen.

When I study a business I go to it, stay in it, and work, to speak from the inside, so a wide range of experience may be available to me. I should say, first that it is important to acquire a good knowledge of the basic technique involved in the industry one is studying. It is a basic defect in most economists' training that technical factors are wrapped up anonymously in the laws of return — where they are so starkly general that they are devoid of all empirical content. Paying proper attention to technical factors enables one to appreciate the technical limits to the freedom of choice of the business man. It will also enable one to appreciate how economic factors limit technical choices. Further, in my experience, a lack of acquaintance with techniques will mean that it will be difficult to get hold of the evidence of the technical men within a business; people will always be hesitant about how far they can go with an explanation and will be afraid that the whole story will come out wrong.

I have drawn the distinction between business biographies and economists' exercises. Whenever I investigate a business, I have some leading question in mind. But I do not follow it too narrowly. In actual investigations it is above all necessary to avoid too close a concentration upon the particular questions one is trying to answer. For one thing, we must try to keep aware of the larger aspects of a business's behaviour if we are to appreciate the quality of its response in the more narrow economic field in which we are interested. But this principle, that, at the present state of our knowledge, we had better make our studies of individual businesses with a broad wedge rather than a narrow chisel, is valid even from the narrow point of view of the studies themselves. First, many of the 'facts' one is handling will not be statistical facts but accounts of the relevant experience of business men. Second, even in the case of statistical and accounting 'facts' their precise meaning can be understood only with the help of advice from the business men concerned. Third, both of these types of facts come in answer to questions.

Now, however much one may be careful to be precise and clear in one's questions, they will be formulated and asked under the influence of one's professional training and interests. Serious misunderstandings are therefore always possible.

The more one can steep oneself in the business one is investigating, the more one can learn how to ask questions in order to get them correctly answered in that particular business, and the more assuredly one can interpret the answers one has got. In some cases, moreover, it may be absolutely impossible to get direct answers to some particular questions, but it may be possible to make a confident inference about the answer in the light of a general knowledge of a business. The first part of any investigation accordingly must be some study of the history and background of a business. Later on, as I have said, I try to work with broad, simple questions which will rather get the business man concerned thinking back through the situations in which I am interested, than get him harassed because he cannot answer a particular question.

I have found it necessary to keep verbatim records of all conversations when working in a business, however irrelevant they may seem to become. Further, to guard against misinterpretations, I prefer not to work on my own but to have an experienced colleague with whom I can argue about the work as it goes along.

Above all, perhaps, it is necessary that one should spend long enough in each business and be able to move around freely. The chain of management may be concentrated, but business experience is not, and the best person to answer one particular set of questions is not necessarily the best person to deal with others. Similarly, I try to get a blanket permission to have access to any documents I want.

In order to be able to work in this way, I give strict undertakings to restrict access to the data I collect, and not to publish, without permission, details which might identify the business, but of course I reserve full rights to publish any general conclusions I may come to.

It is from studies of this kind that my theories of price formation emerged gradually. You will have noticed that all the particular topics I have been investigating have some connection with the competitive relations of the individual business and also with the behaviour of the costs of production. At first, I approached businesses with preconceptions due to my training. I had myself taught the accepted body of doctrine for a generation, and my own theories have not been produced as a deliberate revolt against it. Nor did I see then the methodological critique which I have been adumbrating to you. My ideas have been developed gradually and to a large extent reluctantly in the light of my empirical work. The detailed exploration of the experience of businesses led to my taking a critical standpoint about received doctrine — at first about the history of the cost curve, then I began to be dissatisfied about our approach to the question of demand. The one place where I had most difficulty was my general approach that businesses in some way controlled their sales through their price policy. In one way or another, due to this approach, I was involved in continuous argument over misunderstandings of a business's evidence. In the end, I came to believe that a business in ordinary manufacturing industry genuinely did not think that it was good policy to play about with prices in the search for maximum profit, and that they did believe that their settled policy in terms of their costings did give them about the right answer, subject to emergence of actual competition.

I now turn to the theories which I have evolved as a result of my experience — the broad economic theory with which I myself now approach business problems. I shall have to keep to very simple models and shall not have time to make all the realistic qualifications and explanations which I should have liked to make. I regret this since I think that models are excellent forms of notes for economists, but make bad economic theory when symbols take the place of reality, and precise machines take the place of the shifting phenomena of the everyday world. In my book you will notice that there are only four diagrams and no index — these are not unconnected with the remarks I have just made. There I have tried continuously to refer anonymously to industrial situations which, according to my experience, are fairly typical.

In any theoretical model, we must refer to industries in the abstract. Since I employ analytically a much broader concept of an industry than is customary, I should comment on my definition. The type of research I have had to do has necessarily involved me in studying industries in the practical everyday senses we all employ when we are compiling statistical tables or considering government policy. I have learned that there is a good deal of solid economic justification behind the pragmatic definitions which we use on these occasions.

For the purposes of price theory, my definition runs in terms of processes and not of products. Businesses are in the same industry if they have substantially the same sort of process and equipment. Now, of course, I recognize that our theoretical interest has to centre round the price of a particular product or product class. An industry then consists of all the firms who operate such processes that they could, if they wanted to, turn out the products in which we are interested and offer such goods for sale in the markets which we are studying.

I recognize that there is a certain looseness about this definition, since a business's processes and equipment might, in fact, require a certain amount of adaptation before it could produce such and such a product. That looseness has a great deal of theoretical merit since it calls attention to the area of competition which is most significant for actual businesses in an established and settled industry.

In our traditional models, we are used to defining an industry in terms of firms all producing identical products. This puts a very tight ring fence around the industry and leads us too easily to think in terms of new competitors having to be new businesses. In view of the well-known difficulties of new businesses obtaining adequate capital, this definition takes us half-way towards accepting the ready application of the theory of monopoly, and we go the whole way as soon as we impose a narrow definition of the product. Our model also does not prepare us for the shifting balance of product interest under the influence of profit considerations, and the stress of competition which is the characteristic of reality.

I want, then, our theoretical business to be potentially multi-product. For the purposes of our discussion this morning, however, I shall suppose that in fact it produces only one product. In my article on Industrial Economics I have vindicated the analytical justification for this in terms of the existence of normal-cost-price relationships between products stemming from an industry in the sense I have defined. I shall not repeat my argument now.

For the purpose of my first model, I want to postulate that all consumers of the product in question are other business men — either the product is bought by them as a piece of capital equipment which they will simply use in their business, or they buy it as a raw material for their product, or they buy it for resale to some other customer who may or may not be a final consumer of the traditional kind. This is one of the biggest analytical steps involved in my theories. Economic theory has traditionally been based upon the theory of consumers' demand which is related to utility — a subjective matter. The modern theorists we have been discussing have had no warrant for applying to manufacturing markets generally, the notions about consumers' preferences, which they justify with reference to conditions which can apply only in the markets for consumers' goods sold to consumers.

Yet, of course, buyers' preferences exist for all types of manufactured commodities, and it is rational that they should exist. Accordingly I postulate that, other things being equal, the demand will *not* be distributed at random between suppliers, but that various customers will prefer to deal with particular producers and that each producer will have his circle of customers whose 'goodwill' he enjoys.

We may not, however, assume that such preferences will prevail against known price differentials, since to do so would be to deny the assumption that all business men will seek to maximize their profits, whether buying or selling. And in the case of business men buyers we can presume that their self-interest will lead them to keep a watchful eye upon prices and qualities generally.

Seasonal and other times of pressure of demand will give opportunity for testing the products of wider circle of suppliers. But I shall not repeat all the arguments I have set out in my book. It may take time for buyers to discover the existence of more favourable terms elsewhere, but we have no right to assume that it will take a very long time.

Accordingly, in the case of the longer-term demand in which we are interested in our model, if there is to be equilibrium in the market, the prices of identical products must be identical.

This rule of the identity of quoted prices does not imply any infinite elasticity of demand for the product of the individual business. The existence of buyers' preferences implies that at the given price, each business will at any one time have only a definite demand, which can be increased in given conditions only by the rather slow process of building up goodwill.

In this particular model, we need not allow selling costs any function of adding to the demand which is available to the business. Advertising can be only informative — and in practice for this type of market is usually of negligible importance. The other selling costs are simply consequences of a business trying to sell its particular product at all in the market we have assumed. Accordingly, selling costs may be simply regarded as as much involved in the production for sale of the product, as are production costs themselves.

On this general basis, I construct what I call the price line for the product of any particular business. Its level represents the maximum price which the business can charge if it is to retain its goodwill in the long run. This price will equal the lowest price any potential competitor would charge for a product of identical specification.

At that price, the business would have a definite market, the demand which was determined by its goodwill. If it charged a higher price, then, except in the very short run, its demand would shrink and in the long run it would lose its market. The business's demand will, therefore, be infinitely elastic for a higher level of price. For a lower level of price, demand would be inelastic, except in the very short run — for other businesses will have to lower their prices if they wish to remain in the market for this product, so that our business will simply get its share of any increase in the general demand for this product which is caused by the general fall in price. For practical purposes, and for the kind of commodities strictly covered by our model, I regard market demand as very inelastic, and it is convenient to represent it as definitely limited. In dynamic conditions, as when general demand is rising or falling over the trade cycle, we can interpret this as implying a relatively constant share of the total market, other things being equal.

Despite the consequence of a price cut, it may pay a business to initiate it as a matter of long-run policy — but that will be better understood when we have dealt with costs of production. Similarly, a business may be *forced* to do this as a short-term measure; I shall discuss that later as a matter outside the conditions of our model as we have constructed it.

In our model then, the sales environment of the individual business will be represented by its price line. For an understanding of the forces operating inside a business, we must turn to the question of costs.

I continue to analyse in terms of a single product. I define costs in no special sense, but am content to leave them as in the aggregate including whatever a business chooses to reckon among its costs. We may assume that, at any given time, our business is organized so as to produce a given range of output of its product as efficiently as possible to it. Several realistic considerations justify this assumption instead of the traditional assumption that it is organized to produce some particular output exactly.

How will its costs vary as it changes its output, its organization being unchanged — *short-run costs* — or as it changes its whole organization so as to produce larger or smaller outputs on a permanent basis — *long-run costs*?

For our present purposes, we may take its factor prices as constant, including its overtime rates if it has to work its labour overtime, which will bear a constant relation to normal payments.

Short-term costs are of crucial importance, since they are the costs most immediately within the knowledge of the business man. I distinguish between paying-out and other costs, and between direct and indirect costs.

Paying-out costs are all costs which have to be met currently. They will equal direct costs as I shall define them, plus the paying-out indirect costs. They are relevant to the problem of short-term stability since their existence implies a continuous need for cash, which, unless it is provided by current receipts, must be got from cash reserves or from external finance.

The distinction between *direct* and *indirect* costs follows normal business usage, but I am more strict about the analytical definition than businesses can be in practice.

Direct costs are those outlays which are directly linked to production — direct labour, direct materials, and other expenses directly linked to the processes of production. All other costs are *indirect* costs.

Given factor prices, average direct costs will be constant over the range of output which the business is organized to produce, if we ignore any rise in costs due to working labour overtime. Such rises I classify as *extraordinary* costs, and as irrelevant to pricing policy though not to actual profits or to investment policy — because they are not necessarily entailed by the production of the product, and so their incidence may be a matter of chance as between competing businesses.

The difference between total receipts and total direct costs is the business's gross profit — the fund from which it will have to pay all its indirect costs and get its profits, if any. The difference between price and the average direct costs is the gross profit margin. It will be seen that, given market price and given the business's organization, this will be a constant quantity.

How will the business's costs behave if it meets an increased demand by increasing the scale of output which it is organized to produce, varying its complement of indirect factors accordingly?

Traditional theory asserts that average costs will fall up to a certain point, owing to the effect of economies of scale, but that beyond that point the difficulties of organizing the business on a larger scale will cause average costs to rise.

I find it difficult to accept this simple U-shaped cost curve, although I understand the methodological reasons for it in pure competition analysis. I find it sensible to think of managerial organization in terms of the utilization of managerial techniques varying with the scale of the business, but each being successively applicable over an increasingly large range of scale. Even if we assume that difficulties of management cause a net rise in costs between successive management scales, I cannot see why costs should rise on this account over any such one range of scale. Within any such range, accordingly, I think that the weight of technical costs must make for decreasing costs as a whole.

Leaving this difficult matter of the actual behaviour of long-run costs, when we come to pricing theory and are thinking in terms of the growth of a business by normal increments, then the relevant question is how the business man will expect his costs to behave. I argue that he will expect, given time to make necessary adjustments, not to be less efficient in his organization. Therefore, our pricing theory should postulate a falling long-run average cost curve because of the influence of technical factors. We may expect that such a curve will fall more steeply for increases from a relatively small scale, than it will for increases from a relatively much larger scale. The curve of long-run costs in our model may, therefore, be drawn as falling even more gently. In the limit, it may be taken as approximately constant, but long before that point we should remember the everyday importance of chance factors in the actual level of costs, so that, against that background of uncertainty, costs may be taken as constant. For an established industry in stable conditions, I postulate that all businesses will be beyond the scale of output for their particular products at which their costs would show a marked fall for a moderate increase in scale. (This proposition, of course, has welfare implications, which I have no time to go into now, but which you may care to take up in discussion.)

Our business man, accordingly, will have no cost deterrent to increasing his scale to meet any permanent increase in demand but, equally, for any likely increase in demand he will not expect a substantial fall in his costs.

Given plant etc., average direct costs may be taken as constant. Average total short-period costs may well fall markedly for rises in output up to the limit of practical capacity, but at the extreme end of the range of output they will be below the costs at which such an output could be sustained in the long run — so that for a sustained increase in demand it would pay to extend capacity.

It will be seen that our model postulates no fine marginal balance, except in so far as the business will be doing the best it can, if it meets whatever demand comes its way to the limit of its capacity. Given the cost situation, the individual business of our model will be far from restricting sales in the interest of maximum profits. It will maximize its profits if it keeps price at the level dictated by external competition and produces what it can sell.

This model, then, reproduces a good many features of reality, but before we can understand the precise origin of the price determining competition postulated in the price line, we must leave this simple model. We must recognize two things — that businesses are not single product; and that products, in fact, are not the static things we have taken them to be, but vary in specification even for a single business, and within the limits of its historical market.

In our model, the chief problem of the business man is to estimate the price at which he can sell his product. In a completely static state we might imagine him inferring that directly from experience. To make our model fit the actual world, however, with varying product specifications and with multi-product outputs being normal, it is convenient to see the business man's estimates in terms of the estimated average direct costs of a product, and the margin which he proposes to add in order to get his quoted price — the gross profit margin, already mentioned. Since his direct costs will be given quantities, given the specifications, his pricing problem is to estimate the gross margin which it is safe for him to charge, revising his estimates downwards if he is forced to do so in order to meet competition. He will try to avoid such revisions, because since preferences cut both ways, the lost goodwill may be difficult to recapture.

The costing margins are therefore determined by estimates of potential competition. Now such potential competition may come at any time from businesses with suitable equipment. We have already seen that the cost side will entail no internal obstacle to expansion. It follows that a business will always find it profitable to take on products which it can produce and sell at a price likely to be profitable in the long run.

Here we have to depart from our strict single product model — however narrowly we define our product from the point of view of its marketing there will always be at least a bundle of products sold for the same sort of purpose, and having some close substitution relationships for some uses at all events. For instance, to take rayon — a very standardized product — it would be no good a business offering only 150 denier rayon. Its customers will be wanting several counts of rayon and even with maximum specialization it could not offer a low enough price on 150 denier to induce its customers to acquiesce in the inconvenience of dividing their orders in so extreme a fashion. Besides, considerations of long-run profitability will induce a business to be at least as wide in its product as I am imagining at the moment — there is always a shifting balance of demand, and the business must be able to take advantage rather than lose by it.

Of course we should imagine a typical business as specializing in some part of its range of products, but we must not imagine it as averse to widening the range for the sake of future prospects. We may postulate, therefore, that a business man will try to enter the market for any product whose price seems sufficiently attractive to him — and although he may justify his decisions by more elaborate calculations, the first signal of attraction may be seen in terms of the gross profit margin which it offers, in comparison with similar products. More elaborate calculations will simply allow for the special indirect costs involved by the product.

In a complex industry, then, all businesses may be producing a wide variety of products strictly defined. Each will adopt a pricing policy designed to keep its market in those products. The price which it can maintain will be determined by the competition of others — not only the competition of actual competitors but also by the threat of potential competition from businesses at present producing something else, but who would be tempted to have a lot of its products if its price got out of line.

In an industry, then, where markets are freely open to competition, we may postulate normal price relationships between the prices of the various products stemming from the processes whose existence constitute our definitions of an industry. Such price relationships will be interpreted by producers in terms of normal differences in the gross profit margin. When prices are at such levels they will tend to be stable, given the levels of factor prices and subject to the absence of abnormal circumstances such as I shall mention in a moment.

For any one product, these normal price relationships certainly do not entail that all businesses cover all their costs and make satisfactory products in the case of every product which they make. There is no full-cost theory. It will be quite normal for any business to have a proportion of products which, for long-run reasons or because of the nature of its market, it wishes to keep offering, but which are not its specialities. In these cases the normal costs determining price must be those of other businesses, and by-producers may well make costing losses.

Also in the case of new businesses, if the long-run conditions seem attractive, these may well be making losses, not only over fringe products, but over the whole of their output. So long as others would take a similar view, or so long as more efficient businesses are already in the market, there will be no scope for prices being high enough to cover the costs of such businesses, and we may well have stable market conditions without all businesses being profitable. The chance interflow of competitive forces has the same effect. For England there is important evidence that in quite ordinary years, and for any industry, a substantial part of total output may be produced at a loss.

The price level will change if factor prices change, but will ordinarily preserve its stability. If factor prices fall, then competition under the pressure of informed buyers will soon enforce a general fall of price. If they rise, then sooner or later prices will rise, since the normal costing approach to prices will make such a change seem justifiable. The rise may be delayed longer in the case of material prices than it will in the case of wage changes. The upward revision will be helped usually by the fact that general changes in factor prices occur only in conditions of strong general demand.

The price level may become unstable and subject to drastic falls if, under the influence of a general fall in demand, or, in the case of a developing industry, of the entry of an excessive number of businesses, a substantial number of businesses are making losses. As soon as a business is not covering its paying out costs, there will be the danger of its ceasing to exist for purely short-run reasons, although it may be as efficient as other businesses, who happen to have stronger reserves. In these circumstances, the price cut may very well not be expected to pay in even a moderate period, but if it offers the only chance of paying the wage bill this month and getting by for that period, a weak business may well start a general fall of price. In that case, of course, the fall of prices will hasten the elimination of the weaker businesses. Such instability is liable to happen in contract markets where, in bad times, a particular large contract may be very attractive and spell the difference between life and death to any business. This is one of the reasons for the attempt to establish price rings for such markets.

Price levels, similarly, may depart on the average from normal cost relationships in certain abnormal circumstances which involve great restriction of supply in the face of, or relatively to, a very strong demand. Thus in wartime, many consumer goods industries are drastically cut down and their capacity devoted to other things. Price controls may be imposed for essentials, but for others the market may be left more free. In these circumstances the long-run viewpoint of larger well-established businesses may well lead to their preserving normal prices. Smaller, weaker businesses, however, knowing that competitive relationships will be a long time in re-establishing themselves, since new entry is impossible, may very well charge prices which bear an abnormal relation to normal costs. My favourite example relates to the production of children's lead toys. In Britain, this market is ordinarily well supplied, and is dominated by one or two very efficient large firms offering high quality lead soldiers, animals, etc. at relatively low prices. At the end of the war, these things were attractive exports to dollar markets; so established producers who were large enough to do business in export markets were ordered to place virtually their whole output abroad. Meanwhile there was a pressing home demand which could not be met, and since lead animals can easily be made, and since small enterprises could in one way or another evade legal controls over the supply of lead, many small 'firms' came into being — in some cases even making their moulds from products previously produced by established businesses, illegal though that was. I even heard of a schoolboy who was making £5 a week at this 'hobby'.

Such supplies were sold at prices which were abnormally high, even in relation to the high costs of their producers. Of course, as soon as the established firms could get back to their markets, many of these mushroom businesses were knocked out, but I have no doubt some survived and used their profits to continue in business, either in this line or in some other! Times of high demand, then, may enable new businesses, which have no goodwill to worry about as yet, to come into a market and charge prices seriously out of line with those of others. This is one way in which it may be possible to get new businesses effectively started.

But lead animals are in danger of taking us away from our main theme of high theory! Our model still has certain serious limitations from a realistic point of view, and I want to remove these, or, at least to indicate the effect of removing them.

I shall not spend long over one limitation — that throughout we have been speaking in terms of a business quoting a price for a specified product. In some markets, the position is rather that producers have to work to a price — as with products sold to a chain store, or in the case of consumers' goods generally, where conventional prices apply. In these cases, the theory can easily be turned round to display competition working out in terms of producers having to offer a normal quality of specification at the given price. This model has the nice property that, unless the conventional or fixed prices are revised — as will happen in the case of drastic changes in the general price level — the qualities offered at the given prices will vary inversely with factor prices. In my book I have referred to the length of towels sold in fixed price markets as offering an inverse index of the trade cycle.

The previous paragraph has touched on a more serious limitation of the model — that it is still in terms of products sold to other business men, and not to the final consumer. The model which I construct for the consumers' market is influenced by the fact that, in empirical studies, I find no substantial difference between the attitudes adopted by business men selling products direct to the consumer, and those selling products falling strictly within our simpler model. When looking over the actual experience of business moreover, one is impressed by the way in which carelessness over quality for price, or price for quality, seems to bring the same penalty as it does in the simpler market — namely, the successful growth of rivals and the shrinking of the market. It is true that such a process may take longer and that a business may be able to rely for a longer period upon the protection of its goodwill, but that goodwill seems to depend upon the same factors as before, and is stronger for commodities in the consumers' market only because it takes longer to test quality and to get information about alternatives.

The chief difficulty in analysing such a case comes not from the facts but from the existence of a strong body of theory asserting that advertising may create consumers' preferences not associated with differences in quality, or which are out of line with the normal costs of providing such qualities. I personally do not accept that, for most commodities, advertising can play this magic role. I think that it can attract attention, but whether or not it will bring permanent custom depends upon quality. For most commodities I am impressed with the interchange of experience which goes on between consumers, and find that this leads me to suppose a quality-regarding demand which is consistent with the facts of these markets as I have seen them.

In order to get my theory considered seriously, I have chosen to attack the theory of advertising at its strongest point — the case of commodities such as drugs or medicines, where it may be alleged that preferences may be induced and that these will relate to imagined qualities of the products rather than to any real ones. All right. Let us accept, for a moment, that such selling expenditures do create preferences. Then I hold that normal theory is not justified in treating such preferences as stable and as giving the settled particular demand curves it chooses to imagine. For what one advertiser has done another can do. It follows that the particular demand curve obtained by advertising will be unstable and that such cases should be analysed on the lines of oligopolies — with no determinate solution. I am encouraged in these views to find that, in such cases, producers adopt a severe conventional limit to their advertising expenditure, or even on occasion reach agreements with their competitors.

Coming to more normal commodities, it seems to me preferable, whilst recognizing the attractive force of advertising, to see its normal function as enabling the real competitiveness of industry to be increased. Thus advertising enables manufacturers to compete directly in the consumers' markets with retailers for the goodwill of the consumer, and in relation to those markets I analyse advertising costs also in terms of normal costs.

For producers making consumers' goods, then, my model remains in terms of normal costs, with realistic reservations concerning the instability which

216

advertising expenditure may lead to in the short run. So far from seeing advertising as adding to normal costs in total, I see it as reducing normal costs through enabling producers to be larger in scale in those cases where their increase in scale enables them to offer sufficient quality or price advantages *vis-a-vis* products sold as retailers' brands.

I shall not now go into the arguments which I have put up, in consequence of the above reasoning, in favour of allowing manufacturers to fix individual resale prices for their branded goods.

Nor shall I have time to go into the attack which I have been led to make upon the monopolistic competition approach to retail trade. I have, so far, confined that attack to certain features of retail trade which have been themselves attacked or naively explained on the basis of the theory of monopoly — namely conventional prices, fixed prices, and fixed margins for each type of retail outlet.

Finally, and looking back over my theory as a whole, there are two topics which I should like to refer to briefly. One is the question of cartels. I have made some study of these and am going to embark upon some intensive research into them. Already I have come to the conclusion that we approach these too naively in terms of static theory — for instance the general opinion that such cartels will have to fix their prices so as to cover the costs of the less efficient businesses. I have found the tendency to go in the opposite direction for cartels which have survived, and suspect that when I study cartels which have broken down, or successful cartels which have broken down in the past, I shall find that the cause of their breakdown was precisely that they followed the price policy economists tend to assume. In which case they suffered from the strain of the desire to expand, of the more efficient businesses within the cartel — as a published case of such a cartel I recommend Mr. Marlio's study of the Aluminium Cartel. I find it significant that the British Steel industry, when it came under a regime of government administered prices, after its long experience of not very successful cartels, developed a pricing basis which related to the average of all costs and so penalized the less efficient producer of any particular product. You will find details of this in the book by Miss Brunner and myself. Apart from these internal strains, a cartel which ignores cost positions or in which existing producers have tended to become less efficient will suffer from outside competition. I may give two examples, both involving really small but specialist producers in sections of the electrical engineering industry dominated by large businesses. In the one case, small electric motors, there was an attempt after the first War to form a price ring which included virtually all the principal producers. A small business outside the ring found that at ring prices it could do quite well, so set a price which was below ring price. In consequence it grew, extended its range of products and became more efficient. As it grew it pressed home the advantage of its falling costs until eventually it became as efficient in

217

its line as any member of the ring. It never joined the ring but, in the end, the ring had to set its prices in relation to the costs of this smaller business, since those determined the price which the latter quoted. Similarly, in the case of a certain type of switch-gear, I have found a small business which regularly set the price for the apparently strong ring around the market for its products.

On this view of cartels, we can take a much more optimistic way of how to deal with them — remove all obstacles to other businesses competing — i.e. prohibit tying clauses — and insist on having made public the maximum information about costs and profits by individual products in ring dominated industries. Then, I think we can leave competition to do its work more effectively than any regulation or simple prohibition.

The last question I want to refer to is that of patents — patents are intended to give a monopoly and of course they do so for the life of the patent, subject to one important condition — that in every country patent law is difficult and many patents, when actually tested in the courts, are invalid. It is, however, expensive to test a patent in this way — by infringing it and incurring an action for damages. If, however, the gross margin of the patentee is too high, examples seem to show that businesses will risk prosecution. An example from England is the case of the ball-bearing fountain pen. This was originally protected by world patents and sold in 1945–7 at a really fancy price. Before long, other producers were offering admittedly inferior products, but at sensationally low prices, and at least half a dozen businesses got firmly established. The patent owners started suits for infringement but, in the end, had to compromise, I understand, and issued reasonable licences, and now the ball-pen market is served by products at very reasonable prices, and that long before the expiry of the patent.

I have taken this extreme case to show the pervasiveness (even in very unlikely cases) of competition based upon costs of production in relation to prices. In conclusion, let me say that I am aware that I have covered a good deal of ground in a very short space. It seemed to me desirable, however, to give you the simple model with its admittedly great realistic relevance, so that you could see how my theory differs in essence from the usual approach to manufacturing prices, and then rapidly to indicate how one might break the model down so as to extend its realistic application, and in such a way that you might catch a glimpse of my own approach to business, of which my theory is a by-product. On that I want to make one last methodological observation. I have been very much impressed by the way in which traditional theory has tended to stultify empirical research, in the field in which I am most interested. Even if the theory were right, this might have happened, in so far as it provided the student with rigid models, not set out in terms which would be recognizable when he worked inside a business. I have deliberately avoided too much model building, except of the simplest kind. I have tried hard to leave my theoretical work with the fuzzy edge which belongs to reality — in the sense that, within the simple models which I have constructed, I try always to analyse in realistic manner, and with qualifications and examples given as soon as they become relevant. Arguments with my colleagues are leading me to set out my models in starker terms than I think desirable if I am to keep my theory broadly correct, and so make it easier for it to be corrected and amplified by later empirical research. My chief aim is, and must be, to encourage such research as much as I can — and if I can throw out hints of what direction I think we have to move in, I should say that attention should be paid to the factor markets, especially the labour market, also to capital investment, and perhaps the detailed study of all ordinary business situations which we tend to regard as overt cases of monopoly — such for example as cartels.

Appendix: letters on the marginalist controversy[2]

From ROY HARROD, *26 October 1950*

Dear Philip,
   This is just to warn you that my co-editor has paid you the compliment of reviewing your book at the length of 10 pages. The substance of it is thoroughly critical, claiming that you are expert in practices and stats, but don't really traverse the theory of imperfect competition.[3]
   He pays some tributes to your work and I think I may say that the whole is written without any asperity. Indeed it is couched in language which is quite honourable as regards yourself — tho' he won't have your doctrines. Anyhow its length exceeds greatly what we normally allow! I may say that I have no hand in the allocation of reviews. My colleague deals with that end, and I don't like interfering. But I don't think I could have improved on his choice of reviewer, since criticism is good and a good-mannered critic is the ideal reviewer.

Yours,

ROY [HARROD]

---

(2) Reprinted from the P.W.S. Andrews Papers, London School of Economics, Lomdon. Reprint permissions for individual letters are listed in the Acknowledgements at the start of this book.
   (3) Editors' note: Harrod is referring to E.A.G. Robinson (1950) 'The pricing of manufactured products', *Economic Journal* **60**, pp. 771–80.

To E.H. CHAMBERLIN, *14 February 1952*

Dear Professor Chamberlin,

Thank you for your letter and for the three reprints which have now come to hand. I do intend to get down to the matters between us, and look forward to a friendly discussion with you. As I think I told you, I have on the stocks a book on the development of imperfect competition theories in England, and on Marshallian theory. This is in an advanced state and I have lectured on it twice, but have had to put it by for the moment. All my remarks there about monopolistic competition might give me a chance of making the sort of statement which you will agree is fair to you. At the moment, however, the publication of the Steel book by Miss Brunner and myself, has led to our being inundated with extra work and obligations, so that it is difficult otherwise to do more than keep routine duties going. In addition I have to get ready for an important course of lectures which I am giving in Holland in May, and also for a 'battle royal' kind of seminar which Miss Brunner and I are giving in Wales. Next, behind these priorities, comes an attempt I am making to salvage an important piece of research work done by someone else on a large British business. The person in question has been rather tactless; the business has been rather brusque, and it will need a lot of work on my part to ensure that the interesting book which is there can be freely written and published. So if I am silent for a while you will know that it does not imply neglect.

I think I ought to say that I think you are in danger of misunderstanding some of my remarks, because their social context is not so clear to you as it would be to someone working in this country. For example, I think everyone here would know that my attack on 'monopolistic competition' so far as retail trade goes, is an attack on the work of Mrs. Hall in particular, and also people like Henry Smith. Further, it is dangerous for you, I think, to take very simplified models of my theory put forward in summary form, so as to deal with a particular point of issue, as with the retail trade article and my article in *Oxford Studies in the Price Mechanism*.

At present the main body of my theory is given in *Manufacturing Business*, and some further developments are contained in our Steel book. Had you read these I think you would not find it so simple to say that my theories are simply special cases of your monopolistic competition. Falling cost curves — and the rejection of the U-shaped cost curve — together with the relationship between long-run cost and demand curves for the individual business, play a key part in my theory, which is quite different from the part that similar constructions play in atomistic equilibrium of a traditional kind. However, I shall be coming back to all this as soon as I can, and, meanwhile, thank you very much for your courtesy.

Yours sincerely,

PHILIP ANDREWS

To RICHARD KAHN, *2 April 1952*

Dear Professor Kahn,

Thank you very much for your courtesy in sending me an offprint of your *Economic Journal* article on *Oxford Studies in the Price Mechanism*. I have, of course, already read this, and although I think you completely misrepresent my own position I have much admired some aspects of your article.

I shall not be replying through the *Economic Journal* any more than I did to Professor Robinson's earlier article. I was then informed that editorial policy was to discourage controversy, but that if I insisted I might have a page or two! This would not be sufficient, since any reply, especially to Professor Robinson, whose article has such serious internal inconsistencies, must be point by point; a reply which simply dealt with one or two points would be open to serious misrepresentation — e.g. that I had 'avoided' the other points as Harrod points out. I have decided to wait until I can deal systematically with the whole 'Cambridge' position, in the light of the development of indigenous theories. Meanwhile, I know that some other articles are being published elsewhere which will make my general position with respect to Robinson and yourself clear — I, of course, am not one of the authors concerned.

So far as your own review is concerned, I shall now comment only on your treatment of my pricing theories. My chief complaint is that you treat me as a 'full-costite', with absolutely no authority. The principle of full-cost pricing which the Research Group put forward must be sharply distinguished from the methods of price fixing (namely various methods which can all be interpreted theoretically, given my conclusions about the behaviours of costs and demands, as the fixing of an average gross profit margin to be added to average direct costs) which the Group reported. There is no reason whatever why any individual firm should be able to get a price which covers its 'full' costs, whatever that means. I regret this misleading interpretation of the principle for which its name is responsible; I regret even more the principle itself which must mean that a business determines its own price — i.e. perpetuate the fallacy of atomistic equilibrium. We all, I think accepted this at the time. The introduction by Hall and Hitch of the kinked demand curve prevented us from finding the inconsistencies in our position. My own position now is quite distinct and it is not simply a desire to differentiate my product which has led me to argue in terms of a 'normal' cost principle.

I could wish to have had more of your reactions to my interpretation of Marshall *qua* Marshall.

Sincerely,

PHILIP ANDREWS

From RICHARD KAHN, *16 April 1952*

Dear Andrews,

I am very grateful to you for your kindly letter of the 2nd April. — Absence abroad has prevented me from replying earlier. I am very glad to hear that you intend to deal systematically with the whole question, and I very much look forward to seeing your treatment. It is kind of you to arrange for other contributions to be sent to me.

I would repeat my plea that you should make public use of some of your factual investigations, i.e. give the public some idea of the factual basis of your conclusions.

On the point on which you challenge me — that I treat you as a 'full-costite' — need I do more than remind you of the quotation from you which appears at the top of page 120 of my article? — though I am quite sure that I could find many other similar quotations from your works. I am, however, very glad to learn that I have misinterpreted you.

On the question of the disturbance introduced by Hall and Hitch by the use of the kinked demand curve, I wonder whether you have ever considered my own much more tentative reference to these on pp. 8 and 9 of my Duopoly article (*Economic Journal*, March 1937).

Yours sincerely,

R. F. KAHN

To RICHARD KAHN, *2 May 1952*

Dear Kahn,

I am sorry not to have acknowledged your (unsigned) letter of 16th April, before this, but I am shortly going abroad and have had a lot to get through first.

As regards your plea that I should make public the factual basis of my conclusions, I regard as 'facts' not statistics alone, but facts of situation, and behaviour in a given situation, and *Manufacturing Business*, although a designedly theoretical book, contains such facts. To illustrate what I mean, I have been much amused by the comments of business men who have seen themselves in its pages, even where I have never investigated their business.

I do not think you know enough about my methods of research. In effect, if I investigate a business, I spend a considerable time in it, keep nearly verbatim records of conversations with many different persons in the business, take transcripts of documents etc. This evidence is not publishable in itself — indeed, I undertake not to show to one man what a colleague has said, even within the same business. What I hope to do is to publish a series of studies which incorporate the results of these investigations — which have been both on an 'industry' basis and into particular businesses in a wide range of industry (all sorts of engineering, some sections of the chemical industry, textiles etc.). In a bowdlerized form a good deal of my general conclusions from my researches are tucked away in *Manufacturing Business*. That book was intended to give an account of the general theoretical attitude to business which I have developed on the basis of my experience, and to give it in such a form that anyone who is acquainted with business life can refer it to situations which he himself knows. On that basis, I have no reason to complain of its reception.

On the question of being a full-costite, the quotation to which you refer me at the top of p. 120 of your article, provides a clear example of how you misinterpret my position. You will note that what I say is that business men appeared to adhere firmly to this method of pricing, i.e. the average-cost method. I do not say that they adhere firmly to a price which covers their full costs. The wording of the first part of the quotation--that a general method was to add a margin as for net profit to average short-run costs--might have warned you of your misunderstanding. See, again, p. 164 of my chapter in *Oxford Studies in the Price Mechanism* (p. 149 in this book), and the whole section in *Manufacturing Business*, pp. 163-180. I cannot think why this misunderstanding should have arisen, since I have, as I hope you will now realize, tried to be very careful about my choice of language.

I have, of course, read your interesting article on Duopoly in the *Economic Journal*. I agree that you forestalled Hall and Hitch in some ways. So too did Chamberlin. My own interest in Hall and Hitch remains in the business practices which they reported and in the theoretical ideas which were implied in the business men's attitude.

Yours sincerely,

PWSA

To HAROLD MACMILLAN, *29 May 1952*

Dear Mr. Macmillan,

I have been intending to write to you since my return from Holland, but am only just catching up with arrears of work. I thought that you would be interested to know how I found the situation there.

I had a very busy time, in fact I discovered that I had to give twice as many lectures as I had reckoned on. However, fortunately, I took my portable typewriter and was able to start work at a sufficiently early hour in the morning.

The controversy over marginal theory in Holland has come up quite independently of my work. As you will probably know, most of their economists have strong connections with the practical problems of industry — nearly everyone of standing has some consulting appointment, they therefore have got used, when acting as practical economists, to thinking of pricing in terms of costs. It sounds as though for some time, the leading spirits amongst them have been wishing to teach price theory in these practical terms, but the one or two really pure-pure theorists have seen this as the thin edge of the wedge in the war against marginalism, going on in this country and in America, and have been objecting.

The conference, with which my visit terminated, was largely concerned with the humdrum question as to whether or no economists of a practical bent could be permitted to describe pricing theory in average cost terms. My work has thrown a fairly large-size cat amongst some plump, but middle-aged pigeons, since the Dutch are beginning to realize that I am opening a much more fundamental question: however we describe pricing practice, is it correct to retain a fundamental marginal theory? I had some very lively discussions, and am well pleased with my impact on young Dutch economists. I am quite sure that if the practical men carry on as they intended, their younger men will insist on a more consistent fundamental theory.

I need not tell you, since you know the Dutch, how enjoyable the personal aspect of my stay was. I was able to work really strenuously and keep really fit on a high protein diet, with occasional relaxation in very friendly surroundings.

I have one other piece of news for you; I am founding a new *Journal of Industrial Economics*, which should provide a very good vehicle for work in my field, especially for the writings of economists engaged in industry. Blackwell's will be the publishers, but it is to be an Anglo-American Journal, and my editorial board consists of:

Edward Mason	Professor in, and Dean of the Faculty of Economics, Harvard.
Prof. R.B. Heflebower	Professor of Northwestern University.
Joel Dean	Now on leave from a Chair at Columbia and a very successful economic consultant.

These are my American colleagues; my English colleagues are:

John Jewkes, and

Sir Henry Clay.

Mason is the doyen of American economists interested in industry, and Joel

Dean ranks very closely after him. You will be interested to know that in accepting my invitation without any hesitation, it was made perfectly clear that these American economists were prepared to do so because of respect for my work, and particularly for *Manufacturing Business*.

The condition on which I send you a chatty news-letter of this kind occasionally, is that you do not bother to reply.

With kind regards,
Yours sincerely,

PWSA

To R.B. HEFLEBOWER, *30 June 1952*

Dear Professor Heflebower,

Thank you for your letter. I am glad that Professor Mason and you had the chance of talking to Mr. Hamilton, and that you have been able to make practical recommendations to him. Thank you also for approaching some of your contacts in industry for articles. I expect that for the first number or two, we shall be unduly weighted with English articles, but no doubt this will more than redress itself. However, in my introductory article I shall refer to our intention of being a genuinely Anglo-American Journal, or, indeed, an international journal in the end. From the interest which the news of our *Journal* roused in Holland, when I was lecturing there in May, I should say that we should have quite a number of interesting contributions from there. As you will know, the position in Holland is very much more like the position in the United States than ourselves; at least half of the senior teaching economists have strong connections with industry, and there are many more economists in industry there as economists.

No, I do not think you had told me that you were giving a paper on 'Full-Cost Principles' to the National Bureau Conference, and I shall be very interested to see your article when it is ready. Your last sentence intrigues me. I had hoped that you did not regard me as a full-cost theorist; I am not, but the articles by Robinson and Kahn in the *Economic Journal* have done much to make people read me in this way. I am annoyed about those articles on more grounds than this, and should have liked to do a full scale reply. However, it is not possible for me to reply at all because the editors, wishing to avoid their *Journal* being given up to a controversy, will only allow me a short note of a page or two and, as Roy Harrod himself said, it was hardly worth my while replying on this basis since, if I gave a thorough reply to one or two points — which would be all I could do — then I should be exposed to the suspicion that I had avoided others because I had no answer. I shall myself deal with Robinson fully, and I hope justly, in my book on Marshall. Miss Brunner, my colleague here and former pupil has written what I think to be a very good article, which is to be published in *Economia Internazionale*, in August and November of this year. (It is a pity that they had to split it because the thing is written as a closely interlocking whole.)

I understand a 'full-cost theory' to be one which would assert that prices tend to cover the full average costs of businesses established in a particular market. Hall and Hitch asserted no such theory. In fact, the first part of their famous report from the Research Group, which incorporates their own theorizing, leaves the level of price indeterminate. The full-cost *price* as they report, and certainly as it interests the Research Group, simply reports formally the price which we find established among business men — that for an efficient business prices *ought* to cover the full average costs of the products concerned, plus 'a reasonable margin of profit'. This discussion of the price, together with Hall and Hitch's kinked demand curve theorizing, has rather, to my mind, obscured the main results of the pre-war Oxford inquiry which was the prevalence of an average cost system of pricing and the absence of explicit reference, or, so far as we could judge, implicit reference to particular elasticities of demand. My own theory should rather be seen as taking this practice of average cost pricing, provide an explanation of why it is reasonable, in which the behaviour of costs plays an important part, and then give a theory of the stable price system which will emerge under the influences of competition in an established manufacturing industry; integrated with it is the beginning of a theory of instability, i.e. the conditions in which the stable price set-up will breakdown. For an established industry this is seen as a short-run problem largely due to the uncovering of paying-out costs, but there is also involved a theory of the instability of prices in an industry whilst it is being established, or in an established industry which has become exposed to technical change. This last involves theorizing based upon the shapes of static cost-curves. How clear or interesting this bald statement will be to you I do not know, but I may, perhaps, mention the other element in my theories which interest me, and that is what I have called in later work the theory of the complementarity of competitive firms in an established but settled industry, which takes the form of the competitive survival of small businesses along side the larger mass-production firms which can fully exploit the economies of scale.

I think you will realize that these few remarks of mine are really thrown out at random, since your last sentence was necessarily elliptic. I shall look forward to seeing your paper, and shall see that you get an early copy of Miss Brunner's paper when it becomes available. I am annoyed with *Economia Internazionale* because they promised her publication for May, otherwise we should certainly have taken it for *Oxford Economic Papers*. I was reluctant, however, since the papers were largely written as the result of an invitation from the Italian journal, although I should have liked to have seen them kept together with other articles of their kind.

I shall be sending the Minutes of our Board of Editors meeting about next week — I hope. You will see that we were largely concerned with routine matters, although we did discuss in what way we could facilitate the early development of joint control from our American colleagues; as you know I am keen that this should be so.

I told Sir Henry Clay and Professor Jewkes of the correspondence I have been having, and they were gratified at the friendly interest which you have been taking.

With very kind regards,
Yours sincerely,

PWSA

From R.B. HEFLEBOWER, *9 December 1952*

Dear Mr. Andrews,

Enclosed is a copy of my paper on 'Full costs, cost changes, and prices'. Other copies have gone to George Stigler, the editor of the proceedings volume, and to critics whom you will be interested to know include Mr. Coase.

As you will note I have expanded the title of the paper to indicate that it covers ideas of price-making other than those termed 'full-cost'. I hope I have made an accurate interpretation of your views and appraisal of their significance. I shall look forward to your comments.

Sincerely yours,

R.B. HEFLEBOWER

To R.B. HEFLEBOWER, *1 January 1953*

Dear Professor Heflebower,

Thank you for sending me a copy of your paper on Full Costs, etc. I am afraid that this has reached me while I am in the middle of finishing an urgent article for *The Manchester Guardian*. I have, therefore, not had time to read it; all I have done is turn the pages, so far. I hope to be able to get down to it by Wednesday or Thursday of next week.

May I refer to one minor point in passing? I did just notice the reference to the Saxton studies on page 35.(4) Very privately, I should be glad if you would not couple my name with Saxton's work in any way whatever. I know nothing more about his evidence than that which he gives in his book, and dislike the manner in which he obtained it and his handling of it. The Research Group's Studies, to give the Hall and Hitch researches their proper attribution, were, of course, part of my prewar background, but I do not think that it would have been possible for me to have reached my present theories on the basis of the Research Group's work. We did not go into enough detail then and were too bemused by full-costs. The basis of my work consists of a large number of studies of individual businesses, including those involved in the large scale industrial studies of the British rayon, and boot and shoe industries. Here my method has been to stay with a firm for some time, to have right of access to any documents of whose existence I know and which I think would be interesting, and to have the right of access to any member of the business for private interview, with freedom to refuse to disclose to one member of a business what another has told me. My theories of price were thus reached as a result of a good deal of interrogation about price formation and changes, in the course of my general researches into the efficiency of businesses, and allied problems. However, I won't go into this now, but I do not wish to be coupled with Saxton, and I do think that I owe it to those who have financed my own researches to indicate the independence of my own background and methods from those of the Research Group. My sincere acknowledgement to the Group as an important factor in my experience has sometimes, I fear, been misunderstood.

In view of the date, I should have started this letter with that with which I shall conclude it! My most sincere good wishes for the New Year. I shall try to write to you a proper letter about your article some time next week.

Yours ever,

PWSA

To R.B. HEFLEBOWER, *16 January 1953*

Dear Professor Heflebower,

I am sorry it has taken me so long to get down to reading your article on Full-Costs, Cost Changes, and Prices. I have managed to give it one careful reading now, but term is upon us and I have had no time to do what it deserves, namely, use it as a springboard for an independent discussion, which is always the best way of showing an author what one has got from his work. My general

---

(4) Editors' note: the reference is to C.C. Saxton (1942) *The Economics of Price Determination*, Oxford, Oxford University Press.

impression is that it is a good and very interesting article. I am grateful for the effort which you have made to represent my stuff fairly and, in particularly, that you should, at critical points, call attention to my objection to being classified as a full-cost theorist, and the chief ground for that. At the same time, I think that some of your difficulties with me arise because you are necessarily looking at me against a full-cost background, and so it is difficult to maintain the continuous distinction which I think my theory calls for. What I think I will do in the first part of this letter is just go through the odd notes which I scribbled down as I read. They are, necessarily, more concerned with the first half of the paper than with the second, although I should have liked to have commented especially on the second part, if I had been able to think again and write more fully.

I will not go over the points I made in my previous letter. On pages 1–2, there is a cognate point — your references to Hall's and Hitch's 'questioning' etc. I do not know why there has been so much misunderstanding about the Research Group's work, but Harrod is trying to clear it up in his Introduction to his file of reprinted Essays.

On Page 17 you refer to Hall and Hitch's evidence. The evidence was the Research Group's, and was obtained by general probing. Members of the Research Group included practically every economist of any standing at Oxford — Sir Hubert Henderson, R.F. Harrod, C.J. Hitch, James Meade, Redvers Opie, Jacob Marschak, R.S. Bretherton, E.H. Phelps Brown, Eric Hargreaves, etc, and I think it is wrong to regard Hall/Hitch's evidence as unprobed or unchecked. What you have to distinguish carefully is the evidence as set out in the Hall/Hitch Paper and the enunciation of the Full-Cost Principle which we all thought we had found.

One general point — I think in our discussion of Full-Cost there is a danger of confusing two things: (a) the practice of basing prices on some sort of calculation of average costs, and (b) the explanation which may be offered of that practice. Full-Cost is simply one explanation. Mine runs in terms of a gross profit margin formed by competition. I shall take up later the points that it is not so much demand determined in the ordinary sense, it is determined by the demand for the full products of this business, but such a particular demand is simply a reflection of the costs of other businesses, and derives immediately from the prices at which they would produce and sell.

To some extent it is a great pity that you have to discuss all the 'Full-Cost' pricing theories together. I think it does prevent me from being precise about the theoretical set-up which any one theorist is constructing. Re. page 3, I don't agree with Sweezy that it is of questionable value to mix the analysis of the level of equilibrium price and the conditions of change of prices. He only thinks so because he is too static a man; he is trying rigidly to work out oligopolistic analysis with static tools in the real world. The articles which a business is producing have frequently changed specifications, and the fundamental basic cost conditions are also subject to change (e.g. in wage rates, cost of raw materials etc.) and any theory which explains why and how prices will change in these conditions is also, necessarily, a theory of the equilibrium of price if conditions were not changed.

Pages 5–6: I think it is misleading, despite your explanation, to say that Full-Cost pricing is a short-term price theory — at least it is not misleading for many of the authors which you are discussing, but it is extremely misleading so far as I am concerned, and whilst I am not a Full-Cost theorist, still you are discussing me in this context. Many theories are long-run in the ordinary technical sense and yield a theory of short-term price only if what I call 'stability conditions' are satisfied, and for this there is an underlying theory of the structural development of an industry; so that the industry itself has to have developed, so that most substantial internal economies of scale, etc., have been realized, and demand may not have had a drastic fall from a hither consistent higher level. It is through that, to my mind, my theory does provide the best explanation I could find of actual prices, and of the changes in these, as underlying (short-term) changes in basic cost factors took place. But the essence of my theory is to call attention to the way long-run or normal factors influence short-term prices.

Page 7: I do not regard my incorporation of demand influences as hedging. It is, I think, for Hall and Hitch, for they are preaching full-cost, i.e. full coverage of the individual firm's costs as the basic principle underlying prices. With me the costs of competing businesses are much more crucial, and these necessarily influence the individual business through its demand side; to that extent demand influences are basic to my theories.

Page 8, line 4: I rather *hold* that there is no reason why the gross margin should equal the 'remaining cost of handling the product', so far as any individual firm is concerned.

By the way, I am not sure that you represent my theory correctly in another way. In itself it is a theory of equilibrium of the whole of price. In view of the consistency of direct costs and in view of their influence on the analysis, it is natural for a manufacturer to find his price by calculating the gross profit margin; to this extent it is an integral part of my theorizing that average direct costs are constant in given conditions.

Page 8, bottom; page 9, top: So far as I am concerned, I represent the firm in this way, not because it is a monopolist but because in a settled industry specialities are so important. (This is not monopoly because other businesses could produce these specialities, etc., etc.)

Page 12: I may be wrong, but I have thought that my own discussion of the behaviour of costs was more substantial than most discussions to which you have referred. It is based upon a very considerable experience of business, and I would have thought that the way I handled costs analysis is crucial for an understanding of my theories. I am not suggesting that it would have been relevant for you to have gone into my work here. I am merely putting up a caveat.

Around pages 13–14, I was several times reminded of the point of my distinguishing concept of 'extraordinary costs'. Leaving out that class of costs I can say that in my experience, any non-linearity in actual direct cost curves is small in relation to sheer chance variations in those costs, so does not appear — if it exists at all, I would have given theoretical reasons why it should not exist in the analytical circumstances I presume.

Page 16: I think wartime experience slightly misleads us about business men's attitudes to mark up prices. The rule of thumb which they would use as a first approach to presenting a new commodity would equally be modified by competition, as I explained it, in the actual world, but in wartime conditions it gets crystallized into the fairest way of settling prices, granted that these are to be administratively settled, and competitive conditions cannot arise in that way. It suits the administrator because it is the way to hold prices *down*: the business man accepts it because it conforms to his general philosophy, because there could only be administrative reasons for his not doing so, hence the rigidity of attitudes.

Page 17: I have already commented on what I regard as a misrepresentation of the Hall/Hitch evidence as a whole. Kahn has recently tried to give these a new lease of life. I should go on to say that my own theories certainly arose from what you call 'full blown' studies of particular industries. It is therefore significant, according to your analysis, that I am not a Full-Cost theorist, and I should have thought that my position might have been distinguished a little more in terms of your own thesis. My own theories are not based upon questionnaires or simple interviews of that kind, but are based upon attempts to steep myself in particular industries and, in particular, in trying to understand the markets involved — not simply at one time, but against as much as I can get of the experience of a business over its past. Not only are my withers unwrung by the sort of comments on pages 19/20, but I feel that this is a justification of my type of research work.

Page 27: I do not know whether you saw my discussion of retail trade, which was deliberately restricted to some very narrow questions, which had been put to me by politicians, and about which I felt I could say something: *Oxford Economic Papers*, June 1950; and the subsequent controversy with Margaret Hall and Professor Efoymson, *Oxford Economic Papers*, October, 1951.

Page 36: I have already commented that horizontal average direct costs are an integral part of my theories.

Page 38: I think that we mislead ourselves when we carry over ideas of excess capacity, which are derived from the theoretical discussions of the 1920s and 1930s. The reserve capacity, as it exists in the actual world as I see it, which is planned, would not be there continuously, but can only be there if the reserve is called upon for a short period or intermittently. There is also the point that in an established industry, the fall of costs for any likely expansion of output is small in relation to the uncertainties involved. I am not sure that the reference to the inconsistencies of such conduct with longer-term objectives of the firm is not slightly misleading, against my discussion at all events, but I do not think this is an important point in your context.

Page 40: end of the first paragraph: I should like to say that it is rather difficult to disentangle causes of price changes where there are both changes in factor prices and widespread demand changes. Around correction of these, of course, rigid conditions must affect general changes of price. In any discussion of independent demand changes, I think a good deal of reference will have to be made to the underlying stability conditions, as I define them.

Well, I am sorry to offer you these notes in this scrappy and terse, uncoordinated form. It is a poor return for your courtesy in sending me the draft of your chapter. I do hope you will not regard the reference to my own work as a sign that I am developing the neurosis which you, as well as I, must have found in an eminent contemporary. I cannot help making personal references here since you are concerned with my theories, but in general I do not like this sort of detailed discussion of my own work; I would rather sooner spend the time getting on and doing new work.

To revert to another matter, I have not yet received any articles from your side, although I have had a letter from Mr. W.W. Cooper, of the Carnegie Institute of Technology, in which he said that you had told him that you have sent on his manuscript. At all events, he wrote about the question of reprints; I think we can meet him all right.

With kind regards,
Yours sincerely,

PWSA

6 Some aspects of competition in retail trade[1]

1 Introduction

Most economists would agree that, in some sense or another, modern retailing is a competitive industry. At the same time we have come to stress the extent to which the force of its competition is mitigated by what are regarded as elements of monopoly. In fact, the recognition of these 'monopolistic' factors in the sale of consumers' goods has been largely responsible for the ease with which the modern theory of monopolistic competition has come to be taken as applicable not only to retail trade but to business in general.[2] I have argued elsewhere that, so far as manufacturing industry is concerned, some of the important implications of that theory are false (e.g. the restrictive determination of outputs by reference to marginal revenues and costs), and that some of its basic assumptions are incorrect (e.g. those concerning the shape of the cost-curves, and the way in which differentiation of the market works). In this paper I shall argue that we should also reconsider the present ready application of this body of doctrine to retail trade.

Some recent correspondence about these matters leads me to believe that it may be of interest to consider certain features of retail trade which have contributed to a widespread suspicion of the extent to which it serves the social interest. These features, which are enumerated below, are all present in the case of many branded consumers' goods and, separately or together, are to be found in other sections of retail trade:

1. *Price rigidity*. The exposition of the fundamental features of a 'purely competitive' market, especially in the elementary statements of economic doctrine which have most influenced general thinking on these matters, proceed in terms of a great flexibility of market price, in accordance with the shifting balance between demand and supply. Such flexibility is obviously

(1) Reprinted with permission from *Oxford Economic Papers* 2 (June, 1950), pp. 137–75.

(2) Before these theories appeared it had already become usual to analyse industries as if they were producing consumers' goods sold to the consumers. In England this largely originates with Marshall (see Principles, pp. 92 and 340).

absent from most sections of the retail trade in manufactured products. Further, the income of the retailer proper is obtained from a gross profit margin which remains remarkably constant (for any given section of retail trade) as a proportion of the price at which he resells these products.

2. *Resale price maintenance*. Not only are many retail prices not flexible in this sense, in many cases they are fixed by the manufacturers, and, equally, whether this is so or not, there are many cases where the retail prices of consumers' goods remain remarkably constant over fairly long periods — these last are usually referred to as cases of 'conventional prices'.

3. *Advertising*. This is of especial importance in retail trade, and may make up a substantial proportion of the costs of branded consumers' goods.

Subsequent sections of this paper will therefore discuss how far the 'higgling' of a market, or the flexibility of its price in the short run, are to be required as evidence of its competitiveness; from this we shall turn to the explanation of the inflexibility of the prices of manufactured goods and shall argue that this results from certain basic factors in manufacture and in retail trade which present no obstacle to competition; the next section will consider the question of conventional prices; the following will discuss the economics of branding and of price maintenance by manufacturers; finally, we shall ask how far advertising is a necessary cost in retail trade, rather than a waste which ought to be avoided, and how far it leads to prices which are higher than they would be in its absence.(3)

2 'Higgling' and variability of price as criteria of competition

Strictly speaking, 'higgling' refers to the chaffering between dealers and their customers which takes place in primitive and undeveloped markets — what our language used to call the 'cheapening of the market'. It is probably the sound of the word which has been responsible for it sometimes being used as applying to the short-run variability or instability of price which is a feature of some markets. We shall first consider 'higgling' in the strict sense and shall discuss the question of the variability of market price later on as a separate issue; in each

---

(3) Since I shall wish to argue as directly as possible, I shall not make detailed reference to particular theorists. The theory on which my argument is broadly based has been given in greater detail in its application to the economics of manufacture in my book *Manufacturing Business*. When I refer to the older economists, with whose general industrial analysis I am in sympathy, I am thinking especially of the neo-classical theory which culminated in Alfred Marshall's *Principles* and *Industry and Trade*. I should perhaps note that I have made a more detailed examination of Marshall's theory and of the post-Marshallian development of the theory of business in an essay which I have contributed to *Oxford Studies in the Price Mechanism*, to be published by the Clarendon Press later this year. When I refer to business behaviour, I am thinking especially of the doctrines which had their origin in the discussions in the *Economic Journal*, 1926–1933, to which many economists contributed. These resulted in Professor Chamberlin's *Monopolistic Competition* and Mrs. Joan Robinson's *Economics of Imperfect Competition*. These basic theories have been developed by Mr. Kalecki in his *Essays in the Theory of Industrial Fluctuations*, where the concept of the 'degree of monopoly' in the system has assumed great importance; and by Messrs Hall and Hitch in an article which modified the theory in order to incorporate certain features of the determination of prices in practice, which had been discovered during the research of the pre-war Oxford Economists' Research Group: 'Price Theory and Business Behaviour' (*Oxford Economic Papers* (Old Series), No. 2, 1939). A recent application of these modern theories to retail trade will be found in Mrs. Margaret Hall's *Distributive Trading*; Mr. Henry Smith's *Retail Distribution* may also be referred to. The most important study of advertising in practice will be found in *Statistical Analysis of Advertising Expenditure*, by Messrs Kaldor and Silverman. *Economics of Advertising*, by Mr. F.P. Bishop, states the viewpoint of one with considerable practical experience; this supports the theory that I have put forward. For a very recent factual study of distribution the reader is referred to Mr. Jefferys's *The Distribution of Consumer Goods*, which was published while this article was in the press.

case the question is how far 'higgling' is to be taken as a sign of the competitiveness of a market.

'Higgling' may sometimes be met with in the weekly markets of country towns, where the vendors of underwear and the like and their customers occasionally treat price as a matter to be settled between them. Bargaining here preserves some of the atmosphere of a social occasion, enjoyed with comparative leisureliness, which is still a characteristic of marketing in backward areas of the world. But it is not, and could not be, a regular feature of the selling of manufactured goods — not in an industrial country where production is on a large scale and where retail and other markets are consequently organized for the movement of relatively large quantities of products. Not only would modern business and its customers have little time for 'haggling' and 'higgling'; markets tend to organize themselves on the basis of normal price–cost–quality relationships. In these circumstances a 'higgling' market would make for higher prices because it would increase the costs of trading.

'Higgling' arises, even today, as a normal feature where the particular specimens of a commodity which are dealt in at any one time have each some aspect of uniqueness, their qualities being variable or displaying peculiarities. In such cases strictly equivalent goods come on the market rather infrequently, and such markets are essentially dealers' markets. Horse trading is, perhaps, the best (and proverbial) example of what I have in mind, but 'higgling' is also a normal method of buying and selling the more valuable classes of antiques, pictures, etc. A horse or an old master is 'worth what it will fetch' (4) and the dealer in such a commodity will try to buy it as cheaply, and to sell it as dearly, as he can. But 'higgling' does not usually operate, even in the second-hand market, for articles whose qualities and descriptions are frequently encountered. In large centres of population, at all events, where the dealers of this kind have to meet regular competition, one will find that they behave like the retailers of new goods — selling on a quoted price basis. Given the demand and supply conditions in the market, much the same price will prevail for any one type of article, and its dealers will buy and sell at prices which give them whatever gross profit margin has come to be normal. When prices change owing to changes in the fundamental conditions of the market, dealers will make abnormally low or high profits on the stocks which they already hold, but their buying prices for newly purchased articles will change with the selling price.

Competition, then, tends to make for a uniformity of price and 'higgling' should rather be taken as a sign of an uncompetitive market, or of one whose trading is not sufficiently regular for normal values to become quickly

---

(4) As a second-hand dealer first said to me when I offered *1s. 6d.* for a painting and he stuck out for *2s. 6d.*!

established.

Variability of price[5]

Apart from 'higgling', the markets we have been discussing have another characteristic which is often taken as being a sign of competition: quick variations in price levels with changes in the strengths of demand and supply. It is true that this sort of variability does exist in one sort of competitive market and that it has, apparently, developed with the increase in the competitiveness of such a market. It is, however, no more a general sign of the competitiveness of a market than is the 'higgling' of which we have been speaking.

Short-term price is very flexible in what are often referred to as the great commodity markets — those for primary commodities such as grains and crude oil — as well as those for regularly dealt-in stock exchange securities. The prices for such things are established through the competition of buyers and sellers, but are determined largely through the speculative activities of dealers who will buy or sell according to their view of the market at any given time. It does mean something to analyse such markets on the basis of normal prices, but these take time to control the market. From day to day and over short periods, price will be much more affected by temporary changes in the balance of demand and supply.

This is so because the total supply in existence of such commodities is not so quickly altered as is the case with manufactured commodities. Demand, however, is subject to considerable short-period variation, and, at different times, will press heavily on available supplies or will leave a margin of supplies not taken up. It is an important function of the 'speculative' dealer to take up any such temporary excesses and to hold stocks with which to help meet any temporary deficits of supply. The variability of market price plays its part in inducing him to perform his functions without which markets of this type could not carry on. There is, however, no reason for considering the social justification of this kind of market for the types of commodity with which it is concerned.

The essential points for us to notice are that 'goodwill' cannot arise in such a market; there is no reason for dealing with one trader rather than with another. The essential function of the dealer is to quote a price at which he will sell to any comer and similarly, one at which he will buy. In the short run the supply coming on to such a market is a dealers' supply and they will, by their

---

(5) The strict interpretation of marginal theory will require, of course, that short-term price should be variable both in the case of a pure monopolist and in the case of a pure competitor (subject to demand and/or cost curves not behaving in a very peculiar manner), but discussions have shown me that many economists tend to regard a relative stability of prices as favouring a presumption of the existence of 'monopolies'.

bargaining with one another, fix prices so as to get the highest price which will leave them only with the stocks which they consider appropriate in the light of their knowledge — and judgement — of the market. Market price at any one time will consequently be dominated by short-term considerations, and costs of production will affect price only when they cause changes in supply to occur, or to be forecast by the traders.

That such a market is essentially competitive I do not dispute. The mischief is that all its characteristics have come to be taken as the essence of competition in any market — both by economists and by intelligent laymen whose thinking has been greatly influenced by elementary expositions of the way it works. For this is the 'perfectly competitive market' which is so readily explicable by diagrams of demand and supply. I shall argue that a manufacturing market, however competitive, will not work that way, and that, consequently, a market price which is the resultant of the balance between short-run demand and supply is not to be taken as the touchstone for a competitive manufacturing market.

What, then, is the essence of competition? As I have urged elsewhere, it is simply that *no seller can get a price which is higher than would be taken by any other potential seller of his type of product*. That is obviously true for the kind of market that we have just been discussing; it is no less true for the normal markets of manufacturing industry. This should certainly be admitted for the bulk of manufacturing industry whose products are sold immediately to other businesses (manufacturers or traders), but it is not the normal concept in modern economic thought, where demand is treated as if it were entirely a matter of consumer demands, and the latter are analysed on assumptions which rule out such competition. Further, although the older economists would have accepted it, their view of competition in manufacturing industry has been rejected in the discussion of modern problems because their theories described manufacturing markets as if they were in all respects similar to the commodity markets discussed earlier. In fact, the principal errors in the modern theories of business behaviour have arisen chiefly in the course of attempts to correct this particular mistake — but in my view the modern theory has been much more misleading in its practical implications.

Leaving the bulk of manufacturing on one side, then, there remains the question of manufactured consumers' goods sold to the consumer at prices fixed by the manufacturer, whether directly or indirectly through independent distributors. These are the cases raised immediately by this paper. We shall see that the general position is very similar for these commodities, but a little more argument will be required to establish it. Meanwhile, I am dealing only with the question how far fixity or conventionality of prices, taken by itself, is a sign of the absence or weakness of competition. First, an attempt must be made to explain briefly why the prices of manufactured goods, however keen the competition with which they are produced, will not be flexible in their response to short-period changes in trading conditions, as is the case with primary commodities.

3 The inflexibility of manufactured goods' prices

Quite apart from branded products, whose prices are 'fixed', it is characteristic of manufactured products in general that their prices tend to be inflexible, as compared with the primary commodities from whose markets we derive many of our ideas about competition. Since this results from the way competition works both in manufacture and retailing, this difference between the two types of markets would persist, no matter how much competition increased in the selling of manufactured products. To explain why this is so we must go a little way into the theory of manufacturing prices.(6)

From some points of view it is convenient to recognize that manufactured products fall into two classes, according to their ultimate use: those used by other businesses and those which minister to the wants of personal consumers. (Some goods, of course, would appear in both lists, e.g. motor-cars.) In the case of consumers' goods, we should formally distinguish three price levels: (1) that at which the manufacturer sells his products; (2) that at which they are sold by a wholesaler (where they pass through this stage of distribution); and (3) that at which the retailer sells them.

For the problems with which we are now concerned we need consider only the first and third of these price levels. Further, we shall not miss out a large proportion of the output of this country if we ignore the cases where a manufacturer sells directly to the consumer. That being conceded, we do not need to distinguish the two classes of product at the stage when the manufacturer sells them — it being remembered, once again, that we are going to discuss branded consumers' goods separately. (Retail prices, however, will have to be considered first, before we can take up this deferred question.)

(a) Manufacturers' prices
The price which a manufacturer gets for his product, since it will be sold to another business man, cannot be higher than his customer would have to pay for an identical product from another manufacturer. The rule of competition is, thus, the same here as in the primary traders' markets, but it does not result in the

---

(6) The theory has been stated at greater length in my book, *Manufacturing Business*; in consequence no more detail is given than is required for the present argument.

same short-term flexibility of prices. A manufacturer has to look forward when deciding his price and take a long-run view:

(1) He will have to employ machinery, plant, and buildings which will last for a considerable time. In every line of industry in this country the prices which a manufacturer gets will not allow him to replace these until a number of years have elapsed — equally, of course, these fixed assets of his will give useful service for a correspondingly long period.

(2) Demand conditions work very strongly in the same direction. A manufacturer will lose his customers in the end if his price is too high; he adds to them only by the relatively slow process of acquiring 'goodwill', which is the customers' preference for dealing with him, provided that his price is not out of line with that which would be charged by his potential competitors. Once lost, the goodwill of a customer is not easily regained.

(3) When he is considering producing a particular product, given its specification and the methods by which he contemplates producing it, a manufacturer will be able to calculate only the average direct cost to him.(7) This average direct cost per unit is stable over a wide range of output for an established business. The difference between it and price is the gross profit margin, and that must be sufficient in the long run to cover average overhead or indirect costs if the producer is to survive; it must seem likely not only to do this but also to yield him a reasonable net profit, if he is to start producing a particular product.

(4) The competition in a market limits the price which can be obtained for a particular sort of product, and in a settled market an established business will, therefore, come to estimate price on the basis of a definite gross profit margin for a given class of product. Given the wages and efficiency of labour, the prices of materials, and the methods of production, price will not tend to vary with changes in the sales which a particular business manages to make.

A business will not put up its prices merely because there is a heavy demand for its products. The increase in demand will be met in the first instance by drawing on stocks, until output can be stepped up. If the business were to raise price it would make its product more attractive to a competitor, in accordance with (3) above.(8) Its competitors, or potential competitors, may well have spare capacity and it will, accordingly, be attractive to add to their output;

---

(7) Direct costs are those which vary directly in total with output (i.e. their average remains constant in given conditions). They consist mainly of the wages of process labour and the cost of materials used in the product.

(8) It will be noted that the goodwill factor makes traders in manufactured goods perform the stock-carrying functions which dealers in primary markets are induced to perform by the short-term variability of their prices.

not only will they gain the possible long-run goodwill of their new customers but, in time, such an expansion of output may mean lower costs and enable them further to strengthen their position in the market. Even if the increased demand occurs at a time of general pressure of demand affecting all existing businesses, it does not take long, in normal times, for new capacity to be installed in most lines of industry, and, if the level of gross profit looks attractive at such a time, the market will be attractive to quite new enterprises.(9)

Equally, a business will not reduce price below its normal cost level just because demand is slack. If it does so, the consequence must be to cause its competitors to lower their prices and, in a time of falling or low demand such as is contemplated, this general reduction in price will not usually bring much extra sales. It will, therefore, merely diminish the profits, or increase the losses, which are being made. Nevertheless, it must be noted that at such times price-cutting may occur out of the desperation of weak businesses which cannot hope to cover the costs which they have to pay out, and snatch desperately at this last remedy. Price-cutting of this kind cannot be a normal feature and tends to correct itself by the elimination of the weak businesses, the normal gross profit margin being restored in better times.

(5) If, however, its costs fall, due to technical change or to reorganization following upon expansion, an established business in a settled industry will lower its price. It is in this way that the prices in such an industry tend to be settled by the most efficient firm. To avoid misunderstanding, it should be noted that the identity of the most efficient firm varies from time to time. It is one of the virtues of competitive activity that it provides a continual stimulus to businesses to improve their efficiency and, in the process, industrial leadership often changes its address.

(6) Of course, it follows from the above that prices will alter if there is a general change in the cost position of an industry due to rises in the wages of labour, etc., and in the prices of materials. These tend to change with changes in general business activity which affect the strength of demand in these 'primary' markets. Prices in manufacture will not, however, as will have been seen, rise or

---

(9) It cannot be too often stressed that it is misleading to think of such competition as coming only from brand-new businesses. Factors which I have analysed elsewhere are making it increasingly difficult for such businesses, and in established lines of industry the level of available profits, even at the best of times, may not give much help to the genuinely small new business. But, in fact, businesses established already, frequently in rather remote lines of industry, are effective sources of competition of the kind contemplated. The professional reader should understand that I am not thinking merely of 'cross-elasticities of demand'. The important point is the widespread possession of sufficient technical 'know-how' to make good guesses at the possibilities in disparate lines of manufacture.

fall just because of temporary strength or weakness of demand in the market for the product.

It is in this way that the economics of manufacture cause its prices to be relatively less flexible than those for primary commodities. Competition tends to establish relatively stable prices, given the technical and other fundamental circumstances of the industry. It will be true that the easier it is for a business to enter the production of a particular commodity (this is very much a matter of the size of capital required for economical production in comparison with the risks involved) and the wider the field from which such potential competition can come, the lower will be the gross profit margins, and, more important, the lower will be the net profit margins, that existing businesses will be able to obtain at prevailing prices. As a matter of experience, in established industries neither prices nor gross margins(10) will in themselves offer much attraction to new business. That, accordingly, tends to come in only at times when high pressure of demand makes it seem likely that they will be able to make a living at about the existing prices.

It is worth stressing that, already, existing competition holds prices and profits down, but that the competitiveness both of manufacturing and of distributive industry can be increased by social action. The theories of business behaviour which have become accepted during the last 20 years have made the effectiveness of such social action appear extremely doubtful, since they stressed the possibility of increased competition being frustrated by increased profits at smaller outputs (due to use of 'monopoly' powers, thought to be a characteristic of business economics). This pessimistic conclusion seems to me to be a consequence of errors in the assumptions on which the theories were constructed. The older theory of pure or perfect competition has served economics well by providing a manageable abstract view of the pricing system as a whole. It has, however, led to the consolidation of presuppositions as to the nature of industrial competition in an 'ideal' state, which are misleading when we study industry in practice. Equally, the correction of the assumptions of perfect competition in order to take account of certain features of the real world has inevitably led to mistaken views of their social implications.

The argument so far has sought to establish that the relative stability of manufactured prices, and their comparative equality as between different manufacturers, is no sign of the absence of competition — that, in fact, the latter results directly from the fact of competition, and the former from the

---

(10) A technical point: the 'large group' solution of Chamberlin, of course, makes competing businesses have only reasonable net margins, but the excessively small scale on which his businesses operate would, on my analysis, increase the gross margin, in terms of which new competitors will be attracted.

pricing rules which the nature of manufacturing competition tends to establish in a settled industry in normal times.

Cartels. Before passing on, however, we cannot overlook the fact that business men have been known not to leave this equilibrium of market price to chance and that there have been cases where they have got together and tried to settle agreed prices! Such attempts are especially liable to occur when a severe short-run cutting of price has forced it down substantially below the level of normal costs of production, even for efficient businesses. The fact that, as I have argued elsewhere, such abnormally low levels of price have only a dubious social value is beside the point that we are discussing. The relevant consideration is that, even when this happens, the price that the 'cartel' will succeed in obtaining must depend upon the considerations that we have just been discussing.

It is true that the agreed identity of price in a cartel arises explicitly from attempts to limit competition, but the participating businesses will still have to reckon with potential competition from outside, and experience shows that such agreements will not have a stable basis unless the price is genuinely held down to a level which is justified by costs to reasonably efficient businesses. The agreement will otherwise be vulnerable to competition from new businesses, and to subsequent instability.

These considerations account for the fact that, in my experience, when such cartels persist, their prices come to be determined by the efficient firm, which exerts a continuous downward pressure on price. It is in its interest to do this rather than, as usually thought, to agree to a price which will bolster up relatively inefficient businesses and offer continuous invitation to new business.(11)

If the entry of new business is especially difficult, it may well happen that, even though prices are determined by costs plus only a fair allowance for profit, the fact of the agreement removes a spur to increased efficiency, and costs remain higher than they would otherwise be. There will be a limit to this, as, sooner or later, the industry will become attractive to new entrants on account of the increasing attraction of the established price in the face of technical possibilities.

Once a new business comes in for such a reason, the situation alters; there are numerous cases of such a vigorous new firm, even whilst it remains outside the cartel, becoming in effect the regulator of the latter's price policy. Even granted this view of cartels, there is still a strong social interest against them — as permanent features. Where, as is true in some cases, special circumstances make them desirable, any agreements should be subject to the State's authority and there should be some machinery for governmental oversight of the way in

(11) For an interesting account of the way this has actually happened in the aluminium industry, see Mr. Louis Marlio's *The Aluminium Cartel.*

which prices are fixed. The kind of arrangement which has been made for steel in this country provides an example.(12)

All that these paragraphs on the subject have been concerned to point out is that price-fixing agreements are not the reason for the relative stability of manufacturing prices encountered in normal times — and the apparent scope for such agreements that is afforded by the times through which we have been passing would not normally be offered, and would be removed by a return to more normal relations between supply and demand (i.e. by the ending of the sellers' market induced by war-time regulation and by post-war scarcities).

Finally, I would stress that the most effective counter to private monopoly is not price control. That has always to proceed on the basis of the costs of the manufacturers who are already in the industry; and it is always difficult for an official price-controlling body to set such a level of price as to threaten the disappearance of a proportion of the existing businesses — a situation which frequently arises under the stress of the normal determination of prices. The way out is to increase the possibility of competition —for example, by making it easier for businesses to get capital, by making illegal any agreements to drive out competitors by unfair means or to restrict channels of trade, and perhaps, above all, by not protecting home industry by high tariff walls, but, if tariffs exist and cannot be swept away at once, by adopting a policy of continuously squeezing the protected industries through a steady and foreknown reduction in tariffs. The point to be remembered is that, even with cartels, the situation is always controlled by the degree of potential competition, and that can be increased by social action — never, I think, by State regulation of the kind to which we tend to fly nowadays.

Pricing in abnormal circumstances. Before passing on to consider retail prices, there is one other matter which should be discussed. Market prices have been referred to as tending to cover normal costs of production in the long run. That does not mean that they will normally cover the costs of especially inefficient businesses. Further, it does not mean that they will cover the average costs even of a normally efficient business at all times.

It will be normal for market price to yield very low profits and even losses, in slumps, whilst yielding relatively higher profits in booms. In the latter conditions, of course, even very inefficient businesses may make profits, but that will be because of the increased volume of sales, not because of an upward shift in the basis of price determination. In fact, prices in manufacturing industry tend to remain somewhat higher in slumps and lower in booms than would

---

(12) See Mr. R. M. Shone's paper to the British Association, 'Planning and Competition', *Monthly Statistical Bulletin of the British Iron and Steel Federation*, August 1949.

happen if the market were a pure dealers' market of the kind that was previously described.

Of course, if there should be long-run conditions of great scarcity, and if for some reasons it should be impossible for businesses to add to their productive capacity, then the weaker businesses will find that they can get a price which will, with impunity, yield them a better profit. This should be regarded as a rare situation which normally occurs only in war or siege conditions, but over-full employment, for whatever reason, might produce it. Even when it does occur, the better established businesses will do their best to maintain their usual price policy — cutting up prices only in accordance with rises in basic costs, and rationing not by price but by such means as lengthening delivery dates. It is because they understand such a policy as normal wisdom that such businesses usually are strong supporters of government price control in war-time. Further, it is because businesses estimate their prices in the way that I have described that it is natural for government price control in these conditions to proceed in terms of allowed gross profit margins. Equally, under such price control, it is usually desirable to keep as much capacity in production as possible. For that reason the more efficient businesses will probably find that prices are fixed at a level higher than they would fix on their own. Sentiments of fair play in such times tend to make all businesses adhere to the controlled prices.

(b) Retail prices

A retailer is more than the 'final link in the chain of distribution' of manufactured consumers' goods. If he is to remain in business at all, that is the least he can be — a mere agent, getting his customer what he asks for from manufacturer or from wholesaler. But fully developed retailing involves a much more complex set of activities and can take a great variety of forms, even in one trade; and the variety increases, the larger the population density of the area that we are considering. In general, all forms of retailing provide services other than just the getting of goods for customers, and the latter ordinarily expect, and pay for, much more than that.

The most obvious of these additional services is that of carrying stocks. This economizes the time of the shopper: it also widens his range of choice — both in any particular shop and as between shops. When we walk into a shop we expect to be served quickly with our choice of commodities for our regular needs, from stocks which are already available in the shop. Equally, for needs which arise less frequently, we expect our choice to be helped by the stocks which are present in the shops and the advice of the shopkeepers who carry them. In addition, varying degrees of credit and delivery services have come to be provided.

It is, of course, easy to make play with the irrationality of the (other) consumer, and to attack the system as inefficient which offers such a variety of services, from the little general store or grocer 'just around the corner' to the chain store or departmental store or the specialist shop such as the stamp dealer of the largest towns. A naive view, taking the retailer's service as just passing the goods over the counter, must lead one to despair of customers who manifestly do not choose merely to have that service at the lowest price possible. Looked at from this angle, it is very easy to measure the costs of this variety, less easy to credit any value to the variety itself. Such attacks both overlook the services which are rendered alongside the actual passing of the commodity to the consumer, and make insufficient allowance for the fact that the variety of the service offered is one of the factors which develop consumer rationality; one cannot develop reason without choice.

More important, perhaps, such attacks overlook the way in which retail competition will enforce its own rationalization. In retailing, as in manufacturing, economics, the effects of competition may conveniently be analysed in terms of gross profit. A retailer's gross profit is the difference between his turnover — the receipts from his sales — and the cost to him of the commodities which he has sold. In order to survive, once he is in business, he must be able at least to cover his costs from this fund. For him to decide to start in business he must think that he has a sufficient chance to have enough left, after meeting his costs, to give him a satisfactory reward for his own labour and for the capital which he employs.

The price of a commodity as sold by a retailer thus equals its cost to him, plus the gross profit margin on it. On many articles, where the terms of sale are determined by the manufacturer, this is not within the discretion of the retailer, who simply has to decide whether he will stock and sell the commodity on the terms offered him. Price-fixing of this sort will be discussed later. Apart from these cases the retailer is formally free to determine his gross margin for himself and thus to fix his own price. He will not necessarily place the same margin upon all that he sells. As already noted, it is usual even for specialist retailers to deal in a considerable variety of goods. Some of them will be more expensive or more troublesome to sell than others, and the retailer will tend to take a higher margin on these, for the market will be such that competition in these is normally only at a price higher relatively to their cost. Equally he may shade the margin on other articles, where he incurs relatively less expenses or finds them less troublesome to sell. It is, however, also a well-known feature of retail trade that the trader may set an especially low margin on commodities which will attract his customers' attention, his extra trade in these being used to strengthen his goodwill generally, and thus to increase his sales of other goods. Such commodities are often called 'loss-leaders', because of the relative loss which may be made on these magnets for custom. Loss-leaders are, however, important only for articles which are well known and which generally have a definite price

— and, in fact, they are especially liable to be articles whose general price is fixed by manufacturers. For the purpose of this paper it will be convenient to ignore these aberrations and to look only at the average gross profit margin — imagining, if you like, that our retailer sells only one line of goods.

In fact, when we are studying any particular shop, we shall find that the trader has a definite price policy for any particular type of article, setting a given proportionate gross profit margin upon it. Frequently the majority of the articles in which he trades will bear the same margin — i.e. their prices will be in the same relation to the cost of them to him. Indeed, in any given area we shall often find that retailers of a particular kind of commodity employ the same gross margin in their mark-up. This pricing practice of the retailer is often referred to in terms of 'conventional retail margins'.

It is true that the reason for this way of fixing retail prices must be a matter of historical conjecture, but one can see that the proportionate margin is an easy way of translating a price policy into practice. The retailer normally has to think in terms of a large number of articles and must have some rule-of-thumb for deciding his policy on a new article within his class of trade. The proportionate margin does rough justice, and makes sense, in so far as the more expensive articles of a given type cost more to sell or involve more service or are sold relatively less frequently.

Why the margin should have come to be determined at such-and-such a figure, it is, however, impossible to say. The point that we have to remember is that, given the margins, the development of competition in retailing will enforce a rational basis to them, in terms of the service which the retailer has to provide. The exponents of 'monopolistic competition', however, would probably grant that profit margins are not excessive, but would argue that costs are higher than they need be, because of excessive ancillary services, and that the consumer might prefer to have less service and a lower price but has not the choice. The flaw in this argument is in this last clause — the consumer *has* the choice of many different kinds of retailing, including the cash-and-carry multiple store, at lower prices. If he chooses to go to a more expensive type of retailer it is because he thinks the extra service worth the extra cost, and it will be a rational choice. In any area, and in any line of business, the retailers should be seen as offering their customers both their commodities and the associated services which go with them. It does not follow that the retail prices even of very similar goods will have to be the same, for very different services may be provided by different retailers, and, where the value of the commodity can be greatly enhanced by such services, as with footwear, we must not be surprised to find that prices differ substantially even for similar articles.(13)

What is true is that all these retailers will be competing for the custom of the consumers in their area — and may, of course, set out especially to cater for particular sections of this broad market. It is equally true that customers are not so quickly sensitive to differences in price or in the value of service as would be a business-man customer who was going subsequently to use the commodity for business purposes. But it makes most sense of the history of particular retailers to suppose that there is fairly sensitive competition in the rather longer run. One consideration which tells in this direction is that it only needs a fair proportion of consumers to be sensitive to such differences in the values which they are offered for an equally substantial proportion of turnover to be dependent upon these considerations; a retailer who offered substantially better terms would thus find a marked growth in his trade.(14) This leads to the further consideration that the fact of such customers is of even greater importance than their probable proportion would suggest. As we must all know from our own experience, such discriminating buyers have their effect upon less sensitive persons. It seems wrong, therefore, to analyse retail trade as if it were so irrational an affair as it has become fashionable for many economists to make it appear, certainly not

---

(13) In fact, of course, the commodities to which the higher margins are attached are usually of a somewhat higher quality.

(14) I am indebted to Mr. Ward-Perkins for this point, which is based upon a criticism which he made to me of Chamberlinian theory.

when we are making statements about retail trade in general.(15) It does not make sense, when we study actual retail trades, to imagine the goodwill of a retailer as allowing him to get a higher price indefinitely irrespective of the value of the service which he provides — i.e. of the costs of his commodities.

When we are, as in this part of the paper, thinking about retailing as a whole, we can simplify the picture considerably by analysing the retailers in one line of business *as if they were* selling identical commodities with identical services attached; we thus get a theoretical model whose characteristics can be used to throw some light upon the rationale of the more confused real world. On the assumptions that we have made, each retailer will find that the price which he can get will be determined in the long run by the price at which new businesses would try to get into his market, and competition will thus control the gross profit margin which he can set in the long run. Of course an established retailer will have built up goodwill, and will have customers who will prefer to deal with him, provided his price is right and they can do no better elsewhere. If he charges a higher price, then he will lose customers and their goodwill in the long run. If he cuts price below this level, it will not really pay, because other business men will cut theirs to counter any inroads that he makes on their markets. Thus business men's short-term policy will reflect this situation and gross profit margins will be determined by long-run competition and will be stable except in periods of price-cutting due to temporary distress of

(15) This reservation is made because it must be admitted that there are some goods which apparently are subject to irrationalities — where the appeal of the commodity is on 'snob' grounds, consumers buying them because they are high priced and, therefore, suitable for ostentatious expenditure. I do not think these cases are so important — they are not to be confused with the purchase of better-priced articles, where experience has taught the customer that such price differences represent quality differences. To come back to the former case: even so, it does not follow that prices will not have normal relations to costs; e.g. I remember one business producing a consumers' good *de haute luxe*, where the business man believed that it was bad for his trade to make price reductions — or rather, to advertise them. Nevertheless, any substantial fall in his costs (he was a manufacturer-retailer) was followed by a corresponding cut in price, which he did not shout about; and any minor but persistent fall in costs was followed by an improvement in quality so that the cost of the article went up correspondingly. The reason for this was that too great a gap between costs and prices would attract new entrants into this particular market. Potential competition thus made his business offer normal quality for the money. It is, of course, a question of fact how quickly such competition would arise. One can say only that experience makes established business men attempt, through their price policy, to prevent it arising at all. Recent theory seems to me too prone to assume both serious imperfection of knowledge and a readiness on the part of business men to rely on it.

the kind which we analysed for manufacture.

We have already mentioned that, in any one line of business, retailers will be found offering many different kinds and degrees of service. How does this normal-cost rationale work out there? This will be understood in terms of a realistic example: the development of retailing, partly under the influence of the increasing concentration of our urban population, has led to the development of retail chain stores, which get substantial buying economies by their size, and also selling economies (so far as the actual physical transaction is concerned) by locating themselves at suitable centres of population. They therefore offer cheaper goods and by this means induce customers to come to them from the suburbs. What is the effect of this competition? The smaller, dearer businesses on the periphery must offer more services in order to justify their higher gross profit margin, otherwise the reduction in their turnover will drive them out of business.

It is in this way that competition in retail trade ultimately determines the value which the consumer gets for his money. There is one thing more that must be said about retail trade: where there are no artificial restrictions, it is much the most competitive line of industry. That is because it is easily entered, many persons have sufficient knowledge to be able to make fair estimates of its profitability, and only moderate capital is required. (It should be said in passing that many factors have begun to make this competition potentially less, e.g. town-planning restrictions upon the location and numbers of shops, to mention one. The modern passion for regulation has led to suggestions for further 'orderliness' by the regulation of entry and by the use of clever methods for penalizing 'inefficient' (i.e. small) retailers through tax devices. These should be resisted.) In consequence, the profits available in retailing have been fairly tightly held down; it has been the economic 'frontier' of our country for a long period — to be one's own boss is a good spur to enterprise and retailing has been one of the easiest fields for such would-be new enterprise. In consequence of this we have had our retailing done very cheaply.

One sign of this is the ease with which the small one-man shops, which are still important, can be attacked as inefficient, because so many make losses (especially if a fair value is put upon the market value of the labour of the man and/or his wife) and there is considerable mortality. It is difficult to see why a greater return should be offered, and I do not know why it has become so fashionable in some quarters to attack this part of the capitalist system where the consumer does get a great deal, if not for nothing, then for what the critics regard as a pittance. There would be a lot to be said for trying to increase the ease with which new business could set up in other industries and increase the strength of this 'inefficiency' there! The main conclusion to carry forward from this section is that in retailing, as in manufacture, prices will be controlled by competition and that the levels of normal cost will decide the size of the gross profit margin which is available to a business. Before passing on, it should be noted that the omission of reference to the effects of advertising is deliberate — this is dealt with in the last section of this paper. First, we have to discuss the explanation of conventional prices and the pros and cons of price-fixing of branded goods.

4 Conventional prices

In my *Manufacturing Business* I have already explained in some detail how conventional prices come about, and so the matter can be summarized here. Conventional prices arise for some consumers' goods at the stage when they are actually sold to consumers. There is first the case of semidurable consumers' goods which are in wide demand, and which, therefore, have to be supplied in a considerable range of qualities. Examples are boots and shoes (not of the 'extreme fashion' kind), ties, or towels, sold through the ordinary mass channels of distribution. To take the first-named, the general demand in this country, before the war, took men's shoes at prices which covered as wide a range as from 6s. 11d. to 12s. 11d. or 16s. 11d. In such a case there is, obviously, almost an infinitude of opportunity for quality variation and, if the market worked at random, the consumer would be faced with a literally bewildering variety of qualities of footwear at a corresponding variety of prices.

It is, however, easy to see why things have not worked out that way. Obviously any one shop would find that it paid it to offer shoes at clearly differentiated prices, suiting definite layers of purse or taste. This would enable it to get the maximum buyings and stockholding economies for a given turnover; it would also be found that customers liked it, since the choice was clearer and it was also easier to see something of the difference in quality which was being offered for a given difference in price. The chain stores would naturally have the same policy over their areas. The development of these forms of retailing has been responsible for a considerable strengthening in the habit of shop-window shopping, whereby a consumer collects information about 'the state of the market' at times when no purchase is contemplated, and is enabled to make rapidly a final survey of the situation before he actually enters one or more shops to examine matters more closely. It would be found that to pick upon 'fancy' prices was not of much use, that it 'bothered customers'; this means that subject to minor aberrations, due to beliefs that people did or did not like prices at even amounts but at a penny less or threepence on, the shops in a given area would offer their shoes at the same 'price tickets'.

It will be seen that the development of these conventional price levels has made the market *more* competitive rather than less; they facilitate the more exact comparison of what is being offered and enforce therefore a much closer competition in quality of article or service than would be possible otherwise. The exact points at which different qualities were offered within the price range has no doubt been arrived at as a matter of experience, but it can be seen as corresponding to levels of demand which are largely dependent upon income levels — for such types of consumers' goods, those consumers whose incomes fall within a given range will have a typical price up to which they are prepared to 'go'. This rightness of price from the point of view of monetary convenience and of considerations on the income side has been confirmed by modern marketing research. It does not mean that the consumer is indifferent to what he gets for the money, but that it suits him to allocate a certain sum for a particular purpose, and, generally, to deal in particular units of money — his preoccupation then being to see that he gets the best he can for his money.

It will now be understood why conventional prices in the strict sense emerge — why we find certain articles always being sold at particular prices; a penny for normal boxes of matches, sixpence for the smallest tubes of popular brands of toothpaste, and so on. (The quoting of pre-war prices and customs is deliberate.) In some cases it has been found that a shop offering better value for some fancy price lower than that which has become conventionally established gets less sales than if it puts its price up; and this is a favourite instance of the behaviour of the irrational consumer. But, as already seen, it is reasonable that conventional prices should exist and, to take up again the example in the last sentence, a shop which adopts the 'usual' level of price will need to offer as good a quality as the next one if it is to get and maintain the increased sales, and it will do better in the long run if it can improve its quality.

Meanwhile, perhaps it will be accepted that, for the classes of commodities where experience does give information as to quality, conventional prices do not imply the absence of competition. Otherwise, the costs of manufacturing and selling a particular article sold at such a price fall, then quality will have to be increased. Otherwise, the market will be invaded by new entrants whose competition will be attracted by the increased generosity of the gross profit margins. In this case, then, shops will supply superior goods or more services.

Equally, if costs rise permanently, specifications and qualities will have to be cut or services reduced. If costs rise high enough (which will usually be due to an inflation and hence to a rise in money levels of income), then the levels of conventional prices will be raised (which will suit the new income conditions) and quality will not be cut so drastically as would otherwise have to happen.

As a matter of fact, we also find continuous changes in quality in response to temporary changes in costs (e.g. over the trade cycle) for many goods subject to conventional prices. Some goods, however, such as proprietary goods of rigid description, cannot change in this manner.(16) In that case, unless costs fall very substantially, so that a change in price does become feasible, the price will be lowered indirectly — for example, by the occasional offering of two articles for the price of one in special selling campaigns, the giving of tooth mugs away with a tube of toothpaste, etc., or putting more into selling costs, so that the consumer is offered the greater convenience of finding the article much more widely stocked. (This is a service to him, for, as Professor Lewis has observed, the ideal to the consumer would be to have a shop in his home; it follows that a more widespread system of stocks is at least some gain.)

The kind of indirect cutting of prices to which we have just been referring seems especially wicked if we judge on the basis of a notion of prices which can be fixed at any level, when we may think that a consumer should always be given a direct price cut. But granted the consumers' monetary preferences and conveniences, the more flexible price policy which might naively be demanded might well tend rather to upset the market than to improve it. This question of upsetting the market links on with the question of advertising and selling costs generally, to which we shall return later. Meanwhile it should be said that many of the consumers' goods of the types to which we have been referring, and which are the subject of the kinds of attack which this paper is rebutting, now cost a lot less than they used to, and are much better goods, because they are produced in a modern mass-production fashion. That, in turn, has been possible just because of the orderly development of retail markets on the basis of the preferences and the conveniences of consumers. However, before the subject of advertising leads us on to these wider issues, there remains the question of the fixing of prices by manufacturers for their branded goods.

5 'Branding' and the maintenance of retail prices

Although it has been much attacked, the fixing of retail prices by manufacturers and the enforcement of their policy upon retailers is not the simple monopoly practice that it is sometimes thought to be. However, before a manufacturer can enforce a retail price he will first have had to have established his 'brand'. So before we can consider the question of retail price maintenance we must discuss that of branding — the marking of an article with a trade name or mark to indicate its origin and the popularization of that mark with consumers.

Branding has become of especial importance only in comparatively recent times, the present general significance of brands and trade marks having

---

(16) For example, it would be impossible to produce many commodities economically if continual changes had to be made in packaging, cartons, etc.

developed alongside modern methods of manufacture and commerce. The latter have not only led to, but have also depended upon, an increased remoteness of productive processes from both consumer and retailer. The branding of consumers' goods is a natural complement of this development, as we shall see, and is, equally, tied up with advertising, which will be separately considered in the next section of this paper.

It is possible, and indeed very useful, to think of all the stages of the process of making an article and getting it into the hands of a consumer as complementary to one another when we are looking at the process as a whole. When we look at it from the point of view of an individual business, however, it is important to remember that the functions of manufacturers, wholesalers, and retailers overlap in practice, so that actual businesses are competitive even as between the stages of distribution.(17) Competition is a matter of the behaviour of individual businesses and not of the logical relation between industries.

For example, it is correct to think of manufacture as involving more capital for its successful operation as compared with the typical situation in retail trade; but it is wrong to stress this as a factor necessarily reducing the relative competition of the individual business when we pass over from the latter industry to the former, as though the two departments of industry were cut off by watertight bulkheads. For, in many ways, the manufacturer of consumers' goods has to reckon with competition from wholesalers and retailers — that is to say, from the field where direct entry is regarded as so much easier. Equally, if we think, as people often do, of retailing as being much more imperfectly competitive than manufacture because of the local 'monopolies' of small retail shops, then, even on that view, the retailer of the simple kind that is imagined will have to reckon with direct and indirect competition from manufacturers who are usually thought of as working to finer profit margins.

It is because the whole system of manufacture and distribution forms such a network of complementary and competitive relations that it may have a social justification in terms of the satisfaction of consumers' needs — if not on the hypothetical cheapest terms possible (which is much easier to assert — or to deny — than to assess) then, at least, on competitive terms. In this system, what may seem a very secure quasi-monopoly, viewed narrowly, is frequently open to appreciable competition of an indirect kind. For example, the development of manufacturers' brands, on the one hand, and of chain and departmental stores on the other, may be seen to have greatly increased the competitiveness of modern industry: the one through greatly increasing the amount of standardization of product which consumers will take voluntarily, the

(17) This matter has been well discussed by Professor R.G. Hawtrey in *The Economic Problem*.

other through increasing the degree of standardization of retail service, and both through providing in these ways cheaper or more attractive substitutes to products made or distributed under the older system. The fact that the firms developing these newer methods may be analysed as strengthening their own position by their success is beside the point, since their success is a measure of their effective competition with other businesses.

The full implications of these cross-relationships, and the significance of the practice of branding, will be seen more clearly if we take the case of what we may call the primitive manufacturer-retailer before the development of modern industry. His one business will combine in itself all the functions that modern conditions cause us to distinguish and analyse separately: he will have formal responsibility for deciding exactly what the nature of his product will be; and not only for making and selling it, but also for carrying stocks for his customers' convenience and his own, as well as deciding just what other services he will also be ready to render for the price of his product; which latter, of course, he will formally decide for himself.

Now, all and each of these, except that of merely selling the product as little more than an agent for someone else, *may* be performed elsewhere than at the retail stage or anywhere in the system of manufacture and distribution, and it is the possibility of putting their brand on the product that enables others to take over any of these services so freely, and thus increases the flexibility of the whole system. Branding does this because it provides access to the 'goodwill' of the consumer — the custom of the consumer to come back and ask for more of what he finds satisfactory at its price.

The mere development of modern manufacturing processes made it inevitable that production should no longer be carried on in retail premises, the costs of a bought ready-made article falling so low as to compete effectively with products made on the smaller original scale. A considerable measure of standardization would also tend to be imposed because factory-made goods must go through standard processes — certainly the orders coming to any one factory would have to be relatively standardized. Further, the newer manufacturing had to be relatively more localized than retailing, and once it had become localized, well-known reasons would increase the concentration of manufacture.

These developments initially favoured trading by wholesalers as a means of cheapening the cost of goods still further; wholesalers entering into successful competition with manufacturers and retailers for the performance of their functions. They could combine the orders of their retail customers in such a way as to give larger-scale orders for any particular type of product, and would also save costs through their specialized knowledge both of the retailer's needs and of the manufacturer's specialities. In addition, some of the stock-holding functions of the retailer would pass to them, since with their larger turnover they could economize in what may be thought of as the 'second line of defence' element in stockholding. The retailer could cut his stocks down to the minimum for day-to-day selling and rely upon the wholesaler to meet any unexpected increases in demand at fairly short notice, passing back upon him likewise some of the first effects of an unexpected decrease in trade.

Such wholesalers would be competing with one another for the favour of retailers, and with the development of competition that goodwill would be a very short-term affair liable to be cut off fairly quickly for quite small differences in price, even if these were temporary incidents. Further, however much standardization the mere development of manufacture would impose, there would still be a strong element of differentiation of the product due to particular retailers imposing their idiosyncrasies — and in the competition of retailers, the desire to offer something a little different from others would affect both the product that they ordered as well as the services that they provided with it. The goodwill of the final consumer would be a much more stable factor; the price to him could not reflect the sensitive small changes that might occur in wholesale prices in the short period, and whilst he would tend to go back to his shop for what he had had previously, his shopkeeper was certainly not obliged to offer the same stability to the wholesale supplier.

The self-interest of the wholesaler would naturally tend, then, to make him think in terms of establishing his brand of the commodity and making it known to the final customer. The development of advertisement made this possible since he could inform the consumers directly about his brands and seek to attract their custom. The retailer would then find that his demand was for such-and-such a brand, and a successful sales campaign on the part of the branding-wholesaler would lead to his stocking the product and selling it for what it was. The wholesaler, however, in the long run would be able to hold his position largely because the relatively increased scale of standardization would lead to further production and stock-holding economies.

Still further developments in the scale of industry as a whole, with increases in trade and population, would similarly lead to the development of manufacturers' brands when once some manufacturers had become large enough to be able to produce economically a greater variety of their product — so that they could take on the relatively more varied market of a wholesaler — helping out their own production by buying on a wholesale basis such parts of their trade as were too small in scale for them to manufacture. They also would have as inducement the magnet of the relatively more stable retail and consumer demand. They would succeed to the extent that they were large and efficient enough to produce their product and distribute it as cheaply as could one of their rival wholesalers. Once they had done this successfully they would in fact tend to produce more cheaply than before; not only would their products be relatively more standardized but they would also have the possibility of growing larger and thus getting the benefit of any reduction in costs through so doing.

This last possibility would arise because the wholesaler would tend to disperse his orders to some extent, since he would prefer the insurance of dealing with several manufacturers — thus getting a more continuous direct knowledge of market conditions as well as having a wider area to draw on in times of difficult supply; equally, one who was purely a manufacturer would tend to have a more varied product than one who became his own wholesaler, and, where economies of scale were important, the latter might therefore get lower costs of production. So long as he were large enough to do the wholesaling side economically he would improve his position by greater profits or by lower prices — the development of competition would, in the long run, enforce at least a measure of the latter.

Before turning on to the question of price maintenance by the proprietor of a brand it is interesting to complete the picture of the development of modern business, which we now see in full competition for the goodwill of the final consumer. The growth of urban populations has enabled the business on the retail side to compete with manufacturers and pure wholesalers in the distribution of (un- or own-) branded goods even in those lines where the economies of wholesaling and manufacture are important enough to have facilitated these earlier developments that we have been describing. The growth of the chain store has meant that some retail organizations have been large enough to become their own wholesaler and, in some cases, to concentrate sufficient trade either to manufacture for themselves or to get full economies in the price which they can command from manufacturers. This also has been helped somewhat by the development of advertising, but that is not so important here as it is for the selling of manufacturers' and wholesalers' brands.

Modern trade thus presents its complex picture of independent retailers, chain and departmental stores, manufacturers and wholesalers each providing a variety of services. The same class of product may be sold through any of these channels. Subject to the fuller consideration that we have to give the question of advertisements, the success of any one of these depends upon its efficiency in meeting the needs of the final customers. The manufacturers' brands will have to compete with those of the wholesaler, and, both, with the speciality product for which the retailer takes responsibility. If any one of them is notably cheaper than a rival method of manufacture-distribution it will drive the others out (thus the economies of mass production in soaps and toothpastes have made these a manufacturers' market). Otherwise they will each tend to specialize in that section of the market for which they are at least as efficient as the other methods of distribution.

Here we must observe that the variety of trade has some relevance to social policy in the scope that it offers for the talents of all sorts and conditions of men. Nowadays we concentrate too much upon the economies of large-scale organizations. For one thing these need large-scale talents, and these are relatively more scarce than some of the nationalization proposals would have us believe. Secondly, the costs of production and distribution are only one side of the picture — the consumer buys more than this. In other parts of the field, and for commodities where the economies of large-scale production are not already dominant, there is plenty of room for the, perhaps mediocre, talents of the small-scale man with energy. Many of the services of retail trade in particular are such that they can best be provided by a small man who is literally minding his own business — for example, the provision of credit facilities and the careful attention to likes and dislikes of customers, each of which will require a detailed personal knowledge and judgement. That is one reason why we should lose something if retail trade ceased to be the despair of those who see the world with a planning eye — which is easily acquired, since the kind of information which is readily available makes it relatively simple to judge the cost of everything, but much more difficult to judge its value. Profit considerations in the end lead to the relative success of more standardized methods of production and distribution of commodities where consumers' needs do not seriously differ, yet they leave room for the satisfaction of unstandard wants where sufficient people have them to make this worth while. If we increase the competitiveness of the system — which is feasible — costs will be reduced without the sacrifice of flexibility to standardization. A standard system of distribution of standard goods might certainly have very low costs but it would equally, or more, certainly have to be enforced. It is the virtue of the competitiveness of retail trade that it offers sufficient variety for the consumer to be some sort of judge in his own cause.

Within this complex, brands play a very important part, as we have seen. They enable manufacturers and wholesalers to enter into direct competition for the retail market, thus not only increasing its competitiveness but also enabling manufacture or wholesale distribution to proceed upon a larger-scale, more standardized basis, where the technical gains from this are sufficiently large. They have also played an important part in the maintenance of quality standards for products whose quality is not obvious to the eye, but has to be learned by experience. On the basis of the latter, a consumer can ask again for what pleased him, or equally, shun what disappointed him.

Price maintenance
By itself, branding does not require that the manufacturer should fix the retail price of his product. The brand may merely be a mark of origin to be associated with a certain standard of quality in the case of products whose description is subject to continual change, fashion goods, etc., and also where the industry or

trade is such that the manufacturer produces a great variety of goods. Where, however, the branded products are of standardized description for fairly long periods, the manufacturer will be more or less obliged to adopt the policy of fixed retail prices and to take steps to see that they are observed in order to safeguard his sales position.

A number of causes contribute to this, but the basic position is that a standard branded product whose price is subject to arbitrary variation as between retailers will lose the goodwill both of retailers and of actual consumers, and so will not be able to maintain its position. First, there is the fact, whose recognition has caused such a change in retail trade since the latter half of the nineteenth century, that consumers prefer shops to mark their wares with fixed prices in plain figures. No one minds finding a bargain, but for their ordinary needs consumers do not like to have to haggle — indeed, they would have little time for it — and they therefore resent that the price they pay should depend upon the accident of temperament or of their personal position. A manufacturer by advertising and branding makes himself known as the responsible source in the case of his branded product, and, where this is described as a recognizably standard commodity, consumer sentiment — and that of retailers in general — will expect that its price should be standard and announced. It will be natural on this score for the manufacturer to fix prices. Consumers will certainly not expect, as a rule, to pay more for the same product just because they bought it at one shop rather than another. Since retail values make some sort of sense in the light of experience, consumers will be suspicious of the value that they are getting for an article whose price varies at all noticeably according to the shop that sells it. In consequence the manufacturer will lose goodwill for his product.

But why should there be a noticeable variation in the selling price? As explained earlier, retail margins will in general be determined by normal costs and they should accordingly tend to be comparable for articles which involve similar costs in distribution. That will be true for the majority of retail outlets, but branded goods are especially likely to prove an exception for outlets which are having difficulty in maintaining their position or wish to make an aggressive expansion. We referred earlier to the use of 'loss-leaders' in order to attract custom. Branded goods are especially attractive if they are of the standardized kind that we are discussing. Branded goods will have been generally advertised and tend to become recognized standards of value; to offer these at prices which will be beyond the competition of retailers who depend at all largely on such goods for their living will attract both attention and custom, leading to an increase in trade for other things than the branded goods. The retail shop using them as a loss-leader will get an expansion of trade, but the others who do not cut prices so unduly will lose trade in them. The consequence will be that they will be withdrawn from these, perhaps more normal, outlets, and the price-cutting shop will have gained its advertisement at the expense of the manufacturer of the branded product.

It should be noted that it certainly does not follow that the shops which are especially liable to do this sort of price-cutting will be very important outlets for the kind of goods in question — otherwise they could not make the kind of reduction in price which we are contemplating. They will, in fact, be especially likely to cut prices on goods which will attract buyers' attention in the way that we have described but which are not an important part of their turnover. The effect of this type of competitive advertisement will therefore be to diminish the market for branded goods, not by providing cheaper substitutes but by saddling the manufacturer in effect with the costs of 'advertising', or rather promoting the general trade of the price-cutter at the expense of his own goodwill — and this, as we have seen, is necessary for such goods to be produced on such a large scale.

Once the manufacturer *has* fixed his price, the dangers of such price-cutting become more serious. Price-cutting on an article which has a publicly announced price will make it an even more attractive loss-leader. The manufacturer, therefore, normally makes it a matter of contractual obligation that retailers shall observe the prices that he sets.

This practice of price maintenance has, as we have already said, been seriously attacked, and was considered in the report of the Resale Price Maintenance Committee (1949). The committee concluded against interference with price-fixing as such but recommended that the government should stop certain other practices designed to increase the control of the manufacturer over his price. We shall refer to these wider issues almost immediately, but, first, it seems desirable to review the question of price-fixing by itself. The main burden of the attacks has been that it imposes monopoly control over the retail market and prevents the more efficient retailers, whose costs are lower, from competing with higher-cost outlets because all have to sell the goods at the same price. There is, of course, something in the strict letter of this attack, but, looked at more closely, price maintenance need not mean higher prices for lower-cost goods.

We have already made the point that competition of the loss-leader kind is especially liable to develop in the case of branded goods, and that such competition would in fact prevent branded goods from playing their important part in the process of competitive trading; also that by its nature it has little reference to costs. It is true that the sort of unfair competition that we have in mind is especially liable to come from retailers whose actual costs of trading are low. Such retailers are the large departmental stores situated in the centre of large towns, and chain stores similarly placed. We have already seen that this concentration enables them to get low costs and to attract custom for the kind of goods which it is convenient for the consumer to buy on his shopping expeditions; in other words, they get their low costs at the expense of imposing some extra costs upon the consumer by way of extra fares, the loss of the convenience of being able to make a sudden casual purchase, and also the loss of personal services such as the smaller shops can provide. For such businesses it will be the case that they can take on trade at lower costs than can the smaller retailers, and competition tends to bring them the sort of goods in which they can best deal. It may be thought that the attractions of lower prices for branded goods would concentrate the consumer's demand on these shops, the manufacturer thus probably benefiting from increased trade. In so far as this is possible there is nothing to prevent such large-scale retailers developing their own brands at their lower prices, but, in fact, it would probably not occur. The costs involved in shopping at the low-price shop would mean that the consumer would be forced back on to the more differentiated, unbranded market, which would then be provided by his nearby retailers. Both the consumer and the manufacturer would thus lose the economies of large-scale production based on branding by the manufacturer.

It is, of course, open to these low-price shops to advertise their services and promote their sales by whatever means they can, and relatively heavy expenditure upon advertisement of one sort or another is one of their costs which counterbalance their efficiency in direct selling — which is really a logical complement of their remoteness from the consumer. I therefore see nothing against loss-leaders where those who set the price have the full responsibility for their decisions and bear the whole costs. Although such loss-leaders will be more effective if they consist of price-fixed branded goods, I do suggest that other business men are correct in thinking that this latter is unfair competition — in the sense that its social consequences, as has been argued above, are on balance negative. The consequence, then, is to reduce competition in the long run.

If, as is the case, the types of retailer that we are discussing have lower costs, that should be reflected in their *general* price policy, and they are not prevented from attracting the consumer by low prices there. There is no reason why the economies that they obtain should be concentrated upon branded goods at the expense of margins which are maintained relatively higher than they need be for other goods. Many of these retailers to whose case the critics appeal, on the grounds of low costs, are of such a size that they could well establish their own brands for many goods, and they can determine their own price policy for them. Where they are not large enough it surely means that they cannot carry the branded goods on the cut-price basis as a long-run proposition, and so that the standard branded product of the manufacturer justifies its existence.

There are, however, as the Resale Price Maintenance Committee pointed out, other practices which have grown up, which are understandable from the point of view of the manufacturer of branded goods, but whose social value is more questionable. They all involve the standing together of such manufacturers and the imposing of sanctions upon any shop which has been found to cut prices in any line covered by such agreements. To impose the penalty that the retailer should lose the selling rights for other branded products seems too strong — it means that the powers of the manufacturer of any brand are bolstered up by the advantages of other branded goods and do not have to be sold and stocked simply on their own merits. I must admit that I can see the argument that failure to stand together may mean that some manufacturers will acquiesce in occasional price-cutting and get a temporary advantage over those who stand out against it.(18) If that is so, then the matter should be left to the normal tests of profitability which will adjust the matter in the long run. Freedom here will increase the competitive controls over the prices of branded products, and it seems to be desirable.

Where such manufacturers get together to impose exclusive dealing so that a particular shop may not stock any articles of the kind covered by the agreement unless they emanate from one or other of a particular group of manufacturers and are controlled by price-fixing agreements, it seems quite indefensible. On these matters, then, I am also in agreement with the report of the Resale Price Maintenance Committee to which I have referred, so far as I can see the economics of the matter. In default of clearer proof of social advantage, these ancillary practices might well be forbidden.

There is one other matter to which we should refer — the feeling behind the attack upon branded goods that they automatically give their manufacturer such a monopolistic position that he can get an unduly high price. This is, however, closely tied up with the question of the effects of advertising which has been deferred until the next section, and it does not seem very profitable to disentangle the other consideration separately. This topic will, accordingly, be reviewed later.

6 Advertising

In most of us there is a good deal of instinctive sympathy with Adam Smith's attitude to 'unproductive' labour — the labour which does not result directly in the production of physical articles which we can see, weigh or measure, and handle. So far as concerns personal services performed for us directly, at least we

---

(18) It has been suggested to me that in some lines of trade it might be possible for retailers to remain on a price-cutting basis, taking up another brand when they were forced to drop one, and so doing what might be considerable damage to the whole trade in branded goods.

know that we have had them — although we may well feel that we often pay a man rather a lot just for 'knowing how', as the well-known story has it. Our natural suspicions are much stronger in the case of the services and costs involved in getting products to the shop, holding them at our pleasure, and handing them over the counter. On reflection, however, we are usually prepared to agree that, even here, these services must cost something, but are very ready to believe that, if things were properly organized, these hidden services of the retailer would cost us appreciably less — which is why the term 'middlemen's profits' carries such a sting.

But when it comes to advertising, it seems almost impossible to accept this as anything but a waste. This is quickly seen as the one part of the cost of a commodity for which we get nothing whatever. For we refuse to accept the pleasure that most of us get out of reading advertisements as being any justification for the cost of them in itself. This attitude of the plain man has a considerable echo in the undertones even of nineteenth-century economists. (Note Marshall's attitude to commercial travellers, whose wages he regarded as an advertising cost.) The development of the theory of business behaviour between the wars provided a very convincing rationalization of this attitude. I have discussed this fairly fully elsewhere. Here I need only summarize the position as that, in order to reconcile certain facts about the behaviour of costs of production with the existing theory of the behaviour of an individual business, the latter was eventually analysed on the lines of a quasi-monopolist. Buyers' preferences of an irrational kind (in so far as they would pay more for the product of the business to which they were thus sentimentally attached than the price at which they could get an identical commodity elsewhere) which were required to make the newer theories work, were adduced as the chief explanation of the differentiation of the market which they assumed. Selling costs, of which the leading type was advertising, were produced as the chief explanation of this behaviour of customers and the acceptance of it by producers.

So far as the mass of manufacturing industry is concerned, advertising is not very important, selling costs of other kinds involve services to the businesses who are the direct customers of these typical manufacturers, and the theory demonstrably breaks down; with it goes the chief basis of the theory of business behaviour which was involved, and the way is clear for a theory which takes more explicit account of the method by which such businesses do, in fact, determine their prices. That method — basing price upon normal average costs — is also applied by other types of business: by those manufacturers selling branded consumers' goods and by retail shops. The traditional theory involved is, accordingly, suspect here as well. But the emphasis which it places upon the importance of the persuasive function of advertising remains. In the rest of this section we shall examine what conclusions can be reached about the function and effects of advertising.

It must first be granted that the purpose of advertising is to attract consumers to the commodities which are advertised and persuade them to purchase them in preference to other articles of the same class and to other articles in general. But is it correct to regard advertising as a cost to which there is no limit? — other than that set by a firm's (assumed) calculation of marginal selling costs and marginal revenue — a cost which, in this sense, would be automatically covered by price no matter how slight its real services, the consumer being persuaded to value them accordingly.

Let us clear out of the way one class of goods whose attractions lie entirely in the mind of the consumer — such things as lucky charms. Here it is true that the persuasive function of advertising *may* enable these goods to sell for a price which will cover the advertising cost, no matter to what level that rises; it may be true that advertising can so successfully play upon the fears and hopes of the consumer that he will think that the object which satisfies these wants, themselves partly created by the advertising itself, is worth whatever price will cover the costs of the advertisement. We can dismiss this case because it is relatively unimportant so far as normal industry is concerned. The remedy for it is not so much to discourage advertising but, through education, to help the consumer to know the truth about these matters — and generally to work for a society in which the ordinary man is not subject to the basic fears from which these habits spring. There remains the large class of branded consumers' goods and other objects of advertisement in which the consumer does get something else for his money beside the product of advertising — he may be thought to get more or less, just as the costs of advertising form varying proportions of retail prices. In all cases advertising exercises its persuasive function, which may, perhaps, reach its maximum in the case of certain patent medicines and other nostrums which may border on the lucky-charm type of case, so far as their intrinsic value is concerned.

As has been indicated earlier, the function of advertising is to convey information in order to enable our modern large-scale manufacturing and distributive system to overcome its relative distance from the consumer who, in the end, decides what will be and will not be sold. The small shop in the middle of its customers does not need to advertise in order to inform them (or to attract them); it is, however, a necessity for the larger central shops of a town and for manufacturers and wholesalers of branded goods. Without it they could not obtain the consumer-goodwill that they need to survive; and it is the development of these forms of competition in retail trade that has enabled consumers to obtain at lower prices the goods and services which are more efficiently provided by large-scale trading. From this point of view advertising is a cost which has to be covered if the economic system is to get the benefit of these newer developments where they are most effective. The reservation at the end of the last sentence is significant. It is not correct to go to the other extreme, refer to the low costs of these forms of distribution, and then urge the sweeping away of the small-scale inefficient retailer in order to be able to concentrate, by a measure of compulsory rationalization, the demand of consumers upon the lower-cost outlets. They may have lower costs up to the point of sale, but in the transference from the 'less efficient' forms of distribution the consumer will incur some costs which do not come into the reckoning, such as extra transport, and the giving up of the special services which the other forms provide just because they are small-scale. Free competition in retail trade enables the consumer to choose how far he will go in order to get reduced costs, and the extra costs of advertising are the price that we have to pay for this flexibility of the system. It is only too usual to analyse business life as though all consumers were standardized and as though all business operations could be concentrated. In fact this can be done only at the expense of inefficiency in other parts of the system; the dispersion of businesses must increase the nearer we get to the consumer.

What decides the amount of advertising expenditure that, say, a branded product has to carry? In the case of the majority of consumer goods, I would suggest that experience, both his own and that related by others, does enable the consumer to make some judgement of the relative value to himself of different goods and services sold at various prices. In that case the price of the advertised good cannot, in the long run, be higher than the price of a competing article sold through a channel carrying less advertising, allowance being made for differences in quality and in associated services supplied with it. Advertising will, therefore, justify itself in the long run only if, on balance, it does lead to economies, somewhere in the system, which are sufficient to pay for it. In itself it is a necessary cost of such economies being realized in a society which retains any degree of consumer freedom.

This is even true in the very suspect field of proprietary medicines — by which is *not* meant quack nostrums, but the branded preparations of recognized medical dispensers. Let us first take the case of the standard drugs advertised not to consumers but to doctors. The alternative to their being made by the manufacturer will be their compounding by the local chemist. This is certainly a field where economies of large-scale production and distribution are important; at the same time the advertising costs are not very important and the advertisement is directed at skilled persons; it therefore seems to me likely that, on balance, the prohibition of the use of proprietary brands of such medicines (for example, as a provision under the National Health Service) must in the long run be expected to lead to a rise in their costs — unless they continue to be bought ready-made from the former suppliers, in which case we cannot expect much change in their prices.

There remains the case of domestic medicines such as aspirin. Aspirin is not just aspirin: like any other consumers' good it is an article available in certain places and at certain prices. Now, such a commodity is especially liable to be required to meet sudden needs and emergencies of consumers, and will therefore require to be stocked fairly widely and to be sold in relatively small packages. The heavily advertised brands of aspirin meet these requirements. The advertisement means that consumers will accept them wherever they find them. (This is not so much a case of persuasion as a consequence of the belief that 'advertised goods are good goods' to which we shall return in a moment.) Retailers such as the corner grocers will therefore be willing to stock them, and advertising thus enables a genuine consumer demand to be met. But such aspirins will still have to compete with the cheaper, less advertised brands of aspirin sold through the chain chemists, etc., whose products are recognizably cheaper, and equally trusted, but have to be bought in larger quantities and on the occasion of shopping expeditions to the town centre. In the long run the price and convenience of the more expensive brands must justify themselves against this competition.

But what about the short run? Is it not true that advertising's persuasive function may be much more important here? And is it not the case that there are other commodities where demand is much less stable and based upon shorter-run considerations, so that advertising may play a dominant part in consumer choice? The answer to both of these questions is 'Yes', but we must assay the difficult task of estimating the importance of these considerations. Of course, a well-directed advertising campaign will persuade some consumers to buy the advertised product, and a manufacturer may thus add to his sales in the short run at the expense of rival sellers. When we refer to this situation, however, the mistake that we make is in imagining that such a gain can be permanent. What one has done, the others can do, and a situation analogous to a price-cutting war may develop, with a continual but not very valuable snatching of customers from one to another. In a settled industry, however, this situation is not the normal one; experience leads businesses generally to decide what amount of advertising is necessary for them to hold their own in the market, to limit the amount that they spend by various rules based on experience, and generally to hold advertising down to what is normal for their type of product distributed in their way. Advertising thus does not add indefinitely to costs, and if it did, competition is such that the costs could not be recovered in higher prices, which would favour a rival's sales. Some of the extra profits of a boom may well be put into extra advertising designed to improve consumer goodwill, but it seems doubtful to me to accept the argument that prices will be forced higher by these short-run effects of advertising so that the level of its cost is probably higher than is necessary for the type of distribution involved. Of course, when an industry is newly the subject of branding, and various manufacturers are competing for the goodwill which will enable them to get established in this market, advertising may rise to an excessive level, but this is one of the costs which will have to be borne by the business concerned. In this situation, it certainly cannot put up prices to enable it to wage the struggle more successfully.

There remains the case of the fashion goods, subject to temporary changes in demand, and where the branded manufacturer must squeeze as much out of his market as he can while it is being successful, and use advertising to enable his products to compete for the fickle goodwill of the final customer. All that can be said is that it is the essence of this sort of trade that it is fickle, and that the quality which causes the fickleness is greatly valued by the consumer. Advertising may be expensive, but it is the one condition of large-scale production being at all possible. That the development of large-scale selling and production has enabled great economies in the costs of such goods and made them much more widely available seems generally admitted, and with the admission I suggest that the case for advertising is at least strengthened.

This fickleness of demand and its liability to short-run change is an important element in many markets. For some of us, toothpaste is an article where we like successive variety, and advertisement enables us to find what is available on which to ring the changes of our likes and dislikes. In so far as such a changeable demand is an important element for these commodities (sweets are another example) the manufacturer can, once more, get the stable and large demand which is necessary for large-scale production by advertising, so that he at least holds his own.

One thing which is frequently appealed to as evidence of the irrationality of the consumer is his preference for well-advertised brands, unless the shop where he is purchasing is equally well known. There is, in fact, a lot to be said historically for his attitude. It has been said before, and it should be stressed again, that the long-run success of a manufacturer does depend upon his reputation for fair quality. Those who establish a brand have, therefore, learnt by experience that they must maintain quality. To judge by some accounts of conditions in nineteenth-century trade, in the generality of consumers' goods (such as sugar) hard-pressed competitors were too ready to take something out of the product (or put something into it!). The development of branded goods has resulted in the setting and maintaining of much higher standards of quality. In lines where quality is hidden, because the consumer has no experience or because only actual use of a particular article can tell him what it is like, the consumer is rational in choosing to buy what has been advertised. But even here such goods will have to compete with unbranded goods from retailers whom the consumer has learnt to trust. Nevertheless, the result will be that a new manufacturer wishing to start selling branded goods — and some consumers' goods where the economies of large-scale production are important can only be sold as national brands — will have to incur the heavy costs of initial advertising.

It seems doubtful how important this is as an additional deterrent, where large-scale production *is* required from a beginner. When that is so, competition is really being limited by the general scale required; the price will still be held down by such competition, but may yield rather higher normal profits than would be the case if entry were easier. Here it can only be said that the difficulties of new enterprise coming in to expensive trades — where they are really profitable — has been exaggerated. In normal times there are enough large businesses looking round for fresh fields to conquer to provide some regularly available source of competition. It is feasible to increase that competition, by any social action which will increase the chances of smaller-scale businesses starting up where it is more appropriate for them to do so, and the chances of their being able to grow out of their profits. We can see this if we think of an industry where the large-scale manufacturers of branded goods compete with those who sell unbranded goods through other channels. The efficient manufacturer of unbranded goods may well grow to such a scale that he can put a brand on his product, and, equally, the efficient retailer may enlarge his operations, through the development of a multiple-shop system or in other ways, until he can manufacture in competition with those who previously sold to him.

The picture with which we conclude this theoretical account of some of the main ways in which competition works in retail trade is, then, of the various ways of distribution all competing with one another, and of the margins which they can get as being limited by the fact of actual or the threat of potential competition. On this view, then, in the ordinary lines of retail trade, advertising cannot raise the normal price of a commodity — that will be determined by the level of price which would satisfy the ways of selling that use less advertisement. In a stable situation, advertising costs will have to be paid out of the price which is competitively possible and will justify themselves only in so far as they enable a sufficient reduction in costs elsewhere. It is in this way that I think Mr. Bishop is right when he stresses that, on a dynamic view, advertising has had the social function of making large-scale production possible, in lines subject to the choice of the final consumer, where that would not have been otherwise possible.

7 Conclusions

Two big issues of social policy remain undealt with. On the first, I can only offer an opinion; on the second, I do not think that economic considerations can be the final determinants of social action, for in that particular field much wider political issues are involved and the question must be settled on those wider grounds.

The first issue concerns the cost of this competitive system in terms of the profits which it allows to the business men who are its agents. It will be admitted that the theory that I have presented gives a very different picture from that which it has now become normal for economists to give. The theory of monopolistic competition presents a world where businesses, enjoying monopolies of the conventional sort, determine their prices in such a way as to maximize their net profits. This theory presupposes restriction of output by the individual firms and the twisting of consumers' preferences so as to get maximum profits out of a balance between demand considerations (which penalize increasing outputs) and cost considerations (which may favour increasing outputs, but which in fact have normally been taken as also working in such a way as to penalize outputs). The net profit arising out of such a system would have, accordingly, a strong flavour of social irrationality; given the fundamental assumptions, prices would have no necessary normal relation to costs, and the incentives to restrict output would, the greater the competition in the industry, result in businesses being too small, and enabled to survive by profits which were higher than unrestricted competition would find necessary, and therefore greater than it was in the social interest to allow.

On my view, prices are fixed on the basis of competition and will yield a normally efficient business only the competitive profit margin in the long run. At that competitive price, a business will be keen to sell all it can, and the restrictionist implications of accepted theory are quite misleading. In such a competitive system, prices have a normal relation to costs, such as was believed in by the older schools of economists, even if the nature of manufacturing and retail competition is different from that which they supposed. But what about the net profits? May it not be the case that they are 'high'? It is impossible to say what is 'high', but on the basis of my experience I should not like to call 'high' the standard of net profits which is available over a number of years to an established business in ordinary lines of manufacture or of retailing.

Of course there are speciality trades which are small in scope, which require special knowledge to enter, and where the profitability of existing enterprises may not be obvious to the potential competitor. Such situations are not typical; there are too many looking for them. In the ordinary lines of retail trade, if the profits available to a particular business are high, direct competition will tend to reduce them, when it can appear. When, because of the special services provided or the geographical isolation of the retailer, his gross margin becomes abnormal in relation to the cost of the service which he provides and the costs and qualities of competing outlets, those other outlets will gradually strengthen their position and, unless he justifies his price by still higher services — which will itself force him into a more restricted market — he will have to lower his prices or shrinking trade will gradually drive him out of business. The typical outlets of our urban markets will not be in such a sheltered position, and competition will react both more quickly and more sharply.

Granted that the competitive capitalist system has the sort of rationale that has been provided here, and even granted that the net profits which it yields are nowhere exorbitant, anyone who explains such a system will be expected to face up to the other question whose consideration we deferred — that is, the scope for improving the efficiency of the whole system and for increasing its social value through the conscious direction which nationalization will make possible. It may still be thought, to confine ourselves to the case of retail trade with which this paper has been chiefly concerned, that reasonable though the profits may be, the costs could be lowered through State systems of trading, standardization of products, elimination of advertising, and so on. In this case, the argument runs, the social gain would be great; we should waste less resources upon the processes of distribution and should have more for the purposes of production. This argument is couched in economic terms, but it cannot be settled only on the basis of economic arguments; there are too many presuppositions about the way people will behave under nationalization and also about the 'wastes' of competition — i.e. the scope for improving the situation by standardizing all products and the mechanism of distribution.

The present theory does, if it is accepted, remove the grounds for one view of business behaviour — that it tended to go positively against the social interest — which has been much taken as supplying one very cogent economic argument for nationalization: with private enterprise being considered naturally restrictionist in the determination of prices, and with prices not necessarily relating to normal costs, at least there was a strong reason for trying to impose a greater rationality on the system, and that would require public ownership.

Moreover, the argument is often put that in some goods consumers have never had the choice between a cheap, standardized article and a more expensive, less standardized one, because the former has never been on the market. The sort of example cited is the possibility of a really cheap motor-car if manufacture were sufficiently standardized. It may be true that under a nationalized economy consumers would prefer, if they were sufficiently cheap, the standardized products that they would get, but it is doubtful if the saving in cost would be anything like that envisaged. British manufacturers are limited by the size of the market, and what they would gain on one hand by standardization they would lose on width of appeal, particularly in the export field. Where economies from standardization are large, branded goods have already given us some of the benefits. Retail trade would still have to go through relatively small-scale channels, and to the extent that it did not, other costs would be imposed which would not be without their effect upon the productivity of the society. The efficiency of management might well deteriorate. Moreover, there is still the larger question whether a directed society can provide the same efficiency, flexibility, and capacity for taking advantage of — or rather initiating — new developments as has been shown by private enterprise, whenever it has not been too restricted by outside factors. The new ideas, the inventiveness, which determine the level of a firm's costs must spring from the fertile individual mind, not the committee system.(19) But, as I have said, this is a quasi-political question: I personally have grave doubts about nationalization working successfully in productive and distributive enterprise, but there is no touchstone by which we can be sure of the answer before we have made the experiment.

What remains true is that there is considerable scope for social action to increase the pressure of competition, as I have urged in several places in this article. It should first be said that for the last 10 years and more we have been living in very abnormal times and the system has not been allowed to work effectively, but it is capable of returning to normality, and will do so when the inflationary conditions of the sellers' markets have come completely to an end. This will be enforced by events outside our island, if we are to maintain our position in world trade and our standard of living, based as it is upon our import requirements. For one thing, it would be possible to improve our taxation system so as to remove some of the present difficulties in the way of a successful business increasing its effective competition through growth out of its profits. If competition is made sufficiently strong, we need not worry about the level of profits in successful businesses — they will be the magnet, driving force, and regulator of the whole system — and a larger proportion of output will be produced at very low profits; the whole tone of the system would be improved.

Secondly, the State can help by providing much more relevant information. For example, *prompt* publication of the Censuses of Production and Distribution, with sufficiently detailed breakdown of the figures, will call

---

(19) To take up the motor-car point: had nationalization been imposed in, say, 1927, we might by now be getting 1927 motor-cars at very cheap prices, but would we in such a system be able to get the *modern* motor-car so cheaply, and, failing that, would we be able to maintain output at the rate which is assumed in the calculation of the costs of such a standard motor-car?

attention to those areas where increased competition is likely to benefit both the new entrant and his society.

Thirdly, on the vexed question of branded goods, there may be scope for consumer research councils giving full information on what seem to be the merits and demerits of particular goods when seen by expert buyers. One difficulty here, however, is that these can only refer to quality, not to the comparative value for the price; that will depend upon the other services that are involved in the distribution and sale of the commodity and a technical evaluation of these is not so easily possible.

Finally, it is sometimes urged (largely under the force of what I have tried to argue is an erroneous view of business behaviour) that the State might directly intervene to prevent exorbitant profits or excessive advertising by price control. I doubt the feasibility of this, at all events as being likely to reduce prices below the level at which they ordinarily would stand. The danger would be that qualities and services would be reduced so as to conform to the imposed prices, in so far as they were justified competitively. Such control would also tend to be much more tender to the inefficient business than normal competition would be.

Whilst we have a private enterprise economy, it would seem natural that our policies should rather be directed at increasing competition; and on the theory that I have put forward in this paper, this would seem to be a much more feasible proposition than it has been thought to be in recent years.

7 Competition in retail trade[1]

1 Introduction

This chapter offers a general view of the way competition works in retail trade in the light of the considerations which seem most relevant to the controversy over resale price maintenance (r.p.m.). Emphasis is placed on longer-run tendencies since these, obviously, should be most regarded in the determination of the public policy issues which are involved. In particular, we discuss the impact of innovations in retailing methods which some argue are frustrated by it. Attention will, however, be paid to the conflict of private interests around r.p.m., which to some extent does involve shorter-run considerations. The fact the critics propose that r.p.m. should be banned as a general public policy does enable the analysis to be simplified to the extent that, although it could be extended to take in rural retailing, it concentrates on retail trade in the urban community which is the context within which British retailing predominantly takes place.

For similar reasons, much of the analysis runs in terms of the roles of manufacturers and retailers; the lack of reference to wholesalers where it would otherwise be proper does not imply a view that their important function can be disregarded in a complete analysis of retail trade. The single reference which is made in section 5 will serve as an example of a general point that wholesalers and factors are part of the competitive complex which is retail trade as a whole. But r.p.m. characteristically is concerned with manufacturers' brands, and it is their role which is concentrated on. Our focus is on consumers' goods. Attention is called to the appendix notes which give some of the more detailed argument underlying the analysis, notably that involving the general rationality of consumers.

2 Reference list of trade terms

The following is an explanation of some terms which may be used anywhere in

(1) Reprinted with permission from *Fair Trade: Resale Price Maintenance Re-examined* (London: Macmillan & Co. Ltd., 1960), pp. 40–84. This paper is the second half of the *Fair Trade* pamphlet, the first half of which was written by Frank A. Friday.

273

the subsequent analysis:

Cost of goods (a): total of the purchase prices — 'cost prices' — of the goods
  sold in a retail business;

General, operating, expenses (b): all other expenses of the business;

Turnover (c): total receipts from sales;

Gross profit (= c – a): turnover less cost of goods;

Gross profit margin (= [c – a]/c x 100): gross profit expressed as a percentage of
  turnover;

Mark-up, on an individual article (equivalent to [c – a]/a x 100): the gross profit
  it would bring in if it were sold at the normal or expected price, expressed as
  a percentage of the cost price;

Net Profit (= c – [a + b]): the balance of sales receipts after deducting all costs
  and expenses; more or less the same as profit in ordinary usage;

Net profit margin (= {c – [a + b]}/c x 100): the net profit put as a percentage of
  total turnover;

Discount: abatement of some price (e.g. list price), usually to a particular class
  of customer, e.g. to wholesale customers (one kind of 'trade discount'), or to
  customers paying prompt cash ('cash discounts'), usually expressed as a
  percentage of the basis price.

Some economic analysis of costs and expenses in retail trade will be found in
Appendix Note B.

3 The competitiveness of retail trade

Retailing ought to be analysed on the basis that it is a highly competitive
industry. The main reason for this is not that there are so many shops, although
it is regarded as important that shops are relatively numerous in urban shopping
centres. The industry is not easily analysed in terms of theoretical 'pure'
competition, where mere numbers might be an important consideration.
Subsidiary analyses of demand, costs, entry-possibilities, and of the form the
industry's structure takes, lie behind the choice of analytical method. This
analysis in fact is an extension of one which was first developed for
manufacturing industry, and because of the function which 'normal' costs play,
it may perhaps be termed a theory of 'normal competition', normal gross
margins in retail trade playing the part of normal prices in manufacturing
industry.(2)

A major element in the analysis is the assumed rationality of consumers.

---

(2) For the parent theory reference may be made to P.W.S. Andrews,
Manufacturing Business, Macmillan & Co. Ltd., London 1949.

This does not involve the preposterous postulate that every individual consumer is always 'rational'; nor, at the same time, does it involve the assumption, made explicitly or implicitly in so many theoretical discussions of retail economics, that consumers are 'located', rigidly tied to one place. The detailed argument underlying the assumption of 'rationality' is summarized in Appendix Note A, but attention should be called to two consequences of the assumption that there is a general tendency with any large number of consumers for them to make rational choices between the alternatives, in the way of qualities, special services, and prices, offered them by the shops with whom they come into regular contact as they move around on ordinary journeys as well as on special shopping expeditions. The first consequence concerns the extent of competition between individual shops. All shops in urban areas are enmeshed in a complex chain of competition for patronage which is most intense within any one area but which will have important linkages between adjacent areas as well as between them and regional 'shopping capitals'. For our present summary analysis, the more important patterns within this complex of competition may be put as follows: Shops which any group of consumers may be near at various times are deemed to be in close competition for their patronage in what are later called 'individually important goods'; any shops in shopping centres are in close competition generally with one another for the patronage of consumers passing through such centres, or able conveniently to get to them for shopping expeditions (and to be strong potential competitors, the shops need not actually be selling similar goods so long as they could do so); residential neighbourhood shops are exposed to the competition of all other shops regularly open to the residents except for commodities required in domestic emergencies.

The second consequence of consumers choosing rationally in terms of 'value for money' is that our subsequent analysis may be simplified as though consumers were choosing in terms of prices alone. With this convention, the broad conclusions which are reached in the course of the analysis of demand may be summarized as follows:

(a) For individually important goods — those which are bought at frequent intervals, and any whose prices are appreciable in relation to typical consumer 'budgets', as well as any other goods whose prices in other shops are well-known — a shop whose price for any one of them is lower than any of its competitors are charging will gain turnover in that line and, of course, the competitors charging higher prices will lose turnover. A shop with a higher price will similarly lose turnover, and its competitors will gain;

(b) To have lower prices in such 'important' goods will lead to turnover in other lines increasing, and higher prices will lead to other turnover falling; the effect of (a) is therefore amplified;

(c) A shop whose general price level is low compared with that of competing shops will gain turnover generally; and turnover will be lost in the contrary case.

The general effects of these laws of demand are studied in section 4 below, but one effect is relevant to the other major factor intensifying the competitive tendency of retail trade — the ease of entry of new businesses. The demand laws mean that there are no barriers on the demand side to the new entry of competitive business. Any detailed analysis of ease of entry here and elsewhere requires reference to the formal structure of retailing.

In analysing the structure of retailing, three major characteristics typify a business, and with the sub-classifications of these some ten characteristics are involved altogether. Location is a major characteristic, and within it we distinguish neighbourhood, district, urban centre, and regional capital shops; then there is the scope of the business, distinguishing general, specialist, and departmental shops; thirdly comes ownership class, with its subdivisions of independent, private multiple, and co-operative shops. It is hoped that this terminology is self-explanatory. We note that the 'self-service' 'supermarket' is not from this point of view a distinct class of shop; it represents the impact of a modern innovation affecting more than one of these classes, discussed in section 5. For a similar reason, we do not classify a manufacturing retailer as a distinct sub-class of shop; it represents one method by which a retailer may extend its organization. Entry of competitive businesses is most easy in centres and capitals, but more easy in local districts than in neighbourhoods.

Retail trade requires low capital relatively to turnover. Thus an effective entry may be made with what is, considered alongside the capital normally required in manufacturing, a relatively small venture. One factor in this is the ease with which retail premises can be rented (and, if a business does own its own premises, capital may be easily freed for use elsewhere by arranging a sale and a 'lease back'). Another factor which reduces capital needs is that so much is represented by saleable stock-in-hand, and it is therefore comparatively easy to arrange additional finance through bank overdrafts if necessary, for example, at a time of seasonal pressure. Finance may similarly be obtained by mortgages on the premises. Finally, because cost of goods is generally so large a part of turnover, trade credit can be used freely up to the limit of the periods during which cash discounts are available, and the business's longer-run capital employed can be further increased (although at heavy rates of interest) by foregoing the discounts.

Another factor making for low capital needs is that the minimum unit of enterprise is only one shop. Although really small retailers may have large cost disadvantages, and really large retail businesses may have appreciable advantages, extremes of size in retailing are often associated with significant differences in the classification of the business concerned, which affects the area of competition. In general a moderate-size business has only minor cost disadvantages to overcome as against relatively much bigger businesses in the same general line, so it may equally hope to 'make a do'. Since we have been referring to 'businesses', we should stress that in fact there is no necessity for a new competitor in an area to be a completely new retailer. All that is necessary is a 'new' shop,(3) and a large existing business is quite capable of making this relatively modest venture. This is one reason why recent innovations have shown such competitive strength (see sections 4–6).

In retail trade it is also an important fact that there is a relatively considerable potential supply of managerial talent; any manager of a shop is potentially a retailer, and many of them in fact try (along with people less likely to succeed) because to be a retailer is a relatively easy way of trying to secure an independent position which will be, if not affluent, at least not subordinate. A man from almost any walk of life who has retired early and has some savings may see the attractions of purchasing a livelihood along with living accommodation. It is for these reasons that there is ordinarily such severe pressure from new-entry competition in the smallest size-classes of all, the small neighbourhood shops and the smallest specialists.

The wide geographical opportunity for enterprise which retailing's very ubiquity affords should also be mentioned. If one area seems likely to be unrewarding, there are plenty of other places to look at. And the fact that it is possible to find premises in 'desirable' areas, where shopkeepers and managers would like to live anyway, increases the pressure of competition.

It seems desirable to refer to institutional impediments to entry. First, of course, a shop needs a site and in any one area there is not a limitless choice. Beyond that, however, there are town-planning restrictions on the uses to which sites may be put, which have had a severe effect on the amenities which the inhabitants of new areas can enjoy. The movement of population and other factors have probably led to a relatively easier supply of small retail premises in older urban areas, in so far as this can provide a counterbalance in the retail competition complex as a whole. The controls on expansion for existing retailers are a severe hindrance to certain types of shops (notably department stores). But would-be new entrants to an area can bid for and 'take over' existing businesses perhaps just for the sake of the site and premises. This means that efficient businesses can readily displace the inefficient.

This last sentence leads us on to one other factor not only in the competitiveness of retail trade but also in the details of the balance of

---

(3) The inverted commas around 'new' are a reminder that a new competitor may take an old business — see the remarks below about ease of exit.

competitive power — the ease of exit of existing shops and businesses. In retail trade, we do not find, as we do in some manufacturing industries, businesses dragging on a miserable existence because a large part of their investment is represented by sunk capital of no value to anyone else and involving no current cash outlay. As we have seen, retail assets have a cash value and are relatively easily disposed of. Moreover, exit is not only easy in this sense, it is also rather more easily compelled than in many manufacturing industries because so much of the cost of retailing is cash outlay. It is true that time lags in rents, and in taxes in the cases of businesses owning their premises, may delay the forcing out of businesses whose normal costs are not covered by their turnover (see Appendix Note C on Rent) but this often increases the opportunity for the 'take-over bidder' to buy them out.

4 The balance of competitive power

Retail competition evolves a balance of power between major classes of shops. A fuller classification was outlined on page 276, but the discussion can be simplified by limiting illustrations to shop types which occupy key positions in the analysis of r.p.m.:

(a) neighbourhood shop, e.g., the 'corner' general shop where sweets, tobacco and grocery items usually predominate in a mixed bag of razor blades, stationery, hair nets, etc. Meeting consumers' needs near at home, it gets its turnover from whatever it thinks profitable to stock and sell;

(b) specialist shop, selling, e.g., footwear, blouses, books, photographic goods, etc., offering a wide choice of goods within such a speciality, it adds anything else which can profitably be sold alongside them. Most numerous in the larger shopping 'centres', but also in smaller 'districts' on the one hand, and the large shopping 'capitals' on the other. The range of goods offered within the speciality tends to be larger the 'busier' the location;

(c) department store, a commonly-owned grouping of specialist shops within one building, located in 'centres' and 'capitals'. To encourage consumers to spend time passing between departments, it often provides general 'amenities' to a larger extent than other shops, but the relative importance of these in its costs tends to be greatly exaggerated;

(d) branch of a large multiple organization. Mainly located in 'centres' and 'capitals' but, as with the food trades and newsagents, sometimes also in districts. Organized on the basis of central buying and the application of management routines in the control of individual branches, the core of a multiple is usually some group of specialisms, standardized commodities predominating in the range and so with less choice at particular prices than

278

either of the two preceding kinds of specialized shops;

(e) branch of a co-operative society, which can straddle across any of the previous classes but whose special features of customer-ownership, local organization, and the payment of 'dividends' related to purchases, will call for separate comment.

This classification is somewhat blurred when we look at actual shops and their ownership-organizations, but practical retailers use it when discussing their industry because it does focus attention on the lines of force in the balance of power.

Paradoxical as it may seem, we introduce, temporarily, one more simplification: no reference is made to the fact of r.p.m. in establishing the general economics of retail competition against which the practice of r.p.m. is to be studied. To do otherwise would require replication of generalizations which space will not allow and the deficiency can be made good more simply later.

Let us first think in abstract terms of 'a' shop of a given 'type', competing in a shopping 'centre' with shops of its own type and of practically all other types as well (which implies that the 'neighbourhood' shop will be treated later as a special case). An economic model of 'central' retailing can assume without serious error that all retailers within the same type-class will have the same purchase costs for the goods sold typically by them so that if they were sold by all at identical prices they would individually yield the same gross margins.(4)

Our imaginary retailer will have greater freedom with particular prices than he will have with those of his range of commodities as a whole. To lower his general price level will attract turnover from competitors generally, more severely from those of the same type, and in a cumulative fashion. Close competitors will inevitably retaliate. In the normal case, in an area where competition has existed for some time, such retaliation would drive our retailer back to the re-establishment of former price levels, or the group will be worse off, unless, and occasionally this is important, the lower general prices cause them as a group to make net gains from retailers who are hit but who are sufficiently remote from them in type or location as not to be able to retaliate effectively.

The characteristic occasion for the development of permanent lower price levels in a class of shops is the adoption of some innovation in retailing. This

---

(4) As Appendix Note B argues, the cost of goods is, in general, affected appreciably only by differences in the sizes of turnover which are so extreme that they normally go with differences in type of retailer. The whole of the present argument will explain why we should assume that 'very small' retailers of any particular type-class, those small enough to have appreciably higher costs of goods, could not survive in competition with the general run of their type.

must start with some individual retailer. If our retailer who has cut his price level has found a cheaper way of selling his line of goods, it will pay him to take higher profits from increased turnover at the reduced prices and not worry about the inevitable copying of him by competitors. He can invest his profits in enhancing his goodwill while his competitors' strategies are correspondingly hampered. More, he can consolidate and extend his position by acquiring other shops in which to apply his higher 'efficiency'. But this exceptional case from our present point of view, where we are looking at economics of retailing as at a given time, has led us into two matters to be specially discussed later — 'efficiency' and change in general.

Coming back to changes in price policies in settled conditions, we shall surely not need to argue about the inadvisability of the retailer setting a price level which is higher than that of his close competitors, if he wishes to maintain his competitive position; we must rather be concerned with the limits which will hold down the price levels of the group of competitors as a whole. The freedom with which new competition can arise, from the switching of existing businesses as well as from newcomers, means that if shop price levels for any class of shop are high in relation to costs, others will have a go at this trade. The general level of prices must not be so high as to enable 'outsiders' to compete effectively, or the existing retailers will lose turnover.

These laws of competition mean that, 'if' all retailers of a given type sold exactly the same commodities and in the same proportions, each would tend to have the same, normal, gross profit margin. In fact, retail trade in detail is very varied and the range of goods handled differs from retailer to retailer within the same class, but not without each looking continuously at any opportunities there might be in extending in his rivals' ranges. The general implications of the laws are valid; these competitive forces bear on the individual shop's gross margin and ultimately determine its normal level. Consistently, any substantial differences in gross margins for retailers in the same type-class can usually be explained — for example, as between specialist jewellers and grocers, or as between two department stores (where the higher-normal-cost department may be more important in one than in the other). Because individual retailers in the same type-class do sell much the same range of commodities, retail statistics with all their diversity show a tendency to cluster around typical values (and with relatively small differences between the averages for type-classes). As from inside the individual shops this tendency is reinforced by the retailer's custom of applying the same percentage mark-up on cost for goods of the same general kind, unless he is aware of cost factors tending otherwise or (obviously connected) competition prevents this. This custom makes economic sense because the costs of stocking and selling goods of the same general type are expected to go with price.

An individual shop can, of course, hold its own with its competitors over-all without having all prices at the same level as theirs. Window 'call-birds' and 'special offers' are temporary and changing attractions with only a passing effect on close competitors, if that, since they will be doing the same sort of thing and these are settled weapons in the struggle against other shops in general rather than against each other in particular. What a retailer cannot do for long, is to cut the usual price for what to its competitors is an important good without getting their retaliation. Of course, if there is a price war on, this is the kind of commodity which may be cut for temporary advantage, as also if a shop is finding its survival difficult for any other reason; for this kind of low price will have the biggest and sharpest effect on total turnover. In general, an important good to a class of shops will be important to the consumer. But with the competitive restraint on overall gross margins there is not room ordinarily for one shop to sustain low prices at the heart of its range of goods, and (still excepting the period of an innovation mentioned previously) the prices of such goods will generally be in line as between shops of the same type. If a retailer comes to the conclusion that a particular item is highly priced in relation to properly allocated costs, and especially if its costs to him have been lowered by access to a cheaper supply, then his normal price policy will lead to a lower price, and competitors will have to match him or get out of the line.

Of course, there is no reason why a shop should worry about setting a lower price as compared with other types of retailer. Here, it will pay best to pick goods which are important to them but not so important to it. If such goods are sufficiently standardized, these are the ideal items to 'lead' with in order to get other trade from the questing consumer, and the following suit of close competitors will still leave the whole group with an advantage. In this way, the balance of power between alternative types of retailer is more uneasily held than that between retailers of the same type; the possibility of a type of shop offering low prices on goods which are important to consumers buying from other types is the fulcrum on which innovations turn the balance of competition. So the rule for a settled balance of competition as between types of shops is that the prices of any goods which are important to sizeable groups of consumers shall be in parity right across the board. When such goods are being used as 'leaders', as before, the shops to whom they are in fact important will have, individually or collectively, to find some way of holding their own, or they will have to withdraw from all but casual or 'emergency' sales of the goods concerned, and this means a net shrinkage in the turnover of the losing group. (We shall later see that this is how innovations produce their counter-revolutions!)

If the general freedom of new competition and the rationality and mobility of consumers in the large be accepted, it is probably not necessary to go into detailed analysis from the 'centres' to the 'districts', which in many areas, and

281

especially in certain lines of trade, are having at present to do all they can to stem the tides of successful 'centre' competition — the trend being towards 'High Street Shopping'. Modern transport has greatly intensified the thrust of competition along the chain of shops in urban areas at a time when important changes are working themselves out. Passing on to the question of competition between types of shops, we once more cut detailed arguments and simply state the conclusion, relevant to our main subject, to which we have been led by the same kind of reasoning as has been used so far. This is that the balance of competitive power between types of shops will lead to a shop of a given type, and a given general range of goods, having a normal profit margin at which it can hold its own, not only with other shops of the same type, but also with shops of different types when their prices are similarly at normal levels. But if this be the normal state of affairs, it has been established not only by the experience of orderly development but also by the tests of sporadic local or general periods of warfare with guerilla-like individual actions somewhere most of the time. We have already said that this inter-type balance of power is 'uneasily held' and it is always upset — and properly — when there are any fundamental changes in the basic trading methods which are involved in any type of retailing. Let us look more closely at the differences in the strategic and tactical positions of leading types of retailer from this point of view. To shorten the discussion, we concentrate first on the differences between multiple retailers and other types, and second, on those between multiples and department stores, and the rest. What is said about multiple stores under the first head will also apply under the second.

The key to success in a multiple shop is sheer turnover. Central management itself uses estimates of turnover possibilities as criteria between goods which could equally well fit into its gross margin patterns; then, from the resulting lists branch management selects the goods which it thinks will maximize the local turnover in fact. The success of branch management, of course, is very much judged on a turnover basis. The multiples need fairly substantial gross margins to carry their administrative overheads (and the costs of instalment credit, the bulk of which is done by multiples). They have a considerable advantage in their cost prices and the large multiples generally hold their own on low net margins for the type of goods in which they deal; their success turns on the continued mass sale of the standardized and relatively cheap goods for which they are responsible. Let volume drop or the price level be squeezed, and the margin of profit can swell into a large loss quite rapidly. Given the general pressure of their overheads and the continuously increasing pressure of competition at their end of the industry, to get more customers in and more turnover out of their shops is the ever-present anxiety of the managers. Historically, the continuing development of the multiples is continuously eroding at the base of the range of goods sold by department stores and at the middle of the range of many specialists and neighbourhood shops. It is its normal competition for the multiple to develop standard commodities which compete on a price basis with those sold by others; it is a normal feature of this competitive strategy to 'lead' if it can with commodities which are important to others for the sake of the general turnover which the additional customers will take with them. To say that on a long view the history of modern retailing has been multiples versus the rest has great validity, and the general standard of living owes much to their development, but nevertheless this misses out the changing game which the 'other side' have played, which will concern us in section 5.

On a short view of the struggle, the department store stands side by side with the multiple in the commercial strategy which it employs. The nature of its business means a relatively high proportion of expenses, and its net margins have to reward much heavier investment in relation to turnover than is the case with multiples. The heavy standing expenses go on in season and out of season, and in its trading complex as a whole the rest of its departments are in a way 'overhead' to the activity in any one. The department store generally, because of the kinds of commodities which it sells, attracts by the variety of its stocks, but it increases that attraction by suitable 'leading' on the prices charged for some of its 'own lines' (including its restaurant) generally or at special times of the year. We can see from other countries' experience that department stores, like multiples, will tend to 'lead' if they can with what are standard commodities of importance to others for the sake of their turnover as a whole.

In contrast, the specialist shops and the neighbourhood shops are in a much weaker strategic position. A key function with both is the carrying of relatively large and varied stocks and, since we shall return to the question of other functions performed by the specialist, we can let a discussion of the position of the neighbourhood shop stand for the interests of both for the moment; both have important proportions of their sales which they would lose if there were 'leading' of prices against them.

It is true that some part of the sales of the neighbourhood shop is really to meet the emergency needs of consumers ordinarily buying elsewhere, but a large part of the sales is made in the ordinary way, because those very goods are not likely to be cheaper elsewhere and because their prices (wherever sold) are thought sufficiently competitive with other goods for consumers to be prepared to buy them locally. One implication is that consumers are able to keep lower stocks in the house. For this wider part of its turnover, however, our theory tells us that the neighbourhood shop would lose sales heavily if consumers thought they had a good chance of doing better elsewhere. Perhaps even more important, the shop would take such risks into account and would be less willing to stock goods where this was liable to happen; but to have fewer stocks would itself cause lower sales. With the average turnover lower for both these reasons, the numbers of neighbourhood shops would have to decrease. Doubtless the lower numbers that would be left could exact higher margins on the basis of the pure emergencies they were meeting, but on the average consumers would have to travel farther for these purchases. In addition, they would have lost the convenience of being able to shop locally, emergency or no, at the same prices as elsewhere. The question which really interests the consumer is surely not whether he can occasionally get an ounce of tobacco at a halfpenny cheaper but whether the prices which he pays in general are as low as they would otherwise be. As it is he gets the service of his neighbourhood shop in most cases below full cost. With no advantages of large-scale purchasing and with parity of most prices, the small independent shop has to manage on relatively low gross margins; it gets by because often the owner is content to take less out of the business than he could command as someone else's employee, or the woman of the household runs the shop alongside her home, and so on.

With this last paragraph we have been pushed into the question of the effect of banning r.p.m., which we can tackle systematically only together with the dynamics of change in retailing. In this connexion it is often said that r.p.m. keeps alive relatively 'inefficient' shops and hinders the development of less costly, 'more efficient' methods of retailing. This alleged hindrance to change will be discussed in the next section, but a lot of the dicta about 'inefficient' retailers is rather loose talking. The theory propounded in this paper would lead us to believe that a type of retailer can survive only if it is sufficiently 'efficient' by comparison with competing types for consumers to want to buy enough of its goods to give it the turnover which, collectively, it needs for survival.

As for the especially 'efficient' *individual* retailer, we may surely dismiss any suggestion that he will give his 'rent of ability' away, as it were, 'with a packet of tea'. Why should he reduce his prices more than is necessary to hold his own in his present shop? There will be a limit to its capacity and once that is more or less attained and even before, there is no reason why he should not both enjoy the profits of his superiority and grow. Why should he not rather buy up additional shops, managed now by less efficient people, and take his gains directly at competitive price levels all the way? He will then be untroubled by the fear that his superior efficiency may be only a passing phase, and by thoughts of his own mortality, but take comfort that his larger business will have a fair chance of always being managed with at least average ability. If, of course, his 'efficiency' lies really in his having discovered a new method of retailing, that is a different matter. He will virtually have founded a new type of retail business and will have the maximum chance of gain if he exploits this both price-wise and through taking on additional shops. The history of retailing shows that large fortunes can come from either 'efficiency' exploited in the appropriate manner.

By way of coda to this section, we may remark that our theory has certainly indicated the commercial reasons for at least some types of businesses wishing to retain r.p.m. To the explicit interests of the neighbourhood and specialist shops, we shall add those of manufacturers of standard branded goods, especially where they are small compared with the trade of the largest retailers. Further, although department stores may occasionally look longingly at the increased freedom which an r.p.m. ban would bring, they also often have a general interest in r.p.m. in terms of their own competition with multiples, on at least some part of their turnover. But all such argument is heavily involved with the general question of change in retail trade.

5 Is r.p.m. necessarily an obstacle to progress?

Retail trade is often seen as an unproductive sort of activity. The feeling that to sell something is less useful than to make it goes sufficiently deeply to tinge the thinking even of those of us who are trained by economic analysis to know that there is no warrant for such a distinction — that it is a single economic process from the getting of primary materials right down to the delivery of finished products, in the required quantities, into the hands of the individual consumer. One element in the grudge against distribution is that the 'same' goods are sold by the factory at a much lower price than we have to pay. We can see how much better off we should be at those prices, and forget the necessary condition that other people should still buy through retailers if the special costs of serving us individually are not to affect the standard price of the factory. This fantasy gets some semblance of rationalization in a contrast which is drawn between manufacture and retailing. Of the one, the tale is of advancing technology and falling real costs; of the other it is of the rising proportion of social resources going into distribution. It is easy to exclaim how much more we could have, if only 'wastes' in distribution were cut. This viewpoint is seriously out of touch with reality. The rising proportionate cost of distribution results partly from our choosing to have some of our increased income in additional services, but it mainly results from the greater gains which are possible in manufacture just because distribution does its job relatively well.

Retail distribution is not untouched by progress; there is a continuous adaptation of its organization to match the development of industry. Mass consumption we can never have, but distribution has remained able to move the increasing flow of mass products into consumption whilst still allowing the private consumer to keep the ultimate freedom — of choice. Although the general direction in which retailing is travelling is therefore that of mass-distribution of mass-produced goods, minority preferences are still met so long as sufficient numbers share them to make it commercially worthwhile to satisfy them. In this process, the mass goods of one generation are often such as were the luxuries of their parents, and luxuries themselves tend to follow the trend towards larger-scale production.

Before continuing to describe change from an abstract point of view, we may recall that in one lifetime Marks and Spencer have changed from everything-at-a-penny barrows in a small North of England area to nation-wide 'penny bazaars', and thence to the great multiple chain store organization with its specialization in clothing, whose contribution to the standard of living in Britain no one of working-class origins can overlook. It does not belittle the achievements of their competitors to acknowledge the stimulus which has accompanied Marks and Spencer's own achievements. But the business itself is clearly one which has changed with the changing industrial conjuncture, and this is one more reason why it can stand as an individual instance of the change in the whole complex of retail trade which is still going on.

Although change in retail trade is more or less continuous it seems to make its larger movements in waves following the impact of major innovations, whose success hindsight can frequently see to have been due, no doubt, primarily to the genius — and often persistence — of the first founder himself, but also partly to the circumstances of the times, which in their turn accounted very largely for the success of those who followed him and turned over to the new idea. For such a major innovation there is a pattern, in the beginning and in the subsequent readjustment of retailing in general, which fits both our present thesis of a retail-trade complex which moves in parallel with the expansion of manufacturing industry and the thesis put forward in the last section of the dynamic balance of competitive power, which in its way is the retail-trade complex itself.

The pattern is that the innovation normally appears first in the urban shopping centres where large-scale selling is more easily at home, consists of some means of offering more standardized goods, with less 'frills', at prices which bring to the shops embodying the innovation what, for the time, are large turnovers — which, to complete the circle of success, are needed for the innovation to justify itself. The new form often makes spectacularly quick development at first. There is usually some driving out of existing businesses of older forms, and some conversion of them, especially in the centres, to the new form. In particular, the historic trend has usually been a reduction in the proportionate importance of 'general' independent stores. Those remaining of the older types show the balance of power operating to form the next phase of the pattern of development; these competing forms of retailer modify their own methods of selling or their range of goods to compete more successfully, or at least hold their own, with it. In the final picture the innovating type itself is modified. The successful emulation and competition from followers and from other types of store make it more difficult for the shops of the new type to continue to grow at the rate their private economics requires, if they remain unchanged. Other factors bring some pressure from within the general increase in centre-shop turnovers will pull up site values and ultimately rents, disproportionately perhaps on the kinds of sites they require; there is also the secular trend of rising retail wages. With all other retailers, they are also affected over any long period by the rising demand for additional services which accompanies higher national income.

In the ultimate balance of power, then, the new type of shop will have had to 'trade up' to some extent, to move towards greater ranges of goods, the supply of higher qualities etc., in short, to add 'frills' somewhere, in order to get the increased sales needed for continued success in the new conditions. The obverse, as we have seen, is that the same factors cause the more 'frilly' competitors to change; these tend to 'trade down', moving towards larger-scale distribution. The gains from the innovation in the final pattern, which will be stable until the next major change, thus include not only the enrichment of competition by the thrust of the new type of shop, still especially oriented towards the characteristics which set it off originally, but also the further general move of retail trade as a whole towards larger typical turnovers and an extension of the mass-distribution of goods.(5)

The major retailing innovations during the first half of the period of the development of the modern industrial community were associated with the introduction of new forms of ownership-organization, and came, all things considered, fairly rapidly on the heels of each other. In this century, apart from cross-associations between manufacture and retailing which are discussed below, the broad classification has remained unchanged until recently. Co-operative societies, founded on consumer-ownership, the attractions of dividends bringing a concentration of working-class purchasing power on staple commodities; department stores, founded to sell centrally a variety of goods on a bulk cash-and-carry basis, with limited ranges of goods in each line, low-price mass outlets; multiple stores, carrying the large-purchases, low-prices, massive-turnover principle further by combining the purchasing power of many branches (the 'five

---

(5) We do not imply that in a period of stable pattern there is nothing for the efficient retailer to do except go on with what he is doing; in fact changes, each of which may be minor and local, are always going on, and each produces readjustment in the pattern somewhere. The balance of power in retail trade is therefore never statically at rest even though from the point of view of analysis we may treat it as so.

and ten' or sixpenny variety store being a special development of these from the present point of view); these successively followed one another and brought changes in all predecessor types.(6)

Multiple stores, with their purchasing advantages and their great flexibility of location and capacity for specialization have perhaps been the most persistent pressure group in retail trade since they emerged as a distinct type. The interactions with department stores have been interesting. At first mass providers, department stores were gradually forced into 'trading up' in the face of multiple competition in what had been a special market, and became the collocations of specialist shops of at least moderate quality and large variety within each range which are described in the textbooks on retailing. Under the influence of the newer developments favouring multiples, which we shall be discussing in a moment, department stores are under pressure in this country. The pressure is partly masked by self-ownership of sites or lags in rent charges, partly increased in many cases by the difficulty or expense of converting buildings which changing organization has rendered unsuitable for their purposes; but the trend is there. To get their turnover in the future, a measure of trading down is necessary, and to an outsider it appears that this has already set in. For many such stores the future may well lie in association with a multiple organization so that they may extend into the mass-selling of goods on a better purchasing basis. Is the new trend to be a multiple-type ground floor, with higher grade specialisms upstairs?

In the same way, the present plight of the co-ops is of saddish interest. With large resources, the movement as a whole is barely holding its own against the pressure of the multiples. A pioneer in self-service, the movement generally speaking went into this early because of the pressure of high labour costs. It is now going through a strenuous period of self-analysis, but the chief difficulty remains for small societies, with their main turnovers in lines which now earn lower net margins (and consequent struggle to keep dividends whilst matching prices here), to get sufficient trade in other lines to which mass expenditure has mainly shifted its emphasis. One thing seems certain: the co-operative movement will eventually find how to use its own peculiar advantages, and the resources it has invested behind them (perhaps movement-wide chain stores?) to regain its due share of total trade. When it does so, of course, its exploitation of its solution will at that point have the force of an independent re-sharpening of

---

(6) If more were known about them, we should doubtless have said more here and later about specialist mail order stores and mail order facilities generally. Originally, apparently, of major importance to relatively isolated consumers, their renascence is obviously playing a big, but so far as we are concerned non-measurable, part in modern retailing.

the edge of retail competition. The readjustments in these and in the other sections of retail trade under fire from the multiples make it most interesting to an industrial economist to be an outside observer at this time. Much more could be said, but this is not a kind of specialist *Old Moore's Almanack* and we are more concerned to describe present tendencies from the point of view of the r.p.m. question rather than to prophesy the future gratuitously.

The trends with which we are concerned result from the super-position of present circumstances and an important innovation on the generally strong position which the large multiple had gained before the war. We deal with this last factor first since to do so will bring out the general economic function of brands with associated r.p.m. In clothing and in food the large national multiples were big enough, and had been established long enough, to have become 'household words'. This meant that in the lines standardized to their own orders they had established their own 'brands' whether or not there was a special house name. The standardization of commodities by the multiple meant of course that it could place its own 'cachet' on them; no one else could sell Marks and Spencer garments; but this advantage was founded as always on relative quality and price. Standardization was not only the means of making one's product exclusive, it was also the way in which the multiple maximized its advantages as a large-scale buyer. Such large standard orders brought their advantages in manufacture, and their steadiness in the aggregate also had its attractions. Competition from supplier manufacturers in these circumstances ensured the keen quotations which were the basis of the multiples' fortunes. (It should, moreover, be said that because of their interest in cost, some multiples play an important part in stimulating the adoption of the latest production and cost-control methods in their suppliers' businesses.)

Multiples occasionally achieved such close relations with particular suppliers that even without common ownership there has been virtual integration. Other multiples in some lines of trade went further and bought or established their factories. Here not only was manufacturing completely integrated with retailing but, in industries where there is a great variety in the goods — as with footwear — the manufacturing multiple could do a great deal better than the average manufacturer; it could organize its own manufacture on the most standardized basis possible and keep its factory running full-bore on items where it could place larger orders. The orders to outside manufacturers were smaller-scale, more varied and also more fluctuating, in so far as its own factory had first call. Manufacturing multiples therefore gained a preponderant advantage in many lines. Manufacturers fought back in two ways. Some acquired shops and became manufacturer-retailers themselves. Others developed their own brands to leapfrog distributors and appeal directly to the demand of consumers. A successful brand brought more stable demand, necessarily more standardized, and so lowered costs, so that it could survive on the basis of prices which, quality for quality, were competitive with others.

This example has special features but fairly wide application in sections of the clothing industry. Its main feature, however, applies to all manufacturers' brands — the competitive process before the consumer is extended by their existence. Brand-owning manufacturers and large retailers not only compete between themselves but also, as competitive ways of producing and selling, with each other. This extended competition ensures a greater standardization both of production and of selling methods than if either type survived on its own, whilst giving the consumer a more varied choice. In the retailers' case the standardization is organized primarily in the interests of selling; in the manufacturers' in those of production economy. Retailers as such have their interests in making their brands 'different' and, although they can parcel up orders so as to get the more competitive prices at any one time, those prices may well reflect costs whose normal levels are higher for both reasons. Each manufacturer's brand is, of course, also 'differentiated' but orders for it are necessarily concentrated on the factory where it is a standard. Neither approach is necessarily superior from the social point of view. Free competition may fairly be left to decide between the alternatives, and will usually have so much of each. The point remains that any one manufacturer's brand must win through on price or out it will go.

The conclusion is, then, not that brands in themselves hinder more progressive standardization in modern mass-production, but that the competition of brands actually helps this. It may be objected that manufacturers' brands compete only on the basis of persuasive advertising and thus 'distort' final demand in their favour at the cost of 'wasteful' advertising. The short answer to this is that it overlooks the whole function of 'persuasion' in retail trade and mistakes the permanent effect of advertising besides. A summary guide to a longer answer is given in Appendix Note A.

This conclusion, however, does not dispose of our present questions, for brands also involve r.p.m. and we must consider how far the fixing of retail prices by manufacturers is itself an obstacle to progress. Not all brands are price maintained; where, as in some fashion trades, products change rapidly, brands can be established without r.p.m., which would in fact be difficult to operate. Where specifications are more stable, however, the rule stands that standard goods will have to have standard prices if demand is to run steadily at the level justified by their real qualities in the view of the consumer and, withal, the levels at which prices are standardized must be such that each is fully competitive with other goods. Large retailers obey this rule for their 'brands' by having standard prices at their various branches. The manufacturer must similarly fix standard retail prices if his commodities are to be generally available to the extent to which consumers would otherwise like. An uncertain price will both reduce demand and make retailers generally less willing to stock the goods; a price which is generally observed but cut noticeably by some retailers will lead to those price-maintaining retailers who continue to stock the good simply meeting 'emergency' demands, whilst promoting other goods so far as they can.

Our conclusion is that price maintenance is itself no obstacle to progress in manufacture or in retailing. We may already dismiss the naive view that it is obvious that r.p.m. causes prices to be higher. The conclusion from our analysis is rather that to the extent to which a general ban on r.p.m. weakens the thrust from manufacturers' brands, the whole competitiveness of retail trade will in the long run itself be weakened; such a ban, in short, must itself reduce an important influence keeping prices in general down. A brand does not give a monopoly, it simply gives regular preferences at competitive prices.

Another objection to r.p.m. is more directly concerned with innovation and progress. It runs on the lines that a brand will be stocked by retailers with very different costs, that the margin which the fixed price yields must cover the costs of the least efficient and that it is therefore excessive for the more efficient who are prevented by the fixed price from competing on the basis of their lower costs. We have already uncovered two fallacies in this. The first is that there are great differences in normal cost for similar kinds of shop; the second is that if there were such differences they would be reflected in prices even in perfect competition. A third fallacy arises from overlooking how much of the 'selling' is done by the manufacturer of a brand, partly in his actual preparation of the product (convenient pack etc.), partly in his distribution arrangements (own warehouses etc.), but especially in that persuasion of the customer, whose economic function is so easily misunderstood. What is left for the retailer to do is a much more standard operation and this is a factor which must still further reduce any differences in costs between retailers so far as this product is concerned. The overwhelming objection to this kind of criticism, however, to our mind, is the one we keep stressing — that it overlooks the fact that a mistaken policy will be uncovered by competitors who will get lower costs and can charge lower prices by adopting more appropriate policies. It is no objection to r.p.m. that branded goods are sold by such a wide variety of retailers, where this is the case. If the critics are right and if some 'more efficient' retailers would have much lower costs of selling some particular kind of branded goods, so very much the greater is the competitive opportunity for their own brands. If they cannot drive out the rival brand, surely the critics are mistaken.

Of course, it is true that some retailers would at any one time find it attractive to compete for increased general turnover on the basis of selling some popular brands at lower than the fixed prices, because of the trade which would come to them with the customers for that brand thereby attracted from other retailers. The question is whether or no they would thereby sell more of the branded goods than would otherwise be sold. In the generality of cases, the issue is not in doubt; the manufacturer will already have tried to set the price which gives him the largest sales. The short-run benefit to the price-cutters has to be set against the permanently lessened market for the competitive brand manufacturer and the, from an economic point of view, adventitiously reduced general market opportunities for the retailers who have previously sold the branded goods where prices are subject to price-cutting.

Putting on one side, then, the objections which rely upon alleged differences in efficiencies of established types of retailer, we should consider those which are concerned with the alleged prevention of or hindrance to the development of new, more efficient, types of retailing. Let us not discuss this in the abstract but consider the specific case of the supermarket, the modern general store which has developed on the basis of self-service. Self-service developed first in grocery-general shops, because higher wages costs with the difficulty of getting suitable labour in full-employment conditions had such an impact on the relatively low gross margins typical of this line of trade. Preparation for self-service meant in effect carrying out more processes away from the shop apart from the sheer packing in convenient and attractive forms. One factor in the resulting type of shop was that meat especially lent itself particularly well to the new system and the exploitation of this was in its turn helped by the rising importance of butchery products in higher standards of living plus the contemporary development of relatively cheap and suitable refrigeration (which had already led to the emergence of frozen foods as a new line of trade).

Be the causes what they may, here we have a new type of shop which conforms to our general law of retail dynamics in that it locates itself in the major centres. The discovery in itself was not apparently a cheaper form of retailing in general; there does not seem to have been any revolutionary reduction in average expenses margins as compared with other mass retailers. Put one way, it enabled greater turnover to be got from a given shop-site and if that were forthcoming the general range of goods sold could be sold at competitive prices; put another way, the innovation increased the proportionate importance of overhead expenses. The pressure of this last factor meant that the supermarket needed much greater turnovers in order to survive and it got them in the usual way partly by its general price level but notably by exploiting the attractions of especially low prices on individual items which were important both to its customers and to the shops from which it had to bid customers away.

It is now apparent that in more densely populated urban areas the self-service-supermarket shop has been a successful innovation. Anyone can also see that r.p.m. is no longer enforced in the grocery trades, which cover most of the brands handled by the new shops, and a raggedness of prices of certain notable brands is likewise obvious. Consumers are therefore benefiting by cut-price bargains as compared with the situation before these shops came along. How easy for someone with a short memory to conclude that these are the benefits of abandoning r.p.m.! In fact, the price-cutting came before r.p.m. was abandoned by the manufacturers concerned and at a time when our law had in fact just been strengthened so that it was actually easier for a manufacturer to enforce r.p.m. The point was that the new type of shop soon became a major class of customer for many manufacturers in the grocery trades. Leading brand owners therefore decided that they might well make less sales if they enforced r.p.m.; given this change of policy by some, others decided they had better follow suit. But r.p.m. has not necessarily been given up for good.

The oft-referred-to example of the grocery trades, then, proves our general contention that r.p.m. cannot enforce higher prices than are justified by the fundamental economics of retailing. Moreover, the developments in the grocery trades have not yet fully worked themselves out. Let us once more indulge in prophecy on the basis of our theory. For one thing, costs of supermarket forms of shops will stabilize at higher levels than the present — (1) the rents of suitable sites will rise still further; (2) as more and more shops turn over, the newcomers will get their quotas of sales in the lines which are now the staples of the present shops; these, in the drive for turnover and net profit, will have to extend their lines of goods to cover other goods and services which will not fit so easily into the new type of retailing, and so other expenses will rise; (3) the competitive lowering of present profits with continuing rises in general incomes will lead to some 'trading up' and therefore a trend towards higher general expenses. For another, and this is related to both of the last two points, we have yet to see the full effect of the reactions of those whose trade is so much threatened by the new developments so far; in one way or another, they will find means to compete more effectively and this will be a factor spreading the new type of trade and putting up the expenses of those who have pioneered it.

On this final point we have space only to discuss a move from the independent grocery shops. Wholesalers whose trade with them has been threatened by their weakened position have joined hands with them to form 'voluntary chains', sharing the purchasing advantages of the combined turnover of numbers of independents, helping with the re-development of premises to suit self-service, organizing joint brands which can be sold competitively etc., etc. Co-operative wholesaling is no innovation; private grocers tried it thirty years ago in the South of England, but the newer forms of trading have given it teeth. The new chains will combine many of the qualities of the multiple supermarkets with the peculiar advantage of the private grocer of being well aware of the profit and loss account of his shop and deciding his policy within the group scheme accordingly — an advantage which the manager of a multiple can never have.

The battle is not yet won in this corner of retailing where hasty critics are nevertheless rushing to congratulate the winner of a single round.

What is clear is that the whole balance of trade is in dispute in the grocery trades and ideas of normal competitive margins must await the outcome. But settle down it will and when it has done so, doubtless there will still be several types of shops competing for the consumer's favour. When that happens, unless there is a general ban, we may expect to see r.p.m. re-introduced. The brand-owning manufacturer will have his long-run interest in protecting his distribution from the effects of the casual but deadly forms of short-run price-cutting which the central multiple shops will still find a useful weapon in their day-to-day war with each other and with other types of retailer. The margins covered by maintained prices will be appropriate to the new competitive conditions; in them, the consumer will still have his own longer-term interest helped by manufacturers being able to keep their brands in fair competition before him.

The self-service supermarket could exist, r.p.m. or no. We end this section by discussing a type which could not come into existence on any scale without a background of 'usual' prices which are higher: the 'discount house' selling consumer durables (TV sets, cameras, refrigerators and the like) on cash-and-carry terms with little pre-sales service and none afterwards. Early and abnormal figures from the USA mislead as to the price levels normally achievable as compared with those of ordinary retailers.(7) There is, of course, no doubt about the scope for such enterprise as long as sufficient other shops maintain the price levels and services on which the early spectacular success of the discount shops is based. These are *par excellence* the kinds of goods for which consumers will shop around at considerable inconvenience if there is a chance of any sizeable

---

(7) Early discount houses could use derelict factories etc. (not so easily found in our full-employment community, nor so conveniently near mass concentrations of our less car-based people) at very low rents and sell from bare boards; their low margins needed quick achievement of a large turnover which they got by shovelling the goods out to flocking consumers attracted by their low prices. The dynamics we have expounded have already begun to work: other shops, including discount houses, get near the early ones, crowd the parking spaces they have exploited, are prepared to bid for the premises which consumers are now habitually coming to; rents rise; the increased competition with other shops and the difficulties of maintaining turnover lead to increased amenities and to increased varieties of goods being sold; in the end the older discount houses are well on the way to becoming department stores of the ordinary type (ref. *Cartel*, vol. 10, no. 2, 1960, pp. 48–52). There are correspondingly tighter limits to the cuts they can make on the average, and their prices are being matched more nearly by other traders as the whole system readjusts itself to their presence.

saving in price. But this is not the whole story and further analysis is needed.

The system on which discount houses would impinge is one where the normal pattern is of retailers, located in the centres near enough to each other for consumers to make conveniently the comparisons they need when weighing up alternatives. Usually selling more than one brand, each sells goods which 'belong' with its speciality — either, e.g. the camera shop, because it is convenient to get them at one place or, e.g. electrical goods, because the same expertise is needed in selling and servicing them; and service departments generally handle most brands which come their way, their experience helping the sales advice given to consumers. Competition enforces standards of salesmanship and post-sales service which the consumer takes for granted — just as he takes for granted that goods of good reputation offer him 'much of a muchness' in quality for price until his information adds up differently. But there is, competitively, such great flexibility in detail that it is difficult to write shortly about the service aspect of sales operations.

Apart from guarantee periods and special warranties, separate charges are usually made, although many critics give the impression that this is not so, that the consumer has always a coupled bargain. The repair charges of the shop are made as from an establishment to whose overheads the sales of all equipment (including reconditioned part-exchanged goods, the trade in which eases a problem both for the man who wants new goods and for the one who cannot afford them) and the general repair and service turnover alike contribute. Manufacturers are perfectly free to give margins which assume that the service which they want given with the goods is done in the shops, enforcing this with agency terms etc., or free to set up their own depots and give less margins accordingly. Here again there is greater variety than critics of r.p.m. suggest. So far as the other repairs and service charges are concerned, there is usually keen competition from the little man who specializes in repairs (sometimes, curiously enough, with no overheads because he works in the daytime for one of the shops!).

With this competitive variety, can we not say in short that these shops must get their average margins if they are to continue to compete in offering these services to the consumer? Whether consumers can get them more economically otherwise is a question we must consider. Whether consumers can afford to dispense with the competition in goods and services of which they will be deprived in alternative circumstances is a question for the reader. With our question we are squarely in the subject of the next section — the effects of a ban on r.p.m. It will be convenient to complete the discussion of discount houses as such before moving on.

A great proportion of the goods sold by the consumer durable shops are those which are ideally suited to the price-cutter's requirements. Assuming what has not invariably been true elsewhere, that discount houses will not be allowed flagrantly to mislead people about normal prices in other shops, the balance of trade will move inexorably towards the discount houses. Unless they push their prices downwards, the older shops will lose turnover. During some interim period, the consumer will still be able to make use of the pre- and post-sales services of the very shops he is selecting against in his purchases. Part of selling costs is therefore taken off the discount houses (who will have to make more efforts with resulting higher costs once this period is over). The end result, to cut the story short, must be that consumer durable goods generally will have to sell on the same cash and carry basis and, as the critics of r.p.m. point out, the consumer will now be able to pay separately for the services he uses and know what he is paying for.(8) It is difficult to see how he will be able to appreciate what he saves by going and fetching the thing himself, but, otherwise, the chief reason why the critics' generalization is casuistically true is that two vital services will be greatly reduced in scope; and what the consumer does not have he need not pay for.

On the first, how many shops will carry the same numbers of brands when they are no longer assured against casual price-cutting? The intelligent consumer will not have the opportunity which he has now for close comparisons of rival goods in the light of comments from the expert salesman (the more useful because the consumer will cannily discount them). The odds are that in many more shops he will find but the one brand and a salesman whose livelihood depends on pushing that one.(9) On the second, there will be a tendency to a narrowing of the choice open to the consumer both of goods and of repair facilities. The first point here ties on to the previous paragraph. If r.p.m. is forbidden, manufacturers who wish to maintain standards of service, under guarantees or otherwise, will have an interest in establishing their own repair depots, possibly combining these with their own demonstration showrooms; alternatively, they may prefer to adopt the exclusive agency system under which they can dictate the level of service the consumer is to get and see that he is fairly charged. This system, already in use for some goods, can be fairly easily adopted by the really large manufacturer whose franchise is so valuable in any

(8) But the consumer will still assume until taught by experience, that the manufacturer will give him his usual service; so if any fault develops he will expect the manufacturer to put it right.

(9) Of course, the developing consumer research organizations are a useful complement to this process, their assessments sometimes being helped because they have now a firm price basis to go on. But there is not space to discuss the reasons why their brief reports on unit samples of selected brands, presented away from the goods, and with persistent attempts, for good reasons, to curtail the commercial use of them, cannot quite replace the function of the shop.

area. The small manufacturer will find it impossible to adopt either kind of expedient. At the same time he will suffer from no longer being able to share facilities of which a proportionate part of the overheads are now paid for by trade with his larger rivals. Existing shops will also lose much of the trade which they will need to maintain their present facilities for repairs and service; so will the small repairer. In general, then, the consumer may be well-served when he gets to the specialist depots of the manufacturer or to the exclusive agency shops. But on the average he will have farther to go and will be rather more in the hands of fewer competitors here, as in the supply of the goods themselves.

Looking at the alternatives from the consumer's point of view it is surely possible to argue that, if the critics are right and maintained prices for durable goods cover more services than consumers really want, or consumers are being overcharged for them because of the multiplicity of outlets, the present system is the golden opportunity for the large retailer. The consumer already trusts the quality of the goods backed by such a name; will it not pay such a retailer to initiate the manufacture of his own brand of consumer durables? The outside circumstances appear to be favourable — rising trends of demand with a desire to be 'in' durables as the growth lines for the future, given the expectations of continued general prosperity; to this, if the critics are right, the large retailer has added unto him what, above all, a new entrant to an industry longs for — the opportunity to exploit serious mistakes in the pricing and distribution policies of his competitors. To sell with fewer services, or none, would enhance the initial sales impact because of the large apparent difference in price. Paradoxically, if r.p.m. is banned, we shall be the less likely to see such extensions of competition — again, if the critics are right. For if all are forced by price-cutting to cut out services from the price of the good, there will no longer be this gap for such a retailer to fill.

Our own conclusion, as will have been gathered, is that r.p.m. is not an obstacle to improvements in methods of servicing and distributing consumer durables, any more than it is an obstacle to other kinds of progress.

6 The effects of banning r.p.m.

By the time we started to work on this booklet we had reached the conclusion that there were grounds for suggesting that those who proposed a general ban on r.p.m. had not proved their case. We were impressed by effects of the ban which critics of r.p.m. passed over but which did imply some general social disadvantages to be set against any gain which it might bring, sectionally or socially. We were particularly concerned about the effects on the production and distribution of consumer durables. Beyond that we thought there was a good case for completely exempting from any ban some products whose peculiarities seemed to take them out of the general run of any argument, notably books and gramophone records. In the event, having thrashed matters over and worked our way through to publication, we remain convinced that the critics' case is not proven; more, we find ourselves impelled by our own argument to declare that we think that there is indeed some general case for the retention of individual r.p.m. If the decision to allow it, in 1956, should be revoked provision ought to be made for a very considerable exempted sector and a case must be fully made out before r.p.m. is banned in any industry.

The general basis for our conclusion has been given already and will not be repeated in detail. It stems from the easy competitiveness of retail trade, which should mean that any method of distribution of commodities which, alone or conjoined with manufacture, would bring a lowering of the net cost of a good to the consumer, or a net increase in the benefit he gets from it at present prices, will be able eventually to force its way in open competition. In particular, the larger retailers have no obstacles because of r.p.m. in the way of their developing further in this direction if they choose to do so and bear the risks that may be involved themselves. On the other hand, we are extremely disturbed by the overall reduction in competitiveness in production as well as in retailing that seems likely to follow from banning individual r.p.m. We do not view the lessened choice of service which would follow with the same equanimity as do the critics. The consumer is entitled to get whatever goods or services he is prepared to pay for, so long as each alternative form of organizing production and distribution stands fairly on its own bottom, so that its costs are fairly represented in its prices. To ban r.p.m. would be to load the dice in favour of one particular direction of change — towards the overall organization of distribution being more entirely in the hands of the large retailers than it would be if they compete with each other, and with such manufacturers as choose to support their brands with r.p.m., on the basis of commodities which are unequivocally their own responsibility.

To be particular in a brief summary, the following are the deleterious effects which would seem likely to follow from a general ban on r.p.m.:

(1) So far as *reduction in competition* is concerned, the net effect of a ban would probably be that (a) there would be a decline in the numbers of independent neighbourhood and specialist shops; (b) there would be a reduction in the strength of the competition which large retailers' own brands now meet from manufacturers' brands; (c) there would be a needless general rise in the size of units, through the growth of large retailers, the further integration of large producers with retailing, and the squeezing out of smaller manufacturers from direct competition at the retail level, not justifiable on a normal cost basis; (d) neighbourhood shops which survived would have to

trade more on the basis of the emergency needs which they meet and would in many areas, thanks to planning regulations etc., be in more of a monopoly position than they are now, when they have to reckon with standard prices for many of the commodities which they sell.

(2) So far as *service* is concerned, (a) the consumer would lose some convenience in the decline of the numbers of neighbourhood shops and in the decreased variety of stocks which both they and the independent specialists will offer; (b) he would have less of the specialized services he now enjoys from retailers, in particular he would have greater difficulty in making pre-purchase comparisons for durables and would have to shop around more on the chance of price reductions on standard goods generally; (c) service facilities would be more concentrated in the hands of large manufacturers serving their own products; the post-sales services and repair facilities at present conveniently available for several makes at the same place, the shop or the independent repairer's, would be curtailed and fragmented; (d) in general the shift towards large retailers would mean a reduction in the variety of service offered by retailers.

(3) So far as *prices* are concerned, the general levels at the various types of shops are unlikely to be much affected by a ban on r.p.m. in itself, and, otherwise: (a) there is a probability that neighbourhood shops' prices would tend to be higher (see above); (b) other things being equal, the reduction in overall competitiveness should mean that prices generally would be unlikely to continue to be so low as they are under the present system (especially since on our analysis r.p.m. must bend to any changes in real costs of distribution or break down); (c) whilst no r.p.m. would mean that there would be a greater likelihood of individual prices being cut at some time or another, this in itself would mean that the average prices would tend to rise, for these goods, on occasions when they were not being cut, and for other commodities generally.

(4) So far as *production* is concerned, the weakening of producers' brands would mean a tendency to greater irregularity of output, especially for the smaller manufacturer, and some tendency for costs to rise due to the greater fragmentation of types of product in order to meet the desire to be different on the part of retailers with a stronger market position *vis-a-vis* producers; it is possible that manufacturers would try independently to compete by greater differentiation of individual products.

On the other side of the medal what have we to place? We have made plain the advantages to the larger-scale retailers. For the consumer there would be the short-run advantage of the widespread price-cutting of standard brands which would follow any ban at first. He would thereafter be able no doubt always to pick up more odd bargains than he can now, but in the long run there seems no reason why there should be any general lowering of the prices he pays. He would probably more often have a straight choice between plain goods and goods plus service, but this would not be his preferred position because if it were someone could be satisfying his demand already. Competition in retail trade would be much more in the hands of the large retailers and this would tend to reduce the variety of service from which he can choose rather than give him greater freedom of choice.

Many of the advantages which critics claim for the abolition of r.p.m. are either very short run or they are mistaken. One of the differences between us and the critics is that our section on the advantages of a ban can not include an encomium of all the ways in which it would increase efficiency and competition — just because, on balance, our conclusion is that retail trade is extremely competitive already, and that a ban on r.p.m. is likely to reduce the overall competitive pressure. Of course, there are likely to be many shops after the ban, still competing with each other strenuously enough to earn only reasonable aggregate profits; but competition is more than that, being an affair involving competition between types of shops in which manufacturers themselves play a major part if they are free to choose between complementary and competitive roles *vis-a-vis* the ordinary retailers as their products impinge on the consumer.

These are generalizations. We could wish that we had more space to discuss in detail the impact of a ban on individual trades, but this booklet is already much longer than some competitive products and we should like it to be purchasable by the same consumers. In particular, however, because their organizational problems do present such an interesting variety, we should have liked to have discussed speciality shops rather more fully. Durable goods shops have been at least given some special mention; since this product is going from its publisher through the bookshops it would be suitable to discuss the book trade as a concluding example. We may at least take one aspect of it, confessing our interest as authors and readers.

Most new books are sold at 'net prices' in the shops, these being fixed and maintained by the individual publisher. Leaving aside for the moment the established classics and text-books, the peculiarity of books is that the size of the total market for any one title cannot be more than roughly guessed. It may very well fall into some general class, such as 'light novel' or 'serious biography' and the publisher will have some guide in the normal sales of that class of book when bearing his imprint. That is a very tenuous guide. Books no doubt have the most informed consumers of any commodity but their ranking of the individual title is very chancy. Until it is out, it cannot generally be known whether it is going to do averagely for its class, or worse, or be a best seller — many remainders bear the signs that they were in fact expected to do very well. Despite all this uncertainty, both publisher and bookseller alike have to undertake commitments in advance of publication. Price will depend on the size of the edition, so the publisher has to back his judgement both as to edition and price, and the bookseller in general has to 'subscribe' for copies before publication so that he may have it available in the shop when the public comes for it. For any type of book on the average there must be sufficient shops where the corresponding class of readers are catered for; most being served by the 'general' bookshop.

Obviously there has to be an averaging process here. Books where the publisher guesses right or is pleasantly surprised have to carry the costs of the 'flops' or he goes out of business. He cannot charge extra for the best seller in advance; in fact the general result of his thinking a title will do well is that the price tends to be lower. Similarly, in the bookshops, the margin may seem generous on a best seller being handed out over the counter to a queue of customers who already know that they want it; but the profits from that sort of sale have to help to pay for the service of running the shop as a whole, carrying stocks of books which move more slowly, and tracking down out-of-the-way and inadequately described requirements (by no means confined to 'learned' works!), obtaining a White Paper specially at a net loss, and so on. Even best sellers pass out of the period when they sell 'like hot cakes'. But for a short while to have them is to be certain of large sales.

The mass retailer would be able to sell the known best seller during this brief period profitably on a much lower margin than the bookshop gets; it is argued that r.p.m. is wrong because it stops him from doing so. But this is not analogous to selling large quantities of standard clothing specially produced for the retailer's known market. There is nothing to stop such shops having produced for them special editions of out-of-copyright classics and selling them at whatever price seems right in relation to regular sales and costs. Such cases exist, but they do not make the chain store a publisher in the ordinary way. Nor would it make them a bookseller to take copies of a best seller, once it has become a 'cert', and cream the market, leaving the ordinary houses to handle books with lower sales on margins which necessarily allow for the chance of a best seller in the industry's competitive system of pricing. Someone has to do all the work and pay the costs on the average of the run of books from which the single best seller emerges, before it can appear to excite the interest of the mass retailers. The ordinary bookshop which relies on the swings to make up for the roundabouts, providing a general service to book buyers, and the specialist bookshop would be greatly reduced in numbers, it seems clear; prices of books in general would have to rise — at the publisher, to compensate for the smaller editions and the higher risks with fewer outlets; at the retailer, margins on ordinary books and on specialist publications would have to be higher.

It would be easy, given space, to show that other specialist trades have their own features which offer some good justification for the desire of manufacturers serving them to retain r.p.m. Our discussion of books, however, shows the kind of detail into which the critics of r.p.m. should have gone before they ventilated their sweeping proposals. To know how a particular trade works seems to us far more important than any quibble about whether the manufacturer was behind the retailer, or vice versa, in the introduction of r.p.m. — a question which particularly interests Prof. Yamey in his discussion of books.

Appendix

NOTE A: On the Rationality of Consumers' Behaviour

I. *The general assumptions underlying the laws of demand at the shop level* (pp. 274–8) sum up to the proposition that the general behaviour of any large number of consumers will be of the same kind as if on the average every consumer is rational, not that every consumer is always rational. In general theory we are entitled to look at aggregate effects, but especially here since the proposed ban on r.p.m. is a general policy. We do not extend the argument to fruit and other perishable goods or to fashion articles, since r.p.m. does not usually apply here, although the argument can be so extended.

(1) Some consumers may be irrational all the time, but if only 1 in 10 were normally rational, a very pessimistic assumption, the total expenditure of rational consumers in any urban area would be large in relation to the typical turnover of any shop, so that shops individually would find a large increase of demand if they offered better value for money than other shops. This point is put forward only because theorists who concentrate on assumptions involving a general disposition towards irrational preferences completely overlook it. The present authors assume the general tendency is towards rationality. The case is argued for consumer goods although r.p.m. applies to business goods also (e.g. office stationery). If customers were irrational there, there could be no foundation for any economic analysis, including that which economist critics of r.p.m. use. Our analysis fully applies to them.

(2) We may approach the general problem by considering types of goods. For expensive consumer durables, the effect of heavy initial costs and subsequent expenses more than counterbalances that of relatively infrequent purchase by individual consumers. They use experience and opinions of others to supplement their own knowledge. Hence the success of the Radio Show, *et*

al., the feature columns of newspapers, the expanding circulation of *Which*, *et al.*, and the demonstrations and advice which would-be persuaders must offer to help the consumer make his own comparisons. A full argument would relate to the way information on such goods is collected and spread in the ordinary business of life, the use made of expert friends, the general interest in friends' experiences, etc. Proof of consumers' general rationality here can also be found in the details of the formulation of price policy by manufacturers and large retailers.

For everyday commodities — the large mass of goods bought at frequent intervals at prices which are low relatively to consumers' incomes — it is not assumed that every price need everywhere be the same even in nearby shops. The fundamental law we put forward is the 'law of the basket', that shops must offer competitive, in equilibrium equal, value for money over the average contents of the consumer's shopping basket, or trade will move towards those that offer better value. Here again, consumers are not isolated; there are constant exchanges of experience, especially between the housewives who manage consumers' buying departments. Anyone who keeps a shop for a length of time comes to see 'the public' as a many-headed computer of price-quality relationships, whose operations are effective because its 'input' of information is also its 'output'. One certainly relied on customers to 'tell one', and they told each other.

Within the basket, however, are commodities of individual importance to the consumer: those which bulk large and regularly in the weekly bills; also, the goods which are standardized enough (as with all brands) or whose prices are sufficiently stable over short periods for consumers to become aware of standards of price. Differences in prices here will attract attention. The general sensitivity of demand is increased by the fact that it is cheap to make trial purchases. These types of goods are used as 'call-birds' and 'loss-leaders'; equilibrium is consistent with differences of individual prices so long as the 'basket' law operates — provided that they are not also important goods in the turnovers of nearby shops of the same type; the otherwise avoidless mutual retaliation here makes parity of individual prices prevail.

For the intermediate class of goods — moderately expensive and not individually bought every week or month (footwear, clothing, household goods, shavers) — prices may not be the powerful inducement to research which those of expensive durables are, but they are not cheap; consumers can weigh up a more continuous experience of shops and also of makes. There are the usual signs of rational consumer interest in everyday conversation, the features of newspapers, etc. Institutional signs are the location of shops selling such things near each other in their own sections of shopping centres, corresponding with the observation that many consumers do seem to be shopping around before buying; the conventional ranges of prices for regular clothing items and for footwear which facilitate this process by making possible noticeable differences in qualities.

(3) All this does not mean that the corner shop remote from others could not get higher prices for emergency needs but it does mean that it would have a lot less trade, if its prices were noticeably different for commodities the need for which can be regularly foreseen and which are easily carried home or ordered with usual deliveries. Such goods are a large part of the present turnover of these shops.

II. *The role of persuasion in consumer demand*: the above argument and the laws of demand derived from it have been in terms of the behaviour of consumers satisfying given wants. This is regular procedure in the economic theory of prices and is the best basis for general analysis but gives a misleading approach to the question of advertising, which itself is so much related to branded goods. The 'given' set up of demand is, in fact, always changing — must change if there is to be economic progress; persuasion plays a necessary part. In a fuller argument detailed reference would be made to these characteristics of consumer demand:

(1) consumers will not want new commodities or be prepared to consider alternatives (and economic progress and effective competition depends upon these) unless they find reason to do so;

(2) even for established kinds of commodities demand is very changeable over time: (a) there are large swings in demand for the same group of consumers, e.g. fashions, trends to or against sweetness in foods, and as between chocolates and boiled sweets; the demand from one group of population is very changeable in general — the 'teenagers'; (b) the composition of the population changes. For every age-group each year there are new consumers, and this is especially important in the teenage-group whose incomes have become proportionately much higher than in earlier periods; (c) consumers' demands in general change with rising incomes. There is a steady accession of new groups to those who can afford any 'luxury'. These latter mean that a large proportion of the demand of any group of consumers is 'on the wing' at any given time, and they need information about the alternatives among the commodities towards which they are heading.

(3) We would emphasize what we have called the latentness of demand in general at any particular time. Even with settled wants (leading to regular expenditures over a period), which particular commodity will be bought at any one time is not so precisely determined. 'Something nice for tea', 'something for the house' — these may be objectives on a shopping expedition to be satisfied by one of numerous commodities. 'Get some jam'; 'let us buy a washing machine'; these leave still open the alternatives between makes and suppliers. The latter kind of indeterminacy is involved in ordinary problems of consumer choice, but the former, wider, indeterminacy is also resolvable by the same kind of shopping procedure.

Each of these characteristics means that the consumer is correspondingly in need of affined information, and he uses everything which comes his way. His decision can be put in orthodox fashion as choice according to prices and qualities, but we can put it that the consumer has to convince himself as to the right course of action; seen this way, 'outside' data are persuasively apprehended; they must be persuasively presented in order to impinge on him. The 'persuasion' necessarily involves creating an imaginative apprehension of quality and serviceability of goods in his use.

The persuasive functions of the shop can be exercised quietly in its lay-out and general service; they do not obtrude nor can they be costed independently of what the shop does otherwise. But it is a very real function of retail trade to help the consumer to 'make up his mind'. In the text we allow for the fact that advertised goods reduce the selling costs of the shop. But there is another aspect; without manufacturers' advertisements the shop would be the predominant influence in the whole process of persuasion.

III. *The role of advertising* is to enable brands to have a fair chance of being brought before the consumer's mind when he is choosing, both in his preliminary thinking and, because they are more likely to be stocked, in the shop. Advertising does not so much create wants (certainly so far as detailed categories of wants are concerned) as make the consumer aware how advertised goods can fit into this pattern and endeavour to create a desire on his part to try them. There is much misunderstanding of advertising; as with all other 'outside' persuasions, it can only persuade a consumer to make one try, and any disappointment not only deters him from repetition but will be communicated to others. The initial acceptability of an advertised good is increased by experience that such goods in general are backed by those who have invested in their relative value. A brand can be built up to an initial position of strength by attractive publicity but it cannot sustain its position on this, as an example of a recent brand of cigarettes shows. It is an overlooked fact that many of the most heavily advertised commodities are cheap in unit price so that trial and rejection is cheap. If advertising alone could win the day, the next day the victory would go to a heavier spender. Advertising wars are guarded against by rules to limit total expense; in effect, goods have to sell well on their own merits before they can carry regular heavy expenditure on advertising.

NOTE B: On Retailing Costs[10]

We refer separately to the long-run and the short-run behaviour of costs in retail trade. The first question is how the overall scale on which a retail business is organized will affect its normal costs. For this purpose the cost of goods and the general expenses are considered separately.

In any line of trade or for any given combination of lines (range of goods) the cost of goods will fall with increased order-size, since it is cheaper for sellers to supply in larger quantities, but beyond a certain scale there will be no further substantial reduction over a wide range of further increase in order-size. The smallest business will therefore be at a substantial disadvantage vis-a-vis others, but in most trades a fair range of businesses will be more or less equally well-placed. The very large retailer, however, is likely to find his cost of goods substantially lower in various ways as a result of the very great scale of his general operations, and this whether his turnover is very specialized in range or not. Over the middle ranges of scale the more specialized business will get better terms than one which sells a very diverse range of goods.

The general expenses are to be analysed as the costs of the business's organization itself and their level is very largely determined by what type-class the retailer is in (ref. pp. 278–9). They include rent, rates, Schedule A taxes, heating and lighting, maintenance (the 'occupancy' costs), wages and salaries, etc. (A separate note is appended on some analytical aspects of rent costs.) Using a theory of managerial organization already developed by us, a retail business is to be seen as some particular combination of individual 'activities' — buying, selling, managing, etc. The expense of any one activity will tend to fall as total

---

(10) This note looks at the costs of 'a retailer' in the abstract along lines familiar in the theory of the firm, although the conclusions are in many ways substantially different from those which have often been imported into discussions of retail trade from general analysis. (So far as short-run costs are concerned, Professors Richard Holton and Arthur Lewis should be mentioned as having stressed the importance of overhead costs.) Only the principal conclusions have been adumbrated, without the practical detail against which the analysis has been constructed.

turnover increases, but this percentage expense will tend to flatten out at very large turnovers. Total expenses for activities, combined as managers choose to combine them in the interests of the business (still making the simplifying assumption about the range of goods), will fall rather more sharply than the average of the separate activity curves, and will thus also tend to fall percentagewise with increasing scale of turnover. Again the penalties of very small size, and therefore the gains from further growth, are likely to be more substantial for growth from small size-scales than from scales which are already substantially larger. The more specialist business will be effectively on a larger-scale organization than a more diversified one.

We may conclude, *ceteris paribus*, that increased scale of business will bring increasing advantages of scale. But 'other things' are not equal, by reason of the general assumption about the range of business and, among other things, especially in this industry, because of peculiar supply conditions for management enterprise to the smaller neighbourhood and specialist shops. Even making allowances for this latter factor, the conclusions from the analysis are misleading in so far as (a) at the largest end of the size-scale, to be of such a size and reasonably specialized means that the business is of a different type, viewed marketwise. It does not necessarily therefore compete directly with medium-sized businesses in a simple manner; market analysis brings the conclusion that there is room for a division of labour between different types, and so in this case the balance of power between types may rest on cost advantages for each in the tasks which it actually carries out. Innovations which affect the balance of costs as between size-types will through competition affect the balance of power. (b) At the other end of the scale, it is similarly true that a very small business cannot survive in the same market class because of its cost disadvantages, except with the help of the willingness of people to work at abnormally low costs in the ownership-management of such businesses; in this case this exception to the conditions of analysis must be brought in to explain actual affairs in some lines of trade.

We turn to the short-run question of the behaviour of costs, for a given business with a given organization, when turnover fluctuates. The dominant factor here is the relative fixity of such a large proportion of costs. Not only are total occupancy costs constant at any one time, but retail trade differs from much manufacturing in that a very large proportion of the wages and salaries bill must also be regarded as a fixed expense. Moreover, most of the fixed expenses have to be met currently in cash. Therefore, if turnover falls, the expenses percentage rises rapidly, and once profit is swallowed up the sharp rise in percentage cash expenses causes a cash drain from the business. On the other hand, the more the turnover from a given shop, the lower the proportionate charge for expenses and the greater the net profit, largely spilling over into cash. Success or failure is spelled out in the incidence of a retailer's overheads, and he is therefore under constant pressure to add to his turnover, with consequent tendencies in dynamic conditions to extend his range. A retailer who is not threatened already will add to his turnover in any way not likely to provoke retaliation from rivals of his own type, but a retailer who is threatened by failure will use any weapon he has.

NOTE C: On some Analytical Aspects of Rent Costs

The actual incidence of the charges for rent borne by individual retailers is fortuitous and this variation usually accounts for the greatest part of the variation of profits between otherwise similar retailers. A business may own its site and buildings, which may have been erected a long time ago. In such a case, the accounts may show rather higher maintenance costs, will show no charge for 'rent', and a Schedule A charge which has only a tenuous connexion with actual current rents which would be paid for its particular site.(11) Even where premises are rented, leases will have been taken up at very different dates, and similar shops in similar situations may show very different charges. To make a fair comparison of business expenses it would be necessary to standardize rent charges in each set of accounts. When looking at the longer-run effects of economic forces in retailing, we may avoid these difficulties analytically by assuming that all businesses in fact have to pay the full economic rent of their real property. In long-run analysis, this is fair procedure, witness the recent waves of take-over bids and of sales-lease-backs. As previous comments have shown, however, when looking at the flux of short-period competition, especially as between older and newer types of retail organization, the varying incidence of rents must be taken into account — and it partly explains the time-lag before the newer type has its maximum effect, and why the older type has time to reorganize.

---

(11) In such a case, the age of the buildings may also be responsible for running difficulties which restrict turnover and put up other costs; but this will not be a consequence of the rent position as such, although the favourable actual rent position may in some cases account for time-lags in reorganizing to reduce such difficulties of age.

8   Some aspects of capital development[1]

I was pleased to be invited to come here. In industrial matters generally, I am sure that economists have more to learn than they have to teach and it flatters an academic economist that those practically engaged in industry should think that they will be interested to hear him on a subject about which, in the nature of things, they must know more than he does. I must admit that I have not always seen it this way. When I was very young, economics seemed to me a splendid subject whose general principles were well-established and sufficient by themselves to settle many important practical problems. I remember as an undergraduate going to lecture to the prisoners in Winchester Gaol on the theory of wages! The funny side of this did not occur to me until several years afterwards, but I should now admit that I had not chosen an entirely appropriate subject. At the time I was diffident on quite other grounds — it was my first public lecture; I was reassured that I should find an easy and tolerant audience, since they were only too pleased to have a reason to be out of their cells. I have no doubt that this reassurance embodied a perfectly good theory; but on that occasion the prisoners roused themselves and, in the discussion after my lecture, I soon became aware that my theories were not the guide to practice that I had assumed.

In the last generation, however, there has been an important change in economics, in England at all events, and nowadays, there are many of us whose chief preoccupation is to learn what happens in fact in business, and to confine ourselves to making as valid a set of generalizations as we can about practical behaviour. I suppose that this change of interest is the reason why I have been able during my whole career as a research economist to concentrate upon studying business 'on the ground', as it were, observing individual business men and cross-questioning them as to their conduct of their businesses against the background of the records of their operations. I personally owe a lot to the business men who have been prepared to put up with this!   One question which I have found particularly interesting is what limits the pace of capital development in business. Of course, this is not the sort of question to which a simple answer can be given, and I usually prefer to think in terms of the

(1) Lecture to the Lancashire Section of the Textile Institute, 26 February 1953. Reprinted with permission from the *Proceedings* of the *Journal of the Textile Institute* **44** (September, 1953), pp. 687–97.

individual businesses I have studied. Here, however, I must keep to fairly broad generalizations and, since I do not want to leave these in the air, I shall try to link what I have to say to certain social issues about which much has been heard in recent years.

Speaking on such a general plane, I shall not discuss the purely personal factors which are very important when we consider any particular business. We all know some businesses where the moving spirit is strongly biased in favour of the latest thing in technique — and, surely, others where the opposite is true. I mention this merely to emphasize its importance in practice, but I should like to say in passing that I do not know why we should readily assume that the second type of personal bias necessarily leads to greater inefficiency than the first. Industrial efficiency is the result of a balance of factors, and commercial and strategic circumstances may be quite as important as techniques.

The capital development of a business is a question of changes in the size and nature of its investment in fixed assets. It is trite to say that a business needs access to liquid funds in order to develop. For expansion, of course, it may borrow these or raise them on the capital market. The assets which it already has, however, must be replaced and maintained out of its own cash reserves; no new investor will willingly see his resources go simply to maintain existing earning power. Equally, a prudent business will try to put by sufficient funds to do this for itself. Provided that plant values do not change drastically and permanently, this will normally be more than possible for a reasonably efficient business, aided by the practices of the Inland Revenue which are reasonable enough in such a situation.

There should, therefore, normally never be any question about replacement. But plant values have risen drastically and continuously for years and, with the other calls on business liquidity on account of high prices, we are in danger of not being able to replace our fixed assets over a wide range of industry. A special inquiry would be needed to ascertain exactly how serious the position is, but I do know that the possibility is serious enough in some important businesses to cause a brake on capital development proper.

Of course, many people are already worried about this and suggestions have been made to improve the situation without drastic rises in selling prices. I do not myself favour the idea that the Inland Revenue should change its normal practices and allow wear and tear etc., on a replacement basis. It seems to me far more important that we should stop the insidious inflation which is at the heart of the problem. Then we need only take some special measure to allow for the effect of the step-up in prices since 1939, but it is important that we should do at least this.

Some people are complacent about this great problem just because the position has been broadly held so far; Inland Revenue allowances may not have been adequate but most businesses have probably been able to carry out their replacement from the net profits left after taxation (the position will of course get worse in so far as the steepest rise in capital prices has been during the last few years). I have had it put to me (by some colleagues) that there is no harm in a business just being able to maintain the status quo out of its taxed profits. After all, if it wants to expand, it can go to the capital market (which, as some think, would make the problem of control of capital investment easier than it would be if businesses could expand out of their net profits). It is further pointed out that when an asset is replaced it is usually replaced with one which is superior in efficiency, so that on balance the business will actually have improved its position.

What a narrow view that is! This country does not stand alone. We have to compete with other countries for our continued existence and from our present point of view our industry will have to compete on a much narrower front than in the past. I need not remind an audience from the cotton industry that modern changes in the balance of industrial power, plus our greatly increased needs, have caused us to be mainly dependent for the future upon industries which are based upon modern technology. These are just the industries in which technical progress is maintained in the industries of our competitors. We need, moreover, to look beyond today's equipment to what our rivals will face us with the day after tomorrow. I personally do not believe that central planning wisdom will make so accurate or so timely an anticipation as the efforts of individual businesses in competition using their own resources. Be that as it may, we shall need a continuous improvement in our equipment if we are to stand still in relation to our competitors, and, as I have suggested, a firm which cannot at least stand still from its own resources is on the way out.

It is much more difficult to say *a priori* for any one business or even for an industry precisely how fast the pace of technical progress ought to be. The reason is that techniques really offer several courses and which we should take depends upon cost factors and can be determined only by each business man for his own business. To overlook this can lead to some extremely misleading comparisons between countries. Defining a technical advance as that which brings the substitution of capital equipment for other resources such as labour, it will be obvious that if labour costs more relatively to machinery in one country than it does in another, we should expect the first country to be relatively more advanced in the substitution of machinery for labour. It would, however, be a mistake, just because this involved a more advanced technique, to say that the other country was less efficient.

If I may quote an example of the sort of thing I have in mind, my friend Mr. Seymour Melman of Columbia University in a book to be published later next year, (some of his conclusions will, I believe, be given in the *Manchester*

311

Guardian Annual Survey) says that, generally speaking, British businesses which he visited in 1949 were making the kinds of technical improvements in handling and transporting equipment which had been introduced in the United States in 1940. Further investigation led Mr. Melman to suggest that this was not just because we were nine years behind the USA in our methods. He thinks that the position is rather that the technically older methods were cheaper in this country relatively to the costs of the 'new' appliances until about 1949. By 1949, the relative costs had moved to about the same ratio as was to be found in the United States in 1940. I give this illustration off the record, for I am quoting from memory and without permission, but that was the broad picture. Although this is not the whole story, certainly the relative costs of process labour and of equipment play some part in the technical differences between industry on both sides of the Atlantic.

Of course, technical efficiency does have considerable relevance to economic efficiency; in particular, it helps to set minimum limits to the size of business which can efficiently survive in any given industry. As a general rule, a particular business will usually be able to produce any given product more cheaply if it can expand its output and reorganize suitably. It follows that a small business always tends to be under some technical disadvantage, but the effect of this is lessened by several factors, notably, in our present context, by the fact that technical economies do not usually increase proportionately with scale, beyond a certain minimum size depending on the industry and product, so that they give a relatively slackening advantage to still larger businesses.

Against this, in the actual world, small businesses often have to choose to be less efficient technically than they would like to be in a less changing world. The fixed assets of a business limit severely the types of processes which it can operate, as well as the actual output of any particular products. So, to suit practical conditions, a given plant has to have a certain minimum of flexibility built into it. In particular, equipment must be sub-divided at bottlenecks and there must be standby capacity, to provide for short-term flexibility and for sudden breakdowns. Such considerations may set limits to capacities of individual pieces of equipment below those which would otherwise be ideal. Similar considerations, although they may be less obvious, also operate in the layout of a plant and the design of its buildings. Obviously, a larger business will tend to be able to get a given degree of flexibility in plant etc., at a smaller cost than will a substantially smaller business. (Of course, it does not follow that the larger business will actually be the most flexible from all points of view.)

I shall refer later to the difficulties which smaller businesses find, especially in present conditions, in raising money capital for investment in fixed assets. In so far as smaller businesses tend to be rather starved for money capital, this will

312

operate similarly to the factors we have just been discussing, and will cause smaller businesses to make even less proportionate investment in fixed assets than they would like to do, having regard only to technical conditions and their effects upon costs.

Of course, it would be dangerously misleading to apply all this strictly to actual industries — the greater technical disadvantage of the small unit is not necessarily the dominant consideration from an economic efficiency point of view. We may take, in particular, this question of flexibility. Actual industries, in fact, produce a large variety of products, and businesses specialize in those which suit them best; a small business, therefore, often specializes on the relatively less standardized products and on meeting special needs and emergencies. In this case, its relatively less developed capital equipment does not handicap it. We may further notice that the fact that smaller businesses specialize in this way, in itself, helps to make possible greater standardization of output and economy of capital in the larger business. But a full consideration of this question of size and efficiency for its own sake would take us too far from our immediate purpose. Let us simply recognize that, in themselves, technical reasons mean that growth will bring economic advantages to a business and so serve as one spur to its capital development.

What I have been saying also implies that the variety of output which an industry produces will set limits to its capital development. This is well recognized for example in the Anglo-American Productivity Team reports, and in the earlier reports of the Board of Trade Working Parties. The greater the variety of output which the individual factory produces, in normal technical conditions, the less important relatively will be the gains available from applying larger-scale methods. This is a factor which vitiates comparison, say, between our industries and American industries.

Certainly, one consequence of our greater dependence upon exports is that many of our industries have to produce a greater variety than American industries and, since goodwill goes by the firm, we must expect this to be reflected in a greater diversity of individual outputs. For example, I understand that the USA home market for radio sets is a short-wave market. Since exports of sets are less important to the USA manufacturer than they are to ours, he can concentrate upon a set which suits his home market and simply market his sets to whatever other markets it suits. With our medium-wave home market, if we are to export at all we have to produce for the short-wave market as well. On top of that, to be large exporters we have to serve many markets and each has some peculiarity, even if it be only the fire-prevention fuse which, I understand, Sweden insists on. By the time that this variety is built into our production layout and arrangements we cannot expect to produce on such a large-scale fashion as the larger American producers.

There is, however, no room for complacency. I am not sure that the fundamental national taste for variety to which we often refer would demand all the complicating variety in the British home market if our costing methods were more detailed and we attached appropriate price penalties to demands for non-standard products. We would certainly do more in the way of standardizing components; it is absurd, for example, that fractional horse power motors which are really standardized products should have to be made with the large variety of fitting arrangements which I understand is demanded. A little more care on the part of designers of the equipment into which these motors go would enable the manufacturers to achieve great economies in their production. More thought to this type of consideration on the part of designers generally would probably have a big effect on our over-all costs without penalizing variety in the final product.

Having said that, I must also recognize that we have done a good deal more in this direction than is recognized in many public discussions of the subject. There is another related point: between the wars our standards were affected in many industries by the difficulties of the times. In order to get what orders were going, and with our excess capacity because of the long slump, we had to tolerate what would otherwise have been an excessive variety of output. In the circumstances to do so was more economic than it seems in a time of sellers' markets.

Just because of the difficult times it may well be that we did not get the development of the types of large-scale methods of production which really suited us and which would have been compatible with our fundamental need for variety in finished output. In consequence our ideas of just what large-scale methods are, are too much dominated by those which have been developed to suit, say, the more standard American market. With the pressure on our capacity in recent years, there has begun to appear an interesting new trend in the layout and design of large-scale assembly plants which really suit our products.

So far as I know, the first plant to develop and incorporate these principles was the Austin motor vehicle assembly plant. As you will realize, one disadvantage of producing a variety of output from such a plant has been the locking up of capital in stocks of a variety of components located so that they can be brought into the line when needed; allied to this has been costly congestion on the factory floor and delays in changing over from one model to another. Austins, by using electrical controls based upon the use of punched cards, have been able to design an assembly plant which can be kept going full bore and yet be amazingly flexible so far as changes in product are concerned, without the disadvantages elsewhere which I have already cited. I have been greatly impressed by the opinion of one skilled American observer that this plant meets our own problems without, as he thought, any serious cost disadvantage as compared with the rigidly standardized American assembly system.

If that is true, Austins deserve our gratitude for pioneering a system which will have great applicability elsewhere. Any general application of the idea might well render otiose a good many criticisms of the varied goods which our industries produce, and which they feel they have to produce. I have already heard of at least one interesting application of part of the idea in solving the problems of meeting the variety of output handled by a boot and shoe closing room, which is where the uppers are sewn together. I want simply to make the point again that this sort of development might well have occurred earlier, had times been better and the pressure for high and economical output been more obvious before the war.

Another factor which has been thought to affect the drive for capital development is the competitiveness of the industry within which a business operates. There is some confused thinking here. It is recognized that a competitive industry will make the individual firm sit up and try to keep in line with technical trends. At the same time, because many competitive industries show great varieties of output and less rapid technical development we hear references to the wastes of competition. Similarly, in references to some of the industries liable to come within the purview of the Monopolies Commission because of the concentration of output among a relatively few producers, we hear friends of competition rather sadly recognizing that those industries in this country where technical progress has been continuous and where prices have gone up less than general prices are the so-called monopoly industries. I cannot lay down a general law here, but individual instances suggest, as I have said, some confusion of thought.

For one thing, many of the 'competitive' industries are those which are not easily amenable to marked technical development. Industries where materials make up a large part of costs will not show the same drive towards mass-production methods as those where labour costs dominate the situation. In the former case skill in buying may be far more important than saving the odd halfpenny in production.

At the same time, there is competition, and competition. There are, for example, quite a number of chemicals in which there are only one or two domestic producers. First, that position has often arisen just because economies of scale have been so important that only a few firms could survive the struggle for elimination or growth. Secondly, in quite a few cases the domestic market is only a part of the whole — our domestic heavy chemical industry characteristically exports a very large part of its output, and needs to do so in order to keep its low costs. For these external markets it is in keen competition with foreign producers.

What about cartels? I am sure I cannot mention chemicals without that thought arising. I have not time really to go into this fully and shall simply suggest the change of ideas which I think may be desirable about at least some of these industries. In these 'monopolized' industries, demand at any one time is very inelastic and often shifts drastically with changes in general activity. At the same time, overhead costs are high. In bad times, therefore, in the past, there has been a tendency for weak producers to cut prices without any reference to normal costs. Such abnormally and undesirably low prices surely are not the sort of prices which we hope will come from competition? It is experience of those prices which leads to the appearance of cartels and other forms of restraint of free competition. I should not like to press any generalization, but such evidence as I have of cartels suggests that even if they eliminate one form of competition, nevertheless, and if the cartel is to endure, the pressure for output from the genuinely low-cost producer must be allowed its influence on price, so that competition not monopoly may well remain the clue to *trends* of price, which would appear to explain the facts. For a published discussion of the kind of situation I have in mind, I can refer you to Mr. Marlio's very interesting little book on the Aluminium Cartel.

The mention of price-cutting reminds me of the obvious fact that periods of weak trade are least likely to favour new capital development. As the cotton industry knows, even maintenance may be achieved by robbing idle machines of parts for working ones. One of the points behind the Cotton Industry Reorganization Act of 1939, and which was reluctantly recognized, was that weak selling prevented longer-term reorganization in your industry. It was even more obvious in the British iron and steel industry, which is much more open to technical change and to the economies of large-scale production. The achievements of that industry since its reorganization are a powerful reminder that an industry needs stable and reasonably profitable conditions if it is to develop continuously. The pace of capital development quite as much as the happiness of workers is strengthened by reasonably full employment.

One point about the steel industry's monopolistic price-fixing arrangements is that they did work in such a way as to maintain effective competition, popular mythology to the contrary notwithstanding, and caused consequent reductions in normal costs to be reflected in prices. Such arrangements are necessary only in special cases, but I am sure that, generally, the quality of our capital development depends on our maintaining the competitive strength of our industries. Our tariff programme of the 1930s did a lot of good in the circumstances of the time, but I think we should keep a close eye on tariffs as a permanent feature of the economy. It is true that many industries now depend on successful competition in foreign markets, but, for healthy long-run development, it is not desirable that the home market should be too sheltered. If I may fly a very little kite of my own manufacture, I should like to see all our tariffs reduced by one per cent per annum on a reducing balance method, so that next year's were 99 per cent of this year and the following year's 99 per cent of those. It would take a long time for there to be much to show in the way of absolute tariff reductions, and the reductions in any short period would be so trifling as not to hurt, but the squeeze would be in the right direction and the impact of competitive forces from *outside* our economy would be strengthened.

I have already said that the availability of adequate cash resources is the condition of any capital development; it is also very important from the point of view of maintaining the competitiveness of our industry from within. From both points of view many people are now rightly worried about the future provision of risk capital for industry. British industry has been built up on the basis of ploughed-back profits, the capital market being used only for relatively major stages in a firm's growth. We know that retained profits, even with dividends reduced in real terms, are now no longer adequate for rapid development, owing to the weight of ordinary taxation and of special taxes upon profit.

The capital market is therefore of even greater importance, but the changes in our economics which make it so are also weakening the capital market itself. The taxation of profits and the restriction of dividends are, of course, making the provision of risk capital less attractive to the outside investor. Worse, these same changes, plus our heavy personal taxation, are diminishing the supply of funds to the market as a whole. Here I may perhaps refer you to Mr. Momtchiloff's interesting but disturbing paper in the first number of the *Journal of Industrial Economics*. In our present economic position and with our heavy commitments for social expenditure, we may not be able to do much to improve the position, or not rapidly, but we should be keen that it does not become worse.

I have referred already to the historic importance of ploughed-back profits as the basis for capital development. They are of absolute critical importance for smaller and medium-sized businesses, for the capital market proper is available only for fairly large issues of capital and to businesses which are large and sufficiently well established to be fairly stable in the face of any vicissitudes in their personal management. We all know what has been happening in this sector. As elsewhere, profits taxation is at a penal rate — but, in addition, the director-controlled business is penalized by surtax regulations and by death duty arrangements which, originally inspired in order to prevent revenue frauds, are certainly strangling the further development of even medium-size businesses.

It is a sad thing from the social point of view to see such businesses increasingly subject to semi-forcible mergers with larger types of business. It is sadder when we realize how much they have been the source of effective competition to the largest scale of business and the development of new products. Many of our most significant modern developments have originated with successful businesses of this class, to which, to give only one instance, Courtauld's belonged at the turn of this century. I am *quite* sure that we should take special steps here, and, in 1949, I therefore suggested a very substantial lightening of the burden of taxation on undistributed profits for small and medium businesses, subject to some pretty effective safeguards to ensure that the profits were retained for development, which I shall not elaborate now.

The position would be relatively much more desperate were it not for the recent successful establishment of the Industrial and Commercial Finance Corporation. This is doing very good work in providing longish-term finance for medium businesses. It needs every encouragement, but with the best will in the world, an outside finance agency of this kind cannot stop up the whole gap. For one thing, it is a lot easier to help the development of new technical products and processes than it is to help the development of a good small business in an existing line of industry, where the personal factor of management is alike more important and more difficult to assess. In this sector, above all, however, I want to stress the importance, for development, of retained profits which a management can spend without having to look over its shoulders at outsiders. It is true that industrial progress here has been at the expense of failures and uncertainties which, to say the least, are untidy to the planning mind, but I personally consider the success of one Lord Nuffield to be worth quite a few motor business failures.

I have been stressing the availability of finance rather than its cost because, in my experience, that has been the major factor affecting industrial capital development. Our text-books err in the emphasis which they place on the effects of normal differences in rates of interest, etc.

So far, I have been talking about the pace of development in general, and considering external obstacles to it being as quick as it should be. We should not overlook the fact, here, that sheer management factors set a limit to the rate at which new development can take place. One problem is to introduce new methods etc., without disorganizing present production. Another is to train sufficient skilled management personnel so that the management cadre may grow with the business and its problems. These difficulties increase as we move back from a given industry to its equipment industries. The impact of such dynamic problems at this level is sometimes overlooked when critics comment on the apparently slow re-development of British basic industries after the general tariff gave them a breathing space. How many rolling mills had the equipment industry erected for the steel industry, or how many blast furnaces had been put up, over the period from 1919 to 1932, and how many of the middle range of management in those industries had had responsible experience of the erection of large new works? The textile industries, also, found after the recent war that it takes time for an equipment industry, long starved of major orders, to readjust itself for high outputs. There are managerial limits to the pace of technical progress, and if we force the pace too much then we come up against more physical limitations — such as the sheer number of trained bodies at the drawing boards.

Lags such as these which I have mentioned account for the time which it took for British industry to begin pulling itself up-to-date after the war. Here, there is another contrast with America which should be borne in mind when other comparisons are being made. The full impact of the war came late in America, and her industry could carry out maintenance and development on a more or less normal scale up to practically the end of hostilities. Here, we were on a fully mobilized footing, from 1940 at all events, and, except where urgent war requirements could justify the allocation of resources, new capital development came practically to a standstill, and even maintenance was seriously held back. It was to be expected that it would take us a couple of years or so to get going, bearing in mind the fuel crisis and other set-backs, but a good deal of the sensational rise in industrial productivity from 1948 onwards was simply due to re-equipment getting into its stride.

During the post-war period, our capital development has, of course, been much subject to government control. This has been necessary because all the things which we want to do, or have wanted to do, would have been beyond our resources. If industry has not got all that it would have liked, especially when it faced sellers' markets, it probably has not done badly in the circumstances of the times. Over the five years 1947–1952, for instance, plant, machinery and equipment, including that going to public corporations etc., accounted for three-eighths of our grand total of gross national investment. Industry has had to take its place in competition with all the other social objectives; I personally think that in our position it would have been rational to have given industry rather more, and to have cut down the extent to which we invested resources in other social objectives, but that is a purely personal opinion, and political realities were in the other direction. In some cases, I think we might really have held back more equipment from foreign markets until our home industry had had a little more of its leeway made up, but, here again, the need for exports was pressing and we shall need the foreign markets for our equipment industries in the future. In theory, I could make out a strong case that we should not have been so ready to export generating equipment and should have pushed on with the home electricity programme, since electricity is the key to so many modern methods of production. But, again, in this case, our long disappointment with coal output reminds me that had electricity wanted more coal, domestic consumers would have had to take less. (Coal is the real bottleneck in all national strategy looking ahead.)

Making these concessions to political and other realities, I should still say that we have not been free enough with industrial building, apart from the favoured special areas. It is perhaps part of the explanation that the allocation of building resources has been the easiest control to enforce, quite as much as because of the pressure of our housing needs. The fact is that since 1948, the only period for which I can find figures, it appears that industrial premises make up less than one-fifth of the total new work done by the building industry. I particularly regret this stringency because, as I said earlier, buildings set the most inflexible limits to capital development. The recent periods of high output combined with the installation of so much new equipment offered golden opportunities for the full adoption of modern layouts which would have improved our future flexibility considerably. Modern layouts, however, ideally require new buildings or at least freedom to consider these. A lot has been done, but many firms in the interest of present output, and in the face of delays imposed by building control, have had to botch and make do with buildings which they would have liked to have scrapped in more lenient conditions.

Still thinking of buildings as the long-run limiting factor in the re-development of existing businesses, it has sometimes been said that we tend to build too well, and to put down buildings which will last too long, bearing in mind the demands of changing layouts and technology. That may be so — I am sure that some of your ancestors in Lancashire built too well! To some extent, however, the complaint arises from a comparison of modern buildings with older factory buildings, and there is less to grumble about in modern factory designs. One thing is clear, our taxation system in its allowances does not offer much encouragement to plan buildings on a temporary basis. I have sometimes been impressed with this feature in the design of buildings where technical factors make it more possible to treat buildings as expendable structures from the Inland Revenue point of view — where, for example, the building's framework can be designed simply as a crane track. It is possible that a more generous treatment of buildings as subject to obsolescence would have important and favourable consequences on the trends of design in industrial buildings. I simply put that up as a matter which might well be considered.

This question of hanging on too long to old buildings is related to the general question of how far we are ready enough as an industrial country to scrap equipment before it is worn out and go for what is better. I have suggested already that we may tend to exaggerate this, partly because in full employment and with sellers' markets the economy of up-to-dateness in technology tends to be exaggerated. We also tend to place too heavy a stress on it because of our memories of the conditions in the years of depression. For the rest, it is a matter of personal opinion. If, however, my fears about a capital-short future are correct, and if liquid resources are going to be scarce for new capital development, then we must expect to see a renewed tendency in this direction.

Such conditions will tend to make us economize on such less directly productive assets as buildings, and be more inclined to make do and mend generally. All this simply reinforces what I have said already about the potential seriousness of the money capital position. Certainly, we should do well to be careful that we get the best we can out of our present resources.

I do not want to discuss in any detail the extent to which labour practices act as a brake upon our development. I know that that is so in some cases, but equally it is amenable to good management given a long enough period of favourable general employment conditions. The necessity to save on fixed assets, where we can, lends points to current efforts in cotton to get double-day-shift working extended.

So far, I have touched only lightly on one most important aspect of capital development — the development of quite new commodities, which I have referred to in connexion with competition in dynamic conditions. Nowadays, however, many people are worried about the pace with which new fundamental discoveries in the scientific field, many of them originating in this country, are applied in our own industries. We do well to worry about this. At the same time, I believe we are wrong to appeal to pre-war experience and to post-war experience in the same breath, as denoting a universal tendency towards backwardness on our part. If we think back to pre-war conditions, although we should probably agree that it was only to be expected if many of our industries were relatively backward in this matter, in fact, however, in the 1930s at all events, we did not do badly, especially if we bring the electronic field into consideration.

It is clear, however, that we have slipped a bit since the war in some directions. Again, it is not a universally true story; jet aircraft alone give such a generalization the lie direct. Apart from such specially favoured fields, however, it does seem that we lag in fields requiring heavy initial development. When we probe into some of the cases which are usually mentioned, such as, may I say, Terylene, we become aware that the lags involved have been often a product of our present difficulties — of the controls over buildings for example, and of shortages of essential equipment.

There are, however, institutional factors which are at present unfavourable and to which we should do well to pay attention. One which is often mentioned is a shortage of persons with a basic scientific education. Having been educated in a modern grammar school myself I do not believe that the problem is quite so simple as all that. What has happened is that our industries have moved over to a greatly increased demand for scientists and are straining higher educational facilities etc., which were devised when there was a much lower demand. I think back, for example, to the relative shortage of jobs for those who were scientists at my own University College in the early 1930s. I think the position is

321

righting itself as rapidly as it can, and that as usual we are shouting after we have started doing something about it. What is necessary is to do all we can to increase the output of special kinds of scientists, especially those who are trained in development techniques, and the best place to train these is in developing industries. A larger proportion of the resources going on general science spent in more narrowly specialized channels might have a big effect.

I myself want to come back to the institutional question of the capital market and the availability of profits. New products take a long time to be developed, the failures may well be heavy, and the expense to bring even the winners to fruition will usually also be large. The National Research Development Corporation is doing very valuable work here for fundamentally new ideas, and should be given more scope. We must not, however, think too much in terms of brand new product classes. It is just as important to get continuous innovations in regular products — even if the gains at any one point are less spectacular. For these developments to occur more largely, we need two things — first, a rather greater freedom of current resources, so that the development of new products is not so much at the expense of current output in the businesses where they have to be developed. Secondly, however, in view of the risks and waiting involved, I again come back to my theme that we need to leave rather more money resources in industry. I suggest that from the social point of view this is the most important aspect of capital development to which I have called your attention.

9 Competition in the modern economy[1]

1 Introductory remarks

It is necessary to begin with some explanation as to why this paper is so concerned with economic theory. The first point to be made is that competition in any industry cannot be discussed without the most careful attention to general ideas about what competition is or ought to be. Each speaker at this meeting is exposing his own working set of ideas, selecting from the shifting congeries of facts those which his experience tells him are most relevant to the discussion, in other words, every speaker is necessarily theorizing. Their common experience enables them to make effective communication with each other and their specialized audience but the object is to do more than expound ideas as between colleagues. The Institute is also concerned with communicating them to the outside world and it is necessary to face up to the general ideas which are held outside.

Economists are an important part of the wider audience, for theirs is the profession most concerned with ideas of competition and accustomed to looking at industry from the point of view of its competitiveness. When writing this paper the author had, because of his contacts with industrialists, some inkling of the kinds of facts which speakers from the oil industry would consider relevant to any appraisal of its competitiveness. It seemed probable that there might be some conflict between the general framework of their thinking and that of economists, which might prevent a proper appreciation of what was being said and cause the relevance of the cited facts to be doubted.

In any such conflict of viewpoint it does not follow that the ideas of economists should automatically be given greater weight. The development of theories aiming at critical discussion of the details of industrial situations is comparatively recent and the possibility of error should be considered. As a matter of fact, the author happens to believe that economic theory in this area has gone off on the wrong tack during the last thirty years. Be that as it may, there is no denying that recent trends in economic thought about industry have had enormous practical effect. One regrettable result has been that not nearly

(1) Reprinted with permission from *Competitive Aspects of Oil Operations*, edited by G. Sell (London: The Institute of Petroleum, 1958), pp. 1–42.

enough theorists have made serious studies of the actual workings of industry, being sustained by an apparatus which for long seemed to have all the general factual confirmation that it needed. Conclusions derived from these theories have impinged directly on public policy. The modern development of Anti-Trust Law in the USA and the framework of our own Restrictive Trade Practices Act, with the recommendations of the Monopolies Commission set up under earlier legislation, can all be seen as thoroughly informed by the theoretical ideas of economists even if they have not gone so far as many economists would wish.

Economic theory has also had an important effect through the colouring of ideas about industry which are held by non-economists: for the general public has been readily influenced by the easy popularization to which prevailing theories have lent themselves. To paraphrase *1066 and All That*, Monopoly is a Bad Thing and many of the natural leaders of public opinion in Western democracies have been influenced by authoritative pronouncements that ordinary competitive industry is best seen as 'monopolistic' or at least as imperfectly competitive — backed as these are by positive statements that the effect of such everyday methods of competition must be to achieve prices which are too high, for commodities produced by too many firms, working on too restricted a scale of output (the standard of comparison being a technical state of affairs which apparently merited the name of perfect competition).

Bearing all this in mind, and conscious of professional responsibility, it was decided to attempt two tasks in this paper. First, to give the meeting some idea of the climate of theoretical ideas with which the speakers from industry have to contend so that the discussion might be pointed directly at any conflict of viewpoint that is involved. Secondly, to state the issues as they are seen in order to try to induce those professional colleagues who had not already done so to look anew and critically at basic ideas which are the more difficult to criticize because professional training has made them become presuppositions. In the last ten years much new thinking has been developing and if this paper helps to increase the measure of critical agreement which its author thinks is beginning to emerge it may assist the important papers which follow this to get the attention which is their due.

This is a large task, but it was felt that at the invitation of the Institute the near impossible should be attempted. This paper has therefore tried to set out orthodox theory and criticisms of it in terms which would be comprehensible to the non-economist (under pain perhaps of an occasional wet towel) and yet which would be sufficiently rigorous to stand up to professional criticism. For any errors into which, despite his efforts, he may have fallen the author hopes that no vicarious punishment will be visited on the rest of the report and that it will be welcomed as a valuable contribution to informed opinion.

This paper, however, is not just critical and academic in its approach. All through the author has tried to present also a connected view of industrial competition as one finds it in practice. Much of what is said was new when he first started to say it but it has been argued elsewhere. Perhaps the novel element in the present paper is the stress on the intrinsic competitiveness of large firms. Some ideas about this did play a part in the first general statement of the author's theoretical attitude published as long ago as 1949 but only gradually has their full importance been seen after clearing out of the way negative approaches to competition which were determined by his own earlier professional conditioning. In this general presentation of the paper, it seems fitting to reverse the order and deal first with this topic from the final section.

It is certain that any assessment of the competitiveness of industry must start with a recognition of the truth that modern large businesses are competitive affairs internally. The validity of any generalizations in which such businesses are taken as simple units (as when Business A is seen as trying to dominate the market for X, or as in competition with Business B) can be tested by seeing how far they allow for the consequences of this state of affairs in the relations businesses have with one another. Nothing like sufficient attention has been given to this in theoretical and practical discussion of industry alike. Yet it may well be that it is so true that it will seem obvious to men of practical experience when once it has been stated.

The paradox is perhaps that practical men have not made more of this point themselves. One reason may be that although we all call for competitiveness in industry, our society rather turns its face from the competition between man and man, each for his own personal advancement, which must lie at the heart of this. Business by its very nature is a department of society where such qualities have to be encouraged but we can understand that so little reference is made to it when the lip-service of society runs so strongly in the opposite direction and when our social arrangements (for instance, taxation) do so much to discourage it.

There may be other, more subtle reasons why business men's own theorizings do not give more explicit recognition to this factor. Part 4 of this paper was outlined to a friend who has long held high administrative office. After sitting quiet for a time he said that perhaps the most important part of the argument — the hungry generations threatening to tread him down — had become uncomfortable to think about at his time of life. But he did accept the strength of this factor in keeping a business up to the mark and agreed that in the last analysis it expressed itself in a competitive business outlook.

In the paper it is argued that the generation by efficient businesses of strongly competitive forces from within themselves is not at all incompatible with the fact that such businesses may make arrangements of the kind that we loosely characterize as monopolistic — but that it is incompatible with the persistence of such arrangements if they go against the grain of the basic

325

technical and commercial factors. If such inconsistency threatens, then this vital force from within will fight the outside constraints and will eventually enable the basic factors in the situation to have as full an effect as they could have in more obviously competitive conditions.

The professional conditioning of business men which has been described leads typically to the development of a character-element which can only be described as a sort of integrity which contributes greatly to the social healthiness of practical competition. To give an example, let us consider a pre-war international cartel which the author and a colleague have been studying. At its birth, the industry was cursed with excess capacity hanging over from the enthusiasm with which its basic inventions had been greeted, for it was a young industry. In their price policies the leaders of the cartel, even at its strongest moments, therefore paid great attention to keeping prices low enough to avoid commercial inducements to the setting up of new capacity.

This price policy, however, is not the point at the moment. As techniques developed and knowledge of them spread, it was natural that important markets without their own productive capacity and relatively far from producing countries should ask if they could not do better to produce at home with the advantage of saving the freights involved. It was found that there were one or two countries where such a question had been raised several times and each time turned down on the expert advice of technologists from existing producers. One has to work to keep a suspicious mind on this type of research and it was thought that the reports resulting from such consultations should not be relied upon. Therefore, a man who had been involved most recently in these discussions was asked bluntly how far was he swayed by the fact that it was so much to the interests of his firm that no new plant should be built in X or Y? He went carefully over the details of a report but his patient treatment of his questioners was an evident triumph of self-control. He realized that there was an implicit suggestion that inexperienced foreign governments might be blinded by 'science', so finally he took that bull by the horns and asked if it was really thought that he could give the foreign government advice which would not stand up to critical examination in the light of technical and economic facts. His signature was on the report and so on. That was his real point and more important really than the one which he put forward as more likely to appeal to professional sceptics — that, in the end, independent checks on his advice could be obtained and then, if he had let them down, where would his company be in any negotiations with that government, or with any other which heard about the matter? The author was then as much convinced by the engineer's attitude as by his argument but only gradually has he come round to a theoretical view which requires that such conduct should be accepted as a norm.

Accepting this view of business, how can we accept notions of great firms in large industries sitting down to impose unnecessary restrictive conditions which are repugnant to the whole philosophy by which men succeed within their own businesses? In later sections of the paper, it will be found that this general theoretical attitude prevails in the view taken of the conditions which make possible the stability of any industrial structure, whether or not it is bolstered by what are technically restrictive practices within the meaning of the Act. Greater confidence is felt in this theorizing because it not only seems to fit in with observed historical facts of instability in cartellized and uncartellized industries but also because by holding to it it has occasionally been possible to predict unstable conditions before they manifested themselves to the business men concerned, or at least at the stage when they were only getting round to recognizing them.

The other major theme it is wished to extract from the present paper is that the customers with whom businesses have to deal, even when they are ordinary chaps, are not collectively nearly so likely to create sheer market imperfections as recent economic theory has assumed. Without repeating the detailed argument given later, the important point which emerges is that we should not readily accept parity of prices between producers in industries with very few firms as a sign of the working of monopolistic forces but should recognize that it is enforced by the general pervasiveness of competition for which this paper argues. We can then begin to think, for example and *pace* US Anti-Trust actions, that there may be something in the protestations of the American motor industry that it is really fiercely competitive — and even that the extravagance of motor car design over there reflects genuine preponderant consumer taste as well as the relative cheapness of gasoline.

Why is the international oil industry not cited as an example? Because it would be preaching to the converted. Like any other business men, discussing the industry which they know intimately, most readers in the oil industry will be prepared to believe in its fundamental competitiveness, given all the minor imperfections which they will rightly see as flowing from their having to operate in an imperfect world where improvements take time and may be outdated by the time that they are perfectly accomplished. But there is no doubt that they will be much more suspicious of other industries. It is a sign of the spread of ideas which the more theoretical parts immediately following try to combat, that business men are so ready to believe that other industries are uncompetitive rackets. From contacts with business the author knows how easily such bivalent attitudes are adopted and personal argument will show that more than mere prejudice is involved — the views taken of other industries are supported with theoretical positions that the proponents will fiercely attack when it comes to their own. The cure is practical study and improved theory.

Here, finally, one may touch on the wider functions of conferences such as that at which these papers are being read. Quite apart from adding to the enlightenment of business men and outsiders, this kind of discussion encourages general economic speculation among business men. In Great Britain in the past non-professional economists drawn from the world of practical experience have sometimes had a very honourable position among professionals. There are now some signs of a renewal of confidence among business men that they too can contribute to the development of the subject not only by being guinea pigs or otherwise providing the professionals with practical data but that they may usefully come into the arena of speculative discussion and so can help to extend our understanding of industrial operations. It is hoped to see yet more business men appearing as direct contributors to specialist academic journals but, to keep strictly to the oil industry, any industrial economist must be interested in such attempts as that by Dr Frankel to develop specialized theory which will be peculiarly suited to it, to cite his treatment of the consequences of the elementary fact that oil is a liquid. Anyone who has seen examples of the general handbooks prepared by leading oil firms for use in the training of junior managers must also wish that these were available on the general market, for some are first-rate text-books of industrial organization with the virtue which is difficult for outsiders to achieve, that technological factors are given their due importance. It should be added that in the proper comprehension of technology lies the way to future progress in industrial economics, but to go further into this now would be outside this paper.

2 Ideas of competition

The *Oxford English Dictionary* defines 'Competition' in commerce as 'rivalry in the same market, striving for custom between those who have the same commodity to dispose of.' This follows the sense of ordinary language and stresses the 'striving for custom' which very many business men generally see as the essence of competition for them. It should be said, however, that to the economist's way of thinking it is significant that this aspect of competition in more sophisticated industries is not noteworthy in primary industries however competitive they be. Nor is striving for custom an ingredient in the economist's own basic definition of competition.

Business men in manufacture and distribution whose own thinking dwells on the continuous attempt to displace rivals forced on them under pain of themselves losing ground to competitors are often surprised if they happen to pick up economics text-books to find that in perfect competition, the hypothetical condition which is the quintessence of competition as the economist sees it, there is no mention of this, to them, major aspect of the competitive struggle. Reading on, they may be still more bewildered to discover analyses in which some of their chief competitive weapons do appear, but are then described as characteristics of 'imperfect' or 'monopolistic' competition!

The short solution of this paradox is that the assumptions on which the concept of perfect competition is based imply that any individual business would have the maximum possible freedom to displace rivals — it would merely have to offer a slightly superior product at the same price or undercut by a very small amount their price for the same quality to attract all the others' customers to itself; the very concept of particular rivals which so sharply focuses the thinking of business men becomes meaningless in such a condition.

If one is to understand in what way important features of actual competition have come to be regarded as involving the adulteration of the pure concept with elements of monopoly, it is necessary to go beyond this brief answer and spell out, if only in summary fashion, the assumptions underlying this fundamental economic analysis. It is hoped that the following will make plain where the author and, probably, quite a number of other economists are now unhappy about how economic theorizing usually 'goes on from there'.

The following characteristics of a perfectly competitive industry embody the basic assumptions:

(1) Producers and 'consumers' alike must be so numerous that none of them has any significant effect on the market situation facing him if he withdraws or varies his output or purchases, as the case may be;

(2) Each must act independently and there can be no public regulation which would achieve the same result as collective manipulation of demand or supply (e.g. in brief, no rationing — and no prorating, either!);

(3) Consumers and producers must be rational and perfectly well-informed about prices and qualities in the whole market;

(4) The entry of a new business must be 'easy', not only because, as the above characteristics imply, there are no impediments on the sales side, but also because a new entrant must be able to raise the capital needed for efficient operation without being penalized as compared with established firms.

A perfectly competitive industry, thus defined, will have the following consequential characteristics:(2)

(5) After due allowance for transport costs, there will be only one price

---

(2) It is useful to remember here and elsewhere that in general economic theory price is usually treated as a shorthand phrase for the whole set of terms on which a commodity is offered for sale. Non-price competition ordinarily costs money and it is therefore possible to treat it as the equivalent to a reduction in price, an economist referring to it specifically only where it would have a special significance for his analysis.

throughout the market for a product of a given quality;

(6) At any one time, this price will be at such a level that total demand exactly matches total supplies;

(7) Any producer can sell any quantity he cares to produce without affecting market price (see (1) above); therefore the output of each business will be determined only by costs of production and each will produce just so much that its costs at the margin of production are exactly covered by price; for short periods of time it will be sufficient to recover the prime costs, but, if businesses are to stay in production at a given level of output, the full costs at the margin must be covered (since capital must be replaced, etc.);(3)

(8) It follows that, if for any reason (for example, the fluctuation of national income during a 'trade cycle') the general level of demand for the industry's products should fluctuate, then prices will also fluctuate — and relatively sharply, since any reduction in demand will leave businesses equipped to produce bigger outputs, and prices will fall drastically to prime cost levels; and any rise in demand will tax existing capacities and prices will rise sharply because of the difficulties in the way of increasing outputs;

(9) If a decrease in demand persists, then businesses will be driven out of the industry and prices will rise to the normal level dictated by costs of production; similarly, with a persistent increase of demand, new businesses will come into the industry so long as they may expect at least as good results at existing prices as they could get in any other line. There is thus a normal, long-run limit to prices in perfectly competitive industry and generally they will be determined by costs of production.

A pause is made here to discuss the effect of removing one in particular of the basic characteristics of a perfectly competitive industry, since this will be relevant to some generalizations which are occasionally put forward about the market for crude oil. Suppose, in contradiction to Characteristic (1), that there is not a 'large' number of producers, or, alternatively, that at least some producers control a large proportion of total output individually or in association. Variations in the supplies offered by such producers will therefore significantly affect total market supplies and so the level of market price. It is clear that there must now be some doubts about the validity of continuing to assume that businesses will act independently (Characteristic (2)). Apart from that and if all other conditions are still satisfied, parity of prices throughout the market (Characteristic (5)) will still operate. But it will not now be possible, while

---

(3) If the industry is to be stable and stay fully competitive, (7) implies that a business's unit costs will rise if it increases output, given wages, and other cost prices. This, as will be seen later, is a very important postulate from the point of view of the realistic application of perfect competition analysis.

retaining the other assumptions, to make any generalization about the level at which prices will settle *(a)* at any point of time; because such businesses will be able to raise or lower the price they can get by manipulating their supply; *(b)* in the long run; because we cannot be sure that Characteristic (4) will apply, since new entry may not be 'easy', either because individual businesses have to be of large size to be successful or because newcomers have to face the opposition of large established businesses.

It must be said at once that economic theory has not so far been able to give a firm solution to the problem of the level of prices in an industry containing relatively few firms which are otherwise perfectly competitive. In fact the analyses which have been produced will have to be examined later, but really it all boils down to the conclusion that it all depends on the assumptions about the behaviour of their competitors which individual businesses take as guides to their own conduct. This negative conclusion about what is called a situation of 'oligopoly' is nevertheless very relevant to some statements about crude oil prices.(4) To show that delivered prices at any major point of consumption must be identical, and so on, may rebut suggestions that the oil industry arranges such features of its prices. But it cannot be said *tout court* that the general level of prices is determined chiefly by the competition of numerous smaller producers if a large part of the general supply is in the hands of very few producers (and obviously not, moreover, if supplies from even the 'many' are influenced by systematic prorating which may take the market situation into account). To analyse the formation of prices in such cases it is necessary to know the policies and practices of all who are in a position to influence the market; and, since some of the factors at work must originate in political circles outside the industry, these, also, have to be recognized in any analysis of prices.

If, then, the policies of large business units cannot be taken for granted, it may still be true that they need not be regarded so sceptically as the indeterminateness of 'oligopoly' theory allows. Before that question can be taken up, we must go farther with the main theme, which at the moment concerns the difficulty of applying perfect competition theory to ordinary industry. In the 1920s and early 1930s, economists became greatly concerned about this. To put the story in a few nutshells, they came up against the following facts:

(i) In manufacture, etc., it is quite frequently the case that costs do not rise — may even fall — if outputs increase provided that businesses can organize to produce on the larger scales;

(ii) Plants in many industries, in the depressed conditions of the time, were then running well below capacities and so could produce larger outputs at lower

---

(4) Cf. E.C.E. 'The Price of Oil in Western Europe', 1955, Chapter 2; and O.E.E.C. *Oil: The Outlook for Europe*, 1956, Chapter XI.

costs, even without changing their organization.

Further, even when trade is not particularly depressed it is not unusual for businesses to keep some capacity in hand so that some additional output may normally be possible without rising costs;

(iii) Businesses are normally willing to sell more than the market will actually take from them at ruling prices. (Which fact could be better understood in the light of (i) and (ii).)

In the face of these facts, it was clearly wrong to assume that the output of a business in such industries would be determined solely by its cost position. This meant that the fundamental characteristic of competitive industries, as economists understood them, (Characteristic No (7)), was not to be found in wide sections of industry generally regarded as 'competitive'. Logic suggested that our ideas should be corrected on the demand side and after much discussion in England and America, some brilliant innovations, whilst keeping to the general method of reasoning, incorporated the following characteristics, thought to be observable in many industries:

(iv) Businesses in the kinds of industry under discussion did not produce 'identical' products:

(a) whatever the resemblances, they 'differentiated' their products by the application of brand names and trade marks, supported by advertising and other 'selling costs';

(b) for this and possibly for 'real' reasons, consumers were not indifferent between products from different businesses but had preferences for particular brands. 'Real' reasons might account for some such preferences, but the selling activities referred to in (a), working on consumers' susceptibilities, produced 'irrational' preferences;

(v) Individual businesses thus had their own 'market' with, consequently, some freedom of action regarding prices — if they raised prices relatively to their competitors they would not lose all their customers, while a small reduction in price would by itself attract only a part of the available custom away from their rivals;

(vi) To add significantly to its market, a business would have to incur selling costs, such as advertising;

(vii) Beyond some point, selling costs would rise out of proportion to the extra sales gained and so would be a counter-balancing factor to any reduction in costs which increased production in itself might bring.

Where only a relatively few businesses sold a given type of product, changes in price by any one business (v) might well have such perceptible repercussions on one or more rivals that the latter would be forced to alter their own policies. The level at which prices would settle in this case is, therefore, as indeterminate as in the simple 'oligopoly' case referred to earlier. It was sometimes recognized that this failure of analysis was a defect practically, since such 'oligopoly' industries certainly do exist; but the question was sidestepped in elaborate analyses of the ways in which the situation *might* resolve itself and the theorists (with a whole generation of students after them) rushed with satisfaction to the important area where they could apparently get results from the new way of thinking.

There, the theories which were developed may be summarized as follows: where businesses *were* sufficiently numerous for such interactions to be negligible — cases to which perfect competition concepts had often been uncritically applied hitherto — it now came to be considered that each business, in effect, enjoyed a partial monopoly and, given the general level of its rivals' prices, could adjust its own prices so as to maximize its advantage. Now, the general level of prices which businesses in such an industry could enjoy would be limited by the competition from new businesses which would come in and remain so long as they could get reasonable overall profits in relation to investment opportunities elsewhere; and coming in, these would chisel their own market out a little here and there, from the established businesses. Combining the individual monopoly approach with this long-run competitive effect, the new analyses produced a result of the kind that the theorists were looking for. In such an industry, now, it could be prophesied that one might get a relatively stable general price level which gave individual businesses merely competitive profits on the average but where each settled down with falling costs (in the sense of (i)) and so where businesses which were too small for highest efficiency, and yet which had 'excess' capacities, would be the rule.

These theoretical developments, despite the errors of viewpoint we can see now, undoubtedly led to much progress in economics but it would be beyond the scope of this paper to go into such questions of sheer methodology. Nor is it the intention to discuss in detail the very important practical consequences — not all fully justified — they have had in their generation: but we are concerned with the broad validity of the view of the competitive process which they engendered.

In recent years there has been a good deal of new thinking — largely as economists gradually got around to aspects of the industrial situation which the new *Weltanschauung* itself neglected:

(A) A point which had been recognized early in the new discussions but which had been somewhat overlooked in the development of monopolistic competition analyses (which settled so many other problems but which were not fully compatible with this fact): that, in the actual world, businesses seem quite willing to sell more than they are selling at current prices. See (iii) above;

(B) The 'cost-plus' approach to pricing problems is very general in industry and industrialists generally do not pay the attention to the particular elasticity of their demand that they should according to the theories;

(C) Much evidence began to accumulate about the way costs of production vary with changing output and it became arguable that the whole traditional approach here was wrong — that, outside primary industry, average costs in the long-run will be more or less constant or fall only gradually no matter what the size of the industrial plant once it achieves the main economies of scale; certainly the universality of increasing costs beyond some 'optimal' point — and the idea of an optimum itself — were put in doubt;

(D) Oligopolistic situations are very common in industry so that there is a significant part of the industrial field held for which current theories could not pretend to offer very useful generalizations;

(E) In such situations, and generally, business men, on interrogation, although not calculating elasticities or exploiting demand consciously in the way we expected, seemed convinced that their demands would in general fall off quite sharply if they sustained a price which was out of line with those quoted by their rivals.

The points (C) to (E) in this list mean that a lot of the acclaimed differences between 'monopolistic' and 'perfect or pure' competition would not amount to much in practice. However, other points of criticism have been developed which go to the root of the whole method of economic analysis in either situation. Here a warning must be given that points are being made to which, because of the nature of his researches, the author was one of the first to call attention. In order to try to be uncontroversial in the way in which things are put reversion is made to the note form which minimizes commentary:

(a) For historical reasons, economic theory not only called all customers 'consumers' but analysed their behaviour as if they *were* ordinary people spending their personal incomes for their own enjoyment. In fact, businesses typically sell to other business men and whatever preferences these may have as between sources of supply to treat them as 'irrational' in their behaviour would make it questionable how far all the rest of the theoretical apparatus (on the cost side, for example) can apply;

(b) Similarly, the long-run equilibrium situation was previously described as dependent upon the extent to which the entry of new competitors to the industrial group was 'easy', etc. But these new entrants were usually discussed in terms of their being quite new businesses, with all the difficulties these might have to get the resources which were necessary for minimum efficient scale. In the actual world, however, competition may more easily come from businesses already established in other lines of industry and these limitations need not apply to them;

(c) The types of selling costs of which advertising is a leading example, designed to influence consumers' tastes, affect only a relatively limited field and are important only for a quite narrow sector of consumers' goods properly so-called. For the rest, selling costs may well be a condition of being in a market at all, rather than an expenditure whose variation has great effects on the net preferences and prejudices affecting the custom for an individual business;

(d) The whole approach to prices has been imbued with a static view of cost-possibilities; there has been no analytical scope for innovation and no analysis, in particular, of the way in which the competitive process encourages or discourages this.

This section now concludes with a few final words of commentary. In the revival of economic thinking and controversy to which these recent developments have given rise, there has been a renewed interest in the working of the competitive process. In the present state of economics, as previously indicated, there is certainly not any settled body of dogma in this field. A fresh distinction is now beginning to be drawn between the industries where competition approximates to the old perfect competition model — primary industries with large numbers of enterprises — and the general run of manufacturing and distributive industries where competition may be less perfect but 'workable'. Resulting comparisons are not wholly to the advantage of the former groups of industries. Economists are increasingly aware of the effects of uncertainties in the actual world and of the fact that new investment and development give hostages to fortune. In these dynamic conditions, the 'differentiation' of the market which characterizes non-primary industries is seen as one factor which may help industrial progress; which is itself seen as occurring in contrast to the tendencies to technical stagnation that plague competitive primary industries unless they are assisted from outside. Such views are also leading some economists to plead for a new assessment of the position of industrial 'monopolies' (hitherto the most readily condemned form of industrial organization) especially with the realization that they are potentially exposed to much wider competition than seemed possible when new competition was treated as if it had to come from quite new enterprises.

Finally, there are even re-assessments of organized interference with free pricing. Since oligopoly is so widespread the uncertainties of genuinely free pricing might themselves have unfavourable effects on long-run development. Here, however, we are touching on the most controversial area of all and to pursue this question in any detail must take one into the subject-matter of the following sections.

3 Competition in the modern economy (or 'Oligopoly in practice'!)

No voyage starts from nowhere. Even that of Columbus, made as it was without practical assistance from maps, once the then-known world had dropped from sight over the horizon, had quite definite connexions with the geographical knowledge and speculation of his day. Here also, as we turn to our set subject, we shall find that what we are in fact going to discuss links on to the theoretical problems and analyses we have just laid aside. The implicit analogy with the voyage of Columbus, however, if it thus has a point, is inexact and it would be misleading — as well as immodest — to press it too far; for we are not going to run into any unexpected continent.

What we must talk about is oligopoly of one sort or another and our economists' maps already run all round its frontiers. Our territory, then, is known to exist and its borders are clearly marked whatever the direction from which we approach it. ('Here beginns Oligopolie!') So perhaps, on reflexion, 'In Darkest Africa' offers a better analogy than 'Towards the New World'. Bearing in mind the warnings of the dangers of jungle warfare uttered by most economists who have tried to peer over the frontier, we must later have a closer look at the guesses about the nature of the terrain which some of them have written across the map at this point.

A state of oligopoly exists wherever a few businesses are each large enough for one's policies and decisions to be able to have a perceptible effect on the market situation which all face. There are, however, important differences in structure as between oligopolist industries. In some cases, the 'few' make up a whole industry; in others, there is also a large or small number of other businesses each of which, by itself, has but a negligible effect on the general market, sometimes, some of these individually negligible businesses are associated and act as a unit which does have a significant effect and their association must then be counted among the 'few'. In general, however, theory has not paid much attention to these structural questions but has tended to work with cases where all firms are assumed to be of the same order of size.

It is necessary to give prominence to oligopoly in this paper because it is so much a typical situation in modern industry, and certainly much more prevalent than one would conclude by comparing the proportion of standard general texts given to it with that devoted to the cases where theory can reach more settled conclusions. In fact, oligopoly is extremely prevalent. Clearly the case in those industries where but few firms exist (as in the manufacture of motor cars, rayon, or polythene), it is no less true of very many industries which the various censuses show to have quite large numbers of firms.

Take any such manufacturing industry, and it will be found that at any one time its products fall into groups of specialities and within these will frequently be found individual firms in an oligopoly position. The author was first led to pay proper attention to this in a study of the British boot and shoe industry. When an individual business was asked about competition as it saw it, it always gave a short list — up to a dozen or so of the businesses that it 'bothered about', the businesses it frequently 'ran up against', and within the list, it could name its 'close competitors'. If then firm B, named as a close competitor in firm A's list, was approached it would also give a short list which might differ substantially from A's, but which generally contained A's name (not necessarily among the few that it 'bothered' most about!). Such chains of oligopoly relations were found to be essential elements in the working of competition within this industry, which on the broadest classification was then recorded by the Census of Production as having upwards of 600 businesses.

If the older economists thought it proper to discuss the ordinary run of industry in terms of perfect competition ('long-run' at all events), some of the recent generation, with enthusiasm for the newer theories of the 1930s, have argued for an approach via a 'world of monopoly', pleading that, if any one approach is to be used, businesses are generally better analysed in terms of the monopolistic elements in their situations. The author thinks that it is high time that the prevalence of oligopoly was faced up to despite the difficulties which that places in the way of our using accepted tools of thought. Indeed, it will be argued later that, apart from those maintained by Government fiat, such apparent 'monopolies' (in the strict sense of single-firm industries) as are found in Western economic life are better understood from the point of view of oligopoly.

This is pleading for a competitive approach to industry for, whatever else it is, a world of oligopoly is a world of competition. It is hoped to show that it is possible to make some broad generalizations about the working of oligopolies which promise a useful route towards the better understanding of competition as it is found in practice; and, as the numerous registrations under the British Restrictive Trade Practices Act have shown, competition in practice has come to include quite sizeable doses of cartellization of one sort or another! The author will use his approach to comment on the working of such 'cartels' and restrictive associations as he has experienced them.

There is, therefore, an ambitious programme for the rest of this paper. It will help in this section to use economic theory as a framework of reference. making comparisons and contrasts with what economists generally have said about the probable behaviour of oligopolies.

Parity of prices: All the businesses in a pure oligopoly are assumed to produce identical commodities. It then becomes a postulate that market forces compel a parity of prices everywhere, allowance being made for delivery costs (including any tariffs around sections of the market). This may be accepted where industries produce standardized or easily standardizable commodities, such as for example ammonium sulphate or rayon yarn; it cannot, one would think, be for long that any producer will get, or any consumer pay, a higher price for a given quality than that ruling in some other accessible part of the market, and the qualities of such products are either determined by standard specifications or readily ascertainable by practical tests.

How far does parity of prices obtain when commodities are not standardized even, perhaps, inherently unstandardizable? This is the typical situation in much of modern industry, individual products being made to diverse specifications imposed by customers (for example, generating stations) or having their particular qualities settled by each producer as characteristics of his 'brands' (for example, motor cars). Here, economic theory has gone haring after the 'differentiation' of the market into separate sub-markets which is so apparent on first sight. Even when producers are in an oligopoly such industries are generally analysed in terms of 'consumers' having some degree of preference for particular producers so that a business will hold some customers even if it increases the difference between its prices and those of its competitors. In consequence, not much talk of parity of prices will be found when it comes to oligopolies where the market is differentiated in this apparently quasi-monopolistic manner.

The author would be the last to dispute that buyers' preferences do exist. It is rational that they should where, in the last resort, the quality of the product and service offered by a manufacturer may be tested only by experience. In such cases, everyone prefers to go on dealing where he has been satisfied until there is some reason to switch his custom. But it is irrational for economists to assume that such preferences will persist in the face of price differentials, all other qualities of the goods being unchanged. Let this assertion be taken in two stages.

The first reason for challenging the alleged consequence of dividing a market between distinct brands of product is that economists have generally made a mistake in treating the customer as always the same as the poor ignorant private consumer. In many cases, the customers of businesses are themselves other business men whose profits depend upon the care with which they buy things for business use or for re-sale. Where this is so some special reason must be found, and one has not been adduced so far, for assuming that parity of prices will not be preserved — and if such a reason were found, it would throw doubts on practically all economic analysis of business, which makes the general assumption that business men are rational and maximize profits in a single-minded fashion.

It is not proposed to just confute illogic with mere logic chopping (although that is not unreasonable where analysis is so much a matter of sheer logic). Of course, business men are not always 'rational' and can be affected with prejudice; they certainly value long-continued and well-tried connexions with suppliers. But can it really be believed to be anything like the general case that businesses will continue to buy from their usual sources things which they can get cheaper elsewhere?; surely, not if they learn that this is so.

It is the nature of salesmen to 'sell', and a mere belief that they have some such point of vantage will sharpen the efforts of the representatives of rival sources. The preference to deal with people a business man can trust from experience may stand in the way of casual horse-swapping; but if such a situation continues, although it may take time for the rival salesman to get business, why should he not succeed in the end? Usually he will already be in the trade and his reputation not entirely unknown. It will not be difficult to get trial orders on the occasions, common if only seasonally in all industries, when existing suppliers are fully stretched, or for special requirements which are wanted in a hurry.

Quite apart from such direct pressures there will also be those coming indirectly from the buying business's position in its own market. It will find itself being squeezed out from the keener sections; or the consequences that it has a poorer financial basis for its operations in itself brings pressure to look for ways to improve that (and the idea that they are inefficient in actual production is so repugnant to business men that disadvantage in buying is one of the first things they suspect). Finally, the influence of the professional buying department must not be overlooked, especially when it comes under the 'new broom' who will try changes for their own sake. Looking at all this practically as well as a matter of sheer logic the conclusion is drawn that parity of prices should be presumed to be the normal rule where the customers are business men buying for their own use or for re-sale under their own brands — a not unimportant sector of the economy.

It may be thought that the author has not really addressed himself to the point that businesses are often not making identical products, though he made it himself. Leaving aside for the moment the case of the industries selling to the 'ordinary consumer', this point is very easily dealt with. It is useful in economic analysis to define industries in terms of the production of identical or even very similar goods but it is a mistake to take this too literally. Competition may come more quickly from within such immediate neighbours but few businesses are committed to an absolutely invariable product and few business men would refuse to take on a new line which promised, eventually, comparable profit to what they get already. A business is therefore the source, potentially, of competition with anyone making a product that it itself could conceivably make. Competition comes fairly directly from any businesses with the right sort of equipment already, and economists should follow practical men in defining industries in terms of equipments and processes rather than mere products. The previous conclusion may be restated to take account of this important point:

prices will have to be in parity not only as between existing producers but also with the prices at which others who are not making these particular products already would be prepared to sell them.

Now, to come to the second stage of the argument, what about the case where products *are* sold to ordinary consumers? It is already agreed that people like ourselves can be very foolish, for part of the time at least. There are, however, a number of cases where it is very difficult to agree that this will have a substantial effect on the overall market situation.

First, not all consumers are irrational all the time and even a small minority of really careful, wise buyers will affect the whole market, provided that their purchases are in total sufficiently large for any one business to find that attracting them by lower prices or better quality will bring a relatively large increase in sales. For most industries it is hard to believe that such a minority, at least, does not exist.

Secondly, the problem can be approached in a different way by asking if it is really thought that the average household will be equally irrational over the whole of its expenditure. It seems clear that rational buying should be predicted for at least two broad classes of commodity. In the first place. we may think of the ordinary everyday goods, whose prices are low relatively to typical incomes and which are regularly bought by the household's specialized buyer, the housewife. Logic agrees with the declared experience of the business men concerned that in the end value does tell most decidedly; it is relatively cheap to shop experimentally for this class of commodity and it is a natural subject for the exchange of experience in which housewives indulge. In the second place, there are really expensive and relatively rarely purchased commodities such as motor cars or TV sets. Here, one can readily discover how much thought consumers ordinarily expend, helped by newspaper specialist comments and even more by appeals to the experience of their friends and to any 'experts' whom they happen to know.(5)   Once again, logic suggests that the assertion of manufacturers is correct and that prices cannot stay 'out of line' for long. For the intermediate class of goods not covered by these two cases, there is similar testimony from business but independent logic is more helpless. The author himself believes that rationality goes right through the field to an important

---

(5) The author well remembers, when TV was still very new after the war, hearing how well a small, new firm was doing, although it did not then advertise very much. A clue to the explanation was given when, in a civil service canteen, a post-office engineer was heard holding forth about the value which this particular set offered for its price. It was clear from the context that someone had started him off by asking his advice on sets to buy.

extent.(6)

Saying that is not to ignore the existence of pressure salesmanship and advertising; but that is a difficult thing to lean on for the purpose of the conclusion being rebutted. The case where sales are determined by advertising, etc., whatever the quality of the product, can only cover a very limited range of articles and then, from its very nature, it cannot give a secure position to any business man. For permanent results, he must look to the real qualities on which he competes with his fellows. For the most part experience leads to some confidence in the judgement of even the most exuberant salesmen — that their efforts will be wasted unless the intrinsic qualities of what they sell match what their rivals offer.

It is suggested then, that parity of prices, as it has been defined must be the rule — the general rule — which should be assumed in analysing industrial behaviour. So far the discussion has been about manufacture or business in general and has not touched the thorny question of retail distribution as such. It is not intended to burke that altogether but to discuss the various aspects of retail distribution together later on.

Before turning to the next part of the argument it will be convenient to round off this discussion by saying something about the relevance of what we have been discussing to the case of an apparent monopolist. Where there is a single firm which has for some time enjoyed the position of a monopolist but which is not protected by legal limitations on potential competition, it should be assumed that, since others are legally free to compete, the price of the monopolist is affected by potential competition in much the same way as an overtly competitive industry. There will be many who could adventure in his coverts and to keep them out successfully the business man concerned must set his prices low enough to discourage them whilst still taking care to meet the full demands of his market efficiently. It is not possible to discuss publicly most cases where this generalization has seemed to pass the test of experience successfully, but it is possible to refer to one where the possession of patents

---

(6) Thinking about the belief prevalent among economists that *other* consumers are very irrational, a radio talk is remembered in which a colleague cited her experience when purchasing grapefruit in Oxford market: She said that there were two stalls opposite one another and that the grapefruit were always dearer at one than at the other. She always bought from the cheaper shop but noticed the dearer one always had more customers for its grapefruit. The implication was drawn that people thought the grapefruit there would be better because they were dearer. It was amusing later to hear of a comment by someone listening to the broadcast: — 'How silly! I have tried the cheap shop and its grapefruit are sometimes very poor, over-ripe, and so on. The shop opposite sells larger and generally better grapefruit and I can't now be bothered to risk the cheaper ones.'

seems to have given an illusion of security, or where the business concerned may deliberately have exploited a situation which was too good to last. The history of the prices of ball-point pens, even when the patents were still in force, seems to bear the author out.

When discussing the possibility of new competition it is natural that one should be reminded how very important easy access to new capital must be for the setting up of new businesses and the development of smaller ones. For this reason one must welcome recent experiments in making capital more readily available for medium-size business. The institutions concerned, like all established businesses, have suffered from the stringency of our long-continued controls over the capital issue market and over long-term borrowing. Although one can not now discuss the general role of the capital market in any detail, this factor must lower the potentiality for new competition generally. Nevertheless, when discussing the extent to which existing businesses are subject to potential competition, one must not dwell too much on the difficulties in the path of quite new businesses, of this or any other kind; large established businesses, if they can not always get all the capital they would like, have large total funds to dispose of and they provide an active source of competition liable to impinge in any sector where existing conditions attract them.(7)

Industrial stability: If it is accepted that parity of prices is the rule in oligopoly industries generally (with proper allowance for time lags where products are not standard commodities), then one must accept the general conclusion which economists reach in the case of 'pure' oligopoly — that any one of the 'few', if it lowers its price will (eventually) compel the rest of its industry to readjust prices to comparable levels. Beyond that point, however, economic analysis has been uncertain in its prognosis. Three possible modes of behaviour are distinguished and the choice between them must rest upon our having additional knowledge about any particular industry.

The first of these possibilities, *Case I*, is where competition is quite unrestrained and each of the 'few' pursues its own immediate advantage, regardless of its competitors' reactions and without regard to longer period consequences. Here, it is thought, the general level of market prices will be very unstable; the attractions of individual price-cutting will always be liable to induce one firm to start a price war until all contestants left in the struggle are working their plants full out and prices are down to prime cost level; then, individual efforts to withdraw from the situation may lead to the assertion of a

---

(7) The Leo computer in which J. Lyons & Co. is trading must certainly not be quoted as an example due to its parent having surplus funds, but it is a nice case of competition coming from an established business to an area which one would have said in advance was far too remote from it.

rising trend of prices which, however. will itself be precarious.

As it has been developed, this analysis is vitiated by an unrealistic approach to costs and by the complete disregard of the probable effect of the likelihood of external competition on policies internal to the 'few'. Readers may also think that it is unrealistic to assume that business men will compete 'regardless' — so do most economists!, but that matter will be considered later on. For the moment, it is convenient to pursue the present topic a little further and to ask what are the circumstances which will tend to produce unstable markets in ordinary everyday competition, while still assuming the validity of the conclusions put forward earlier about the genuine scope for competition in most industries. There is not time to go fully into these circumstances but those which it is important to distinguish can be listed with a brief commentary on each.(8)

First, an industry may have an *inherently unstable structure*: this exists wherever one business can have reasonable hopes of driving some competitors right out of production whilst not becoming hopelessly unprofitable itself. Such a possibility exists when efficiencies are so diverse that one or more businesses would still be profitable at prices which would choke some of its, or their, competitors — the 'squeeze' commencing once prices fall below the level of the latter's 'paying-out costs', so that they have to exhaust their cash reserves to continue in production; the pressure will be absolutely effective when prices are below the prime costs of such less efficient businesses. This state of affairs is particularly likely to happen in the early days of a new industry when businesses generally are too numerous and too small for the full application of available technology. The condition may be disguised if there is extreme pressure of demand but the fluctuations that may be expected in more mature conditions generally uncover the situation and the unstable structure must eventually disappear and be modified to one that can persist. (An example of the kind of situation in mind may be found in either the rayon yarn industry or the domestic radio industry in the late 1920s and early 1930s.)

Technological developments may themselves produce such a situation, if they bring decisive advantages to larger businesses. A stable industry so far may thus become unstable. (An example here is the development of modern press-shop methods in the 1930s with the consequent decimation of firms and departments making motor car bodies.) Here again, the process of readjustment may be easier and less violent in periods of moderate prosperity, delayed in periods of extreme boom, and much more violent in times of inadequate demand.

---

(8) Structural questions, in particular, have been gone into in rather more detail in an article in *Revue Economique*, January 1956, 'Limites economique a la dimension et a la croissance des entreprises individuelles'.

Given time, however, the history of all industries suggests that a structure which is inherently unstable cannot endure under competitive conditions; the number of businesses will adjust itself to technological facts (which is how many 'oligopolies' have developed) under the force of the competition from any business which finds it can exploit its more favourable position. It should, however, be noted as a corollary that it is folly to expect all businesses always to be equally efficient; for practical purposes a range of actual costs is fully compatible with survival even without any business making exorbitant profits.

Next, *a stable structure may become temporarily unstable*. The situation in mind occurs whenever overall effective demand is not sufficient to employ the available productive capacity. If there is chronic underemployment of plant, then the stage is beautifully set for a price war reminiscent of the theoretical case described earlier; that is, any one of the 'few' may be provoked to a trial of strength in an effort to keep its facilities going more nearly full bore, with the chance of permanently improving its market position. It must be said, however, that this kind of instability is quite likely to be brought about by what happens at the 'tail' of the industry. The case, generally, is not that a strong business chooses a price war to improve its position in bad times, but rather that weak businesses snatch after even very temporary relief in order to postpone the day when they must shut their doors, and minor recessions, as distinct from 'bad times' may be sufficient to spark the price-cutting off. This is made the more easy of occurrence, the wider the range of sizes of firm in an industry, for the very small firms, likely to be in the weakest position, can hope to attract quite sizeable market gains before they make any appreciable inroads on the market of the large firms; although they may individually be in this position, their collective effect may be large enough to provoke a prompter retaliation than one expects. One should also mention briefly the difficulties which can arise in industries where substantial parts of the output are sold by competitive tenders, and where, therefore, a price cut may secure a large order.

This kind of instability is, of course, more likely to occur if industry has had any long-continued period of unusual prosperity, such as during and after a war. In such circumstances, with continuous excess demand, and failing tight price control, the parity of prices rule becomes inoperative; less efficient businesses may exploit the possibilities for premia for prompt delivery of badly wanted products and if the better-established firms do not follow them deliberately in short-run exploitation of the market (and after a time it does irk to see the other fellow 'getting away with it') they become careless about their own costs, which has much the same effect — and is one way in which even tight price control fails to prevent the situation.

A similar instability arises whenever there is *major innovation of process or product*. The case of a process change will be similar to that discussed two

344

paragraphs ago. A major innovation in product may be even more powerful in its disruptive effects — especially in a genuine few-firm industry. If the new product renders older products even partially obsolete, the struggle to get established in the new markets will be intense. It may not however show itself in overt price warfare but may have similar effects through selling costs and other inducements to buy (prices generally being set at what is expected to be a fair long-term price). The industry will not settle down to a stable state until its capacity is broadly adjusted to demand, until the latter has itself settled down a good deal (is not increasing violently, etc.), and until the industrial structure corresponds once more to the fundamental requirements for stability.

These are the reasons for market breakdowns in competitive oligopoly industries and the conclusion drawn is that what has been called Case I does indeed describe a kind of breakdown to which such industries are prone but that it is generally wrong in its presumption that such open warfare is likely to break out spontaneously, as it were. Generally speaking the instability results from *real* factors external to the individual firm;(9) some readjustment would be called for in any form of industry but in this case the period of adjustment may be rather painful. The history of industries does contain instances of what look like personal wars between strong men fighting for supremacy in their markets (the early oil industry is often referred to in this connexion), but in the cases studied, when one gets down to the facts of the situation one finds just how important were underlying factors; the contestants, like any other good generals, waged an extended campaign only when each had some real grounds for hoping for success in battle, or just had to fight back to test the position of those who thought that they were themselves so favoured.

In contrast to the Armageddon which would result from the assumptions of Case I, competitive industry, no matter how few the 'few', is not such a very militant unstable affair in ordinary circumstances. Economists have therefore come to attach increased importance to the other theoretical possibilities. It will be recalled that the crucial assumptions of Case I were that businesses compete with absolute independence of policy and with an eye on short-term consequences

---

(9) Where the industry conforms most closely to oligopoly theory — where there are standard products — is where one is most likely to find a great instability of the kind under discussion; but when these cases are looked at more closely it is found that quite frequently the real cause of the breakdowns does not originate with the producers of the goods concerned (with whom theory is perhaps unduly preoccupied) but in the distribution sector. Something more will be said about this later when monopolistic arrangements are discussed and in the short discussion of distribution proper.

only.(10) The theoretical alternatives to Case I abandon the assumption of independent competition and assume that individual businesses will harmonize their policies with those of their competitors.

Case II, 'Canny' Competitors, which logically comes next, simply assumes that a business will still determine its own policy, but that it will take account of any foreseeable reactions by its competitors. This change of assumptions is attractive to common sense and, stated as generally as this, it is a valid basis for generalization. Classical and neo-classical theorizing on this basis has, however, led to very different results according to the precise way in which the assumptions are interpreted. There is no need here to go into details of these different approaches nor to enlarging this section by discussing the more recently expounded, so-called, 'Full-Cost' doctrine, with its use of the 'kinked' demand curve. The only stable solution in pure theory leads to the conclusion that businesses may achieve prices which are higher than those which would be normal in perfect competition and which would get closer to text-book monopoly prices the smaller the number of businesses among the 'few'.

No time need be spent on the details of this reasoning, for it can be easily upset by realistic criticism. A major point is the assumption of a constant number of businesses exploiting their 'cosy' position and the lack of regard for any possibility that new competitors will be attracted by prices which are 'higher than the competitive level'. Another point which has already been put in connexion with Case I is the lack of allowance for competitive forces arising

(10) For the present purpose, this diagnosis of temporal myopia has probably been sufficiently argued but there is an additional reason which is rather technical in character but which, perhaps, should be mentioned at some point: — The demand curves used in oligopoly analysis (and, indeed, *any* demand curves — cf. Marshall Book III, or any standard text) are defined with reference to the short-run positions of fundamental data; tastes, incomes, and all other prices being unchanged, etc. Some apologists have expressed the opinion that, in fact, demand curves should be interpreted in a 'long-term sense' but this seems to be methodological nonsense. It is true that the demand curve for any one firm *may* be supposed to be drawn to incorporate the net effects of the interactions between that business and its competitors — but only on the basis of very simplified assumptions about such reactions; the point still remains that even these sophisticated curves would be short-run in so far as their environment of tastes, national income, and prices set outside the particular oligopoly, must be taken as constant. Yet, as was indicated earlier, the fundamental policies of the competitors and their reactions to a given move from within their circle must be largely affected by what is happening to them from the outside, as it were. A truly 'long-run' generalization about demand, say, as seen by the individual firms would have to be couched in terms of their reactions to movements in, and their beliefs about normal levels of, these important parameters which are not explicitly brought into orthodox theory.

under dynamic conditions from within the industry; similarly in the working out of competition under dynamic conditions some importance must be attached to the existence of the 'tail', to be found in many industries, of businesses which are too small to be counted among the 'few'.

In some recent discussions of these kinds of competitive situations there has been much talk of the role of 'price leaders'. This idea may be found in business men's own description of competitive situations in oligopoly industries and to recognize the phenomenon is an important step towards more realistic analysis. Unfortunately, much of the discussion has been as vague and 'mystical' as are some of the most difficult pages of Nietzsche. For the concept of price leader to have any use more stringent analysis must give it greater operational value.(11)

A Happy Nest of Monopolists? Case III. Alternative to the cases previously discussed, is the possibility that oligopolist industries may achieve stability by giving up the troublesome independence of policies, that the business men involved cease to compete either openly or in hidden fact, that they get together in associations or cartels to organize their market. The pure theory of this case usually goes on to handle it simply as a text-book monopoly, with monopoly prices as a result. There are, however, some more realistic discussions of the behaviour of such associations which pay due regard to the ways in which extraneous circumstances may frustrate and limit the monopolistic intentions of their members.

A glance has already been taken at the fact of the 1700 or so agreements which were registered under the British Restrictive Trade Practices Act (and one should add the unknown number of agreements whose restrictive practices were abandoned before the critical date for registration, if one wishes to get a fair measure of the prevalence of this situation before the Act). Clearly then Case III 'has something', and no discussion of competition in practice can overlook the restrictive associations with which we are so abundantly blessed. The author has some fair experience of the actual working of agreements and associations of this kind and will refer to that later. Here, a summarization of one criticism of Case III analysis as so far developed, is that it does not discuss at all sufficiently the

---

(11) To forestall and deal with a possible criticism of this remark by practical business men: There is no denying the importance of personality and other economically unanalysable factors in explaining fully any actual business situation with all its uniqueness. Economics, however, has to generalize and to generalize is both a respectable and a necessary task. Since there are clear similarities between the behaviour of industries it follows that one ought to be able to produce fruitful analysis of them without short-circuiting one's reasoning with a *deus ex machina*. To describe the price leader in terms of what he does and the circumstances which enable him to do it is the limit of the economist's task; the rest is for the psychologist, sociologist, etc., or plain biographer.

competitive forces which quite frequently are at work in such bodies. A useful theory here will have to pay a good deal of attention to the circumstances which bring such competition into being.

4   Competition in practice: some conclusions

Up to this point general economic ideas about competitive behaviour have been examined in the light of various aspects of competition in practice. Within this framework, these practical considerations have been developed in such a way as to suggest a more positive approach to the general questions of what 'competition' implies and how far ordinary business is 'competitive'.(12) In this section it is desired to face these questions more directly in order to suggest some general conclusions for consideration.

When thinking about everyday business life the author is impressed by a feeling of the general pervasiveness of competition which has, he hopes, been communicated already. But it is necessary to say that something seems to be missing in abstract analyses of industry which, just because they have to generalize in a broad fashion, make competition at best a rather impersonal force which comes to discipline businesses from the outside, as it were. The point which gets pushed into the background is that all drives to compete have their origin somewhere *inside* individual businesses. Here is the clue to the point at which fresh thinking must start. If one starts here, one can deal directly with one large question which people have in mind when they talk about 'the problem of competition in the modern economy' — the role of the large business on which so much of modern industry is centred. This approach will also be found useful in considering the other major questions, of the effect of businesses ganging up in collective rather than competitive dealings with the economy.

To take the first question first, if one stays inside a modern, large-scale business for any length of time one sees what a competitive affair even an ordinarily efficient business is in itself. Internal competition expresses itself in many ways but it is brought to its most intense focus in the personal drives for

(12) Anyone who knows the author's *Manufacturing Business* will have realized already that he adheres to the basis of generalization there put forward. In the decade since that book was written he has continued to study not only individual businesses as such but also cartels and other price-fixing arrangements, in each case getting as near as he could to an 'inside' position. Confidence has been gained in the use of his general ideas even in these formally monopolistic contexts. Orthodox economic analysis has been too ready to treat 'big' businesses as monolithic units. This section of the paper calls attention to the external, dynamic implications of the way in which such businesses organize their internal affairs.

348

promotion inside the management. These bring to individual points within the business much the same zeal as is easily assumed to operate in enterprises which are small enough for the intimate control of one man — the *entrepreneur* of classical economic theory.

By and large, the dynastic age is over in big business. We live in the era of professional managers. It misses the point to say that the success of top managers depends on, when it so directly affects their personal comfort if they fail in, the recruitment of subordinate managers of the right calibre. At this conference there is no need to dwell on the competitive conditioning which a young manager undergoes from his early days in business, nor stress that a feeling for that sort of life is one of the things that make a man go in for managerial office. At each stage in his career the condition for further success is that he displace his contemporaries. A business runs down if other factors are allowed to sway the choice and the criteria which the young manager is trained to use, and by which he must preponderantly be judged, may all be reduced to the requirement that he should establish greater promise than his rivals in the making of better or cheaper products. The result is a pressure which is transmitted right to the top of the firm, whence in turn, should continually flow the stimulus injected by new promotions and appointments.

As for those at the very top level of management the spirit which emerges from this selective process should be, and usually is, reinforced by the wider vision of the large responsibility that they bear to and for the whole business. Their especial drive, besides determining the tone of the business which they run, is directed outwards towards the whole business retaining its position which means trying to keep a step ahead of possible competition.

A fish, proverbially, decays from the head and trouble in a business may often start at the top. The vision of the dominant personality may become blurred by complacency or some other failing; in that case, if his colleagues are of one kind of manager they will try to 'carry him' if they cannot get rid of him, and the overall drive may be little affected. Sometimes, however, the whole of the top echelon become ineffectual, especially where they are but complementary to a particular personality and decline in effectiveness with him. In this case powerful pressures build up from below and are reinforced by outside competitive pressures in the ordinary sense.

A business which does not mend its ways will lose the best of its junior managers to other businesses, including rival concerns, so directly sharpening the external competition. Meanwhile, the progressive loss of confidence on the part of junior managers leads directly to a worsening of internal efficiency and in the last resort the business's evident inability to earn normal returns will lead to the replacement of its management by those who can make better use of its resources. However much 'fat' its previous success may have built up against just such a winter, in the end the process of exhaustion becomes obvious and rejuvenation is enforced. ('Takeover' operations thus have a necessary part in the competitive scheme of things and it is no coincidence that so much should have been heard about them after an enervating period of inflation.)

A surprising number of businesses will be found to have had 'a bad period' in their history and the author has great confidence in the general direction of his argument from the strength of the correctives that he has found to come into operation. Most businesses do not get into the parlous state described but snap out of it in time. In general, top managements are of a piece with the hierarchy that they lead and co-operate with; and they are so sustained and renewed by younger managers that the pressures from the latter become part of an all-embracing drive energizing the entire business.

It is part of this beneficial process that young men are 'young men in a hurry' to be convinced that apparent improvements are unnecessary or impracticable. Great importance may be attached to the hypersensitivity to signs of room for improvement commonly displayed by the idealists who provide some of the very best managerial material. All managers have a natural tendency to resent and fight whatever they think lies in the way of their doing their own job and, idealism apart, such tendencies get the greater impetus because success or failure will be correlated with the chances of personal advancement.

The influence which buying departments have on the competitiveness of industries supplying their businesses with materials and equipment (see pages 338–9) may now be seen as an example of the kind of generalization which needs to be personalized for its real strength to be appreciated. One can underpin it with a consciousness of the personal drives which keep a buying department going — the managerial competition within, and for the supervision of, itself (and quite apart from the sporadic influence of 'new brooms').

There is one type of systematic competition within a business which is so important that it should be mentioned here, even though proper allowance must be made for it in connexion with a later topic. This is the healthy tension, arising from their different viewpoints, which exists between the technical and production side and the commercial or sales side. Each is in its own way guardian of an aspect of the long-term interests of its business against short-term interests which may occasionally pre-occupy the other. There is space to mention only one example of such a conflict of viewpoint; general argument about cartels must be reserved for the moment but, where they adopt a policy restricting production, etc., the technical side of the managements of the more efficient businesses fight on what most of us would regard as the side of the angels. Sheer restriction stands too obviously in the way of the opportunities they can see to be within their economic grasp. In the author's experience, it is only when real conditions in the industry present genuine checks to these drives for competitive expansion (13) that the commercial side can succeed in efforts to stabilize prices with restrictions that impinge on the production side. (To be fair, it is also only in such circumstances that the commercial side in efficient businesses would themselves for long accept any such limitations.)

When one is considering the social effects of this internal managerial competition, the general drive towards mere economy in itself should not be despised. That it is substantial and continuously in operation must be conceded when one remembers the importance of departmental costings in the assessment of managerial efficiencies by superior managers. This drive, then, ensures directly that less of society's resources have to be devoted to existing products and, by setting resources free for use elsewhere, it promotes one sort of competitive pressure of a pervasive kind. The accompanying improvement in productive and commercial techniques also has important indirect advantages because so often the new procedures can be adopted outside the industries where they originate. The social benefits of the improvements of products, as distinct from their cheapening, are also clear.

Where products are used for further productive operations, any improvement is generally also a virtual equivalent of lower prices. Where they are used by consumers, it must at least be true that they do get better products but there remains the question suggested by the subtleties of economics, how far products may be wastefully improved. The answer to this question depends how far one can accept this view of the all-pervasiveness of competition, and so cannot be dealt with quickly in an abstract fashion. When, however, any generation compares its situation with that of its grandparents', will it not seem as a general rule that improvement of products has usually gone hand in hand with cheapening (expressed for example in terms of the proportion of a week's labour that the average man must devote to needs which appeared in his forebears' budgets)? The only general exception which the author is glad to admit is the disappearance of really shoddy products bought previously because low incomes did not admit of economical laying out of money. So even here it is felt that the nose of experience can detect the general answer long before we can establish it with our reasoning. In such general reasoning the space given in this paper to competitive pressures from within large businesses is justified because of their great importance in establishing and maintaining the competitive tone of our society. This point could be elaborated in some further detail but now we must turn to the larger questions which have just been raised.

These are: the question of the prices charged by ordinarily competitive

---

(13) As for instance when the industry is already chronically endowed with excess capacity and when low prime costs mean that the inefficient can hold on in battle for a long time.

businesses, and the related question of the speed with which the competitive process argued for achieves its alleged benefits. A discussion of the first and major question is going to take up most of the rest of this paper. So far as the second is concerned, the lines on which an answer may be sought will be implicit in the way the first question is tackled; and part of the answer has already been hinted at — that the speed is generally fairly fast measured against the time-span of the average management. Two general points which are relevant to any considered answer should be made. First, if sufficiently general competitive pressures are shown to exist in the environment of business then these can but accelerate the working of the internal competitive forces we have been discussing, since a business will accordingly have to strive the harder to keep its place. If the point about the drives which normally prevail in large businesses is accepted, then one must remember that the environment of any business is but a shorthand concept for the ways in which other individual businesses will impinge upon it. Secondly (and this is relevant to Utopian criticism of the speed with which other people do what the critics consider to be the right thing) the author is not impressed with the speed at which authoritarian alternatives to individualistic management achieve correct results, but he readily admits that it is more difficult to convict them of error.

We turn now to the question of the prices and terms which the general run of industry manages to exact for its services. The author's view of the behaviour of demand impels him to the observation that a business will generally have done the best it can for itself, in any established industry, if it charges as high a price for its products as it can consistently get away with. In other words, he shares a 'theory' found commonly among business men that the shortest way to maximize profits is to maximize prices and it is believed that it is possible for business men to find practical procedures to help this object to be realized without their having to bother explicitly with the complicated calculations which economic analysis has found convenient. After these last two sentences, and with experience of tendentious reviews, a warning is given against them being quoted out of context, for it does require further explanation if it is to be rightly understood.

In short, this statement does not mean that it will pay a business man to rack-rent his market — to 'exploit it' in any sense which that term conveys to the man in the street.

To go into further detail in this question of the levels at which prices will settle it will be useful to think in terms of a very efficient business, of which the briefest relevant definition is one whose costs are appreciably lower than those of the general run of businesses in its industry and whose *elan vital*, the

352

'drive' we were talking about just now, is no less compulsive.(14) We may suppose it to be a 'large' business in the sense of producing a large proportion of the total output of its type of products, but not necessarily the largest, nor the most efficient business. Like any other business it will have its 'specialities' which may or may not be produced by competing businesses.

It will be seen that our business is assumed to be in a leading position in the kind of oligopoly situation which is believed to be typical, with its own circle of customers (plus, probably, a casual fringe). The question is, how does the assumed drive to compete show itself? Not, assuredly, in the careless cutting of prices for the sake of purely temporary gains. The discussion in Part 3 of the potential instability of prices in such a situation will not be repeated and it can be assumed that a large business will look beyond the immediate consequences of its actions.

In general, so far as its main products are concerned, the only solid basis for growth will be that which comes gradually in the inner core of its customers while taking full advantage of any favourable trend in the general movement of demand. It would be normal for its management to take as a test of achievement that the business should at least maintain its share of the general market. Serious departure from this standard will be a signal for managerial review of the situation.

In such an oligopoly for such a policy to succeed, the business must set competitive prices, low enough to hold its customers against the offers of direct competitors and not so high as to attract other businesses by making it seem worth any short-term trouble to 'have a go' at its sub-market. On the other hand, the business must be assumed to find attractive any products whose prices seem to offer attractive margins at its own level of costs. Remembering the discussion

---

(14) This definition is very compressed and since 'efficiency' is such a vague term, perhaps it should be spelt out a little for economist readers. In the context the definition, although qualitative, is not operationally vague. For a business to be reckoned efficient in actual industrial conditions, it should have two characteristics: (a) at any given time, it should be able to stand up to price warfare for as long as may be necessary, which implies that its costs should, at worst, be average if it were making products identical with those produced by any *other* business in its industry — an industry, of course, is a group of businesses all operating similar processes, etc. (see page 339); (b) over a period of time it should display to at least the normal extent a fundamental drive to sustain and improve its position. The first quality, (a), is theoretically capable of statistical test; the second, (b), calls for comparative historical analysis. The second is probably more important than the first in the sense that a sufficiently drastic improvement in drive will usually make a fairly rapid improvement possible on the costs side, which will itself deteriorate with great rapidity if the drive should go.

in Part 3 and without making any extended analysis here, one may conclude that as a general rule not only must prices be in parity with one another as between directly competing businesses, but also that they must be mutually compatible from the standpoint of efficient businesses right across the markets of the whole industry. 'Cosy' positions where that is not so, which offer any reasonable volume of potential orders, will eventually break down under the force of the competitive pressures they set up. The nearest firms in terms of product-types may be cautious but they can compete with non-price terms fairly easily and more remote firms will be less reluctant to make direct 'across the border' raids on straight price terms. The characteristically multi-product set-up of large businesses is in itself one sign of their pervasive influence in our society.

It is a very relevant point that this compatibility of prices must be maintained in a world where cost prices are constantly changing. Each business, at least in industries where commodities are not fully standardized, has to act more or less on its own in the first instance and find a basis for sales quotations which will not be to any serious disadvantage when the full competitive situation has emerged. This is achieved by using past experience to establish margins which the business can usually get away with, product by product. These do not, of course, imply satisfactory profits for each business on all its products. Smaller firms and those in weaker positions will generally have to pitch their effective margins lower. In this way, the more efficient businesses virtually establish themselves as price leaders. Price leadership is more obvious where products are standard; there, others' prices often wait openly on announcement of the leader's intentions.

Such stable readjustment of prices has been attacked on irrelevant grounds. Effective competition need not mean that prices are constantly 'all over the shop' — even in theory such a result is expected only because businesses *might* make temporary gains by cutting prices. Normal levels are not higher just because business routines eliminate unnecessary circular motion and are in fact usually set by an awareness of the potential competition of other businesses — all the sharper because in such an industry as is postulated businesses are not competing in a vague general market.

In multi-product industries there is usually quite a lot of minor readjustment going on. Individual costs may move divergently so that a business here and there gets the wrong result and has to realign its prices. Actual prices also have to accommodate temporary maladjustments — as where some trader has to get rid of stocks which he has had to pile up. Such minor corrections of position are obscured by official price quotations but become clear when invoices are examined. The point is that the chosen level is usually very nearly right so that workaday shocks are absorbed without serious disturbance and without adverse effects on the orderly progress of the industry. Any such system of prices has possibilities of a more substantial movement of prices when underlying conditions change at all drastically. If a business gets substantially ahead of its rivals sooner or later the pressure with which it exploits its advantage will lead to readjustment of the normal level of prices. It may at first use to the full all non-price weapons but in the end the response of competitors driven to the wall will bring price weapons into the open. Businesses with sufficient experience forestall such situations by pricing routines regularly applied. Critics are too much pre-occupied with sheer price competition anyway, and it should be realized from what was said earlier that compatibility of market prices is no sign that competition has not done its work, rather the reverse.

The pure theory of oligopoly, however, is correct when it calls attention to the dangers of more serious instability of prices and in Part 3 we have already looked at realistic circumstances which may call this into being, with a resulting open price war — the 'cut-throat competition' of everyday language. It is characteristic of such a struggle that it achieves no permanent results of itself — for if it could, the parties who would be advantaged will refuse any settlement. It is out of such circumstances that there comes the apparent negation of all competitiveness — the development of price rings and the like. It is natural that so apparently cosy a situation should be attacked because of the potentialities for holding customers to ransom, prices being thought likely to rise so as to accommodate the sense of proprieties in the matter of profits on the part of the weakest businesses in the cabal. There is no denying that weaker businesses do appeal to such 'reasonable' requirements. The question is how far such predatory notions are kept in check by the working of economic forces within the cartellized organization of the industries concerned.

The fact should first be noted that even prices fixed in such bodies do seem to set appreciable limits to the rise of price levels, even in seriously inflationary times. It is no accident that they can so often be shown to have moved upward in a far less extreme fashion than those of industries whose behaviour and structure are closer to the perfectly competitive industries of economic theory — and whose products are important ingredients of cost in many of the industries under discussion. The announcement of settled prices seems to impose limits on the ability of any business to take a bit more when the market would apparently gladly pay it. But behind the announced prices is the influence of the stronger, more far-seeing firms.

In the author's experience, the working of the beneficial competitive influences of such businesses is not suspended by such pricing arrangements. They are not moved only by considerations of public policy. One powerful reason comes out of their past experience in the desire to avoid unnecessary inducements for the building up of temporary high-cost capacity which will overhang the markets indefinitely without seriously increasing the total of supplies in the periods of greatest scarcity. More positively, there is often a strong sentiment against setting prices simply to satisfy businesses whose efficiencies do not justify long-term respect. Whatever the motives, it can be said that time and again evidence is found that increases in prices, which weaker businesses can well justify on the grounds of their higher costs, are resisted strenuously by more efficient businesses whose outlooks correspond to their own stronger positions in the industry.

A suspicion is held that in times of greatest shortage of supplies some such view of the situation is widely accepted, to judge from the tolerance shown by political parties and governments. Where one is more doubtful about them is in more normal times when it is easier to expand production. May it not be the case that in their huddles around a table business men will go for the security of prices which buy off the dangers from weaker businesses and tolerate restrictions on their own freedom to push ahead? This possibility cannot be denied; there *have* been attempts to hold the situation in this way. The history of cartels has many cases where they have broken down and often the reason for the breakdowns seems to be that they were run on some such lines. Which leads to the point that a major factor in such breakdowns is quite usually that leading businesses will not tolerate the restraints of their colleagues and prefer to fight.

What should concern us are not the cartels that have failed but those which apparently succeed. From the cases examined it could be said that to survive in normal times a price ring must make way for the pressures of low-cost firms with a dynamic urge to expand. If it does not, and more efficient firms mistakenly acquiesce, then the cartel will be exposed to just the kinds of disruptive pressures that have been examined as the normal processes of competition. Inside the stronger firms, the younger generation of managers, themselves remote from the circumstances that led to the price fixes, will themselves be pressure groups urging a new policy and requiring the existing one to be justified if their loyalty is to be engaged. Outside the cartel, capacity will build up and it will break down unless prices and procedures become more reasonable.

In the inter-war rayon yarn industry Courtaulds explicitly enforced prices which came down with their costs and curbed any installation of high-cost capacity. Two other publicly known cases which illustrate the points can also be mentioned. The first is the international aluminium cartel whose story has been ably told by Louis Marlio. In this cartel, as in others, in order to have a firm check on secret price-cutting it was found necessary to agree quotas for members' outputs. The cartel broke down regularly in weak times until more frequent revisions of quotas allowed the most efficient businesses to get the continuous increase in output they required and market prices had to keep moving in the direction that would accommodate the pressures of their outputs. Walter Higgs in

Starting from Scratch, his autobiographical essay, gives an account of his position *vis-a-vis* an alleged price ring for small electric motors which shows another way in which an obdurate cartel may be forced to comply with the drives of efficient businesses — through the level of its prices having to be compatible with those quoted by a dominant outsider. The author has no knowledge of the alleged cartel to which Mr. Higgs refers and has not checked his view, but it is entirely compatible with the story of another price ring in the electrical industry of which he has some knowledge.

In any case, failing some such conformity with the economic facts of life, the author is now reasonably sure that it is wrong to see price rings, etc., as easily maintained stable organizations. The destabilizing forces of excess capacity, of internal price-cutting by weaker businesses, etc., all have their influence in normal times. Many agreements have been abandoned recently not because of the threatened review by the Restrictive Practices Court but because their situation was already untenable because of changed trade conditions and members' reactions to them. The Court may have affected the situation in some cases because the parties that were left would have little cause to ask to maintain a clearly ineffective agreement merely because, as 'last time', these few businesses thought it better to preserve some organization against the day when it could be properly formed. With all the talk about the rise of price rings in depression, it is no accident that so many date their effectiveness from the recent periods of prosperity (during which period, as already suggested, *some* virtue may be detected in them).

It is therefore the case that the pervasiveness of competition affects even ostensibly monopolistic arrangements. That is not to say that they should necessarily be approved. The recent Act reasonably requires proof of direct public benefit and even then much might be said for further regulation to supervise the details of approved cartels' operations, to require greater publicity in their affairs, to enforce that any fixing of prices should be based on fully disclosed costs, and above all to look carefully at our tariff policy as affecting such industries. There are no grounds for condemning such price arrangements out of hand.

It should have become clear that even this brief space has not been given to price-fixing arrangements because they are directly relevant to the case of the international oil industry. The author well remembers an interesting talk in the New Forest with a specialist in cancers who explained that his particular research object was to see what light cancers threw on the workings of normal body tissue and how far normal processes were carried on in cancerous tissues. Even from this point of view, which would be openly biased if the analogy were pressed in the case of cartels, much study of these and similar bodies would be profitable to anyone wishing to understand the working of normal competitive forces in free situations.

357

The question of price rings, however, does bring up one feature which is also present in uncartellized prices, for example, where there is price leadership, and which is wrongly criticized. This feature is the greater stability of prices. The argument runs something like this: artificially stable prices give the benefits of stability only at the cost of even greater fluctuations in effective demand, and therefore in employment and in overall activity, than would occur with more freely moving prices; lower prices in the boom lead to an excess of demand and the processes of inflation are in fact encouraged; prices are artificially held up in the slump and demands and activities are thereby harmfully curtailed. This argument represents a quite uncritical application of very elementary economic theory and there is a major fallacy in it.

The fallacy consists in equating effective demand which will show itself in orders descending on an industry with the real, underlying demand such as is represented in theoretical demand curves. In the latter, demand is properly shown as a function of current price, but such curves quite leave out of account the speculative movement of actual demand which is determined by the way prices are expected to move, and which is usually the direct reflection of how they have recently moved. In booms such addition to basic demand would add quite unnecessarily to the inflation which is therefore effectively reduced by reason of the curtailment of speculation. In the slump, on the other hand, speculative demand will carry employment even lower than justified by the drop in genuine demand. It may therefore be a real virtue of stabilized prices, when properly analysed, that they diminish the pressures of inflation in peak periods and increase available employment in depression. This argument takes no account of the effects of less stable prices on businesses' investment and development programmes; nor does it rely on the fact that underlying demand is little affected by ordinary changes in prices so that there is by so much little room for significant values to be attached to the harmful effects claimed by the critics.

This reference to the effects of speculative activity can lead into the last major topic: the distributive system seen in the light of competition generally and its own sector of the economy. To get a relatively minor point out of the way, while recognizing that it may be a major one in some industries, let us note that the disturbing effects of speculative changes in stocks held down the distributive chain is one reason why well-organized industries have frequently sought to bring this sector under their own aegis, setting up their own distribution depots, concentrating necessary reserve stocks under their own control, replacing freely competing wholesalers and retailers by controlled agencies.

In the distributive trades generally, economic analysis has rather concentrated on the obstacles to the free working of competition and the opportunities for quasi-monopolistic exploitation of customers' preferences. On sheer factual grounds some of the analysis seems doubtful in its validity, as for example in its neglect of the great importance of overhead costs at all points in retail trade, and the effect of this on the drive to compete. Once again, a historical survey would bring economic thinking into better balance than is reached by concentrating on what appear to be the most important facts at any point of time. On the one hand, the large-scale retailers (departmental stores. chains, and multiples) have come along and in the variety of service that they offer one can see the competitive development of cheap mass distribution of staple items as well as the easy provision of 'luxury' goods and services. How much of this would have been thought feasible by a reader of modern texts living say at 1900 (if such a combination of theoretical knowledge and time were possible)? On the other hand, there is the exploitation of brands (helped by the much criticized advertising industry) enabling large-scale manufacture to make certain of mass demand for its products in the shops and to control the terms on which they are sold. Between the two levels has come very real competition in the wholesale field, with here the manufacturer, there the retailer, extending his frontier to take in territory where the wholesaler was previously sovereign, with the result that everywhere intermediate traders are on the defensive in an active world of competition.

Oligopoly is, it is believed, once again the most appropriate basis on which to analyse the working of retail trade, each locality having but a few shops in direct competition but each being in a chain relationship with each other and with more distant shops. For working clothing, for example, Oxford shops are in active competition with neighbouring market towns and middle class shoppers use cheap day trips to Town to bring London shops into the competitive picture. A good deal of the economic analysis of retailing seems applicable only to a world where all consumers are paralysed and confined to their back gardens and not to one where we all have to move around regularly and where regular shopping expeditions are themselves part of the standard of living. The irrationality and even the sheer convenience of the consumer (so that there is always a point and a time when it is really not 'worth bothering') are obstacles to the full and vigorous flowering of competition but surely one should be impressed by the ways in which competitive forces do assert themselves in not very long periods of time.

Clearly, one of the problems of distribution is that there is room for such a variety of types of organization, but there is much less room for inflexibility and rigidity of prices over the retail system as a whole than some strict theorizing would suggest. The general analysis of retail trade too often runs narrowly in terms of monopolistic competition.

The most fruitful approach to the problem is to start from the habits of consumers, rather than rigid classifications of commodities. When this is done, proper allowance can be made for the working of competition at each point and the precise function of each major type of shop. One approach to modern retailing, which at first sight approximates to that on page 340, does recognize that consumers will tend to buy regular 'shopping goods' fairly carefully. It makes. however, a misleading distinction between these and so-called 'convenience goods' — defined as those that are wanted quickly and near at hand, such convenience outweighing a few pence difference in price. Instead of thinking in terms of goods, one would do better to think in terms of 'convenience shops' and of 'convenience buying' (to meet emergencies, etc.) In fact any examples which are given of convenience goods make it clear that most consumers buy a substantial proportion on their regular shopping trips and not with any sense of urgency; they are moreover just the kind of commodity used by large-scale retailers as loss-leaders in order to attract the passing customer. All that this distinction does is to remind us that a consumer may rationally pay more on occasion in order to get something quickly — and the small corner shop earns its keep by meeting this need over a good part of its trade. Prices here may not be at all uncompetitive when one makes proper allowance for the special costs involved. The distinction also does not recognize the importance of less continually bought, more expensive 'capital' goods in the competitive scheme of things. (Cf. the remarks about TV sets on page 340.) Looking at the trade as a whole in most urban areas one finds the consumer well catered for both in price and services and the continual flux of new and defunct businesses in the small shop sector shows that there is active, if optimistic, competition always at work in this area which is in some ways most remote from the influence of general price competition. The conventional profit margins applied in some sectors do not in themselves indicate lack of competition. Since overhead costs are so important, retail trade is very multi-product and within any one class of shop it is difficult to make use of the concept of the 'low cost' shop for particular types of goods, although some analysis does run in these loose terms. As between types of shop, conventional margins are not fixed; if they are and do not move with changes in the opportunities offered by technical developments, new types of shops altogether appear and compete on appropriate lower margins. The historical development of Marks and Spencer, for example, may be seen in this light, based as it is on the firm's own brands whose margins are directly amenable to their view of the competitive effect.

One sign of the basic competitiveness of retail trade is the survival of smaller shops against a regular pattern of bankruptcies and where incomes of proprietors in ordinary times are low by comparison with the salaries they could earn. Fixed prices for 'convenience goods' may well be a condition for such shops surviving at all. Another sign is that few manufacturers enter or stay in the field themselves, and yet at any one time there is always some large business nibbling at the bait of the greater assurance of stability that would be given by going right through to the final consumer.

In retail trade then, one simply cannot think in terms of competition between a set number of shops of a given type. One has to think of shifting forms of retail trade with all types in direct competition somewhere in the market. Nor must one erect artificial barriers between 'manufacturing', 'wholesaling', and 'retailing'. Because distribution is a necessary activity at all levels, all forms of enterprise struggle in competition in it and the great obstacles to swift victories for efficiency that economic theory detects are matched within a reasonable period by the competitive pressures which come from so many directions.

The author has refrained from any special analysis of the oil industry.(15) The papers that follow look at competition specifically in oil and the task here was to comment on the general economy within which the oil industry has to operate. It is interesting, however, in the present context that such a variety of enterprise is to be found in the industry and especially interesting is the way that the big firms are involved at all levels in the chain from the oil well to the tank of the private motorist and the reception bay of the chemical works. The history of the retailing end for gasoline, lighting oil, and lubricating oil is interesting for the various ways in which large firms have appeared in the sector and for the balance between their own direct activities and those of competitive businesses also distributing their products.

It seems that, on the present position at all events, one can see where the system of separate private ownership has proved strong and where the general methods of distribution have been forced to accommodate this and to develop alternative methods of achieving the control over quality and services which producers need in order to maintain brand standards. Even with the recent development of large-scale demands for lighting and fuel oils, it has proved economical to hand the actual trade to private owners working on contract. In oil as in other trades one can see signs of the competitive efficiency of the smaller separate transport organization working also under contract, in competition with larger centrally organized transport systems. When one gets down to the end of the chain of distribution even large demands reduce themselves to small speedy deliveries and the history of this and other trades has shown that full efficiency seems to be quite compatible with free competition between numerous kinds of enterprise, however untidy that may look to the planning mind.

It will be realized from the rest of this paper that one need not be greatly

---

(15) Editors' note: Andrews's former colleague Tom Wilson presents a related perspective on the OPEC cartel in his 1979 article 'The price of oil: a case of negative marginal revenue?' (*Journal of Industrial Economics* 27, pp. 301–16).

puzzled by, for example, the emergence of a relatively few grades of petrol sold everywhere for much the same prices. A lot of evidence would be needed before the oil industry had to be seen as a special case where the forces of restriction and monopoly could prevail against the competitive forces which are evidently at work. If the function of the large firm and the strength of the internal drives to competition have been stressed, one reason is that occasional visits to the oil industry have convinced the author that its large firms are to be given full marks in this respect.

10 Business profits and the quiet life

(Co-authored with Elizabeth Brunner)[1]

This note discusses some matters which are relevant to the view that business men are more concerned with securing a quiet life than with the maximization of their profits. Before this, however, we summarize the background out of which the question arises. The question is an important one for economics. In order to come to grips with the organization of productive resources, the determination of price levels, etc., at the macro-level of the economy as a whole, economics needs a unifying postulate governing the behaviour of 'firms', the individual businesses which are the decisive agents. Abandon the profit-maximization assumption and general analysis seems impossible.

That business will tend to act so as to maximize profits accordingly remains the basic assumption, not only of the text-books but also of the more advanced work of general theorists when they turn from the analysis of social aggregates to the underlying behaviour of business entities. Even in general text-books, however, there may often be noted signs of uneasiness about the validity of this universal presumption — e.g. in discussions of 'oligopoly'. Uneasiness is much more evident in specialized discussions of the theory of the firm or the analysis of the behaviour of individual industries, where the question of the individual business necessarily holds a central position.

Briefly, three factors involving interplay between theory and empirical knowledge account for contemporary uneasiness about the profit-maximization postulate. First, developments in oligopoly theory have led to apparent indeterminacy on the one hand, or on the other to a determinacy which would be achievable only by some sort of collusion. Indeterminate solutions tend to get rejected not only because they are abhorrent to the drives which make men economic theorists but also because the oligopolies of the real world typically behave in fairly stable regular ways. Yet, accepting collusion businesses do not appear to exploit the situation to anything like the extent of maximum profitability — profits of supposedly collusive oligopolies do not differ sufficiently between themselves nor are they out of line with profits in other

(1) Reprinted with permission from *Journal of Industrial Economics* 11 (November, 1962), pp. 72–8.

industries. Second, empirical researches into the details of business decisions have shown that business men often do not consciously look at, or even know, the marginal cost and revenue quantities which would come into any explicit calculations of maximum profits. Third, and under the influence of the other two factors, economists have attended to remarks by business men, in which these latter rebut suggestions that they are chiefly concerned with shareholders' profits and discuss business life in terms of other acceptable social objectives.

The reactions to these factors have been diverse. One can find 'pure' theorists who have said: 'It does not matter what business men say or look at; since they must be trying to maximize their profits, their actions must in the end come to what we describe in terms of equating marginal cost and revenue.' A wilder school, perhaps, adopts the attitude: 'Business men do what they want to do; therefore they can be represented as maximizing *something*, so the general structure of our analysis is untouched.' There are yet others who take the empirical evidence at its face value and are concerned to reform business habits, so that, given, for example, better cost accounts, the business man *will* come to maximize his profits according to theoretical economic ideas.(2)

The above reactions preserve a theoretical standpoint. In his note we are rather concerned with a reaction which is anti-economic-theory in its very nature, because it tends to throw 'economic man' overboard altogether and would

---

(2) Our colleague, Mr. C.L. Lloyd, has helpfully suggested that he could imagine that some economists would say 'Why should not a genuine quiet-lifer maximize his profits but just not put too much work into doing so. I never teach that business men maximize profits strenuously.' This particular position is not represented in the literature which we have been discussing. We are not surprised because we do not think it should arise. It certainly does not arise in connection with the quiet life in the oligopoly context. There the problem is, as we have said, that determinate economics suggests collusion but in so many instances they would appear to be collusions without fruits. If businesses are not taking advantage of the opportunities for more profits than under competitive conditions, which a genuine quasi-monopoly surely gives according to orthodox economic theory, they cannot be said to be making maximum profits in any sense acceptable within such theory. Nor do we see how the position could arise, e.g. with regard to empirical data on business men's pricing. First, the business man who maximized profits in the sense which would fit in with orthodox economic analysis, but just not 'strenuously', would surely report the use of procedures involving marginal criteria. The examples would then appear certainly as cases of businesses who were maximizing profits — just how strenuously would not have been relevant in the context. Secondly, too much attention to ease or strenuousness of work on the part of a manager, surely carries a hangover from an over-concentration on the single entrepreneur which economic theory uses as a procedural simplification but which, as we explain below, has led to fallacious reasoning.

364

suggest that economic analysis should be steered by reference to psychological or sociological factors which are independent of, and so economically irrelevant to, any particular economic situation.(3) Any such tendency must surely trouble those who believe in economic theorizing about economic entities in economic situations.

We have not space to criticize in detail all important manifestations of this reaction, but may perhaps pause for a moment to take up two. The first, which has had influential support, is worth mentioning because it is related to that 'quiet life' concept which is our preoccupation later. It is that business men are to be divided into those who snatch at quick profits and those who take a longer-term view (not unconnected with a feeling that empirical researches tend to get the co-operation of well-heeled 'established' businesses, so that their attitudes tend to get over-represented). This might, by itself, appear to lead to two rival 'theories' of business behaviour, but surely it is anti-theory to stop there and not inquire what are the economic circumstances which make men decide usually for 'safe' profits and what circumstances will make them think it pays to 'snatch'. This reflection is reinforced by observation that, although individual business men seem to differ in their psychological make-up quite as much as the rest of us (indeed, perhaps, more than very selective professions such as the academic), the general lines of conduct do not vary notably from business to business in the same industry — and any variation usually seems on examination to be related to significant differences in the particular industrial environments.

Similarly, the location of a particular factory *may* have been precisely determined because it suited the managing director's desire for convenient access to a certain golf-course, or because his wife wanted their week-end home to be in the Lake District. The question is not whether such a factor is or is not important in the individual case, but whether any particular factors of this kind have systematic effects upon economic variables — in which case, of course, they would come quite naturally into economic analysis of the ordinary kind. It seems in fact to make most sense to discuss location theory in terms of costs and market opportunities and to treat other considerations as relevant only when economic criteria are not decisive.

As suggested earlier, what we are primarily concerned with is the larger tendency, in areas of economics where business decisions are discussed for their

---

(3) It should be clear that psychological factors are slow to change and that sociological changes need to be large to have serious economic effect. Much of economic theory is concerned with the reaction of economic entities to changes — and comparatively small and continuous changes — in their immediate environment. One must, therefore, it seems to us, continue as a matter of methodology to look to economic forces in the analysis of economic reactions.

own sake, to see business as not very concerned with profits, or not, at least, when enterprises are well established and large. 'Live and let live' tempers, it is suggested, that competition between businesses. Individual managers are thought not to pursue profits so far as prestige or social position. A certain minimum of profits may be required for the comfortable continuance of a business; beyond that lies the 'quiet life', both for it and for its managers. Correspondingly, not-too-strenuous pursuit of economy of operation may be thought consistent with going along with organized labour. And so on.

These factors, and such a view of them, are often linked to changes in business organization which have become apparent. The big corporation which dominates the industrial scene and the professionalization of management may be linked together. The old idea of 'the entrepreneur' has come to be seen as rather remote from reality. Instead of owner-managers bearing themselves the direct risks of their decisions, we have a large part of the economy being run by managers whose shareholdings are negligible, and the accent is on co-operation between managers with little reference to any very clearly specified economic drives.

We suggest, however, that this approach to the facts is inherently fallacious. It is in itself a sound methodology for general analysis to run in terms of businesses conceived as unitary affairs, run by a single decision-taker of last resort, because that enables economic theory to concentrate upon decisions and the relevant data upon which these are taken. But reality has always been more complex. Complexities which can be overlooked in a hypothetical world of perfect competition, because of the pervasive simplicity of its market controls, must not be so simply assumed away in analysis which choose to be more realistic about the markets within which businesses operate, or one will inevitably pass over an important area in which market forces are at work.(4) Realistic analysis must take into account what happens *inside* the firm.

The single-entrepreneur simplification makes it too easy to concentrate on top-management decisions, with too little attention to the lower-level management activities *and* decisions which play a large part in the determination and organization of the internal data on which top management takes its decisions. True, top-level *policy* decisions set a framework within which subordinates have to work but these often leave a good deal of play at what may too-mechanistically be called the 'cog' level, and 'subordinates' have a good deal to do with the evolution of policies.

Let us leave maximization of profits on one side for the moment and look at

---

(4) Much the same comments may be made on the single-product assumption which also suits the perfect competition model, but which is dangerous if taken too simple-mindedly in a model where buyers' preferences are explicitly recognized.

the minimization of costs which is one of its elements. This certainly cannot be left at the top-management level. 'Costs' at any one management level are the result of activities at other levels. Cost accounts come together successively in shop, departmental and branch accounts, if we may simplify matters into this tripartite structure. At each point, a separate group of managers is held responsible for results, and watches results below it as important elements in its own costs for which it can hold others responsible. And there may be 'upwards' and 'sideways' glances as well (e.g. the well-known sparring between production and sales, the one wanting greater standardization, say, than the other believes suits the market, and that other pressing for lower prices than costs will stand — a way in each case of making their own jobs easier). On this basis arises that internal competition(5) within businesses which economic theory has not so far taken into account, and which, under the influence of the mores of our age, spokesmen for business often do not choose to dwell upon.

What other consistent basis for further promotion is there, after all, than how a man has done in his present job, and 'his' profits and costs play a large part in his superiors' judgements? Of course, from the point of view of the business as a whole, other factors will play their part in the judging of the performance of a department, but how important the criterion of profit and loss must be can be seen by the efforts which young managers make to resist going into departments which, for reasons of overall policy, are relatively less profitable. To come back to management as a profession, our definition of a *typical* manager for the purpose of general economic theory would be one who had gone through this testing at successive stages, and enjoyed the complementary supervision of others, right the way to the top.

When 'management' is rolled up into 'the entrepreneur' of pure theory, an allowance must surely be made for there being typically at least a strong bias towards minimization of costs — and towards maximization of profits at subordinate levels, at least. (There is a limit to the quiet life which under-managers can enjoy.) Even accepting for the moment that a Board of Directors might like to go along quietly with profits which were 'just right', those discussions of the subject which have taken this view have not met the difficult point of just how the Board could ensure the success of its policy. Even in full employment conditions, individual industries have their marked ups and downs, and within industries it is no less obvious that individual businesses differ greatly in this respect. One causal factor here is often the external competitiveness which we have not discussed, but, whatever the reason, the

---

(5) This concept was first discussed in P.W.S. Andrews's essay 'Competition in the Modern Economy', in *Competitive Aspects of Oil Operations* (ed. Sell) 1958, where attention is drawn to its *external* consequences.

result must be that any nicely checked profit can easily become a blatant loss. It would probably also be readily admitted that it would not be easy for a Board to turn a business round from the quiet life to saving the bacon.

To have a loss or small profits when competitors are doing better carries certain sanctions: there are adverse effects on the supply of capital, and the activities of financial commentators, investment analysts, etc., will be remembered here; rival managements may be interested in the possibility of a take-over; customers look more doubtfully at a business which is 'not doing well'; and so on. General economic discussion has not faced up to this, perhaps because in abstract models businesses are treated rather ambiguously as in the same general economic position, so that neither short- nor long-run differences between businesses have received sufficient attention. (6) Businesses too often are thought of as competing from scratch.

The factors which have just been mentioned are external ones but they will be strongly reinforced by internal ones, and probably preceded by them in a business which is at all healthy. The sheer self-respect of management should be mentioned first, but, if a business is doing badly, one should not overlook the pressures from within and below for a reshaping of policies. This internal pressure to shape policy will make itself felt at Board level, and in the end, if a Board does not bend, it will get broken.

The development of managers is determined by what a firm is like. If the keen technician cannot get his new equipment he will get dissatisfied and leave. If young managers are not offered expanding opportunities, so that promotion is slow, again the brighter ones will leave. Not to have the reputation of a good firm will mean that young talent will go elsewhere. If this kind of thing happens at the younger, mobile end, older managers in responsible positions do not put up with the situation and will force a change.

Of course, businesses do get into difficult circumstances, and mere external adversity, e.g. due to drastic secular change, can produce short-term inefficiency of a high order. Economic commentators tend to be impatient in their discussion of such cases; one forgets too readily that secular change means long-run readaptation. A recent notorious take-over bid in England brought into the open just how long beforehand it was that a business whose low profitability had caused it to be referred to as 'the slumbering giant' had taken effective steps to meet the changes which it faced. It may be objected that the considerations which we have adduced are 'long-run'; although we would not accept that the internal competition to which we have referred is not an always-present factor, the relevant point here is that much of the theoretical discussion which we have been criticizing by implication is in fact formally concerned with long-run

---

(6) *Op. cit.* p. 21 ff. [or pages 348–51 in the present volume].

equilibrium.

If businesses are to avoid getting into difficulties, we suggest that a devotion to a quiet life will not help them and that they have to have a zealous regard for profits — but not necessarily for profits in the short term. It will be noticed that we have concentrated on internal competition and not discussed competition from outside the firm. That does not mean that we do not consider the latter kind of competition quite as important as the former in practice. To go into this, however, would require closer examination of the formal tools with which economic theory approaches the maximization of profits. The trouble is that strictly short-run considerations are built into orthodox analyses and considerable reshaping will be necessary to come to grips with the long-run determination of business behaviour in which maximization of profits surely has a part.

We believe it is necessary to revise ideas of what are the relevant cost and revenue functions. Although it would be true that, under any profit-maximization assumption, the simple abstract structure of economic analysis would be *formally* unaffected ($\partial R - \partial C = 0$), the conclusions about business behaviour will clearly be of a very different kind from those reached on existing assumptions, and the details of economic methodology must be radically affected. We shall return to this in an essay on the theory of oligopoly, meanwhile it is hoped that the points now raised will help to prevent too quiet an acceptance of the 'quiet life' approach to business profits.

11 Industrial economics as a specialist subject[1]

Industrial economics is often, mistakenly, thought of simply as an 'applied' subject. To some extent, this results from a belief that the theoretical side of the subject is, or ought to be, adequately dealt with as part of general economic theory, and especially in the theory of value, the traditional core of economics.

It is true that the theory of value proceeds in terms of 'firms' and 'industries', and generalizes about the behaviour of these in certain assumed conditions and in relation to such economic quantities as selling prices, wages, costs and outputs. It is equally true that 'firms' and 'industries' must be the main entities in any theory of industrial economics. It would, however, be wrong to assume that industrial economics must *simply* be a field for the application of the general theory of value. In fact, I shall argue that the boot is on the other foot at the present time, in so far as general economic theory seems to me to be waiting on developments which are more likely to come about from the work of industrial economists following their own proper preoccupations. To make clear exactly what is implied in these assertions, it will be necessary to go into some questions of economic methodology and take a view of certain aspects of the history of the development of modern theories.

The theory of value is one of the oldest departments of economic theory. We may define it tersely as the theory of the influence of non-monetary or 'real' factors upon prices and outputs. It may, on a first approach, be divided into a theory of prices and outputs of commodities, or 'products', and a theory of the prices and employment of productive resources, or 'factors of production'. Since, however, human services are the only factors of production which are not themselves products, value theory may be said broadly to discuss the prices and outputs of *products* and the wages and employment of *labour*; wage theory, so far, has been very largely a secondary theory derived from the 'product' sector of value theory, and we may for the moment concentrate upon the latter.

Until a generation ago, price theory had developed two main branches: the theory of monopoly, where 'monopoly' was so strictly defined that it could ordinarily have no application to industrial products; and competitive theory. The

(1) Reprinted with permission from *Journal of Industrial Economics* 1 (November, 1952), pp. 72–9.

latter developed into the theory of 'perfect' competition; allowances might well be made, and usually were made, for various 'imperfections', but these were simply qualifications and had little effect upon the trend of the analysis, especially of long-run conditions. Competitive theory was constructed upon some rather severe assumptions, notably that, in any one industry, commodities were quite homogeneous, and that no individual business could influence the market price at which a commodity could be bought or sold.

A theory should, strictly, be judged by its results and not by its assumptions, for it is a mistaken view of scientific procedure to imagine that this demands that assumptions must be 'realistic'. Where realism is required is in the conclusions, and, at that level, a better name for the quality in question is 'validity'. The validity of a theory is entirely a matter of the extent to which it is a better predicting instrument than any alternative theory. This is as true for the descriptive parts of economic theory as it is for any other scientific activity.

The general validity of the theory of value in perfect competition was shown in the success with which economists came to be able to forecast the effects of the major influences at work in commodity markets. The fact that its doctrines had to be modified, in application, by doses of practical wisdom is not, in itself, a criticism; it was the theory's general validity which made it possible for economists, as such, to get their practical wisdom.

In its modern forms, however, theoretical economics has long included other types of analyses which purport to describe or predict phenomena with which it is less easy for an economist to get the sort of practical acquaintance which is broadly possible with commodity prices. The theories of wages and of the distribution of income are examples, but the most important instance from our present point of view is undoubtedly 'welfare' theory. This is the branch of economic analysis where economic situations are considered in order to formulate policies which might be recommended as tending 'to increase economic welfare'.

Whatever the justification for such extensions of value theory, it is, surely, clear that the validity of these secondary analyses must depend upon the validity of the assumptions from which they start. These assumptions were embodied in a theory of the behaviour of individual businesses in perfect competition. Using a fundamental method of economic analysis, this theory studied a hypothetical individual business on the assumption that it always moved to a position of equilibrium, getting to the best possible position according to its own interest in the face of the various economic forces at work in its economic environment.

Now, the full development of such a theory of the firm had not been strictly necessary to product-value theory. In the work of Alfred Marshall, certainly, it had proved possible to restrict the assumption of full equilibrium to forces working at the industrial level and to avoid assuming that *businesses* always tended to be in the optimum position theoretically available to them. But, as

371

Marshall's own work shows, when it came to secondary analyses derived from value theory, it was necessary to work in terms of the individual business; that was the basic unit of economic activity and the one which the secondary analyses necessarily had in common with the value theory from which they were derived.

The result was that, in academic teaching, this theory of the individual business in perfect competition came to have a logical primacy in value theory as well as in secondary analyses. This made possible the logical integration of the whole of 'pure' economic theory and enormously simplified the teaching problem. The result was that even value theory itself appeared to be *based* upon a particular theory of the firm, whereas the latter was really simply a reworking of certain elements of value theory.

Seen from this standpoint, the theory of value in conditions of competition as developed by Marshallian economists, appeared to lead to serious logical inconsistencies; which was why Marshall had not based it on the idea of full equilibrium in the individual business. In particular, Marshall's theory of competitive prices was general enough to include both ordinary manufacturing industry and primary industry. It, therefore, recognized cases where costs of production would fall with sustained increases in output. These came to be seen as having considerable practical importance. Since the theory of perfect competition with full equilibrium in the *individual business* could not incorporate an assumption of falling costs (for, in this case, in the assumed conditions, a business would never get to any equilibrium but would always be expanding) theoretical economics until very recently has abandoned any general approach to manufacturing industry through competition theory.

What has happened is that we have retained the basic notion of individual equilibrium and have altered our assumptions so as to permit of falling costs in this case. Because of the continued use of other assumptions, this has entailed a general approach to individual businesses and to manufacturing industries in terms of individual 'monopolies', and of outputs being limited, despite falling costs, because of the fall in profits which would occur if expansions were forced on the marketing side. This theoretical revolution has not so far succeeded in producing a theory of such broad application as the older competitive approach to industrial values. Meanwhile, the approach *via* the individual business has so blurred the older generalizations that economists now seem to have little confidence in them even as a first approximation to practical problems.

Fortunately, matters have not stood still. The introduction of 'realism' into the theory of the firm has made it vulnerable to further injections. Empirical work has begun to make us realize that there are important competitive relations between businesses which are not taken into account in the static particular equilibrium theory we have just been referring to. Any positive step forward is still a matter of acute controversy and the possibilities need not be discussed here. What is relevant is that, although the 'atomistic' theory of business still seems dominant if we look only at the positive theorizing of modern texts, we can yet see the breach in the wall in the admission of the existence of widespread elements of 'oligopoly' — competitive relationships involving relatively few businesses. Now, oligopoly theory has long been something of a technical toy just because no general theoretical solution can be found, and the admission of its importance is consequently the first sign of the breakdown of a theoretical approach to prices in practice via the assumption of a determinate full equilibrium in the individual business.

It seems reasonable to suggest that a new start has to be found. For one thing, economics needs a workable approach to prices in general; for another, it needs a workable theory of the behaviour of the individual business. I venture to suggest that this approach will only be found through empirical work on actual businesses. To get the theory we need we cannot continue to tinker 'realistically' with what was originally a derivative of theorizing at a different level. We need to approach the matter in a more truly scientific manner. If we wish to theorize fruitfully about individual businesses, we must find out what are the facts of their behaviour and then construct a general theory especially in order to take account of those facts. As I have already said, much new thinking is already going on, and it is significant that it has been stimulated by empirical research work, especially in England and America. If this is not the occasion to enter upon a lively controversy, one may at least observe that industrial economics seems to be coming into its own.

To return to the point made at the beginning of this article: industrial economics is most certainly not just an 'applied' subject. Few, if any, would now seriously maintain that existing theory provides the industrial economist with a box of 'tools' which he has only to apply in his own sphere. His main task, of course, is the scientific one of giving valid generalized descriptions of industrial phenomena.

It is significant that, in some recent discussions, would-be protagonists of existing theories have said, in effect, 'if this is not how the industrialist behaves, it is how he *should* behave in his own interest'. Even from the point of view of private welfare theory, this evades an important point raised by empirical research, that the industrialist does not generally know, and, it may be argued, could not find out, some of the important criteria in terms of which he would be assumed to assess his gains. For our more objective purposes, however, the important thing to notice is the tacit admission that industrialists do not, in fact, behave as predicated.

Further, if it were true that economic theory already offered an adequate general theory of the firm and of the industry as units of activity, whilst that would be of very great help to the specialist, his work would still have a theoretical side. He would still have to do more than test, verify and apply theories produced elsewhere. The sharpening of his focus must necessarily make him more interested in details than would be relevant for general economic theory, and he would need correspondingly more detailed theories. It should certainly not be assumed that he could simply derive these detailed theories from any more general theory. When an analysis changes its level of abstraction there is no reason why the character of the analysis should remain unchanged.

If we agree on the importance of a continuous development of theory, there is little doubt concerning the way in which it may be encouraged. The kind of economic theory which is most useful to industrial economics as a specialist subject will be best helped forward by concentrating attention on empirical studies. This also, as we have argued, will be of the greatest possible service to economics in general. If physical sciences move forward in the laboratories, economics, and especially the economics of industry, will advance in proportion as it is possible to hasten the assembly and discussion of empirical experience which is relevant to its theoretical needs. Accordingly, it is no paradox that, after having been so concerned with theoretical issues, I should end by urging the importance of empirical work.

Just as the theory of industrial economics must start with that of the individual business, so the subjects of specialized interest are bound to be headed by those which have direct relevance to the conduct of individual businesses; among these are: the pricing of products; the development and marketing of products; the location of new enterprise; the organization of production; the payment and organization of workers; the planning, carrying out, and control of expenditure upon capital assets; the supply and use of financial resources; and the general organization of management in the individual enterprise.

This list calls attention to the fact that, because so many of these subjects are of direct management interest, in its efforts to improve efficiency and lower costs, they are nowadays studied also by persons who give professional advice about them. Industrial economists themselves, because of their experience, are increasingly proving of service to businesses in this manner, even if not always as professional advisers. Nevertheless, the direct interest of industrial economics in these matters has a different orientation. It will be interested, of course, in the work of such advisers to the extent to which they are building up systematic views of the methods by which the dynamic efficiency of businesses can be improved. Above all, however, as a branch of a social science, industrial economics will be interested in what actually happens, as distinct from what should happen in hypothetical or ideal circumstances.

This interest may not be met by 'organizational' descriptions of the present positions of individual enterprises with respect to any one of these subjects, although a comparative study of the differing positions of a number of

374

enterprises, properly selected, will help us to answer the question how the position in any one business, on the average, tends to change with changes in other relevant factors. Such questions are answered more directly in case studies, which bring out the factors or circumstances through or in which the changes in question have been brought about.

Our list so far has been directly concerned with the individual business as such. The subjects listed will, however, have reminded us that industrial economics has a lively interest in the relationships between individual businesses. (It would indeed be a poor study of even an individual business which neglected to look at such questions.) One thinks at once of competitive relationships — of the ways in which many prices, for example, emerge out of the competitive struggle between businesses. But, in fact, even in very competitive industries it is important not to overlook the complementary relationships which exist as well; and in other cases relationships between businesses would, of course, be more formally regulated by collective action. Here again we shall be helped by the making of empirical studies of the changing positions of individual businesses. Indeed, these are essential if we hope to get at the influence of the general economic factors which, to continue the example, may effectively set limits to the prices which can be realized, but which may be lost in the background of a view of the position at any one time.

One of the difficulties with which we have to contend is that detailed case studies of many of these topics involve the elucidation of intimate details affecting individual businesses and full publication of an identifiable character may not be possible. The industrial economist may well get confidential access to such facts, and he can contribute directly to our subject by generalizing from the cases which he has studied. So can the professional advisers already mentioned.

In the present state of our knowledge, and even in the interest of industry itself, it is, however, very desirable that more should be known about the way in which industry sets about even its most intimate tasks, as well as about the facts of industrial experience generally. With the reduced secretiveness of industry, unnecessary obstacles to these studies are passing away. Much more can be done in the way of direct publication than has been done so far. The real obstacles can be met in various ways. Often, it will be possible to discuss a case with practically all the detail which an economist requires, if it is subjected to a 'bowdlerization' which removes identity or generalizes about really confidential details. For all this, our subject depends upon the co-operation of business men. They can also help by contributing directly to the discussion of industrial problems, drawing generally upon their experience.

These references to our subject as being advanced by publication and discussion bring us directly to the part to be played by this journal. The *Journal of Industrial Economics* has been established by its editors and publishers in the belief that it will be of value as an academic periodical specializing in the economics of industry in the widest sense. As such, it must aim at being international in scope. Its Anglo-American foundation seems especially fitting, in view of the extent to which industrial economics has developed as an academic study in the United States, and of the traditional importance of the subject in the curricula of both countries.(2)

From what has been said already, it will be seen that this new journal may be expected to have a detailed and empirical interest. Even its theoretical articles will usually be concerned with some particular problem, and will for that reason usually carry practical implications. On the other side, as has also been indicated, it is intended that the empirical articles shall be acceptable on the basis of their relevance to the theoretical tasks before us. We intend to offer a medium of publication for the increasing academic research into industry and commerce. Equally, we hope that a good many of our articles will arise from within industry itself. In this way, we hope to make available some of the material and experience arising within businesses which is normally lost both to academic researchers and to other business people.

A journal run on this basis may reasonably hope to have business men among its readers. It is hoped that they will also appear in the more active capacity of authors, being encouraged to make their contribution to the discussion of the detailed problems in which the *Journal* will be interested, and on which they, being the subjects of our theorizing, have so much that is relevant which they can tell us.

This reference to business men as such may remind us of a most important point: much has been said in the abstract of 'the industrial economist'; it would be unfortunate if this left too clear a picture of such persons as necessarily being academics. Nowadays, we have increasing numbers of trained economists working in industry, a growing proportion of them as economists. Here trained persons are acquiring practical experience in the best possible way. Although the position seems to be better in the United States than it is in Great Britain, far too few of these alumni of economics have contributed to the wider development of our subject from their own experience. Their silence during a generation in which the theory of business has been so much discussed may be a tacit tribute to the remoteness of much of the discussion itself from the actual problems and

---

(2) That we have only one American article in our first number is due to a production time-lag (the *Journal* having been mooted on this side of the Atlantic before the possibility of the joint enterprise was discovered) and not to any expressed lack of interest on the part of American authors. We hope gradually to redress the balance.

situations of businesses. Be that as it may, it is time that the position changed and that economics began to draw upon them for its own development and progress.

There is one final point which should be made. The discussion so far has been almost entirely in terms of problems of some permanent theoretical interest. A fair proportion of our space should certainly go to these, but industrial economists must also be interested in what is going on in their subject-matter generally. We shall, therefore, publish articles of a more contemporary interest dealing with some of the important problems of industry today.

Having thus passed from our strict subject to the question of the *Journal* itself, the author bows to the instruction of the General Editor — that he should leave the *Journal* to speak for itself, having first commended it to the indulgent favour of the reader.

12 Industrial uses of economic theory(1)

The terms and purposes of the Bley Stein Memorial Lecturership necessarily make any lecturer, but perhaps especially the first, worry a little about his choice of subject. Feeling bound, as will become clear, by reason of my academic interests and experience to speak on a topic which is rather narrowly rooted in economics, I nevertheless had an hour in which I contemplated alternative topics which might have lain nearer to specific interests of business men. I assembled a list which ranged from 'Computers — Profits, and Losses, Therefrom' to 'Space — The Industrial Impact of Otherworldliness.' With a little more effort, I stretched my alphabet from A to Z; quite easily and naturally at one end: 'A is for Anti-Trust ... (I do not think I shall risk a subtitle here!); more artificially at the other end to 'Z is for Zollverein', which you will doubtless spot at once as a clumsy party dress for a possible talk on the Common Market.

As you see, I put all those temptations behind me and decided to begin much nearer home within the economic and business worlds. At the end of the road, however, it seemed to me that what I wanted to discuss with you under my present title had implications for practically all the topics on my list, and in fact I hoped to have time to touch on one or two of them anyway. In other words, I have to confess that I find it practically impossible to discuss anything of general interest in the business world without beginning to get involved in questions about industrial structures and behaviours which interest me as a theoretical economist. So, in effect, I should have wanted to have given a good deal of my present lecture as a preamble to any other that I might have given. And, especially since I speak at the beginning of this memorial lecturership, for whose future I offer my own sincere good wishes, I hope that my contribution will prove to have a number of links with those which will eventually follow it.

My choice of subject did not spring out of academic parochialism, although it is true that I have spent practically all my working life with the theory of the 'firm' — a term used to denote any sort of individual business when considered in the abstract — and with the theory of the firm's industrial environment; and I shall on this occasion, also, have most to say about that particular branch of economics. I chose in fact to speak on the industrial uses of economic theory

(1) First Annual Bley Stein Memorial Lecture, 18 April 1963. Reprinted with permission of the Graduate School of Management, University of California, Los Angeles.

because I happen to believe that there should be far more intellectual interpenetration of the worlds of economics and business. With your indulgence, I hope, I shall comment on both ends of this statement of faith because to do so will lead me most conveniently into a brief review of economic theory which I shall use as the main gateway to my subject proper.

So far as the business end of the matter goes, I think that it is concerned with the study of mankind in the ordinary business of life (perhaps, in view of some developments in economics, we should nowadays add 'ultimately' to this famous definition of Alfred Marshall!). *A priori*, then, one might expect, since so much economics is formally concerned with business behaviour, that the more reflective kinds of business men would be keen students of economics. More — one might expect even to find some of them contributing to the development of the science itself. We must all know how rare an event this is, yet my experience is that relatively large numbers of those in responsible business positions do reflect on their activities in a very relevant fashion.

It may or may not be the case that our culture, and perhaps especially in the United States, discourages the public expression of any such reflexions. It is probably true that technical developments within economics have by now made it difficult for the business man's reflexions to impinge cogently on the thinking of economists. I should like to say here that I think that any teacher in my own field might find it useful to consider very carefully in what ways he can get business men to contribute their experience in his classroom. I can say, from some years' experience in graduate teaching at Oxford, that it can be very rewarding to experiment towards this end, and the recent work of Miss Brunner and myself with the Faculty of the Graduate School of Business at Pittsburgh has shown, as you, of course, would expect, that American business men can contribute as much as their opposite numbers in Europe.

Turning to the economic side, to my own profession, the theory of the firm and of the industry is clearly basic to any analysis of the economics of Western capitalism. If, therefore, one were to come in proverbial fashion from Mars, surely one would expect to find not merely many economists specializing in this field but also a very widespread interest among economists in general in what happens in practice in this Heartland of economics. I venture to say that the published literature shows that this is not the case, once one gets away from — disallows — the broadest and haziest (and sometimes the most misleading) of generalizations.

There is not nearly enough contact between those who are developing economic theories in which firms and industries are the operational entities, however abstract the treatment of them may be, and the actual business world whose activities are thus allegorized. If one's glance stays within the academic economic profession, the position there seems to be still worse. In the Western world generally there is a division, an unnatural canyon, between pure theorists and those economists who get down into the factory and market place.

In the United States, the subdivision of labour just referred to, between theorists and those who conduct empirical researches, is sometimes made to appear respectable by an ostensible division of territory between liberal arts faculties of economics and the business schools. In many cases, a business school, which is so set up as to make no provision for basic teaching in the general theory of the firm, has no way of drawing on the fundamental work in the economics faculty — and that latter has little to restrain it, as the customer needs of business students would, from curtailing work in the industrial economics area.

I think that I may properly refer to this in a university which is one of the few whose business schools have not made any clear cutting off of theoretical activity but, in fact in your case, the business school has rather been a home for economists with a strong theoretical bent which is exercised in the industrial economics area. Perhaps it would not be out of order here for me to make a plea that, if the theory of the firm and of the industry should be being given much less place in the liberal arts' economics discipline, the business schools should try especially to develop teaching and research in this field just because it clearly has such direct relevance to what they themselves are doing.

I should like to go on and add that I owe it to one of your own theorists, probably, that I got my own particular attachment to the practical business area as the starting point for my own theorizing. My appointment in 1937 as Secretary of the then-flourishing Oxford Economists' Research Group, where *all* the Oxford theorists of the day combined to research into business decisions, owed much to the personal interest of Professor Marschak. I have always been grateful to him and his colleagues for having drawn me to such an interesting way of life — which leads me to admit that there is something unusually altruistic about the title of this lecture.

Looking at the matter through my title — the industrial uses of economic theory — I have some slight feeling as of looking through the wrong end of the telescope. 'Wrong', of course, is not the right word to use when one is referring simply to a different attitude of mind; but I myself ordinarily do look at business rather the other way round — in terms of its interest for economic theory. It is, no doubt, very academic for anyone to consider that an improved understanding of the working of business is of the highest order of usefulness. Recognizing that there are other possible pre-occupations, even for an academic economist, I should, nevertheless, be prepared to defend the position behind my attitude, that this is an area where a more developed body of theory — the technical term for an improvement of understanding — is urgently required for the general purposes of economics. I should also maintain with no less vigour that such a development would be very much in the interests of business itself. A higher level of academic research in this area would mean that individual industries would have at least some economists who knew them in some practical detail; and even if they were not to be called on as committed-friends in any public difficulties which an industry had to face, they could be relied on to challenge any critical views which were based on actual misapprehensions of fact. I should like to add that the occasional use of economists as consultants, which is relatively common in the USA, does not at all meet the same needs. Such consultations are on too narrow a basis and the resulting acquaintanceship with the business making them is far too restricted.

The polemical position which has just been taken up is very close to what, for me, is a major purpose behind this lecture — to interest business men in the advancement of academic research into the economics of individual businesses in relation to their market — and general industrial — environment. I discuss economics only very broadly and in general terms from the point of view of the uses which business makes, or could make, of it. For present purposes, economics may be divided, perhaps a shade too neatly in view of the interconnexions between them, into two levels of analysis — the macro-level, and the micro-level. At the macro-level, economics is virtually studying the social environment of business decisions, in order to disentangle the factors which cause changes in that environment; it is also interested in those basic environmental factors themselves and in the interactions between them. At the micro-level, economics deals with the decisions and activities of individual businesses and of industrial groupings of businesses, and generalizes about the ways in which they will react to changes in their environment, of the kind whose causes are analysed under macro-level economics — more particularly the changes affecting demand for the products and the costs of supplying them.

There are, of course, clear links between micro- and macro-level theory: the quantities studied at the macro-level (the national income, price levels, foreign trade, consumption and investment, and so on) are proximately determined by what individual businesses and industries do. The decisions-conduct of other businesses therefore makes important elements in the economic environment of any one business or industry; and any changes in the economic-social environment will achieve their ultimate effect very largely through the reactions in business decisions.

In its origins, economics was essentially a macro-level subject. Only in our own times has it developed so that the individual business became anything more than one term in an argument relating to an industry or to society as a whole, and only so recently has it been realized that the quirks of individual businesses and industries could not be smoothed out in that way when one was concerned with actual markets.

The most ancient part of economics is monetary theory, which has its roots in generalizations learned the hard way in the inflations which spread from Spain, as Europe digested the silver she had prised from the New World — and re-learned equally hardly in subsequent inflations. Not until our own day, and the process is by no means complete, has monetary theory been integrated with the general body of economic theory — 'real' or non-monetary theory. But his vision in the currency and banking world has long been a valued, if separate, part of the good economist's qualities.

The origins of real general theory lie back through Adam Smith in the French Physiocrats' work. Quite clearly in Smith, one can see the characteristic of economics which is of the greatest value to business and to society generally. Indeed, the history of economics from its earliest times has been one of the progressive development of a kind of vision of economic society as a whole, yet with an awareness of the working of the parts. Adam Smith's much-quoted reference to the 'hidden hand' will be seriously misunderstood unless it be read as bearing the emotive equivalent of whatever cry stout Cortez gave as his eyes encompassed the view from Darien (for I do not myself believe that the Spanish adventurer remained silent on that historic peak!). Smith had discovered intellectually what the physiocrats had presumed — the interlocking of the activities of individual men, pursuing their self-interests in the market, into an unconsciously co-operative whole society.

This classical vision of the economic machinery of our society reached its peak so far with the perfectioning of the theory of perfect competition, the work of distinguished European economists in the second half of the nineteenth century. No one who learned this theory during its long hey-day can have forgotten the power of that vision, especially on the side of costs. The cost-prices of materials and other factors of production, which the individual business had to take as a basis when determining its own outputs and prices, were shown to reflect the values of consumers of the other good things which could have been produced but which were foregone in the production of any one industry's commodities. The process of competition ensured thus that what any industry produced would tend to be worth at the margin what society gave up for it elsewhere.

I shall later refer to the developments which were to cause a regrettable faltering in this particular vision, but just when these were beginning to take effect, not long before the last war, the pricing-process vision was excitingly complemented by another which encompassed the level of economic activity in society as a whole which the older body of analysis had had to take for granted. In taking that for granted, price theory had totally failed to come to grips with the problem of mass unemployment. The existence of heavy involuntary unemployment, where and when that occurred, meant that it was conceivable that society was going without some commodities which it could have had without sacrificing others at all. From 1936 on, economists added the Keynesian vision of the interactions between general economic activity and activity in its consumption and investment sectors.

This revolution in our thinking produced basic ideas which spread very rapidly into informed public opinion, but the overall effects on economics have been very large, spilling over, as they have done, into many areas in studies of economic relationships at the macro-level, and they have produced the first general corpus of quantitative economic theorizing. The resulting extension of the economist's bailiwick has had valuable effects on and for economics. For one thing, it brought a large and important area which economists could explore with a high degree of self-confidence. The whole subject of growth and economic development is virtually a new line of development for economics itself.

It is relevant to our subject to stress that the Keynesian extension of economics has had important practical effects: When one considers both the mildness of inflation during the last war and after in any of the belligerents (and, if someone were to raise a cry of 'France', I should counter that it is a fact that French economists began to read Keynes only after the war), and when one realizes what a long period we have had without a major depression, surely one can not but conclude that here economics has something to its credit. After all, politics is an ancient profession which has always had its share of talents at the top. There seems no reason to believe that it has but recently got some sensational increase in its share of innate wisdom. Does it not appear probable that governments have got better advice from somewhere? And the extension of the employment of economists by governments shows where they think they are getting it or where lies the expertise which their advisers need to call on.

The comparative success of our still necessarily crude attempts to keep the general economic environment of business on course, but on a more even keel, may perhaps be reckoned as one use of economics which is of great value to business, and which could be of greater value, even if many business men are unappreciative of it. If business men generally come to grips with Keynesian ideas, not only might the efforts of governments be more successful, especially in securing the economic co-operation which is required for a more complete achievement, but the working out of stabilization policies could be carried out in ways which were easier on business. The stops and starts, the relatively sharp short-term reversals of official signals, would appear to tell their own tale of the lack of sufficiently continuous feedback, and the major source of any improvement in the latter must come from business.

Governments generally have developed new ideas of their economic responsibility and have been pushed into exercising them. The resulting extended seeking after better economic understanding, administration and control has led to an enormous growth in their employment of economists as such. These same activities, as I have already hinted, have encouraged the newer interests of outside academic economists not only by reason of the increased job opportunities for their pupils but also by reason of the greatly increased flow of published economic information. Alongside this has come a marked growth in the population of academic economists and in the output of trained men from them. Where does business fit into all this new development?

Of course, there are many people in industry nowadays who have had *some* sort of training in economics. With the growth in numbers of students of this subject which we have experienced, such an increase would be to be expected, unless business men had found that to have studied economics at all was a positive hindrance. But we are not thinking of such people, but of the much more limited number of trained economists doing economists' work. In England and, so far as my impressions go, in the United States as well, only a small proportion of working economists are in business. By far the larger proportion of our output goes into government or other institutional bodies, the higher levels of journalism or into teaching. Even of those working in the business field, only a proportion are in businesses in the ordinary sense; large numbers relatively are in advertising agencies, market research firms, and in other consultant businesses.

What is most definitely true, in England at any rate, is that business in general does not get any significant numbers at all of the very highest flight of students. I know that we for our part do all we can to persuade them that they should stay in academic life. We fail sometimes so far as the competition from government is concerned and we should lose out to business at least on occasion if business came to realize more clearly than it does the potential value it is missing. There certainly is room in business for the trained economist with the highest quality of speculative mind, even if only in limited numbers. Given that he should have other qualities as well, the better the theorist the business man can hire the better the business economist he will get, and the more valuable the material which he will have to develop for higher management. Of course, to get such a man, business must make the job attractive to him intellectually. If that were to happen, there would be no need to grieve over an occasional loss to our academic profession, because such a man, enjoying the right kinds of job opportunities, would I am sure continue to contribute to economics. And his presence would help to sharpen the cutting edge and improve the job opportunities of the other economists in business.

Outside the ranks of the A+++ man, even if business does not employ what I should consider to be its fair share of economists, there has nonetheless been a relatively large growth in the numbers of economists which it does employ, and what I have been saying is not to deny that there has been a proportion of very good men among them. The economists whom business does employ are, as is perhaps to be expected, concentrated in the relatively large firm. To discuss the uses which businesses make of them is perhaps the best way of commencing the discussion of the uses which business makes of economic theory.

It is the macro-level of economic theory which is most relevant to the jobs which these people mostly do as economists. This, in itself, means that, excepting where the business man himself is a trained economist, he will generally make only indirect use of economic theory. It is his economists who use economic theory and whose whole approach to their work is decided by their training. I add that later in this lecture I shall be concerned with micro-level theory and shall suggest that here is an area where the business man himself *needs* a theoretical approach — and should do all that he can to help to develop better economic theory.

If we could assemble in this room a fair sample of economists from business and then stick a random pin among them, the odds would be heavy that our victim had at least some responsibility on the marketing side, even if he did not come from the advertising or market-research agencies which, as I have said, have been important employers of economists. The marketing side of practically every business calls for — certainly it can use — the kind of approach which an economist is trained to use and this not only in orthodox sales or commercial departments or the research departments which serve them. The need for such talents also appears on the desks of those who control capital expenditure as well as at the highest level of all where corporations assess their position as a whole — which should be served directly from the desk of the Economic Adviser, in the few cases where such an exalted office has been distinguished.

One should expect to find this special market interest among economists in business. Sales happens to be the point where the environment most impinges on the individual business, and so somewhere on the sales side is the place where large businesses have begun to feel an economist to be a necessity, not a luxury. Business ordinarily takes an appraisal of this impact at two main levels — at the top, where the general position of the business is reviewed, and down below, where appreciations of the market position and trends are used by the various departments in the routine assessments framing their day-to-day operations as well as for the policy proposals which they send upstairs and the reviews of operations which accompany them.

In corporations where the use of economists has some long standing, one finds that they have often come to be engaged on the formulation and appraisal of capital expenditure proposals, also, in some cases assisting technical committees in their assessment of new commodities or the adaptation of old, and the provision of facilities for them. Clearly, their expertise on the market-research side is generally what gave them their original foothold in these areas.

385

Because their training causes them to take a more all-round view of a situation and to look at it from a different point of view from that taken by other specialists, economists have also been engaged in operational research divisions, in work study and labour planning departments and they have made special contributions to the linear programming of industrial operations. (Alongside this, especially in business schools, the training of economists has extended to take in the corresponding subjects although in themselves these newer tools of management might well not have been specially connected with economics.)

All this extended employment of economists taken altogether has not been a bad achievement in the comparatively short time involved, especially when one considers the depths of feelings with which business men used to regard economists in the abstract;'used' is perhaps somewhat too much a past tense, for traces of older habits, like the sleeve-buttons on men's dress, are still to be detected. Too theoretical the economist may still be thought to be, but the macro-economic training given him by his theoretical upbringing has evidently enabled him to prove his usefulness wherever he has been given sufficient opportunity.

In view of the time available, I do not think I should say any more about economists' achievements in this area, and I shall not do more than notice that even businesses which do not employ economists or which are so misguided as to keep them entirely for low-level work, even such businesses are getting into the habit of calling in professional advisers — or even just asking professional economists in for lunch, so as to 'pick their brains' — on the general impact of outside events. Such 'events' vary from periodic changes in taxation associated with yearly budgets, through the less frequent major changes in governmental policy often associated with a change in Government itself, down to the really large outside event such as the setting up of the European Common Market. I have not mentioned one important area for outside advice here, that needed in connexion with anti-trust proceedings, because I shall come on to that in some detail later.

What I shall do is comment on aspects of the position where I feel some cause for concern. The first one arises from what I have tried to suggest as one of the great virtues of employing an economist — that he enforces, if he is allowed to do so, a more thoroughgoing and detailed appraisal of alternative proposals than untrained men, each looking at the matter from his own business viewpoint, are likely to do. One place where economists have had a most valuable impact of this kind is the planning and control of capital expenditure. As every business man knows, earnings criteria are not always decisive but it is essential to look at the earning side. Older procedures, developed in businesses themselves, started with what an expenditure was estimated to earn, when it came into effect, and the total cost. Where a business man was choosing between projects on the basis of their earnings, he generally used a very crude 'cut-off' procedure based on the number of years in which the expenditure would be paid off if the estimated earnings were realized.

The modern discounted-cash-flow procedures for evaluating earnings have been largely developed under the influence of economists because, through these, they could force top management to look at details which they knew to be relevant and which management itself often took into account of course, but unsystematically, notably the probable length of life of plants and equipments and the riskiness of the market outlook and of other factors on which any forecasts of earnings were implicitly based. One should also mention, even if one can not find the time to illustrate, the gains which have come from the increased objectivity of these more centrally-controlled procedures.

In professional comment and in other reporting of these procedures by economists who have been engaged on them, however, I smell some dangers of which they seem to be unaware, probably, as it seems to me, just because here is a rare instance of a business procedure which fits the kind of process envisaged by abstract micro theory. The actual procedures are described in too cut and dried a way and the discounting procedure is advocated with an enthusiasm which I can only describe as rather naive. I know that in fact those responsible for top policy make allowances for the defects of the procedure by applying subjective non-standard rates of discount to the final figures yielded by the procedures, and so on; but there are serious dangers of too great a standard systematization here making it more troublesome for the business man to apply the general scepticism which his older, cruder, pay-off procedures made a routine. There are, perhaps, even greater dangers for our subject, if the audience for the kinds of description to which I have been referring, come to think that businesses using them are behaving just as they 'ought' to do according to theory and that businesses not using them are necessarily liable to be making serious mistakes. I regret anything which suggests no necessity for further research in the one sort of case or which suggests that the mere advocacy of different procedures will make it unnecessary to do further research in the other sort of case.

Of operational research I shall say nothing except that it involves just the kind of evaluation of alternatives which the economist feels born to, and that I could wish for more sustained research by outside theorists into its applications in business. Linear programming brings up other considerations. The economist here has a job to which he can apply the mathematical-statistical techniques which are often part of his stock-in-trade; and linear programming, on certain types of operations, has yielded results which have convinced business men that it is worth developing. But this is a case where the techniques involve assumptions which often conflict with basic assumptions which the economist is trained to make about the situations in which the techniques are applied. I should like to see many more economists who are engaged on this work worry about this conflict between practice and assumptions. It also seems desirable that academic teaching in this area should be more closely in contact with ordinary theoretical teaching so that the contrast might stimulate more intellectual inquiry outside business. I personally do not think that there would be found to be much need to change the linear programmer's assumptions about cost functions, say; but the further researches which I am urging could make some contribution to economics itself at the micro level and perhaps help us in the further development of academic theory.

I am much more worried about the sub- or partial-optimalization procedures employed in these techniques. It may sometimes be the case that the circumstances which are excluded from the calculations are of the order of minor importance; I wish I did not so frequently suspect that the main point is that they are difficult or impossible to quantify. It seems to me to be of poor service to management to leave the matter with the calculations and I could wish that economists participating in such exercises felt, or were encouraged to feel, it their duty to make the kind of qualitative analysis of the impact of the excluded areas which seems to me to fit in with their fundamental training. It does sometimes seem that practitioners get blinded by the fact that here is a procedure which yields quantitative results and positive recommendations on the basis of which they can take a firm part in management deliberations. I recognize that to go further must take business economists to areas, for example, of market strategy, into which academic theory has not so far pushed firm roots; but once again this is a measure of the opportunity which business economists have to contribute to our subject.

Mention of all this newer work in industry reminds me of one virtue of the economist which I have not mentioned so far — he is lusting to be used and given a chance to prove that he can make a contribution to management. Alongside this I put another fact which has been borne in upon me by my own contacts with industry: economists in industry are not, generally speaking, a happy lot. One cause of this unhappiness I shall deal with briefly, although it is an important point: Too often, economists are kept at low-level routine procedures organizing data, writing technical reports, and so on, which are taken by higher-level men to those meetings where policies are decided. Often, of course, some particular advice which the economist would have given is not taken, but that is to be expected in the balancing of all considerations and I do not think that that in itself is a fundamental cause of malaise. The point is that, all too often, the economist of some experience in a business (I am not here discussing the use of young graduates) is not 'in' on the top-level decisions. He is debarred from the opportunity of contributing directly to business thinking at that level and I am as sure as he often is that the approach of such an experienced man can be of great value. If I may come back to my admittedly narrowly professional point of view, such an economist is also refused the chance of seeing at first hand the way in which economic factors really impinge within the business, and this further restricts the opportunities for him to develop the bases for theoretical contributions to our subject.

A second, really professional, cause of unhappiness may seem to cut in the other direction but it is related to all this — I have found economists in business to have become very discontented with the micro-level theory on which they have been trained. This makes it convenient for me to pause here and make my promised reference to this matter.

I have already referred to the old theory of perfect competition and the valuable vision of economic society as a whole which that gave economists. You will not find much nowadays of that vision among academic economists, not as reflecting actualities anyway. What is left is but a dream of a perfect, 'promised' sort of land which can be used to make trenchant welfare criticisms of actual industrial conditions. As descriptive theory, the vision began to break down around the middle of the inter-war period, as economists tried to come to grips with apparent facts — of falling costs as businesses expanded outputs, of prices which did not move sensitively with every breath of wind in a market, of advertisement and other selling costs which could not be handled in existing theory, and of commodities which were so differentiated from others of the same kind that the general market was fragmented into sub-markets which at first were thought best analysed as kinds of monopolies. For a time some sort of macro-level theory of the industry survived on the basis of assumptions that the 'monopolies' would be limited by an all-pervasive competition from new entrants and that the industries concerned had a really large number of businesses within them. In such a world prices would be higher than they need be and businesses less efficient, because smaller; but at the end of the day there would be some sort of systematic connexions between prices and costs and some sort of social integration of markets remained analytically conceivable.

It can not be pretended that this (large group) monopolistic competition view of industry has survived although echoes of its specific implied criticisms of the outcomes of ordinary everyday business competition linger in the minds of economists who are not in any close contact with industry and affect their writings and their teaching. What drove that compromise out was the recognition of oligopoly as the prevalent situation — of the fact that businesses were so few in many industries or markets that any genuine competition *along the lines so far conceived by economic theory* would be always liable to lead to severe if sporadic price–cutting. Since industries do not regularly behave in this way, many economists have settled for some sort of collusive conduct as the explanation, so that a more formal kind of monopolistic organization is

389

assumed; but the hard fact remains that analytically the whole micro-level position is indeterminate.

What this means is that our young men going into business feel — in strong contrast to the position at the general social, macro-level — that they have no firm framework of theory to fall back on, where the most immediate environment of business is concerned, for all the matters which most closely affect pricing and market policy, and competitive relationships with other businesses. On the other hand, firmly settled into business, the economist finds a prevalence of pricing procedures which seem to have very little theoretical basis, but he gradually learns to understand them darkly as he apprehends the business experience behind them. He comes to adopt something so like the old perfect competition outlook, because he finds it workable, that he is professionally rather ashamed of doing so, since the critical theorizing to which he has earlier been subject in that regard has been so devastating even though it prove to have given nothing usable in its place.

I have referred to the analysis of general industrial markets which the trained economist can make in industry. This break-down of our theory at the micro-level means that the economist in industry has no formal analytical link which he feels he can trust between macro theory at the industrial level and what goes on at the individual business level. Moreover, the ideas about industries as economic entities which older theories took for granted and which he finds that he must continue to use in everyday business life are indeed themselves ideas which he has been taught to feel to have very little theoretical substance. I must add that, on this last point, the economist in industry having taken on a practical job does not seem to worry very much but gets on with analysing his industrial conditions. Where he does worry is at the next stage from that, as I have indicated.

Of course, the good economist does not remain, or grow into, a sterile business man — if he gets up the ladder he gives advice on prices and so on which, in form of argument, is practically indistinguishable from that of his other business colleagues, but once again he brings to it his trained awareness of outside factors and trends. But what all this boils down to is that business men are having to be their own theorists in this micro-level area. They have to form views about the immediate industrial environment and about the impact on it of what they can learn of other businesses' results and policies.

I suppose, looking at the overall result, one must say that the mind trained in business can not make such a bad micro-level theorist of its possessor, judging by results. Yet I am sure that such practical situations would be better handled if we could offer business minds trained in thinking about them in the abstract, the very kind of theoretical mind which we develop in economics. For one thing, business men are not much given to discussing their immediate environmental problems in any terms but those of the present. The mores of their class and experience are against 'philosophizing' in such a way that one might be tempted to take a particular decision too readily in advance and without having a good look for all the factors which are individually too minor to be mentioned in a short answer but any one of which may well turn out to be major in a particular case. In the end academic economics must develop, so that conceptual help comes from outside; but business could do more to get this area looked at from within if it brought economic expertise right up into top policy discussions and encouraged its economists to question all principles and sort out the underlying factors in the way that they have done on the capital investment front.

To put the matter that way is to bring out some of the difficulties of micro-theoretical training from within business. It is however, urgent that business should do something positive about this. As you may have come to expect, I stress the urgency from the point of view of economics itself. We need urgently a micro-level theory which we can rely on. Now, I do not feel called on to say anything about any micro-theorizing which I myself have been associated with; what is relevant is our experience that one can get at least some sort of workable beginnings of such theories out of actual business experience and that even these beginnings may be useful to business.

One reason why better theory is essential to economics is that we are committed to government attempts to control the broad direction of our economies and no modern government can avoid a good deal of intervention in economic life even if its efforts stop far short of the economic planning which some advocate. I have already referred to the comparative success of our experiments with employment and income stabilization but they could be much more successful if we had a surer footing of micro theory beneath us, especially when dealing with the heavy capital goods industries and their difficult pricing and investment problems. There are other social policy areas, too, where such an improved analytical basis is essential.

The most important one from a business point of view is probably that of anti-trust where governments prohibit some practices and regulate others. This is also important from the point of view of economics — for many of the ideas used in criticism of business practices and in the evaluation of practical remedies derive from ideas in economics whose only firm basis lies in the world of competition theory whose application to the real world in fact causes us such great difficulty. The business man himself has begun to realize that he needs someone to come and take a look at micro-level behaviour, if only because all his training disqualifies him from looking at this from a broader social point of view and his isolated defence of particular practices can, very easily, be brushed aside just because the defence is not part of a wider, testable, vision of how the

391

business world actually moves at this level.

Here I should like to make two points. The first is that I am not going to discuss the American anti-trust situation. For one thing, I have not worked in that area; for another, your legal background is such that on some matters the kinds of things I want to discuss are in the highest degree academic. It is possible that there will be some applicability in, say, Federal Trade Commission proceedings. But your law settles some important issues which in many European countries are still open to economic argument even in anti-trust litigation. It would seem regrettable if the effect of legal prohibitions should be to rule out the development of economic analysis of the effects of the law. From my own experience in the USA, I feel bound to say that there does not seem to be nearly enough professional discussion of the economic aspects of anti-trust against the background of the detailed economics of the industries concerned. Too many ostensibly factual discussions seem never to raise the curtain of allegations made in legal indictments and *ex parte* pleadings. All is on too general a level and industry might well encourage more intimate scientific research in this area. It is, however, not my job tonight to start any detailed discussion of this kind, and I should want to have stayed in the United States and to have worked in American industry for a far longer period before I should feel qualified to take on myself the task of belling this particular cat.

My second point is that although I have been involved in several very heavy anti-trust cases in England, I got into them because of academic work. A little discussion of this background might be useful as suggesting ways in which business might both help micro-level economic research and get some benefit from the process. I have mentioned the old Oxford Economists' Research Group which started asking business men what they actually did and why they did it. My colleague, Elizabeth Brunner, and I have developed research which stems directly from that approach and have made a number of studies of actual individual businesses in their environment so far as we could understand it. Where our work differs from the pre-war work is its depth and that we work for fair periods inside businesses going wherever it is necessary to be alongside the decisions in which we are interested or the decisions which contribute to them or follow from them.

One point which may be of interest is that, so important are what are too often dismissed in economic discussion as matters of detail, we find we can not work on industry until we have learned enough about its techniques to be able to talk to technologists about their side of the business; when, of course, they acquiesce in our discussing the economic and business aspects of techniques with their managements and in fact continue to help us to keep matters straight. I think that there are lessons here for the use of economists in business. I am sure that exposure to techniques should be a far more regular matter than it is, and I have already mentioned the area of capital expenditure control which is one which would greatly benefit by this kind of background training. The economic analysis of the cost side of business is of course a much more detailed affair when one has the necessary technical background, but one's whole approach to the market situation of a business is transformed when one can sort out the cost factors in some detail according to the time period involved in one's analysis, and one does need to be much more *au fait* with technical factors and less in the hands of settled accounting procedures than economists usually are.

Despite the reference to techniques, what I have just been saying will have indicated to the trained economist that we do start from some familiar theoretical territory in the analysis of the individual business. Because we found that this was so, over ten years ago we decided to develop our teaching of graduate students along the lines of our researches. We have now a regular seminar where they can begin to think about the micro-economics of the individual business on a sort of limited research basis — confronting business men with their theoretical problems and listening to the business men describe, under questioning which the students have thought out, their approach to parallel problems as they find them in reality.

So, in our research and in our teaching, we began to establish at least a framework of questions which we found were good starting points in the discussion of the economics of the individual business. They were good starting points just because, although stemming from a theoretical attitude of mind, they took little for granted, and we try always to ask them in such a way as not to lessen the chance of our finding the business which really does turn out to be exceptional — perverse, if you like — in its behaviour as compared with what we find to be the usual run. Our experience has convinced us in fact that there are sufficient broad similarities in approach and behaviour for one to have hopes of a theoretical framework in which behavioural differences between businesses can be explored in terms of factual differences in their intrinsic circumstances or in the circumstances confronting them from without.

I have already hinted at the necessity of attempts to construct generalizations about costs which lie as near as possible to the cost curves of traditional theory. We ask also about the structure of costs in ways which that theory, because of its generality, has not usually got down to. For example, one is not simply interested in the relative importance of overhead costs; one inquires how far and in what circumstances elements of overhead cost involve a necessary drain of cash and how far such consequences can be deferred for more, or less, long periods. Then one gets into the structure of an individual industry — the relative sizes of businesses against the background of their relative specialization or diversity of output and of markets, including diversity of distribution methods. One does what one can, even if working only as from within one business, to

393

get some idea of the structure of costs, not only in aggregate but also in terms of components, as between businesses; and the work on techniques is of great importance here. The questions which we have always at the back of our minds, and they are perhaps our principal questions even though the approach to them is deliberately indirect, are concerned with the stability and instability of markets and of the positions of individual businesses within them. What factors make a market unstable and how do they work? How far ahead can one spot the beginnings of an unstable market? What are the effects of periods of unstable markets? Specifically, what effects do periods of high, rising, or low. falling, prices have on the conduct of individual businesses and of their industries?

Here, I hope that business men in the audience will recognize questions which, however theoretical the purpose behind them, are worth discussing. Our business men have found it interesting enough to encourage us to poke about in their affairs after any formal research contact was over, and we do so just so that we may keep an eye on changing circumstances. Perhaps even more to the point, we have had a very lively and interesting cooperation from any resident economists in the businesses concerned — where there have been any such. Perhaps one consequence of this kind of research has been that the senior resident economist tends to be a little more involved in higher policy discussions as an economist after the researchers have gone.

If the general body of research has been done for our own purposes, it is perhaps the anti-trust work which has brought the greatest responsibilities towards business. We got into that kind of work originally because we could not refuse to help business men present their case when they had over the years done so much to help our pupils and ourselves. Confining my present attention to work done in connexion with the Restrictive Trade Practices Act, which is the major British anti-trust statute, the terms of this Act have eventually been found to call for a more thoroughgoing analysis of the individual industries concerned than is usually germane in the United States under its legislation. There has been a gradual development here which I can not comment on in detail but the course of events has probably been influenced by industries who rather courageously, as it may have seemed at the time, gave their advisory economists freedom to work as though they were engaged on academic research rather than *ex parte* litigation.

The point which I wish to make is that the Court has eventually become willing to let an economist testify in very theoretical terms about the kind of model which he would apply in his analysis of an industry, not debarring that evidence because it related apparently to factors which the Court had the duty of judging nor ruling it out because the economist lacked the strict qualifications of business experience as legally recognized. In effect, the most recent developments have shown the Court prepared to hear such evidence from an economist whose expertise in the field it was prepared to recognize and then judge it against the factual testimony of business men and other witnesses. In the most recent case on which I can report, the Net Book Agreement case, the Court was helped by the business witnesses adopting all details of the theoretical model so far as it generalized about matters which were factually within their experience and then being prepared to be cross-examined on it as though it were their own evidence. The Court there had a 78-page document from the economist which was theoretical in its structure, reaching conclusions about the behaviour of the publishing and bookselling industries with and without resale price maintenance on the basis of generalizations about economic elements entering into business decisions and the environments in which these were made, which were themselves conclusions derived from independent study of the industries.

One consequence of this development has been that businesses with agreements which have to be defended before the Court have now been given some very practical reasons for wishing that more economists did the kind of economic research to which I am referring, and it would seem reasonable to expect that economic evidence against such agreements may be encouraged to be based more on detailed study of whatever industry is concerned, and rather less on generalizations about the effects of competition and of restraints on competition in a theoretical world where practical differences between industries are blurred over and time and chance seem not to exist. Our Act will continue to impose the circumstances of public benefit to which the Court shall pay regard but in the examination of the factual evidence and in the assessment of economic argument, the Court has lately given encouragement to much more sensitive appraisals of industrial characteristics and situations. This can not be without its long-term consequences on economics itself.

As you may imagine, a good deal more could be said about this kind of economic analysis of industries, and indeed a general review of the way the economic side of the case for and against industrial practices has been presented in our Court might be full of fascinating detail, even if one did not go on to discuss the working of our Monopolies Commission which has ostensibly had greater freedom of inquiry. For our purposes tonight, however, I shall confine myself to general points arising from two cases, including the one which I have just spoken about. They may have some special interest for an American audience because the economic details in the case to which I have not so far referred, that of the Water-Tube Boilermakers' Agreement, involved an industry which had some characteristics in common with your own heavy electrical generating industry whose affairs were the subject of Court action and Senate Committee hearings not so long ago. And the Net Book Agreement case, of course, involved the whole question of the economic effects of fair trade in the matter of books.

Briefly, the legal background to this litigation is that our Restrictive Trade

Practices Act forbids (*inter alia*) any restrictive business agreement affecting prices or terms of trade unless the parties can show to the satisfaction of a special Court, where laymen of suitable experience participate in the adjudgment of factual issues, that it confers one at least of a small number of very tightly defined specific public benefits, such as preventing exploitation of the industry by a monopsonist customer, or bringing a substantial gain in exports, or conferring some other particular benefit to the public, outside the industry itself, which is both specific and substantial. Finally, if one of the specified gateways is passed, the Court must also be satisfied that there is no countervailing consideration from the point of view of public welfare. The onus of proof is on the industry.

In discussing these two cases I shall keep as closely as I can to the economic aspects and shall try to bring out how the general approach of the prosecution differed from the viewpoint of the defence which was accepted by the Court. As my wording indicates, I shall not go into matters which are of legal interest and which would have to be considered in any full account of the two cases — notably, in one case, a discussion of the reasons why the Court might have chosen with apparent inconsistency to reject under one head economic argument which it seems to have accepted under another. Since that case was won under the other head, the argument involved will be summarized without regard to other aspects of the judgment.

Water-tube boilermakers make steam-raising plants for electrical generation. Under the agreement there was no price-fixing of the ordinary kind. In effect, all producers were left free to determine their own prices for any tender or inquiry; the parties agreed on a method of trying to influence the sharing out of work according to quotas which were themselves based upon recent but past shares of the market. If the business which was entitled under the agreement to get preferential treatment had in fact decided to quote a price which turned out not to be the lowest price, it was permitted to lower its quotation to match the lowest price.

This agreement had of course important indirect effects on prices. A business which was relatively falling behind with trade would know that the system would at worst give it an equal chance with others at the lowest price and so, in times of poor aggregate demand, had the less incentive to embark on any reckless price-cutting. Equally, important customers could not, in such circumstances, get lower prices by dangling the chance of a renegotiated contract after tenders had gone in. On the other hand, the system did allow businesses which wanted more orders, but who were not doing so badly as to be likely to get preferential treatment, to try to get their tender in at the lowest level of price at the first stage.

The economic argument of the prosecution kept to a very general level. The best results for public welfare were always brought about by free competition and anything which interfered with that was bad, and in particular would keep in being businesses of lower efficiency than could survive otherwise. Free competition brought the lowest prices. It was admitted that the industry was first-rate technically. There was some suggestion that the industry had not exploited all the overseas markets it might have had. Because there had not been free competition, there might be too many firms in the industry and the introduction of free competition by banning the agreement would again adjust this in the best way. In Court, the suggestion that prices could be too low was countered with the argument that since it was universally acknowledged that high quality research backing was necessary in this industry, it would pay firms to put money into such things anyway.

The factors to which the Court looked in its verdict were as follows — to list them will suggest the general economic model used by the defence, even though it runs in terms of generalizations about established facts: There are few customers; in the British market, practically only one, the nationalized electricity authority. In foreign markets the parties to the agreement have to meet very keen competition from business located elsewhere and prices have to meet that competition. There were important competitors even in the British market. The demand presented itself characteristically in very large contracts which were getting larger and a single large home contract would be sufficient to keep the smaller businesses occupied for a long time. The construction period was about 2 years. There was a good deal of sub-contracting and small firms could take a large contract and get help in carrying it out from the bigger businesses as well as other sub-contractors. In normal times overheads were a very important part of total costs and these involved heavy continuous money expenditure whatever the level of output, since they were largely made up of salary and labour costs; the burden of overheads would increase correspondingly with any fall of activity. The industry had made important technical discoveries and spent large sums in co-operative research from which smaller firms, in particular, benefited.

At the time of the hearing, the industry was at the beginning of a severe depression, so that total demand was nothing like enough to keep occupied the capacity and establishment of all the businesses. Prices and profits were only reasonable, when viewed against the general industrial background. If prices fell, the industry would have to contract. The smaller businesses would go out. The longer-run prospect was that demand would revive to a level which would require at least the existing establishment of the industry. In foreign markets the Court had clear evidence of buyers trying to renegotiate tenders so as to force prices down.

The Court found that in these circumstances in this industry it would not be possible for the industry to get fair prices in free competition for the custom of the predominant home market buyer. The fact that it refused to sanction the agreement on a technical point on this account had no effect since the Court found that the agreement brought in higher earnings in foreign trade than would be obtainable otherwise. Despite the suggestions of outside commentators, it did not find that foreign prices were 'subsidized' by home prices.

Factors brought out in Court which were not reviewed by the economic side of the prosecution were the effects of a preponderant buyer (monopsony) on competition in an oligopoly in times of depression, the importance of the structure of overheads (the economist in fact argued that it was not essential to cover these), the effects on competition of a very disparate industrial structure, and the effects of the presence of competitors not adhering to the agreement. The prosecution entirely failed to convince the Court that, in these circumstances, businesses could so rest on the agreement that they could charge unreasonably high prices. The Court heard detailed evidence on the making up of tender prices.

The net book agreement between publishers also leaves them quite free to determine at what prices their books shall be sold and whether any book shall be published at a 'net' price (i.e., fair traded at a specified retail price) or not. But, if they do fix a net price, they agree to see that it is kept and mutual assistance is available for any prosecution. The agreement also establishes standard 'discounts' from net prices for sales to libraries by booksellers and for certain other special classes of customers. I note that individual fair trade is permissible and technically enforceable under English law. It was, however, conceded by the prosecution that, without the agreement in this particular industry, fair trade could not be enforced by individual businesses and that the system of individual resale price maintenance would break down in this industry. The case therefore resolved itself into a general trial of the economics of fair trade in books.

The economic case against the agreement held that prices would be lower on average without the agreement. The prices of a few might be higher — the implication brought out in argument was that 'mass sale' books would be lower in price and that the books wanted by only a few would cease to be, as it was alleged, subsidized by the mass-sellers. Second, it was urged that retail prices should be determined by the retailer at point of sale. The discounts, which were at present effectively the retailers' margins at the fixed prices, for various classes of books were not related to the costs of selling those classes of books, and booksellers would select mass-sellers in preference to other books. (There was a curious but serious error in the detailed argument here which I shall not go into.) The industry, by penalizing unorthodox methods of distribution had become fossilized and unresponsive to change. The number of firms in the industry, both publishers and retailers, and the methods of distribution, were not necessarily the best.

These counts of course recur in any discussion of the case against fair trade and I shall not go into details. It may be interesting to observe that the general drift of such argument by concentrating upon distribution, and in the light of the benefits alleged to flow from a banning of fair trade, implies that producers making such agreements must be mistaken, do not understand their real interests. A consequence of this, in the prosecution's economic argument before the Court as well as in the general economic discussions to which I have referred, is that the benefits which producers may get from such agreements were not adequately considered, and so the prosecution failed to appreciate the public benefits which might have their origin in economies at the publishing end.

I should perhaps say that I am concerned in what follows only with the case of books and not with other commodities which might be fair traded. I am also concerned only with the English conditions which the Court reviewed, and not with the circumstances, say, of the American book industries at this time. May I be allowed to add that, if I were an American book reader or author I might be tempted to envy the English their book industries, whatever the actual reason for any disadvantages on the American side.

The economic characteristics of the industry established in Court were as follows: There are a large number of firms both in publishing and in distribution. Entry is free and easy. There are not necessarily any substantial economies of scale as between larger and smaller businesses, any businesses being taken as a whole. The costs of publishing a title fall markedly with increases in the size of edition. The demand for books will be greatly affected by the size of the stocks of books actually visible in the retail market. People going in for one book frequently come out with another and there is a substantial proportion of impulse buying. The demand for individual titles varies enormously; the out and out best-seller, of which the prosecution made much, is very rarely predictable until actual sales show that it is such a book. Publishers' methods of settling prices are such that if they expect a larger demand they print more and fix the price at a lower level. If the agreement went, publishers would not be able to maintain their prices but they would still be forced to continue to issue list prices, (which would provide benchmarks for price-cutting). If there were no agreement, price cutting was likely to develop on certain types of books, notably (a) books which became best-sellers, (b) academic text-books of a particular kind, and at certain times of the year, (c) widely-stocked cheap series and widely-demanded works of reference. Discounts would develop for large buyers, libraries, institutions, etc., but this would not be on a basis of cost savings but on the bargaining power of such buyers in relation to individual distributors. The stocks at bookshops would be greatly reduced, and with the consequent reduced sales shops would cut down their pre-publication orders.

It was found that, as it was, booksellers were not making excessive profits and that a large proportion of good smaller bookshops were making very low profits or losses. With fewer sales and lower estimates of sales typically expected for individual titles of any class, publishers would print smaller initial editions and have higher costs. Prices would go up and fewer titles would be published. List prices would go up even more, because of pressure from booksellers to have increased nominal discounts to allow for price-cutting. If discounts for libraries were a matter of bargaining, their trade would go in the short run to library suppliers and away from ordinary bookshops.

The industry is intensely competitive and there is nothing in the agreement to prevent new methods of distribution being tried. (Evidence showed the willingness of publishers to experiment, with appropriate variation of their trade terms.) The competition from non-specialist retailers who might feature price-cut lines of books would drive many of the smaller businesses out although they were giving a real service to the community. In such a multi-product industry retailers have to average their costs and the discounts for different classes of books do tend to reflect the differing ease with which those classes are sold and the special risks that may be involved in stocking them. The buyers who would get lower than list prices or increased nominal discounts would be worse off than they are with the agreement because other factors would cause a rise in prices which would more than cancel out these apparent beneficial changes so that they would suffer a net rise of prices.

In view of the controversy over fair trade, it is interesting that in the judgment of the Court there were no public detriments at all in this agreement. But, of course, the points of highest economic interest are that the Court's analysis refused to treat retailers as being high- or low-cost for the sales of particular books taken in isolation, that it recognized the over-all effect of stocks on demand at point of sale, and that it brought in the effects of the increased uncertainty and lower sales which publishers would encounter on sizes of individual editions and therefore on costs. Discounts had to be related to the kinds of sales that might be expected and should not be expected to be right in retrospect for every individual commodity in an industry where there was so much risk and variability. The fact of a large number of low profit retailers was no sign that these were inefficient at doing their job. The type of distribution which an industry has cannot be discussed as though it is only the relatively inefficient which would be affected adversely by the pressures of short-run competition. In assessing the effects of any changes on an industry, the Court in this case began to adopt the view that one should take a rather longer-run standpoint.

Consistently with what you may have gathered to be my general attitude, what I like about the position in this English Court, if these trends go on, is that one should not think that one can forecast the decision in any future case on general grounds in advance of evidence — and that industries will be encouraged to offer a more thorough examination of their working details. I welcome this development just as much as I deplore that any industry should be attacked on general *a priori* grounds without reference to the details of its circumstances and working. I anticipate that the prosecution will be forced to move to more realistic ground.

As a theoretical economist working at the micro-level, I welcome the prospect that the co-operation between business men and economists in these matters will continue to provide examples of the kind of economic analysis of individual industries which I think economics needs. I also welcome the prospect of economists being compelled to get down to studying the industry whose agreements and practices they may be criticizing. Out of this I see real prospects that the interesting material which such litigation will provide will create an inducement for a more adequate development of micro-level economic theory, which will be of use to the business men concerned not only for litigation but also their everyday problems. It ought to be possible for economics to give them a much better framework of reference than most industries can draw on today.

I may add that I put the matter in these impersonal terms because I myself hope in the future to get on with longer-term research and to cease to be involved in these exciting but time-absorbing battles. Perhaps I should add one point which seems very much in keeping with the spirit of the foundation of this lectureship: that, in the cases which I have been discussing, the business men concerned have left the Court, even before the judgment, feeling that they understood in general terms the working of their own industries better than they had done before. That seems to me to be the role of economic theory, not so much to show the business man how to run his own business, but to give him a better understanding from which he can get down to the details of his business which only he can decide.

Epilogue: Whatever happened to P.W.S. Andrews's industrial economics?

Peter E. Earl[1]

Introduction

Philip Andrews occupies an unusual position in the history of economic ideas. It would be easy to claim that he is a significant twentieth-century economist on the basis of his appointments during his career (the long stint at Oxford, followed by the Chair at Lancaster), his setting up a successful journal, and on the 'objective' evidence of the interest that his work has generated. Under the last heading a variety of facts can be noted:

(a) His key book *Manufacturing Business* generated much discussion in the years immediately following its publication in 1949 (for a blow-by-blow account, see Irving, 1978).

(b) It appears from the *Social Science Citation Index* that during the twenty years following the publication of Andrews's other major book, *On Competition in Economic Theory* (1964), his work was being cited around seven or eight times a year.

(c) Those who initially got to grips with industrial economics via the top-selling British texts of the late 1970s and early 1980s (Pickering, 1974; Hay and Morris, 1979; and Devine *et al.*, 1985) should have seen his name mentioned more than a few times — indeed, in the opening page of the first chapter of Devine *et al.*, Andrews is credited with coining the term 'industrial economics'.

(1) This chapter is based on a revision of a paper that was originally written for the 1987 conference of the History of Economic Thought Society of Australia at the University of Newcastle, NSW. Revisions to it have come far later than I intended, partly because other projects intervened but also because I needed to incorporate many constructive comments offered by conference participants and later by Alan Bevan (who sent several letters and an eight-page commentary), John Davies, John King, Fred Lee, Brian Loasby and an anonymous referee. Given this, an apology for being so tardy appears to be in order, along with my thanks and the usual disclaimer.

(d) The late Anna Koutsoyiannis also made extensive use of Andrews's thinking on pricing in the chapter entitled 'A "Representative" Model of Average-Cost Pricing' in her highly successful text *Modern Microeconomics* (1979). This is hardly surprising, for she developed the book at Lancaster on the basis of Andrews's own course structure, though the chapter in question did involve a dilution of her original plan, which had actually been for a very strongly Andrews-based chapter on normal-cost price theory (Bevan, 1987).

(e) Andrews received major attention in a variety of monographs and academic papers. These range from the published thesis of his graduate student Harry Edwards (1962) (whose career in economics was cut short by his movement into political life in Australia), to well-known contributions of Modigliani (1958), Sylos-Labini (1969) and Bhagwati (1970) to the literature on oligopoly.

Yet, despite all this, and despite Andrews having been recognized as sufficiently noteworthy to deserve at least a brief entry in the *The New Palgrave* (Eatwell, Milgate and Newman, eds, 1987), I concur wholeheartedly with Fred Lee's suggestions in this book's Introduction about the limited impact of Andrews's work: in the United States few industrial economists seem to make much use of his work these days; he has certainly failed to influence significantly the mainstream of modern industrial economics and many economists who *have* heard of his work appear not to take it very seriously .(2)

The present paper is not primarily concerned with why Andrews's work has had a rather limited, uneven impact: this issue has been dealt with at length elsewhere (Irving, 1978; Earl, 1983a) and so will be dealt with relatively briefly towards the end. Rather, my primary intention is to argue that many notions which are seen as important post-war advances in the area of industrial organization and the theory of the firm, and which are not credited as having originated with Andrews, can be seen as important elements in earlier work by Andrews. In other words, *his ideas appear to have been reinvented*. This seems an inefficient use of scarce scholarly resources and serves to reinforce the idea that there is much to be gained from studying classic and/or heretical texts rather than concentrating on the most recent publications that happen to be highlighted in modern databases.

Before proceeding to the main body of the chapter, however, it is appropriate to note the relationship of Andrews's work, and the paper itself, to the earlier work of Alfred Marshall. Andrews (1951) was quite explicit about the Marshallian roots of his way of thinking (he also noted the connecting link

---

(2) Two notable exceptions that themselves deserve more attention are by Reid (1979) and Andrews's former colleague, Tom Wilson (1984, Chapters 10–12).

provided by his reading of D.H. MacGregor), and, unlike many, he was well aware of how different Marshall's original work was from versions of it that were finding their way into the conventional wisdom. Misapprehensions of Marshall may well be significant factors in explaining the neglect of Andrews; if so, Andrews-enthusiasts should be thankful that the nature of Marshall's view of economics has been clarified in recent years. Thus it is that the title of the present paper is a deliberate allusion to the earlier essay by Loasby (1978) which explores some of the ways in which Marshall's ideas were distorted and reinvented, such that on being re-read they could appear 'so old-fashioned as to appear avant-garde.' Loasby rightly lists Andrews along with G.B. Richardson (another unjustly neglected scholar) as rare examples of economists following the truly Marshallian theme that markets are 'information structures'.

Andrews and the American behaviouralists on costs and pricing

Like Marshall, Andrews was not content to engage in armchair theorizing — the activity which H.A. Simon (1986) puts at the heart of his critique of much modern research. Both Andrews and Marshall are to be regarded among the pioneers of the behavioural methodology normally associated with Cyert, March and Simon and Carnegie-Mellon University. Long before Cyert and March (1963, p. 1) announced that their idea was 'to make detailed observations of the procedures by which firms make decisions and use these observations for a theory of decision making within organizations', Andrews (1951, p. 172) — in urging the abandonment of the concept of static equilibrium — had observed that the alternative patterns of analysis 'will have to be built up out of empirical studies, just as Marshallian concepts were largely informed by their founder's studies of historical processes. No amount of spinning-out of logical chains of analysis based upon static concepts will help in this task'. In addition to as yet unpublished case studies of the boot and shoe industry of the British Midlands, Andrews engaged in in-depth business history work with Elizabeth Brunner (1951, 1955, 1965) and consultancy investigations of the building and water-tube boiler-making industries (see Andrews and Brunner, 1975, Chapters 4 and 5). These practical investigations played a vital role in the formation of his views of what an industrial economist should consider as necessary to study (see Andrews, 1952, pp. 76–7 [page 374 in the reprint in this book]) , as well as inspiring his theoretical picture of the working of businesses more generally.

Of course, this wealth of knowledge did not result in him writing a work which looked anything like Cyert and March's *A Behavioral Theory of the Firm.* In his analysis of the operations of the *Manufacturing Business* (Andrews,

1949b), there were few diagrams, no formal notation and certainly no computer simulations. What he produced was an analysis in prose, that outlined the situational complexities with which businessmen saw themselves as having to cope, and which then proceeded to make its theoretical contribution by uncovering the decision rules that it would be reasonable to use in such situations. The parallels with Cyert and March should seem obvious when Andrews's work is characterized in this manner, and it was in precisely these terms that, in his obituary note, Farrell (1971) outlined the approach to theorizing that Andrews adopted.

For Andrews, the complexities of the business environment were not matters that he felt it appropriate to deal with in asides. Rather, as Farrell (1971, p. 11) put it, they became 'sources of illumination and the true basis of an incisive theory ... [which was] at once simple and amazingly sophisticated.' In this respect his empirical research led to a much more subtle view than that of the behaviouralists, who remained surprisingly close to the neoclassical view in some respects. For all the attention the behaviouralists give to internal aspects of the firm, they tend to be vague about the nature of the market contexts in which they assume firms to be operating or treat them as having discretionary power due to large size (cf. Andrews and Brunner, 1975, pp. 35–6, and Lee, 1984, especially p. 1122). Andrews noticed that businessmen usually recognized the presence of few actual, but many potential producers of their products. When deciding what prices to put in their catalogues, they were mindful of the potential for frequent changes in rates of orders, in input prices and in prices of substitutes, factors which implied considerable costs in calculating optimal prices, particularly since firms typically produced, or could consider starting to produce, many products. As Farrell (1971, p. 12) observed, Andrews concluded that 'the firm must keep in step both with its existing competitors' prices and with that which would render its product attractive to new entrants. So long as the optimal technique did not change, the normal-cost rule gave an accurate answer [for pricing problems].'

Andrews's normal-cost pricing rule envisaged a firm as setting its prices with reference to actual and potential competitors' costs of invading its market, with the firm's knowledge of its own cost structure and standing relative to its rivals being used to gauge a safe, but not unduly cautious, price. The theory dispensed with downward-sloping marginal revenue curves and upward sloping marginal cost curves. With respect to the former, Andrews stressed that customers would not keep coming if the firm set unduly high prices and induced rival suppliers to enter swiftly with better terms, so demand curves were not pertinent to pricing planning, even though sales estimates at normal-cost prices would affect the capacity expansion plans of the firm. As far as costs were concerned, Andrews's fieldwork had convinced him that, except in the short run,

405

firms' cost curves did not turn up as they increased their rates of output. In the short run, firms would generally be planning to have some spare capacity in order to be able to satisfy unexpected increases in orders without having to ration regular customers. Such thinking would ensure they were not normally operating in the range which forced them to incur rising marginal costs as a result of getting their staff to work overtime, stressing their machinery more frequently to the point of breakdown, or recommissioning outmoded equipment that had been mothballed rather than scrapped.

In short, his empirical studies had led him to reject the idea of the optimal size of the firm and end up with an analysis in which the current turnover and sales of a firm depended on its success in marketing and selling and in access to finance to construct capacity to deliver goods in the quantities for which it could drum up orders. On this basis, and because of his emphasis on pricing rules, Andrews's work ought to have found favour with the American behaviouralists. The closest he seems to get with Cyert and March (1963, p. 12) is being referred to as editor, with Tom Wilson (1951), of the volume in which there is a reprint of the classic paper by his colleagues Hall and Hitch (1939) on full cost pricing and the kinked demand curve. There is no reference to Andrews's own, very Marshallian essay on the nature of competitive processes from that volume (reproduced as Chapter 3 of the present book). Simon makes no reference to Andrews when lamenting the fact that 'The most widely used textbooks use the old long-run and short-run cost curves to illustrate the theory of the firm' (1986, p. 23), despite the fact that 'empirical studies show the firm's cost curves not to be U-shaped but in fact to slope down to the right and then level off, without a clearly defined minimum point' (1986. p. 24).(3) I suspect that it is only as a result of ignorance of Andrews's work that American behaviouralists never commend it as an alternative to the conventional treatments. Such an error of omission is disheartening to Andrewsians, but it is far less disturbing than the orthodox economist's continuing tendency to deal with a hypothetical world of optimally-sized firms.

Andrews and the Post Keynesian theory of pricing

Like modern Post Keynesians, Andrews saw economics in terms of processes that were often irreversible: trade took place in his models through time, so if a firm upset and lost the goodwill of a regular customer the loss of future revenues arising from a 'never again!' attitude on the part of the customer could be

---

(3) For a more detailed paper on the empirical limitations of neoclassical production assumptions, see Cyert and Simon (1983).

considerable. However, many Post Keynesians give his work short shrift: citation is usually very brief, often comprising no more than a footnote mention (usually of his 1949b, Chapter 5 analysis; his 1949a article seems totally ignored by them), and I know of no instance in which attention is drawn to the careful analysis of the business cycle in the final chapter of Andrews's (1949b) book. Such citations list Andrews alongside other writers in the 'normal-cost/mark-up pricing' tradition, such as Sylos-Labini or Kalecki, without conveying the particular richness and distinctive features of his analysis; indeed they are often made by scholars who have developed a parallel analysis totally in ignorance of Andrews's work.

Two case studies can serve to illustrate this phenomenon. The first is brief and concerns work on pricing and the trade cycle by Godley and Nordhaus (1972) (see also the subsequent book by Coutts, Godley and Nordhaus, 1978). Godley and Nordhaus (1972, p. 853) note that one view of industrial price behaviour 'is that prices move with normal costs, i.e. they do not react to temporary changes in demand or costs; this is the "normal price hypothesis".' But they do not merely go on to ignore the final chapter of *Manufacturing Business*; they fail to mention Andrews at all, referring instead to Kalecki, Means and Hall and Hitch.

Secondly, consider the wording of a footnote by Eichner (1976, p. 304) to an appendix — on 'Antecedent formulations of the entry factor' — to Chapter 3 of his book *The Megacorp and Oligopoly*:

1. Bain (1958, 1956). A parallel line of development in Great Britain, though resulting in a less formal treatment of the entry factor, can be traced though the work of Harrod (1952, ch. 8), Andrews (1949, ch. 5), Hicks (1954) and H. Edwards (1955).

Eichner (1978) subsequently paid due tribute to the pioneering importance of Andrews's work on pricing, but it certainly had no role whatever in the development of his analysis of the megacorp. In fact, Eichner developed his theory of pricing — which argues that the mark-up is set with a view to generating the cash-flow to pay for investment projects — in ignorance of Andrews's work, after noticing a parallel between the way Soviet planners used the proceeds of the turnover tax to finance investment, and the explanations that Western executives gave of how they financed their investments from their profit margins. As I discovered from Jan Kregel (in conversation in 1981), it was only as a result of Kregel's knowledge that Andrews came to figure in Eichner's footnote. Kregel, an avid collector of books, happened speculatively to buy a secondhand copy of Andrews's (1964) book in a Cambridge market for a few pence, around 1971. Some years later, having thus discovered Andrews, Kregel acted as publisher's referee to Cambridge University Press, to whom Eichner had sent the manuscript of his Post Keynesian analysis of oligopoly. This had been written some years before but, as Eichner (1976, pp. xi–xii) explains in the preface, its appearance had been retarded by hostile reports from mainstream economists acting as referees for other publishers. Kregel liked the book, but insisted that Andrews at least deserved a footnote in it.

In noting how Andrews has often been given short shrift by Post Keynesians I am not trying to suggest that their contributions do nothing more than repeat Andrewsian ideas. For it is the case that some of Andrews's ideas were in need of further development and progress is evident in the work of scholars such as Eichner. Most important, perhaps, is the issue of whether Andrews over-estimated the power of potential entry as a deterrent to anti-social corporate practices. Although Andrews had a view of entry that was rather broader in vision than the view of most industrial economists — for example, he and Brunner saw product differentiation as often providing a way of getting into a market, rather than a barrier to entry (Andrews and Brunner, 1975, pp. 38–41) — his views on the merits of entry-deterring strategies can sometimes appear naive. Shaw (1974) has shown how, in the case of petrol retailing, it can be a very expensive policy indeed to aim for long-run profits at the expense of short-run earnings, since difficulties in obtaining good sites may mean that entry takes a few years to become effective and in the interim very substantial short-term margins can be earned. If is not costless for a firm to defend its long-run market position, Eichner's (1976) refinement of an entry-deterring analysis via the introduction of a managerial preference for more immediate profits over more distant ones sounds like something of an improvement on Andrews's idea — particularly once one recognizes the possibility that product life-cycles may be unexpectedly truncated by shifts in technology. The question of the interaction between the lengths of product life-cycles and corporate pricing policies in general deserves more thought, since a price that deters entry by potential producers may be sufficiently inconvenient to incumbent rivals to make them bring forward their plans to revamp their products (see Earl, 1983b, pp. 46–50, for a more detailed discussion).

Potential competition and the revolution in monopoly theory

Scholars of Andrews's work have been suffering acutely from feelings of deja vu in recent years, feelings made all the more troubling by thoughts that what they were seeing was rather more insightful in its original Andrewsian guise (see Wilson, 1984, especially pp. 226–30; Lawler, 1985, p. 37). The source of such feelings is the proliferation of research on the 'contestability' approach to industrial structure, associated particularly with the work of Baumol, Panzar and Willig (1982; see also the Presidential Address to the American Economic Association given by Baumol, 1982). Similar reactions might be expected from other industrial economists such as Caves and Porter whose work on strategic groups and mobility barriers also predates Baumol *et al.*'s contributions and is both consistent with and a development of the notions of potential competition and cross entry, as well as providing a practical framework for analysing competition between firms (see Caves and Porter, 1977; Porter, 1979, 1980, Ch. 7). A useful commentary on what is not so new about contestable markets has already been provided by Shepherd (1984), but his focus is largely on American contributions and fails to note the relevance of Andrews's work.

According to Baumol (1982, p. 2), the key theme in his team's 'new' work is that

> ... in the limiting case of perfect contestability, oligopolistic structure and behavior are freed entirely from their previous dependence on the conjectural variations of *incumbents* and, instead, these are generally determined uniquely and, in a manner that is tractable analytically, by the pressures of *potential* competition to which Bain has directed our attention so tellingly (italics in original).

The emphasis on the power of potential competition is, of course, the foundation of the work of Andrews and Brunner, which predates that of Bain. In the Andrews analysis, it is argued that if existing producers engaged in policies of collusion, whether explicit or implicit, these would tend to founder if they involved prices sufficiently high as to attract others into their market. Andrews's fieldwork had brought home to him the great awareness of this risk amongst businessmen. After all, in seeking to expand their own operations, they were themselves constantly on the lookout for markets which they could enter on the basis of their established know-how and capital investments. Such a basis for entry, if strong, would mean that few new costs would have to be sunk in an experimental foray into a market where existing suppliers seemed incompetent or to be pushing their luck: in the limit, one could use one's existing sales force and capital equipment, both of which might be exhibiting spare capacity, and not need to invest in additional training or capital (cf. the extension of Andrews's analysis by Moss, 1981). If firms were looking for opportunities to raid other markets in this way, it was not surprising that they lived in fear that raiders from other markets might find it attractive to invade their own territory.

This is also the sort of thinking that underlies the revolution in monopoly theory: the *perfectly* contestable market is one in which *both* entry *and* exit are costless, there being no sunk costs. In such a market, the ability to exit without having made any capital commitment guarantees freedom of entry, and the fear of hit-and-run raids concentrates incumbents' minds wonderfully against the idea of pursuing socially undesirable pricing policies. Hence, whether there is one firm or a multitude of firms actually operating in it at any time, a perfectly contestable market never offers the incumbent(s) more than the normal rate of profit.

Baumol and his latter-day revolutionaries have succeeded in capturing the imagination of industrial economists where Andrews failed, despite — or more likely, because of — the fact that the 'new' exposition concentrates on the theoretical ideal in a highly formal, equilibrium manner. Wilson (1984, p. 227) describes the formal theory as 'another exercise in comparative statics, with all the problems of inadequate information, risk, and uncertainty largely ignored'. Goodwill, a concept central to Andrews's analysis of the determination of market share, figures nowhere in Baumol *et al.*'s treatise. Nor, indeed, would we expect to find a logical place for it in the first 370 pages, since the concept concerns the empirically significant phenomenon of repeat business and it is only on page 371 that the analysis is broadened to take account of the passage of time. Since they lack the goodwill factor to provide a limit to the size of the firm (only a short-run restraint in Andrews's process analysis), an Andrewsian is not surprised to see Baumol *et al.* (1982, p. 113) note that their 'powerful analysis of the number of firms that minimizes industry costs' was 'made possible by the assumption that average costs first decline, achieve their minimum and then rise'. Once again then, it seems that 'armchair theorizing rules, OK?' Of course, Baumol *et al.* do not claim that their world of perfect contestability is anything more than an approximation to reality, yet, unlike the somewhat less precisely specified approximation of Andrews and Brunner, it throws up implications about industry policy with the aid of assumptions that simply do not stand up empirically.

Costs and the competitive process

The analysis of costs that Andrews presented in *Manufacturing Business* is a sophisticated integration of themes which most modern industrial economists should find remarkably familiar. It is convenient to deal with these themes separately in a series of subsections, with extensive quotations to document the claims that are being made.

The hiring of workers

Andrews's analysis of the demand for labour is not unusual merely because it recognizes an oligopsony problem, the possibility that it may be futile for firms to engage in wage competition against other employers of the required kind of labour in their area (see Andrews, 1949b, pp. 226–7). It also stands out because it treats labour as a 'quasi-fixed factor'. Such a view of labour is one normally associated with the work of Oi (1962), whose inspiration was the work of J.M. Clark (1923) and who makes no mention of Andrews's work. The following extract gives a flavour of this side of Andrews's thinking and, in its stress on corporate idiosyncrasies, anticipates some of the work of Williamson (1975) (who refers to neither Oi nor Andrews) about which more will be said later:

> The personnel employed will be much more valuable to the business, in so far as they acquire an increasing familiarity with its methods of production, with its particular product, and with its particular market. To let them go means parting with trained and experienced personnel who will, perhaps, not be available if subsequently the business wishes to re-expand, thus leading not only to the strict cost of hiring newcomers but also to the inconvenience and bother which necessarily arise with the introduction of new personalities into the organization of a business, which, at its best, has to function as a team of people who know one another (Andrews, 1949b, p. 97).

Management and the growth of the firm

The final remarks in the passage just cited should leave students of the work of Penrose (1959) wondering to what extent Andrews anticipated her analysis of the short-run restraints on the growth of the firm. Andrews (1961) actually wrote a somewhat unsympathetic review of her book, in which he argued that, in concentrating on managerial limitations to the pace of corporate expansion, she was neglecting the barrier to rapid growth caused by the time it takes for firms to pick up customer goodwill. This reaction is odd, given his view that innovatory product differentiation and diversification — both of which Penrose highlighted — could provide an alternative to going for growth in one's existing market via market-share competition. His reaction to Penrose reads all the more strangely in the light of the following extracts from his own (1949b) work:

> [The manager] will certainly not let output expand at so fast a rate as to disorganize his factory and lower the general standard of work which he has established (p. 107). It is in this way that the growth of a business is most limited — the extent to which decisions can be delegated (p. 125).

The latter passage leads on to a discussion of the different 'levels' of management in terms of which a firm could be run (pp. 130–2), which notes how these levels (or management modes) were applicable to discontinuous ranges of output and would therefore only be appropriate to change at discrete

411

intervals. Such changes are one of the things we would expect to be implemented in the periods when the growth of a firm seems to reach a Penrosian plateau and consolidation is undertaken; they also remind one of Chandler's (1962) 'chapters' of corporate evolution.

Competition within the firm

Like Coase (1937), Andrews recognized that the contracts by which workers are tied to their employers are only partially specified. He was therefore drawn to consider the question of *how* productivity levels are determined. His answer centred on the idea that employees usually are aware of the fact that they work in competition with one another (see especially Andrews, 1958; Andrews and Brunner, 1962; in addition to Andrews, 1949b, Chapter 3). Workers who have only recently been hired are likely to be on some kind of probation: if they fail to deliver the kinds of results that incumbents in similar job-slots deliver, then they will be returned to the labour market and be replaced by others. Once established within the firm, workers who desire to earn more and be accorded higher status and responsibility may win promotion if they can to demonstrate their superiority over others on their present level. From the standpoint of the modern literature, we would recognize that Andrews was thinking in terms of internal labour markets with limited ports of entry, as in the work of Doeringer and Piore (1971), and was presuming that the internal market is sufficiently free from 'small numbers problems' arising from 'task idiosyncrasies', of the kind discussed by Williamson (1975, Chapter 4), to be classed as broadly contestable. To Andrews himself, however, his analysis of 'internal competition' was simply an obvious generalization of his theory of potential competition and competitive oligopoly.

The oligopolistic perspective that Andrews introduced to the analysis of worker productivity should be of especial interest to those familiar with Stephen Jones' (1984) *The Economics of Conformism*. Needless to say, Andrews figures nowhere in this book, but Jones makes much of the classic sociological investigations of the 1930s known as the Hawthorne Experiments. In their report on these studies, Roethlisberger and Dickson (1939, p. 522) noted the widespread belief among manual workers that '(1) You should not turn out too much work. If you do, you are a "ratebuster". (2) You should not turn out too little work. If you do, you are a "chiseler".' In other words, there were social pressures to produce within what an Andrewsian would call some kind of 'normal' band. Andrews certainly saw productivity as having a social side, though he stressed that normal rates of output would also be affected by what seemed physically sustainable:

... the newcomer who is much more efficient than average will generally settle down to the pace of work which prevails in the factory. Quite normal forces will restrain any tendency on his part to show excessive zeal which might jeopardize the established position — which may be justified as the working pace which workmen are to keep up day in and day out at the given rate of wages (Andrews, 1949b, pp. 106–7). ... the tendency for a regular pace of work to show itself ... will always be present when men work in groups: it does not arise only from deliberate ca'canny, but, to some extent, no doubt arises from an inclination among a group to establish a general rhythm, which can usually be overcome only by a strong enough incentive to individuals to break away (1949b, p. 105).

The need for a strong incentive to break away is particularly apparent if one focuses less on 'social pressures' and more on the logic of a process of internal competition. For the ambitious worker, promotion often depends upon being able to demonstrate relative superiority, not upon being able to reach some absolute standard. Such a demonstration is not a costless undertaking. If zealots do make conspicuous deviations from normal rates of output, it must be because they judge that the opportunity costs of shooting for promotion are not uniform, and that relatively few workers are prepared to incur them; for if most workers were equally capable and keen to be promoted, zealous behaviour would simply provoke what we might call an 'effort war'. In the latter situation, it would pay everybody to conform, and promotion decisions would be very much a lottery.

Had Williamson been familiar with Andrews's work when writing *Markets and Hierarchies*, I expect he would have wished to point out that, in situations where the requirements of jobs at different levels are difficult to compare, the actions of zealots at each level play a decisive role in determining the minimum standard of output. This is because it may be somewhat difficult for an incumbent at a lower level to provide a credible demonstration of his or her ability to match or better the 'value for money' offered by those already employed at a higher level. (Note that this applies also with respect to the unemployed versus those already employed: see Earl and Glaister, 1979.) Such a view takes us somewhat away from the idea of strongly contestable internal markets, for it is suggesting that actual, not potential, suppliers of particular kinds of labour services will set productivity precedents. This is a qualification that Andrews would only recognize for the short run: sooner or later, competitive pressures from the product market will make those nearer the top of the firm start listening to the allegations from, as he (1958, p. 29) called them, 'young men in a hurry', concerning scope for improvements at intermediate levels.

Organizational slack and X-inefficiency

Devotees of the theory of contestable markets doubtless will not be surprised to discover that Andrews was openly hostile to suggestions that firms do not engage in optimizing, profit-maximizing behaviour and that members of corporate coalitions can often get away with the pursuit of their own sub-goals (cf. Baumol's, 1982, p. 4, remarks on perfect contestability and efficiency). It was indeed the case that Andrews's views on the role of organizational zealots and the power of competition from potential producers led him to take issue with the work of Cyert and March (1963), despite his own essentially behavioural methodology. His troubled reading of Cyert and March — 'So far as I understand their position ...' (Andrews, 1964, p. 39) — led him to construe their view of 'organizational slack' as pertaining to something which arose in situations where competition was lacking (situations his fieldwork suggested were probably the exception rather than the norm) and where there was no need to strive to take high quality decisions: satisficing was a concept that he disliked intensely (see Andrews and Brunner, 1975, p. 1, where he described theorizing along such lines as 'evading economic analysis').

But despite these attacks, and despite his emphasis on the long-run power of competition, it is clear from his work that, like Cyert and March, he certainly did not believe that firms always operate on some objectively given cost curve. For example, consider the following extracts:

> The very ups and downs of the trade cycle contribute their own element making for the increased efficiency of business over time, but the individual business will also get its share of minor setbacks. Something always remains from the enforced ideas of economy and novelty to which business men are driven by such forces. Innovation and the rest of such factors will mean that the forces of competition ... will cause the level of the normal-cost price always to fall (1951, p. 172). Sometimes ... the whole of the top echelon become ineffectual, especially when they are but complementary to a particular personality and decline in effectiveness with him. In this case powerful pressures build up from below and are reinforced by outside competitive pressures in the ordinary sense. ... However much 'fat' its previous success may have built up against just such a winter, in the end the process of exhaustion becomes obvious and rejuvenation is enforced (1958, p. 29).

Further discussions of the process of search and the uptake of slack are found in Andrews and Brunner (1975, p. 158). There one can see that Andrews had his own jargon phrase — 'plasticity of costs' — for organizational slack and did believe it had some bearing on the determination of costing margins.

Related to these passages is the highly innovative analysis of efficiency that Andrews (1949b, pp. 113–23) presented, which seems to concern what, following Leibenstein (1966), we nowadays call X-inefficiency. Andrews distinguished between 'technical' (or 'non-managerial') and 'managerial' costs. By the former, he meant the outlays that would be necessary if all workers and machines were working at their theoretical level of 100 per cent engineering efficiency. Managerial costs are the difference between these (theoretical) technical costs and the larger, actual costs of non-managerial factors of production in a business which is producing at a given scale of production. He called this difference 'managerial costs' since changes in the difference between theoretical and actual technical costs would correspond to changes in the relative efficiency of management, and was under no illusion that there would necessarily exist some firm in an industry which was so well managed as to incur no managerial costs, thus defined (1949b, pp. 114–15). This terminology is certainly somewhat perplexing: the worse the management, the greater the managerial costs of production, for management's ineptitude imposes costs on the firm. But it is difficult to differentiate its content from X-inefficiency.

There is no inherent contradiction between holding such views about managerial processes and believing that the world of business is not a place where the quiet life is the norm. Despite the similarities between normal-cost analysis and contestability theory, Andrews's vision was not equivalent to the equilibrium philosophy of 'perfect contestability'. Rather, he had in mind processes of 'open competition' (Andrews, 1964, p. 15) akin to what J.M. Clark called 'workable competition' (note the similarities between Andrews's works and those of Clark, 1940; see also Downie, 1958). This being so, it is a pity that Andrews never seemed inclined to reconcile his vision with that of the behaviouralists. He shared with them not merely his desire to let empirical knowledge precede the construction of theories but also his recognition that decision-makers do not enjoy the perfect rationality often assumed in neoclassical economics. Where he differed with them seems to boil down to the issue of how much insight lies behind the rules that are chosen as means of simplifying the process of decision-making. His view was more sophisticated but it does not entail a return to global rationality.

Cyert, March and Simon tended to portray rule-based pricing as a *reactive* activity undertaken as if managers pay little attention to the competitive contexts in which they are operating. However, through his field studies, Andrews uncovered widespread fear of perceived rivals and a recognition by managers that if they failed habitually to think ahead they would have little prospect of surviving in business in the longer run. Bevan (1987) sums up Andrews's position rather neatly by saying that 'Andrews's theory is about the firm as an integral part of its industrial and market environment. It is just this environment which mercilessly imposes competitive constraints on the firm regardless of any particular managerial, labour or any other problems the individual firm might experience.' Firms that fail to sort out internal problems which raise their costs above those of their actual and potential rivals will be squeezed out of existence before very long, not least of all because their inferior profitability will make it difficult for them to invest in cost-reducing techniques and hence keep pace with

415

rivals in engineering terms. Managerial solutions to problems may involve renegotiating the distribution of inputs and outputs among different interest groups (in the words of Cyert and March, the uptake of organizational slack) and/or it may involve the discovery of a better method of doing things, that represents a Pareto improvement for members of the corporate coalition. These changes may enable a lagging firm not merely to match its rivals but to move ahead of them, at least for a while.

It is possible to recast Andrews's broad vision of costs and pricing in rather more subjectivist terms. This seems particularly worthwhile since subjectivists of the Austrian school are another group who have made surprisingly little reference to Andrews's work. Andrews had started out with his roots in trade unionism but then became very sympathetic to business as a result of his fieldwork discoveries about the pressures of competition. We might therefore expect typically pro-business Austrians to feel an affinity with normal-cost theory even though it was the product of many years of the kind of detailed research and observation that many of them would be inclined to eschew as superfluous. A subjectivist version of normal-cost theory begins by pointing out that although competitive environments may be pretty merciless, they do not *determine* the behaviour of participants in economic processes (cf. the characterization of the neoclassical theory of the firm as 'situational determinism' by Latsis, 1972). Fear may concentrate the mind wonderfully, but it does not tell decision-makers where problems lie or which solutions are appropriate. On this basis, normal-cost theory should not portray firms as having to set identical profit margins, merely to set prices mindful of their conjectures about the opportunity costs of whoever they see as potential producers of similar products. Likewise, the theory of internal competition should not be seen as predicting that people in identical job slots will put in an identical performance to that which would be offered by those by whom they could be replaced; they merely have to offer at least what their superiors will conjecture to be the opportunity cost output.

The activity of guessing what one *can get away with* seems inherently to involve keeping in mind the strong possibility that if one achieves conspicuous abnormally high returns or imposes significant costs on others, one's actions may be seen as an incentive to search for an alternative supplier or to acquire similar skills as a means for sourcing the product (or a substitute for it) more cheaply inhouse. To the extent that agents sometimes set out to achieve supernormal returns that prove unsustainable in the long run, this may be due to them having made poor conjectures about what would be sufficiently moderate a demand as to preserve their positions for the future, or it may arise because they prefer to discount distant returns somewhat and accordingly have chosen to exploit their temporary advantage in full recognition of the risk of encouraging entry. This analysis would imply an accord with the view of Littlechild (1981) that there is no reason to condemn abnormally high short-run earnings as *necessarily* implying a loss of consumer surplus, since without the lure of such earnings agents may not have bothered to invest in the knowhow from which these earnings were derived: deviations from perfect contestability are part of the dynamic by which the competitive process progressively reduces costs.

Consumer behaviour and the role of the retailer as an intermediary

Andrews felt it essential to make sense of consumer decision processes before jumping to conclusions about appropriate policies for corporate survival and the kinds of industrial structure that these might imply. Although he never published a systematic alternative to orthodox Hicksian consumer theory a careful reading of his work on retailing (Andrews, 1950, 1964, part IIB; Andrews and Friday, 1960) indicates that the analysis with which he worked did not run along conventional lines. Its roots are, as ever, more in the tradition of Marshall, a tradition to which, in this context, Hicks himself later came to wish he had adhered (see Hicks, 1976, pp. 137–8). But it goes beyond Marshall and seems best characterized as resembling a prescient bridge between the 'utility tree' notion associated in the mainstream literature with the work of Strotz (1957), the characteristics analysis proposed by Lancaster (1966), and the essentially behavioural analysis of contributions to consumer theory made in marketing.

It is clear that Andrews saw consumer choice as an hierarchical process; he did not see consumers as if they possessed well-defined brand preferences in an n-dimensional goods space. Having engaged in a good deal of enjoyable yet purposeful window-shopping, the Andrewsian consumer decides the budget range within which to look seriously for a particular kind of product — that is to say, the consumer initially is concerned with tradeoffs among broadly defined commodity categories, or a particular category to be traded-off against general purchasing power foregone from other unspecified uses. Such budget ranges would be discrete, 'conventional' constructs; consumers would not choose between many marginally-overlapping rival plans of feasible financial allocations. The budgeting process would leave the consumer with an upper bound for the particular product category, which would exclude as 'too expensive' some brands that might otherwise be candidates for serious evaluation and comparison with rival means of meeting the ends in question. The range's lower bound would exclude cheaper goods as likely to be of inadequate quality.

The use of such attention-confining price bands by consumers — which is empirically well documented (for example, see papers in part B of Taylor and

Wills, eds, 1969) — was something that Andrews saw as placing firms under competitive pressures to offer products that could safely (in Andrews's normal-cost sense) be priced within conventionally popular ranges. The fact that brand evaluations would be carried out with respect to goods that consumers actually encountered as possible means of producing desired ends led Andrews to emphasize the role of stocks as demand-generating devices, and to be critical of the depiction of incompletely planned consumer spending as irrational 'impulse buying'. Although Andrews saw consumers as having to focus their attention to cope with potential information overload and uncertainty, he did not see them generally as inconsistent in their underlying wants or incompetent as shoppers.

In Andrews's view, consumers, like industrial buyers, would give particular suppliers their goodwill. In embarking on a particular shopping expedition, they would make what we might usefully call 'primary patronage choices', according to their assessments of stores' relative competitiveness in respect of the broad mix of things with which they intended to fill their shopping baskets — not with regard to marginal choices of particular commodities. If relative competitiveness did not seem to have changed, they would go to their 'usual' store. Having made such decisions and entered particular stores, consumers would then buy as many of the items on their shopping lists as were available and seemed unlikely to be cheaper elsewhere. They would purchase only the residual items in alternative stores. To the extent that this is how retailers also see things, economists should not usually see price competition on particular brands among general stores and supermarkets as means of boosting net earnings on the lines in question. Rather, such competition should be seen as aimed at changing primary patronage choices on shopping expeditions. Here, then, as throughout his work on price formation, Andrews did not engage in a reductionist focus on individual commodities.

Andrews's views on what precisely one should think of consumers as purchasing led him to be unusually open-minded about resale price maintenance and to his becoming embroiled in debates with those who advocated a legal presumption that such policies were against the best interests of consumers (see Borts, 1961, for a useful review article). Consumers were not, in Andrews's view, simply buying a product to take home and consume; they were also buying information about rival ways of meeting their needs and often they would require after-sales servicing facilities and advice on how to get the best performance from what they had purchased. Manufacturers who try to control their prices by refusing to supply dealers who failed to offer before- and after-sales facilities should not necessarily be seen as trying to push up market prices against customer interests. Rather, they could be seen as trying to win business by reducing customers' transaction costs and risks, and guarding against the possibility of market failure. In his contribution to the *Fair Trade* pamphlet

(Andrews and Friday, 1960), Andrews highlighted the possibility that discount retailers who sought to offer lower prices by failing to offer the additional services would only be able to free-ride on approved retailers so long as the latter could generate enough sales to stay in business. If resale price maintenance were abolished and widespread discounting led to the demise of full-service retailers, consumers would have to look elsewhere for back-up services. If resale price maintenance were allowed and some manufacturers thought they could win more business in the long run by unbundling the physical product from the back-up service, consumers could then show what kind of retailing deal they preferred: to give choice to the manufacturers about which intermediaries they use does not necessarily close off choice from the consumers; it might actually widen the range of choice.

This view of the interaction between consumers and manufacturers and the role of franchised intermediaries is close to modern thinking in marketing and remains relevant to policy debates in this age of increasingly deregulated markets (for example, the case made in 1992 by the New Zealand vehicle assemblers' trade association against policies that permit easy imports of used cars and non-franchised imports of barely-used vehicles had much in common with the analysis just outlined). It is a rather paradoxical analysis when seen in the context of Andrews's broader vision: on the one hand he portrays consumers as canny shoppers as a result of their day-to-day mobility or enjoyment of shopping as an activity; on the other hand, he is highlighting the complexity of the problem the consumer faces and casting the manufacturer's appointed intermediary in the role of an agent who helps the consumer cope. His thinking anticipates that of some of Scitovsky's (1985) recent work on buyers' markets and price-making behaviour, which fails to refer to Andrews (though it is evident from Scitovsky's earlier contributions that he was aware of *Manufacturing Business*, if not of Andrews's subsequent work on retailing).

The right ideas at the wrong time?

The experience of discovering and coming to terms with the work of Andrews was, in my own case, a thought-provoking one in respect of the process whereby contributions to knowledge achieve academic standing. It was only the work of Loasby (1976, 1978) that finally triggered my decision to read Andrews's major (1949b, 1964) books, even though my initial training in industrial economics had involved me in reading many of the textbooks and other sources that mention his work. It then took a considerable effort to get on top of what he had to say, and to realize quite how rich and ahead of its time his view of the competitive process was. I later discovered that most economists that I encountered who admired his work tended also to have been his or Brunner's students (or former colleagues at Lancaster University) or taught by their former students. Several lessons seemed to be implied by this experience.

First, the processes whereby scholars screen sources of potential relevance to their work may have a major influence on the kind of research they use and themselves produce, with cumulating impacts on the fact of particular contributions. Reviews, reputations and personal connections affect this process, as does the way in which contributions are discussed. During his lifetime, Andrews failed to receive glowing endorsements of his work from other leading economists, so snowball effects were naturally rather limited. Later generations of students could easily miss his work: if their teachers had already got them to read, say, Godley and Nordhaus, Sylos-Labini, and Cyert and March on non-mainstream views of the firm and they saw Andrews referred to as just another mark-up theorist in a brief discussion or footnote, they would be unlikely to see much point in tracking his work down, particularly if this would involve an inter-library loan. His books would thus continue to gather dust.

Secondly, the packaging of ideas may affect the reception that they achieve. Andrews's style of writing can often be quite hard to follow, despite its non-technical style. He seemed reluctant to trumpet the existence of his other works or papers by Brunner which were far more transparent: the closing sentence of his 'Note to the Second Impression' of his 1964 book was hardly the best place to mention that he and Brunner had elsewhere set out an alternative theory to that which he was criticizing, and, as Irving (1978) points out, some reviewers of the first impression of his critique seemed to have no idea of the existence of his earlier work, despite the controversy that *Manufacturing Business* occasioned in its own reviews fifteen years earlier. Nor does the earlier work highlight Andrews's non-equilibrium philosophy. It was a major marketing error to present his theoretical contribution as though its departures from the mainstream were both obvious and likely to be accepted without question, and then to write his critique of the conventional wisdom so long after his theoretical contribution. A volume integrating his analysis of manufacturing business, investment decision-making and retailing in an accessible style and against a critical backdrop was, and remains, badly needed.

Thirdly, Andrews failed to grasp the need to build marketing coalitions, and instead of seeking to integrate compatible elements from the work of potential intellectual allies such as the American behaviouralists and Penrose, he chose to attack them. His personality may have limited his opportunities for building coalitions: following the hostile reception to his work, he was seen by some as 'having several chips on both shoulders'. This being so, he was lucky to have on his side R.H. Barback who, uniquely, was converted to a supporter after setting out to refute normal-cost theory by empirical study (Barback, 1964). He might also have enjoyed a better reception — if not from mainstream economists — and better understood Cyert, March and Simon had he worked in a business school, and seen how the use of business ratios in management control systems and business appraisals is neatly represented by the idea of satisficing that he disliked so much. Certainly, the subject matter of his vision of industrial economics (Andrews, 1952, pp. 76–7 [p. 374 in this book]) calls to mind the curriculum of a business school far more than industrial economics as nowadays practised, and he chose to write *Manufacturing Business* in the language of the business manager, not the economist. His work did not, therefore, look like rigorous economic analysis.

Though Andrews's choice of language certainly contributed to the hostility that his work provoked (see Irving, 1978), he was bound to have a rough time at the hands of a profession of economists who were following the lead of Joan Robinson's (1933) *Economics of Imperfect Competition* and concentrating on building rigorous equilibrium models. Andrews appeared to be clinging to the Marshallian research programme which, in the immediate post-war period, seemed rather obviously to be degenerating. Unlike Robinson, Andrews did not insist on the necessity of exchanging the world for a model, or that the principle of rational self-interest had to be construed as entailing equality between marginal costs and marginal revenue. His rejection of the demand curve concept at the level of the individual firm further contributed to his work being construed, erroneously, as rejecting profit maximization and, with it, rational choice. His work inevitably makes little sense in terms of an equilibrium framework because it is not cast in terms of static equilibrium analysis: potential competition provides the basis for a steady state in which short-run decisions are taken in the shadow of the long run. Goodwill serves to explain market share in Andrews's model but it has no logical place in subsequent models of a perfectly contestable equilibrium whose formal equilibrium structures are readily comprehendible from the mainstream perspective. Despite their more technically challenging nature and empirically more questionable assumptive structures, such models thus have an appeal that Andrews's analysis lacked.

Concluding comments

It has not been the intention of this paper to claim that 'It's all in Andrews', or that he left behind a vision that he had *fully* integrated and detailed for his readers. All I hope to have done is alert readers to the fact that quite a lot of the supposedly novel themes of modern industrial economics certainly are present in works by Andrews that often sit gathering dust in libraries around the world. Some of these ideas were not even original to Andrews's work: the influence of

Marshall on Andrews is considerable, but some of Andrews's themes are also to be found in work in the United States which he tended not to cite, by scholars such as J.M. Clark (1940) and Gardiner Means (1935).

This exercise in consciousness raising was not something I decided to undertake simply to establish Andrews's place in the history of the discipline or as a cautionary tale about the processes by which intellectual reputations snowball or fail to take off. It can also be justifiably claimed that although the 'reinvented' ideas have found acceptance in many quarters, Andrews's works still repay careful scrutiny, for two main reasons. The first is due to the fact that it is rare to see anybody using these ideas in an integrative manner: for example, scholars of industrial structure typically do not concern themselves with the internal organization of firms, or vice versa. Thus Andrews's works are worth reading because, although they may not explore individual themes in the kind of depth found in the later treatments, his breadth of coverage, his feel for the subject at large, is uncommon in modern writings: his writings thus encourage and facilitate attempts at integration. Secondly, scholars of the modern literature are in the main still preoccupied with equilibrium states and could therefore find it invigorating to examine the work of someone who thought in terms of non-equilibrium processes and yet did not end up getting lost in a fog of complexity. So long as orthodox scholars are forewarned, they should not suffer the same bewilderment that afflicted many reviewers of Andrews's works.

It must be said, however, that despite Andrews's very broad vision of the subject matter of industrial economics, his coverage does display some gaps which would justifiably concern those familiar with the latest developments in the field. It may therefore be useful to end by noting some of these lacunas.

Andrews's output appears distinctly thin on what modern-day industrial economists would call strategic diversification and internalization. Diversification possibilities are certainly seen by Andrews as at the forefront of the entrepreneurial mind: the notion that a firm can transfer its existing resources to other markets is, as we have seen, central to his analysis, and Moss (1981) has made much use of it in his theory of business strategy. However, Andrews did not consider potential dangers of such synergy-seeking policies. Hence he did not go on to note that the question of what might constitute an appropriate entry-preventing pricing policy would be made even more problematic by a desire on the part of some firms to hedge their bets by breaking into areas where their skills were, as yet, poorly developed (see Kay, 1982, 1984, on the hedging versus synergy issue). Of course, Andrews did recognize a basic point stressed in modern internalization theory (Williamson, 1975, 1985), that vertical integration may be construed by managers as a cost-effective alternative to subcontracting: 'do it yourself' in the face of of uncompetitive performances — in price and/or quality terms — by incumbent suppliers and distributors is an obvious variation on Andrews's basic potential competition theme. However, unlike Williamson (whose inspiration came largely from Coase, 1937), Andrews did not argue that such forms of integration arose primarily as a result of problems in drawing up suitable contracts between buyers and sellers.

References

Andrews, P.W.S. (1949a) 'A reconsideration of the theory of the individual business', *Oxford Economic Papers* 1 (New series), pp. 54–89.

Andrews, P.W.S. (1949b) *Manufacturing Business*, London, Macmillan.

Andrews, P.W.S. (1950) 'Some aspects of competition in retail trade', *Oxford Economic Papers* 2 (New series), pp. 138–75).

Andrews, P.W.S. (1951) 'Industrial analysis in economics', in Wilson, T. and Andrews, P.W.S. (eds) *Oxford Studies in the Price Mechanism*, Oxford, Clarendon Press.

Andrews, P.W.S. (1952) 'Industrial economics as a specialist subject', *Journal of Industrial Economics* 1, pp. 72–80.

Andrews, P.W.S. (1958) 'Competition in the modern economy', reprinted from Sell, G. (ed.) (1958) *Competitive Aspects of Oil Operations*, London, Institute of Petroleum.

Andrews, P.W.S. (1961) 'Review of E. T. Penrose, *The Theory of the Growth of the Firm*', *Oxford Magazine*, pp. 114–16.

Andrews, P.W.S. (1964) *On Competition in Economic Theory*, London, Macmillan.

Andrews, P.W.S. and Brunner, E. (1951) *Capital Development in Steel*, Oxford, Basil Blackwell.

Andrews, P.W.S. and Brunner, E. (1955) *The Life of Lord Nuffield*, Oxford, Basil Blackwell.

Andrews, P.W.S. and Brunner, E. (1962) 'Business profits and the quiet life', *Journal of Industrial Economics* 11, pp. 72–80.

Andrews, P.W.S. and Brunner, E. (1965) *The Eagle Ironworks, Oxford*, London, Mills & Boon.

Andrews, P.W.S. and Brunner, E. (1975) *Studies in Pricing*, London, Macmillan.

Andrews, P.W.S. and Friday, F.A. (1960) *Fair Trade: Resale Price Maintenance Re-examined*, London, Macmillan.

Bain, J.S. (1956) *Barriers to New Competition*, Cambridge, MA, Harvard University Press.

Bain, J.S. (1958) 'A note on pricing in monopoly and oligopoly', *American Economic Review* **48**, pp. 448–64.

Barback, R.H. (1964) *The Pricing of Manufactures*, London, Macmillan.

Baumol, W.J. (1982) 'Contestable markets: an uprising in the theory of industrial structure', *American Economic Review* **72**, pp. 1–13.

Baumol, W.J., Panzar, J.C. and Willig, R.D. (1982) *Contestable Markets and the Theory of Industrial Structure*, San Diego, Harcourt Brace Jovanovich.

Bevan, A. (1987) 'Private communication, 10 July', London, Monopolies and Mergers Commission.

Bhagwati, J.N. (1970) 'Oligopoly theory, entry prevention, and growth', *Oxford Economic Papers* **22**, pp. 297–310.

Borts, G. (1961) 'The recent controversy over resale price maintenance', *Journal of the Royal Statistical Society* **124** (General), pp. 244–9.

Caves, R. and Porter, M.E. (1977) 'From entry barriers to mobility barriers', *Quarterly Journal of Economics* **91**, pp. 241–61.

Chandler, A.D. (1962) *Strategy and Structure: Chapters in the History of the American Industrial Enterprise*, Cambridge, MA, M.I.T. Press.

Clark, J.M. (1923) *Studies in the Economics of Overhead Costs*, Chicago, Chicago University Press.

Clark, J.M. (1940) 'Toward a concept of workable competition', *American Economic Review* **30**, pp. 241–56.

Coase, R.H. (1937) 'The nature of the firm', *Economica* **4** (New series), pp. 386–405.

Coutts, K.J., Godley, W.A.H. and Nordhaus, W.D. (1978) *Industrial Pricing in the United Kingdom*, Cambridge, Cambridge University Press.

Cyert, R.M. and March, J.G. (1963) *A Behavioral Theory of the Firm*, Englewood Cliffs, NJ, Prentice-Hall.

Cyert, R.M. and Simon, H.A. (1983) 'The behavioral approach: with emphasis on economics', *Behavioral Science* **28**, pp. 95–108.

Devine, P.J., Jones, R.M., Lee, N. and Tyson, W.J. (1985) *An Introduction to Industrial Economics* (4th edn), London, George Allen & Unwin.

Doeringer, P.B. and Piore, M. J. (1971) *Internal Labor Markets and Manpower Analysis*, Lexington, MA, D.C. Heath.

Downie, J. (1958) *The Competitive Process*, London, Duckworth.

Earl, P.E. (1983a) 'A behavioral theory of economists' behavior', in Eichner, A.S. (ed.) (1983) *Why Economics is Not Yet a Science*, Armonk, NY, M.E. Sharpe, Inc.

Earl, P.E. (1983b) *The Economic Imagination*, Brighton, Wheatsheaf.

Earl, P.E. and Glaister, K. W. (1979) 'Wage stickiness from the demand side', University of Stirling Discussion Papers in Economics, Finance, and Investment, No. 78, December.

Eatwell, J., Milgate, M. and Newman, P. (eds) (1987) *The New Palgrave: A Dictionary of Economics*, New York, Stockton Press.

Edwards, H.R. (1955) 'Price formation in manufacturing industry and excess capacity', *Oxford Economic Papers* 7, pp. 94–118.

Edwards, H.R. (1962) *Competition and Monopoly in the British Soap Industry*, Oxford, Clarendon Press.

Eichner, A.S. (1976) *The Megacorp and Oligopoly*, Cambridge, Cambridge University Press (reprinted, 1980, by M.E. Sharpe, Inc., White Plains, NY).

Eichner, A.S. (1978) 'Review of P.W.S. Andrews and E. Brunner (1975) *Studies in Pricing*', *Journal of Economic Literature* 16, pp. 1436–8.

Farrell, M.J. (1971) 'Philip Andrews and Manufacturing Business', *Journal of Industrial Economics* 20, pp. 10–13.

Godley, W.A.H. and Nordhaus, W.D. (1972) 'Pricing in the trade cycle', *Economic Journal* 82, pp. 853–82.

Hall, R.L. and Hitch, C.J. (1939) 'Price theory and business behaviour', *Oxford Economic Papers* 2, pp. 12–45 (reprinted in Wilson and Andrews, eds, 1951).

Harrod, R.F. (1952) *Economic Essays*, London, Macmillan.

Hay, D.A. and Morris, D.J. (1979) *Industrial Economics: Theory and Evidence*, Oxford, Oxford University Press.

Hicks, J.R. (1954) 'The process of imperfect competition', *Oxford Economic Papers* 6, pp. 41–54.

Hicks, J.R. (1976) 'Some questions of time in economics', in Tang, A., Westfield, F. and Worley, J. (eds) (1976) *Evolution, Welfare and Time in Economics: Essays in Honor of Nicholas Georgescu-Roegen*, Lexington, MA, Lexington Books.

Irving, J. (1978) 'P.W.S. Andrews and the unsuccessful revolution', unpublished Ph.D. thesis, Wollongong University, Wollongong, NSW.

Jones, S.R.G. (1984) *The Economics of Conformism*, Oxford, Basil Blackwell.

Kay, N.M. (1982) *The Evolving Firm*, London, Macmillan.

Kay, N.M. (1984) *The Emergent Firm*, London, Macmillan.

Koutsoyiannis, A. (1979) *Modern Microeconomics* (2nd edn), London, Macmillan.

Lancaster, K. J. (1966) 'A new approach to consumer theory', *Journal of Political Economy* 74, pp. 132–57.

Latsis, S.J. (1972) 'Situational determinism in economics', *British Journal for the Philosophy of Science* 25, pp. 207–45.

Lawler, K.A. (1985) 'The revolution in monopoly theory', letter to the editor, *Lloyds Bank Review* No. 157, pp. 36–7.

Lee, F.S. (1984) 'The marginalist controversy and the demise of full cost pricing', *Journal of Economic Issues* 28, pp. 1107–32.

Leibenstein, H. (1966) 'Allocative efficiency versus X-inefficiency', *American*

Economic Review, **56**, June, pp. 392-415.

Littlechild, S.C. (1981) 'Misleading calculations of the social costs of monopoly power', *Economic Journal* **91**, June, pp. 348–64.

Loasby, B.J. (1976) *Choice, Complexity and Ignorance*, Cambridge, Cambridge University Press.

Loasby, B.J. (1978) 'Whatever happened to Marshall's theory of value', *Scottish Journal of Political Economy* **25**, pp. 1–12.

Means, G.C. (1935) Industrial Prices and their Relative Inflexibility, Senate Document No. 13, 74th Congress, 1st Session, Washington, D.C., 17 January.

Modigliani, F. (1958) 'New developments on the oligopoly front', *Journal of Political Economy* **66**, pp. 215–32.

Moss, S.J. (1981) *An Economic Theory of Business Strategy*, Oxford, Martin Robertson.

Oi, W.Y. (1962) 'Labor as a quasi-fixed factor', *Journal of Political Economy* **70**, pp. 538–55.

Penrose, E.T. (1959) *The Theory of the Growth of the Firm*, Oxford, Basil Blackwell.

Pickering, J.F. (1974) *Industrial Structure and Market Conduct*, London, Martin Robertson.

Porter, M.E. (1979) 'The structure within industries and companies' performance', *Review of Economics and Statistics* **61**, pp. 214–27.

Porter, M.E. (1980) *Competitive Strategy: Techniques for Analysing Industries and Competitors*, New York, Free Press.

Reid, G. C. (1979) 'An analysis of the firm, market structure and technical progress', *Scottish Journal of Political Economy* **26**, pp. 15–33.

Robinson, J.V. (1933) *The Economics of Imperfect Competition*, London, Macmillan.

Roethlisberger, F. J. and Dickson, W. J. (1939) *Management and the Worker*, Cambridge, MA, Harvard University Press.

Scitovsky, T. (1985) 'Pricetakers' plenty: a neglected benefit of monopoly capitalism', *Kyklos* **38**, pp. 517–36.

Shaw, R.W. (1974) 'Price leadership and the effect of new entry on the UK retail petrol supply market', *Journal of Industrial Economics* **18**, pp. 65–79.

Shepherd, W.G. (1984) '"Contestability" vs. competition', *American Economic Review* **74**, pp. 572–87.

Simon, H.A. (1986) 'The failure of armchair economics', interview in *Challenge* **29**, November/December, pp. 18–25.

Strotz, R.H. (1957) 'The empirical implications of a utility tree', *Econometrica* **25**, April, pp. 269–80.

Sylos-Labini, P. (1969) *Oligopoly and Technical Progress* (revised edn),

Cambridge, MA, Harvard University Press.
Taylor, B. and Wills, G. (eds) (1969) *Pricing Strategy*, London, Staples.
Williamson, O.E. (1975) *Markets and Hierarchies*, New York, Free Press.
Williamson, O.E. (1985) *The Economic Institutions of Capitalism*, New York, Free Press.
Wilson, T. (1984) *Inflation, Unemployment, and the Market*, Oxford, Clarendon Press.
Wilson, T. and Andrews, P.W.S. (eds) (1951) *Oxford Studies in the Price Mechanism*, Oxford, Clarendon Press.

A bibliography of the writings of P.W.S. Andrews

Books and monographs

Manufacturing Business, 1949, London, Macmillan & Co. Ltd.

Oxford Studies in the Price Mechanism, 1951, edited with Tom Wilson, Oxford, Clarendon Press.

Capital Development in Steel: A Study of The United Steel Companies Ltd. (with Elizabeth Brunner), 1951, Oxford, Basil Blackwell.

The Life of Lord Nuffield: A Study in Enterprise & Benevolence (with Elizabeth Brunner), 1959, Oxford, Basil Blackwell.

Fair Trade: Resale Price Maintenance Re-examined (with Frank A. Friday), 1960, London: Macmillan & Co. Ltd., translated into German in 1962.

Industrial Uses of Economic Theory, 1963, Los Angeles, University of California Los Angeles.

On Competition in Economic Theory, 1964, London, Macmillan & Co. Ltd.

The Eagle Ironworks, Oxford: The Story of W. Lucy and Company Limited (with Elizabeth Brunner), 1965, London, Mills & Boon.

Studies in Pricing (with Elizabeth Brunner), 1975, London, The Macmillan Press Ltd.

Articles and other published papers

'Post-war public companies: a study in investment and enterprise', 1937, *Economic Journal* **47**, September, pp. 500–10.

'Summary of replies to questions on effects of interest rates' (with James Meade), 1938, *Oxford Economic Papers* **1** (old series), October, pp. 14–31.

'A further inquiry into the effects of rates of interest', 1940, *Oxford Economic Papers* **3** (old series), February, pp. 32–73.

'Food rationing and the present emergency', 1940, *Oxford Institute of Statistics: Bulletin* **2**, July, pp. 2–7.

'Development-projects in Great Britain during the war', 1941, *Oxford Institute of Statistics: Bulletin* **3**, 1 February, pp. 22–5.

'Food policy', 1941, *Oxford Institute of Statistics: Bulletin* **3**, 22 February, pp.

428

48–51.

'A survey of industrial development in Great Britain planned since commencement of the war', 1941, *Oxford Economic Papers* 5 (old series), June, pp. 55–71.

'A reconsideration of the theory of the individual business', 1949 *Oxford Economic Papers* 1 (new series), January, pp. 54–89.

'Productivity and the businessman' (with Elizabeth Brunner), 1950, *Oxford Economic Papers* 2 (new series), June, pp. 197–225.

'Some aspects of competition in retail trade', 1950, *Oxford Economic Papers* 2 (new series), June, pp. 137-75.

'A Reply', 1951, *Oxford Economic Papers* 3 (new series), October, pp. 249–58.

'Industrial analysis in economics — with especial reference to Marshallian Doctrine', 1951, in *Oxford Studies in the Price Mechanism*, pp. 139–72, edited by T. Wilson and P.W.S. Andrews, Oxford, Clarendon Press.

'Industrial economics as a specialist subject', 1952, *Journal of Industrial Economics* 1, November, pp. 72–9.

'Some aspects of capital development', 1953, *Proceedings* of the *Journal of the Textile Institute* 44, September, pp. 687–97.

'Review of *Capital Budgeting* by Joel Dean', 1953, *Economic Journal* 63, December, pp. 882–5.

'Sir Henry Clay', 1954, *Journal of Industrial Economics* 3, December, pp. 1–8.

'Limites economiques a la dimension et a la croissance des entreprises individuelles', 1956, *Revue Economique* 1, Janvier, pp. 39–67.

'The business enterprise as a subject for research: a comment', 1957, *Kyklos* 10, pp. 70–74.

'Competition in the modern economy', 1958, in *Competitive Aspects of Oil Operations — Report of the Summer Meeting of the Institute of Petroleum, held at Scarborough, 4th–6th June 1958*, pp. 1–42, edited by George Sell, London, The Institute of Petroleum.

'The Registrar's report', 1961, *The Lawyer* 4, Trinity, pp. 15–20, 44.

'Review of *The Theory of the Growth of the Firm* by Edith Penrose', 1961, *The Oxford Magazine* 2, 30 November, pp. 114, 116.

'Business profits and the quiet life' (with Elizabeth Brunner), 1962, *Journal of Industrial Economics* 11, November, pp. 72–8 (also published in 1963 in the *Pittsburg Business Review* 33, pp. 1–4).

'The recent controversy over resale price maintenance: a rejoinder' (with Frank A. Friday), 1962, *Journal of the Royal Statistical Society, Series A* 125, pp. 592–5.

'Mr Sutherland's bad books', 1964, *The Solicitor Quarterly* 3, pp. 260–4.

'Economic aspects of the Net Book case' (with Elizabeth Brunner), 1966, in *Books Are Different*, pp. 75–85, edited by R.E. Barker and G.R. Davies,

London, Macmillan.
'P.W.S. Andrews: proof of evidence', 1966, in *Books Are Different*, pp. 513–607, edited by R.E. Barker and G.R. Davies, London, Macmillan.

Some unpublished papers and lectures

'The real costs of house building', 1941, Nuffield College Social Reconstruction Survey Papers, Nuffield College, Oxford.
'Estimate of the quantity of building labour needed to carry out the building involved in certain proposals for educational reforms, together with some tentative estimates of the demand for teachers in England and Wales in 1945', 1942, Nuffield College Social Reconstruction Survey Papers, Nuffield College, Oxford.
'International economic conditions needed in connection with full employment in Great Britain' (with M.P. Fogarty), 1943, Nuffield College Social Reconstruction Survey Papers, Nuffield College, Oxford.
'Report from the "accountancy" side of the pilot inquiry into the relative efficiency of small- and large-scale manufacturing', 1944, Nuffield College, Oxford.
'The legacy of the 1930s in economics', 1952, P.W.S. Andrews Papers, British Library of Political and Economic Science, London School of Economics, London.
'The Netherlands lectures', 1952, P.W.S. Andrews Papers, British Library of Political and Economic Science, London School of Economics, London.
'Fundamental errors in the orthodox theory of the firm', 1965, P.W.S. Andrews Papers, British Library of Political and Economic Science, London School of Economics, London.

Name Index

Subject Index

434

Economists of the Twentieth Century

Monetarism and Macroeconomic Policy
Thomas Mayer

Studies in Fiscal Federalism
Wallace E. Oates

The World Economy in Perspective
Essays in International Trade and European Integration
Herbert Giersch

Towards a New Economics
Critical Essays on Ecology, Distribution and Other Themes
Kenneth E. Boulding

Studies in Positive and Normative Economics
Martin J. Bailey

The Collected Essays of Richard E. Quandt (2 volumes)
Richard E Quandt

International Trade Theory and Policy
Selected Essays of W. Max Corden
W. Max Corden

Organization and Technology in Capitalist Development
William Lazonick

Studies in Human Capital
Collected Essays of Jacob Mincer, Volume 1
Jacob Mincer

Studies in Labor Supply
Collected Essays of Jacob Mincer, Volume 2
Jacob Mincer

Macroeconomics and Economic Policy
The Selected Essays of Assar Lindbeck, Volume I
Assar Lindbeck

The Welfare State
The Selected Essays of Assar Lindbeck, Volume II
Assar Lindbeck

Classical Economics, Public Expenditure and Growth
Walter Eltis

Money, Interest Rates and Inflation
Frederic S. Mishkin

The Public Choice Approach to Politics
Dennis C. Mueller

The Liberal Economic Order
Volume I   Essays on International Economics
Volume II   Money, Cycles and Related Themes
Gottfried Haberler
Edited by Anthony Y.C. Koo

Economic Growth and Business Cycles
Prices and the Process of Cyclical Development
Paolo Sylos Labini

International Adjustment, Money and Trade
Theory and Measurement for Economic Policy, Volume I
Herbert G. Grubel

International Capital and Service Flows
Theory and Measurement for Economic Policy, Volume II
Herbert G. Grubel

Unintended Effects of Goverment Policies
Theory and Measurement for Economic Policy, Volume III
Herbert G. Grubel

The Economics of Competitive Enterprise
Selected Essays of P.W.S. Andrews
Edited by Frederic S. Lee and Peter E. Earl

The Repressed Economy
Causes, Consequences, Reform
Deepak Lal

Economic Theory and Market Socialism
Selected Essays of Oskar Lange
Edited by Tadeusz Kowalik

Trade, Development and Political Economy
Selected Essays of Ronald Findlay
Ronald Findlay